PRIMARY MATHEMATICS
Integrating Theory with Practice

Fourth edition

Primary Mathematics: Integrating Theory with Practice is a comprehensive introduction to teaching mathematics in Australian primary schools. Closely aligned with the Australian Curriculum: Mathematics v. 9.0, it provides a thorough understanding of number, algebra, measurement, space, statistics and probability.

The fourth edition provides support for educators in key aspects of teaching: planning, assessment, digital technologies, diversity in the classroom and integrating mathematics content with other learning areas. It also features a new chapter on the role of education support in the mathematics classroom.

Each chapter has been thoroughly revised and is complemented by classroom snapshots demonstrating practical application of theories, activities to further understanding and reflection questions to guide learning. New in this edition are 'Concepts to consider', which provide a guided explanation and further discussion of key concepts to support pre- and in-service teachers' learning and teaching of the fundamentals of mathematics.

Written by a team with extensive experience in mathematics education, *Primary Mathematics* is an exemplary resource for pre-service teachers beginning their career in education.

Penelope Baker is Professor of Mathematics Education at the University of New England.

Rosemary Callingham AM is Adjunct Associate Professor in the Faculty of Education at the University of Tasmania.

Tracey Muir is Professor of Education at the Australian Catholic University (Brisbane).

Cambridge University Press acknowledges the Australian Aboriginal and Torres Strait Islander peoples of this nation. We acknowledge the traditional custodians of the lands on which our company is located and where we conduct our business. We pay our respects to ancestors and Elders, past and present. Cambridge University Press is committed to honouring Australian Aboriginal and Torres Strait Islander peoples' unique cultural and spiritual relationships to the land, waters and seas and their rich contribution to society.

Penelope Baker
Rosemary Callingham
Tracey Muir

PRIMARY MATHEMATICS
Integrating Theory with Practice

Fourth edition

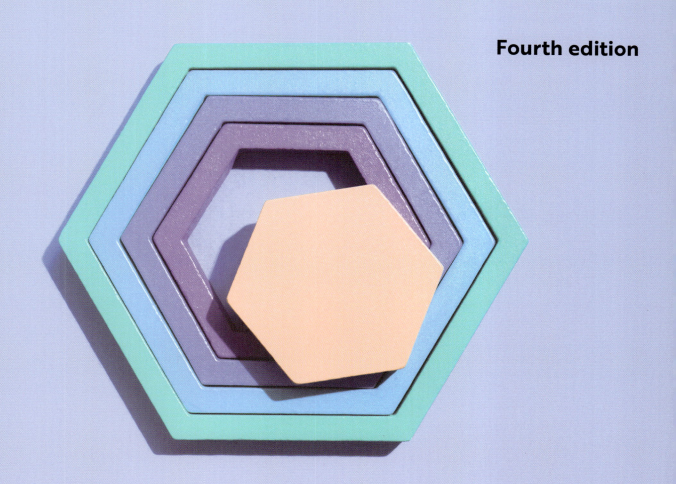

Shaftesbury Road, Cambridge CB2 8EA, United Kingdom

One Liberty Plaza, 20th Floor, New York, NY 10006, USA

477 Williamstown Road, Port Melbourne, VIC 3207, Australia

314–321, 3rd Floor, Plot 3, Splendor Forum, Jasola District Centre, New Delhi – 110025, India

103 Penang Road, #05–06/07, Visioncrest Commercial, Singapore 238467

Cambridge University Press is part of Cambridge University Press & Assessment, a department of the University of Cambridge.

We share the University's mission to contribute to society through the pursuit of education, learning and research at the highest international levels of excellence.

www.cambridge.org
Information on this title: www.cambridge.org/highereducation/isbn/9781009265171

© Cambridge University Press & Assessment 2014, 2016, 2019, 2023

This publication is copyright. Subject to statutory exception and to the provisions of relevant collective licensing agreements, no reproduction of any part may take place without the written permission of Cambridge University Press & Assessment.

First published 2014
Second edition 2016
Third edition 2019
Fourth edition 2023

Cover designed by Bec Yule, Red Chilli Designs
Typeset by Integra Software Services Pvt. Ltd
Printed in Malaysia by Vivar Printing, June 2023

A catalogue record for this publication is available from the British Library

A catalogue record for this book is available from the National Library of Australia

ISBN 978-1-009-26517-1 Paperback

Additional resources for this publication at www.cambridge.org/highereducation/isbn/9781009265171/resources

Reproduction and communication for educational purposes

The Australian *Copyright Act 1968* (the Act) allows a maximum of one chapter or 10% of the pages of this work, whichever is the greater, to be reproduced and/or communicated by any educational institution for its educational purposes provided that the educational institution (or the body that administers it) has given a remuneration notice to Copyright Agency Limited (CAL) under the Act.

For details of the CAL licence for educational institutions contact:

Copyright Agency Limited
Level 12, 66 Goulburn Street
Sydney NSW 2000
Telephone: (02) 9394 7600
Facsimile: (02) 9394 7601
E-mail: memberservices@copyright.com.au

Cambridge University Press & Assessment has no responsibility for the persistence or accuracy of URLs for external or third-party internet websites referred to in this publication and does not guarantee that any content on such websites is, or will remain, accurate or appropriate.

Please be aware that this publication may contain several variations of Aboriginal and Torres Strait Islander terms and spellings; no disrespect is intended. Please note that the terms 'Indigenous Australians', 'Aboriginal and Torres Strait Islander peoples' and 'First Nations peoples' may be used interchangeably in this publication.

CONTENTS

About the authors	xi
How to use HOTmaths with this book	xii
Acknowledgements	xvi

1 Teaching mathematics today with tomorrow in mind — 1

Today's classroom	2
Approaches to teaching mathematics	3
Summary of chapters	7
How to use this book	10

2 Exploring early mathematical development — 12

Introduction	12
Early childhood mathematics pedagogy	14
Transition to school	14
The importance of play	15
Early number concepts	16
Numeracy progressions	19
Linking with curriculum documents	19
Early number activities and strategies	22
Early operations with number	31
Extending early mathematical development beyond number	35
Conclusion	38
Guided student tasks	38
Concepts to consider	38
Further reading	39

3 Exploring measurement — 41

Introduction	41
Learning sequence for measurement	41
Establishing formulae for areas and volumes	46
Estimation	47
Conservation	51
Measurement topics	52
Using inquiry to develop an understanding of measurement	65
Conclusion	67
Guided student tasks	67
Concepts to consider	67
Further reading	68

4 Exploring geometry — 69

- Introduction — 69
- Geometric concepts — 70
- Theoretical framework — 72
- Geometry in the primary classroom — 76
- The van Hiele teaching phases — 90
- Conclusion — 96
- Guided student tasks — 96
- Concepts to consider — 96
- Further reading — 99

5 Exploring whole number computation — 100

- Introduction — 100
- Developing number sense — 101
- Properties of numbers — 103
- Operations with whole numbers — 103
- Conclusion — 118
- Guided student tasks — 118
- Concepts to consider — 118
- Further reading — 120

6 Part-whole numbers and proportional reasoning — 121

- Introduction — 121
- Background — 122
- Parts and wholes — 123
- Conclusion — 138
- Guided student tasks — 138
- Concepts to consider — 138
- Further reading — 140

7 Exploring patterns and algebra — 141

- Introduction — 141
- Linking with curriculum — 142
- Pattern and structure — 142
- Developing an understanding of relationships — 149
- Equals and equivalence — 151
- Generalisation in upper primary — 156

Conclusion	163
Guided student tasks	163
Concepts to consider	164
Further reading	164

8 Exploring data and statistics — 166

Introduction	166
Development of statistical understanding	168
Asking questions (problem)	169
Collecting and recording data (plan, data)	170
Analysing and representing data (analyse)	175
Telling a story from the data (conclusions)	182
Conclusion	186
Guided student tasks	186
Concepts to consider	187
Further reading	189

9 Exploring chance and probability — 190

Introduction	190
Why is probability important?	190
Understanding probability	192
Developing understanding of uncertainty	194
Conclusion	208
Guided student tasks	208
Concepts to consider	209
Further reading	211

10 Capitalising on assessment for, of and as learning — 212

Introduction	212
Assessment	213
Quality of student responses	217
Construction of assessment tasks	223
National testing	223
Designing assessment items for different levels of complexity	230
Conclusion	231
Guided student tasks	231
Further reading	232

11 Planning for mathematics teaching in the 21st century classroom — 233

- Introduction — 233
- Planning considerations — 233
- Preparing your lesson — 240
- Teaching online — 241
- Adapting games to the online environment — 243
- Developing an understanding of place value — 246
- Planning for an integrated unit — 249
- Conclusion — 255
- Guided student tasks — 255
- Further reading — 255

12 Diversity in the primary mathematics classroom — 256

- Introduction — 256
- Why is it important to recognise diversity? — 256
- Differentiating the mathematics curriculum — 258
- The impact of teachers' understanding and beliefs — 259
- Practical aspects of addressing diversity in the mathematics classroom — 261
- Conclusion — 277
- Guided student tasks — 278
- Further reading — 278

13 General capabilities and cross-curriculum priorities — 279

- Introduction — 279
- General capabilities — 280
- Cross-curriculum priorities — 293
- Conclusion — 295
- Guided student tasks — 296
- Further reading — 296

14 STEM in the primary setting — 297

- Introduction — 297
- STEM in schools — 298
- STEM and primary mathematics — 299
- Problem-based learning and STEM — 301
- The United Kingdom experience — 303
- Implementing STEM in the primary classroom — 304
- Conclusion — 313

	Guided student tasks	313
	Further reading	314
15	**Surviving as an 'out of field' teacher of mathematics**	**315**
	Introduction	315
	Community beliefs about mathematics teaching and related issues	317
	Secondary lesson structures	319
	Issues to think about in the secondary context within each strand	324
	Conclusion	329
	Guided student tasks	330
	Further reading	330
16	**Teaching mathematics beyond the urban areas**	**331**
	Introduction	331
	Rural and remote areas	332
	Considering classroom structures	337
	National testing	340
	Conclusion	347
	Guided student tasks	347
	Further reading	348
17	**Digital technologies in the mathematics classroom**	**349**
	Introduction	349
	The TPACK framework	350
	Auditing your digital technology skills	351
	The SAMR model	352
	Leading teaching with digital technologies within your school	356
	Conclusion	363
	Guided student tasks	363
	Further reading	364
18	**Education support roles**	**365**
	Introduction	365
	What are education support workers?	366
	Working with ESWs	370
	Working with other ESWs	378
	Conclusion	380
	Guided student tasks	380

| | Further reading | 381 |
| | Acknowledgement | 381 |

19 Becoming a teacher of mathematics — 382

	Introduction	382
	Mathematics anxiety and the challenge of tests	383
	Evidence-based teaching	390
	Professional learning and communities	395
	Classroom observation	397
	Conclusion	399
	Guided student tasks	400
	Further reading	400

| References | 401 |
| Index | 414 |

ABOUT THE AUTHORS

Penelope Baker is Professor of Mathematics Education at the University of New England. She has worked on various development projects in Pacific Island contexts and is actively involved in research in the areas of primary, secondary and pre-service mathematics education. Penelope's research interests include assessment for learning practices, making the most of available tools in the mathematics classroom to actively engage students, and providing community-focused opportunities for teacher education in remote locations.

Rosemary Callingham AM is an Adjunct Associate Professor at the University of Tasmania. She has an extensive background in mathematics education in Australia, at school, system and tertiary levels, including mathematics curriculum development and implementation, large-scale testing and pre-service teacher education. Rosemary's research interests include teachers' pedagogical content knowledge, statistical literacy, mental computation and assessment of mathematics and numeracy. In 2020, she was honoured as Member of the Order of Australia for services to Mathematics Education, Teacher Development and the Community.

Tracey Muir is Professor in Education at the Australian Catholic University (Brisbane). Her teaching expertise has been recognised through a number of awards, including an Office for Learning and Teaching Award for Teaching Excellence and a VC Teaching Excellence Award. Tracey is an Executive Member of the Mathematics Association of Tasmania, and a previous editor of *Australian Primary Mathematics Education* and the *Mathematics Teacher Education and Research Journal*. Her research interests include effective teaching of numeracy, student engagement, making mathematical thinking visible, and teacher knowledge. Tracey regularly conducts professional learning for teachers and has delivered workshops, presentations and keynote addresses at state, national and international conferences.

HOW TO USE HOTMATHS WITH THIS BOOK

Once you have registered your HOTmaths access code, found on the inside front cover of this book, for subsequent visits the below navigation instructions provide a general overview of the main HOTmaths features used within this textbook.

Log in to your account via www.hotmaths.com.au.

Upon logging in you will automatically arrive at your Dashboard. This screen offers you access to your last viewed lesson, the next topic of that lesson and any tests, tasks or classes you've created. The toolbars on the left-hand side of this and any HOTmaths lesson page offers quick access to the platform's features, including the Dashboard, course content, **Games** and the HOTmaths **Dictionary**.

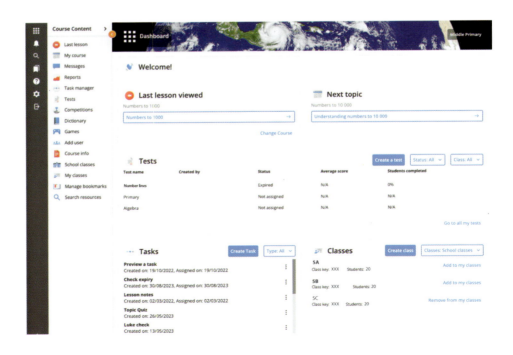

Different HOTmaths streams can be accessed via the Course list dropdown. You can change the **Course list** and **Course** (year level) using the dropdown on the left-hand side of the toolbar. You can then select a **Topic**, and finally a **Lesson**.

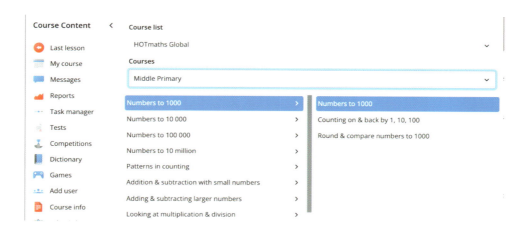

Most lessons contain a number of interactive and printable activities, which can be accessed via the links on the right-hand side of the page. These include: **Resources, Walkthroughs, Scorcher** and **Questions**.

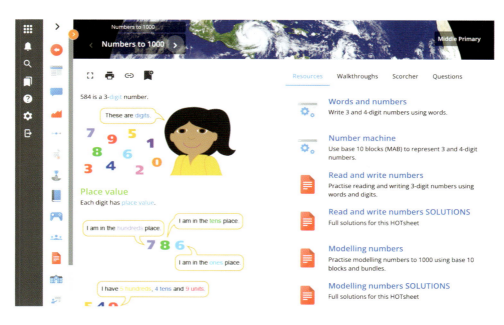

The Resources tab within lessons contains **widgets** (animations) and **HOTsheets** (activities). By clicking on the 'Words and numbers' link, you will access the widget below. Clicking the 'Read and write numbers' link will give you access to the HOTsheet below.

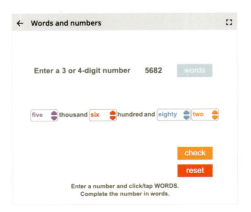

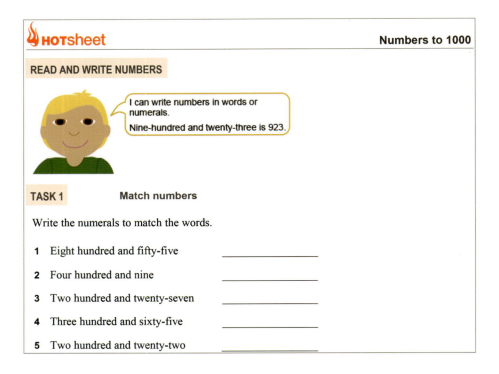

The toolbar at the left-hand side each lesson page is also the location for the **search** function, where you can enter the name of any widget or HOTsheet for quick access. The results page will automatically display widgets based on the keywords searched, indicated by the widgets tab being highlighted in blue. If you are looking for a HOTsheet, simply click onto the required tab and the results will appear. Using the above HOTsheet as an example, searching 'Read and write numbers' and clicking on the 'Hotsheet' tab will provide you a link to the Read and Write Numbers HOTsheet. You can also narrow your search results to a specific topic using the additional dropdown.

Throughout this textbook you will find numerous references to resources from HOTmaths. Please note that given its nature HOTmaths is constantly being updated. All resources mentioned are live as of May 2023 and every effort has been made to provide you with an accurate picture of the functions within HOTmaths. More detailed information about HOTmaths's features and functionality can be found via the Help tab at www.hotmaths.com.au.

ACKNOWLEDGEMENTS

The authors and Cambridge University Press would like to thank the following for permission to reproduce material in this book.

ACARA material: © Australian Curriculum, Assessment and Reporting Authority (ACARA) 2014 to present, unless otherwise indicated. This material was downloaded from the ACARA website (www.acara.edu.au) and Australian Curriculum website (https://v9.australiancurriculum.edu.au/) and was not modified. The material is licensed under CC BY 4.0 (https://creativecommons.org/licenses/by/4.0/). ACARA does not endorse any product that uses ACARA material or make any representations as to the quality of such products. Any product that uses material published on this website should not be taken to be affiliated with ACARA or have the sponsorship or approval of ACARA. It is up to each person to make their own assessment of the product.

Figure 2.1: © Getty Images/Amy Bader. **Figures 2.12** and **7.2**: Scootle images licensed under CC BY-SA 3.0 AU, https://creativecommons.org/licenses/by-sa/3.0/au/. **Figures 3.1** and **13.1**: © Getty Images/JohnnyGrieg. **Figure 3.2 (top left)**: © Getty Images/Tim Grist Photography. **Figure 3.2 (top right)**: © Getty Images/Fernando Trabanco Fotografía. **Figure 3.2 (bottom left)**: © Getty Images/Carolyn Hebbard. **Figure 3.2 (bottom right)**: © Getty Images/Lacy Washburn. **Figure 3.14**: © Getty Images/Annabelle Breakey. **Figure 7.3**: This material may be used in accordance with the Creative Commons Attribution-ShareAlike 3.0 Australia (CC BY-SA 3.0 AU) licence, https://creativecommons.org/licenses/by-sa/3.0/au/. **Figure 8.11**: © 2022 The Concord Consortium (concord.org). This material was downloaded from the concord.org website (accessed August 2022) and was not modified. This material is licensed under CC BY 4.0 (https://creativecommons.org/licenses/by/4.0/). **Figures 10.5–10.10** and **19.3**: © Australian, Curriculum, Assessment and Reporting Authority (ACARA). Permission to reproduce obtained. ACARA does not endorse this publication or make any representations as to its quality. This publication should not be taken to be affiliated with ACARA or have the sponsorship or approval of ACARA. **Figure 11.7**: © Jamboard™ electronic whiteboard is a trademark of Google LLC. This book is not endorsed by or affiliated with Google in any way. **Figure 11.12**: The software is provided 'as is', without warranty of any kind, express or implied, including but not limited to the warranties of merchantability, fitness for a particular purpose and noninfringement. in no event shall the authors or copyright holders be liable for any claim, damages or other liability, whether in an action of contract, tort or otherwise, arising from, out of or in connection with the software or the use or other dealings in the software. **Figure 13.3**: © Australian Curriculum, Assessment and Reporting Authority (ACARA) 2020. This material was downloaded from the (lpofai.edu.au/) website (accessed August 2022) and was not modified. This material is licensed under CC BY 4.0 (https://creativecommons.org/licenses/by/4.0/). **Figures 14.2** and **14.3**: Scratch is developed by the Lifelong Kindergarten Group at the MIT Media Lab. See http://scratch.mit.edu. Images licensed under CC BY-SA 2.0, https://creativecommons.org/licenses/by-sa/2.0/.

Table 2.1: © State of New South Wales (Department of Education), 2019. This material was downloaded from the (education.nsw.gov.au) website (accessed August 2022) and was not modified. This material is licensed under CC BY 4.0 (https://creativecommons.org/licenses/by/4.0/)

Every effort has been made to trace and acknowledge copyright. The publisher apologises for any accidental infringement and welcomes information that would redress this situation.

TEACHING MATHEMATICS TODAY WITH TOMORROW IN MIND

CHAPTER 1

CLASSROOM SNAPSHOT 1.1

Mr Brookes held his grand-daughter's hand and proudly walked into her Year 4 classroom. It was Grand-Friends Day, and he was looking forward to seeing what Bonnie was achieving – particularly in mathematics, his favourite subject while at school. He remembered the feeling of achievement when his page was filled with a column of ticks.

Mr Brookes looked around the room, and already he was feeling a little uneasy. On one wall he saw a display of some contextual addition problems with different techniques such as a jump method, split method and compensation method. He thought, what is wrong with lining up the two numbers, beginning with the units column, and borrowing and pay-back? Next to the strategies that were already disturbing him, he saw the formal strategy with which he was familiar; however, it was labelled with words such as 'trade'.

On closer inspection of the displays, he observed that the students had made their own metre rulers, they had traced around their feet on grid paper and used string to find the perimeter, and they had built as many different rectangular prisms as they could with 24 small cubes. There were group results on the wall of throwing dice and tabulating the results, and another activity that involved strips of paper that were as long as the height of each student, which were used to find the average height of the class by breaking the strips into pieces until they were approximately the same length. In another display, he saw patterns being explored on the 100 chart. He couldn't believe his eyes when he saw times tables presented next to rows and columns of dots.

Mr Brookes was about to ask Bonnie whether he could look in her exercise book when he noticed an electronic board of some kind on the wall where he expected to see the chalkboard. On this board – which Bonnie called the interactive whiteboard – a group of students were predicting the shape that would be made (the cross-section) when they cut an object at particular positions. After choosing the shape, they cut the object with a virtual knife and checked their solution. On another table, two students were sharing an iPad, creating as many different four-sided figures as they could, and then exploring everything they could find out about the shapes. On the far side of the classroom, three students sat at computers and were entering the data about the area and perimeter of the student's feet in the class into a special program. When he turned to see what three other students were doing on computers at the back of the room, he noticed that they were completing a series of review questions against the clock.

> The changes that had occurred in the classroom since Mr Brookes had visited his own children's classroom were undeniable. He could see that the students had been doing mathematics, but he was astounded by the variety of the concepts covered, how the tasks were accessible to all students, the level of engagement in the class, and the use of concrete materials with computers and mobile technology. Bonnie proudly shared her achievements, but they weren't about the number of ticks in her maths book. Instead, she showed her mathematics discoveries and the interesting findings she had recorded electronically in her maths journal, accessed through google classroom.

Today's classroom

Teacher education, at all levels, requires a resource that will address issues surrounding the teaching of mathematics within the broad and ever-changing context of particular classroom settings. To meet this need, this book is grounded in empirically evidenced developmental models and linked closely to practical classroom practice. While many classrooms have been resourced with equipment such as base-10 materials, counters, shape kits, mobile devices, dice kits, drawing tools and interactive whiteboard technology, and even a laptop trolley in some cases, extensive professional development is required to enable the range of classroom resources to be transformed into teaching tools. The difficulty faced by the teaching profession is in integrating a wide range of teaching approaches and resources to weave a pedagogically sound learning sequence. This book provides mathematics teachers and pre-service teachers with detailed teaching activities that are designed and informed by research-based practices. The aim is to provide you with a sensible and achievable integration of available educational tools, with research-based approaches to mathematical development that provide for the mathematical needs of all learners. As such, it is intended for primary pre-service teachers, and teachers looking for ways to enhance their teaching of primary mathematics, to assist them to design student tasks that are meaningful and to use educationally sound ways to improve their mathematics teaching.

In writing the book, we were guided by a moral imperative: we wanted students to be engaged in tasks designed to develop mathematical conceptual understanding in purposeful ways. Pre-service teachers are asked to consider the wealth of strategies and resources available to enhance students' learning. It is hoped that this book will encourage you to teach school children to become successful learners who are prepared for and responsive to the dynamic demands of the future.

As the expectation of accreditation increases, teachers around the world are being asked to consider issues such as student diversity, behaviour management and assessment for learning techniques within the key learning areas. Another contentious – but very real – issue is the impact of external assessment 'of' learning, in the form of national testing. Mathematics teachers are asking, 'How can we use this information to enhance the mathematics learning in our classroom?'

In many countries, we have reached a crisis point in relation to staffing schools with mathematics teachers in rural and remote areas. The problem is not being addressed, and 'out of field' teachers of mathematics – such as primary-trained teachers working in the secondary setting – need a tool kit to assist them to design student-centred mathematics activities. As in any teaching area, if the appropriate knowledge base is not strong, teachers resort to teaching in the manner in which they were taught in an effort to survive the situation. Australia and the wider Pacific region are not in a position to fill these vacancies with qualified teachers of mathematics. We need to accept this situation and to consider ways of supporting 'out of field' teachers while the workforce in this area grows.

More recently, there has been a shift in some state-level education departments to mandate teaching styles and strategies that are in conflict with the student-centred teaching strategies that are explored in the following chapters. We challenge readers to reflect upon the nature of external directives and the impact these have on mathematical learning in your classroom and future classrooms.

Throughout the remaining 18 chapters of this book, the contents of each chapter are informed by evidenced-based research into how students develop mathematical concepts and how to create teaching environments conducive to engagement in mathematical learning. You will come across a wide variety of teaching approaches throughout the book, with the aim of integrating theory with practice while the student remains the centre of the learning process.

Approaches to teaching mathematics

There are many ways to teach mathematics. They lie on a continuum from teacher-directed to student-centred. In teacher-directed approaches, the teacher makes all decisions about what to learn and when to teach it. The curriculum takes precedence and student needs are discounted.

Student-centred approaches, as the name suggests, place the student as a learner at the centre of decisions about teaching. The teacher is sensitive to the needs of individual students and plans learning experiences for each student accordingly. In practice, most teachers use some mix of these extremes. Broadly speaking, student-centred teaching is based on **constructivism** which has its roots in the work of Piaget (1936) and Vygotsky (1978).

In contrast, teacher-centred approaches are based in **behaviourism** (Skinner 1968) where the teacher maintains total control over the classroom and teaching consists of transmitting knowledge in various ways. Students work individually on exercises and are passive learners. Rote learning and practice are important reinforcers.

Both constructivism and behaviourism have led to teaching methods that are heavily criticised. Although it is beyond the scope of this book to examine approaches to learning and teaching in detail, the different ways of thinking about teaching mathematics impact on classrooms and teachers. Some of the teaching methods advocated are examined here with particular reference to learning and teaching mathematics. It should be noted that the Australian Curriculum: Mathematics F–10 v. 9.0 does not advocate any single approach to teaching mathematics. Rather it emphasises the content, processes and expected standards that students should experience and acquire across the years of schooling.

Constructivism the notion that individuals *construct* new knowledge based on prior experiences and social interactions. Knowledge is actively developed rather than passively acquired

Bahaviourism an approach to understanding human behaviour that assumes that learning develops from stimuli in the environment reinforced by reward or punishment

ACTIVITY 1.1

Link 1.1 Australian Curriculum, Understand this learning area: Mathematics

Go to the Australian Curriculum: Mathematics F–10 v. 9.0 and read 'Understand this learning area'.

1. Summarise the Rationale in 100 words so that you could explain it to a Year 6 student.
2. Read the section on Proficiency in Mathematics, including the explanation of each proficiency. Which of these proficiencies did your own mathematical education nurture?
3. Read the sections on Mathematical processes, Mathematical modelling and Computational thinking. As you read the rest of this section on Approaches to Teaching Mathematics, consider how each approach supports the development of both the proficiencies and the mathematical processes, modelling and computational thinking.

Make notes on each of the three activities above and share your thinking with a colleague.

The approaches to teaching mathematics suggested in this book are broadly constructivist and student-centred in nature. Collaboration, discussion and investigation with and between students are emphasised. Such an approach is not, however, 'anything goes'. The activities suggested are all carefully planned by the teacher to ensure that appropriate learning outcomes are met.

You will meet, while on practicum and in your teacher education, a number of terms to describe teaching. Many of these are strongly advocated for particular situations, and all have attracted criticism. Some of these teaching and learning ideas are described here as they apply to mathematics.

Discovery learning

Discovery learning was strongly advocated by Bruner (1961) who argued that students who 'discover' concepts for themselves are more likely to remember them. Discovery and investigations work closely together. The role of the teacher may appear to be minimal, because students are expected to 'struggle' with the ideas. There is considerable debate, however, about how effective it is to let students work on their own with no guidance. Unstructured discovery may lead to frustration, especially if students do not have the essential underpinning knowledge required to complete the task. Carefully structured tasks, however, can lead to students developing deep understanding of the target concept. As an example, consider Activity 3.8, which addresses the relationship between perimeter and area. This is a carefully structured investigation about the areas of rectangles with a given perimeter (16 cm) that will lead to the 'discovery' that different shapes with the same perimeter do not necessarily have the same areas.

Classroom Snapshot 14.2 provides a different kind of discovery. The students are provided with a carefully developed design brief in an integrated STEM setting. The mathematics outcomes are less clearly targeted, and may not be the same for all groups or individuals. Such open outcomes should not negate the mathematical learning experience. Rather the discoveries can provide a basis for more targeted mathematics learning activities.

The teacher's role is critical in discovery learning. Through the tasks chosen, responses to student questions and guidance during the activity teachers can draw attention to the ideas at the heart of the learning intention – that is, what the students need to learn.

Investigations

Not all investigations are linked to discovery. Some are integral to the domain within mathematics. For example, the PPDAC (Problem, Plan, Data, Analysis, Conclusion) cycle (see Chapter 8) is at the heart of learning statistics. This approach to teaching and learning statistics mirrors how statisticians work. Students are involved in working like statisticians, albeit using simpler statistical tools. For example, look at Classroom Snapshot 8.2, in which students discuss how to collect data for the investigation. Rather than discovering a concept, they are developing the habits of working statistically.

Mathematical modelling

Mathematical modelling is emphasised in the Australian Curriculum: Mathematics v. 9.0. In Year 1, for example, students

> use mathematical modelling to solve practical problems involving additive situations, including simple money transactions; represent the situations with diagrams, physical and virtual materials, and use calculation strategies to solve the problem. (AC9M1N05)

By Year 6, students

> use mathematical modelling to solve practical problems, involving rational numbers and percentages, including in financial contexts; formulate the problems, choosing operations and efficient calculation strategies, and using digital tools where appropriate; interpret and communicate solutions in terms of the situation, justifying the choices made. (AC9M6N09)

Modelling approaches make explicit links between mathematics and real problems, and this emphasis has implications for teaching mathematics. Although abstract mathematics still has a place, the application of mathematics takes greater precedence. Solving word problems such as 'Tom has five marbles and Jemma has seven marbles. How many marbles do Tom and Jemma have altogether?' are not modelling a real situation, whereas setting up a shop, using play money and asking students to record the amounts of money and goods changing hands is building a simple model of transactions that young children are aware of. Answering questions such as 'Can I afford it?' and 'How much do I need to save each week to buy … ?' are examples of real problems that mathematical modelling can help with. The Think Board shown in Figure 6.6 is another type of model.

Explicit teaching

Explicit teaching means having clear goals for teaching and sharing these with the students. In Classroom Snapshot 12.3, for example, the aim of the lesson is to develop understanding of the relationship between the diameter and circumference of the circle. This is shared with the students at the start of the work, making the learning intentional, but the activity involves an open investigation in which students explore the relationship in different ways. Typically, an explicit teaching sequence always includes some form of summary or wrap-up, where students share what they have learned with respect to the intention expressed at the start. The actual activities used during the explicit teaching sequence may vary and be quite open-ended. They are not limited to teacher directed drill and practice.

The ending summary used in explicit teaching is a useful technique for any approach to teaching because it provides a time when students have to consolidate their learning. This summary may take the form of a discussion, a report, a video, a diagram or picture and so on.

Direct teaching

Direct teaching has similarities to explicit teaching in that there is a defined goal but the steps towards that goal are standardised and taught in sequence, and do not allow for different student understandings. Developed initially for literacy, there are now many programs based on this idea. Some of these have a script for teachers to follow, and each mathematical procedure is broken into very small components. Students often have to repeat out loud what the teacher says, and they follow the procedure exactly. For teaching specific algorithms this process is very effective, and research indicates that students improve when tested using narrow, algorithmically based assessments (Przychodzin et al. 2004). Ewing (2011), however, provided an overview from an Australian perspective concluding that 'a direct instruction approach to the teaching and learning of mathematics is strongly associated with student non-participation and disengagement in mathematics' (p. 84).

Another form of direct instruction is provided by commercial web-based programs. The teacher becomes a 'tutor' as each student works through an individualised program. Such programs are also limited to developing mathematical skills, although they are somewhat more tailored to individual student needs.

Targeted teaching

Targeted teaching uses an evidence base to plan programs and activities that will meet the needs of students in a defined group. Prior to starting a set of lessons, the teachers assess the position of each student in relation to the target concept or 'big idea'. Planning aims to provide a set of rich tasks or activities that every student can attempt and which will move their understanding forward, regardless of their starting point (Goss et al. 2015; Siemon & Callingham 2019). At the end of the teaching sequence, assessment focuses on growth rather than what students have failed to learn.

In many ways, targeted teaching and explicit teaching share some characteristics. Both have clear learning intentions, but targeted teaching is more focused on the evidence base and growth against a defined concept or 'big idea'. Both can use open-ended approaches including investigations, mathematical modelling and discovery learning. Both require skilled teacher input.

Activity 18.1 shows another approach to targeted teaching. The quick, on-the-run assessments made by the education support worker under the direction of the teacher provide a basis for planning for mathematics learning.

> **PAUSE AND REFLECT**
>
> Think about the approaches to teaching described here. How do these fit with your own views and philosophy of teaching? Which approaches would you be comfortable using? Which would be challenging to you?
>
> As you read further in this book, you will meet many examples of teaching in different situations. Consider how these would impact on you as a teacher.

While this book is relevant to the teaching of mathematics in many nations, particular reference is made to the Australian curriculum documents. However, the content can be related to most primary mathematics curriculum structures. The Australian Curriculum: Mathematics F–10 v. 9.0 has six content strands: Number, Algebra, Measurement, Space, Statistics and Probability. The syllabus includes stage outcomes, stage statements, content outcomes, content descriptions, elaborations and links to the Numeracy Progressions. Curriculum documents are under development and will include updated support materials such as assessment and teaching mathematics for children with special needs. Readers are encouraged to relate the ideas explored in this book to their own context and curriculum structure.

The next section provides the reader with an advance organiser that presents a summary of the key objectives of the remaining 18 chapters in the book.

Summary of chapters

Chapter 2: Exploring early mathematical development examines the key ideas associated with learning early number concepts. Readers will become familiar with counting principles and how they underpin number understanding. The capacity of learning frameworks and curriculum documents to guide teaching early number concepts is explored. The effective use of technology to develop an understanding of early number concepts is examined through active engagement in a number of different activities designed to help you think about and evaluate the role of technology as a teaching tool.

Chapter 3: Exploring measurement presents the measurement sequence used to introduce and develop an understanding of each measurement attribute – that is, length, area, volume and capacity; angle, mass, time, temperature; and money and value. The principles of measuring with units will be explored and the importance of developing estimation skills and meaningful benchmarks emphasised. Strategies for utilising varied classroom resources to support, develop and extend students' measurement experiences are addressed.

In *Chapter 4: Exploring geometry*, we consider the breadth of concepts included in the geometry section of curriculum documents generally, and in the Australian Curriculum: Mathematics v. 9.0 in particular. The chapter presents a theoretical framework, known as the van Hiele theory, as a lens through which to view students' geometrical thinking and a pedagogical framework that is useful for designing sequential student tasks to assist students to grow in their understandings of geometrical concepts. The important role of language and maintaining 'student ownership' of the geometrical ideas is explored, as is the use of technological tools to enhance our teaching of geometrical concepts for the e-generation.

The difference between additive and multiplicative thinking and the appropriate use of drill and practice activities are both explained in *Chapter 5: Exploring whole number computation*. This chapter explores various representations that teachers can use to illustrate different ways of thinking and the effective use of the range of technological tools available to explore whole number computation.

Chapter 6: Part-whole numbers and proportional reasoning investigates the importance and representation of part-whole numbers such as fractions, decimals and percentages. The importance of understanding proportional reasoning concepts in daily life is explored, together with strategies for using technology effectively in this domain.

Underpinning *Chapter 7: Exploring patterns and algebra* is an understanding of the central importance of patterns in early childhood and primary school mathematics, and the importance of mathematical structure and its relevance to children's learning of mathematics. The chapter explores the process of using sequences effectively to find and justify rules and to explain phenomena. Strategies for representing and resolving number sentences, equivalence and equations are presented. Effective teaching approaches to explore algebraic situations where students are encouraged to describe relationships between variables are investigated.

Chapter 8: Exploring data and statistics examines suitable statistics questions for investigation by children of different ages, using a cycle of problem, plan, data, analysis and conclusion (PPDAC) (Wild & Pfannkuch 1999). The importance of variation in data and different types of variables and the difference between a population and a sample are investigated. Readers will explore different ways of displaying data to 'tell a story'. The importance of drawing inferences from data and the uncertainty associated with these inferences are discussed. Readers will engage in activities that use technology to support the development of statistical understanding.

Chapter 9: Exploring chance and probability begins with a consideration of the difference between objective and subjective views of probability. A range of tools for investigating probability are explored, and applications of probability in daily life are provided. Strategies for using technology effectively to develop ideas about uncertainty in the primary classroom are presented.

Chapter 10: Capitalising on assessment for, of and as learning focuses on the notion of assessment 'for', 'of' and 'as' learning, and how these forms of assessment work together in the mathematics classroom. A developmental framework to assist in designing an assessment item and assessing the quality of a student's response – the Structure of the Observed Learning Outcome (SOLO) model (Biggs & Collis 1982) – is presented. Issues surrounding national testing data are raised in the light of positive ways to support growth in mathematical understanding. Readers will engage with various educational tools that can assist in creating valid assessment items.

Chapter 11: Planning for mathematics teaching in the 21st century classroom outlines the considerations that need to be taken into account when planning effective mathematics lessons. The chapter explores different teaching approaches, lesson phases and teaching practices that facilitate thinking. Activities in this chapter include suggestions as to how technology can be incorporated into classroom routines and how classroom-based lessons can be adapted for online learning.

Chapter 12: Diversity in the primary mathematics classroom raises issues concerning the complexity of primary mathematics classrooms and a range of potential barriers to learning mathematics experienced by many students. Strategies for planning for diversity in the mathematics classroom are explored; these utilise the potential of technology to meet all learners' mathematical needs.

Chapter 13: General capabilities and cross-curriculum priorities describes the seven general capabilities and three cross-curriculum priorities that are named in the Australian Curriculum v. 9.0 and suggests ways in which they can be addressed through appropriate mathematics teaching. A range of contexts is presented that demonstrate how the general capabilities and cross-curriculum priorities can be accessed through mathematics, and vice versa.

Chapter 14: STEM in the primary setting explores the nature of STEM in the primary context and considers issues and debates pertinent to the implementation of a STEM strategy. Teaching strategies such as coding and robotics are presented, alongside practical real-life mathematical scenarios that link STEM-related careers and primary students' life experiences.

In *Chapter 15: Surviving as an 'out of field' teacher of mathematics* we identify issues pertinent to 'out of field' teachers of mathematics. Strategies are offered to assist 'out of field' teachers of mathematics while considering the invaluable knowledge a primary-trained teacher can bring to the secondary mathematics classroom. Examples are presented of teachers' critical pedagogical content knowledge that has a high impact on students' growth and development across the main strands of the curriculum.

Chapter 16: Teaching mathematics beyond the urban areas delves into the challenges and rewards of working in remote areas of countries such as Australia and New Zealand, and small Pacific nations. Teaching strategies are presented to assist in maintaining a positive learning environment in remote and small Pacific-nation classrooms. The importance of the relationships among and between parents, students, teachers and other community members is explored, along with practical suggestions for making the most of the available resources. The chapter demonstrates that, even with limited or no internet access, information and communication technology (ICT) can still be utilised as a tool to enhance and extend upon more traditional classroom materials; it is about making the most of the tools and resources that are available.

Chapter 17: Digital technologies in the mathematics classroom reacquaints readers with pedagogical frameworks that support the use of ICT as a teaching tool and the different types of teacher knowledge required for effective teaching for numeracy. It provides opportunities to develop strategies for evaluating and reflecting upon teachers' own use of technology. The notion of a community of practice is explored, as are ways to establish one within your school. Strategies are presented for evaluating the use of online resources, and insights are provided into the change process and how school-wide approaches to teaching mathematics with ICT can be sustained.

Chapter 18: Education support roles considers the range of possible education support roles in the mathematics classroom that a teacher may work with. This chapter presents effective ways of working collaboratively with education support workers and explores positive planning of learning experiences which considers the affordances of various education support workers' roles.

Chapter 19: Becoming a teacher of mathematics addresses the challenges associated with moving from being a pre-service teacher into being a member of the teaching profession. It explores ideas associated with testing and the pressures this can place on students and teachers; collecting evidence of teaching effectiveness for both accreditation and personal development; keeping a professional portfolio; and becoming a full member of a professional learning community. At all times mathematics, and its teaching and learning, is at the centre of the discussion.

How to use this book

Each of the chapters includes common key components that provide different ways to consider the material.

- *Learning outcomes* describe the learning that is expected as a result of engaging with the different components of the chapter.
- *Key terms* identify and define the common terms that are used throughout the chapter.
- *Classroom snapshots* are short vignettes of real classroom situations that exemplify some pedagogical principles, including technology use.
- *Pause and reflect* sections are points where the reader is asked to think deeply about some specific issue or dilemma.
- *Activities* present a task or short investigation to enable the reader or students to become familiar with a tool or way of presenting mathematics in a technological environment.
- *Tips for online teaching* highlight ways of working productively with students in the online and mixed mode teaching environment.
- *Concepts to consider* provides reference to important mathematical concepts and background material that relate to the relevant content strand and ideas explored.
- *Guided student tasks* present practical tasks and questions at the end of the chapter to further explore mathematics education concepts and issues.
- *Further reading* sections at the end of each chapter provide some of the research background, as well as places to find other ideas and material.

As with all texts, the more engagement there is with the ideas and activities presented, the better the learning is likely to be. Educational resources are changing so fast that this book can present only what is available at a single point in time. Teachers starting their careers will find that what is new and cutting edge when they first enter the classroom is obsolete before they are ready to retire. Bonnie's grandfather probably used a slate and chalk when he started school. Bonnie's parents used a ballpoint pen and saw the introduction of whiteboards instead of chalkboards. In three generations, we have changed teaching from literally 'chalk and talk' to a dynamic and creative endeavour, in which the teacher and students are co-learners and partners. It is difficult to predict what skills and knowledge school students will need in the future, but it is hoped that this book will provide teachers with ways in which they can apply educational research to inform teaching practices that inspire mathematical development.

Online resources

Visit the book's online resources at www.cambridge.org/highereducation/isbn/9781009265171/resources to find links to a range of useful resources. This margin icon is used throughout the book to indicate that a weblink relating to the content under discussion or websites for exploration are available online. The weblink number and descriptor can be used to help you easily identify the link in the materials.

CHAPTER 2
EXPLORING EARLY MATHEMATICAL DEVELOPMENT

LEARNING OUTCOMES

By the end of this chapter, you will:

- have gained an understanding of early childhood mathematics education and relevant philosophies and approaches that underpin it
- be able to identify key ideas associated with learning early number concepts
- have become familiar with counting principles and how they underpin number understanding
- understand how learning frameworks and curriculum documents can be used to guide teaching early number concepts
- be able to use technology effectively to develop an understanding of early number concepts.

Introduction

While some may question whether mathematics can or should be explored with young children, a significant body of research provides compelling evidence that young children can and do explore complex mathematical ideas as part of their everyday lives (MacDonald 2018). While not necessarily engaging in formal mathematics, we believe that young children are capable of developing mathematical skills from a very young age and that young children have already engaged with a range of mathematical concepts and processes prior to beginning school.

Everyday experiences can 'provide many opportunities to engage with mathematical concepts and processes through play, exploration, routines and activities' (MacDonald 2018). Young children explore mathematics all the time – for example, when setting the table or sharing food – but often the mathematics in these situations may go unnoticed and unexplored. There has been a focus in recent years in early childhood education on 'play', and this is reflected in the Early Years Learning Framework for Australia (EYLF) (DEEWR 2009), which states that play is a context for learning that:

- allows for expression of personality and uniqueness
- enhances dispositions such as curiosity and creativity
- enables children to make connections between prior experiences and new learning
- assists children to develop relationships and concepts
- stimulates a sense of well-being. (DEEWR 2009, p. 9)

This chapter looks at appropriate early childhood pedagogy, particularly as it applies to the early learning of mathematics. The importance of play and recognition of children's prior learning is emphasised throughout. Although many of the experiences and learning documented focus on number, we acknowledge that children's early mathematical learning extends beyond number into areas such as geometry, measurement and spatial awareness.

Both the terms 'children' and 'students' have been used throughout this chapter according to the context in which they are discussed (i.e. it is more appropriate to use children in before school situations).

CLASSROOM SNAPSHOT 2.1

Two children, Anne and Sam, were playing on the class's road mat (see Figure 2.1).

Figure 2.1 A road mat

They had lots of different coloured cars and animals that were placed all over the mat. Anne was 'driving' her car down one road, and then she stopped when there was an elephant on the road. She said, 'I'll have to go back now and turn down that other street'. Sam then 'drove' his car into Anne's car, creating a crash. He then got a tow truck to come and take the car away. Anne got an ambulance and drove it quickly to the crash site, going down several different roads and making lots of turns. Later, Anne and Sam carefully parked the cars near the garages of the houses, so that all cars were allocated to a house.

PAUSE AND REFLECT

If you were a teacher observing the situation in Classroom Snapshot 2.1, what mathematics would you 'notice'? What opportunities are there for exploring the children's mathematical skills and understandings? What prior experiences might the children have had that enabled them to engage in this mathematical play?

Early childhood mathematics pedagogy

Early childhood the period from birth to 8 years of age

Recognition that **early childhood** educators require a range of pedagogical practices that particularly apply to educating young children has resulted in qualification and accreditation requirements in this sector. The National Quality Framework, which was developed by the Australian Children's Education and Care Quality Authority (ACECQA), provides a national approach to regulation, assessment and quality improvement for early childhood education and care across Australia. According to ACECQA (2018), the early years are 'critical for establishing self-esteem, resilience, healthy growth and capacity to learn'. These developments can be achieved through:

- improved educator to child ratios
- educators with increased skills and qualifications
- better support for children's learning and development through approved learning frameworks
- consistent, transparent information on educators, providers and services in the national registers. (ACECQA 2018)

In their position paper on Early Childhood Mathematics (AAMT & ECA 2006), the Australian Association of Mathematics Teachers (AAMT) recommended that early childhood educators should adopt a range of pedagogical practices that included the following:

Play a context for informal learning that allows for expression of personality and creativity

- Engage the natural curiosity of young children to assist in the development of the children's mathematical ideas and understandings.
- Use accepted approaches to early childhood education such as **play**, emergent, child-centred and child-initiated curriculum to assist young children's development of mathematical ideas.
- Recognise, celebrate and build upon the mathematical learning that young children have developed and use the children's methods for solving mathematical problems as the basis for future development.
- Provide appropriate materials, space, time and other resources to encourage children to engage in their mathematical learning.
- Focus on the use of language to describe and explain mathematical ideas, recognising the important role language plays in the development of all learning.

Link 2.1 AAMT and ECA: *Position Paper on Early Childhood Mathematics*

(For a full list of the practices, see the *Position Paper on Early Childhood Mathematics* available through the AAMT website.)

MacDonald (2018) has identified that part of an educator's role is to notice, explore and talk about mathematics with children. There are lots of opportunities for talking about mathematics, keeping in mind that the conversations should be as natural and playful as possible.

Transition to school

Early childhood research has recognised that early mathematical development begins before children enter formal schooling, and that it involves much more than just being able to count. Many children know a great deal of mathematics before they come to school, and they are likely to have developed a sense of what's 'fair' when sharing, and they can recognise a range of numbers and shapes. Along with capitalising on children's prior mathematical knowledge, the early childhood educator also needs to consider each child's mathematical disposition and help to promote their confidence, creativity and playfulness (MacDonald 2018). The term 'funds of knowledge' has been used to describe the skills and knowledge that have been historically and culturally developed to enable an individual or family to function within a given culture (Moll, Amanti, Neff & Gonzalez 1992). We believe that being aware of each child's funds of knowledge and integrating them into classroom activities creates a richer and more highly scaffolded learning experience for students.

HOME SNAPSHOT

Isaac's father was a builder. Isaac watched and helped his father with his work and the conversion of their home, together with all aspects of joinery, measuring, writing, plumbing and construction. Isaac's dad had a large toolbox in the kitchen, and Isaac also had his own workbench and tools. For more than two years, Isaac's favourite bedtime reading had been a builders' trade catalogue. Isaac often went camping with his father. His father was also very interested in maps and had hung some large old maps of Britain and New Zealand on the walls of their home. Together they often pored over the details of contemporary maps, relating them to the city in which they lived and the journeys that they would make.

Source: Adapted from Worthington 2018

PAUSE AND REFLECT

What funds of knowledge can you identify from the Home Snapshot? How would you as an early childhood educator gain access to these funds of knowledge?

The importance of play

Play is regarded as a significant feature of effective early years' pedagogy and has a focus on *how* children learn rather than *what* children learn (Tucker 2014). Play can take many forms and may include 'free-flow play' (Bruce 1991), where play is freely chosen by the child and is characterised by:

- child-initiated activity in a meaningful context
- child control and ownership of the activity by imagining, making decisions and predictions
- experimenting with strategies and taking risks in a safe context
- showing curiosity
- seeking pleasure from the essence of the activity.

According to Fisher (2010), to fully support mathematical development, playful activity requires adult involvement at some level; a balance of practitioner-led, practitioner-initiated and child-initiated activity is desirable. Others (e.g. Worthington 2018) warn against the 'pedagogization of play' that is 'planned' or 'structured' to meet curriculum targets (Worthington 2018, p. 254), resulting in play being marginalised and misunderstood. She argues that spontaneous and sustained social pretend-play that occurs in contexts that are meaningful to young children provide an ideal opportunity to promote mathematical behaviour.

Early number concepts

Together with general mathematical skills and understanding, children come to school with many ideas about number on which the teacher can build to develop understanding through making connections between home and school communities. The concepts of number and number operations can be understood through building a network of cognitive connections between concrete experiences, symbols, language and pictures. This assists children with *constructing their own knowledge*, which is the basic tenet of **constructivism** (von Glasersfeld 1996). The general principles of constructivism are based primarily on Piaget's notions of assimilation and accommodation. Assimilation refers to the use of an existing schema to give meaning to new ideas. Sometimes this requires restructuring of that network in order to *accommodate* the new experiences (Haylock & Cockburn 2008). Researchers have also recognised the importance of both the individual's construction of meaning and the social context within which this occurs (e.g. Simon 2000), leading to the realisation that children are actively contributing to their mathematical development.

It could be argued that counting and understanding number are at the heart of mathematics, and while many children will begin school knowing how to count, it is likely that they will vary considerably in what they know and how it can be demonstrated in practice. It is also important to recognise that learning to count requires a considerable background of experience, including the ability to be able to sort and categorise, the notion of 'more or less' and even the ability to distinguish between small numbers such as 1, 2, 3 (Haylock & Cockburn 2008). While the recitation of the number sequence up to 10 or even 20 is one indicator of a child's counting ability, there are a number of other understandings that are required. Siemon (2007, p. 2) identifies that early numeration involves:

- recognising one-to-one correspondence
- recognising that '3' means a collection of three, whatever it looks like
- recognising that the last number counted represents the total number in the collection
- recognising small collections to five without counting (**subitising**)
- matching words and/or numerals to collections less than 10 (knowing the number naming sequence)
- being able to name numbers in terms of their parts (**part-part-whole**)
- identifying one more, one less, what comes after and what comes before a given number.

Other authors have also agreed that there are a number of principles that can help us to understand how children have mastered this knowledge or assist us in supporting those

Constructivism a theory of learning whereby new knowledge is constructed on the basis of past experiences

Subitise recognise how many are in a set without counting

Part-part-whole the relationship between the parts of something and its whole

children who have not. While there are variations, the following principles, originally developed by Gelman and Gallistel (1978), have been identified as underpinning counting:

- *The one-to-one principle.* A child who understands the one-to-one principle knows that we count each item once.
- *The stable order principle.* A child who understands the stable order principle knows that the order of number names always stays the same. We always count by saying 1, 2, 3, 4, 5 … in that order.
- *The **cardinal** principle.* A child who understands the cardinal principle knows that the number they attach to the last object they count gives the answer to the question, 'How many … ?'
- *The abstraction principle.* A child who understands the abstraction principle knows that we can count anything – they do not all need to be the same type of object. So we can count apples, we can count oranges, or we could count them all together and count fruit.
- *The order irrelevance principle.* A child who understands the order irrelevance principle knows that we can count a group of objects in any order and in any arrangement, and we will still get the same number (Cotton 2010, p. 55).

Cardinality the understanding that the last number said in a count of objects is the same as the number of objects in the group

Cardinality is discussed further in 'Concepts to consider' at the end of the chapter.

ACTIVITY 2.1

Access the 'Every Child Counts' video, available through YouTube. It contains a number of examples of children struggling with correctly demonstrating the five counting principles. Try to identify which examples relate to which counting principles. What would you do as a teacher to develop these principles?

Link 2.2 'Every Child Counts'

Trusting the count

The term 'trusting the count' refers to the situation where children believe that counting the same collection again will produce the same result (Siemon et al. 2015). Children who have difficulty with counting large collections (e.g. 40 or more) might not understand that counting is a strategy to determine 'how many' and/or that the last number counted gives the answer to the question, 'How many?' (the cardinal principle). Trusting the count is an important precursor to learning more about place value and recognising, for example, that '10 of these' is 'one of these' (10 ones make ten, 10 tens make a hundred, and so on). Trusting the count is one of the 'big ideas' in number as identified by Siemon (2007), along with place value, multiplicative thinking, partitioning, proportional reasoning and generalising. For more about the big ideas, see Chapters 5, 6, and 7 in this book.

Number frameworks

The ways in which students demonstrate an understanding of the **counting principles** are commonly described using number or learning frameworks.

Counting principles the principles that govern and define counting: the one-to-one principle, the stable order principle, the cardinal principle, the abstraction principle and the order irrelevance principle (Gelman & Gallistel 1978)

Learning frameworks or learning trajectories provide a guide to the developmental progression through an area of learning. According to Clements and Sarama (2021), in mathematics, learning trajectories typically have three parts:

1. A mathematics goal which would include the big ideas of mathematics
2. A developmental path that learners progress to achieve that goal
3. Teaching practices matched to the levels of thinking in the developmental path.

For example, the First Steps Framework (Department of Education and Training WA 2004) includes a diagnostic map in which terms such as 'emergent', 'matching' and 'quantifying' are used to describe the phases through which students typically pass in developing a sense of number and operating with numbers.

The Count Me in Too Learning Framework in Number was initially developed by Wright (1994) and outlines how students move from using naïve strategies to adopting increasingly sophisticated strategies in order to solve number problems. Although the framework was developed more than 20 years ago, the description of the stages still provides a useful reference for developing children's arithmetical strategies (see Table 2.1).

Table 2.1 Model for development of early arithmetical strategies

Stage	Brief description
0: Emergent counting	The student cannot count visible items. The student either does not know the number words or cannot coordinate the number words with items.
1: Perceptual counting	The student is able to count perceived items and build numbers by using materials or using fingers as replacement markers to find the total count. The objects or fingers must remain constantly in view of the student. The student may also hear or feel the items when counting.
2: Figurative counting	The student is able to count concealed items and will typically visualise the items that he/she cannot see but always starts counting from 'one'. For example, when presented with a collection partitioned into two parts (both screened), told how many in each part and asked how many altogether, the student will count from 'one' instead of counting-on. However, when the total of two screened partitioned parts is greater than 'ten', the student may also use fingers as a crucial sensory link to represent the concealed items. For example, in solving 9 + 4; the student may count to 'nine', starting from 'one' while simultaneously raising his/her fingers. The process would be repeated when counting the 'four' and again for the total starting from 'one' each time.
3: Counting-on-and-back (Advanced count by one strategies)	The student counts-on rather than counting from 'one', to solve addition or missing addends tasks. The student may use a count-down-from strategy to solve removed items tasks (e.g. 17 – 3 as 16, 15, 14; answer 14) or count-down-to strategies to solve missing subtrahend tasks (e.g. 17 – 14 as 16, 15, 14; answer 3).

Source: Count Me in Too Learning Framework in Number (State of New South Wales Department of Education 2019)

The Count Me in Too resources also include a number of assessment and diagnostic tools that can be utilised to determine children's stages of development. For example, a very basic task requires the child to count a set of counters (e.g. 8, 15 or 27), with the aim being to observe whether the child correctly coordinates the number words with the items. Diagnostic tasks such as these are usually conducted through one-on-one interviews and can also be conducted online (e.g. The Early Numeracy Research Project conducted in Victoria).

ACTIVITY 2.2

If you can, conduct the following activity with a young child, aged 3–5 years.

Place a pile of 20 teddies (four yellow teddies, five red teddies, three green teddies and eight blue teddies) in front of the child in a scattered pattern. Ask the child to do the following:

Can you please put the yellow teddies together?
How many yellow teddies are there?

Next, place a group of three green teddies together near the four yellow teddies (giving two different small groups). Ask:

Are there more green teddies or more yellow teddies?
How many green and yellow teddies are there altogether?
What did you notice about how the child completed these tasks? What other questions could you ask?

Numeracy progressions

The National Learning Progressions (which are referred to more explicitly further on in this chapter in relation to the Australian Curriculum: Mathematics v. 9.0) also provide a framework or trajectory related to students' learning of key numerical concepts. The National Numeracy Learning progression outlines a sequence of observable indicators of increasingly sophisticated undertaking of and skills in key numeracy concepts. While the progression does not advise on how to teach, plan, program or assess, it does recognise the importance of the need to sequence numeracy development. Similar to the other frameworks discussed here, the progressions describe the learning pathways along which students typically progress in numeracy. For example, in number and place value (v. 3), sub-elements describe how a student becomes increasingly able to recognise, read, represent, order and interpret numbers within our place value system. Early indicators of pre-place value understanding include instantly recognising collections up to three without needing to count and using language to describe order and place. The next level of this indicator (developing place value) includes ordering numerals to at least 10 and demonstrating that one ten is the same as ten ones.

Linking with curriculum documents

National curriculum frameworks in Australia cover the early childhood years from ages 0–8. *Belonging, Being & Becoming: The Early Years Learning Framework for Australia* (DEEWR 2009) provides a holistic approach to learning and development and covers children from ages 0–5. The Australian Curriculum: Mathematics v. 9.0 (ACARA 2022), which is directed at school-aged children (ages 5–8), is focused on content and proficiencies, with more specific learning outcomes identified.

The Early Years Learning Framework

The EYLF outcomes and key components that are particularly relevant to mathematics are not explicit as specific learning areas are avoided (Perry, Dockett & Harley 2012). However, the following two outcomes and their components can be linked with mathematical development.

Outcome 4: Children are confident and involved learners
Components:
- Children develop dispositions for learning such as curiosity, cooperation, confidence, creativity, commitment, enthusiasm, persistence, imagination and reflexivity.
- Children develop a range of skills and processes, such as problem-solving, inquiry, experimentation, hypothesising, researching and investigating.

Outcome 5: Children are effective communicators
Components:
- Children begin to understand how symbols and pattern systems work.
- Children resource their own learning through connecting with people, places, technologies, and natural and processed materials.
- Children use ICT to access information, investigate ideas and represent their thinking. (DEEWR 2009)

The EYLF also makes reference to the use of technology and its role in supporting mathematical development: children 'use information and communication technologies (ICT) to investigate and problem solve' (DEEWR 2009, p. 37).

The implications for educators are that: children need to be provided with access to a range of technology; the technology needs to be incorporated into children's play experiences and projects; and skills and techniques need to be taught in order for children to use technologies to explore new information and represent their ideas (DEEWR 2009; Muir, Callingham & Beswick 2016).

The Australian Curriculum: Mathematics v. 9.0

The stable order principle, which refers to the key understanding that the number names are said in sequence and must be said in a particular order, is one of the first connections children make when counting. The ability to rote count and then extend to rational counting is fundamental to early number development. While many children will come to school able to rote count to 5, 10 or beyond, they are expected to further develop this in the Foundation Year of the Australian Curriculum: Mathematics v. 9.0. The descriptors related to Number for the Foundation Year are as follows:

- Name, represent and order numbers including zero to at least 20, using physical and virtual materials and numerals (AC9MFN01).

- Recognise and name the number of objects within a collection up to 5 using subitising (AC9MFN02).
- Quantify and compare collections to at least 20 using counting and explain or demonstrate reasoning (AC9MFN03).
- Partition and combine collections up to 10 using part-part-whole relationships and subitising to recognise and name the parts (AC9MFN04).
- Represent practical situations involving addition, subtraction and quantification with physical and virtual materials and use counting or subitising strategies (AC9MFN05).
- Represent practical situations that involve equal sharing and grouping with physical and virtual materials and use counting or subitising strategies (AC9MFN06).

Each content description includes a link to elaborations which provide suggestions of ways to teach the content description and connect it to the relevant general capabilities and cross-curriculum priorities. For example, the elaboration for AC9MFN02 includes: Recognising how many objects are in a collection or in images on a card with a quick look and saying the associated number without counting.

As explained in Chapter 13, many of the content descriptions contain links to the general capabilities, including numeracy. In version 9.0. of the Australian Curriculum: Mathematics, the numeracy icon links directly to the Numeracy Progressions. By providing a comprehensive view of numeracy learning and how it develops over time, the progression gives teachers a conceptual tool that can assist them to develop targeted teaching and learning programs for students who are working above or below year-level expectations (ACARA 2022). As an illustrative example, the numeracy link for AC9MFN02 aligns with the following numeracy learning progressions at level 2:

- Numeral recognition and identification: For example, identifies and names numerals in the range of 1–10 (e.g. when asked 'which is 3?' points to the numeral 3; when shown the numeral 5, says 'that's 5')
- Developing place value: For example, orders numbers represented by numerals to at least 10 (e.g. uses number cards, or a number track and places the numerals 1–10 in the correct order).

ACTIVITY 2.3

The extract above outlines the alignment of the learning progression for AC9MFN02 at level 2. Can you predict what the Levels 1 and 3 progression statements would include? Access the progression statements through the Numeracy icon link for this content descriptor and see how accurate you were. Familiarise yourself with the other progression statements across the different content areas.

The first section of this chapter has looked at appropriate pedagogies for developing early mathematical thinking in children, and early mathematical development as described in frameworks and curriculum documents. The next section of the chapter will focus on what experiences, strategies and approaches you can use as an early childhood educator to foster children's mathematical development, particularly in the domain of number.

Early number activities and strategies

Rhymes and stories

Nursery rhymes, number poems and counting books offer an engaging way to expose young children to numbers and how numbers are used. The stable order principle can be introduced and reinforced through rhymes and songs, and through counting story books such as *One is a Snail, Ten is a Crab* (Sayre & Sayre 2003) and *Ten Out of Bed* (Dale 2010). Rhymes and songs can be accompanied by actions, which also help to reinforce the principle of one-to-one correspondence, such as in the following songs:

> One, two, three, four, five
> Once I caught a fish alive.
> Six, seven, eight, nine, ten
> Then I let it go again
> Why did you let it go?
> Because it bit my finger so.
> Which finger did it bite?
> This little finger on my right.

and

> One little, two little, three little, four little,
> Five little birds so small;
> One little, two little, three little, four little,
> Five little birds on the wall.
> Kitty Cat came from a nearby bush … MEOW!
> Gave the garden gate a push … SQUEEEEAK!
> And one little, two little, three little, four little,
> Five little birds went WHOOSH!

Link 2.3 All Nursery Rhymes
Link 2.4 EFlashApps: 'Five Little Monkeys Jumping on the Bed'

As you sing, you can role-play using children or stuffed animals.

Many examples of rhymes and songs can be sourced on the internet – for example, on the All Nursery Rhymes website. A number of sites provide interactive elements, such as audio-recordings and video clips – for example, the animation of 'Five Little Monkeys Jumping on the Bed' at eFlashApps. YouTube has literally thousands of examples of animated rhyming songs for children. Simply enter 'counting songs for children' into the search field to begin exploring.

Many counting activities and games are also available as apps and can be downloaded for free or cheaply from the iTunes Store or its Android equivalent. 'Counting Bear' is an example of an application that is compatible with iPhones and iPads, and it focuses on consolidating the correct sequencing of counting numbers to 10.

Sequencing activities

One commonly used strategy that is popular in many early childhood classrooms involves the use of a clothesline where numbers are 'pegged' to designate their correct sequencing. This activity is extremely versatile, as the end numbers can be varied to represent, for example, 0 and 10, 0–20, 10–20 and even 0–1 for older children. Once the numbers have been placed in order, further teaching opportunities can occur such as looking at which number comes before and after, one more, one less, and what number comes between. Versions of this activity can also be found online and can be used either as substitutes for the real materials in the classroom or as follow-up activities to provide both reinforcement and individual consolidation. For a variation of this activity, see the Topmarks website which has an activity called Caterpillar Ordering where children can place the numbers in the correct order to form a caterpillar.

Link 2.5 Topmarks: Caterpillar Ordering

ACTIVITY 2.4

Access the Placing Numbers on a Number Line activity (see Figure 2.2) from the Mathsframe website.
- Play around with placing the numbers on the line. What happens when you place a card incorrectly?
- Do you think this activity would assist with developing an understanding of the correct ordering of numbers?
- What would be the advantages and disadvantages of doing this activity online as compared with using real materials in the classroom?

Link 2.6 Mathsframe: Placing Numbers on a Number Line

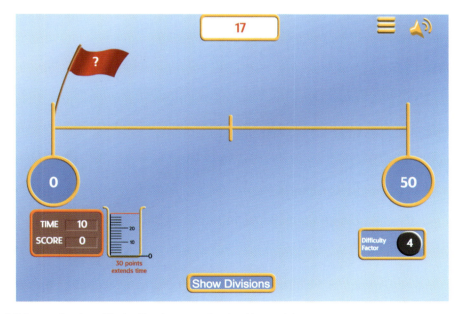

Figure 2.2 Screenshot from Placing Numbers on a Number Line activity
Source: Ted Burch/Mathsframe <https://mathsframe.co.uk/en/resources/resource/37/placing_numbers_on_a_number_line>

Opportunities for reinforcing sequencing and developing the stable order principle can also be found in picture books. While many picture books explicitly involve counting 1–10 (e.g. *Ten Black Dots* by Donald Crews (1996)), also look for picture books where the mathematics is implicit or unintended such as *Six Dinner Sid* (Moore 1991) or *The Very Hungry Caterpillar* (Carle 1994).

CLASSROOM SNAPSHOT 2.2

Ms Bragg chose the picture book *Six Dinner Sid* to read to her Foundation class. The story is about Sid, an insatiable cat, who lives at six houses on Aristotle Street and is fed six dinners a day unbeknownst to his different owners. One day Sid becomes ill and his secret is revealed. Ms Bragg selected the book as a stimulus for consolidating the stable-order principle, and because she noticed that some children in the class had difficulty with one-to-one correspondence. During and after the reading of the story, Ms Bragg asked key questions and encouraged active engagement in the story. Some examples are below.

- How many different people think they are Sid's owner?
- How many different names does Sid have?
- Let's count the different beds he sleeps in.

In order to encourage an understanding of ordinal numbers, she also asked:

- Who lives at the fifth house?
- What is Sid's third meal?

After reading the book, children were given the opportunity to role-play the story. Six children represented the six owners and lived at their respective houses (desks labelled 1–6). Each child placed a dinner bowl out for Sid and filled it with blocks to represent food. Children were then encouraged to count from 1 to 6 for each house, owner, food bowl and behaviour.

PAUSE AND REFLECT

Read Classroom Snapshot 2.2 and answer the following questions.
- How engaged do you think the students would be in the lesson?
- What difficulties could you anticipate students having with the activity?
- Where would you take the learning next?

Linking numbers with quantities

Classroom Snapshot 2.2 also demonstrates an experience that could be used to develop children's ability to recognise the relationship between the number name and the quantity it represents. Children need to understand that the numeral 5, for example, which can also be represented as 'five', can be used to show there are five objects. They also need to understand that a set of objects can be counted in any order or arrangement, and the result will be the same each time (order-irrelevance principle). Activities that reinforce this concept typically involve 'matching' experiences or drawing tasks that focus on the number words, symbols and visual representations. Often referred to as the Concrete, Representational, Abstract (CRA) sequence, teachers can help students to develop these understandings by moving from concrete representations that encourage learning through movement or action, to representations of drawings or pictures, and then on to learning through abstract symbols (symbolic) (Flores 2010). There are a number of interactive online resources that encourage children to make these links. For example, the Illuminations activity Concentration requires the user to match the numeral and name with representations showing various quantities. Similarly, Counting Birds (see Figure 2.3) in HOTmaths shows representations of these concepts and includes support materials in the form of HOTsheets (Collection Cards and Using Numbers to 10).

Link 2.7 Illuminations: Concentration

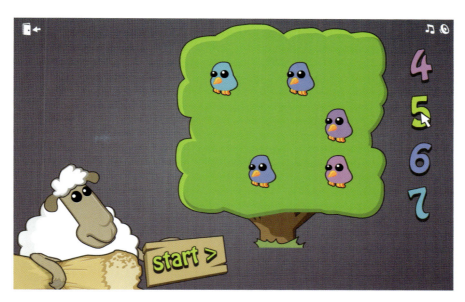

Figure 2.3 Screenshot of HOTmaths Counting Birds FUNdamentals activity

Drawing programs such as Kid Pix could be utilised for children to design their own representations, providing an alternative to the labour-intensive task of drawing and writing. If real materials were utilised, digital photographs could be used to record what was done physically, and these could be accompanied by audio-recorded verbal explanations.

Subitising

Subitising refers to the ability to recognise how many objects are in a group without counting. It is a fundamental skill in the development of number, and one that needs to be developed and practised through experiences with patterned sets and dot patterns. Subitising is a useful skill as it saves time, reduces cognitive load, develops number sense (particularly in terms of understanding the relative sizes of numbers) and accelerates addition and subtraction skills. Clements (1999) distinguishes between perceptual subitising, which is the immediate recognition of numbers up to four, and conceptual subitising, where groups can be recognised in terms of their subitised parts. The part-part-whole relationship that is developed through conceptual subitising is an important forerunner to both number and computational sense.

Appropriate materials to use in pattern-recognition activities include dot plates and 10-frames. Both can be made cheaply by using paper plates, cardboard and round sticky

Subitising is discussed further in 'Concepts to consider' at the end of the chapter.

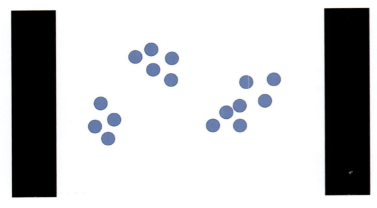

Figure 2.4 Dot patterns on a PowerPoint slide

dots. Alternatively, PowerPoint can be used effectively to produce a series of patterns that can be flashed up for a short, predetermined period of time (see Activity 2.5). When designing the aids, include variations of arrangements and gradually increase the number of dots shown (see Figure 2.4). When using the activity with children, ask questions such as the following.

- How many do you see?
- How do you know?
- Who saw something different?
- How many more do you need to make … ?

Interactive websites that support and reinforce subitising can also be used to complement and extend whole-class activities.

ACTIVITY 2.5

To create subitising flash screens using PowerPoint follow these steps:

1. Open PowerPoint.
2. Begin with a blank slide.
3. Click on the 'Select shapes' icon and select circle.
4. Copy the circle and paste in desired formation (e.g. see Figure 2.4).
5. Click on 'Insert new slide' and repeat as desired.
6. Begin with one formation, then extend into different variations and combinations.
7. To transition, select all dots and put a box around them.
8. Select 'cut' or 'fade' and 'advance slide' after one to three seconds (or select 'on mouse click' if you want children to explain what they see).

In her book *Number Sense Routines* Shumway (2011) discusses how 'quick images' can be organised in such a way as to enhance and extend children's subitising skills. She recommends using a variety of configurations and models to encourage children to think flexibly, and to consider selecting combinations that help to consolidate and reinforce mental strategies. For example, if you were encouraging children to use double facts (use of doubling, such as 8 + 8 = 16) to assist them with adding number combinations such as 8 + 7, this could be built by using dot cards or slides to visually display 7 + 8 as being two lots of seven and one additional dot (see Figure 2.5). Sequences to encourage this strategy can be devised using similar facts, such as 4 + 5, 6 + 7.

10-frames an array of two rows of five used to provide a visual representation of the base-10 number system

10-frames

10-frames are also useful tools for encouraging children to subitise and to build up an understanding of the part-part-whole relationship. Activities and routines with 10-frames

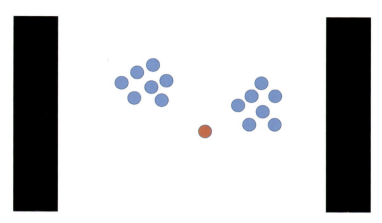

Figure 2.5 Dot formations to demonstrate doubling strategy on a PowerPoint slide

encourage students to think in groupings, and foster their development in using the five- and 10-structures of our number system (Muir, Callingham & Beswick 2016). The structure of the frame always shows a quantity's relationship to 10 and assists students with composing and decomposing 10, and hence the addition or subtraction combinations of 10 (Shumway 2011; Muir, Callingham & Beswick 2016). Classroom Snapshot 2.3, taken from a transcript of a lesson conducted with a Year 1 class, demonstrates how the teacher used 10-frames and an interactive whiteboard (IWB) to teach children how to use the strategy of bridging 10.

CLASSROOM SNAPSHOT 2.3

Teacher: We're going to talk about a different strategy that you can use today. So you could use knowing your doubles facts, you could use counting in ones or you could use this other strategy as well. And that's what we are going to learn today. Just to give you another way of working out maths problems. How does that sound?

Students: Good.

[Displays two 10-frames side by side on the screen, one showing eight and one showing seven.]

Teacher: So do you know what these are called?

Jake: Um, counters.

Teacher: Well, we do use them with counters, but we call them 10-frames. So the first step in using bridging 10, which is the strategy we're finding out about today, is to imagine these 10-frames in your head. So imagine an eight in your head and imagine a seven in your head. Do you think you can do that? Close your eyes and see whether you can see an eight in the frame in your head, or a 10-frame with an eight in your head. How many dots is it missing?

Jake: Um, two.

Teacher: Great. Now see if you can imagine a 10-frame with seven counters in your head for me. Cover up, your eyes are meant to be closed … How many are missing?

Students: Three.

Teacher:	Fantastic! Okay. This is what we do when we bridge 10. We make one of the 10-frames up into 10 by moving the dots. Which one would be the sensible one to move the dots in up here? [Referring to the two 10-frames showing eight and seven.]
Amit:	What do you mean by sensible?
Teacher:	So that you don't have to move too many dots.
Sarah:	From the yellow frame [showing seven] to the purple frame [showing eight].
Teacher:	Yes. Would you like to do that, Jack? Fill up the 10-frame showing eight from the 10-frame which shows seven.

[Jack uses his finger to move two counters from the frame showing seven, and fills up the other frame, leaving five counters in the right-hand frame.]

Teacher:	So, what have we got?
Sarah:	Five and 10, which makes 15.
Teacher:	Let's move them back and do it again. Sarah, would you like to do that – move the two dots back to the yellow frame?

[Sarah goes to the IWB and moves two dots from the first frame to the right-hand frame, leaving the original eight.]

Teacher:	Thank you. Roy, would you move those two dots over to the frame showing eight? So we're bridging 10 by moving two from the seven.

[Roy moves the two dots into the frame showing eight, filling it up.]

Teacher:	That's it. So we bridged 10 by moving two over on to the eight. What did we turn the eight into now?
Students:	Ten.
Teacher:	Yes, so we've got 10 and … ?
Sarah:	Five.
Teacher:	Makes … ?
Jade:	Fifteen.
Teacher:	Beautiful. Roy, could you put us onto the next slide?

PAUSE AND REFLECT

After reading the lesson transcript in Classroom Snapshot 2.3, reflect on the following:

- In what ways did the teacher capitalise on the features of the IWB to demonstrate and model the bridging 10 strategy?
- Do you think the lesson would have been as effective if each child had their own individual 10-frame in front of them and placed counters on it according to instructions? Why/why not?

There are also a number of websites that use 10-frames to reinforce the part-part-whole relationship, and their use can serve to reinforce the concepts discussed or modelled in class. A math learning app (see Figure 2.6) allows students to select ten frames and a range of different counters to place on the 10-frame. Whole-class discussions could occur around: How many do you see? How many more do we need to make 10? The selection of the 10-frame also provides for extension to 20, 30 and so on.

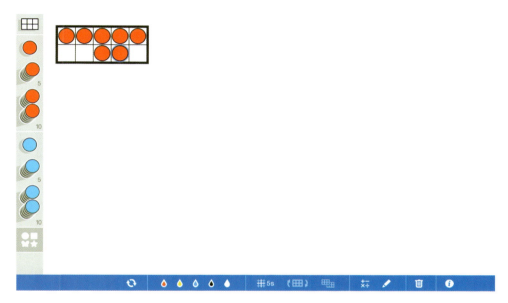

Figure 2.6 Screenshot from The Math Learning Center's Number Frames tool
Source: The Math Learning Center <https://apps.mathlearningcenter.org/number-frames/>

Extending counting beyond 10

As children develop increased facility with counting, they will learn to associate the name of the number with the numeral (e.g. one – 1, two – 2) and extend their counting beyond 10 to 20 and so on. The **hundreds square** (see Figure 2.7) provides a useful visual representation of the numbers 1–100, and it can assist with counting numbers up to 100. The spatial arrangement of numbers emphasises the ordinal aspect of number and the relationships associated with place value. Numbers are defined by their position in the chart – for example, 47 is in a square that is in a row between 46 and 48 and in a column between 37 and 57. Along with being an excellent tool for identifying patterns in the number system and demonstrating place value concepts, the hundreds square is often used in early childhood settings as an opportunity to engage in group counting and class discussions about the counting of numbers up to 100.

HOTmaths has a version of a 1–100 square activity called Hidden Numbers (see Figure 2.8), in which incorrect answers are noted and there are options to try again.

Hundreds square an array of 10 columns and rows depicting the numbers 1 to 100

1	2	3	4	5	6	7	8	9	10
11	12	13	14	15	16	17	18	19	20
21	22	23	24	25	26	27	28	29	30
31	32	33	34	35	36	37	38	39	40
41	42	43	44	45	46	47	48	49	50
51	52	53	54	55	56	57	58	59	60
61	62	63	64	65	66	67	68	69	70
71	72	73	74	75	76	77	78	79	80
81	82	83	84	85	86	87	88	89	90
91	92	93	94	95	96	97	98	99	100

Figure 2.7 Hundreds square

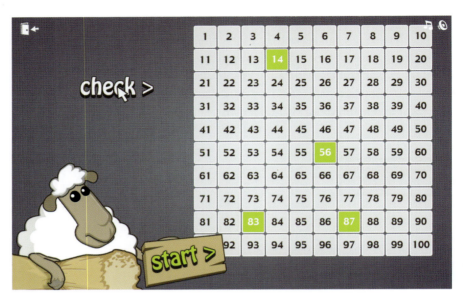

Figure 2.8 Screenshot of HOTmaths Hidden Numbers FUNdamentals activity

ACTIVITY 2.6

Link 2.8 Crickweb
Link 2.9 ABCya.com: Number chart

Investigate the range of interactive number charts that are available on the internet. Each of the examples below have different features and functions, and they each require different levels of interaction:

- Crickweb
- ABCya.com.

1. Consider how you would use the charts within the context of a lesson.
2. Would you incorporate the IWB and engage the whole class in modelling and demonstrating skip counting?
3. Would you encourage students to access the charts individually, in pairs or in small groups?

Counting strategies

Counting strategies such as counting on, counting back and skip counting are essential for developing skills to operate with numbers. Counting on occurs when children are given a particular number and asked to count on from there. They need to develop the ability to count on, and not begin from zero. For example, counting on from 5 (6, 7, 8, etc.), or when given the sum 6 + 3, begins counting on 3 from 6. This strategy is an appropriate one to use when beginning to add numbers, but it is only efficient if adding on 3 or less (see **mental computation** strategies section further on in this chapter). Counting back is the reverse of counting on and requires children to identify what comes before any given number. Counting back helps children with developing subtraction skills and, like counting on, is only efficient when subtracting 3 or less. Skip counting involves counting in multiples of any given number other than one. It encourages children to recognise patterns in number sequences and helps to develop children's multiplication and division skills.

Mental computation performance of mathematical computations in the mind without the aid of pen and paper or calculator

> **PAUSE AND REFLECT**
>
> Were you ever told not to count on your fingers? Have you ever told children not to count on their fingers? Neuroscience research has actually shown that an area of our brain 'sees' fingers, leading to recommendations that we should actually be encouraging students to use their fingers in mathematics classes and that it may well even be essential for mathematics achievement (Boaler & Chen 2016).

Early operations with number

According to Siemon (2007), the idea that the numbers up to 10 can be conceptualised as units in their own right is fundamental to establishing 10 as a countable unit. As children learn about number in terms of the part-part-whole relationship, these ideas can be related to addition and subtraction, with the numbers being seen as *composite units*. Similarly, multiplication and division require students to think about numbers as units (Van de Walle et al. 2013) – for example, in 4 × 3, each of the four threes is counted as a unit. The Australian Curriculum: Mathematics v. 9.0 expects that by Year 1, students will be able to recognise, represent and order numbers to at least 120, partition one-and two-digit numbers in different ways, and add and subtract numbers within 20. Specifically, the Year 1 Content Descriptions for Number in the Australian Curriculum: Mathematics v. 9.0 (ACARA 2022) are as follows:

- Recognise, represent and order numbers to at least 120 using physical and virtual materials, numerals, number lines and charts (AC9M1N01).
- Partition one- and two-digit numbers in different ways using physical and virtual materials, including partitioning two-digit numbers into tens and ones (AC9M1N02).
- Quantify sets of objects, to at least 120, by partitioning collections into equal groups using number knowledge and skip counting (AC9M1N03).
- Add and subtract numbers within 20, using physical and virtual materials, part-part-whole knowledge to 10 and a variety of calculation strategies (AC9M1N04).
- Use mathematical modelling to solve practical problems involving additive situations including simple money transactions; represent the situations with diagrams, physical and virtual materials, and use calculation strategies to solve the problem (AC9M1N05).
- Use mathematical modelling to solve practical problems involving equal sharing and grouping; represent the situations with diagrams, physical and virtual materials, and use calculation strategies to solve the problem (AC9M1N06).

ACTIVITY 2.7

In addition to the six content descriptors listed above for Number, the Australian Curriculum: Mathematics v. 9.0 also contains two content descriptors for Algebra for Year 1. Access the Australian Curriculum: Mathematics v. 9.0 and look at the Algebra content descriptors for the early years. Are any included for Foundation Year? Many of the descriptors for Algebra refer to numbers and counting – why do you think they are included under Algebra and not Number?

Addition and subtraction

Addition and subtraction are related: addition names the whole in terms of the parts and subtraction names a missing part (Van de Walle et al. 2013). Researchers have separated addition and subtraction problems into categories based on the types of action or relationship described in the problems (Carpenter et al. 1999). Cognitive guided instruction (CGI) describes four basic classes of problems that can be identified for addition and subtraction: join, separate, part-part-whole and compare. Within these structures there are different quantities involved and various actions that are undertaken to solve the problem. For example, the following problem involves a situation where the two quantities are *joined*, and the result is unknown.

- John had 3 toy cars. Michael gave him 6 more toy cars. How many toy cars does John have now?

Consider how this structure is different in the following problem.

- John has 3 toy cars. Michael gave him some more. Now John has 9 toy cars. How many did Michael give him?

In the second problem, the result and the initial amount are known, but the change is unknown.

Similarly, separate problems also involve different actions, whereby the result, the change or the initial amount can be unknown. Can you identify the different structures in the following problems?

- Oscar had 9 toy cars. He gave 3 toy cars to Dong. How many toy cars does Oscar have now?
- Oscar had 9 toy cars. He gave some to Dong. Now he has 7 toy cars. How many did he give to Dong?
- Oscar had some toy cars. He gave 3 to Dong. Now Oscar has 6 toy cars left. How many toy cars did he have to begin with?

This focus on different problem structures, the analysis of story problems and the importance of teachers' interpretation of student responses are key components of the CGI program, which is highly regarded in the United States. Developed by Carpenter and colleagues (1999), the program provides a framework for teachers to consider students' mathematical thinking, and workshops demonstrate how to put this framework into practice in the classroom. A number of resources (including examples of video footage of children carrying out activities) are available to help teachers with developing their own pedagogical content knowledge in this area.

> **PAUSE AND REFLECT**
>
> Think back to the types of problems you were asked to solve in your mathematics classes. How many of them were typically of the 'result unknown' type? What do you see as the limitations in teachers providing students only with these types of problems? What are the benefits of exposing students to a variety of problem types?

Mental computation strategies

As children are exposed to a variety of situations that require them to use addition and subtraction, they should be encouraged to make use of mental computation strategies to assist them to solve these types of problems. As demonstrated earlier in this chapter, bridging 10 was an appropriate strategy to use to solve 8 + 7. McIntosh and Dole (2005) endorse this strategy, as well as others, as suitable ways to solve basic addition and subtraction facts. The strategies that they endorse are:

- *Commutativity (addition).* Reversing the order of the numbers so that the larger comes first (e.g. to solve 2 + 9, it is easier to begin with 9 and add 2).
- *Counting on and back in ones.* Efficient for adding 1, 2 or 3, but not for adding larger numbers.
- *Doubles/near doubles.* Many children find it relatively easy to double numbers (e.g. 'to add 5 and 6, I know 5 + 5, so 5 + 6 is one more').
- *Bridging 10.* Knowledge of pairs of numbers with a sum of 10 is very valuable and can be used to derive other facts (e.g. 8 + 5; 8 + 2 = 10, + 3 = 13).

These strategies are also effective when adding and subtracting larger numbers. Sometimes the addition of other tools, such as an empty number line, can be used to informally record the thinking process. Figure 2.9 shows an example of one way the empty number line could be used to add 46 and 33.

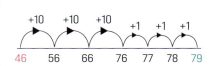

Figure 2.9 Empty number line used to add 46 + 33

ACTIVITY 2.8

Make an empty number line strip (see Figure 2.10). Fold horizontally along the dotted line so that the numbers 0–10 are hidden and the strip showing 0–10 is displayed. Ask the student to place a peg where they think 6 might go. When they have placed the peg, flip to turn the strip over to see how close they were. The strip can also be used for adding and subtracting numbers and can be adapted to include different numbers at the start and end (e.g. 50–100).

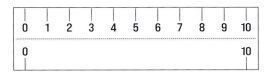

Figure 2.10 Number line strip

Multiplication and division

Like addition and subtraction, there are problem structures that represent different multiplication and division situations. When the number and size of the groups are known, multiplication is the process to use, whereas division is used when either the number of the sets or the size of the sets is unknown. The terms multiply and divide are first directly referred to in the Australian Curriculum: Mathematics v. 9.0 at Year 2 level, in the following content descriptor:

> Multiply and divide by one-digit numbers using repeated addition, equal grouping, **arrays**, and partitioning to support a variety of calculation strategies (AC9M2N05).

Reference is also made to multiplication in the Year 2 Algebra content descriptor:

> Recall and demonstrate proficiency with multiplication facts for twos; extend and apply facts to develop the related division facts using doubling and halving (AC9M2A03).

Array an arrangement of rows and columns

Because children need to be familiar with the addition process, it seems logical to base early multiplication experiences around situations that require 'repeated addition'. For example, 5 × 3 can be seen as 'five groups of three' and the answer can be found by adding three five times (3 + 3 + 3 + 3 + 3 = 15). Links can also be made with tools that were useful in learning about place value, addition and subtraction, such as the hundreds chart. The interactive hundreds chart referred to previously is a great source for demonstrating skip counting and investigating patterns. The calculator can also be used to link multiplication and addition and to demonstrate skip counting, as the following activity demonstrates.

ACTIVITY 2.9

Counting on the calculator

- Choose a number to count by (e.g. 4).
- Key this into the calculator then press + +. Now press the = sign. With each subsequent press of the = sign, the calculator will 'count' in 4s (4, 8, 12, etc.).
- Ask children to predict what the next number in the sequence will be before pressing the = sign.
- Try it with different numbers and try predicting what numbers will be in the sequence (e.g. Will we get to count 64? To 83?).

Broken multiplication key

To extend students and to demonstrate the link between addition and multiplication, ask children to use the calculator to find the answer to various multiplication problems without using the multiplication key. For example, 5 × 3 can be found by using the constant function feature (as above) or by keying in 3 + 3 + 3 + 3 + 3 =. Variations on the broken key can include a broken division key (e.g. find 15 ÷ 5 without using the ÷ sign) or a broken number key (e.g. find 6 × 4 without using the 4 button).

Scootle an online repository of digital resources for Australian teachers

Multiplication as arrays

Arrays are useful models for moving children from additive thinking to multiplicative thinking. An array is an arrangement of rows and columns, such as a rectangle of square blocks. The array can be turned around to demonstrate the commutative property of multiplication.

Scootle has a learning object The Array, which requires students to use an array-building tool to help solve multiplications (see Figure 2.12). The activity requires students to create and solve multiplication problems, such as 4 × 2, and examines the relationships between rows, columns and areas in arrays.

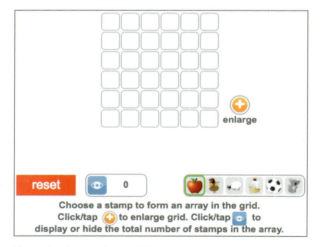

Figure 2.11 Screenshot of HOTmaths Arrays widget

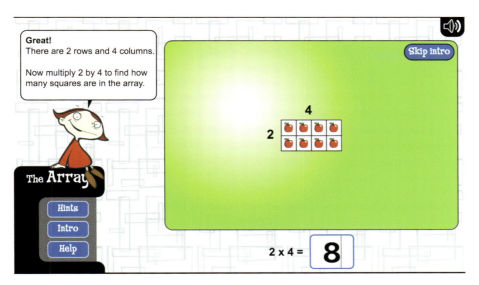

Figure 2.12 Screenshot of Scootle learning object The Array (TLF1-ID L106)
Source: Scootle

Link 2.10 Scootle: The Array

Place value

Early number development activities, such as those outlined in this chapter, can provide the foundation for understanding the base-10 numbers, or that collections of 10 (hundreds, thousands and so on) can be counted. For example, a collection of 25 counters can be seen as 25 individual counters or as two groups of 10 counters, and five additional counters. The development of place value is addressed in more detail in Chapter 5.

Extending early mathematical development beyond number

Children's early mathematical development is not (and should not be) restricted to number. This chapter has focused on the development of early number skills to reflect the general emphasis that is given to the importance of early number development. The next section of this chapter provides an overview of children's early mathematical development and appropriate learning experiences in the other mathematical domains, which are further extended upon in Chapters 3 and 4.

Space and geometry

Research has shown that babies can recognise shapes and navigate spaces, and by 2–3 years of age, children can recognise and use symmetry, identify a variety of shapes, and learn about positional concepts and relationships (MacDonald 2018). Evidence of children's spatial awareness can be seen in everyday experiences, such as when they identify the wheels of a car as 'circles' or place the right shapes in the appropriate holes in the classic Tupperware shape-sorter ball. Recognition of the importance of developing young children's spatial awareness is reflected in the EYLF (DEEWR 2009):

Outcome 3: Children have a strong sense of wellbeing

Component: Children take increasing responsibility for their own health and physical wellbeing.

This is evident, for example, when children:

- combine gross and fine motor movement and balance to achieve increasingly complex patterns of activity including dance, creative movement and drama
- use their sensory capabilities and dispositions with increasing integration, skill and purpose to explore and respond to their world
- demonstrate spatial awareness and orient themselves, moving around and through their environments confidently and safely.

Outcome 4: Children are confident and involved learners

Component: Children develop dispositions for learning such as curiosity, cooperation, confidence, creativity, commitment, enthusiasm, persistence, imagination and reflexivity.

This is evident, for example, when children:

- express wonder and interest in their environments
- use play to investigate, imagine and explore ideas
- participate in a variety of rich and meaningful inquiry-based experiences.

Children's geometric thinking is believed by some to be developed by moving through discrete stages of reasoning. These stages are referred to as the 'van Hiele' levels of thought, and young children would be expected to be operating at Level 0 (pre-recognition) and Level 1 (visual). The levels of van Hiele are further discussed in Chapter 4. While the levels are useful for identifying the different elements of children's geometric thinking, their linearity may limit our capacity to understand the fluid ways in which children acquire spatial and geometric knowledge (MacDonald 2018).

Early geometric experiences often focus on shapes and their properties. The Australian Curriculum: Mathematics v. 9.0 requires students at Foundation Level to 'Sort, name and create familiar shapes; recognise and describe familiar shapes within objects in the environment, giving reasons' (AC9MFSP01). Similarly, Year 1 students are expected to 'Make, compare and classify familiar shapes; recognise familiar shapes and objects in the environment, identifying the similarities and differences between them' (AC9M1SP01). Simple activities such as going on a shape hunt outside and placing a variety of different shapes in a 'feely bag' for children to describe through touch can help students to develop these outcomes.

ACTIVITY 2.10

Prepare a number of cards with the names of different shapes on them. Ask a child to volunteer to come up the front. Without revealing the name of the shape to the child, place the card on top of the child's head so that the rest of the class can see the name of the shape. The child then has to ask a number of questions with yes/no answers in order to identify the name of the shape (e.g. Am I round? Do I have straight sides?)

Measurement

Measurement is essentially the assignment of a numerical value to an attribute of an object or event. Research shows that understandings of measurement begin to develop in the early years. As with other mathematical areas, young children are likely to come to school with lots of informal measurement understandings. They would often know, for example, that length and mass exist but may not be able to measure them. They are likely to describe objects as long, short, big, and so on; and they might even be able to compare objects (e.g. I am taller than you). The measurable attributes are length, area, volume and capacity, mass, time, temperature and value (money); these are discussed in Chapter 3. Early measurement experiences should focus on developing children's capacity to 'identify the attribute' and comparing and ordering activities in line with the 'sequence for teaching measurement' (see Chapter 3).

Earlier in this chapter and elsewhere throughout this book, we have provided examples of how children's literature can be used to stimulate children's interest in mathematics and as a vehicle for teaching important mathematical concepts. Story-telling can also be equally effective, particularly with young children. Classroom Snapshot 2.4 describes how the telling of a story led to children exploring concepts about capacity.

CLASSROOM SNAPSHOT 2.4

Mrs Jones told the following story to her prep class:

> Once there was a poor woodcutter and his wife. They were so poor they had holes in their clothes, holes in their shoes, and no food in the house.
>
> One day, the woodcutter was asleep in the forest. Lucky Bird Huma flew by, looking for someone to help. She landed beside the poor woodcutter and laid a beautiful egg as a present. The woodcutter took the egg home to his wife. He asked her what they should do with this precious egg.
>
> His wife said: 'If only Lucky Bird Huma would live with us, she would lay us lots of eggs, not just one.'
>
> The next day, when Lucky Bird Huma flew by, the woodcutter called out to her 'Please, Lucky Bird Huma, won't you come to our house?'
>
> To begin with, the woodcutter and his wife treated Lucky Bird Huma well. But every day they wanted more and more eggs. Lucky Bird Huma laid jewelled eggs patterned with bright colours. She laid shiny stone eggs. She laid smooth wooden eggs. Every day the woodcutter and his wife collected the eggs in baskets and boxes and counted how many eggs they had to take to market to sell.
>
> One day, Lucky Bird Huma stopped laying eggs. Her feathers grew dull, and lost their colours.
>
> 'What's wrong, Lucky Bird Huma?' asked the woodcutter.
>
> 'I am ill,' said Lucky Bird Huma. 'I need to go outside in the fresh air.'
>
> So the woodcutter took Lucky Bird Huma outside. At once she spread her wings and flew away. And the woodcutter and his wife never saw her or her eggs again.

After telling the story, Mrs Jones put two baskets filled with lots of different eggs made from different materials, including paper mache, dyed hard-boiled eggs, and painted stones that were egg-shaped. She also had a variety of baskets and boxes to place the eggs in. The challenge for the children was to work out which boxes or baskets would hold the most eggs. Lots of discussion took place on where to place the biggest eggs and whether they could actually work out which boxes or baskets would hold the most eggs as they were all different sizes.

Source: Adapted from Leeper & Muir 2019

PAUSE AND REFLECT

What key ideas or understandings would you decide to focus on if you were implementing the activity with your class? The story had the potential to explore several different mathematical concepts. How do you decide what to explore? Is it better to focus on one concept or link several concepts in one lesson?

Conclusion

This chapter has provided you with an overview of early childhood mathematics pedagogy, along with the importance of recognising the prior mathematical experiences that young children bring to their formal schooling. Prior to attending school and early childhood centres, children are likely to have experienced a range of opportunities for learning about mathematics and it is important for us educators to capitalise on these experiences. While many of you may never teach young children, it is hoped that this chapter has provided you with insights into early mathematical development and learning, which is likely to impact on students' engagement and learning with mathematics in the primary years.

GUIDED STUDENT TASKS

1. How important do you think it is to consider children's earlier mathematical experiences? How can early childhood educators capitalise on the mathematical knowledge that children bring to school?
2. Think about your own early schooling and the approaches your teachers used to teach mathematical concepts. How much focus was placed on engaging the learner? What role do you see technology playing in engaging the learners of today?
3. In this chapter, you visited several websites aimed at developing early mathematical concepts. Think about which website appealed to you most. What features made it appealing? Did it incorporate mathematics that was important to learn? Did it offer affordances beyond what could be achieved with traditional classroom materials?

CONCEPTS TO CONSIDER

Unfortunately, some pre-service teachers may believe that their own mathematical content knowledge is not strong, but that is all right as they will only be teaching mathematics in the early years. All students, regardless of their age and year level, deserve a teacher who has a strong robust understanding of key mathematical concepts and processes, is confident with being able to apply mathematics to a variety of situations and can help students understand the mathematics at the level in which they are required to teach. LANTITE (Literacy and Numeracy Test for Initial Teacher Education students) was established in part to address concerns with the quality of Initial Teacher Education and successful completion of LANTITE is required for all graduating teachers, regardless of the grade level they will be teaching (see Chapter 19 for more details about LANTITE). While the actual mathematical content of this chapter would not be challenging to most prospective graduates, we believe that our graduates need to look beyond knowing enough mathematics to teach the intended grade level. After all, if we used literacy as a comparison, we would expect our Year 2 teacher to read beyond the level required for a Year 2 student. We recommend, therefore, that in alignment with LANTITE expectations, that every graduate should be confident with the content of Year 9 mathematics.

There are aspects of your pedagogical content knowledge that are particularly relevant to this chapter. First, it is important that you are familiar with and understand how to develop the counting principles with your young learners. This does not mean that you state these as learning intentions with your students, but rather that you can engage in professional dialogue about the difference between the principles and their importance in providing the foundation for future number work. Second, you would not necessarily use problem structure terms with your students (such as initial, result unknown), but rather that you are aware of what the different problem structures are, provide a variety of them for your students and recognise when students have difficulty with particular types of problems.

Cardinality

Cardinality refers to the number that is obtained after counting something. A cardinal number is a number that is used to label how many is in a set (MacDonald 2018). The cardinal principle is so named because it refers to the last counting word being the total of the number in the set. For example, when a child counts a group of toys: 1, 2, 3, 4 – they recognise that there are 4 toys in total.

Subitising

Subitising is foundational to children's number sense. Being able to quickly identify a set of objects without counting helps to develop understanding of a quantity and as children's ability to visualise develops, their number sense also improves (Shumway 2011). Daily practice with using 'quick images' such as the PowerPoint slides showing counters discussed earlier in this chapter can help to consolidate children's ability to subitise. When preparing or selecting suitable images for encouraging subitising, initially choose images which show familiar arrangements, such as those found on dice faces.

FURTHER READING

This chapter provided information about the different problem types associated with addition and subtraction. For further reading about these, and problem types for multiplication and division, see:

Carpenter, TP, Fennema, E, Franke, ML, Levi, L & Empson, S 1999, *Children's mathematics: Cognitive guided instruction*, Portsmouth, NH: Heinemann.

For further reading about learning trajectories, see:

Sarama, J & Clements, DH 2009, *Early childhood mathematics education research: Learning trajectories for young children*, New York: Routledge.

Clements, DH & Sarama, J 2021, *Learning and teaching early math: The learning trajectories approach*, 3rd edn, New York: Routledge.

For ideas on how to use stories to develop early mathematical concepts, see:

Leeper, M & Muir, T 2019, *Developing early maths through story: Step-by-step guide for using storytelling as a springboard for maths activities*, Strawberry Hills, NSW: Teaching Solutions.

Websites for exploration

For ideas on incorporating regular number sense routines, including subitising and 10-frames, see:

Shumway, J 2011, *Number sense routines*, Portland, ME: Stenhouse.

CHAPTER 3

EXPLORING MEASUREMENT

LEARNING OUTCOMES

By the end of this chapter, you will:

- be familiar with a measurement sequence used to introduce and develop an understanding of each attribute
- have an understanding of the attributes of length, area, volume and capacity, angle, mass, time, temperature, and value and money
- understand the importance of developing estimation skills, spatial awareness and meaningful benchmarks
- understand the principles involved when measuring with non-standard units
- understand how technology can be integrated and utilised to support, develop and extend students' measurement experiences.

Introduction

Measurement is an aspect of the mathematics curriculum that has wide usage in everyday life. A basic level of knowledge, skills and confidence in measurement is very much part of being numerate. An analysis of the measuring process suggests that children learn to measure first by becoming aware of the physical attributes of objects and how they compare with other objects. Estimation is a significant aspect of measurement and should be seen as an integral part of the measurement process. The ability to estimate is enhanced when students have strong spatial awareness and are able to visualise and represent measurement situations in their heads. Students therefore need to be given plenty of opportunities to engage in measurement activities that focus on developing a sound understanding of the attribute being measured, along with the act of measuring.

Learning sequence for measurement

When developing an understanding of measurement with children and students, we find it useful to follow a specific learning sequence that can be used to develop effective measuring processes (e.g. Van de Walle et al. 2013; Booker et al. 2010). This sequence, which is detailed below, enables the building of understanding in all the measuring topics (**length**, **area**, **volume**

Length a measure of something from end to end

Area the amount of space contained within a closed shape

Volume the amount of space occupied by a three-dimensional object

41

and **capacity**, **angle**, **mass**, **time**, **temperature**, and **value** and money). There are five stages in the learning sequence.

1. Identifying the attribute

The first and most important stage in the sequence is for the **attribute** to be identified – that is, are we interested in finding out the length of an object, the area of an object, how heavy something is or how much space it takes up?

Children need to be given lots of opportunities to explore what different attributes mean before being asked to measure in standard ways. For example, if asked to find the height of something, do children realise that this essentially means length? Confusion often occurs with the attributes of area, perimeter (length) and volume, so it is vital that a robust understanding of the attribute is developed before moving on in the sequence. Involving children in lots of experiences that require them to cover surfaces, for example, will help them to distinguish the concept of area from perimeter and volume.

2. Comparing and ordering

While comparing and ordering will no doubt be part of children's experiences of identifying an attribute, the second stage in the sequence focuses on these aspects and will help to consolidate an understanding of the attribute. Comparing and ordering activities should focus on an attribute and initially involve direct comparison: Who is taller? Whose pencil is the longest? Which tile would cover the most area? Which ball is heavier? Indirect methods may be necessary for some attributes, such as comparing the volume of two boxes, and this can lead to the introduction of non-standard, or informal, units.

Figure 3.1 Who is taller?

> **Capacity** the measure of how much a three-dimensional object can hold
>
> **Angle** a measure of the amount of turn between two lines; a figure made of two rays with a common endpoint
>
> **Mass** the amount of matter in an object
>
> **Time** the duration of an event from its beginning to its end
>
> **Temperature** the measure of how hot or cold something is
>
> **Value** the measure of a cost placed on something
>
> **Attribute** a property or characteristic of something
>
> **Non-standard units/informal units** everyday materials or objects that can be used to measure various attributes – for example, hands, feet, straws, tiles, marbles

3. Using non-standard units

Non-standard, or informal, units are essential for developing the concept of measuring and for children to see the need for standard units. These units should utilise everyday objects that are familiar to children and should primarily be uniform in nature and resemble the standard unit. For example, straws, paper clips and pencils are all suitable materials for measuring the length of objects, as they can be laid end to end along the length of something. Playing cards, dominoes and tiles are useful for measuring area, as they can be fitted together to cover a surface without leaving gaps.

Most attributes have suitable non-standard units that can be used, although non-standard units for time and temperature are not as readily identifiable. When students measure with non-standard units, important aspects about measuring or measuring

Figure 3.2 Examples of non-standard units

principles can be introduced and consolidated. The following understandings should be developed with students as they participate in measurement activities using informal units:

- The unit must not change – for example, we should select one type of informal unit, such as straws, to measure the length of the table, rather than a straw, a pencil and a rubber.
- The units must be placed end to end (when measuring length), with no gaps or overlapping units.
- The units need to be used in a uniform manner – that is, if dominoes are being used to find the area of the top of a desk, then each domino needs to be placed in the same orientation in order to accurately represent the standard unit.
- There is a direct relationship between the size of the unit and the number required – that is, the smaller the unit, the bigger the number, and vice versa.

These understandings need to be explicitly taught and practised. It is also helpful to measure the same objects with different non-standard units to develop the understanding that there is an inverse relationship between the size of the unit chosen and the number of units required to measure that object. Non-standard units are also useful in their own right – as adults, we often use them as benchmarks for estimating in everyday situations, such as using our height to determine whether or not the new fridge will fit in an allocated space.

While students should be involved in physically selecting units and measuring with them, there are a number of interactive sites and applications that can be used to supplement and consolidate classroom experiences, and which focus on developing the understandings associated with measuring with informal units. HOTmaths, for example, offers widgets that

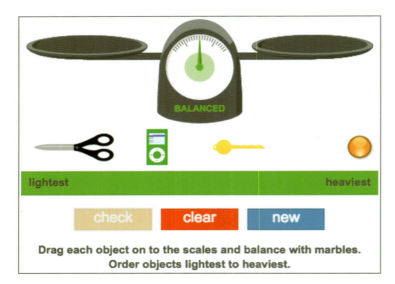

Figure 3.3 Screenshot of HOTmaths Lightest to Heaviest widget

include opportunities to measure length, mass and capacity using informal units. Figure 3.3 shows a screenshot from an activity that requires users to order the objects from lightest to heaviest, using a pan balance and marbles as informal units. While not advocating this as a substitute for gaining a sense of the mass of an object through hefting, the widget does provide a visual representation of how the scales are balanced when the mass of both sides is the same.

4. Standard units

Once students have had considerable experience with using non-standard units and understand the principles behind measurement, they can be introduced to standard units. Encourage students to discuss and think about the limitations of non-standard units and the usefulness of having standard ways by which to communicate measurements. For example, it might be interesting to see that it takes 100 pieces of A4 paper to cover the floor in a room, but this would not be helpful if we were ordering carpet to cover the floor. Similarly, discussion around the different sizes of students' feet can highlight the need for standard units if measuring and communicating the length of the tennis court. The use of measuring instruments needs to be taught explicitly and their construction discussed. A useful task involves students constructing their own ruler (see Activity 3.1), whereby students are encouraged to make connections between the iteration marks (centimetres/millimetres) and the unit, and to view the ruler as a convenient tool that assists in the measuring process. Students need to develop an understanding of the relationships between units such as millimetres, centimetres, metres and kilometres, and later to explore the relationships between different units such as millilitres, cubic centimetres and grams, and cubic metres and litres.

ACTIVITY 3.1

- Decide on a convenient unit to use (e.g. pen top, pen, mobile phone).
- Cut out pieces of paper that are the length of your unit.
- Stick these along a strip of cardboard to make a ruler.
- How would you allocate numbers on your ruler?
- Use your ruler to measure:
  - the length, width and height of your table
  - the length of an A4 page
  - the length of someone's arm.
- Compare your answers with those of another group/friend. What do you notice?

Reading instruments and scales

Ryan and Williams (2007) found that confusion about the 'ticks' and 'intervals' on measuring devices was a common error made by students across all ages. Other common errors involved always interpreting the end number on the ruler as being the 'answer', regardless of whether or not the ruler was lined up with 0 to begin with, and misinterpreting the scale markings, believing that each interval or marking was one complete unit.

Figure 3.4 shows a broken ruler and a segment to be measured. This is a task that is commonly used on test items, and it requires students to use the ruler to measure the length of the segment. Broken Ruler is a useful assessment item in that students who do not have a solid understanding of what the intervals on a ruler represent are likely to indicate that the segment is a bit more than 7 cm long. It would be useful to project a broken ruler on an interactive whiteboard (IWB) and discuss how it could be used to measure different objects. It would also be valuable to provide students with a number of incorrect responses to the question and to have a class discussion on possible reasons for the incorrect responses.

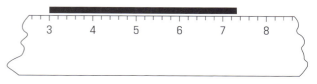

Figure 3.4 Broken ruler

There are many interactive sites that provide opportunities for students to focus on reading instruments and scales. The ICT Games website, for example, includes a scales reader activity called Mostly Postie, in which students can read and record the weight indicated by the scale. It is quite challenging in that students need to work out what scale is being used and then accurately read and record the measurement (which is sometimes between intervals).

Link 3.1 ICT Games: Mostly Postie

5. Applying formulae

When students become proficient at measuring correctly and with selecting and using appropriate standard units, they can be provided with opportunities to use measurement applications and formulae. Students should be encouraged to construct their own methods for calculating areas, perimeters and volumes before being introduced and/or instructed to use 'rules' or formulae. For example, covering the surface of a desk with playing cards can demonstrate the relationship between arrays and multiplication as well as the concept of multiplying the number of units along the length by the number of units placed along the width (see Figure 3.5).

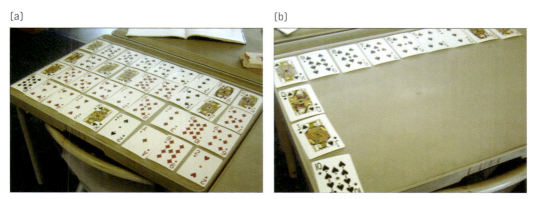

Figure 3.5 (a) Cards covering desk; (b) Cards partially placed

Establishing formulae for areas and volumes

According to the Australian Curriculum: Mathematics v. 9.0 (ACARA 2022), students in Year 7 are expected to use units of measurement according to the following descriptors:

- Solve problems involving the area of triangles and parallelograms using established formulas and appropriate units (AC9M7M01).
- Solve problems involving the volume of right prisms including rectangular and triangular prisms, using established formulas and appropriate units (AC9M7M02).

In Year 8, these expectations are expanded to include the following descriptors in relation to units:

- Solve problems involving the area and perimeter of irregular and composite shapes using appropriate units (AC9M8M01).
- Solve problems involving the volume and capacity of right prisms using appropriate units (AC9M8M02).
- Solve problems using the circumference and area of a circle using formulas and appropriate units (AC9M8M03).
- Solving problems involving duration, including using 12- and 24-hour time across multiple time zones (AC9M8M04).
- Recognise and use rates to solve problems involving the comparison of 2 related quantities of different units of measure (AC9M8M05).

There are a number of interactive sites and resources that can be used to develop an understanding of the above concepts. The Illuminations website contains area, volume and capacity tools that can be used to investigate, for example, how the base and height of a figure can be used to determine its area.

Angles and triangles

In version 9.0 of the Australian Curriculum: Mathematics, the study of angles is included in the Measurement content strand. For example, students in Year 4 are expected to:

> Estimate and compare angles using angle names including acute, obtuse, straight angle, reflex and revolution, and recognise their relationship to a right angle (AC9M4M04).

As referred to earlier in this chapter, and elaborated further on, angle can be considered an attribute about which understandings can be developed through applying the learning sequence to teach measurement. In relation to angle, the final stage in the sequence, application of formulae, can be demonstrated through investigating the sum of the angles in a triangle.

ACTIVITY 3.2

Students are often told that the sum of all the angles in a triangle is 180 degrees, but how many of the students have developed an understanding of why this is the case? HOTmaths has a useful widget that demonstrates clearly why this occurs, without focusing on manipulating the numbers (see Figure 3.6). The activity can also be undertaken in class, using paper triangles and tearing off the corners.

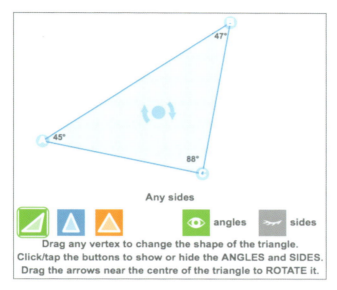

Figure 3.6 Screenshot of HOTmaths Exploring Triangles widget

Area and circumference of a circle

The relationship between the circumference of a circle (distance around the outside or perimeter) and the length of the diameter can be investigated at a number of levels. The circumference and diameter of circular items such as lids, cans and jars can be measured and entered into a table. Plots can be made of the data using CODMap or graphic calculators. The plot should show that most ratios would be approximately 3:1 or 3:2, with a straight line showing through the origin. The ratio (pi) is an irrational number that is about 3.14159. There are a number of online resources that demonstrate the origin of pi and how it was derived. It is useful to share some of these descriptions with students, particularly if they demonstrate the rearrangement of a circle's segments into eight or more parts.

Khan Academy is a website that is popular with students in the older years. It contains a number of video presentations in the form of tutorials demonstrating how to carry out various operations and procedures. The Khan Academy website has a tutorial based on finding the radius, diameter and circumference of a circle. It needs to be emphasised that the application of formulae occurs late in the measurement learning sequence, and students need to be provided with lots of opportunities to discover formulae for themselves.

Link 3.2 Khan Academy: 'Circles: Radius, diameter, circumference and pi'

Estimation

Estimation is an integral part of everyday life, as many measurement situations do not require exact measurements (Hodgson et al. 2003). The significance of estimation as an everyday and natural aspect of measurement needs to be conveyed to students, yet many students

Estimation an approximation or judgement about the attribute(s) of something

tend to view it as a difficult technique where success is dependent upon how close their estimate is to that of the teacher (Muir 2005). Muir (2005) outlines eight principles that can be used in classrooms to enhance the value of measurement estimation experiences for students:

- Estimation is useful.
- Estimation should be related to real life.
- Estimation saves time.
- Estimation experiences should be purposeful and relevant.
- The ability to estimate is enhanced through practice and over time.
- Personal benchmarks are useful referents for estimation.
- Sometimes it is better to over- or under-estimate, depending on the context.
- Estimation is used to validate measuring tools and methods.

CLASSROOM SNAPSHOT 3.1

The following is adapted from an article (Muir 2012a) based on a lesson conducted with a Year 5/6 class.

The lesson began with the whole class sitting in front of the whiteboard. It was introduced by posing three questions, one at a time, to the class and soliciting three different responses to each question.

The questions were:
- How far is it from Launceston to Hobart?
- How far is it from the earth to the sun?
- How old is your teacher?

Three responses for each question were recorded on the board and students were then asked to vote for the most reasonable answer. Discussion then occurred on the reasons for the vote, what referents were used to make estimates, which questions were 'easier' to estimate and why. The activity was particularly useful for gauging which referents were used by students. For example, students indicated that they found it easier to estimate the teacher's age because they could gauge whether she was older than their parents, whereas distances posed more of a problem.

How big, how tall, how many?

The next activity required the students to provide (and receive) answers to a number of questions that did not have an obvious answer and involved larger numbers. For example: How high is Mount Everest? What is the population of China? How tall is the world's tallest man? How long would it take you to count to a million? The *Guinness World Records*, Google and the Australian Bureau of Statistics website are all useful resources for questions. Cards containing the questions were placed on the students' backs without the question being revealed to its wearer (see Figure 3.7). Each student then asked three people to provide an answer to the question and, in turn, they provided answers to others' questions. The responses were recorded on a pro forma. After everyone had recorded three responses, the class regrouped and answers were discussed. Before the students were allowed to look at their questions, they first had to decide on an appropriate answer, based on the responses received, and then they had to identify an appropriate question that would 'fit' the answer. The students were very curious about what their questions were and about the 'correct' answers.

Figure 3.7 Reading the question

One student, Susan, received three responses to her question, 'How high is Mount Everest?' Is it 1000 m, 2000 m or 500 000 m?' She chose '2000 m' as a reasonable answer (the correct answer is 8848 m) and predicted that her question was 'How far is it from somewhere to somewhere?'

PAUSE AND REFLECT

When the activities above were conducted with the class, the teacher was surprised that many students did not demonstrate a 'sense of the relative and absolute magnitude of numbers', and did not utilise a 'system of benchmarks' with which they could operate to make reasonable estimates (Muir 2012a). How would you capitalise on the experiences from this lesson to develop these aspects? How could information and communication technology (ICT) be utilised to demonstrate the magnitude of numbers?

ACTIVITY 3.3

Classroom Snapshot 3.1 referred to sources such as *Guinness World Records* and the Australian Bureau of Statistics website as useful resources for generating questions and investigations. Visit the *Guinness World Records* website and then use either the 'Explore Records' or 'Search Records' tab to locate records related to size. Search for the world's tallest man and view the linked YouTube clip. Either during or after watching the clip, try to answer the following questions:

- How tall do you think Sultan Kösen is?
- How tall do you think the waiter is? The driver of the car?
- What would be the height of an average doorway?
- How close would Sultan's head be to the ceiling in your house?

Now pause and reflect on how you came up with your answers. What benchmarks did you use to make your estimates?

How did you use your ability to visualise situations to help you make reasonable estimates? How do you think not having this ability would affect students' capacity to make reasonable estimates?

Further explore the site to identify three examples of pictures or reports that could be used as source questions for a lesson similar to that outlined in Classroom Snapshot 3.1.

Making estimation meaningful

As mentioned earlier, many students tend to view estimation as a 'guess', and they fail to see it as a useful or meaningful experience. One way to make estimation more meaningful is to allow students to revise their estimates. Try the following activities:

- Choose a distance to estimate – for example, the length of your classroom.
- Choose an informal unit to measure with – for example, your foot.
- Estimate how many of your feet (end to end) it would take to measure the classroom from one end to the other and write it down.
- Next, take five steps (placing feet touching), then pause. Look at your estimate and adjust if necessary.
- Take five more steps in the same way. Pause and adjust your estimate if necessary.
- Keep going in this way – you can revise your estimate as many times as you like.

Through engaging students in similar experiences, you can maintain their interest throughout the measuring process and facilitate the understanding that estimation is useful, purposeful and has real-life applications.

Figure 3.8 How many chocolates will fit on a plate? Allowing students to revise their estimates can make estimation more meaningful.

ACTIVITY 3.4

A website that encourages you to revise estimates and develops an appreciation for the magnitude of numbers is Estimation180 (also referred to in Chapter 13).

The website is particularly valuable in that it requires users to think of an estimate that is too low and too high, and to justify how the estimate is reached. Try out the different activities and see how good your estimation skills are.

Conservation

Many of the common misconceptions that students display in relation to measurement involve the concept of conservation. Young children, for example, might not recognise that the length of a given piece of string does not change according to whether it is curled up or laid straight. Similarly, the conservation of capacity can be demonstrated by recognising that four cups of water is still the same amount, regardless of the height and width of a container. Many middle primary and older students do not readily understand, for example, 'that rearranging areas into different shapes does not affect the amount of area. Cutting a shape into two parts and then reassembling it into a different shape can show that the before and after shapes have the same area, even though they are different shapes' (Van de Walle et al. 2017, p. 384). The tangram activity in Activity 3.7 could also be used to help develop students' awareness of this. NZ Maths also has an activity where students can develop spatial awareness skills through making pentominoes from five one-centimetre cubes (see Outlining Area).

Link 3.3 NZ Maths: Outlining Area

ACTIVITY 3.5

HOTmaths has a widget called Measuring Capacity (see Figure 3.9), where users are required to fill three different-sized containers with cups of liquid. Do the activity three times. What do you notice about the number of cups taken to fill the containers? In the screenshot, the tallest container actually holds the least amount of liquid. How could you capitalise on this teaching opportunity with students?

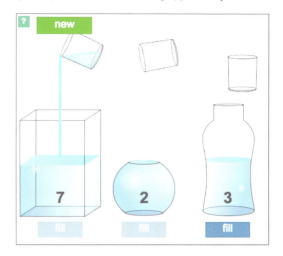

Figure 3.9 Screenshot of HOTmaths Measuring Capacity widget

Measurement topics

The measurement learning sequence explained earlier can be used to develop an awareness and knowledge of the attribute being measured, and it can be applied to the measurement of any attribute, including measures of length, area, volume, angle, mass, time and temperature, and value and money. This section looks at these attributes in detail and their development as guided by the Australian Curriculum: Mathematics v. 9.0.

Measurement is one of the six content strands in the Australian Curriculum: Mathematics v. 9.0. Throughout their schooling, students are expected to develop an increasingly sophisticated understanding of size and shape, including making meaningful measurements of quantities and choosing appropriate metric units of measurement.

Beginning in the early primary years, and extending through to Year 10, the Measurement strand in the Australian Curriculum: Mathematics v. 9.0 (ACARA 2022) includes the following aspects as being indicative of the teaching emphases in the early primary years:

- Identify and compare attributes of objects and events, including length, capacity, mass and duration, using direct comparisons and communicating reasoning (AC9MFM01).
- Sequence days of the week and times of the day including morning, lunchtime, afternoon and night time, and connect them to familiar events and actions (AC9MFM02).
- Compare directly and indirectly and order objects and events using attributes of length, mass, capacity and duration, communicating reasoning (AC9M1M01).
- Measure the length of shapes and objects using informal units, recognising that units need to be uniform and used end-to-end (AC9M1M02).
- Describe the duration and sequence of events using years, months, weeks, days and hours (AC9M1M03).

Interestingly, while many descriptors are general in nature and particular attributes are not mentioned every year (e.g. only length, mass, capacity and duration are referred to in Year 1), time is mentioned frequently, and there is an emphasis on telling time and using units of time. Metric units are first mentioned in Year 3 in relation to measuring everyday items incorporating the attributes of length, mass and capacity. Measurement of perimeter and area of shapes and enclosed spaces, using appropriate formal and informal units, is referred to in Year 4 (AC9M4M02). Formulae are first mentioned in Year 6. Money values are also included in the Measurement content strand. For example, in Year 3, students are expected to:

> Recognise the relationships between dollars and cents and represent money values in different ways (AC9M3M06).

Within the Australian Curriculum: Mathematics v. 9.0 (ACARA 2022), the proficiency strands should also be incorporated to engage students in understanding measurement concepts and solving problems involving measurement contexts. Many of these contexts require students to engage in spatial thinking, such as indirectly comparing the lengths or areas of different objects.

Each of the measurement attributes mentioned earlier and referred to in the Australian Curriculum: Mathematics v. 9.0 will now be discussed.

Length

Length refers to the measurement of something from end to end and is usually the first attribute introduced to children. Children should be given frequent opportunities to investigate length measurements, initially with straight lines, and then extending into curved distances and length around plane shapes. Because length is often the first attribute encountered by children, teachers need to capitalise on both developing the concept and building an understanding of what it means to measure and estimate. Activities that help children to develop an appreciation of comparing and ordering, and discussion of appropriate vocabulary, are particularly valuable in the early years of schooling. The following are examples of length activities that could be used with Foundation to Year 1 to develop the concept of length:

- In small groups, ask each child to make a play dough worm. Compare the length of each worm to determine who made the longest worm.
- Make class books based around the attribute of length (e.g. the title of the book could be: 'I am tall enough to ... ' or 'The gate is wide enough to ... ') (Department of Education and the Arts, Tasmania 1994).
- After reading *The Gingerbread Man*, provide students with gingerbread family members and ask them to place them in order from shortest to tallest (see the NZ Maths website for lesson plan based on the story).

Link 3.4 NZ Maths: The Gingerbread Man

ACTIVITY 3.6

Go to the *Guinness World Records* website and look up the world's longest snake. Think about how you could use the picture of the snake to develop the first three stages in the sequence of measurement: the attribute of length, comparing and ordering length, and measuring with informal units.

PAUSE AND REFLECT

A class of Prep children (aged 5 to 6) were asked to bring in their teddies from home, with the aim being to find out who had the 'biggest' teddy.
- What discussions might be stimulated by such an activity?
- Would this be an appropriate activity for developing an understanding of the attribute of length?

Area

Area is a two-dimensional concept that refers to the amount of space within a closed region. Experiences that encourage children to investigate covering surfaces should be provided early on and, where possible, direct comparisons should be made. Where such direct comparisons cannot be made, Van de Walle and colleagues (2013) recommend activities in which one area is rearranged. Cutting a shape into two parts and reassembling it into a different shape can show that the 'before' and 'after' shapes have the same area, even though they are different shapes. This notion is often not readily apparent to younger children, and it relates to the ability to conserve area. The following are examples of activities that could be undertaken to develop an understanding of the attribute of area.

Hand prints

Give each child a piece of A3 paper and ask them to estimate how many of their hand prints it would take to cover the paper. Have children make prints of their hand and cover the surface of the paper. Discuss how many it took, compare with other children's answers and discuss the notion of 'gaps' remaining between the hand prints, and whether or not spread out or closed fingers made a difference to the results.

Icing the cake

Give children three different-shaped 'cakes' made from cardboard: rectangle, square and circle. Ask them to predict which cake would need the most icing to cover its top. Discuss ways in which the areas could be compared and/or the use of non-standard units.

Tangrams

Tangram an ancient Chinese dissection puzzle comprising seven flat shapes

Tangrams, or dissection puzzles, are a useful resource for investigating size and shape concepts. Provide students with the outline of several shapes made with some tangram pieces and encourage them to use the pieces to decide which shapes have the same area.

ACTIVITY 3.7

Link 3.5 Math Playground: Tangrams

Visit the tangrams site at Math Playground (see Figure 3.10). Complete three or four of the activities. How could you use the experiences to develop students' conservation of area?

Figure 3.10 Screenshot of Math Playground Four Piece Tangrams activity
Source: Math Playground <http://www.mathplayground.com/tangrams.html>

Area and perimeter confusion

Students tend to confuse the concepts of area and perimeter. This may be attributable to the tendency to teach the two concepts in tandem – particularly in the older grades – and a heavy reliance on memorising formulae to calculate the area and perimeter of different shapes. In the Mathematics Assessment for Learning and Teaching (MALT) project, researchers found that 32 per cent of 13-year-old students calculated the perimeter of a shape, rather than the area, to find a missing dimension (Ryan & Williams 2007). They also found that while 60 per cent of 14-year-olds could calculate the 'distance a referee ran around a rugby pitch 90 m long and 60 m wide', 14 per cent of them calculated the area, and another 12 per cent simply added 90 and 60. In her seminal study, Ma (1999) found that many practising teachers believed there was a constant relationship between the area and perimeter of a rectangle, and that whenever the perimeter of a rectangle increases, the area also increases. Livy, Muir and Maher (2012) also found that this was a misconception held by many pre-service teachers.

> This confusion with area and perimeter is further addressed in the 'Concepts to consider' at the end of the chapter.

ACTIVITY 3.8

Mary says that whenever you increase the perimeter of a rectangle, the area also increases. John says this is not true. Who is correct – Mary or John?

Use geoboards and rubber bands to make rectangles with different areas and perimeters. What do you notice about the shape of the rectangles that have bigger perimeters and smaller areas? Investigate making a number of different rectangles that have the same perimeter measurement.
- Which one has the largest area?
- What do you notice about the shape of the rectangles (remember that a square is a rectangle)?
- What conclusions can you draw about the relationship between the area and perimeter of a rectangle?

Many students will think that the rectangles in Figure 3.11 support Mary's conjecture. How would you convince them otherwise?

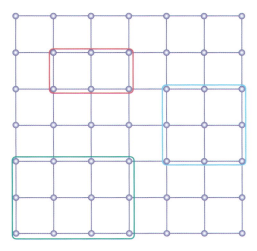

Figure 3.11 Geoboard showing different rectangles

If you do not have access to geoboards, then visit the National Library of Virtual Manipulatives website and access the virtual geoboard.

A focus on activities that involve covering a shape with tiles and counting the tiles within it can help to reinforce and consolidate students' understanding of the attribute of area.

Link 3.6 National Library of Virtual Manipulatives

CLASSROOM SNAPSHOT 3.2

After reading *Zack's Alligator* (Mozelle 1989), the teacher showed her Year 3/4 class a 'growing creature' that she had purchased from a novelty shop. On the packet it claimed that the starfish would increase 600 per cent when placed in water for 72 hours. This provided an ideal opportunity to investigate area as an attribute, and to introduce students to square centimetres as the standard unit for measuring area. Each day, one of the students placed the starfish on the grid paper and traced around it. If the claim was correct, after three days the starfish should have reached its maximum size. The class decided to keep measuring for five days to ensure maximum growth had been achieved. The tracings were compared informally and then students counted the squares to more accurately record the results. The tracings were projected on an IWB, which clearly showed the grid squares and raised the issue of how to count partial squares (see Figure 3.12). Different colours were then used to match up partial squares with the counting and recording of squares modelled with the whole class. The class found that the starfish grew in area from approximately 44 cm^2 to 204 cm^2 – an increase of about 400 per cent rather than 600 per cent.

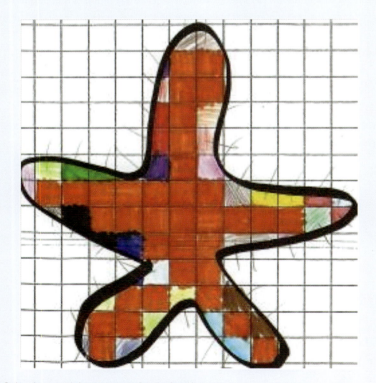

Figure 3.12 Colouring partial squares to determine the area

Classroom Snapshot 3.2 demonstrates the practical nature of measurement and how technology can be incorporated to enhance measurement experiences. In addition to investigating the change in the area of the starfish, the class was also immersed in other experiences that focused on the attribute of area. As the result of a number of practical activities and experiences, students were able to make connections between the multiplicative nature of arrays to discover the formula for area for themselves. Through covering objects with tiles, for example, students were able to determine that a quick and efficient way of counting all the tiles was to count the tiles across the top and bottom and multiply them together (see Figure 3.13).

Figure 3.13 Covering a surface with tiles

Volume and capacity

Volume refers to the three-dimensional space that a figure or object occupies, while capacity is a measure of the amount of something that a three-dimensional object can hold. In primary school, most of the experiences that students encounter are really about measuring capacity, and involve the comparison of different containers. As with area, some students will not have developed an understanding of the conservation of volume – believing, for example, that a taller container will always hold more than a shorter container, even if the volume of liquid in each is the same. Water, sand, rice and beans are all appropriate non-standard units that can be used to compare and measure the capacity of various containers. Activity 3.9 is indicative of the types of experiences in which young children should be involved to investigate capacity.

ACTIVITY 3.9

Provide students with a series of five or six labelled containers of different sizes and shapes, with the task being to place them in order from least to most volume (or capacity). This can be quite challenging. Students should be encouraged to work in groups to come up with a solution and to justify the reasons for their order.

Figure 3.14 Measuring liquids

Angle

The attribute of angle can be described as 'the spread of the angle's rays', as angles are composed of two rays that are infinite in length with a common vertex. Angles are also a measure of rotation, which are measured in degrees. In practice, there is a tendency to leave the study of angles until later in primary school, where students' first encounter often involves the use of protractors, rather than activities that help them to identify the attribute of angle. However, young children can be introduced to the attribute of angle and be involved in comparing and ordering activities that may then result in a more conceptual understanding of the attribute when they are exposed to more formal experiences further on in their schooling. Activity 3.10 is an example of an activity that would be appropriate to use with younger children to explore the concept of angles.

ACTIVITY 3.10

Angles in the environment

Take the class on an angle hunt. Discuss what an angle is and where we see them in the environment.

Angle turner

Using two different-coloured circles, make an angle turner (see Figure 3.15). Use the angle turner to represent different angles – for example, ask students: 'Show me what angle is made when it is three o'clock on an analogue clock' or 'Show me the angle of the open door.'

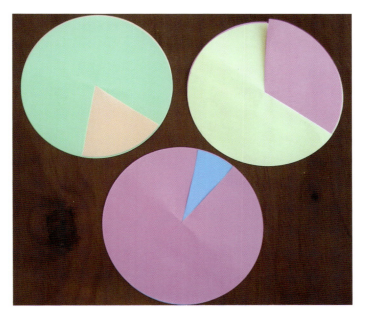

Figure 3.15 Angle turners showing different angles

As with the other attributes, the use of standard units and formulae should occur later in the measurement sequence. In a similar way to using non-standard units to measure the length and area of different objects, students should also be given the opportunity to measure angles with non-standard units. Van de Walle and colleagues (2013) suggest that a wedge can be made from a piece of cardboard and used to measure different angles by counting the number of times it will fit into a given angle. Students could then use their individual wedges to measure similar angles and discuss the reasons for different results that are related to the size of their unit.

PAUSE AND REFLECT

Many students have difficulties with measuring angles and reading a protractor. What do you think contributes to these difficulties? There are a number of websites that provide online protractors and require the use of protractors to measure angles. One example, at TeachableMath provides a protractor and activities suitable for interactive use (see Figure 3.16). Identify how you would model the use of the protractor through this site.

Link 3.7 TeachableMath: Interactive protractor

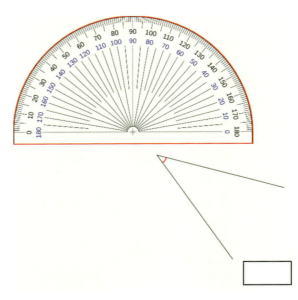

Figure 3.16 Interactive protractor from TeachableMath
Source: TeachableMath (teachablemath.com)

ACTIVITY 3.11

Link 3.8 'Wax Paper Protractor'

Follow the directions in the video 'Wax Paper Protractor' by Talent Development Secondary, available on YouTube, to make your own protractor. What would be the benefits of having students complete such an activity? Use your protractor to measure some different angles drawn on a piece of paper. What do you notice?

Mass

Although the terms 'mass' and 'weight' are often used interchangeably, it is important to remember that they are different. Mass is the amount of a substance, while weight is the pull of gravity on that substance. Having said this, on earth the measures of mass and weight are about the same, and measurement experiences in primary school generally involve measuring weight. One of the earliest understandings to develop with students is the notion that mass is not necessarily proportionate to volume, and that an object's mass cannot be calculated by looking at it. Early experiences should require children to compare the mass of two objects by holding one in each hand (**hefting**) in order to demonstrate what 'heavier' means. Balance scales can then be used to demonstrate how one side of the scale lowers when the object is heavier. Non-standard units such as marbles, cubes or washers can be used to measure the mass of different objects before introducing children to standard units such as grams and kilograms. As mass is a physical measure, children need opportunities to be physically involved in weighing different objects, and also comparing and ordering the mass of these objects. The following activity is an example of a suitable experience to engage young children in focusing on the attribute of mass.

Hefting estimating the mass of objects by holding them in the hands

Play dough animals

In small groups, ask each child to construct a worm using play dough. Discuss whether the longest worm would also be the heaviest. Try different ways to determine this, including hefting and comparing with non-standard units. Place the worms in order of lightest to heaviest.

Ask the children to now make their worm into a cat. Will their cat have the same mass? Why/why not? Now get them to make the cat into different-sized balls. Which ball is the heaviest? What would happen if all the balls were placed on the balance scale? Would they have the same mass as the cat? The worm?

Making and using a scale

Bathroom and kitchen scales are compact devices that produce a number to indicate the weight of an object placed on them. Simple spring scales can be made using rubber bands, paper cups and weights to calibrate the scale. Full instructions are provided at the Lyncean Education website. Learning opportunities here should focus on choosing appropriate informal units and constructing a scale that accurately distinguishes between the mass of different objects.

Link 3.9 Lyncean Education: A toy spring scale

Time

Time can be thought of as the duration of an event from its beginning to its end, and it differs from most other attributes in that it cannot be perceived through sensory experiences in the way that other measurement concepts can. Time is also subjective according to context – something can take a long time or a short time, depending upon the situation and people's perceptions – for example, one hour can seem a long time when you are waiting for a bus or a short time if you are playing a game.

There is a tendency in classrooms to focus instruction on time around reading the time on an analogue clock face. As the clock represents an instrument for telling time, which uses the standard units of minutes and hours, focus on this aspect should occur later in the measurement sequence. We do not, for example, expect young children to measure with a ruler or scales, yet many children are expected to be able to tell the time from a very early age. As with the other attributes, children need to be given plenty of opportunities to develop an understanding of the attribute of time, as well as experiences in comparing and ordering time and measuring time with non-standard units, before being introduced to standard units. Experiences that require students to order the duration of events can be used to establish a feel for how long something takes, and activities such as placing events in their correct order according to length of time can help develop the concept of time as a sequence. Non-standard units can involve the use of hand claps, pendulum swings and sand running through a bottle. Students often show confusion with reading analogue clocks, which can be related to the different actions and functions of the two hands. Van de Walle and colleagues (2013) recommend the use of a one-handed clock, which allows a focus on approximate language (e.g. it's about seven o'clock; it's a little past nine o'clock) (see Figure 3.17).

Figure 3.17 (a) A bit past nine o'clock; (b) Halfway between three and four o'clock; (c) About 11 o'clock

ACTIVITY 3.12

Try this yourself to see how accurate you are with estimating the length of a minute.

Stand up and press start on a stopwatch. Sit down when you think a minute is up and stop the timer. How close were you? Repeat the process three times. Did you improve your estimate each time?

What are some other activities you could engage students in to emphasise the attribute of time, rather than focusing on reading a clock face?

ACTIVITY 3.13

Ready for the bell

Give students a recording sheet with a set of blank clock faces. Set some timers to go off at different times during the lesson. When the timer buzzes, students should look up and record the time on the clock face in both analogue and digital form.

Source: Adapted from Van de Walle et al. 2017

ACTIVITY 3.14

Look at this screenshot from the HOTmaths What's the Time? widget (see Figure 3.18). How helpful do you think this would be in assisting students to tell the time?

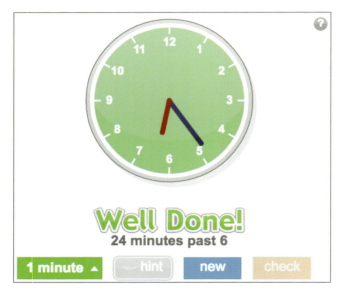

Figure 3.18 Screenshot of HOTmaths What's the Time? widget

Investigating times and time zones

World time zones can be accessed through The World Clock website. This site can be used to determine the respective times of cities throughout the world. Cross-curricular links could be encouraged through mapping the zones on a world map and using some of the information to predict which cities would be 'ahead' or 'behind' Australia in time. Further investigations could involve the use of travel websites to plan trips, and to calculate distances and travel rates. Other activities could involve research into other aspects of time, such as why there are 60 minutes in an hour, why October is the tenth month instead of the eighth, and how other cultures measure their years.

ACTIVITY 3.15

HOTmaths has some excellent time zone widgets and associated activities (see Figure 3.19).

(a)
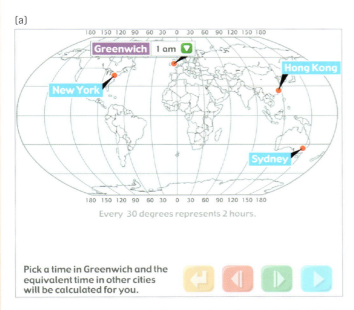

(b)

Figure 3.19 (a) Screenshot of HOTmaths Times Around the World widget; (b) Screenshot of HOTmaths Time in Australia widget

Temperature

Temperature is the measure of how hot or cold things are, with the judgement of this being dependent upon people's perceptions or feelings. Children will typically use terms such as 'cold', 'warm' or 'hot' to describe the weather, food and drinks, and it is likely that the interpretation of these terms will vary among the children. There are no non-standard units for temperature, and the use of standard units to describe temperature is complicated by using different scales (Celsius or Fahrenheit) and the inclusion of negative numbers. Students' experiences with temperature should begin with a focus on the attribute and development of the understanding that describing temperature is based on sensory experiences – for example, a surface may feel hot because your hand is cold. Before introducing students formally to the thermometer, it is useful to have them design their own thermometers and include descriptions of their own developed scales to designate a range of temperatures.

Value and money

Money is the unit used to measure the value or cost of something. As with the other attributes, it is important to establish an understanding of what value means rather than beginning with a focus on operating with currency. In the primary grades, students typically are required to:

- recognise coins and notes
- know the value of coins and notes
- create equivalent coin and note collections
- make change
- round money amounts up or down.

In the early years, many worthwhile experiences and learning opportunities can be provided through the establishment of a class shop, which can be used for free and directed play. The relative value of items can also be discussed, and games such as *The Price is Right* can be played to compare and order the cost of various items. Non-standard units can take the form of counters or stickers before formal units are introduced. In the Australian Curriculum: Mathematics v. 9.0, money and value are included as part of the Measurement strand, but also referred to in the Number strand in relation to solving problems including simple money transactions (e.g. AC9M1N05). Where possible, provide lots of opportunities for students to calculate and give change using real money before expecting them to carry out purely written computational tasks. Interesting investigations can be carried out with older students about currencies used in other countries and exchange rates. A currency converter can be found at XE Currency Converter.

ACTIVITY 3.16

The value of money is relative. To adults, $100 may not seem like very much but young children typically think it is a lot of money. If you asked a young child what they could buy with $100, their answers might range from a house to a car, to lots of groceries. The picture book *Sophie's Prize* by Jennie Marston can be used as a stimulus to explore what can be bought with $100. In the book, Sophie wins $100 in an art competition and must decide how to spend the money. After reading the book, students could be given copies of catalogues with the prices removed and asked to select items that would total $100. Another version of the catalogues could include the prices to extend students to figure out the totals.

CLASSROOM SNAPSHOT 3.3

While the picture book 'Heads or Tails?' (Muir 2018) has a strong probability focus, one Prep teacher used the story as a stimulus to explore coins, and subsequently used money to learn about lots of different mathematical concepts. Over a series of lessons, the students engaged in activities ranging from recognising and sorting Australian coins to estimating and accurately counting a group of objects (coins), measuring the mass of coins, and using coins as an informal unit to measure length. They then extended their investigation to recognising the difference in money from other countries, and even learned to make 'friends of 10' using heads and tails to show the part-part-whole relationship. ICT was also incorporated as they used Bee-Bots and mapping to locate a treasure of coins.

Using inquiry to develop an understanding of measurement

Inquiry is a teaching approach whereby students respond to ill-structured, open-ended questions that reflect the authentic problems we encounter in 'real life' (Allmond, Wells & Makar 2010). Measurement situations provide authentic contexts that can be used to engage students in inquiry-based experiences. Classroom Snapshot 3.4 demonstrates how a measurement problem was used to engage students in a rich inquiry experience.

CLASSROOM SNAPSHOT 3.4

Having taken digital photos of 'Mr Splash' (see Figure 3.20), Mrs Jones, a Year 7 teacher, projected the images on the IWB and introduced the following problem to the students by saying:

I have a photograph of Mr Splash. I wonder if we can work out how tall he might be?

(a)

(b)

Figure 3.20 (a) Mr Splash; (b) Measuring Mr Splash
Source: Photos courtesy of Sharyn Livy

▶▶ Students were asked to volunteer their estimates of the height of Mr Splash, and they were encouraged to explain how they decided their predictions. They were then asked to compare their predictions with their own heights and those of other people in the class. In order to more accurately determine class heights and measurements, they then worked in small groups to measure heights and some body dimensions. The data were entered into a spreadsheet, with data recorded for every student. Each group was then allocated one relationship to investigate and subsequently produce a graph – for example, height compared with head length, arm span or leg length (this can be done by hand or using technology).

PAUSE AND REFLECT

Using the data collected in Classroom Snapshot 3.4, what other relationships could be investigated? In what ways do you think the use of technology would contribute to students' ability to complete the task? How do you think students could have undertaken the investigations without the use of technology? Would it have been as effective?

Common Online Data Analysis Program (CODAP) is an example of a program that can be used to graphically represent data. It is described more fully in Chapter 8, and would be a useful resource for the upper primary and early secondary years. Data can be sourced from students' own investigations (e.g. 'People say you are as tall as your arm span – investigate') or from the New Zealand CensusAtSchool site.

TIPS FOR ONLINE TEACHING

While we have emphasised throughout this chapter that measurement experiences need to be practical and hands on, they do not necessarily have to take place in the classroom. Students can be provided with many activities and experiences that require measurement in the home or outside environment. For young children who need guidance with the act of measuring, particularly with non-standard units, the teacher could provide 'how to' videos to illustrate measuring principles such as lining up the units in a straight line or not leaving any gaps. In turn, students could then video themselves measuring objects in their environment and return the footage to their teacher as evidence of their learning.

While not always an appropriate substitute for physically measuring with real materials, there are many suitable virtual manipulatives and websites that focus on measurement. Activity 3.8 and Activity 3.9 provide two examples that provide students with authentic online measurement experiences. Students could also be encouraged to conduct their own investigations. For example, to investigate capacity and the use of standard units, students could be encouraged to keep a record of how much milk their family consumed in a week. The class could then collate their results via a Zoom session and a class graph could be constructed online, facilitated by the teacher.

Conclusion

This chapter has provided an overview of the main factors that need to be considered when teaching measurement concepts. Examples of teaching approaches, including ones that incorporate ICT, have been provided to introduce, develop and extend students' understanding of the different attributes of measurement. Measurement is such a practical activity, so the use of ICT and virtual measurement experiences should be used judiciously, to supplement and complement what can be done physically. As with the other learning areas, there are endless resources that are accessible online, and, as teachers, we need to be aware of the affordances and constraints of these resources and select from them accordingly.

GUIDED STUDENT TASKS

1. Read the book *How Big is a Foot?* (Myller 1990) or view it on YouTube. In the story, the king measures the queen using his feet and orders a bed that is 6 feet long and 3 feet wide. The carpenter's apprentice makes the bed using his own feet, which results in the bed being too small. How could you use the story as a stimulus for demonstrating the need for standard units?
2. It is recommended that non-standard units should resemble the standard unit. Can you identify appropriate non-standard units for each of the attributes discussed in this chapter?
3. Select a year level from the Australian Curriculum: Mathematics v. 9.0 and identify an appropriate measurement activity that matches the content descriptor. Not all attributes are mentioned in each level – does this mean that you would not teach those attributes every year?

Link 3.10 'How Big is a Foot?'

CONCEPTS TO CONSIDER

As mentioned earlier, students often confuse the terms area and perimeter and will use the perimeter formula instead of the area formula when finding a missing dimension (Ryan & Williams 2007). This is likely attributable to not having a good conceptual understanding of what both these attributes are, along with introducing the formula as a procedure to be memorised. To avoid confusion, think of the perimeter as being the outside or fence around a paddock, while the area is the space inside the paddock. Imagine the area divided up into little squares of land, and to calculate the area, you would need to count all the little squares. Our knowledge of multiplicative arrays means that we can apply the area formula to multiply the dimensions of the length and width of the paddock to work out the area.

As students start to calculate with units of area measure, conversion between square units can become very difficult. For example, if you calculated the area of a rectangle was 10 000 cm squared, how would you express this in square metres? 1, 10 or 100? If we think of the sides of the rectangle as being, for example, 100 cm × 100 cm (yes, a square is a rectangle), then that would be the equivalent of 1 metre by 1 metre, which would then mean the rectangle was 1 square metre. We can then use this knowledge to convert other square centimetre measurements to square metres. For example, to convert 500 square centimetres to square metres, we would divide 500 by 10 000, giving us an answer of 0.05 square metres.

FURTHER READING

Websites for exploration

Austin, R, Thompson, D & Beckmann, C 2005, 'Exploring measurement concepts through literature: Natural links across disciplines', *Mathematics Teaching in the Middle School*, vol. 10, no. 5, pp. 218–24.

Battista, M 2003, 'Understanding students' thinking about area and volume measurement', in D Clements (ed.), *Learning and teaching measurement*, Reston, VA: NCTM.

Lott, JW & Lott, CJ (eds) 2014, *Mathematics lessons learned from across the world*, Reston, VA: NCTM.

Muir, T 2005, 'When near enough is good enough: Eight principles for enhancing the value of measurement estimation for students', *Australian Primary Mathematics Classroom*, vol. 17 no. 1, pp. 21–8.

EXPLORING GEOMETRY

CHAPTER 4

LEARNING OUTCOMES

By the end of this chapter, you will:

- understand the breadth of concepts included in the geometry section of curriculum documents generally, particularly the Australian Curriculum: Mathematics v. 9.0
- be familiar with a theoretical framework used as a lens through which to view students' geometrical thinking, known as the 'van Hiele theory'
- have a pedagogical framework that is useful for designing sequential student tasks to assist students to grow in their understandings of geometrical concepts
- understand the important role of language and maintaining 'student ownership' of the geometrical ideas
- be familiar with the use of technological tools to enhance our teaching of geometrical concepts for the e-generation
- consider geometrical concepts in light of student group understanding.

Introduction

Educationally, we are in an exciting time in terms of geometrical investigations in the classroom. While the manipulation of concrete materials to enable student construction of two-dimensional figures and three-dimensional objects has been readily available for many years, there are a growing number of mathematics classrooms that have access to dynamic geometry software and interactive sites that enable real-time creation and exploration of geometric figures and their properties. In fact, in some pockets of society, students' access to a mobile device is in a similar manner to how classrooms of the 1980s used pen and paper as a resource. While, in jest, mobile devices may be referred to as 'an extension of the brain', in its regular use as an instant source of information and exploration there is an element of this use that can be exploited for positive gain in the mathematics classroom. There is sometimes confusion when comparing curriculum documents in relation to using the words 'space' or 'geometry' or 'shape'. Geometry is often described as the exploration of space. The Australian Curriculum: Mathematics F–10 v. 9.0 (ACARA 2022) has adopted the term 'space' to describe one of the six content strands allocated to study of geometry. This involves an investigation of shape, size and place. This chapter explores the development of geometrical concepts and the manner in which we can facilitate exploratory experiences to assist students in their development.

Geometric concepts

The previous version of the Australian Curriculum: Mathematics (ACARA 2016b) had a structure that combined the Geometry and Measurement content areas. In line with the current Australian Curriculum: Mathematics v. 9.0 (ACARA 2022), this chapter is devoted to the principles and practicalities of teaching geometry in the primary years (approximately 5–12 years of age) and moving into lower secondary (approximately 12–13 years of age). While the content issues are dealt with separately, it is not possible to ignore the specific links that geometry has with other content areas, in particular measurement (as it is clearly linked within the Australian Curriculum: Mathematics v. 9.0) and number and algebra. The activities in this chapter are not age-specific and should be used in the classroom according to students' levels of understanding.

For the development of students' understanding of any mathematical concept, the selection of the type of task is critical. It is essential that activities promote student engagement in the task, provide an element of decision-making, and provide opportunities to discuss and explain students' mathematical thoughts. Investigations that promote inquiry are particularly important when targeting geometric concepts in the primary classroom, as too often activities merely require students to identify shapes or geometric processes, rather than investigate and explore geometric ideas.

As the writings of van Hiele (1986) elaborate, and are explored later in the chapter, geometric tasks should promote engagement in the activity, require the students to find their own way to a solution and take ownership of the mathematical ideas. These key components will assist in creating a rich learning environment that adopts effective pedagogical practices. Sometimes there is a need for teachers to let tasks get a little 'messy' while students explore different geometrical concepts; hence, some of the activities in this chapter ask the teacher to let go of preconceived ideas of exactly where the student will travel during their learning journey in the sequence of the activities.

The activities in this chapter centre around geometrical content covered in primary curriculum documents. Internationally, these documents tend to include an investigation of relationships among and within:

- two-dimensional figures and their properties
- three-dimensional objects and their properties
- relevant positions, movements and transformation of shapes
- representations and interpretations of locations.

Each of these concept groups is explored through recognising, describing, comparing, constructing, classifying and developing geometrical arguments.

Visualisation is a key component of this strand as the visual perception of shapes and their properties changes as the learner's conceptual focus develops. The relationship-building among these geometrical concepts builds to a focus on the interrelationships among the properties and their figures through student-centred tasks. To get to this point, learners

---

Visualisation a mental image that is similar to a visual perception

have a long journey to take with specific hurdles along the way. The journey begins with 'sort, name and create familiar shapes: recognize and describe familiar shapes within objects in the environment, giving reasons (AC9MFSP01)'. In the latest version of the curriculum, an emphasis on creating and providing reasons is a welcomed addition. This goes beyond the previous terminology of describe and name.

The familiar shapes to be sorted, named and created are rectangles, triangles, squares and circles; however, this is not an exhaustive list, and should include any shapes of interest. Geometry tasks lend themselves to draw upon students' real-life experiences as the context and base from which to deepen their understanding of geometric concepts.

Taking geometry outside the classroom

There are many geometry activities that are suited to the outdoors. If we are going to build on children's everyday experiences, a large selection of learning tasks may include outdoor activities. These can be as simple as:

- going for a shape walk around the school, and asking students to record the shapes they see and where they found them
- making a circle outside using a string and chalk
- designing and constructing a mini-basketball court
- designing and drawing a map for an outside obstacle course
- 'exploring string games used in story telling by First Nations Australians' (content elaboration of AC9M1SP01)
- exploring the common shapes used in bridge and building designs (this leads nicely into an indoor activity where the students work in pairs using spaghetti or drinking straws and Blu-Tack to make a bridge that can hold a certain object between two tables)
- making wet tennis ball angles (see Figure 4.2).

To assist in the exploration of geometrical concepts, a developmental model will form the discussion.

Figure 4.1 Geometry and everyday objects

 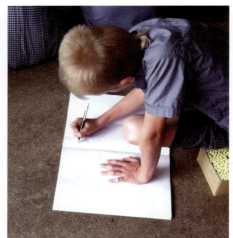

Figure 4.2 Wet tennis ball angle activity

> **TIPS FOR ONLINE TEACHING**
>
> Each of the geometry tasks described above can be adapted to online learning where students are engaged in mathematical tasks at home. These tasks can be introduced through online learning platforms, such as Zoom. When students are confident in going offline to complete the task, it is essential that students have time to explore the task and present their findings to the group. This can be done in various formal and informal ways. Through the online discussion, students will develop the mathematical language with meaning.

Theoretical framework

A range of theoretical frameworks assist in interpreting students' understanding of mathematical concepts. Teachers have at their disposal a developmental theory particular to geometry that has been researched (Serow 2007a) since the 1950s, known as the van Hiele theory (van Hiele 1986). As in most areas of mathematics education, there is considerable debate concerning the validity and nature of the developmental models and their associated features. However, putting this debate aside for now, the van Hiele theory provides a practical lens that enables teachers to view their students' conceptual development and the targeted design of their teaching and learning tasks.

The van Hiele theory characterises five hierarchical levels and two transitional levels of geometric thought that provide a window for viewing students' growth and understanding in geometry concepts. The chosen descriptions of three of the five van Hiele levels of thinking (evident in primary and secondary settings), alongside more recently identified transitional levels of thinking (Pegg & Baker 1999; Serow 2007b), are explained within the context of students' growing understanding of the relationships among figures and their properties. As the context of the curriculum begins with describing and sorting and spirals through any mathematics curriculum, sorting, classifying and describing properties and figures constitute the type of student task referred to. The van Hiele levels of thinking, that are relevant to primary and early secondary contexts are outlined below:

Level 1: Figures are judged by their appearance. A figure is recognised by its form or shape. The properties of a figure play no explicit role in the identification of a figure.

Transitional Level 1/2: Properties are perceived as 'features'. When grouping shapes, students complete this spontaneously upon the identification of similar features. For example, students at this level will be aware of the number of sides and angles of a shape.

Level 2A: Figures are classified on the basis of one property. This property is treated as a unique signifier of the shape and is used to describe groupings.

Level 2B: Figures are classified on the basis of more than one property. Students will make links among different groups of shapes when the links are supported by visual cues. Students will use more than one property as unique signifiers when attempting to provide minimum descriptions.

Level 3: Thinking at this level is characterised by a focus on the relationships among the properties and figures.

Transitional level 3/4: Students focus on a single relationship that is two directional.

Level 4: Further conditions are placed upon class inclusion and general overviews of different relating concepts are formed.

> The van Hiele levels of thinking are elaborated in relation to geometrical concepts in 'Concepts to consider' at the end of the chapter.

CLASSROOM SNAPSHOT 4.1

A casual teacher, Mr Walker, was allocated a Year 4 class for two teaching days. The usual teacher of the class left the following lesson notes for the mathematics lesson. 'We are finishing a unit on comparing and describing shapes. Year 4 has finished quadrilaterals. In the mathematics lesson time, please ask the students to identify a square, parallelogram, rhombus, kite, trapezium and rectangle by holding up the shape cards on my desk. The students can then draw each shape and write a description of each one.' Mr Walker found the cards, sat the students on the floor at the front of the room to have a class discussion, and began what he thought would be a quick recap of quadrilateral identification and some descriptions using features and properties. As the cards were held up, students volunteered the following responses:

Ming-Le: That is a rectangle.

Mr Walker: What can you tell me about it?

Ming-Le: It has two sides the same, and the other two sides the same but different to the other two.

Mr Walker: Can anyone tell me anything else about the rectangle?

Abdul: It has four right angles like the square does.

[When the rhombus card was held up, all the children in the class put their hands up as high as they could.]

Mr Walker: Wow, we are all keen to answer this one! What is it?

Jessica:	It is a rhombus because it looks like a square that has been 'rhommed' by a bus.
Mr Walker:	Can you tell me anything else about this shape?
Jessica:	If you straightened it up it would be a square again.
[The teacher turned the card to a different orientation.]	
Mr Walker:	What can you tell me now?
Leon:	When you have it that way, it is a diamond.

PAUSE AND REFLECT

The classroom discussion concerning the quadrilaterals provided a window through which to view students' conceptual understanding.
- What do you know about Jessica and Leon's understanding?
- What activity would you choose to target the properties of the rhombus?
- What technology might you use to assist you, and how could you use it?

Features of the theoretical framework

There are seven key features that directly impact on the pedagogical practices we use when targeting geometrical concepts in the classroom. Teaching points that stem from the van Hiele theory are discussed below.

Hierarchical nature

The levels of thinking are hierarchical in nature – that is, a student cannot proceed to a particular level of thinking without understanding the previous level. For the teacher, this means it is not possible for a student to skip a level. Progression to the next level depends more on learning experiences than it does on biological maturation. These experiences require investigation, exploration and discussion.

Different level, different language

Each of the levels of thinking has its own language. While the words we choose to use may be common at different levels, the meaning attached to the words will be different. Once we have achieved a particular level of thinking, it is not possible to return to that level. This highlights a barrier that can exist in the classroom – not only between students at different levels, but also between students and the teacher. One positive lies in the fact that students' conceptual understandings can be determined through the uniqueness of the language used at each level. The students' classroom talk is a window through which to view their conceptual development.

ACTIVITY 4.1

Consider the following four student descriptions of a pair of parallel lines. How would these align with each student's level of thinking in geometry?

- Student 1: Parallel lines are like railway tracks.
- Student 2: Parallel lines are lines that will never meet if they keep going.
- Student 3: Parallel lines are always the same distance apart.
- Student 4: The perpendicular distance between a pair of parallel lines is the same at any point.

Crisis of thinking

The movement from one level to the next is not a simple process. When students make the transition in one area of geometry, they need to pass through what is called a crisis of thinking (van Hiele 1986). This requires a mental reorganisation. For example, a student moving from Level 2 to Level 3 needs to move from viewing the properties of shapes as isolated bits of information to focusing on the relationships among the properties and their figures. Humans tend to avoid a crisis at all costs, this avoidance is the same for a crisis of thinking. To assist students in surmounting this crisis of thinking, as opposed to avoiding it, teachers can implement a pedagogical framework to assist in lesson and unit design. This is known as the van Hiele teaching phases and will be explored further later in this chapter. A sample teaching sequence incorporating technology will also be provided.

Level reduction

Level reduction involves introducing knowledge via a procedure or trick that allows the learner to solve a task without reaching the required level of thinking for the task. When geometrical concepts are taught in this fashion, ownership of the mathematical idea is not maintained by the students, and they are not equipped to complete unfamiliar questions at a similar level. Introduction of level-reduction techniques at an inappropriate time in the classroom will usually set students up for failure every time they come across problems relating to the particular concept that requires variations of the process to be applied. Level reduction takes only one meaning when initiated by the student.

Progression requires instruction, exploration and reflection

To move students from one level to the next requires the teacher to construct an environment in which the students move to the next level and leave behind the structure of the previous level – something about which they have come to feel comfortable and secure. It is necessary for students to make more and more links to the next level, which means providing opportunities that place the students in a situation where it is necessary to make the change. This requires an exploration of the new structure and a general exposure to the language necessary to communicate effectively within the structure. Students need time to reflect upon the generalisations formed.

Implicit and explicit understanding

Growth through the levels requires learning experiences that facilitate the analysis of elements of the lower levels. Van Hiele (1986, p. 6) describes the attainment of the higher level as evident when 'the rules governing the lower structure have been made explicit and studied, thereby themselves becoming a new structure'.

Discontinuity

> The theory behind discontinuity is discussed in 'Concepts to consider' at the end of the chapter.

Discontinuity has always been controversial, particularly when students have been identified as transitional (between the original five discrete levels of understanding). It is evident that each new level requires a new language, which implies a sudden leap rather than a gentle progression.

Geometry in the primary classroom

> **Three-dimensional (3D) objects** having three dimensions, requiring three coordinates to specify a point
>
> **Two-dimensional (2D) figures** having two dimensions, a flat surface with no depth, requiring two coordinates to specify a point

Three-dimensional (3D) objects, also known as solid shapes, require the same amount of attention as **two-dimensional (2D) figures**. There are many opportunities for extended explorations from the early years of primary to upper primary. According to many curriculum documents, including the Australian Curriculum: Mathematics F–10 v. 9.0, students should cover aspects of the following:

- Sort, name and create familiar shapes; recognise and describe familiar shapes within objects in the environment, giving reasons (AC9MFSP01).
- Make, compare and classify familiar shapes; recognise familiar shapes and objects in the environment, identifying the similarities and differences between them (AC9M1SP01).
- Recognise, compare, and classify shapes, referencing the number of sides and using spatial terms such as 'opposite', 'parallel', 'curved' and 'straight' (AC9M2SP01).
- Make, compare and classify objects, identifying key features and explaining why these features make them suited to their uses (AC9M3SP01).
- Represent and approximate composite shapes and objects in the environment using combinations of familiar shapes and objects (AC9M4SP01).
- Connect objects to their nets and build objects from their nets using spatial and geometric reasoning (AC9M5SP01).
- Compare the parallel cross sections of objects and recognise their relationships to right prisms (AC9M6SP01).

The spiralling nature of the process of exploration or revisiting the same geometrical concepts over a period of time is lost if the outcomes are interpreted literally and in an unrelated fashion. For example, it would be appropriate to continue sorting 3D objects and providing reasoning for the categories in upper primary. The outcomes need to be viewed holistically. While the drawing of 3D objects is not included in the Foundation Year outcome above (AC9MFSP01). It makes sense to ask students in the first year of school to build interesting towers with a range of concrete materials and then ask them to draw what they have built. It is also a lost opportunity if the students are not asked to name and describe the shapes that they have used to build their tower. This activity could also link to a measurement activity, where the students compare the heights of the different towers and how they are represented in their drawings.

Three-dimensional shapes

Students may begin describing the features of 3D objects as those that are pointy, those that roll, those that slide, those that have curved **edges**. They will begin to identify the 2D shapes on the **faces** of 3D objects. As with our 2D discussions, it is essential to use the correct terminology for the features of 3D objects when referring to them. In relation to 3D objects, you may hear students describe the cube as having six sides. After affirming the student in identifying this, the discussion could move to the fact that they are called faces on a 3D object. In fact, the cube has six faces, eight **vertices** and twelve edges. These concepts are continually revisited in their explorations, even in the upper primary years, where students may complete a task where they tabulate the number of faces, edges and vertices on various 3D objects, and then search for any patterns and relationships they can find. It is a pleasant surprise when students identify Euler's theorem in various forms (sometimes referred to as Euler's rule). A nice connection to patterns and algebra is forged in this type of activity. While there are many online videos, apps and freeware to explore 3D objects in varied contexts, providing primary students with avenues to build their own 3D objects, record these in diagram form with annotations, and then move to digital drawings is a valuable learning sequence.

Edge the interval where two faces of a solid meet

Face a flat surface of a polyhedron

Vertices plural of vertex: a point on a 3D object where three or more straight edges meet to make a corner

ACTIVITY 4.2

Tabulate the number of faces, edges and vertices on 10 known 3D objects (e.g. cube, rectangular prism, triangular-based pyramid). Can you find a rule that connects the number of faces, edges and vertices on any 3D object? In how many different ways can you write this relationship?

As in all areas of mathematics, it is important to keep the explorations as open as possible. For example, instead of asking students to match the cube with its corresponding net from a selection of nets, ask them to come up with as many different nets of the cube as they can on 1 cm^2 grid paper. There are several interactive sites that can be used following this exploration to consolidate the concept of the net as a 2D representation of a 3D object. This interactive net exploration is an activity from the Illuminations website (National Council of Teachers of Mathematics).

ACTIVITY 4.3

Find as many different nets for the cube as you can. How do you know when you have found them all? What do you need to be careful about?

Try this same activity with other 3D objects.

How can you use concrete materials and digital devices to assist you with a class discussion of the nets found by the students?

What are the advantages of using different exploration mediums?

CLASSROOM SNAPSHOT 4.2

Isometric projection a corner view of an object

Link 4.1 Maths300
Link 4.2 Mathematics Centre: Four Cube Houses

Mrs Penson was looking for an interesting way to introduce her students to **isometric projections**. She searched high and wide for a contextual teaching strategy. She came across an activity on the Maths300 website, which is a mathematics teaching resource where you can find complete interactive lessons for early primary to upper secondary mathematics classes.

The activity was called Four Cube Houses and involved the students taking on the role of an architect to design as many house designs as possible using four cubes with various defining instructions. An important component of the lesson involved the students drawing their designs on isometric paper. At the end of the first lesson, the students were thoroughly engaged in finding all possible designs. As they were packing up the items on their desks ready for recess, one student was heard telling another, 'I thought we were doing maths before morning tea today.'

In the upper primary years, as students are constructing prisms and pyramids using various commercial and everyday materials, they will benefit from tasks that draw their attention to the cross-sections of these objects. This is the key to higher-order classifications that begin to move away from a focus on the shape of the faces only. When objects are considered in conjunction with their cross-sections, students will begin to differentiate between the classes of prisms, pyramids, cones, cylinders and spheres.

ACTIVITY 4.4

Link 4.3 Maths300: About

Go to the Maths300 website and read the 'About' page. This page lists features of mathematics lessons that are applicable across the curriculum. This site has an annual subscription to enable access to the lessons and associated downloadable software.

PAUSE AND REFLECT

How would you best describe the characteristics of groups of figures named prisms, pyramids, cones, cylinders and spheres? How would you describe the cross-sections of each of these groups of shapes?

Figures 4.3–4.5 tell the story of an experienced teacher integrating interactive whiteboard (IWB) technology into the mathematics classroom for the first time. It is evident that the teacher integrated IWB technology into the teaching/learning sequence within a myriad of practical and discussion-promoting tasks. This teacher acknowledged the gradual introduction and development of mathematical language and followed the van Hiele teaching phases as a guide to do this. The students did not perceive the IWB as the teacher's tool, and instead viewed it as a class tool that was shared freely.

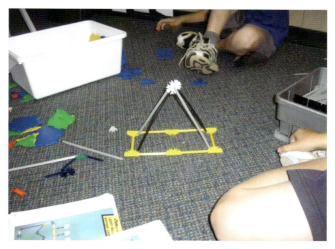

Figure 4.3 Using concrete materials to construct pyramids

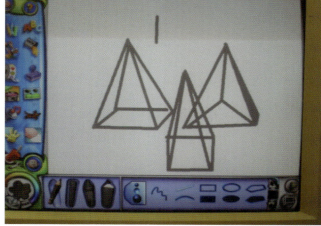

Figure 4.4 Representing pyramids using IWB technology

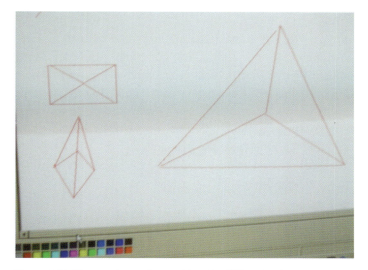

Figure 4.5 Different views of pyramids using IWB technology

While technological tools provide interesting avenues to explore geometrical concepts, it is important to utilise the affordances of everyday materials and contexts that do not involve information and communication technology (ICT) tools. The structure of the New Zealand Mathematics Curriculum provides elaborations to the unit level, and many of these use everyday materials throughout the lesson sequences. Within the shape units of work for GM2–4, titled Foil Fun (NZ Maths 2010), which targets 'explore and describe faces, edges, and corners of 2D and 3D objects' and 'make, name and describe polygons and other plane shapes', the activities require the students to manipulate packages, various solid shapes found in everyday life, nets, foil covers, and 3D representations from magazines.

Link 4.4 NZ Maths: Foil Fun

Two-dimensional shapes

The van Hiele framework clearly articulates a developmental pathway that shapes our teaching of geometry. The level structure, which moves from identifying figures based on overall appearance to focusing on the properties as unrelated elements to focusing on the relationships that exist among the properties, is evident in many national mathematics curriculum documents. The Australian Curriculum: Mathematics v. 9.0 is no exception and centres on the following outcomes in the primary context:

- Sort, name and create familiar shapes; recognise and describe familiar shapes within objects in the environment, giving reasons (AC9MFSP01).
- Make, compare and classify familiar shapes; recognise familiar shapes and objects in the environment, identifying the similarities and differences between them (AC9M1SP01).
- Recognise, compare, and classify shapes, referencing the number of sides and using spatial terms such as 'opposite', 'parallel', 'curved' and 'straight' (AC9M2SP01).
- Recognise line and rotational symmetry of shapes and create symmetrical patterns and pictures, using dynamic geometry software where appropriate (AC9M4SP03).

It is not until the early secondary years that students are expected to explore two-dimensional figures in relation to equality of sides and angles, and angle sum. Later, they explore concepts concerning **congruent figures** that involve **transformations**, conditions for congruency of triangles and solving problems using congruency as a tool.

> **Congruent figures**
> figures that are the same size and shape
>
> **Transformation**
> shifting or modifying a shape, including reflecting, enlarging, translating and rotating

As discussed earlier, while recognition and naming of 2D shapes in the environment is fine in the early years, 2D shape explorations gradually build a focus on the relationships among the properties and figures. Table 4.1 illustrates the properties of the parallelogram that students need to begin to know before the relationships become the target. The findings are described using inclusive property descriptions.

Table 4.1 Quadrilateral property descriptions

Shape	What can you tell me about the …	Your findings!
Parallelogram	Equality of sides	Opposite sides are equal.
	Equality of angles	Opposite angles are equal.
	Parallelism	Opposite sides are parallel.
	Diagonals	Diagonals bisect each other.

> **Bisect** divide into two equal parts
>
> **Dissect** divide into two parts

When exploring diagonals, you will notice that students often confuse the words '**bisect**' and '**dissect**'. These need to be made explicit. As discussed earlier, students will progress from exclusive to inclusive property descriptions. Students who are operating at Level 2, where the properties are known but exist in isolation, will often include no axes of symmetry for the parallelogram, hence not allowing the sub-sets of square, rectangle and rhombus into the class of parallelograms. This is a difficult hurdle to overcome, and in doing so is a target outcome in the secondary setting. It is important for primary teachers to be aware of the importance of the early property explorations; otherwise, concepts such as symmetry and diagonal properties could possibly be overlooked.

ACTIVITY 4.5

Design a similar template (as Table 4.1) for exploration of all the triangle and quadrilateral figures. What would be the differences between students' descriptions of their findings at Level 1, 2 and 3 thinking?

It is common for some students at Level 1 and Level 2 to describe the square as if it is the 'king of the quads'. At Level 1, students may describe all other quadrilaterals as a morphed version of the square. This is evident in Classroom Snapshot 4.3.

CLASSROOM SNAPSHOT 4.3

Peter's teacher showed him all the quadrilaterals, one after another, on flashcards. He very quickly told the teacher the name of all the quadrilaterals. When the teacher asked Peter to describe the shapes he replied:

> The rectangle is a stretched out square, the parallelogram is a pushed over rectangle, the rhombus is a pushed over square, the kite is a stretched diamond and the trapezium is a rectangle with bits chopped off.

The use of the word 'diamond' is an example of the use of inappropriate language that hinders students' progression in identifying the properties of figures. Teachers should take every opportunity to explore the same figures in different orientations to reinforce the notion that a change in position does not alter the properties of a figure. It is not appropriate to use 'diamond' for a square in a specific orientation. In fact, there is no need to use 'diamond' for the square or the rhombus. After exploration of the properties of 2D figures, it is useful to ask students to complete a table where they choose all the properties that belong to each class of figures.

Teachers in the primary years may have the rewarding experience of teaching students who begin describing classes of quadrilateral figures with sub-sets. Figure 4.6 shows an actual higher-order student response to Activity 4.6. Note the inconsistent response where the student states that the 'rhombus is a special square'.

ACTIVITY 4.6

Draw a tree diagram or a flow chart that shows how all the quadrilaterals are related to each other. You must justify the groups and links that you make.

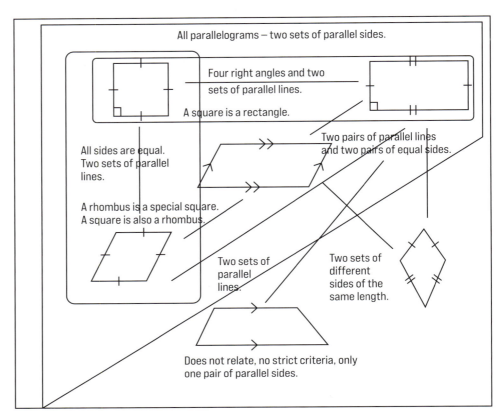

Figure 4.6 Student work sample of quadrilateral relationships and justifications

TIPS FOR ONLINE TEACHING

There are many interactive online games that enable manipulation of figures in an engaging environment. HOTmaths has a growing number of interactive games that can act as catalysts for further classroom discussion of geometric ideas. The first of these, named Peanut Bridge, requires the students to rotate and alter the sizes of shapes to complete the bridge so that a trio of elephants can cross it safely (see Figure 4.7). This is

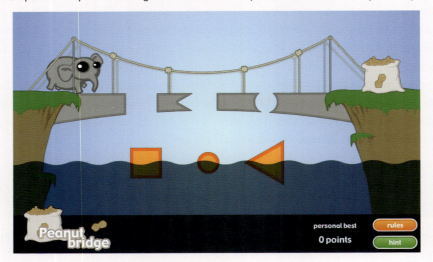

Figure 4.7 Screenshot of HOTmaths Peanut Bridge game

an excellent example of an ICT tool that explores aspects of shape orientation in a context that is of interest to young learners. This game is suitable for individual, small-group or whole-class situations. The platforms of accessibility enable it to be explored on desktops, laptops, tablets, and students' reflections after the task can be shared via an online learning platform.

Another interesting game included in the HOTmaths material is called Shape Sketch (see Figure 4.8). This game is suitable for upper primary students and is one to keep revisiting as it targets the language associated with triangle and quadrilateral figures and properties.

Figure 4.8 Screenshot of HOTmaths Shape Sketch game

In response to the recognised difficulties caused by the cognitive hurdles encountered by many students through the characterisation of the development of relationships among figures and those among properties, we need to consider suitable teaching strategies to assist students to meet and rise above the hurdles.

One readily available tool to counter cognitive hurdles is known as dynamic geometry software (DGS). DGS tools provide teachers with the opportunity to explore the relationships among figures and properties, both intuitively and inductively. Primary-age students have found DGS to be accessible and engaging as the multiple (and formerly tedious) drawings required to identify relationships among figures and properties are carried out with just the drag of the cursor.

GeoGebra is described as a form of dynamic mathematics software (DMS) that is open-source. GeoGebra combines DGS tools and computer algebra systems that together have the potential to target the relationships among the concepts of geometry and algebra. Originally, the tools were designed for the middle-school and secondary years; however, further developments have resulted in a primary version, known as GeoGebraPrim, that is more accessible to primary-aged students. Many DMS programs, including GeoGebra,

TIPS FOR ONLINE TEACHING

can be used in a variety of ways in the classroom, face-to-face and online. For example, the student activity can solely involve student constructions and explorations, or the teacher can initiate exploration through design of templates before the lesson.

When introducing any form of DGS into the classroom, it is usual to start with the segment tool. This becomes a lesson on its own, as the students, through their need to choose the appropriate tool, work through the terms 'line', 'ray' and 'segment'. These tools will have meaning after you work through Activity 4.7.

ACTIVITY 4.7

Go to the GeoGebra website and download the DGS. You will notice that there is a primary version. You may also use any form of DGS to complete this activity, such as Geometer's Sketchpad, and even the iPad version of Sketchpad. To familiarise yourself with DGS, complete the tasks outlined below in separate windows or on separate pages. In this case, we learn by getting our hands dirty.

- Write your name using the segment tool.
- Draw a house using all the quadrilaterals you know.
- Create a picture that uses the reflection tool. You might like to start with a person performing a certain action.
- Construct a robust square (one that is constructed using the properties of the square and that, when dragged, will remain a square). This task can be repeated with any quadrilateral, triangle or regular polygon.
- Construct an **irregular** quadrilateral, then mark the mid-points on each side of the quadrilateral and join the mid-points to form another quadrilateral. What shape have you made? Drag your shape to see whether it changes. How can you prove what you have made?
- Use the circle tool to construct an equilateral triangle.

Irregular shape a 2D shape with all its sides and angles not equal. A regular 2D shape has all sides and all angles equal.

Figure 4.9 shows a student work sample of a rectangle constructed using GeoGebra software.

The student work sample in Figure 4.10 is part of a larger sample created in response to designing a quadrilateral starter game using Geometer's Sketchpad. The students were asked to design the diagonal structure of each of the quadrilaterals they know for younger children to guess the figure and put in the required sides. It proved to be a wonderful way to engage students in diagonal explorations. As with many constructions, it is important to ask students to use the textbox facility to consolidate their ideas and gradually formalise the language used.

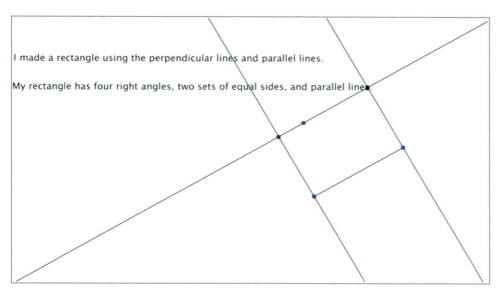

Figure 4.9 GeoGebra construction
Source: GeoGebra

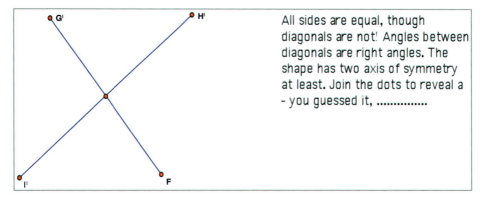

Figure 4.10 Diagonal starter construction
Source: Serow 2007a, p. 396

Angles

In any exploration of their world, students are faced daily with angles around them. Angles are used to explain location, directions, slopes or gradients – even movement in dance. Keeping this in mind, it is essential that we include elements of the environment as stimuli for our investigation of angles in many different contexts. This is where the challenge lies when teaching about angles. The concepts explored in the middle primary years have been described by the NSW Department of Education and Training (2003, p. 8) in several main areas as:

- identifying two-line angles
- identifying the arms and vertex of one-line angles
- comparing angles using informal means such as angle testers
- describing angles using everyday language and the mathematical terms 'right', 'acute' and 'obtuse'.

Interestingly, content related to angles concepts is included in the measurement strand of the Australian Curriculum: Mathematics v. 9.0 (ACARA 2022). It is not until the upper primary years that students begin to do the following:

- Estimate, construct measure angles in degrees, using appropriate tools including a protractor, and relate these measures to angle names (AC9M5M04).
- Identify the relationships between angles on a straight line, angles at a point, and vertically opposite angles; use these to determine unknown angles, communicating reasoning (AC9M6M04).

As with mental computation requirements in the Number strand and Algebra strand, it is essential that students are provided with the opportunity to develop 'angle sense'. This is where they become automatic in their ability to visualise, estimate and compare angles, and eventually relate angle properties to other properties of 2D shapes and 3D objects. Time needs to be devoted to identifying angles in everyday life, such as on furniture, body parts, scissors, clock hands, body turns and opening doors, and in classroom resources such as pattern blocks. Students may construct angles at a point using straws, an activity that relates nicely to the development of fraction concepts.

Location and transformations

Spatial awareness the ability to be aware of oneself in space; it involves the organised knowledge of objects in relation to oneself in that given space and an understanding of the relationship of those objects when there is a change of position

The exploration of location concepts begins well before young children start compulsory education. This strand of the curriculum targets **spatial awareness**, a term used to describe children's understanding of their location and the location of objects in relation to their bodies. This awareness begins to develop as soon as children are able to explore the world around them. It can be observed from a very young age, such as when a baby begins to reach for objects and becomes mobile. As an adult, we rely on spatial awareness daily, whether it be navigating, finding your car in a large car park, or maximising space when packing, to name a few examples. In the primary classroom, it is essential for teachers to seize opportunities to discuss locations of objects/people/places, to use comparative terms such as 'closer to' or 'further than', to talk about relationship among items such as 'under' or 'beside', to measure distances (which is different from measuring the length of an object), and to practise giving directions. The development of spatial structuring links to the Measurement, the Number and the Algebra strands through the structuring of rectangular figures, which also links to arrays. Like mathematics curriculum documents elsewhere, the Australian Curriculum: Mathematics v. 9.0 (ACARA 2022) begins this area of geometry with the following concepts:

- Describe the position and location of themselves and objects in relation to other people and objects within a familiar space (AC9MFSP02).
- Give and follow directions to move people and objects to different locations within a space (AC9M1SP02).
- Interpret and create two-dimensional representations of familiar environments, locating key landmarks and objects relative to each other (AC9M3SP02).
- Create and interpret grid reference systems using grid references and directions to locate and describe positions and pathways (AC9M4SP02).

- Construct a grid coordinate system that uses coordinates to locate positions within a space; use coordinates and directional language to describe position and movement (AC9M5SP02).
- Describe and perform translations, reflections and rotations of shapes, using dynamic geometry software where appropriate; recognise what changes and what remains the same, and identify any symmetry (AC9M5SP03).
- Locate points in the 4 quadrants of a Cartesian plane; describe changes to the coordinates when a point is moved to a different position in the plane (AC9M6SP02).
- Recognise and use combinations of transformations to create tessellations and other geometric patterns, using dynamic geometry software where appropriate (AC9M6SP03).

NZ Maths (2010) includes similar outcomes; however, the activity and unit example exemplify contextualisation and student-centred activities. The initial outcome related to the sub-strand of location is 'give and follow instructions for movement that involve distances, directions, and half or quarter turns' (GM1–3). A sequence of activities is provided that takes the students on a 'follow me' journey using the children's picture book *A Lion in the Night* by Pamela Allen as a stimulus to explore early location concepts. The unit also makes use of digital cameras, with the young students taking on the role of 'director' as they photograph various positions described in the story. Visual representations of vocabulary are available for the teacher, which illustrate 'across', 'into', 'over', 'under', 'through', 'out', 'past' and 'around'. This is a good example of literacy activities across the mathematics curriculum involving children's literature.

It is important to note the interconnectivity in the mathematics outcomes of any syllabus. The notion of half- and quarter-turns relates closely to this topic, as well as to angles and fractions. All the transformations (translations, reflections and rotations) are also part of the exploration of 2D shapes and 3D objects. The interconnectivity is evident in the three Year 1 children's floor plans of their homes in Figures 4.11–4.13. Each of the diagrams provides information about where the students are situated on their developmental journey in geometry.

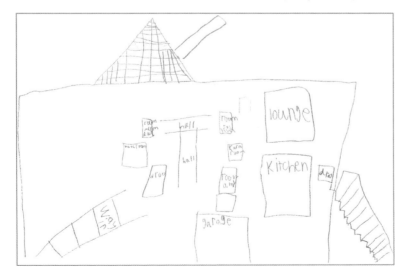

Figure 4.11 Sample floor plan 1

Figure 4.12 Sample floor plan 2

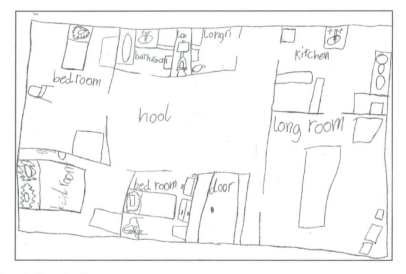

Figure 4.13 Sample floor plan 3

ACTIVITY 4.8

What are the characteristics of each child's floor plan in Figures 4.11–4.13?

What do the diagrams indicate to you about the developmental pathway leading to the ability to draw accurate floor plans of a well-known place? (See Callingham 2008 for further information.)

The teaching of geometry provides some wonderful opportunities to integrate with visual arts in the mathematics classroom. One example of this is the exploration of tessellations. The study of tessellations draws together concepts such as properties of 2D shapes, including interior angles, angles at a point and transformations of 2D shapes, thus providing an opportunity to further explore a group of upper primary geometry concepts. It is not unusual to walk into primary classrooms around the world and be entertained by beautifully coloured tessellating designs made with pattern blocks and other templates. It would be a real shame to spend so much time exploring shapes that create regular and semi-regular tessellations and to never take the time to explore why they do so. For some students, it is a light-bulb moment to realise the connection between the interior angles of the tessellating shapes and the factors of 360 degrees. In addition to the beautiful display, one needs to walk into the classroom and see the students' responses to finishing the statements:

These patterns use one shape to tessellate because …
These patterns use two shapes to tessellate because …

One of the most significant roles of the mathematics teacher is their ability to make the mathematical ideas developed by the children explicit.

Tablet applications (apps) provide a motivating avenue for transformation explorations. Math Doodles has some interesting challenge activities. One game, named Symmetry Shuffle, provides many hours of problem-solving for students at primary level, and older students (see Figure 4.14). The app combines the concept of symmetry with transformations (translations, rotations and reflections). The modes include solving and racing, and the activities enable exploration of line and rotational symmetry, congruence, similarities and transformations. The problem-solving context targets mathematical reasoning, and the game element is motivational. Apps such as these are a good way to extend early finishers. It is good idea to ask the students to record the maths they have used using a combination of diagrams and words. Some interesting insights into students thinking are often forthcoming.

Link 4.5 Maths Doodles: Symmetry Shuffle

Figure 4.14 Symmetry Shuffle game
Source: Carstens Studios <http://www.carstensstudios.com/mathdoodles/symmetryshuffle.htm>

The van Hiele teaching phases

While many experienced teachers confidently use technology as display tools in the mathematics classroom, it is not uncommon for teachers to struggle with finding ways to effectively use ICT as a teaching/learning tool. One teaching framework, based on the work of Dina van Hiele-Geldof, supports teachers in using ICT to promote conceptual development through a scaffold of five teaching phases. The phases aim to assist in moving students from one level of understanding to the next due to the premise that 'help from other people is necessary for so many learning processes' (van Hiele 1986, p. 181).

The structure of the van Hiele teaching phases facilitates students' opportunities to display insight, described as essential in van Hiele's geometrical thinking framework. These opportunities enable students to maintain ownership of their mathematical ideas. Just as the phase framework supports students in transitioning from one level to the next, it also provides a structure to address the concern that 'teachers often feel reluctant or uncomfortable because their pedagogical knowledge perhaps does not include a framework for conducting technology-based activities in their lessons' (Chua & Wu 2005, p. 387).

The phase approach promotes 'maths talk' in the classroom, and students are encouraged to seek clarification from each other and their teacher as they gradually move from teacher-directed tasks to student-directed tasks. Interestingly, despite the initial phases being teacher-directed, they remain student-centred throughout the five phases. A key component is the development of language, which gradually becomes more technical and formal. A description of the phases is provided in Table 4.2 with an emphasis on the changing role of language as the student progresses through them.

Table 4.2 Descriptions of the van Hiele teaching phases

Phase	Description of AIM of phase
1. Information	For students to become familiar with the working domain through discussion and exploration. Discussions take place between teacher and students that stress the content to be used.
2. Directed orientation	For students to identify the focus of the topic through a series of teacher-guided tasks. At this stage, students are given the opportunity to exchange views. Through this discussion, there is a gradual and implicit introduction of more formal language.
3. Explicitation	For students to become conscious of the new ideas and express these in accepted mathematical language. The concepts now need to be made explicit using accepted language. Care is taken to develop the technical language with understanding through the exchange of ideas.
4. Free orientation	For students to complete activities in which they are required to find their own way in the network of relations. The students are now familiar with the domain and are ready to explore it. Through their problem-solving, the students' language develops further as they begin to identify cues to assist them.
5. Integration	For students to build an overview of the material investigated. Summaries concern the new understandings of the concepts involved and incorporate language of the new level. While the purpose of the instruction is now clear to the students, it is still necessary for the teacher to assist during this phase.

Source: Serow 2007a, p. 384

The phases provide a means for defining and aiding progression from one level of understanding to the next. This does not mean that each time a student passes through the five-phase process within concept development they have reached the next level. The phases do, however, provide students with the opportunity to come closer to moving to the next level. It is interesting to note that this teaching process is not centred upon one specific form of instruction. The five-phase process lends itself to many teaching styles, and each phase has a specific and important purpose.

The five-phase teaching approach provides a structure on which to base a teaching/learning sequence using a variety of available classroom tools. It promotes the integration of technological tools while still enabling the use of other hands-on materials. As can be seen, the phase approach begins with clear teacher direction involving exploration through simple tasks and moves to activities that require student initiative in the form of problem-solving.

Sample teaching sequence

The following teaching sequence was designed with two main elements in mind: the developmental framework and the embedding of technology. This sequence focuses on exploring triangle properties. Please note that the teaching sequence is in order of delivery, with students moving both forwards and backwards within van Hiele phases during the various activities presented for the learning and teaching of this geometric concept. The teaching phases are spiralling in nature. While it is not appropriate to skip levels, it is appropriate to go back to previous phases and continue from each phase before finishing at Phase 5. This may occur more than once as shown in the following teaching sequence.

Phase 1: Information

Activity: Play a game of celebrity heads with three triangle cards.

Activity: Class IWB activity where the students need to move shapes into two groups: triangles and non-triangles.

Phase 2: Directed orientation

Activity: Students make 12 different triangles on geoboards (pinboards) using rubber bands, and then draw them on dot paper. Students may use 1 cm grid and isometric dot paper if needed.

Phase 3: Explicitation

Activity: Students share examples of the triangles they have made using an electronic geoboard (HOTmaths Pinboard widget) (see Figure 4.15).

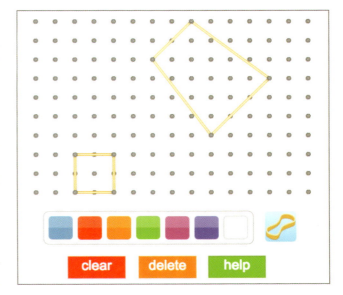

Figure 4.15 Screenshot of HOTmaths Pinboard widget

Phase 2: Directed orientation

Activity: Finding triangles in tile patterns (HOTmaths Triangles in Shapes HOTsheet) (see Figure 4.16).

HOTsheet

TRIANGLES IN SHAPES

TASK 1 **Tile pattern**

Label the different types of triangles used in this mosaic floor pattern.

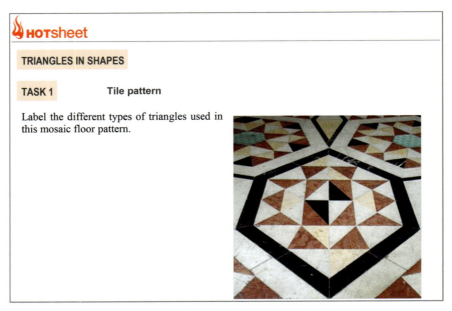

Figure 4.16 Finding triangles in tile patterns from HOTmaths Triangles in Shapes HOTsheet

Activity: Folding squares and rectangles to make triangles (HOTmaths Triangles in Shapes HOTsheet) (see Figure 4.17).

TASK 2 **Folding a rectangle and a square**

Cut out this square and rectangle separately. Make folds along each diagonal then open out the shapes so they are flat.

Describe the number and types of triangle you can now see in each shape.

Square:

____

____

Rectangle:

____

____

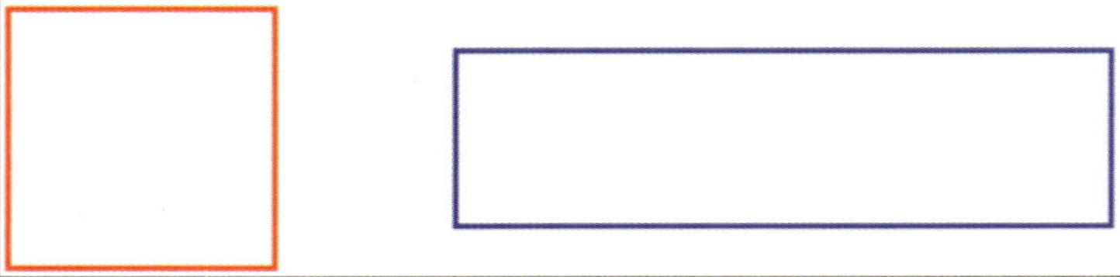

Figure 4.17 Folding a rectangle and a square from HOTmaths Triangles in Shapes HOTsheet

Phase 3: Explicitation

Activity: Students cut out the 12 triangles they have made. Using a protractor and a ruler, they measure the sides and angles on each triangle. Students are encouraged to use paper folding to find any axes of symmetry and to mark them on the appropriate triangles.

Activity: Students complete a spreadsheet with four columns headed 'triangle', 'sides', 'angles' and 'symmetry'.

Phase 4: Free orientation

Activity: In pairs, with 24 triangles for each pair, students are asked to sort their shapes into appropriate groups and record their groups. They need to provide a detailed description of each group and a description of any relationships across groups.

Activity: Draw a detailed concept map indicating how the triangle groups are related to one another.

Activity: Students use the circle tool in DGS to create an equilateral triangle.

Activity: Use DGS to create an example of each of the triangle types possible. Students could discover these triangles: equilateral, right-angled isosceles, acute-angled isosceles, obtuse-angled isosceles, right-angled scalene, acute-angled scalene and obtuse-angled scalene. The HOTmaths Sorting Triangles HOTsheet has an emphasis on students describing different triangles and can provide useful consolidation (see Figure 4.18). Some students may provide a higher-order response and begin noting that the equilateral triangle is a sub-set of the isosceles class of triangles with additional properties. If this happens, it is the right time to ask the child why, and to congratulate them on their mathematical thinking.

Phase 5: Integration

Activity: Students present their DGS diagrams and description of each triangle type and create an information pamphlet. Students add their own summary page at the end of the pamphlet explaining what they know about triangles.

It is important to note that, throughout this teaching sequence, assessment is embedded seamlessly into teaching/learning activities. There is ample opportunity to observe and gather information concerning students' individual understanding of geometrical concepts. The notion of assessment for learning will be addressed in detail in Chapter 10.

Suggested geometry tablet applications to explore

There is an expanding wealth of mathematics apps available on mobile devices. Geometry is one content area that is particularly open to manipulation of objects. To make the most of the app as an opportunity for conceptual growth in terms of geometrical understanding, it is essential for the app to be placed thoughtfully within the teaching and learning sequence.

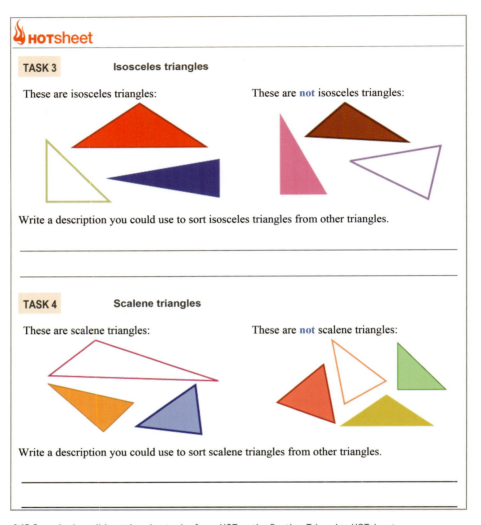

Figure 4.18 Sample describing triangles tasks from HOTmaths Sorting Triangles HOTsheet

Examples of apps include:
- Geometry Pad by Bytes Arithmetic LLC (available via searching on iTunes)
- Geometer's Sketchpad by KCP Technologies
- Tangram XL Free by NG (available via searching on iTunes).

In addition to free and purchasable apps on mobile devices, many of the available tools provide media for investigation and catalysts for discussion. One example of this is the digital camera on many devices – even the most basic mobile phone. Classroom Snapshot 4.4 describes an interesting teaching moment in a Year 3 classroom where a pre-service teacher was beginning a lesson targeting investigating symmetry in the environment.

CLASSROOM SNAPSHOT 4.4

It was Week 2 of a three-week practicum, and Miss Hope was about to teach a mathematics lesson targeting symmetry. She decided to begin the lesson with an introductory activity that involved taking a photo of one student on a mobile device, displaying it via the IWB and using the curtain tool to cover up half the face with a vertical line down the centre of the nose. She requested a couple of students to draw in the outline of the missing half of the face and any of the main features of the face. Miss Hope then asked a student to reveal the whole face and see how well it matched up. The teacher went on to ask the students, 'What did you notice?'

A very rich discussion followed concerning symmetry, axes of symmetry, whether a human face has symmetry, where we find symmetry in our environment and what makes a shape symmetrical. The entire discussion flowed from the students' observations during the introductory activity.

Miss Hope then stated that today they were going to explore items in their environment to determine whether they were symmetrical. As a whole class, the students did one example of a flower together.

The students were provided with six laminated diagrams, including tile patterns. The students were asked to record any symmetry they could find in any way, to say how they knew this, and to illustrate in a diagram the symmetry that was observed. The following day, the students constructed their own nature-inspired design using DGS (see Figure 4.19).

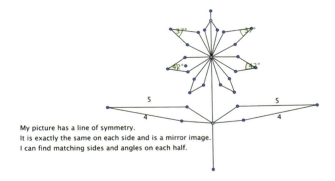

Figure 4.19 Sample of reflection using dynamic geometry software
Source: © 2013 Australian Institute for Teaching and School Leadership Limited (AITSL) <https://www.aitsl.edu.au/tools-resources/resource/dynamic-geometry-software-illustration-of-practice>

Teachers will find that the geometry tasks in the test generator have a range of applications in the classroom. While they may be used to generate a sample of questions to identify where the students are at and store this information, the questions can be used to facilitate class discussion, in an introduction to a lesson or even altered and extended to create more open-ended tasks. Often just adding the question 'Why?' makes all the difference to a geometry task.

Conclusion

In reading this chapter and completing the activity tasks, you will have explored samples of the breadth of content in the Space strand, and other elements of the field of Geometry that are located within the Measurement strand (ACARA 2022). This can be placed broadly in overlapping 2D, 3D, angles, location and transformations categories. The van Hiele theory has been described as a means for viewing students' level of thinking in geometry and providing a window to more accurately target the next student task in an attempt to meet individual student needs. ICT tools have been discussed; however, this is an ever-expanding field that needs to be considered in a flexible manner to enable new and emerging technologies to be placed in teachers' tool kits. To assist planning in geometry, the van Hiele teaching phases have been presented as a suitable pedagogical framework that is open to a wide range of teaching strategies and available resources.

GUIDED STUDENT TASKS

1. Ask five primary age children (ranging from 5 years to 12 years) to describe a square, a rectangle and a triangle to you. Record their answers. What van Hiele level would you assign to their descriptions? Think about a suitable activity for each child to assist them in moving to the next level.
2. Download the free primary version of GeoGebra. Explore the terminology of the software, such as segments, angles, points, bisect, midpoint and parallel. Explore how you could use the terminology in the software to assist students in moving from informal language to formal language when exploring two-dimensional shapes.
3. Find five logos in Google images or magazines that have symmetry in their design. What shapes are used in these logos? Are there any similarities? Why do the graphic artists use particular shapes? Design a complete lesson sequence around this task.
4. Visit the National Council of Teachers of Mathematics website and consider the design of different tessellating patterns that could be used to decorate different components of a house. How could you incorporate samples from a tiling shop as stimulus for an introductory activity?

Link 4.6 National Council of Teachers of Mathematics: Tessellation Creator

CONCEPTS TO CONSIDER

In this section, the focus is on the hierarchical structure as it relates to geometrical concepts, and not the many definitions and descriptions related to 2D shapes, 3D objects and transformations. As reflected in the curriculum content and sequencing, and in the earlier discussion in this chapter, students begin their space journey in the context of grouping and describing figures. While the conceptual understanding elaborated in Table 4.3 conveys student responses at varying degrees of complexity, this is different to being described as a misconception (Pegg & Baker 1999; Serow 2007b).

Table 4.3 Van Hiele levels of thinking in the context of grouping and describing figures

Level 1	**Definition** Figures are judged by their appearance. A figure is recognised by its form or shape. The properties of a figure play no explicit role in the identification of a figure (Taylor, Quinn & Eames 2015). **Sample student responses at this level** 'The pyramid is a pointy shape.' 'A square is like a box.' 'When a square is rotated with the diagonals vertically and horizontally positioned, it will be called a diamond.' 'A rhombus is a pushed over square.' **Teaching focus to promote development** Any activity that involves constructing, building, sorting, drawing and discussing two-dimensional and three-dimensional figures will assist students in moving to Level 2.
Transitional level 1/2	**Definition** Properties are perceived as 'features'. When grouping shapes, students complete this spontaneously upon the identification of similar features. For example, students at this level will be aware of the number of sides and angles of a shape. The students may look at a shape and tell you which sides are equal, etc., but it is merely a feature of that specific shape and not something that is recognised as a signifier of a class of shapes. This is what distinguishes a 'feature' from a 'property'. **Sample student responses at this level** 'A square has four sides and four corners.' When prompted to discuss the sides the student may add, 'All the sides are the same.' A student will be happy to group pyramids and triangular-based prisms together because 'they both have triangles on them'. **Teaching focus to promote development** Students require a selection of hands-on activities that explore each of the properties of figures. Based upon the properties investigated, at this level the students require classification activities where the focus is on the selection of properties which are characteristic of each group, and the identification of group (class) names. Class refers to the group of shapes according to their properties.
Level 2A	**Definition** Figures are classified on the basis of one property. This property is treated as a unique signifier of the shape and is used to describe groupings. **Sample student responses at this level** 'The equilateral triangle has three sides equal.' 'I have put all the pyramids together because they all have triangles going up to the point.' **Teaching focus to promote development** At this stage, the focus is on the collective class of figures, as opposed to specific examples. This begins with a complete isolation of classes, and gradually shifts to recognition of similar properties across classes that are supported by visual cues. To enable this shift, students need to be encouraged to communicate recognised property differences that prevent relationships, and to be directed to find similarities across classes of figures.

Table 4.3 (cont.)

Level 2B	**Definition** Figures are classified on the basis of more than one property. Students will make links among different groups of shapes when the links are supported by visual cues. Students will use more than one property as unique signifiers when attempting to provide minimum descriptions. **Sample student response at this level** 'I think the square and the rectangle are linked to one another because they both have four right angles and opposite sides are parallel. They can't go in the same group because the rectangle has to have two different sides to each other.' **Teaching focus to promote development** It is essential to focus on the domains of student language use at this level. Students would benefit from the introduction of inclusive property descriptions. An example of an exclusive property description is 'two sides are equal and the other two sides are equal, but the two pairs are different from each other' (when describing the properties of a rectangle). An inclusive property description for the same property would be 'the rectangle has opposite sides equal'. Exclusive descriptions hinder relationships among classes of figures, whereas inclusive descriptions enable relationships among classes of figures. Activities that involve materials with moveable parts, and student-created figures using dynamic geometry software showing different figures that may belong in the same class of shapes, are suitable here. The classroom environment should be conducive to focusing upon relationships that exist between classes that are not supported by visual cues.
Level 3	**Definition** Thinking at this level is characterised by a focus on the relationships among the properties and figures. Links are made between classes of figures that are not supported by visual cues. At this level, the links are often described in a manner that is 'one way'. In other words, there is an ordering between two properties. **Sample student response at this level** 'Yes, the rectangle and rhombus are linked to each other because they both have opposite sides equal and opposite sides parallel.' **Teaching focus to promote development** Students would benefit from tasks requiring them to formulate descriptions/definitions of figures incorporating sub-sets. This may include tasks requiring the development and discussion of geometrical concept maps and flowcharts.
Transitional level 3/4	**Definition** Students focus on a single relationship that is two directional. Students will begin at this level by making tentative statements with regard to class inclusion. As students focus on multiple property relationships, they will accept notions of class inclusion; however, their justifications may not be consistent. Levels 3/4 and 4 are included here, although they will rarely be targeted at the primary level, to flag the next level of geometrical understanding.
Level 4	**Definition** Further conditions are placed upon class inclusion and general overviews of different relating concepts are formed. Students are able to succinctly and spontaneously use interrelationships among properties and figures to solve deductive problems. This level is evident in the secondary setting, and student responses involve deductive reasoning. Students are able to find their own way through a deductive proof when thinking at this level. An example of Level 4 thinking could involve applying congruency theorems and relationships among quadrilateral properties to solve a problem.

This notion is also observed in Activity 4.1, in the context of students' understanding of concepts related to parallel lines. While the student responses depict four levels of understanding:

1. Parallel lines are like railway tracks.
2. Parallel lines are lines that will never meet if they keep going.
3. Parallel lines are always the same distance apart.
4. The perpendicular distance between a pair of parallel lines is the same at any point.

Each of the responses above are correct; however, they each depict different levels of understanding in relation to overall structure, language used to describe the concept of parallelism, and focus on overall appearance, features, properties or relationships among properties.

In the area of 3D objects, it is important for upper primary students to begin describing the similarities and differences of cross-sections of groups of 3D figures, after they have developed 3D language use, as described earlier, such as faces, sides, vertices and edges. Once these are observed and explored by the students, it is reasonable to begin using definitions such as:

- prisms and cylinders have congruent cross-sections when cut on a plane parallel to the base
- pyramids and cones have similar cross-sections when cut on a plane parallel to the base.

FURTHER READING

Flewelling, G, Lind, J & Sauer, R 2013, *Rich learning tasks in measurement and geometry for primary students*, Australian Association of Mathematics Teachers.
State of NSW, Department of Education and Training Professional Support and Curriculum Directorate 2003, *Teaching about angles: Stage 2*.
Swan, P 2013, *Geoboard gems*, Australian Association of Mathematics Teachers.

Websites for exploration

CHAPTER 5

EXPLORING WHOLE NUMBER COMPUTATION

LEARNING OUTCOMES

By the end of this chapter, you will:

- be able to recognise the difference between additive and multiplicative thinking
- be able to plan for appropriate use of drill and practice activities
- choose appropriate representations to illustrate different ways of thinking about the four operations of addition, subtraction, multiplication and division
- use technology effectively to develop understanding of whole number computation.

Introduction

Developing computational skills and the concepts that underpin proportional reasoning is a large component of the primary mathematics curriculum. Moving children's thinking towards proportional reasoning will be covered in more detail in Chapter 6. The research base about the development of number concepts in individual students goes back many years and is too large to address in detail (e.g. Björklund et al. 2020; Whitacre et al. 2020). In this chapter, the focus is on effective teaching to enhance learning: developing computational skills, the relationships between different operations and moving from additive to multiplicative thinking.

Across the primary years, the mathematics curriculum places considerable emphasis on computation and the development of more complex conceptual understandings of the ways in which numbers work. Computation includes all those actions we use to add, subtract, multiply and divide numbers of many different types. We use mental computation, technology such as calculators or computers, and a variety of pen-and-paper methods. These activities are part of the domain of mathematics we call arithmetic. With the development of sophisticated technology tools, it is more important than ever to ensure that children receive a good grounding in the operations, and can calculate effectively and efficiently, choosing methods and tools appropriate to their situation. Children will need a well-developed sense of place value and a conceptual understanding of parts of a whole to deal with the ideas in the curriculum.

Teachers should aim for a balanced program that addresses both **procedural** and **conceptual understanding**. Such a program needs to include use of concrete materials, mental computation strategies, traditional pen-and-paper approaches and sensible use of appropriate technology to help develop students' understanding.

Students throughout the primary years need opportunities to 'play', or work informally, with numbers of all types: large and small **whole numbers**, fractions, decimals and percentages, all expressed in a wide variety of ways and presented in diverse contexts. The more opportunities students have to become familiar with numbers, the more fluent they will become when working with them, and this in turn will help develop their understanding, improve their mathematical reasoning and support their problem-solving. McIntosh (2004) stresses the importance of children developing their own informal understanding, which can be built on to develop the foundational ideas that are needed to progress mathematically.

A key component of the mathematics curriculum is to develop students' understanding of the four operations of addition, subtraction, multiplication and division. Initially, students learn to use these with whole numbers; later, the operations are applied to part-whole numbers such as fractions and decimals; and, in the early part of high school, negative numbers are introduced.

This chapter addresses whole number understanding and operations, building on the early number work from Chapter 2. Key ideas are developed about appropriate pedagogy for working with primary-age children, using a wide range of approaches effectively to enhance understanding.

> **Procedural understanding** being able to choose and use the rules and routines of mathematics, such as using an algorithm to undertake addition, subtraction, multiplication or division
>
> **Conceptual understanding** comprehension of the underlying mathematical relationships, such as the inverse relationship between addition and subtraction
>
> **Whole number** a number that has no fractional parts; an integer (e.g. 71 is a whole number but 71.5 is not)

Developing number sense

Building on from work in the early years of schooling (see Chapter 2), children need to continue developing a sense of number. There are many activities to help develop children's understanding. For example, NRICH has an activity called Eightness of Eight in which eight counters are arranged in different ways and a photograph taken each time. This is then made into a short video. Such an activity develops both creativity and understanding of numbers. Another activity is to ask children to make their age in as many different ways as possible. As children get older, they should be encouraged to move beyond addition and subtraction facts into more complex mathematical equations and operations. Children at all ages need to recognise that numbers can be represented in a variety of ways. Figure 5.1 shows a Year 4 child's representation of numbers using a representation of MAB blocks with corresponding number sentences.

As they progress through the primary years, children should experience larger numbers, into the hundreds and thousands. It is a useful skill to be able to read and say large number names, and it is surprising how many adults have trouble doing this. Try Activity 5.1.

Link 5.1 NRICH: Eightness of Eight

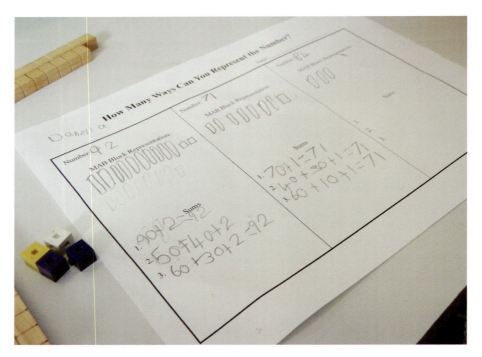

Figure 5.1 Different representations of numbers below 100

ACTIVITY 5.1

Link 5.2 Australian Government Style Manual: Choosing numerals or words

Write some large numbers in symbols. Use the comma ',' to designate 1000s (APSC 2021), although the convention of leaving a space between the thousands and the hundreds (e.g. 10 500) is sometimes used for large numbers.

Make sure that you include some numbers with zeros in them. Make sure that you can write the number in words and that you can say the numbers out loud.

Examples could be: 1037; 125,098; 1,657,832; 10,670,923

Show a symbolic representation of one number at a time to some adult friends and colleagues. Ask them to say the number names. How many stumbled or made mistakes?

Link 5.3 NRICH: Ordering Journeys

Recognising number names is important. There is a big difference between one thousand and ten thousand! We tend to be rather casual about number names, talking of house prices as 'six hundred and fifty' or 'six fifty' when we mean six hundred and fifty thousand dollars. Naming large numbers is not intuitive and is a skill that should be explicitly developed in primary classrooms. Continuing to develop a sense of number is important throughout the primary years. Students in Year 3 are expected to 'recognise, represent and order natural numbers using naming and writing conventions for numerals beyond 10 000' (AC9M3N01). This knowledge will not develop unless it is explicitly taught. Activities such as NRICH's Ordering Journeys, possibly adapted to show distances from your state capital or home town, provide useful practice. Note that the suggestion for teaching this activity is to 'say as little as possible' when introducing the task and to discuss the different approaches taken by students at the end. This instruction allows students to develop their own understanding through informal discussion, questioning and comparing their own ideas with those of their peers. Emphasise the need for students to justify their solutions.

Properties of numbers

Integers (whole numbers) are of different types, including negative numbers, having recognisable properties. Most people will recognise odd and even numbers, but primary-age children also need to explore composite numbers, prime numbers and numbers that can be explained as shapes, such as square numbers. Prime and composite numbers are discussed further in the section on arrays. Perfect squares are those that are the product of an integer multiplied by itself, such as 9 = 3 × 3. These numbers can be represented pictorially as a square as shown in Figure 5.2.

Figure 5.2 Square numbers

Knowing that 16 = 4 × 4 = 4^2 and so on provides useful tools for problem solving, and this is an expectation of the curriculum by Year 6. Upper primary and lower secondary students may enjoy researching other numbers that can be shown as 2D shapes, such as triangular, pentagonal and hexagonal numbers. Such exploration can be linked to the Algebra strand by looking for the generalisations of the patterns formed (see Chapter 7).

The theory behind our number system is discussed in 'Concepts to consider' at the end of the chapter.

Operations with whole numbers

In the middle primary years, there is a focus on developing children's **computational** skills, beginning with addition and subtraction and moving to multiplication and division. Traditionally in schools there has been an emphasis on pen-and-paper approaches to computation. In our daily lives, however, we tend to use mental strategies and informal recording to keep track (Northcote & Marshall 2016). That is not to say that children should not recognise and understand standard **algorithms** for addition and subtraction, but that there should be a balance between written, mental and technology-supported computation. Today, there is less emphasis on developing standard procedures, or algorithms, and children need a well-developed sense of number to understand the different processes, including the commonly encountered algorithms for written computation. Children need to experience a variety of approaches to operations in a range of different situations.

Computation all operations on numbers that are used to calculate a result or answer

Algorithm a step-by-step procedure for undertaking a computation

When computation is written in mathematical text, there should be an emphasis on horizontal rather than vertical recording, especially when written algorithms are introduced because children become confused by the vertical representation (Fernandez & Valazquez 2011). For example, 14 − 6 is a better way of presenting that problem than the traditional vertical structure:

$$\begin{array}{r} 1\ 4 \\ -\ \ 6 \\ \hline \end{array}$$

This kind of problem is best calculated mentally using a variety of strategies, such as counting on from six to ten then adding the four to give eight as the answer. Often children

Number bars concrete or virtual manipulatives that provide a visual proportional representation of numbers – that is, a two bar is twice as long as a one bar. They can be used to model operations with the bars representing known or unknown quantities.

get lost in recording the formal written calculation, having trouble 'lining up' the appropriate numbers, so that the importance of the actual calculation is lost. Instead, children should be encouraged to undertake the calculations initially using their own strategies and informal recording to develop confidence in their capacity. Later these informal approaches can be refined to become closer to the formal algorithms. The aim should always be to develop efficient and effective computation skills that are transferable to different situations.

Addition and subtraction

Figure 5.3 Addition as the merger of two groups

Addition involves joining 'two or more numbers (or quantities) to get one number (called the sum or total)' (Eather 2018). Addition problems are of two types. In *merger* problems, two groups are combined to create a new group. An example of a merger problem is 'I have 12 green marbles and I am given 7 red marbles. How many marbles do I have now?' In *parts-of-a-whole* problems, the questions are about parts of a group. A typical problem of this type is 'I have a bag of marbles. Twelve of these are green and seven are red. How many marbles do I have altogether?' Mathematically, the solution approach is the same: $12 + 7 = 19$. From a representation point of view, however, these two problems look different. The merger type requires two separate sets of objects to be combined (see Figure 5.3).

The parts-of-a-whole problems require the whole to be identified and can be represented effectively by **number bars** or Cuisenaire rods, including interactive number bars such as the HOTmaths Number Bars widget shown in Figure 5.4.

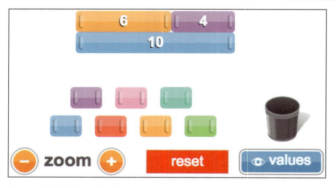

Figure 5.4 HOTmaths Number Bars widget

Several sets of interactive number bars are available online which could be used to model the processes for children to follow using concrete materials. These resources can be used effectively with an interactive whiteboard, or computer and projector, where children can drag the bars to complete the appropriate problem.

Addition is **commutative** – that is, it may be done in any order. For example, the mathematical sentences could be written as $4 + 3 = 7$ or $3 + 4 = 7$; and $4 + 6 = 10$ or $6 + 4 = 10$. This not true of subtraction (see next section). The commutative law is an important principle for children to recognise because it can make addition more efficient by starting with the largest or most convenient number. It should be modelled in different ways including concrete materials, informal recording by children and virtual manipulatives. An example of this convenience is when summing data, as shown in Classroom Snapshot 5.1.

Commutativity addition and multiplication problems can be written and calculated in any order (e.g. 5 + 7 is the same as 7 + 5)

CLASSROOM SNAPSHOT 5.1

Jody's Year 5 class is undertaking a STEM unit on sustainability. As part of the unit, the class collects some data about the amount of litter in the schoolyard. Students record the numbers in a table on the whiteboard. They add the numbers of different pieces of litter together to find the total number of pieces of litter. Their teacher, Jody, decides to use the activity as a practice in computation, emphasising different ways of summing the data. Before they start, Jody asks the students to record their estimates of the total number of pieces of litter. As the students undertake the task, Jody walks around the room talking to the students and identifying their strategies. She asks particular students to come to the front and explain how they did the computation.

Table 5.1 Table of litter collected

Kind of litter	Number of pieces
Icy-pole sticks	11
Chocolate wrappers	12
Milk cartons	20
Chip packets	18
Hamburger wrappers	29
Straws	14

Tara started with the largest number (29) and found compatible numbers to build to groups of 10. She says, '29 + 11 makes 40, which is a "friendly" number because it is a multiple of 10. Adding on 20 (another "friendly" number) to the 40 makes 60 pieces'. Sam then pointed out that 18 + 12 also makes a 'friendly' number: 18 + 12 = 30. He said, 'Add this on to 60 to give 90. Now the only number left to add is 14. So, 90 + 14 = 104. In total, 104 pieces of litter were collected.'

Mick used a standard algorithm, adding all the units, regrouping into tens and then adding the tens. Sara used multiples of 10 by splitting some numbers up and then making tens from the units. She wrote 20 + 20 + 10 + 10 + 10 + 10 + 1 + 2 + 8 + 9 + 4 = 80 + 10 + 10 + 4 = 104.

Knowing that addition can be done in any order provides a starting point for developing a variety of ways of solving a problem. Sara's approach also made use of place value understanding. Jody discussed each of these approaches with the class but deliberately did not single out one way to do the problem. She also asked students how close the final answer was to their original estimates, which led to further conversations about sustainability.

PAUSE AND REFLECT

Jody is using the litter collection activity to provide incidental practice at computation. It is well below the expectations of the curriculum for Year 5 students but any opportunity to reinforce computation skills is valuable. Think about occasions that you might use to provide incidental mathematical activity for a group of children at home or in school. Write down some advice about incidental activities that you might suggest to parents who wanted to help their children with mathematics.

Subtraction is the opposite of addition. This means that for every addition fact there is a related subtraction fact. Children need to experience these related number facts and to be reminded about them. Number bars or Cuisenaire rods can be very useful ways to represent the related facts. In Figure 5.4, it is clear that if 6 is removed from 10, then 4 will be left, and similarly if 4 is removed from 10, then 6 will be left. Consider, for example, a lesson in which a teacher leads the students through a simple problem using a set of interactive number bars. Only the teacher's voice is presented in Classroom Snapshot 5.2, so you can focus on the teaching approach and the teacher's language.

CLASSROOM SNAPSHOT 5.2

Michael, please will you come and make a number bar with the value of 10? You can choose any colour.

Sally, choose another colour and make a number bar underneath to the 10 bar. You can make it any value.

Now we have a blue 10 bar and a pink 5 bar. What is the difference between 10 and 5? How can we find out?

Let's hide the values – Lisa, tap on the value sign.

Who thinks they know the answer?

James, you think that the difference between 10 and 5 is 5. Come and make a bar that would show whether or not you are correct.

Wait a minute, James, before you drag the bar out. Who thinks that James made a good choice by choosing the same colour as Lisa?

Ben, you agree with James and think the answer should be 5 so the bars should be the same colour. Okay James, let's check it.

This is an explicit teaching sequence that draws the information from the students. From this starting point, the teacher could go on to set problems for the children to complete using concrete materials, or discuss 'doubles', or different meanings of subtraction, or different strategies used by the children to arrive at their answers or other ways of recording the problem. The choice of what the teacher does next will depend on the class, their prior learning and what the objective of the lesson is.

Note that the same lesson could be undertaken with concrete materials (see Figure 5.5). It is more difficult, however, to ensure that every child can see the smaller concrete rods and this approach may be more effective for small groups. In Figure 5.5 the 10 small cubes are included as a reference, and for young children this is helpful in establishing the relationships.

Subtraction can also have several meanings. The common 'take away' includes problems of the type 'I had 16 marbles, but I lost 5. How many marbles are left?'

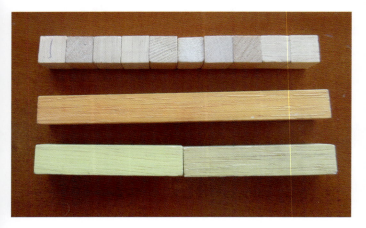

Figure 5.5 Using concrete materials rather than technology

Other meanings are 'difference between', such as 'I had 16 marbles and now I have 11. How many marbles have I lost?' Finally, there is the 'how many more' meaning, such as 'I have 11 marbles. How many more will I need to have 16 marbles?' This last meaning initially looks like an addition problem, but it is actually solved by undertaking a subtraction. It is a missing addend problem: 11 + 5 = 16, and it makes use of the interrelationship between addition and subtraction.

Children may also 'over-generalise' and apply the commutativity principle to subtraction. This misunderstanding leads to the common error of subtracting the smaller number from the larger one in every situation. Teachers may inadvertently add to the difficulty by making remarks like, 'You can't take a larger number from a smaller one' when children are setting up their own subtraction problems. This statement is incorrect and although negative numbers do not come into the curriculum until Year 6 (AC9M6N01) making statements that could mislead students later is unhelpful.

One way to begin to address the over-generalisation is to set up all of the related number facts. For example:

$$6+7=13 \quad 7+6=13$$

Related subtraction facts are:

$$13-6=7 \quad 13-7=6$$

But

$$7-13=-6 \quad 6-13=-7$$

showing that subtraction, unlike addition, is not commutative.

Children could be given answers, such as 13 in the example above, and asked to find all the related number facts. Practice activities such as these are useful to reinforce number knowledge as part of a balanced program.

Even though children are not expected to understand negative numbers until they are older, children in the primary years can understand that the answer to the reversed subtraction problem is different. Complex explanations are not necessary to illustrate this point. For instance, by using the examples of temperature, or going below the sea, children can understand that commutativity principles cannot be applied to subtraction. This activity also lends itself to the use of interactive technology, with children involved in dragging the digits to create the equation.

It is vital to stress the **place value** aspects of the numbers involved in addition and subtraction. Learning to decompose numbers into component parts is important. Empty number lines are particularly useful (see Figure 5.6). They provide strong visual imagery for children and can be used to develop discussion and class involvement.

Place value the value of a digit depends on its place in the number – for example, in the number 361, the 3 has the value of 300 or three hundreds, 6 has a value of 60, or six tens, and there is one unit

The theory behind place value is discussed in 'Concepts to consider' at the end of the chapter.

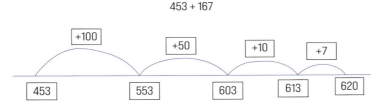

Figure 5.6 Using a number line

When subtracting on a number line, the actions can go backwards from right to left or forwards from left to right, as in 'how many more' problems. Number lines for subtraction, however, become quite complex when decomposition is required. Often the best way to use a number line for subtraction that requires decomposition such as 453 – 167, is to turn it into a 'how many more' problem. The visual and physical representation supports ideas about the relationship between addition and subtraction, and also helps to develop place value understanding, but choose problems carefully depending on the lesson objective.

A summary of the different meanings of addition and subtraction is provided in Table 5.2 with examples.

Table 5.2 Meanings of addition and subtraction

Addition (merger or join)	I had 3 stickers and I was given 5 more. How many stickers do I have altogether?
Addition (combine)	I have 3 glitter stickers. I also have 5 plain stickers. How many stickers do I have?
Subtraction (separate; takeaway)	I have 8 stickers. I gave 4 to my friend. How many stickers do I have left?
Subtraction (combine; missing addend)	I have 8 stickers. Three stickers are glitter stickers, the rest are plain. How many plain stickers do I have?
Subtraction (compare; difference between)	I have 8 stickers, but Ian has 12 stickers. How many more stickers does Ian have than me?
Subtraction (missing addend; how many more)	I have 8 stickers. How many more stickers do I need to have 12 stickers?

ACTIVITY 5.2

Build number sentences that show all of the different meanings of addition and subtraction. Turn your number sentences into 'word problems'. What words did you use that meant addition or subtraction? Make sentences of the type 23 = 10 + 13 as well as the more common 10 + 13 = 23. Why is it important to show different ways of making number sentences?

PAUSE AND REFLECT

Although the mathematical sentences may look the same, word meanings can be very different. What implications are there for teaching because of this situation? There are also different words for the operations. For example, addition can be described as add, plus, combine, join and so on. In schools that you have visited, was there an agreed language for mathematical ideas? What would be the advantages and disadvantages of such a policy? There is no correct answer to this question – it is posed to stimulate thinking about how school policies can impact on teaching.

Curriculum aims for computation are to develop confident, flexible thinkers who can take a variety of approaches to completing any computation. Underpinning computational strategies must be a sound understanding of place value. Being able to use place value partitioning of numbers is a powerful strategy. There are many resources and activities available to develop place value and number understanding. Good, easy-to-find online sources are Australian Association of Mathematics Teachers Top Drawer, NRICH, reSolve: Maths by Inquiry and NZ Maths. Sharing children's ideas is very important, and use of a document camera with a screen provides an efficient and effective way of sharing children's work. The Australian Curriculum: Mathematics v. 9.0 is underpinned by the mathematics proficiencies of understanding, fluency, problem-solving and reasoning. It is important when teaching mathematics to keep these proficiencies in mind and to consider ways in which they can be developed further. The sources suggested earlier all have an underlying approach that encourages children's active engagement in their learning.

ACTIVITY 5.3

Search some of the sources suggested earlier. Find a resource for each year of schooling from Year 3 to Year 6 that addresses place value and/or computation strategies. Choose a different type of activity for each year level or explore the same activity at different year levels.
- Which activities support the fluency proficiency? Do any activities help to develop reasoning, understanding or problem-solving?
- How would you use any of these activities in your classroom to develop the proficiencies?

Multiplication and division

Young children often have an intuitive sense of multiplication and division through grouping and sharing activities, although these activities may not necessarily lead to useful mathematical ideas without some intervention (Mulligan & Mitchelmore 1997). Effective teaching identifies and builds on children's intuitive understanding.

Multiplication is the process by which one number is scaled up (or down) by another number – that is, it is a stretching (or contracting) process.

ACTIVITY 5.4

Use a word processing or drawing program. Go to 'Insert shapes' and choose a square. Insert the square into your document. Copy the square exactly (click on the square, then copy and paste). You have *added* one square. You can do this as many times as you wish to create, ultimately, an infinite number of squares. Now select one of your squares. Grab one corner of the square and drag it to make the square bigger. You have now *multiplied* the square size by increasing the length of both sides. The square has been scaled up.

Additive thinking is characterised by a series of repeated operations in which the same element is added on each time, as in repeating the squares. **Multiplicative thinking** involves stretching (or contracting) the element – the relationship between the quantities is the crucial determining characteristic – that is, the dragging process. Additive thinking characterises 15, for example, as 10 + 5, or 20 – 5 and so on. Multiplicative thinking symbolises 15 as 5 × 3 or 30 ÷ 2 and so on. When whole numbers are involved (as in tables facts), repeated addition – adding on the same number each time – will lead to the same answer as 'stretching' the number; that is, 5 + 5 + 5 + 5 gives the same result as 4 × 5. It is limiting, however, only to see multiplication as repeated addition. Multiplication is about the relationships between numbers and being able to recognise these, that is think multiplicatively is critical for students' future mathematical development.

> **Additive thinking** thinking and reasoning about quantities in absolute terms (e.g. 10 is 8 more than 2)
>
> **Multiplicative thinking** thinking and reasoning about more than one quantity or value at once (e.g. doubling the side length of a square means that the area quadruples)

Multiplication is often associated only with 'times tables', but these are simply a summary of a specific set of number patterns that are useful to aid computation. The Australian Curriculum: Mathematics v. 9.0 expects that students in Year 4, for example, will 'solve problems involving multiplying or dividing natural numbers by multiples and powers of 10 without a calculator, using the multiplicative relationship between the place value of digits' (AC9M4N05). This expectation goes beyond recall of number facts and requires teachers to explicitly develop understanding of the relationships that underpin multiplication and division.

There are several ways in which multiplication and division can be approached in the classroom, and there are many resources that can help, including technology-based resources. Children should not be expected simply to 'learn their tables facts'. To do so is to reduce potentially rich mathematical ideas to a series of disconnected, and often half-remembered, facts. Instead, tables facts need to be presented in a variety of representations including arrays, patterns on a 100 grid, concrete materials, and informal and formal representations. Wherever possible the related division facts should be emphasised.

One useful representation of multiplication is found in arrays (Hurst & Hurrell 2021). An array provides a picture of the ways in which a number can be shown: objects are arranged in rows and columns, such that every row is the same length and every column is the same height. The number 12, for example, could be represented as shown in Figure 5.7. It is important that children have opportunities to see and experience all of these arrangements and to realise that they represent the same number in different ways. These kinds of opportunities also emphasise the commutativity of multiplication. Commutativity is often referred to as 'spin-arounds' when helping children to learn 'tables' facts.

> Further information about arrays is discussed in 'Concepts to consider' at the end of the chapter.

Ask children to make arrays of numbers chosen by them using a variety of concrete objects such as bricks, pebbles, leaves, shells or counters. Then ask them to record their arrays on squared paper, together with the related multiplication and division fact. Activities such as this will also lead to discussion about the kinds of numbers that can be represented as multiple arrays in contrast to prime numbers, for which there is only the horizontal or vertical array – for example, 1 × 7 and 7 × 1. As children move through school, they should be encouraged to think about arrays not as a collection of single objects organised in a particular way, but rather as a rectangle, and using squared paper representations can help with this development.

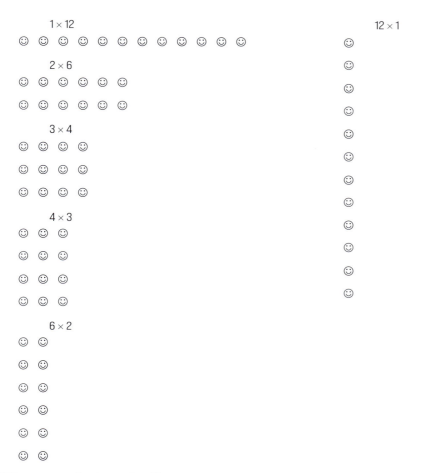

Figure 5.7 Different arrays for the number 12

The reSolve activity Fruit Shop provides opportunities for students to address the Year 2 curriculum outcome 'multiply and divide by one-digit numbers using repeated addition, equal grouping, arrays, and partitioning to support a variety of calculation strategies' AC9M2N05. This activity also leads to recognition of repeated equivalent groups where multiplication is represented as a repetitive addition of the same group. Similarly, division can be understood as repeated subtraction. The Fruit Shop activity could be easily extended by asking students to share fruit into trays using equivalent groups.

The array representation can foster skip counting, which can be a useful strategy for small numbers only (up to 5) of groups. For example, skip counting by 5 to 3 × 5 = 15 is a sensible strategy but attempting to skip count with larger numbers – for example, 8 × 7 – can be problematic. Often children using this strategy lose count of the number of skips and are out by a **factor** – for example, answering 49 or 64 to 8 × 7. Skip counting is an additive approach and does not emphasise the underlying mathematical structure. It should be used in a limited way.

Link 5.4 reSolve: Fruit Shop

Factor a whole number that divides exactly into another number or a whole number that multiplies with another whole number to make a third number (e.g. 3 and 4 are both factors of 12)

The Balloon Bunches widget in HOTmaths (see Figure 5.8) provides an opportunity to develop ideas about equivalent groups and skip counting. Flower Bunches (HOTmaths) is similar but allows for larger numbers.

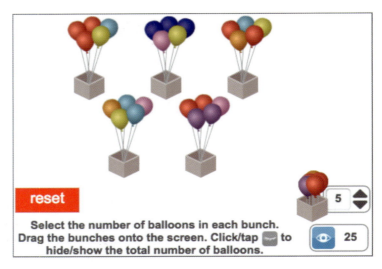

Figure 5.8 Screenshot of HOTmaths Balloon Bunches widget

Link 5.5 Illuminations: Factorize

A more powerful approach is to develop ideas about factors. Older primary-age children should become familiar with using the term 'factor' and be able to explain what it means. The idea that 24 has factors of 1, 2, 3, 4, 6, 8, 12 and 24 provides powerful support for dealing with a range of computations and can be developed from array representations. This understanding is important for later algebra activities. A helpful interactive web-based activity is Factorize on the Illuminations website.

Division has the same relationship with multiplication as subtraction has with addition. It is the inverse operation, and 'undoes' multiplication operations. This understanding is important for children, and when learning tables facts they should also experience all the related division facts. For example, 7 × 6 = 42 should also be written as 6 × 7 = 42, 42 ÷ 7 = 6 and 42 ÷ 6 = 7 to emphasise the interrelated nature of the operations.

Division has two main meanings. First, there is a *sharing* (or partition division) meaning, in which a given number is partitioned into equal groups. Second, there is a *grouping* meaning, in which a given number is divided into a given number or quota. This grouping meaning is sometimes called quotition division. Although the mathematical meaning and operation are the same, for children the different ways in which a problem is worded can make it difficult to recognise the operation needed as division. As an example, think about the subtle differences in the following two problems.

1. There are 54 biscuits packed into 6 equal packets. How many biscuits in each packet?

This problem requires 54 to be portioned or shared among six equal groups. The answer is the number of items per group.

2. There are 54 biscuits which have to be divided into equal packets of 6 biscuits. How many packets would be needed?

This problem requires 54 to be divided into equal groups (packets), each of six biscuits. The answer is the number of groups. The mathematical solution in both instances is 54 ÷ 6 = 9. The answer, however, refers to different physical entities. In the first problem there are nine *biscuits* in each packet. The second problem has nine *packets* each containing six biscuits.

Issues such as those outlined in the two problems make division problems difficult for children. They understand sharing intuitively, but mathematical text and notation can interfere with their understanding. There are several ways of representing division as shown in Figure 5.9.

Figure 5.9 Different ways of showing division

These representations tend to be used in different situations such as 12 ÷ 4 means 12 divided by 4, whereas $4\sqrt{12}$ is often described as 4 'goes into' 12. Reading the bracket notation as 12 divided by 4 in effect means reading it backwards – that is, reading from right to left rather than left to right. To counteract this the third representation is sometimes used, especially in overseas countries, and may be more familiar to some students. The fraction notation will be discussed in Chapter 6. Finally, the 12/4 has become more common because the / is used in spreadsheets for division. This is an informal notation and should be discouraged. Students will, however, come across all of these notations at times and need to recognise them as division. This understanding is best dealt with informally – students do not need to practice all the ways of representing division.

In order to develop understanding of division, children need a lot of work with sharing and grouping, and informal recording, so that they develop an understanding of the division process. The relationship between multiplication and division is crucial, and children should be able to use all of the related number facts to solve problems.

Take, for example, the number 48.

Six lots of eight make 48	6 × 8 = 48
Eight lots of six make 48	8 × 6 = 48
There are six groups of eight in 48	48 ÷ 8 = 6
There are eight groups of six in 48	48 ÷ 6 = 8
If you share 48 things among six people, they will each get eight	48 ÷ 6 = 8
If you share 48 things among eight people, they will each get six	48 ÷ 8 = 6
If you group 48 things into eight groups, each group will have six	48 ÷ 8 = 6
If you group 48 things into six groups, each group will have eight	48 ÷ 6 = 8

Building up this understanding takes time but using a range of concrete materials will help.

Williams and Shuard (1982) suggested that there were three stages in learning division:

1. grouping and sharing as different operations using concrete materials to solve problems
2. recognising the relationship between grouping and sharing
3. using related multiplication facts to solve division problems.

Step 2 is often neglected but without this fundamental understanding, children may continue to struggle with division problems (Back 2012). Activities such as Grouping Goodies, Share Bears and Lots of Lollies available from NRICH support this development.

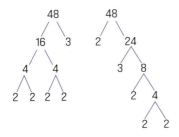

Figure 5.10 Two factor trees of 48

Prime factor a factor that is also a prime number

Prime number a whole number that can only be divided by itself and one, such as 11

Activities that emphasise the relationship between multiplication and division include factor trees. These are a way of representing numbers using its factors. A useful challenge is to reduce the number to its **prime factors** – that is, the factors of that number which are **prime numbers**. Figure 5.10 shows two factor trees of 48. How many more can you find?

Factor tree activities can be easier for children if they know something about divisibility rules. These are rules that govern division of whole numbers without any remainder. Finding these rules can be a worthwhile challenge for children in the upper primary years. The easiest to recognise is division by 2 because all numbers are even; that is, they end in 0, 2, 4, 6, or 8. Division by 5 is also easy because all numbers divisible by 5 end with a 5 or a 0. Table 5.3 shows the basic rules useful for primary age students.

Table 5.3 Divisibility rules

Divisor	Rule	Example
1	All whole numbers (integers) are divisible by 1	39 875 ÷ 1 = 39 875
2	Even numbers end in 0, 2, 4, 6 or 8	486 ÷ 2 = 243
3	Sum of the digits must be divisible by 3	117 1 + 1 + 7 = 9 117 ÷ 3 = 39
4	The last two digits must be divisible by 4	27 9**16** Last two digits are 16, divisible by 4. 27 916 ÷ 4 = 6979
5	Number ends in 5 or 0	475 ÷ 5 = 95
6	Number is divisible by 2 and 3	108 ÷ 6 = 18

There are rules for other numbers as well, which you can find easily using an internet search, along with the mathematical ideas underpinning these rules. Using the simple rules for divisibility can help in starting off a factor tree and in reinforcing the multiplication–division relationship. These ideas can be developed over time as a way of making division easier, whether mental, written or technology-aided.

A word about calculators

Few topics have engendered as much discussion and dissent as the use of calculators in the classroom. This technology is widely used in everyday life – think of cash registers or petrol pumps, for example. In the classroom, however, there is a concern that using a calculator will reduce arithmetical skills. Research into calculator use has repeatedly emphasised the potential benefits of using calculators, although much of that research was completed in the 1980s and 1990s (e.g. Ruthven 1998). In the Australian Curriculum v. 9.0 there is an expectation that technology – including calculators – will be available in schools. As with all tools, outcomes depend on what kind of use is made of calculators.

Many people claim that using a calculator, or other forms of technology, makes children lazy and that it will cause them to avoid learning basic number facts. These views are most common among parents and systems, rather than schools and teachers (Banks 2011). Using a calculator does not replace the need for children to develop fluency and instant recall of basic number facts. Rather, calculator use emphasises the need to have mental tools for simple, straightforward computations, and high-level estimation skills in order to decide whether the answer arrived at is reasonable. Students should be able to make informed choices about whether an answer is best obtained using a mental, written or technology-based approach (Higgins 1990; Sowder 1990) and this approach is echoed in Australian Curriculum: Mathematics v. 9.0. In Year 5, for example, students should 'solve problems involving multiplication of larger numbers by one- or two-digit numbers, choosing efficient calculation strategies and using digital tools where appropriate; check the reasonableness of answers' (AC9M5N06).

> **PAUSE AND REFLECT**
>
> A Year 5 teacher has given a worksheet to her class so they can practise number operations. Alex has provided this answer to the problem: 13 × 6.
>
> 13 × 6 = 52   'I doubled it three times.'
>
> The teacher looks at the answer and says, 'You've got that wrong. Use a calculator to check.'
>
> What has Alex done wrong? What message is Alex getting when he is told to use a calculator? How could the teacher have built on Alex's incorrect answer to develop the understanding needed? Discuss these questions with another person, and write down what you would do to help Alex.

Many commercially produced worksheets instruct students to 'Use a calculator to check your answer'. On the face of it, this appears to be sound advice, but when teaching school children, it is easy for them to avoid the thinking processes that are so important.

If children know that they can 'check' their answers, they may simply fill in the worksheet with little thought, knowing that they can write in the correct answers after they have 'checked'. In addition, the implicit message, reinforced by the teacher's comment 'You've got that wrong', is that the calculator is always correct, and that computation is not a personal skill that matters.

Calculators must be used appropriately. They are a very useful form of technology to develop understanding of patterns and skip counting, for example, and they can be used to remove the computational load when the lesson focus is on some other concept, such as interpreting data or solving a complex problem involving measurement.

Drill and practice

Along with calculators, there is considerable discussion about the role of practice when learning new skills. Many people (e.g. Allen 2011) lament the passing of 'chanting' tables and think that today's children are not expected to memorise number facts. The research of Cowan (2011) clearly indicates that rapid recall of number facts aids mathematics proficiency, but that conceptual understanding of the ways in which numbers work is critical for continued success. The understanding of number relationships leads to the development of multiplicative thinking (Siemon et al. 2012) that provides the foundation for later mathematical development. The Australian Curriculum: Mathematics v. 9.0 expects children to 'recall number facts and demonstrate proficiency' across the primary years. In Year 2, recall applies to addition facts to 20 and multiplication by two; in Year 3, multiplication by 3, 4, 5 and 10 and related division facts; in Year 4 multiplication facts to 10 × 10 with related division facts. Demonstrating proficiency indicates that recall of number facts must go beyond rote recitation to a deeper understanding of the four operations with whole numbers to develop the proficiencies of fluency, reasoning, understanding and problem-solving. It is not that drill and practice with number facts are not needed; rather, the focus should be on the nature of that practice, which should develop deep, connected knowledge of the number system.

Practice and developing efficient computational strategies should not always consist of drill. Jody in Classroom Snapshot 5.1 is making use of an activity in another learning area to provide incidental practice of addition. Consider the ways in which Veena in Classroom Snapshot 5.3 is working with her class to develop number sense, based on multiplication.

CLASSROOM SNAPSHOT 5.3

Distributive property
when multiplying one number by another number, the result is the same as multiplying its addends and summing the products; it can be expressed as $a(b + c) = ab + ac$ (e.g. $5 × 17 = 5 × 7 = 50 + 35 = 85$)

Veena is a teacher with a Year 5 class that is developing strategies for multiplication with larger numbers. The class works in small groups selected by Veena so that there are different abilities in every group. She reminds the children that they may not tell anyone how to do a problem, but they should help each other by asking questions. Each group is given a set of three, word problems involving three-digit by two-digit multiplication. The questions are graded in difficulty and each group can choose the question that they think will challenge them best. The questions are set in the context of a computer game where for every treasure collected there is a reward. The numbers were deliberately chosen to provide messy problems: 127 × 15, 254 × 36 and 598 × 87. The aim is to develop further understanding of the use of the **distributive property** that all the children know about and can use confidently with smaller numbers. The children work on their problems for about 15 minutes, while Veena walks around and asks questions of the children such as 'What is the meaning of the 1 in 127? and 'What are the different ways that you could split up 254?' She calls the class together and asks each group in turn to come to the front with its work. Several different solutions are shown and recorded on the board, including a standard written algorithm and different ways of using the distributive law. Each solution is explained by one member of the group. Many different solutions are presented such as:

$127 × 15 = 100 × 15 + 20 × 15 + 7 × 15 = 1500 + 300 + 105 = 1905$

$127 × 15 = 100 × 15 + 20 × 10 + 20 × 5 + 7 × 10 + 7 × 5 = 1500 + 200 + 100 + 70 + 35 = 1905$

$127 × 15 = 100 × 10 + 100 × 5 + 20 × 10 + 20 × 5 + 7 × 10 + 7 × 5$
$= 1000 + 500 + 200 + 100 + 70 + 35 = 1905$

When the range of solutions has been shown, Veena encourages a class discussion of the ways in which the approaches work, and how they rely on the distributive property. Each child is then challenged to try the problem again in their mathematics book using a different method from the one that their group presented. Veena collects the books at the end of the lesson for later review and ends the lesson with a quick round-up, during which the children say what they have learned during the lesson.

There are many ways to use technology to provide practice, develop understanding or consolidate learning. It is not the technology itself that enhances learning, however, but the nature and quality of the interactions between the children, and the teacher and children, as exemplified in Classroom Snapshot 5.3. Problems need to be posed carefully and with thought to provide different levels of challenge. It is important to have discussion both during the learning activity and, particularly, at the end of the lesson. Asking the children to solve the same problem in a different way ensures that the students engage with new ideas. The brief review at the end helps both the children and Veena reflect on the lesson and sets up a platform for the subsequent mathematics lesson.

PAUSE AND REFLECT

There are sound reasons, backed by research, for students needing to be able to recall number facts automatically (e.g. Pegg, Graham & Bellert 2005). What is the best way to achieve this?

Some common approaches include:
- 10 quick facts at the start of a lesson
- timed tests of basic facts
- competitive games such as Sherrif (Swan & Marshall 2009)
- worksheets with many repetitions of a previously taught procedure
- conceptual games such as Numero™ (Asplin, Frid & Sparrow 2006)
- the use of programs such as *Math Blaster*
- Scorcher activities in HOTmaths.

Discuss which of these approaches you have seen in classrooms. What approaches do you think are helpful to students? What is the role of technology in providing practice opportunities? What resources will you use when you are teaching?

TIPS FOR ONLINE TEACHING

There are many activities in this chapter that could be used for online teaching. The NRICH Eightness of Eight and reSolve Fruit Shop could both be given as online activities with students taking photos of their representations. Making arrays with any kind of object (coins, dried peas, pebbles, LEGO®, etc.) that children may have access to is not only a valuable activity, in itself, but also stresses that you do not need to use expensive, specialised equipment to do mathematics. Activities that ask students to make a given number in as many ways as possible are also appropriate. There are many drill-and-practice activities available online but set a time limit – 10 minutes of focused practice is worth more than 30 minutes of unthinking work. Don't forget that you can ask students to find out how their family members carry out a particular computation. Ask students to explain the methods or write a short report about what they found.

Conclusion

Operating with whole numbers is a key aspect of the primary curriculum. In parallel with the development of these skills, it is important to ensure that students build foundations for proportional reasoning through developing multiplicative thinking and understanding number relationships, including those dealing with parts of a whole, such as fractions, decimals and percentages. Children need time to develop understanding and consolidate new concepts, and teaching should focus on both conceptual understanding and procedural fluency. Providing a range of problem-solving practice activities and opportunities for discussion supported by good use of technology will help to support children's mathematical development.

GUIDED STUDENT TASKS

1. Make a list of all the calculations you have performed in the last few days. Classify these into mental, written or technology use. Which was the most common?
2. Think about how you learned your 'tables'. Over the years how has your understanding changed? Are there ideas that you have now that might have been useful to you when you learned these?
3. Write some mathematical stories to illustrate the relationships between addition and subtraction or multiplication and division.
4. Read the article by Jenni Back (2012) about teaching division. Try some of the activities suggested. Which of these might you use in an upper primary classroom? Why would you use them?
5. Think about some occasions when you have watched children undertaking number calculations on a computer. Were the activities investigations or drill? Was there discussion with the teacher or an aide about strategies to carry out the calculations? How useful is it for children to work on mathematics games or activities on a computer when supervision and discussion is limited? Why do you think this?

Link 5.6 NRICH: 'Difficulties with Division' by Jenni Back

CONCEPTS TO CONSIDER

This chapter contains many of the specialised content ideas, such as types of subtraction. Some additional information is provided here to address some specific concepts.

Number system

Numbers are fascinating and our number system has developed over millennia as our society has become more complex. The Hindu–Arabic system that we use is based on nine digits (1–9) and zero. With these 10 symbols, every possible number can be represented making the system efficient and effective. Zero is critical to being able to compute as fluently as we do. There are many easy-to-read books about numbers, and it is useful to have some of these as reference books to provide 'mathematical gossip' – interesting information about numbers to share with your class. Some suggestions are provided below.

Place value

Understanding place value is critical to mathematics. The position of a digit in a number provides information about the value of that digit. We are used to the 100s, 10s and units, or 1s, but may forget that this system is not completely intuitive and children need to develop understanding.

The largest number sits to the left because this is the way we read the number. In whole numbers, the ones, or units, column is at the far right. There is a mathematical relationship between the numbers that can be expressed in index notation. The index is the small number at the right-hand side of the 10: it is called an exponent. The value of 10^0 (or any other number having an index of 0) always is 1. 10^1 has the value of 10; 10^2 is 10×10 or 100, and so on. Our familiar number system has a base of 10 – that is, we work in 'bundles' of 10. This means that the largest digit that can appear in any column is 9. Once a number reaches a value of one more than 9, it has to appear in the next column to the left as one ten and zero ones, 10. As you move to the left, each column has a value 10 times the preceding column. In the number shown in the table, 5 means 5 ten thousands, 4 is 4 thousands, 3 is 3 hundreds, 8 is 8 tens and 6 is 6 ones (or units). The number is read as fifty-four thousand, three hundred and eighty-six. Note that the words we use do not exactly mirror the mathematical structure.

Ten thousands	Thousands	Hundreds	Tens	Units (1)
10^4	10^3	10^2	10^1	10^0
5	4	3	8	6

This structure also holds for numbers in bases other than 10. Computers use a 'binary' system that has a base of 2. Try to work out a table for the binary system. What would 5 look like if you wrote it in the binary system? It is useful to have some knowledge of the underlying structure of the place value system. There are many sources of information available if you search for 'place value'.

Arrays

Arrays are a powerful visual representation of multiplication. How arrays are named, however, has been the subject of comment (Hurst and Hurrell 2021). In multiplication, the first number describes the number of objects in the group and the second number describes the number of groups. Hence, 2×3 indicates three groups of two objects in each, and 3×2 indicates two groups with three objects in each. In an array, it is a convention that it is described as the number of rows by the number of columns. Hence 2×3 looks like:

It is worth noting that this convention, while easy to read, is tricky to describe in words if we want to preserve the same order. Saying 'there are 2 objects in each group and there are 3 groups' is a relatively complex sentence. It also does not follow other mathematical conventions used in mapping, for example, horizontal location by vertical location or identifying points on a plane (x, y). It is useful, however, to recognise the convention. From the perspective of young students, the critical issue is for them to be consistent when describing an array, and to develop an understanding of the commutativity of multiplication.

For more information and practice, see Chapter 3 in Hilton, A & Hilton, G 2021, *Making sense of number*: *Improving personal numeracy*, Port Melbourne, Vic: Cambridge University Press.

FURTHER READING

Allen, E 2011, 'Scandal of the primary pupils who can get full marks in maths without even knowing their times tables', *Mail Online*, 7 September, <http://www.dailymail.co.uk/news/article-2034442/Pupils-passing-maths-exams-good-marks-dont-know-times-tables.html>.

Back, J 2012, *Difficulties with division*, NRICH, <https://nrich.maths.org/5450>.

Rowlands, T [1997] 2021, Divisibility tests, Article number 1308, NRICH, <https://nrich.maths.org/1308/>.

Seife, C 2000, *Zero: The biography of a dangerous idea*, Chicago, IL: Souvenir Press.

Siemon, D, Bleckly, J & Neal, D 2012, 'Working with the big ideas in number and the Australian Curriculum: Mathematics', in B Atweh, M Goos, R Jorgensen & D Siemon (eds), *Engaging the Australian Curriculum: Mathematics – perspectives from the field* [e-book], Mathematics Education Research Group of Australasia, pp. 19–45, <https://www.merga.net.au/common/Uploaded%20files/Publications/Engaging%20the%20Australian%20Curriculum%20Mathematics.pdf>.

Websites for exploration

Spencer, A 2018, *Big book of numbers: Everything you wanted to know about the numbers 1–100*, Fitzroy, Vic: Brio Books.

PART-WHOLE NUMBERS AND PROPORTIONAL REASONING

CHAPTER 6

LEARNING OUTCOMES

By the end of this chapter, you will:

- understand the importance of part-whole numbers such as fractions, decimals and percentages
- choose appropriate representations to illustrate different ways of thinking about fractions, decimals and percentages in a range of contexts
- be able to recognise the use of proportional reasoning in daily life
- understand how technology can be used effectively to develop understanding of part-whole numbers.

Introduction

We use proportional reasoning every day, often without being aware that we are reasoning in terms of two quantities that vary in relation to each other – that is, as one quantity increases or decreases, so does the other. I may decide to buy two tins of tomatoes. The price of each tin is the same, so if I purchase double the number of tins, the amount I pay also doubles. Despite using this thinking informally quite regularly, it is surprising how many people have trouble with this concept. Doubling or trebling a quantity is one thing, but what about wanting one-and-a-half times, or only needing one-fifth of something? These calculations can become very tricky. Often we make some kind of estimate and end up with either too little or too much of something.

Proportional reasoning is used widely to solve a range of everyday problems from 'best buys' to understanding data presented in tables. It underpins scaling problems such as scale drawings of house plans and currency conversions, and appears in many other situations, including the Australian electoral system.

ACTIVITY 6.1

Think about what you do each day. Identify times when you may have needed to use proportional reasoning where you scale a quantity up or down. Examples might be in cooking, crafting or building, house decorating, shopping, going on a journey … there are many possibilities. Make a list and identify as many different situations as you can. For example, if you have to increase a recipe serving four people to feed 10 people, each of the ingredients will need to be increased $2\frac{1}{2}$ times because $10 = 2\frac{1}{2} \times 4$. Compare your list of everyday activities using proportional reasoning with that of another person, and comment on the similarities and differences.

Background

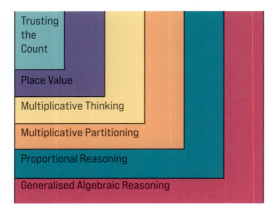

Figure 6.1 The big ideas of number
Source: Adapted from Hurst & Hurrell 2014

Proportional reasoning reasoning about relationships (e.g. 6 being two threes or three twos rather than one more than 5) or comparing quantities or values (e.g. 1 km is 1000 m)

Moving from additive to multiplicative thinking is one of the great challenges in the primary years of schooling. There is considerable research on this topic (e.g. Malola, Symons & Stephens 2020), and being able to recognise key behaviours and capitalise on 'teachable moments' is an important skill of all good primary teachers.

Hurst and Hurrell (2014) discuss 'big ideas' in number (Siemon et al. 2012) – key concepts that are core to developing children's mathematical reasoning and understanding. The big ideas are represented in Figure 6.1 as a set of nested concepts, each building on the earlier ideas.

These 'big ideas' underpin the Number strand of the curriculum and are closely associated with the other strands. Developing multiplicative thinking is fundamental to proportional reasoning, and the shift from additive to multiplicative thinking is a focus for the upper years of primary schooling. The notion of multiplicative proportionality, that is creating equal parts of a given whole or collection, underpins fractions, decimals and percentages. Such thinking lays the foundation for the development of **proportional reasoning** during the secondary years. The importance of fractions, decimals and percentages is endorsed by Australian mathematics curriculum documents, which describe a progression of fraction understanding from understanding the nature of one-half as two equal parts in the early years of the primary school (AC9M2N03), to representing unit fractions (AC9M3N02), to recognising and representing equivalence (AC9M4N03), moving between representations of fractions, decimals and percentages (AC9M5N04), and carrying out straightforward operations (AC9M6N05) by the upper primary years. There are several frameworks for thinking about the development of part-whole reasoning. Investigate some of these in Activity 6.2.

ACTIVITY 6.2

Search online for the Learning Assessment Framework (e.g. Siemon 2017). This framework has eight zones that show increasing sophistication of part-whole thinking. Also search for *Teaching Fractions, Decimals and Percentages* (Book 7) from NZ Maths. This book includes a set of 'strategy stages' ranging from emergent to advanced proportional part-whole. Compare these two frameworks. How do they complement each other? In what respects do they differ? List ways in which these frameworks could support your teaching of fractions, decimals and percentages. Are there other frameworks that you have found? If so, how do these compare with the two suggested here?

PAUSE AND REFLECT

What do you remember about learning fractions, decimals and percentages at school? Jot down all the words that come to mind. What helped you to comprehend these numbers? What was difficult to understand? From your reflection, think about how you can translate your experience into positive learning events for the children you teach. Discuss your thinking with a colleague or friend.

Parts and wholes

Fractions, decimals and percentages are different representations of **part-whole numbers** that are most commonly met in the primary school years. Although these representations are interchangeable, initially they are usually taught separately. Later in the primary years, children begin to recognise that these different representations are simply different ways of showing the same number.

Part-whole numbers representations of number that relate a part to the whole, such as fractions (e.g. $\frac{3}{5}$ is three parts taken from five parts of a whole), decimals (e.g. 0.6 is six-tenths of a whole) and percentages (e.g. 35% is 35-hundredths of a whole)

Fractions

The fraction one-half $\left(\frac{1}{2}\right)$, and its decimal (0.5) and percentage (50%) equivalents are widely experienced by children, and most children develop intuitive understandings of half. They also frequently recognise the ratio representation of 50:50. Many children, however, don't have a lot of experience of other fractions outside the classroom, so care should be taken to ensure that teaching materials use fractions, decimals and percentages that go beyond halves and quarters.

Fractions are notoriously difficult for children to understand. Children need a lot of experience with a range of fraction representations in the early years of primary school. They need to understand that a fraction can represent part of a whole and part of a group and can be a number in its own right.

For children in the early years, a key idea is that the parts into which the whole is divided must be equal in size, whether represented as a whole or a group. One third, for example, means that a whole is divided (or shared) into three equal parts and one part is taken to

Fractions are discussed further in 'Concepts to consider' at the end of the chapter.

give $\frac{1}{3}$. Activities such as folding paper into halves and half again or sharing objects such as blocks into two and then four equal groups, together with the use of the language of fractions, will help young children develop the conceptual understanding. It is important to identify the whole, separate that whole into equal-sized parts, and then take a given number of those parts. Note the links to division here – that is, both sharing and grouping. Figure 6.2 shows different representations of fractions: as part of a whole using an area model, as part of a group, and as a number on a number line.

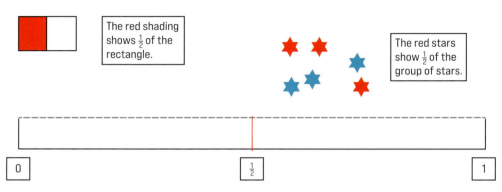

Figure 6.2 Fraction representations

The difficulty that children have with representing fractions other than half was described by Gould, Outhred and Mitchelmore (2006). They found that children in Year 7 still used naïve representations of one-third and one-sixth, most likely based on seeing a fraction as two whole numbers unrelated to each other. This finding is a reminder that diagrams or drawings that adults take for granted may be interpreted quite differently by children.

CLASSROOM SNAPSHOT 6.1

Mr Hay wanted his Year 4 class to develop understanding of fraction 'families' such as thirds, sixths and twelfths. The students were having to study online which Mr Hay recognised as being less than ideal. He created a short video story of the 'Lost Fraction' and modelled the story in the video with cardboard shapes. 'One-third had lost its family. It was wandering around looking for other fractions to join with. One-third met three quarters. "Come and see if you fit with us", the three-quarter siblings said. But when they joined together, One-third was too big to fit into their whole. Next one-third met three fifth family members. "Maybe you fit with us", said the fifths. But one-third was too small to fit into their whole. Then one-third met four-sixths. "Try us", said the sixths and one-third fitted right in.'

Mr Hay asked the students to watch the video and ask any questions about it at the next class meeting, or through the chat line. Once he was sure that all students understood the story, he asked them to choose a different fraction and to write a story or make a video about their fraction, explaining why the fractions fitted together. He provided several templates in different shapes and fractions that could be downloaded and printed. The students' stories and videos were uploaded to the class portal.

Mr Hay has recognised the challenge of teaching online but has developed an interesting and engaging activity. Although he cannot monitor the children directly, the stories and videos they produce will give him a lot of information about their conceptual understanding. The activity is one that is engaging for students and reinforces fraction concepts such as the importance of equal parts and equivalence.

ACTIVITY 6.3

Go to the Australian Association of Mathematics Teachers Top Drawer resource and open the fractions drawer. Read about the different meanings of fractions and explore the activities. Write explanations for the different meanings of fractions in your own words, and then explain these to someone else. Developing a language to explain fractions in a variety of ways is important for teaching. Why would it help to have a variety of explanations ready to use? Compare the 'big ideas' in this drawer with those identified in Activity 6.1. How are they the same? How do they differ?

Link 6.1 Top Drawer: Fractions

Different meanings of fractions

There are different ways of thinking about fractional numbers. As children progress through school, they need to experience both part-whole and part-part representations, as well as fractions as a ratio, a number on the number line, and as an operator. For example, in Figure 6.3, the red section can be thought of as one part out of four, a part-whole notion, because the whole is the large rectangle that has been divided into four equal parts. Usually this is written in traditional fraction notation as $\frac{1}{4}$. It could also, however, be described as one red part to three white parts, a part-part idea, because it describes how the different parts of the large rectangle are related to each other. This idea can also be written as a ratio such as 1:3.

The same idea can be applied to fractions as represented by groups or sets (see Figure 6.4). In the first array shown here, the box contains $\frac{1}{4}$ of the group of ☺. The second array shows the ratio of ♦ to ☺. For every one ♦ there are three ☺, and this can be written as 1:3.

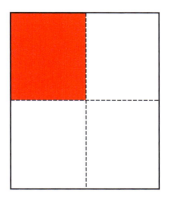

Figure 6.3 1:3 ratio

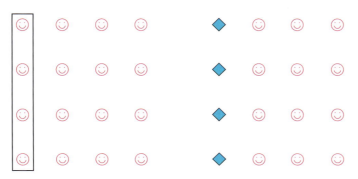

Figure 6.4 1:3 ratio sets array

Representations of fractions are the focus of the downloadable resource Fractions, Pikelets and Lamingtons (Department of Education and Training, NSW 2003). The difference between 'continuous' models, such as shapes and paper strips, and 'discrete' models, such as collections of objects, is important to understand because these may be useful in different situations.

ACTIVITY 6.4

Fractions can also be thought of as division. Consider, for example, dividing three pizzas among five people. How much pizza would each person receive? Solve that problem in any way you like. You can draw or use concrete materials if you want to. Now ask several other people of different ages and experience to solve the same problem. What different solutions did you see?

Each person gets $\frac{3}{5}$ of a pizza. Children will solve these kinds of problems in a variety of ways, and they may represent their answer as a fraction. Often they will start by dividing the three pizzas in half and allocating half a pizza to each person. Then they have to deal with the leftover half of a pizza. Some children will divide this half into five parts and allocate each person one part. Often they cannot resolve this into a formal fraction solution. Other children will divide each pizza into five parts and share these parts among the five people so that each person gets three parts out of five from a pizza. These informal solutions provide important experiences for children and, more significantly, give teachers considerable insight into their thinking and understanding.

A key idea from the middle primary years onwards is that of equivalence. If this is well developed and understood, many of the difficulties with fraction operations that arise later can be avoided. Equivalent fractions are those that are the same size but have different denominators. The idea that $\frac{1}{3} = \frac{2}{6} = \frac{3}{9} = \frac{24}{72} = \frac{100}{300}$ and so on is powerful. Any fraction can be written in different ways. Children should be encouraged to explore equivalence and develop their own 'rule' to make equivalent fractions from any starting point, and then share and test out their rules for accuracy and applicability.

One useful way of starting to develop ideas about equivalence is with a fraction wall. There are many different versions of the fraction wall available, but they are also easy to make using a table in Microsoft Word. Create a table with a single column and as many rows as you want. Then use the Split Cells feature under Table Tools – Layout to split each row into as many cells as you wish. Make sure that initially you have fraction families: halves, quarters, eighths, sixteenths and thirds, sixths, ninths and twelfths. Ask children to find and colour in all the different ways to make $\frac{1}{2}$ and $\frac{1}{3}$ and so on. Initially, use only unit fractions – that is, those fractions with 1 as the numerator. Extend into $\frac{2}{3}$, $\frac{3}{4}$ and more complex fractions as children develop more understanding. There are several interactive fraction walls available (e.g. Visnos's Fraction Wall) that could be used using a computer or tablet with small groups or a whole class.

Link 6.2 Visnos: Fraction Wall

Older children can also be challenged to think about the relationships among different fractions, and how these fractions change if a different whole is specified. In the fraction wall shown in Figure 6.5, if A = 1, then B = $\frac{1}{2}$, C = $\frac{1}{3}$ and so on. But if B is specified as the whole (that is, B = 1), then A = 2, D = $\frac{1}{2}$ and F = $\frac{1}{3}$. Naming C and E when B is the whole can become a challenge, and discussions with children about how they could find out how big C is if B = 1 can lead naturally to discussions about common denominators, which can make use of the equivalence between two lots of F and C, and three lots of F and B. NRICH has a Fraction Wall investigation that upper primary children could undertake.

Link 6.3 NRICH: Fractional Wall

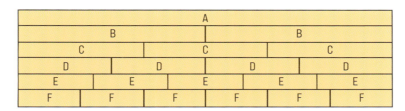

Figure 6.5 Fraction wall

Development of fraction understanding takes place over time and through many different experiences. It is important that children have concrete experiences using activities such as paper folding and cutting. They should also use a variety of shapes – circles, rectangles, squares, hexagons – and paper streamers. By cutting and folding, matching shapes and placing one piece over another, children develop a feel for equivalence that can be transferred to a virtual environment. They should also name the fractions created and write these names to help consolidate their understanding of the underlying relationships.

If children understand equivalence, operating with fractions becomes much more intuitive, and children are less likely to try to rely on half-remembered rules. Adding $\frac{2}{3}$ and $\frac{1}{2}$, for example, can be visualised as a fraction wall such as in Figure 6.5. If A = 1, then $\frac{2}{3}$ can be seen as four lots of F or $\frac{4}{6}$, which has to be added to three lots of F or $\frac{3}{6}$, making $\frac{7}{6}$. Then, it is easy to see that this is one lot of A and one lot of F or $1\frac{1}{6}$. Not only does the addition become more intuitive, but also an understanding of mixed fractions can be developed.

Fractions can also be thought of as operators. When used in this way, fractions can expand or contract a number and are forms of mathematical functions closely associated with patterns and algebra. For example, $\frac{2}{3}$ of 15 could be seen as 'input 15, multiply that by 2 and divide the answer by 3 to get 10'. Making connections with early algebra concepts creates links and provides further rationale for learning about fractions in a metric world. Multiplying by the fraction $\frac{2}{3}$ is, in this instance, shrinking 15 down to 10.

This section has focused more on developing conceptual understanding of fractions than on procedural calculations with fractions. Developing a sound conceptual understanding provides a platform for future development. One way of assessing how much children understand about fractions is to use a 'Think Board'. Versions of Think Boards for use with mathematics are available online. The target idea, which may be from any domain of mathematics, is written in the centre and children are asked to write a story, draw a picture or diagram, show real objects and write symbols or number sentences (as appropriate to the central idea) in the quadrants. They can be encouraged to be as creative as they like. The board can be adapted to any level of understanding by changing the number or idea in the centre. Year 6 children could be given non-unit fractions such as three-fifths, whereas Year 1 children could be given one-half or one-quarter. A similar idea can be used with decimals. Figure 6.6 shows a Year 1 child's Think Board of one-quarter, together with a fraction wall constructed by the same child.

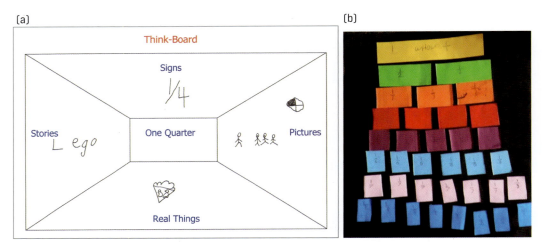

Figure 6.6 Year 1 child's fraction work: (a) Think-Board; (b) Fraction wall
Source: (a) Think Board adapted from PAT Resources Centre, © 2014 Australian Council for Educational Research

These artifacts are interesting for several reasons. The Think Board (a) shows that this child has grasped common mathematical representations, including the shaded circle and the part-of-a-group, in the 'pictures' segment, and the $\frac{1}{4}$ shown under 'signs' or symbols. The child has not, however, translated this understanding into the idea of a 'story', although the L is at a distance from the other three letters. The 'real thing' shows a slice of pizza, but the child has not included the rest of the pizza and the slice does not show one-quarter of a circle, even though he is apparently confident with this representation. The fraction wall (b) shows a similar emerging lack of understanding. Although the child has carefully constructed equal pieces for each part of the wall, again the child has not recognised that these pieces should make up a bar the same size as the whole (yellow). Fractions always need to relate to the relevant 'whole', and unless this idea is explicitly developed, there is a danger that this child will miss this important fundamental concept.

Activities such as these are valuable for teachers to pick up evolving issues of understanding. It is not unusual for children to have difficulty translating the mathematics they experience in the classroom into everyday life. Encouraging children to write stories or identify 'real things' begins to make these links and is a basis for developing the idea of a mathematical model. A mathematical model is developed from a process that involves representing a real-world problem mathematically in order to solve it. Models may be simple, such as using a number sentence to show a subtraction problem, or very complex requiring the problem to be identified, including underlying assumptions and constraints, and a solution to be developed using a variety of mathematical ideas and concepts. For example, models predicting weather, or the spread of disease, are complex models used by experts to help our society make decisions about difficult issues. If several children in the class showed similar behaviour, the teacher would know that this was an area that needed to be addressed. Similar comments could be made of the fraction wall activity which allows children to demonstrate what they understand far more effectively than colouring-in pre-determined images.

Decimals

Decimals are a group of fractional numbers expressed in a different way. In some places they are termed decimal fractions, which emphasises the close relationship. Decimals can be written as fractions with denominators that are powers of 10 (10, 100, 1000, and so on).

A key understanding about decimals concerns the extension of place-value understanding to parts of a number less than 1. You can find quite a good explanation of this for your own understanding at the Khan Academy website under decimal place value. However, to develop this understanding in children requires more than an explanation – however good this may be. Children need to experience a range of ways of representing decimals.

Link 6.4 Khan Academy: 'Decimal Place Value'

Using a strip of paper divided into 10 equal parts, students can explore tenths and represent these as both fractions and decimals. This is a precursor to using squared paper where 10 by 10 squares represent one whole. Each small square is then $\frac{1}{100}$, or 0.01. Children need these concrete experiences before modelling them by using interactive representations such as the HOTmaths Representing Decimals widget.

Decimal number expanders (see Figure 6.7) are another resource. There is an example of a decimal number expander at the Teaching and Learning About Decimals website, and this

Link 6.5 Teaching and Learning About Decimals

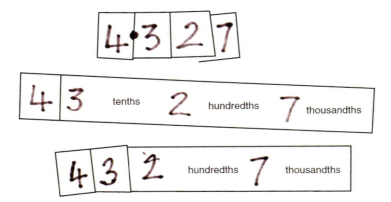

Figure 6.7 A decimal number expander showing different ways of presenting the same number

site also has templates for printing. Representations of this kind help children to visualise decimal numbers and begin to understand the relationships among the decimal parts of a number. This site also has a lot of information about common misconceptions regarding decimals and background information.

Multibase arithmetic blocks are used sometimes to represent decimals. However, these should be used with some care. If children are used to seeing the small cube as a unit, they may have difficulty seeing the flat or large block as a unit. There are various interactive representations available to show this approach.

A better approach is to use linear arithmetic blocks. This concrete model has a long rod as the unit, which can be covered by 10 pieces of poly pipe, or 100 smaller pieces of poly pipe, or 1000 washers (see Figure 6.8). Commercial versions are available, but it is relatively easy to make your own. This model appears to be less confusing for children, and if it is made fairly large, it involves more children in physically manipulating the equipment.

Figure 6.8 Linear arithmetic blocks representing the number 0.143

Link 6.6 NRICH: Spiralling Decimals
Link 6.7 NZ Maths: My Decimal Number

As with fractions, decimals can be represented on the number line. Many children do not believe that there are numbers between the counting numbers represented on a number line. They need practice and experience to understand that, for example, 2.7 lies between 2 and 3. As they move through school, children begin to experience decimal numbers that are more fine-grained, such as to the 100th and 1000th place. Many children develop the idea that the longer the decimal, the larger it is. For these children, 0.678 is larger than 0.75. This notion needs to be addressed through place-value activities, such as Spiralling Decimals from NRICH or My Decimal Number from NZ Maths, and a range of representations.

Building a conceptual understanding of decimals is important before beginning to operate with decimals. The earliest operation is usually multiplication by powers of 10.

CLASSROOM SNAPSHOT 6.2

Kim wants to teach her Year 5 class about multiplying a decimal number by 10, with an emphasis on the aspects of place value. She hangs cards with digits on them over some children's backs. One child receives a card with a large black dot – the decimal point. The children line up to make the number 4.356. The child with the decimal point is asked to sit down, still in her position in the line, and hold her card up high. The other children remain standing with their backs to the class so that the class can see the number clearly. When another child waves the magic × 10 wand, all the standing children take one step to the left. The class see the digits move one place to the left and the decimal point remains stationary. The class reads the new number, 43.56, aloud and children describe what they saw.

They repeat this activity with new numbers and different children modelling the process. Then, they return to their desks and make number slides (see Figure 6.9) to create different multiplications by 10, and then 100. The children write their own rules for multiplying decimals by powers of 10. The following questions are discussion starters:
- Why did Kim first model the activity using the children?
- Why did she place the numbers on the children's backs?
- Why is it important for children to realise that the numbers move – not the decimal point?
- Where is this representation seen in daily life?

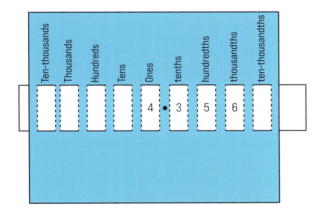

Figure 6.9 A number slide

Calculators are a useful technology for developing ideas about decimals. They could be used to reinforce Kim's lesson, for example. They are particularly valuable for developing ideas about the expansion and contraction of numbers when they are operated on by a decimal. Many children believe that multiplication always makes a number bigger. Challenging this notion by setting up situations where this is not true can be a powerful learning experience.

ACTIVITY 6.5

Use a calculator to complete these computations:

$$25 \times 3, \quad 25 \times 0.3, \quad 25 \times 0.03$$

Predict your answer to the problem 25 × 0.003. Were you correct?

Describe in your own words what is happening. Predict what you think would happen if you divided a number by a decimal. Set up some calculations of your own to test your conjecture.

Money and decimals

Money is often suggested as an introduction to understanding decimals. There is evidence, however, that money is of limited use when introducing decimals (e.g. see the Teaching and Learning about Decimals website).

Children see money as separate from the decimal numbers with which they work in classrooms. Money is concrete, whereas decimal numbers are abstract in nature. Today, money in Australia is rounded to the nearest 5 cents. Using money as a model for decimals may convince children that decimals can only be written to the nearest 0.05 or 0.10, or two decimal places (Steinle & Stacey 2001). Problems of the type 'I purchased a toy for $4.37 and some lollies for $1.24. How much money did I spend?' are unrealistic and do not provide context-based practice in adding decimals. There are many resources available that use such approaches, but they simply reinforce children's ideas that school mathematics is not related to their everyday lives.

Percentages

Percentages are another form of fractional number. Per cent means 'out of one hundred', and percentages are probably more common in daily life than fractions. A percentage means that the number or quantity has been divided into 100 parts. In the Australian Curriculum: Mathematics v. 9.0, percentages are first found in Year 5, where familiar percentages are associated with decimals and fractions (AC9M5N04). It is a logical and relatively straightforward step to recognise that percentages are decimal numbers and fractions of 100.

Children should begin to develop an intuitive sense of the size of a percentage, using 50% as a benchmark initially, and then 25% and 75% as halfway points between 0 and 50%, and 50% and 100%, respectively. As with fractions, it is essential to identify the whole. Describing something as 30% makes no sense unless the whole is defined.

One representation that can help develop percentage understanding is a double number line. In this representation, one line is divided into suitable divisions to show percentages, and the other line shows the quantity or number on which the computation is performed, divided into appropriate divisions. Figure 6.10 shows a representation of a double number line where the top line is divided into 10% intervals and the bottom line represents $45. The mid-point of $45 is marked as $22.50. This represents a discount of 50%. To find a discount of 25% it would be necessary to draw a line at the mid-point between the 20% and 30% marks. This would be halfway between the 0 and $22.50, or $11.25. Try some examples for yourself.

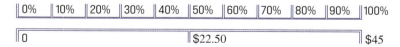

Figure 6.10 The double number line

The strong visual representation of the double number line can be helpful for children developing a sense of common percentages. This approach should not, however, be seen as an algorithm for calculating percentages, or for working with rates and ratios. The visual support that the double number line provides is only one way of developing the deep understanding that is required, and, like every other teaching approach, it needs to be part of a balanced program in which a wide variety of representations are presented and experienced by children of all ages.

The Australian Curriculum: Mathematics v. 9.0 has an increased emphasis on modelling situations using mathematics. For example, the Achievement Standard for Year 6 states (ACARA 2022):

> Students connect fractions, decimals and percentages as different representations of the same rational number and order common fractions giving reasons. They use different representations of rational numbers when solving problems. Students apply knowledge of place value, multiplication and addition facts to operate with decimals. They use equivalence to solve problems involving the addition and subtraction of fractions with related denominators. Students use estimation and substitution strategies when appropriate to find approximate solutions to problems involving rational numbers and percentages. They model situations, including financial contexts, using number sentences that involve all four operations and the use of brackets with natural numbers and interpret them in context.

To reach this level of proficiency, students will need to experience a variety of representations of different types of numbers throughout the primary years. For example, calculating a percentage discount such as 25% off is much easier if students can recognise and use the fraction or decimal forms. With 'friendly' numbers, such as $20, this task becomes relatively trivial. With real-world examples, however, the task is more difficult. For example, a 10% discount on a large item that would cost $1073 is $107.30. For adults who are familiar with such calculations, this is still fairly easy, but for Year 6 children it is less so. Teachers need to remember that they cannot expect the same levels of reasoning and familiarity with short cuts and everyday examples in primary age children but should aim to develop the skills in their students that will allow them to become flexible and efficient users of mathematical information.

PAUSE AND REFLECT

Why is it useful for children to experience a range of different representations of part-whole numbers? Think of different ways of representing the same fractional number. Why might children become confused between fraction, decimal and per cent notation of the same number (e.g. one-quarter and 25%)? Reflect on your own usage of these different representations. When is it easier to think in terms of fractions? What about decimals or per cents?

Recognising that a fraction may be interchangeable with a decimal or a percentage is useful because it makes computation easier later on. Percentage calculations are very common, and developing quick and easy equivalents in fractions and decimals is potentially powerful. In the primary years, the focus is on the common percentages and equivalents, such as 10%, 25%, 50%, and multiples of these, such as 20% and 75%. Remember to emphasise the interconnectedness: if children can recognise 50%, they can halve this to get 25%, in the same way that they deal with halves and quarters. People who have a well-developed sense of these relationships can move effortlessly between the different representations, choosing the one that makes most sense to them or that is most useful for a given purpose. Children should be encouraged to use mental strategies for common percentages. For example, finding 50%

of a quantity is a halving activity, which most children deal with reasonably easily. In the primary years, developing these intuitive understandings is more important than learning algorithms.

There are many games and activities that can be used to develop a facility with using percentages, decimals and fractions interchangeably. These include Bingo-type games, matching games and puzzles, and many different online resources. Choose these carefully. Most involve some kind of drill activity. Choose resources that show fractional numbers in different ways. For example, if the resource uses area models only, make sure that these are not all circles or squares. The widespread use of pizzas as a model has led to some adults believing that fractions are pizzas! Be creative and think of other ways of representing fractional numbers.

Link 6.8 Illuminations: Fractions Models

The Illuminations site has some interactive activities that could be used to support developing understanding. For example, try Fractions Models, which allows a variety of representations and shows the fraction, decimal and percentage equivalents. Use of a virtual manipulative like this allows children to calculate quantities that might otherwise be too complex. From a teaching perspective, though, it is important to be purposeful about the use of such tools. Use them to help children to identify the relationships between the whole, the part and the percentage, and to relate these to real situations. Ask them to explain these relationships to develop reasoning and understanding.

Children need to come to terms with these important numbers, fractions, decimals and percentages. They should not, however, be rushed into computations with these numbers before there is a sound conceptual understanding. Developing this understanding is an ongoing process throughout all the years of schooling, and it is unreasonable to expect young children to have the understanding of an adult who, knowingly or otherwise, works with these kinds of numbers on a daily basis. The underlying thinking is multiplicative and lays the foundation for proportional reasoning that is a critical component of the curriculum in the middle years. These numbers are used frequently in other areas of mathematics, and also in other subjects where their mathematical complexity may be less well understood.

Proportional reasoning

Proportional reasoning can be understood in different ways and is difficult to capture in a short definition. The key to thinking proportionally is to identify the relationships between numbers and quantities. For example, a piece of paper is three pegs or five USB drives long. Another piece of paper is two pegs long. How many USB drives long is the piece of paper? Try solving this problem before reading further.

A problem such as this one can be solved in a variety of ways. You could find out how many USB drives make one peg and then double the answer to find the length of the smaller piece of paper in USB drive units. You might say the new piece of paper is $\frac{2}{3}$ of the old one so the number of USB drives long is $\frac{2}{3}$ of 5. Children should be encouraged to find answers to problems of this type using whatever resources they have. With concrete materials, even children as young as Year 4 level can attempt problems like this – providing an opportunity to develop their problem-solving proficiency.

Proportional reasoning has strong links with algebra, and early activities working with patterns are important in building understanding.

CLASSROOM SNAPSHOT 6.3

Children in a Year 6 class were working on a pre-algebra task. They were using square tiles to model the number of people who could be seated at a series of square tables. They worked systematically through a series of questions that asked about the number of people that could be seated at two tables, four tables, five tables and ten tables. Then they were asked a challenge question: How many people could be seated at 99 tables?

The number of tables was too large to model with tiles, so the children had to find alternative approaches.

- Sam drew the picture shown in Figure 6.11 and counted the number of people.
- Min said, 'It's a pattern going up by two each time. I can skip count by two, 99 times, starting from 4 because that's the beginning number.'
- Jan said, 'It's easy. You just double the number of tables and add one for each end.'

All three children got the correct answer (200 people).

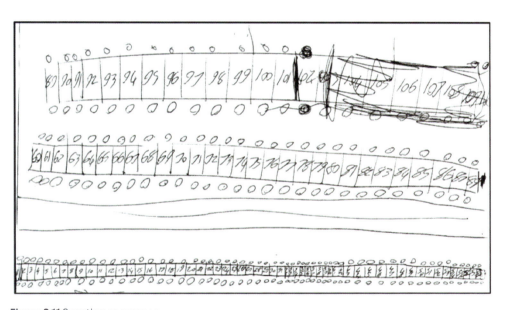

Figure 6.11 Counting on process

The three children in Classroom Snapshot 6.3 demonstrate diverse ways of calculating their answer.

Sam is using counting strategies and needs to recognise that there are more efficient approaches. To provide suitable teaching for Sam, you may need to go back to early number work and provide age-appropriate resources to develop more effective strategies, such as counting by fives or tens. Sam is not yet ready to use the underlying relationship. Rather, he needs to develop more efficient counting strategies so that he can solve more complex problems. So, setting up further learning opportunities to recognise patterns, will help to, ultimately, lead him to the relational understanding.

Min has recognised a pattern and has used that to help her skip count. However, skip counting is not efficient when large numbers are involved, and it is easy to lose count of the number of skips. She needs to begin to use patterns more effectively, recognising the underlying proportional relationship. Min's thinking is still essentially additive – she adds on two each time to get to the answer – but it is more sophisticated than Sam's approach. Min needs to begin to recognise the multiplicative relationship involved so that she can arrive at the answer more efficiently. She would benefit from activities such as making patterns and recording the growing patterns as a table, or activities such as Function Machines (e.g. see NRICH).

Link 6.9 NRICH: Function Machines

Jan is using multiplicative thinking. He has recognised a relationship between the ways in which the tables are arranged and the number of people who can be seated, and he is using multiplication to arrive at the answer efficiently. He needs now to recognise and write rules for a variety of number pairs. Function Machines are also useful for Jan, but different outcomes are expected. For Jan, the emphasis should be on recording the relationships rather than recognising the relationships, because he is moving towards abstraction.

Multiplicative thinking is an underpinning concept for algebra, and activities such as writing rules for number pairs provide a useful base upon which to build. (See Chapter 2 for early number ideas that provide a foundation and Chapter 7 for more ideas on patterns and algebra.)

CLASSROOM SNAPSHOT 6.4

Tina is a beginning teacher, teaching a Year 5 class. She is one of a group of teachers in her school who are working together to explore and improve the ways in which they use technology in the classroom.

Before the lesson began, Tina asked the children to work in pairs on a class laptop. She asked them to log into Kahoot! and then to set the devices down.

The focus of the lesson was developing early proportional reasoning. Tina posed a starting problem on the screen as a warm-up, anticipating that most children in her class would be able to solve this.

In a Year 1 class, Ruby makes a line of bricks that is 7 bricks long. Walt wants to make one twice as long. How many bricks will he need? What if he made it three times as long? Or 10 times as long?

The children worked in pairs to solve the problem. Tina saw that most children were able to solve the problem, so she led a class discussion in which she encouraged children to share their approaches to solving it, asking different pairs to share their thinking. Eventually the class came to the realisation that they were using the seven-times table. Tina posed a few problems based on other numbers such as 3, 5 and 8 to consolidate this idea, recording the children's answers manually on the computer and projector.

She then asked the children to return to the Kahoot! page and gave them the necessary log-in PIN to access a quiz that she had prepared earlier. The quiz used multiple-choice questions and displayed the answer and the number of people who got the answer correct after 30 seconds' thinking time. The children were excited and engaged, talking about the problems and keeping track of what they had got right.

At the end of the lesson, the children returned their devices to the storage facility, and the technology monitors checked that all the tablets and computers were correctly docked so that they could recharge.

Several discussion points arise from Tina's use of technology. All the sharing is anonymous, so children who are less confident can participate knowing that if they get an answer incorrect, then other children in the class don't know. Tina, however, knows her class well and by watching the children's reactions when the solutions are discussed, or their responses to the quiz answers, is able to identify those children who will need some additional help. The quiz is motivating but not competitive, because individuals are not identified. The children are working in pairs and their goal is to get the answer, not to beat the rest of the class. Tina can save the children's answers and the summary from the quiz for later thought and planning. There are good routines in place for using the technology. The class understands how to access the devices, how to log on to the sites requested and how to input their answers. Establishing good routines is an essential classroom-management technique when technology is involved, to avoid unnecessary delays or frustrations from laptops or tablets not being charged, and to minimise damage. This activity is a productive drill activity that provides an opportunity for children to consolidate their understanding.

PAUSE AND REFLECT

In this chapter, various ways have been suggested to support children's developing understanding of fractional numbers. These approaches include concrete materials, role playing, visual imagery, and the use of technology. Look back through the chapter and identify as many different approaches as you can. What similar ideas have you seen or used yourself? For some materials, especially technology, you will need to develop new skills. Why should you invest your time and energy into this learning? How can you incorporate variety in your teaching approaches?

Introducing the ideas of part-whole numbers in an online environment can be tricky. The numbers are relatively abstract and young children may not grasp the essential concept that the parts must be of equal size. Making short videos showing yourself, as the children's teacher, paper folding or separating groups of objects may be helpful. It is important that you do this because primary students react more positively to their own teacher explaining activities or concepts online than watching a stranger. The relationship with their teacher is crucial. Classroom Snapshot 6.1 shows a teacher using an innovative approach in an online environment. This activity could just as easily be done in the classroom.

TIPS FOR ONLINE TEACHING

Many of the activities suggested in this chapter can be undertaken in an online environment. Students can be encouraged to upload photographs of concrete activities, keep mathematics blogs about fractions, decimals and percentages, create stories about their favourite fractions, or go on a fraction hunt around their house and report back at the next class meeting.

Conclusion

Fractions, decimals and percentages will continue to challenge teachers and children in the primary years. However, developing a sound understanding of the characteristics of these numbers is critical for mathematical development. You should have noticed that in this chapter the emphasis has been on concepts rather than procedures. In the primary years, operating on part-whole numbers should arise naturally from the discussions about the kinds of numbers that these are, rather than a focus on computation and algorithms. Given a sound platform of conceptual understanding, the later complexities of proportional reasoning will be minimised and children will develop confidence in their mathematical capabilities.

GUIDED STUDENT TASKS

1. Some people say that fractions aren't used anymore so children don't need to learn them. What would you say to this comment? Find arguments in favour of children learning fractions.
2. Make a list of children's books that address part-whole numbers and proportional reasoning. Develop a lesson plan based on one of these books.
3. Try the Think Board activity for the same number written as a fraction, a decimal and a per cent. How did changing the notation change the representations that you used? Why do you think this occurred?
4. It is fairly straightforward to find a 10% discount. It is a lot more complicated to work out the amount an object has been discounted by. Try some problems of the type 'I paid $50 after a 10% discount. What was the original price?' to work out the answer. The answer is greater than $55 by a small amount ($55.55). Does that small amount matter? What if it was $500 after a 10% discount? Or $5000?
5. How is proportional reasoning used in the Australian Electoral system? Check out Senate voting in the Australian parliament.

CONCEPTS TO CONSIDER

This chapter already contains many of the specialised content ideas about part-whole numbers. Some additional information is provided here to address some specific concepts.

Common fractions

Common or vulgar fractions (vulgar from the Latin vulgaris meaning common) are those that we deal with most such as $\frac{11}{12}$ or $\frac{5}{7}$. The bottom number is the *denominator* because it names (nominates) the number of parts into which the whole is divided. The top number is the *numerator* because it sets the number of pieces taken. One of the biggest difficulties with fractions is that these names used to describe the different parts of the fraction are difficult words. The line separating the numerator and denominator is the *vinculum*, also from Latin meaning a chain or bond. An online search for *vinculum* will give you some of the history of the usage in mathematics. This kind of incidental information provides both a deeper understanding of the mathematics and a source of interesting facts for your students.

Decimals

Decimals are an extension of the place value system to numbers smaller than one. They were first used in China at the end of the fourth century CE. Because they are relatively easy to use, they have become the basis for measurements and currency in most parts of the world.

The value of a decimal is analogous to place value – that is, as you move to the right, the number becomes smaller by a factor of 10. The decimal point is placed between the unit (ones) and the tenths place. Decimal numerals can also be written in index notation where a negative sign before the index shows that the number is divided by the multiple of 10 (see 'Place value' in the Concepts to Consider section in Chapter 5). Hence, the number 6.5438 indicates that there are 6 units, 5 tenths, 4 hundredths, 3 thousandths, 8 ten thousandths and 4^{-2} means $\frac{4}{100}$.

Units (1)		Tenths	Hundredths	Thousandths	Ten thousandths
10^0	.	10^{-1}	10^{-2}	10^{-3}	10^{-4}
6	.	5	4	3	8

The words used to describe the decimal parts can be misheard – the th on the end is important, but many people miss this important clue to the size of the numeral.

Equivalent fractions

The idea of equivalence is a powerful one. If you understand this concept, many of the operations on fractions become easy. An equivalent fraction is created when both the top (numerator) and bottom (denominator) are multiplied by the same number. So, $\frac{5}{7} = \frac{5 \times 2}{7 \times 2} = \frac{10}{14} = \frac{15}{21}$ and so on. The proportion remains the same although the fraction itself may change. This fact can make adding and subtracting fractions reasonably easy because if you turn them into equivalent fractions they can be operated on directly. To add $\frac{3}{4}$ to $\frac{1}{6}$ we recognise that 4 and 6 are both factors of 12. Hence $\frac{3}{4}$ is $\frac{9}{12}$ and $\frac{1}{6}$ is $\frac{2}{12}$.

$$\frac{9}{12} + \frac{2}{12} = \frac{11}{12} = \frac{3}{4} + \frac{1}{6}$$

Try some addition and subtractions of fractions yourself.

For more information and practice, see Chapter 7 in Hilton, A & Hilton, G 2021, *Making sense of number: Improving personal numeracy*, Port Melbourne, Vic: Cambridge University Press.

FURTHER READING

Website for exploration

Department of Education and Training, NSW 2003, *Fractions, pikelets and lamingtons*. Sydney: Department of Education and Training Professional Support and Curriculum Directorate.

Ministry of Education 2008, *Teaching fractions, decimals, and percentages*, Wellington, NZ: Ministry of Education.

Siemon, D 2017, 'Targeting "big ideas" in mathematics', *Teacher Magazine*, <https://www.teachermagazine.com.au/articles/targeting-big-ideas-in-mathematics>.

CHAPTER 7

EXPLORING PATTERNS AND ALGEBRA

LEARNING OUTCOMES

By the end of this chapter, you will:

- understand the central importance of patterns in early childhood and primary school mathematics
- understand the importance of mathematical structure and its relevance to children's learning of mathematics
- use sequences effectively to find, explain and justify rules
- be able to represent and resolve number sentences, equivalence and equations
- be able to describe relationships between variables
- be able to use technology effectively to explore algebraic situations.

Introduction

Until recently, algebra was regarded as the domain of the secondary school years in most countries. In addition, it was often regarded in quite narrow ways by non-mathematics teachers, parents and students as being concerned with the manipulation of symbols according to tightly prescribed rules. Recent attention to algebra in the primary school has not regarded it as appropriate that such a narrow view of algebra be taken, leading to the use of terms such as 'pre-algebra' or 'early algebra' to describe the mathematics involved.

In this chapter, it is recognised that students' understanding of algebra in the secondary school rests on foundations that are laid in the primary school, as reflected in the Australian Curriculum: Mathematics v. 9.0. These foundations are concerned with key algebraic ideas about patterns and generalisations, rather than with symbolic representations of these, such as x and y. This chapter explores developmental models associated with patterns and algebraic concepts, with a focus on developing algebraic thinking.

Recent research in Australia (Day, Stephens & Horne 2017; Siemon et al. 2018) has identified an eight-zone hierarchy of algebraic reasoning. In the lowest zone children can explain a simple generalisation from a physical situation, such as recognising that a pattern of two red blocks and one blue block has the same structure as a pattern of stamp, stamp, clap, or square, square, circle. By Zone 3, children can tell stories using words, materials and symbols to explain straightforward generalisations, and by Zone 5 children can develop rules to explain a sequence. For example, if children are considering a growing pattern such as that shown in Figure 7.5 in Zone 3, they might describe this as 'two more boxes each time', whereas in Zone 5 the children might say 'the rule to find how many boxes is double the number and take one away because the first box only needs three sides'. Although these zones relate closely to curriculum expectations, the focus is on the reasoning used rather than the mathematical content, and hence this approach addresses the Reasoning proficiency. For a full overview of a table of the eight zones, see Day, Stephens and Horne (2017).

Linking with curriculum

In the Australian Curriculum: Mathematics v. 9.0 (ACARA 2022), Algebra is one of the six content strands. The Foundation and Year 1 content descriptions both refer to recognising, continuing and creating pattern sequences:

- *Foundation:* Recognise, copy and continue repeating patterns represented in different ways (AC9MFA01).
- *Year 1:* Recognise, continue and create pattern sequences, with numbers, symbols, shapes, and objects, formed by skip counting, initially by twos, fives and tens (AC9M1A01).
- *Year 1:* Recognise, continue, and create repeating patterns with numbers, symbols, shapes and objects, identifying the repeating unit (AC9M1A02).

In the later years, the descriptors focus more on number patterns, identifying number properties, sequencing and the formulation of rules. By the end of Year 6, students are expected to recognise and use rules that generate visually growing patterns (AC9M6A01) and find unknown values in numerical equations (AC9M6A02). Links are made with the Number content strand through reference to brackets and order of operations, number sentences and numerical equations. In addition, algebra is critically related to the proficiencies embedded in the content strands. In particular, when students identify a **pattern** and look to **generalise** it, inductive thinking is involved, and conjectures need to be made: will this pattern continue in a certain way? Conjectures need to be tested (was the prediction correct?) and if found to apply consistently, reasons need to be found to explain why. The kind of reasoning that explains the origins of a pattern and justifies why it must always be true is endemic to mathematical thinking.

Pattern a set of objects or numbers in which each is related to the others according to a particular regularity or rule

Generalisation the formalisation of general concepts; general statements that can be used to form conclusions

Pattern and structure

Virtually all mathematics is based on pattern and structure, and there are many indications that an understanding of pattern and structure is very important in early mathematics learning (Mulligan 2017; Mulligan & Mitchelmore 2009). Mulligan and Mitchelmore (2016) developed the Pattern and Structure Mathematical Awareness Program (PASMAP) which focuses on developing children's awareness of the patterns and structures that underlie the concepts and processes common to the Australian Curriculum: Mathematics v. 9.0 content strand of Algebra. A mathematical pattern may be described as any predictable regularity, usually involving numerical, spatial, or logical relationships (Mulligan & Mitchelmore 2009). The idea of a pattern is central to thinking about algebra, so it is unsurprising that the Algebra content strand of the Australian Curriculum: Mathematics v. 9.0 consistently refers to patterning throughout the primary years. Although patterns occur throughout mathematics (including geometric, statistical and probabilistic patterns), the focus here is on patterns related to numbers, because of their close connection to the Number content strand.

In its broadest sense, a pattern is a regularity of some sort and may range in sophistication and familiarity from the observation that odd numbers and even numbers alternate:

1	2	3	4	5	6	7	8
odd,	even,	odd,	even,	odd,	even,	odd,	even …

to rather more unexpected observations, such as if three numbers are in a line on a calendar, the sum of the end two numbers is twice that of the middle number.

For millennia, people have been fascinated by surprising patterns and relationships, such as adding up successive odd numbers produces square numbers, as is shown here:

$$1 = 1^2$$
$$1 + 3 = 4 = 2^2$$
$$1 + 3 + 5 = 9 = 3^2$$
$$1 + 3 + 5 + 7 = 16 = 4^2, \text{etc.}$$

Children need opportunities during the primary years to engage with a variety of patterns, make sense of them, describe them clearly, make suitable use of them, understand where they come from and be able to confidently explain why they will continue.

Patterning in the early years

Many young children's early experiences of patterning occur through activities that require them to use informal materials to identify, make, compare and extend repeating patterns. A repeating pattern has a core that contains the shortest string of elements that repeat. For example, in Figure 7.1, the core is the oval and the rectangle.

Figure 7.1 Oval and rectangle

Early childhood educators advocate that the most meaningful patterning activities involve the use of physical materials that children can manipulate to create and extend patterns, and use trial and error. Activities that are presented in a static form, such as colouring patterns on a worksheet, tend to restrict children to a given number of elements and lack the creative aspect of physically creating one's own patterns. Virtual patterning experiences are readily accessible to children and – like physical materials – can easily be manipulated to develop children's abilities to search for, and extend, visual and even auditory patterns.

Scootle has several interactive activities that focus on repeating patterns. For example, the learning object Musical Number Patterns: Music Maker (see Figure 7.2) asks students to:

Link 7.1 Scootle: Music Maker

> Test your understanding of counting rules by building up rhythms for four musical instruments. Make counting patterns by following the given rules, or use the musical patterns to work out what the counting rules are. Then, make your own music by creating rules to make the counting patterns. View and print a report of your results.

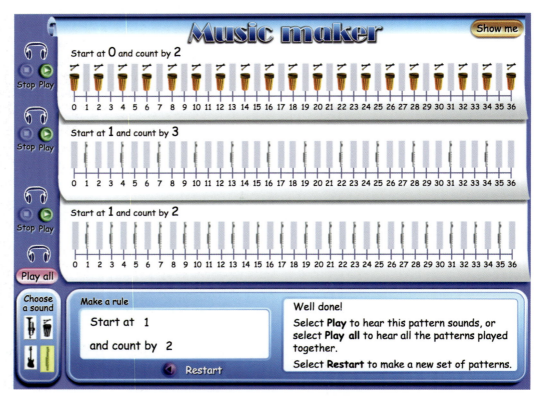

Figure 7.2 Screenshot from the Musical Number Patterns: Music Maker activity
Source: Scootle

Link 7.2 Fuse: Monster Choir – Making Patterns

Similarly, on Fuse, Monster Choir: Making Patterns focuses on matching oral patterns with visual patterns, using symbols and sounds (see Figure 7.3).

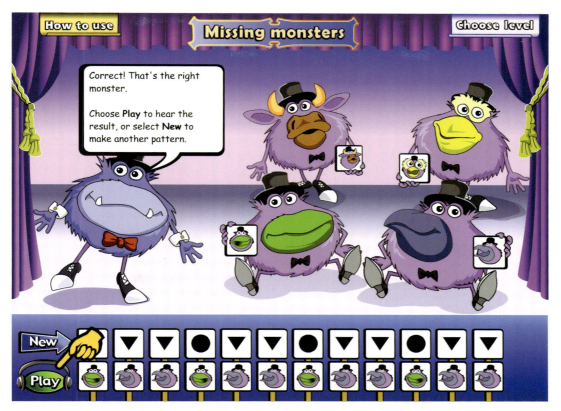

Figure 7.3 Screenshot of the Monster Choir: Making Patterns activity
Source: Fuse © Education Services Australia Ltd, 2017

ACTIVITY 7.1

Access Musical Number Patterns at Scootle and/or Monster Choir at Fuse.
- Look at the learning objectives for each of them. Do you think the learning objectives are achieved?
- What questions would you ask the students either before, during or after doing these activities?
- How would you extend students' skills beyond creating repeating patterns?

There are also several apps that focus on repeating patterns. For example, the Bugs and Buttons app contains a number of repeating pattern activities that can be used to reinforce the concept of patterning and looking for regularity (see Figure 7.4).

Figure 7.4 Screenshot from the Bugs and Buttons app
Source: Snap Two Studios LLC

Growing patterns

It is important for young children to be exposed to growing patterns, and to understand the difference between a repeating pattern and a growing pattern. Experiences with repeating patterns lead to the development of multiplicative thinking, whereas experiences with growing patterns lead to functional thinking (Siemon et al. 2012). When children work with repeating patterns, the focus is on identifying regularity and extending the pattern. With growing patterns, however, the aim is not to extend the pattern, but rather to predict what the next element will be, and then to predict any missing term. Figure 7.5 provides an example of a growing pattern.

Figure 7.5 Growing pattern

Patterning with number

Algebraic thinking thinking that considers the general relationships between numbers, rather than the manipulation of numbers

In order to develop **algebraic thinking**, children need experiences that will enable them to see regularities in the ways that numbers work. According to MacGregor and Stacey (1999), students find algebra difficult to learn unless they have a good knowledge of number and basic operations. These authors consider that there are five aspects of number knowledge that are essential for number learning:

- understanding equality
- recognising the operations

- using a wide range of numbers
- understanding important properties of numbers
- describing patterns and functions.

The hundreds chart is often used as a tool in early childhood classrooms to assist students with counting and place value, and to identify patterns in the number sequence. However, it appears that this tool is only useful if students can understand the structure of the chart, and according to Thomas and Mulligan (1994), many children tend to represent the numbers 1–100 in unconventional ways.

ACTIVITY 7.2

In their article, 'Dynamic imagery in children's representations of number', Thomas and Mulligan (1994) include many examples of how children have constructed unconventional images of the 1–100 chart. Figure 7.6 shows one example.

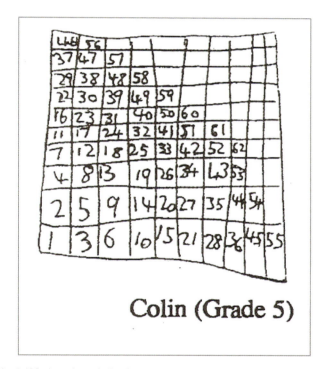

Figure 7.6 Image of the 1–100 chart from Colin (Grade 5)

1. Can you provide an explanation for how Colin has constructed the chart? How would you help him to form a more accurate image of the way the chart should be constructed?
2. Revisit the sites in Chapter 2 that made use of the 1–100 chart. How could you use these sites to help Colin appreciate the structure of the chart?

ACTIVITY 7.3

Link 7.3 NRICH: Coded Hundred Square

In order to further demonstrate how pattern and structure may not be obvious for all students, visit the NRICH website and access the Coded Hundred Square (see Figure 7.7). Print out the pieces of the puzzle, cut them out individually and try to piece the puzzle together.

- What strategies did you use to try to reconstruct the chart?
- What clues did you look for?
- Did you find it difficult to identify a pattern to assist you?

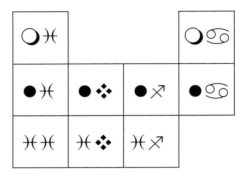

Figure 7.7 Coded Hundred Square
Source: NRICH, University of Cambridge

ACTIVITY 7.4

Make a copy of the 1–100 chart and project it onto the interactive whiteboard (IWB). Use features such as screens or curtains to cover numbers, and have children name the hidden numbers. Question children about how they know what numbers are hidden, encouraging them to focus on the structure of the board (e.g. numbers 44 and 54 because the rows go down in tens). Hundred grids (interactive and static) can be found in many places and HOTmaths also has a Hundred Grid widget (see Figure 7.8).

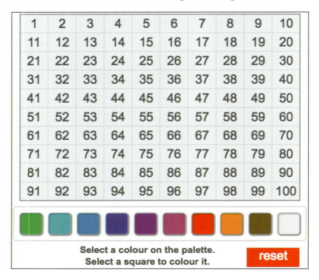

Figure 7.8 Screenshot of HOTmaths Hundred Grid widget

Developing an understanding of relationships

Recognising relationships between pairs of numbers, or between variables, may not be simple. Consider how you would write an equation for the following problem using the variable S to represent students and P to represent professors: 'There are six times as many students as professors at this university' (Fisher 1988, p. 260).

Did you write 6S = P? If so, you are not alone – about one-third to one-half of most educated people are unable to solve the problem correctly (Clement, Lochhead & Monk 1981). The correct response is 6P = S, with the likely explanation for the error occurring attributed to reading S as students and P as professors, rather than S as the number of students and P as the number of professors (Fisher 1988). Together with avoiding the 'fruit-salad' approach to algebra (i.e. referring to 3a as 3 apples and 4b as 4 bananas), developing students' ability to understand relationships between variables can help avoid errors such as the above. Formal algebraic processes are normally not introduced in primary school, but it is appropriate to introduce students to algebraic thinking and develop their ability to identify patterns and relationships between numbers and variables.

Even young children can be encouraged to look for patterns and consider variables. Books such as *Ten in the Bed* by Penny Dale (2007) can be used to explore the relationship between the number of people in the story and the number of eyes (or feet, hands, etc.) they have. Classroom Snapshot 7.1 describes how a teacher used a similar idea to explore patterns in numbers.

CLASSROOM SNAPSHOT 7.1

Using an IWB, the teacher shows a class of Year 2 students the *Sesame Street* song 'Eight Little Spiders', found on YouTube.

In the song, eight spiders are eventually reduced to zero, due to a set of unfortunate circumstances. At the beginning of the clip, the link is made between the number of spiders and the number of legs.

After watching the clip, the teacher asks the children to recall how many legs a spider has. She then draws up a table and asks the children to help complete it to show the relationship between the number of spiders and legs.

1	2	3	4	5	6	7	8
8	16	24	32	40	48	56	64

Link 7.4 *Sesame Street's* 'Eight Little Spiders'

The teacher then asks the students to describe the patterns in the table. The following responses are received:

James: The top numbers go up in ones.

Robert: You just add 8 each time to the second row.

Susan: You times the top number by 8 to get the bottom number.

> ### PAUSE AND REFLECT
>
> After reading Classroom Snapshot 7.1, consider what each student's answer revealed about their thinking. Which students showed evidence of algebraic thinking? Which student's answer would be most useful for determining how many legs 100 spiders have?

Classroom Snapshot 7.1 demonstrates an activity that can be used to encourage students to identify mathematical relationships and to specify a functional relationship as a general rule. A function 'machine' can be used with younger children to look at the relationship between two **variables** instead of just looking at changes in one variable. The picture book *Two of Everything* (Hong 1993) provides a great stimulus for investigating the idea of a function machine. In the story, two farmers unearth a large brass pot that doubles everything that is placed in it. Muir, Bragg and Livy (2015) provide an account of how the story was used with an upper primary class (but easily adaptable to an earlier grade level) to develop functional thinking. Activity 7.5 also provides an example of how a context can be created for exploring functional thinking.

Variable a value that can change within a problem or set of operations

ACTIVITY 7.5

Professor Mad Maths created a machine called the 'Number Cruncher'. If he sets a rule on the machine and feeds numbers in at one end, different numbers come out at the other end.
- What is happening to the numbers as they go in, if they come out like those in the following table?
- Can you identify the relationship between the 'in' and 'out' numbers?

In	Out
4	17
7	26
2	11

Link 7.5 Math Playground: Function Machine

An interactive function machine can be accessed at Math Playground. It provides different levels of difficulty and allows students to input numbers and then identify the function.

If students need help with identifying the 'rule' some scaffolding may be useful. For example, a strategy of listing the out numbers and then filling in the missing numbers may be useful in determining the pattern. In the first example above, the missing numbers could be filled in (1, 2, 3, etc.) with their corresponding out numbers. Students could then see that the out numbers increased by 3 each time.

Equals and equivalence

The concept of equality is one of the five aspects of number knowledge essential for algebra learning as identified by MacGregor and Stacey (1999). Students, however, often literally interpret the equals sign as 'the answer is' (Assessment Resource Banks 2011), or as a command to take an action, rather than as a representation of a relationship. This could partly be attributable to teaching practices that tend to present number sentences in which the answer goes at the end.

Consider Classroom Snapshot 7.2. It comes from teaching resources provided by the Australian Mathematics Sciences Institute, which supports the enhancement of mathematical capacity and capability through a range of mediums. One of these is online support materials. An example of these is a document titled 'Addition and subtraction: the learning and teaching directory', prepared by Janine McIntosh and Michael O'Connor. It includes a student transcript provided by Dr Max Stephens from the University of Melbourne. This transcript is the stimulus for the following snapshot.

CLASSROOM SNAPSHOT 7.2

Students were asked to find the missing number in the open number sentence
$$7+6=\square+5$$
The following responses were given by students:

Luke: $7+6=13+5$

Teacher: Luke, what number did you put in the box?

Luke: 13

Teacher: How did you decide?

Luke: 7 and 6 are 13.

Teacher: What about the 5?

Luke: It doesn't matter. The answer to 7 + 6 is 13.

Teacher: What is the 5 doing then?

Luke: It's just there.

Teacher: Cameron, what number did you put in the box?

Cameron: 18

Teacher: How did you decide?

Cameron: 7 and 6 are 13 and 5 more is 18.

Teacher: Does 7 plus 6 equal 18 plus 5?

Cameron: 7 + 6 is 13 and 5 more is 18.

Teacher: Fiona, what number did you put in the box?

Fiona: 8

Teacher: How did you decide?

▶▶	Fiona:	7 and 6 gives 13 and I thought what number goes with 5 to give 13. 7 + 6 is 13 and 5 + 8 is 13.
	Teacher:	Chris, what number did you put in the box?
	Chris:	8
	Teacher:	How did you decide?
	Chris:	[points to numbers] 7 + 6 = 8 + 5. 5 is one less than 6, so you need a number that is one more than 7 to go in the box so it all balances.

PAUSE AND REFLECT

1. What do you notice about the responses given?
2. How do Luke's and Cameron's responses contrast with those of Fiona and Chris?
3. What would you do to assist Luke and Cameron?

In order to encourage students to develop a more algebraic view of equality, they should be given lots of exposure to various number sentences that do not include the equals sign at the end (e.g. $8 = ? + 5$). In addition, the concept of balance can also be used to reinforce the idea of equality. A set of simple balance scales can be used with different-coloured blocks to visually demonstrate the equality of relationships. Alternatively, string bags containing different objects can be suspended from each end of a coat hanger to visually represent the concept.

Equation a number sentence that states two quantities are equal

While many of the interactive websites that use balance scales to model **equations** are more suitable for older students, the Learning Today website uses simpler equations to demonstrate equality.

Patterns can be made in a variety of ways, including by applying geometrical transformations such as rotation or reflection. Children in the middle years of primary school should explore these options. We use patterns of this type for aesthetic purposes, and this presents an ideal opportunity to link mathematics with, for example, art. The Patch Tool on the Illuminations website provides an opportunity for children to design their own square patch and see whether the design will repeat.

Link 7.6 Illuminations: Patch Tool

Older children could benefit from exploring design ideas from other cultures, and from looking at repeating patterns in friezes, railings, floorings and fabric designs.

In the middle primary years, the curriculum emphasis on patterns shifts from recognising and making patterns with objects to recognising patterns in numbers. There are strong links here with developing computational skills, and children should be encouraged to use patterns as a way of solving computational problems. In Year 3 of the Australian Curriculum: Mathematics v. 9.0, children are expected to 'recognise and explain the connection between addition and subtraction as inverse operations, apply to partition numbers and find unknown values in number sentences (AC9M3A01)'; by Year 4, this is extended to finding unknown values in numerical equations, involving addition and subtraction. Demonstration of proficiency with multiplication facts up to 10 × 10 (AC9M4A02) now sits within the Algebra content strand, rather than the Number content strand. Activities that look for patterns in addition problems, such as 7 + 5, 17 + 5, 27 + 5 and so on, are important experiences for the middle years of primary school.

As previously mentioned, using patterns in the hundreds chart is a useful way to help children see the uses of patterns and to develop ideas about multiples and factors.

ACTIVITY 7.6

Log into HOTmaths and access the Hundred Grid widget (see Figure 7.8) or find a similar interactive widget on the web.
- Colour all the multiples of 3 in green.
- Write a few sentences to describe the pattern that you see. There may be different ways of looking at the pattern.
- Now colour all the multiples of 4 in red.
- Write down all the numbers that are coloured green and red. A new number pattern has been created. Describe a rule for the new number pattern. What would be the next number after 100?
- Activities such as this one can be used in a variety of ways. The new pattern is that of multiples of 12. Why is this pattern created from multiples of 3 and 4?
- Try some other multiples. What can you say about all multiples of 5? What digits do they end with? Using that information, what might you say about the number 375? Or 4980?

Going one step further, such as asking children what they now know that could tell them something about a new number, allows children to engage in a range of approaches to learning and doing mathematics that develop their understanding of and fluency with concepts, procedures and processes (ACARA 2022). While the Australian Curriculum: Mathematics v. 9.0 describes this as a Year 4 outcome, not all children will be able to work from the rule they have found – such as all multiples of 5 end in 5 or 0 – to draw an inference about new numbers; however, it is important to give children the opportunity to develop this sense of working like a mathematician.

CLASSROOM SNAPSHOT 7.3

Children in a Year 3 classroom were exploring patterns using their calculators. The teacher asked them to start at any number and count by nines. They recorded each new number on a long strip of paper. The teacher asked them to record as many numbers as they wished and then to write two interesting facts about the patterns they saw.

Jay started at 1 and recorded 10, 19, 28, 37 … He wrote, 'The pattern goes down by 1 each time.'

Sam started at 714 and recorded 723, 732, 741, 750, 759, 768 … She wrote, 'The last number goes down by 1s to 0, and then it goes to 9 and starts again. The middle number goes up by 1 each time to 5 where it stays at 5, and then goes up next time.'

Asking children to develop rules for patterns is a staging post on the way to generalisation and the beginnings of the mathematical concept of a function. Jay is looking only at the last digit of each

▶▶ number. He is not working with the number as a whole, so he needs to be encouraged to consider the place value inherent in the numbers he is generating. Sam is somewhat more sophisticated in her number sense. She chooses to start with a larger, three-digit number and is looking at the tens and ones places. Her pattern description is still focusing on separate digits, however. She could be encouraged to consider the pattern more holistically by focusing on the idea that when she adds on 9, it is the same as adding 10 and subtracting 1.

The notion of using a rule to describe a pattern is one that becomes increasingly important as children move into the more abstract thinking required for algebraic manipulations in secondary school. In the middle years of primary school, rules will generally look at the growth or contraction of a number sequence, rather than at a relationship between an input and an output number. Nevertheless, activities such as 'think of a number' are useful 'fillers' – educationally sound activities that stand alone as experiences and provide a basis for the development of more complex ideas when children have the necessary skills and knowledge to progress. For example, a starter question on the IWB as children arrive might be, '[Name of child] in the class is thinking of a number. If he adds 7 to the number, he gets 13. What is [name's] number?' Such activities can be varied according to the level of understanding of the class.

There are also a number of activities that could be used to generate questions around the ideas of patterns and algebra. ReSolve: Maths by Inquiry has several inquiry-based resources, as does NRICH, that encourage children to use relationships to describe patterns and make generalisations. Another way of developing relationship ideas through the application of rules is to illustrate 'think of a number' activities with diagrams. For example:

I am thinking of a number.	■
I double that number.	■ ■
I add 6.	■ ■ ☆ ☆ ☆ ☆ ☆ ☆
I divide by 2.	■ ☆ ☆ ☆
I take away the number I first thought of.	☆ ☆ ☆
My answer is 3.	

These activities can be tailored to suit different classrooms and levels of thinking, and children find these 'puzzles' motivating.

ACTIVITY 7.7

Use a word processing program or a stamp tool to create some 'think of a number' diagrams of your own. What might you need to consider when generating these diagrams for children? What happens, for example, if you add an odd number and then choose to divide by 2?

Classroom activities with which the children may be familiar, such as 'Today's number is … ', in which they make the target number in as many creative and different ways as they can, are useful to develop ideas about patterns and relate these to computation.

CLASSROOM SNAPSHOT 7.4

Ian's Year 4 class is working on 'Today's number is … '. Ian has placed 11 as today's number on the IWB. He asks the class to find addition patterns such as 10 + 1. Chloe says, '5 + 6'. Ian puts this on the board below the 11, leaving space above for other suggestions. Tim contributes, '9 + 2' and Ian writes this immediately under 10 + 1. He then asks for subtraction suggestions. Ben says, '12 – 1', and Ian writes this immediately above the 11. Jo then says, '13 – 2, 14 – 3 …' and Ian puts these two suggestions above 12 – 1.

With no further comment, Ian then asks the children to find as many combinations as they can in 10 minutes. Mark quickly completes all the additions to 11 + 0 in a sequential fashion and then continues with –1 + 12, –2 + 13, –3 + 14 … When Ian asks him to explain his answers, Mark says, 'Look, it's a pattern. You just put a minus sign in front. It's the same as 12 – 1 but the other way round.' Ian congratulates Mark on his interesting find and suggests that he now looks for other patterns that make 11.

Sally is struggling with the task. She has written 7 + 4, 1 + 10 and nothing more. Ian draws her attention to the IWB and says, 'We have 10 + 1, 9 + 2. You have found 7 + 4. Is there something that we could put in there between 7 + 4 and 9 + 2?' Sally still looks confused, so Ian asks, 'What number comes between 7 and 9 when we count?' After some time, Sally says, '8'. Gradually, Ian leads Sally to writing 8 + 3 and points out the pattern.

After the 10 minutes is up, Ian brings the class together again. Starting with the subtraction patterns, he gets individual children to contribute their ideas, gradually building the patterns. He then does the same thing with the addition patterns, including Sally, who adds 1 + 10, and Mark, who offers –1 + 12.

Ian then leads a discussion about the links between the addition and subtraction number patterns, but he focuses on the patterns developed. The lesson ends with Ian asking the children to write two interesting things that they have learned during the lesson in their maths journals. While they complete that task, he saves the IWB page that has been created as a starting point for the next day's lesson that will focus on equivalent expressions.

There is a lot going on in this classroom, and other children would also show diverse understandings. Mark has a strong sense of pattern and extends this logically, even though he has not been taught negative numbers. Although he was not expecting Mark's pattern, Ian accepts the understanding that Mark is displaying. Sally has some specific difficulties, and Ian uses some questioning as well as explicit teaching to help Sally begin to recognise the number patterns in the task he has set.

The lesson finishes with a session that pulls together the ideas that Ian wanted to develop about patterns and using patterns to help with computation, and he offers an opportunity for children to articulate their personal understanding through their journals.

Ian uses technology to collect children's ideas in a systematic way and then saves the page created as a starting point for the next lesson.

Ian is demonstrating good pedagogical understanding in how he interacts with the individual children, by asking questions at their level and being explicit when needed; in his organisation of the information, he elicits from the class in a systematic way so that the children can see the developing patterns; and in his intention to use the information the next day to develop the concept of equivalence. Ian's use of IWB technology makes it easier for him to use the class-generated material as a starting point.

PAUSE AND REFLECT

Ian's students have mathematics journals. Whenever they use the journals, Ian provides a prompt or scaffold for the day's entry. Sometimes he asks the children to write down one problem they can do now that they couldn't do before. At other times he might ask them to indicate something in mathematics with which they would like more help or, as in the lesson described in Classroom Snapshot 7.4, to reflect on something they have done.

What do you think of the idea of a mathematics journal? How does the use of a journal help children to develop mathematical understanding? What might be the advantages or disadvantages of this tool?

Equivalence a state of being equal or equivalent; balanced

By Year 4, children are expected to use the ideas of **equivalence** (AC9M4A01). Children need to begin to recognise that there are different ways to express numbers, and that different numbers can be used to make equivalent expressions – for example, asking children to find unknown values in numerical equations such as:

$$\heartsuit + 5 = \square - 4$$

Using a guess-and-check approach and working in small groups, children in Years 3 and 4 are well able to solve these kinds of problems, drawing on their problem-solving proficiency. Developing these ideas to explore unknown numbers also provides powerful opportunities for learning, such as:

If $\star + \blacksquare = 12$, and $\blacksquare$ is less than $\star$, what can you find out about $\star$ and $\blacksquare$?

These kinds of activities lay the foundations for the notion of a variable, which becomes more of a focus in the upper years of primary school.

Generalisation in upper primary

Generalising requires an idea of a variable, now recognised as a subtle and difficult concept that cannot be taken for granted. In secondary school, variables generally are represented by letters, although the available research makes it clear that many students do not interpret the letters in this way. In the primary school, the use of letters to represent variables develops only slowly, although children need to experience the idea of variables being a key to understanding a general property of numbers or to representing a relationship succinctly.

As well as understanding patterns and their representations, primary children need to acquire a good grasp of the key mathematical idea of equivalence, referring to two quantities being the same in some sense, and its representation in mathematics. In the early years, this idea manifests in seeing that there are several different, although equivalent, ways to pair numbers adding to 10 (the base of the decimal number system).

The importance of the correct use of the equals sign is discussed in 'Concepts to consider' at the end of the chapter.

This, in itself, involves a subtle shift in meaning for an expression such as 7 + 3 from being an *instruction* (add 3 to 7) to being an *object* (the result of adding 3 to 7, which is 10). While sophisticated learners in secondary school may have mastered the idea that equivalence is represented using an equals sign, as previously mentioned, young children may at first interpret an equals sign as a reference to the 'answer'. That is, 7 + 3 = 10 is often interpreted (almost literally) as 7 + 3 *makes* 10, although it is perfectly sensible to also write 10 = 7 + 3, indicating that 10 and 7 + 3 are equal to each other. Further, representations such as 7 + 3 = 6 + 4 also represent an equivalence correctly, although young children who are interpreting an equals sign as 'makes' will not find this at all sensible.

The ideas of equivalence lead naturally into the idea of an equation, which requires children to find which values (if any) make a number sentence true. Again, in the early years this may be described quite informally (such as 3 + ? = 12), while in the later years more sophisticated notations and procedures are needed.

It is interesting to note that the Algebra content strand lends itself to targeting multiple outcomes during the same task. Often these tasks include data collected from physical or concrete manipulations related to real experiences. The matchstick activity in Classroom Snapshot 7.5 demonstrates how the same activity can target each of the outcomes listed below:

- Find unknown values in numerical equations involving brackets and combinations of arithmetic operations, using the properties of numbers and operations (AC9M6A02).
- Recognise and use rules that generate visually growing patterns and number patterns involving rational numbers (AC9M6A01).
- Create and use algorithms involving a sequence of steps and decisions that use rules to generate sets of numbers; identify, interpret and explain emerging patterns (AC9M6A03).
- Formulate algebraic expressions using constants, variables operations and brackets (AC9M7A02).
- Solve one-variable linear equations with natural number solutions; verify the solution by substitution (ACM7A03).
- Generate tables of values from visually growing patterns or the rule of a function; describe and plot these relationships on the Cartesian plane (AC9M7A05).

The use of 'x' as a pronumeral is discussed in 'Concepts to consider' at the end of the chapter.

The formation of generalisation can be investigated in numerous settings. Headless matchstick patterns, for example, provide a useful context for exploring patterns and forming generalisations. A sample sequence is provided in Classroom Snapshot 7.5.

CLASSROOM SNAPSHOT 7.5

Sample headless matchstick activity sequence

- Brainstorm patterns noticed in daily life.
- Create and continue the matchstick pattern for five terms:

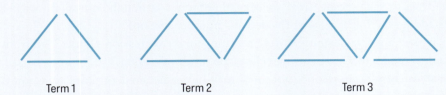

Term 1   Term 2   Term 3

Figure 7.9 Matchstick patterns

- Represent the pattern in a drawing (similar to Figure 7.9).
- Tabulate the data.

Number of triangles	Number of matchsticks
1	3
2	5
3	7
4	9
5	11

- Ask students to describe a rule for the identified pattern in words. You will notice a developmental structure in the quality of the responses. Common responses will include:
  - 'It is going up by 1s'.
  - 'In that column, you just add 2 each time.'
  - 'To get the next one, you just double it and add 1.'
  - 'The number of matchsticks is equal to two times the number of triangles plus 1.'
- Write the pattern in algebraic notation (often described as shorthand for primary students). The students may start with:

$$m = 2 \times t + 1$$

- The students will find it interesting that we do not need to use the multiplication sign when dealing with pronumerals, and instead they may write:

$$m = 2t + 1$$

- Draw a graph to represent the pattern by plotting the points. This can be done with pen and paper or with software such as GeoGebra, as in Figure 7.10.

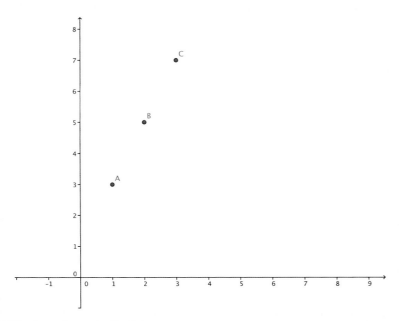

Figure 7.10 Plotting points using GeoGebra
Source: GeoGebra

Students may then graph the relationship in GeoGebra and finally superimpose it over the plotted points as a final step. Graphed function ($m =$) appears in Figure 7.11).

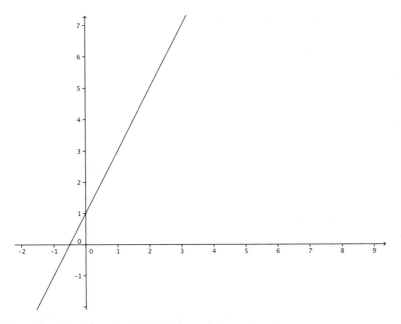

Figure 7.11 Graphing a function using GeoGebra
Source: GeoGebra

Primary aged children can demonstrate a surprisingly sophisticated understanding of relationships and functions if a suitable task is used. Blanton and Kaput (2004) used a task about the number of heads and tails of dogs in the dog pound and showed that children from Kindergarten to Year 6 could solve the same problems using methods appropriate to their level of development.

ACTIVITY 7.8

Design a sequence similar to that described in Classroom Snapshot 7.5 using the pattern in Figure 7.12. How many different matchstick pattern ideas can you find that will be suitable for upper primary investigations? Complete the questions on the HOTsheet shown in Figure 7.12.

HOTsheet

TOOTHPICK PATTERNS

You will need toothpicks or headless matchsticks for these tasks.

TASK 1 — Describe a pattern

1. Complete the table for this pattern which was created by repeating this shape:

Number of ◇ shapes	1	2	3	4
Number of toothpicks used				

2. Use toothpicks to build the next part of the pattern. Add a column to the table for your new design.

3. Describe the link between the number of shapes and the number of toothpicks used.

_____
_____
_____

4. Use your description to predict how many toothpicks would be needed to complete the design with:

   a 6 shapes _____   b 20 shapes _____   c 100 shapes _____

5. How many shapes could you build with:

   a 40 toothpicks _____   b 100 toothpicks _____   c 48 toothpicks _____

Figure 7.12 HOTmaths Toothpick Patterns HOTsheet

The patterns and algebra explorations cannot be viewed in isolation from the other content strands, no matter what syllabus structure is being utilised. While algebraic concepts are often structurally arranged in syllabus documentation alongside number concepts, algebraic concepts are an integral component of all strands, including measurement, space, statistics and probability. Classroom Snapshot 7.6 demonstrates this in the area of measurement.

CLASSROOM SNAPSHOT 7.6

Mrs Kirby, a Year 5 teacher, was teaching a unit on area. The children had explored area 'as a measurement of a surface', they had demonstrated finding areas using informal units and formal units, and they were ready to explore a formula for finding the area of any rectangle.

Mrs Kirby was considering the design of the lesson for the next day and thought she might begin with area revision questions, then give the children the formula and show them how to use it. The students could then complete a series of questions using the given formula to find the area of various rectangles. She reflected upon what had happened in previous years when she used this approach. She remembered the students often confused the perimeter formula with the area formula. Many students found it difficult to identify the 'base' and 'height' of the rectangles they needed to substitute into the formula.

On the basis of these past experiences, Mrs Kirby decided to try something different this year. She decided to use technology to facilitate student ownership of the mathematical ideas involved with the formula for finding the area of a rectangle. The lesson went as follows.

Introduction

Students were supplied with 1 cm² grid paper on which they were asked to draw six different rectangles using the grid lines as sides of the rectangles. They were then asked to label the dimensions of the rectangles and record the area of the rectangle on each one. (Keep in mind that they have already covered repeated units and formal units of area by counting the number of units covered.)

Development of the idea

Students then created a rectangle using GeoGebra and used a table to record the area of the rectangle as the dimensions were changed. The students were asked to find any patterns and relationships, and then to express them in words. They came up with responses such as:

'When the two different sides are larger, the area is larger.'

'To get the area, I always multiply the two different sides.'

'You can multiply the sides that are at right angles to each other to get the area each time.'

In a class discussion, the students shared their findings, and the teacher recorded them on the IWB. The students were prompted to think about a way of expressing how to find the area of any rectangle using symbols. They started with:

> Area = one side length times the different side length

The teacher asked them to think about the square, and whether it also worked for that shape (a few students had an understanding of the square as a rectangle with additional properties). The students decided that 'different sides' wasn't needed, but instead it was always the sides at right angles to each other. This was an important phase of the lesson, and Mrs Kirby was glad that the idea came from the students. A discussion followed, in which Mrs Kirby introduced the convention of using the terms 'base' and 'height', and 'length' and 'breadth'. The students decided as a class to use the terms 'base' and 'height', and they came up with the formula:

$$\text{Area} = \text{base} \times \text{height, or}$$
$$A = b \times h, \text{ or}$$
$$A = bh$$

Application
The students drew two rectangles on grid paper and found the area using the formula they had derived. Mrs Kirby then drew two more rectangles on the board in different orientations and asked the children to find the area using the strategy they had discovered that day.

Drawing conclusions
The students summarised in a diagram, in their own words and in symbols, how to find the area of any rectangle.

Follow-up lesson ideas
- Design a spreadsheet for finding the area of an area. Creating a formula in the formula bar is another excellent strategy for enhancing algebraic concepts. These concepts have been around for a long time, and their affordances are rarely realised in the primary mathematics classroom.
- Students could find the area of larger rectangles outside by working with a trundle wheel to measure the dimensions of the rectangles, then using estimation and the student-designed spreadsheet.

ACTIVITY 7.9

Link 7.7 'The Handshake Problem'

Explore the range of contextual stimuli that can be incorporated into a similar lesson design as in the matchstick pattern example in Classroom Snapshot 7.5. Some ideas to explore are:
- 'Handshake Problem' – a video, available on YouTube, demonstrating solutions with unifix cubes and a calculator
- 'Garden Beds' – an excellent Maths300 lesson
- 'Tower of Hanoi' – an oldie but a goodie, in which patterns arise from the exploration of an ancient game of moving different-sized disks on three spikes, always having a smaller disk on top of a larger disk. The students will develop a rule that will enable them to find out the number of moves required to move to another spike with n number of disks. Complete a search for the Tower of Hanoi. Find interactive software for whole-class investigation on the IWB, lesson plan suggestions and solutions to the problem.

In each of the contexts described above, not only do the student tasks lend themselves to the development of the notion of a variable and relationships, but they also lend themselves to the early investigation of equations. For instance, in the Garden Beds example, the students may develop the relationship, 'The number of pavers is four times the length of the garden bed plus four.' The power of equations is developed when students begin exploring questions such as, 'If I have 424 pavers, what is the length of the largest square garden I could pave?'

> **TIPS FOR ONLINE TEACHING**
>
> Many of the activities referred to in this chapter emphasise the importance of listening to students' responses and encouraging them to justify and explain their reasoning. These important opportunities can still be achieved when teaching online. During COVID-19 lockdowns, many teachers met online with their class using Zoom or Microsoft Teams first thing in the morning like they did in their regular primary classrooms. Students could then be assigned tasks to do throughout the day with another online session scheduled for later in the day. An example of a task that could be readily adapted to this approach would be Activity 7.5, described earlier in this chapter. Students could design their own number crunching machines and then challenge their classmates to identify what the 'rule' is. Students could work in groups in break out rooms to collaboratively identify rules and try different numbers to see if they worked.

Conclusion

This chapter has looked at the breadth of algebraic concepts explored in the primary classroom, with reference to the Algebra content strand in the Australian Curriculum: Mathematics v. 9.0. Over the past few years, we have seen a growing emphasis on the development of algebraic concepts in the early years of schooling, leading to many students being able to formulate algebraic generalisations in the upper primary years. As shown in the examples provided in this chapter, it is definitely a case of 'not throwing the baby out with the bathwater', and instead enjoying the timeless nature of hands-on algebraic tasks within a technological environment.

GUIDED STUDENT TASKS

1. Using headless matchsticks, design three different patterns that will form a straight line when graphed. You will need two changing variables. Describe the relationship algebraically and draw the relationship on the Cartesian plane to check that each one does form a straight line.
2. Consider an activity in early primary, where students explore agricultural contexts, such as gardening and animal production, and use these as a stimulus for activities. What whole class, small group and individual tasks can you devise that use these contexts as stimulus for the patterns and algebra explorations?

3. Algebraic equations assist us with solving many problems in daily life, but we are often unaware of using them as we solve problems. Think about one situation students would be familiar with, where applying simple equations would be useful. Model the equation and possible sample tasks and solutions.
4. In upper primary, algebra links closely to measurement when developing formulae via the observation of relationships. Consider how you would move from drawing a diagram of a rectangle to creating a table of values and describing the relationship between length and breadth in a formula for the area of a rectangle.

CONCEPTS TO CONSIDER

What is x?

There are two generally accepted meanings for 'x' (or any letter used as a pronumeral) as it is used in school algebra. First, it is used to name an unknown number or set of numbers; second it is the name given to a generalised number or variable (Ryan & Williams 2007). It is perhaps unfortunate that 'x' is the commonly used pronumeral, given that it is used in different contexts and has a variety of meanings. For example, it can mean 'times' or 'multiplied by'. Historically, Greeks used letters as names for numbers to count with, instead of the Hindu–Arabic we use today (Ryan & Williams 2007). This, in itself, can cause confusion, as students may think that $m + 1$ must be n because n comes after m in the alphabet (Ryan & Williams 2007). Similar misconceptions can occur when using a pronumeral that is related to the item it represents (e.g. t for the number of tiles). This can lead to a misconception that $2t$ is two tiles, not twice the number of tiles, or that no two variables can have the same value (e.g. incorrectly reasoning that x and y cannot have the same value).

The equals sign

Equations show the equality of two quantities in a relationship, and the equals sign indicates equality between the two quantities. The equals sign does not mean 'the answer is', but rather denotes an expression in which the two sides of the equation are equal. By over-representing number sentences where the answer goes at the end, teachers may inadvertently reinforce this misconception. Students who can solve $6 + 2 = ?$, for example, may have difficulty with solving $? = 6 + 2$, or write $6 + 2 = 8 + 2$ as if the number sentence was simply $6 + 2$.

FURTHER READING

Day, L, Stephens, M & Horne, M 2017, 'Developing learning progressions to support mathematical reasoning in the middle years – algebraic reasoning (Symposium: Learning progressions to support mathematical reasoning in the middle years – introducing the Reframing Mathematical Futures II Project)', in A Downton, S Livy & J Hall (eds) *40 years on: We are still learning!*, Proceedings of the 40th annual conference of the Mathematics Education Research Group of Australasia, Melbourne: MERGA, pp. 663–6, <http://www.mathseducation.org.au/wp-content/uploads/2020/11/Algebraic-Reasoning-Learning-Progression.pdf>.

Muir, T, Bragg, L & Livy, S 2015, 'Two of everything: Developing functional thinking in the primary grades through children's literature', *Australian Primary Mathematics Classroom*, vol. 20, no. 1, pp. 35–40.

Mulligan, J 2017, 'In search of mathematical structure: looking back, beneath and beyond – 40 years on.)', in A Downton, S Livy & J Hall (eds) *40 years on: We are still learning!*, Proceedings of the 40th annual conference of the Mathematics Education Research Group of Australasia, Melbourne: MERGA.

Siemon, D, Callingham, R, Day, L, Horne, M, Seah, R, Stephens, M & Watson, J 2018, 'From research to practice: The case of mathematical reasoning', in J Hunter, P Perger & L Darragh (eds), *Making waves, opening spaces*, Proceedings of the 41st annual conference of the Mathematics Education Research Group of Australasia, Auckland: MERGA, pp. 40–9.

Websites for exploration

CHAPTER 8

EXPLORING DATA AND STATISTICS

LEARNING OUTCOMES

By the end of this chapter, you will:

- understand how to conduct a statistical investigation and be able to choose suitable questions for investigation for children of different ages
- understand the importance of variation in data and different types of variables
- understand the difference between a population and a sample
- be able to recognise different ways of displaying data to 'tell a story'
- understand the importance of drawing inferences from data and the uncertainty associated with these inferences
- be able to draw on technology to support the development of statistical understanding.

Introduction

We experience uses of statistics every day. Some of these uses are obvious – in sports reporting or finance news, for example. Others are more hidden – for instance, supermarkets decide which items to stock and where to place those items on shelves as a result of data gathered at checkouts. Our society has been described as 'data-drenched' (Steen 1999). It is becoming increasingly difficult to make informed decisions without understanding statistical information. This reality has been recognised in the Australian Curriculum: Mathematics v. 9.0 by having one strand focused on **statistics** and another on probability.

Underpinning any understanding of statistics is the notion of variation. People are diverse, events vary, objects differ, and without these differences there would be no need for statistics. Young children intuitively understand differences when they make comparisons – for example, 'I am bigger than Walter' or 'This red brick is bigger than the blue brick'. The notion of variation is not difficult for children to understand. When used in a statistical way, however, it can seem very complicated. In a class of 25 children, there will be a variety of heights, eye colours and shoe sizes. Often, we want to know 'what is typical' of the class, year group, school or population. We have developed a variety of techniques to summarise data, including the mean, median, mode and range, as well as more complex measures such as the interquartile range and standard deviation. Often, applying some common sense and intuition will tell you which of these is most appropriate.

> **Statistics** the collection, analysis and use of quantitative data to describe or draw inferences about a particular situation or to solve a problem

Statistics is about problem-solving. Children need to recognise, or set up, a problem that they wish to solve, which requires data to be collected in order to solve it. This problem may be simple, such as 'How do children get to school?', or more complex, such as 'Do people who play sport have better balance than those who don't play sport?' Once the problem is defined, children must plan to collect the data. They need to develop an understanding of the ideas behind sampling, and of the importance of being systematic and collecting the data in consistent ways.

There are practical considerations as well. How will the data be collected, or how were the data collected if children are using an archived data set? What kinds of analyses will be undertaken? How will the data be displayed to tell the story?

Finally, the findings must be interpreted and communicated to others. This cycle of problem, plan, data, analysis and conclusion has become known as the PPDAC cycle (Wild & Pfannkuch 1999). PPDAC provides a framework for statistical investigations, which is a key approach to learning statistics (see Figure 8.1).

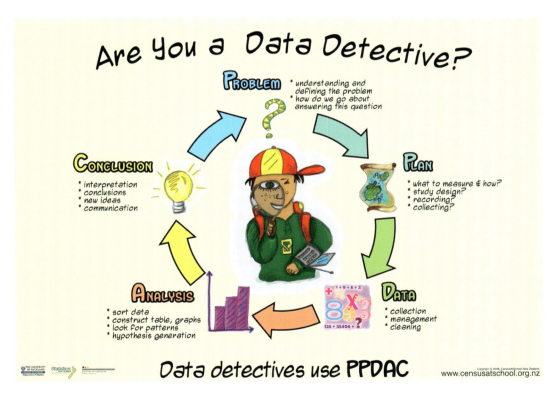

Figure 8.1 PPDAC cycle
Source: CensusAtSchool New Zealand <http://new.censusatschool.org.nz/resource/data-detective-poster/>

The Statistics strand of the mathematics curriculum in the primary years focuses on making meaning from statistics rather than the mechanics of calculating particular statistics. In Australia, the key ideas are related to posing questions, data collection and interpretation, and these ideas appear at every year level. From Year 3, students are expected to conduct complete statistical investigations (AC9M3ST03) that become increasingly sophisticated as they move through school. This strand of the mathematics curriculum links to many other subjects including science, geography, and health and physical education. These other curriculum areas provide opportunities to collect and explore data of interest to children and to create a platform upon which statistical understanding can be built. Children respond to questions of interest to themselves, and about themselves. By the upper years of primary school, they also need to engage with and critique data presented by others – in the media, for example (AC9M6ST02).

> **PAUSE AND REFLECT**
>
> As a teacher, you will be provided with a range of data and will also collect your own data. How will this information affect your planning and programming? What statistical understanding will you need to make decisions based on the variety of data available?
>
> Do you agree that we have a 'data-drenched' society? Why is it important for children to develop statistical understanding and intuitions?

Development of statistical understanding

In the early years of primary school, the skills developed in measurement, such as choosing the appropriate attribute and developing an understanding of standard units, are those that will be used when dealing with **statistical** tasks. Even young children can decide on a question to ask or respond to simple yes/no questions. Asking a Foundation class, for example, 'Do you like bananas?' can be the starting point for a simple collection of **data**. By the middle primary years, children are beginning to develop a sense of collecting data systematically and displaying this in ways that 'tell the story' to someone else. By the upper primary years, children should be developing a critical sense about data. They are starting to summarise data in appropriate ways and to analyse the data they have collected, as well as data from elsewhere. They will also begin to look for associations between variables and to compare groups such as Year 5/Year 6. The ideas of **population** and **sample** will also develop over time. By the end of primary school, children should recognise that their class is not the total population of Year 6 children in the school, the state or the country. They will argue about whether the class is a representative sample, or whether the size of the class as a sample of the population under investigation is sufficient.

At all levels of schooling, children need to explain their thinking and justify their views, demonstrating the earliest ideas of statistical inference. This step is crucial for developing statistical reasoning and can be linked to writing persuasive texts or writing scientific reports.

The role of language and communications is critical. Children must be able to explain and justify their conclusions. Even very young children can have opinions and ideas relating to cause and effect. All children must be given opportunities to explore, analyse and present data in ways that make sense to them, and to explain why they have drawn their conclusions by referring to the data they have used.

Statistic characteristics of a sample of a population derived from data

Data information collected in a systematic way

Population the entire group of interest – for example, all Year 3 students in the school

Sample a sub-group of the population, often intended to be representative of the whole group – for example, Ms Pitt's Year 3 class is a sample of the population of Year 3 children in the school

The nature of data and different data types is discussed in 'Concepts to consider' at the end of the chapter.

Using technology to develop statistical understanding

The use of technology is important for developing an understanding of statistics. Spreadsheets allow us to manipulate data in ways that were tedious and difficult before information and communication technology became so widespread.

There are often good reasons, however, for doing an activity with concrete materials before moving to a technological approach. With technology, children sometimes lose sight of the aim of the activity and instead become caught up in the technology itself. Collecting data from the class using some form of concrete material, undertaking some initial analysis using concrete displays, and then transferring the information to technology may help children see the links from the initial question, through to the data collection and analysis, and then on to drawing conclusions. In this chapter, examples are provided of this process.

Children learn statistics by doing statistical investigations. This chapter is presented around the PPDAC cycle to illustrate how this cycle can be used to support the development of statistical understanding.

Asking questions (problem)

The question posed is of key importance because it determines the nature of the data to be collected. A variety of data displays and manipulations are used with different kinds of data, and understanding the opportunities and limitations of ways to deal with data is important in order to identify misrepresentations and interpret data presented by others.

Teachers must have clear intentions for the lesson or unit of work or important concepts may be missed. For example, if you want children to understand a **pictograph,** the activity chosen must lend itself to the use of a pictograph. Similarly, if older children are to begin to understand the use of summary statistics, such as the mean (Year 7 AC9M7ST01), appropriate data must be collected. In the early years, the data will be **categorical** (AC9M1ST01), such as favourite colours. As children develop understanding of measurement, the data will become **continuous** (AC9M6ST01), such as student heights or arm spans. Categorical data are counted whereas continuous data are measured.

Even young children can ask good questions, so children in all years of schooling should be encouraged to pose questions that they can answer by collecting data. In the early years, the children will pose questions such as 'How many children in our class walked to school today?' To find out the answer, children have only to respond to a yes/no question: 'Did you walk to school today?' As children progress into the middle primary years, their questions will become more complex, such as 'How did children in our class travel to school today?' These questions require data across several categories, such as walk, car, train, bike and bus, and may be expanded into broader, more inferential questions, such as 'What is the most popular form of transport to school for our Year 4 class?' By the upper primary years, children will be able to pose questions about numerical variables, such as 'How long did it take for children in this class to travel to school?' As their questions become more complex and sophisticated, children's natural curiosity will lead to questions comparing groups, such as boys and girls, or questions about what is typical for the class or the year level. They may also

> **Pictograph** a column graph that uses pictures or symbols to show the data
>
> **Categorical data** are identified as different groups and may be counted (discrete data). (e.g. blue eyes/brown eyes)
>
> **Continuous data** have units of measure associated with them such as height or time

want to look at associations, such as whether children walking to school take less time to travel than those who ride bikes.

Children's questions may seem trivial from both a statistical and a substantive perspective – that is, the questions children pose are not necessarily those that statisticians would ask or that adults would find interesting to investigate. Children are more likely to learn, however, if they are able to explore questions of interest to themselves. The teacher needs also to keep in mind that there are statistical ideas that children need to develop, so the questions posed by the children will need to lead to the appropriate outcomes. A skilled teacher will choose broad topics of interest to the class that will still allow the children to pose questions of interest to themselves and, with guidance, pose questions that will allow the relevant statistical ideas to be developed.

Try Activity 8.1 to practice posing questions to children.

ACTIVITY 8.1

Children are intrinsically interested in themselves. Hence it makes sense to choose an attribute that relates to them as a basis for data collection. Consider foot length. Pose a question that children in the early, middle and later years of primary school might want to know about. In the early years, this question should be able to be answered by 'Yes' or 'No'. As children become more familiar with measurement units, it could be a measurement question. By the upper primary years, the question could also draw on other attributes so that associations and comparisons can be explored.

Go to the Statistics strand of the Australian Curriculum: Mathematic v. 9.0. Decide which outcomes your questions could potentially address.

Finally, develop a short 'script' that you could use to introduce the idea of posing questions about foot length to a class at each level. Try to imagine what children's responses might be and develop your 'script' to lead children towards questions that will allow you to develop the statistical ideas that are targeted in the curriculum.

It is important to know your students before you start posing questions. Personal characteristics, such as height or weight, can be difficult for students who are outliers – that is, exceptionally tall or short, or over- or under-weight. Asking children what they had for breakfast excludes those children who don't eat breakfast, or considering lunchbox contents may be problematic in some schools. Although comparisons between boys and girls is common, and there are examples in this chapter, gender is no longer as clearly defined, and teachers must be sensitive to their context when collecting data.

Collecting and recording data (plan, data)

Once children have posed a question, they need to collect and record data. It is important to emphasise the systematic nature of the collection process, and to ensure that the information collected is not ambiguous. For example, children have to learn that they may need to choose only one item from a list, rather than saying they want two or three choices. This requirement has social benefits as well, teaching children about making choices. Consider the teaching that is happening in Classroom Snapshot 8.1.

CLASSROOM SNAPSHOT 8.1

Lee's class of 6-year-old children is sitting on the mat. He asks the children, 'What question would you like to answer today? Should it be about food, or animals, or … ?' Several children say they would like to know about favourite animals. Lee asks the children to suggest some animals. As they say some animal names, Lee writes these on the whiteboard and then suggests the snake as something different. The class settles on four animals: dog, cat, snake and bird. Lee gives each child a sticky note and asks them to draw their favourite animal and to write the name of the animal underneath.

While they do this, Lee creates a table on a piece of butcher's paper and puts this on the easel. He then asks each child to place their sticky note picture in the appropriate place in the table. Through a class discussion that forms a reflection on the lesson, Lee asks the children for their comments about what the table shows and indicates that they will revisit the data the next day.

In the next lesson, Lee goes to the HOTmaths Data Tables widget (see Figure 8.2) where he has created a table with the four categories that are the same as the table drawn on the butcher's paper. Then Lee asks the children to vote for their favourite animal by raising their hands. He makes it clear that they can only vote for one animal.

As they vote, two children who are not voting for that animal count the number of hands raised. Another child enters the number of the count in the table using the computer and data projector. Lee asks the children to look at the table that they created the previous day. He asks them if the two tables are the same or different. The class has a discussion about the most popular animal and what had changed from one day to the next. Snake had one vote on the butcher's paper (Lee's) but no votes in the data table. Lee leads a discussion about why this had changed, and the importance of recording that there were no votes for snake. Lee saves the page created by taking a screenshot so that he can remind the children of their discussion later. He also prints the page using the 'Print' button in the widget.

Figure 8.2 Screenshot of HOTmaths Data Tables widget

Lee had a clear objective for the lessons. He wanted to emphasise that there is no guarantee that data collected on one day will be identical to the same data collected at a different time. Although it will be many years before these children encounter formal links between probability and statistics, he is setting up the foundational knowledge they will ultimately draw on. He also wanted to emphasise that it is important to record empty sets (snake) – the category doesn't vanish when there are no responses. He deliberately suggested snake, anticipating that no child would choose this as a favourite, so that he could start the discussion about recording empty categories. Young children often leave out categories where there are no data, because for them zero means it does not exist.

Lee used concrete materials and technology effectively to achieve his objectives. The children were actively involved in recording the information by counting and entering data on the butcher's paper and the whiteboard. Lee allowed the children to suggest their own question, but also made sure that the animal categories were some of those available in the widget. The data that was collected twice in different ways provided opportunities for discussion about the nature of data and incidental learning about different ways of recording data. Finally, he saved the page for possible future use. This ability to be able to recall what happened earlier is a powerful use of technology.

Collecting data

When collecting data, it is worth having a discussion about the conditions under which the data should be collected. This is an aspect of the work of statisticians that frequently is overlooked. Consider the discussion in Classroom Snapshot 8.2.

CLASSROOM SNAPSHOT 8.2

Teacher: We've decided to investigate how well students in our Year 6 class balance on one leg with their eyes closed. Okay. What data do we need to collect?

Linh: How long each student balances on one leg with their eyes closed.

Teacher: Yes, but is there anything else we need to think about?

Mark: Which leg?

Neema: Yes – it should be the strongest leg.

Teacher: Would that be the same for everyone?

Adib: No – some people kick with their left leg and some with their right and some can kick with both. I think it should be both legs. That way it's fair. [General agreement from the class]

Teacher: [records 'both legs' on whiteboard] Okay. What does it mean to balance on one leg?

Aiden: You take your other foot off the floor.

Grace: But how high off the floor does it have to be? [Grace demonstrates lifting her foot just off the floor and then high off the floor]

The discussion continues in this manner for some time, as the children try to come up with conditions that would be fair to all people that could sensibly be enforced. They consider whether arms can be used for balance, what constitutes the end of timing, whether hops are allowed, whether shoes should be off or on, and other factors that might affect the outcome, such as being right- or left-handed, what sport is played and so on. This time is not wasted. Rather, it is developing a sense in the children of how difficult it is to collect data under consistent conditions, and the need to be sure to consider factors that might impact on the attribute to be measured. Once they have decided on all the conditions, the children collect the data in threes – one balancing, one timing and the third acting as a referee to see that all the conditions are complied with. As the members of each group finish collecting and recording their individual data, the students enter their own data into a spreadsheet via a computer linked to a data projector. This is saved in the class folder so that all children can access it later for analysis. Having each child or group responsible for their own data entry develops a sense of ownership and is easily managed with either a data projector or an IWB. The electronic data set can then be used at a time convenient to the teacher.

One quick and efficient way to collect data is by using a data card. An example of a data card used to collect information about litter at a school is shown in Figure 8.3. Each child in the class completes one or two cards, and then enters the data into a pre-prepared spreadsheet. Data cards have been used to collect data from a variety of situations (Callingham 1993; Watson & Callingham 1997). Using tools such as this together with appropriate technology allows for the best of both concrete experiences and the efficiencies technology can bring. The nature of the information can be adjusted for the age group or interests of the class.

Litter Survey

Day: Wednesday

Area of school: Top Oval

Kind of litter	Number of pieces
Icy pole sticks	7
Chocolate wrappers	4
Milk cartons	2
Chip packets	6
Hamburger wrappers	0
Fruit box straws	9

Figure 8.3 Data card for litter collection

Recording data

Collecting and recording data is not intuitive. Many adults do not recognise the complexity of this task, and planning for the data collection process is important. This task also links to the approaches to be used for data analysis. In the early years, using yes/no questions, children could be asked to vote by lifting a hand, showing a thumbs up or thumbs down, or putting a smiley face on a chart, for example. In the middle primary years, children might 'interview' each other, collecting responses using a list or in a table using tally marks. Older children with access to technology might set up a poll using one of the many free survey creators available on the internet.

Often, data are collected by hand and then entered into some form of technology to transform them into useful information, using tables, graphs or other graphic organisers. Initially, data will be recorded on an individual basis and then the individual information will be combined to create a data set. Consider, for example, a series of simple surveys collecting categorical data about favourites: food, activity, colours – the possibilities are endless. Create a sheet with a limited selection of favourites on it – usually five or six favourites with up to five categories in each. These can be organised so that each child has a strip with the categories on it (see Table 8.1). The children tick their own favourites and then cut the strips into the separate parts and place each part in the appropriately labelled container. This activity could be undertaken with children from the middle primary years upwards.

Table 8.1 Suggested categories for a 'favourites' investigation

Favourite sport	Favourite fruit	Favourite colour	Favourite food	Favourite activity
Football	Strawberry	Pink	Pizza	Reading
Cricket	Banana	Blue	Fish and chips	Dancing
Hockey	Apple	Green	Burger	Playing sport
Swimming	Orange	Orange	Sausages	Computer games
Basketball	Pear	Red	Fried chicken	Hanging out with friends

Link 8.1 NZ Maths: Which Graph?
Link 8.2 NCES Kids' Zone: Create a Graph

Pie chart a sector graph based on a circle, with each sector in proportion to the percentage of the whole

Column or bar graph a way of displaying categorical data using vertical columns or horizontal bars and frequency counts

In small groups, children then summarise the data by counting the number in each category. Using technology, the same activity could be used to create a spreadsheet that could then graph the data. A New Zealand resource from the NZ Maths site called Which Graph? has useful master sheets with clear instructions for using Excel to create graphs. Another possibility is to use the online Create a Graph tool from the National Center for Education Statistics (NCES) Kids' Zone. The children can then prepare a poster, PowerPoint or a report about their findings. Discussion with the class should focus on the appropriateness of the display, whether produced by hand or using technology, to represent the data and answer the question posed about 'favourites in our class'. Because the data are frequency counts of categories, the best representations are **pie charts**, or **column or bar graphs**. A similar activity is 'This Goes With This', which can be found online as a downloadable pdf file.

One of the most common ways of recording data by hand is by using tally marks. The use of tallies for counting data links to the Number strand and counting by fives. A variety of resources is available online to develop the notion of tally marks. Young children intuitively use marks to keep track of numbers but using the familiar ⦀⦀ tally by fives is something that children need to learn. Children should be allowed to make their own recordings in idiosyncratic ways to start with, gradually refining these to more conventional representations. Although there is a range of online tools for making tally marks, learning is more effective if children begin with a personal concrete representation. Use online resources to consolidate the ideas of tallies. HOTmaths has some useful widgets, as do many other free and commercial resources.

Analysing and representing data (analyse)

Data alone do not tell a story. Having been collected, the data have to be analysed and represented to make sense to other people. This process of 'telling the story' from the data is very important. Statistics only make sense if they are related to the social context in which the initial problem was posed.

Approaches to data analysis

The question that children need to consider is 'What story does the data tell?' For teachers, the key aspect is the nature of the statistical understanding developed from the data collected. The focus might be simple counting of categories or the development of summary measures of the data that would differ depending on the nature of the data. The story told needs always to relate back to the original investigative question posed by the children.

In the early primary years, the focus of the analysis is counting. In this way, strong links can be forged to other parts of the mathematics curriculum, especially the Number strand. Counting up categories following data collection provides another opportunity to reinforce counting strategies. Recording the count numerically allows children to practice their number work and assign meaning to the symbol in a real context.

Young children are egocentric and like to see themselves in the data. They may not appreciate that summarising data is important, or they may focus only on the category in which they feature. For these reasons, young children need also to experience data that is of interest to them but not directly associated with them. For example, children may be shown data about the topic of interest from another class.

By the middle years of primary school, analysis may still focus on counts but could include questions such as 'How many more people liked oranges than bananas?' Again, these approaches link to the Number strand and provide incidental practice of calculations. Children are becoming less egocentric, at this stage, and may be interested in comparing groups, such as blue eyes and brown eyes, but are likely still to focus on simple comparisons of counts. The groupings chosen may not be helpful, but children need to come to the realisation that not every attribute is useful.

In the upper years of primary school, children can move beyond counting. They can recognise the usefulness of summarising data, appreciate the distribution of the data, and begin to appreciate the need to use percentages, for example, as a basis for comparisons. Even in these years, however, many children will want to make lists of data, and they will continue to focus on attributes or characteristics that adults or statisticians would dismiss as trivial.

> The concept of a distribution is discussed in 'Concepts to consider' at the end of the chapter.

Different representations of data

Even young children have quite sophisticated understandings of how to display information. In the two pictures shown in Figure 8.4, Year 1 children were recording the birthdays in their class in a way that would make sense to their parents or someone who was not in their class. They worked in small groups to record the information and were free to choose whatever representation they wished. They had not previously had any formal teaching about graphs, but were able to show the information in lists, tables and pictographs.

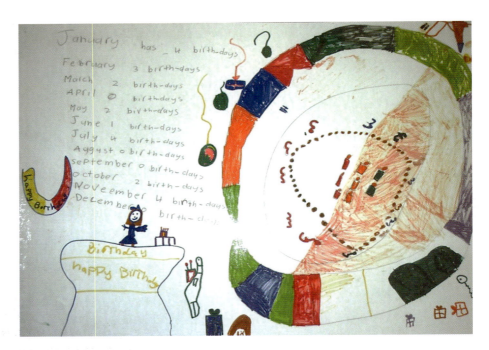

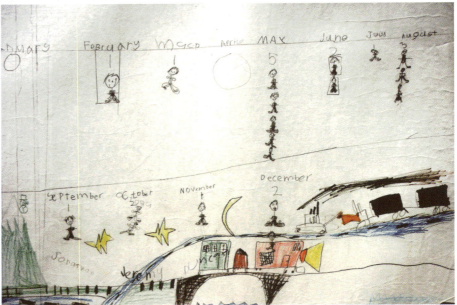

Figure 8.4 Year 1 children's informal recording of data

If you look closely at the pictures, you will see that they don't have the same information. This is because the children were collecting the information from birthday cards that they had made for themselves and hung up across the room. They removed the cards each time they wanted to record the information, and as a result some were missed out and others were counted more than once. This situation led to a discussion in the class about the importance of being accurate and systematic about recording data. The freedom that the teacher gave the children led to a greater range of types of data display and brought up issues that had not been anticipated. Often, we constrain children to recording in a particular way. Although it is important to develop conventional formats for displaying data, if we never give children opportunities to make decisions for themselves, we reduce opportunities for them to display what they know.

PAUSE AND REFLECT

In the birthday activity, children first made birthday cards, and these were displayed on a string hung across the room, grouped by months. How important do you consider this concrete activity to be? How would the learning experience change if the teacher had decided to use technology to collect the information? Refer back to the earlier section 'Using technology to develop statistical understanding' for a discussion.

NRICH has an activity for young children called Ladybird Count. In this activity children are asked to consider some data about the number of ladybirds collected by different children, pose a question and make a graph or picture to show the data. The data displays created could provide a basis for discussion similar to that of the Birthdays activity.

Creating and using different representations of the same data is a useful activity for children. They may be asked, for example, to show the information in two different ways. The diversity of representations becomes a basis for discussion about which is more effective, and this in turn begins to lead to the critical appraisal of data that is needed to develop statistical literacy (Watson & Kelly 2006). For example, the two representations shown in Figure 8.5 are of pets owned by families in a class, created using HOTmaths

Link 8.3 NRICH: Ladybird Count

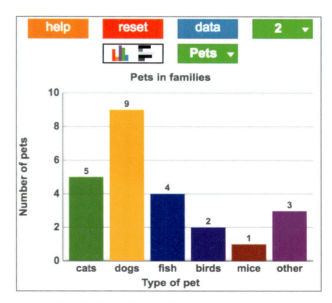

Figure 8.5 Different ways of displaying the same data using HOTmaths widgets (Data Tables and Column Graphs)

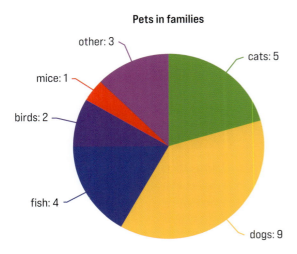

Figure 8.6 Pie chart showing pets in families data

widgets (Data Tables and Column Graphs). They show the same data in different ways – as a table and as a column graph. There are also many freely available interactive graph plotters that could be used.

Older children might create a pie chart of the same data, as shown in Figure 8.6. The advantage of using technology for this purpose is that complicated calculations are not needed. Because the purpose of the activity is to compare data displays, focusing only on the display and not on the computation behind it facilitates the discussion. Later, children will need to understand how to create such displays and be able to articulate how the pie chart segments relate to a circle, but in the primary years, familiarity with different types of representation, without the distraction of calculating the necessary angles in a pie chart, meets curriculum goals. The pie chart in Figure 8.6 was created using a free chart-maker program with the colours customised to match those shown by the widgets. There are many different free resources available.

Asking different groups of children to create these representations and showing them together to the class – which is possible using technology – provides an opportunity to discuss which presentation might be appropriate for a particular purpose. For example, for a fruit shop, it is easier to plan orders using numbers, so a table might be more helpful, whereas a report to fruit growers might want to emphasise the visual image of strawberries being least popular using a pie chart. Children from the middle years of primary school upwards are able to discuss these kinds of ideas and to understand the power of different displays of data. They could be asked to produce a piece of persuasive text targeting a particular audience, or a video 'advert', using data representations to get their message across, hence developing cross-curriculum competence in literacy through mathematics.

Read Activity 8.2 and answer the questions for a creative use of different types of display, built into a classroom routine. Discuss this approach with a teacher or compare it with routines that you have seen in classrooms.

ACTIVITY 8.2

Ang has a mixed Year 3 and Year 4 class. All the children have a personal icon that they have created using their initials by using a drawing program. These are stored in a special folder accessible from the class tablets. Every Tuesday morning, the children come into the class to find a question on the whiteboard and the beginnings of a data display, such as labelled axes or two overlapping circles, with a heading. The topic often relates to whatever the class is focusing on at that time, such as pocket money or travel. The children decide where their own icon should go and position this in the appropriate place. The display is saved and used as a basis for discussion later. The discussion doesn't always focus on the display. Sometimes the aim is to discuss the topic of the question, such as the local show. At other times, the discussion is used to focus on aspects of the data display, such as the meaning of the overlapping section of the two circles.

1. What features of this routine make it educationally useful?
2. What kinds of questions might Ang have used?
3. What preparation is needed to make this activity successful?
4. Why doesn't Ang do this on Monday mornings?
5. How does technology support this activity?

This is a productive routine that Ang uses to create discussion starters for whatever topic she has in mind for the week, or simply to get to know the class better. The technology use is efficient, but it also allows the children to have control over their own information, and it leads to later discussion about statistical concepts.

It is particularly important that concept development – such as ideas about the middle of the data, which lead to statistical notions about summarising data using **mean**, **median** and **mode** – happens slowly so that children develop a deep understanding of the concept and don't simply use technology unthinkingly for computation of statistics that are not well understood. The emphasis should be on developing the concepts of summarising data in meaningful ways so as to answer questions posed in an investigation rather than calculating averages.

In the Australian Curriculum: Mathematics v. 9.0, children in Year 7 not only calculate the different summary statistics – mean, median and mode – but also have to describe what happens to these measures in relation to the distribution of the data (AC9M7ST01), for example, how adding or removing data may impact the measures. In order to reach these outcomes in Year 7, children need to begin to appreciate the importance of the 'middle of the data' to set up the foundation for the **measures of central tendency** that are expected in Year 7. The activity described in Classroom Snapshot 8.2 is particularly good for developing these ideas, including the notion of an outlier. Many children are ready to understand the implications of outliers earlier than Year 7, so exposure to these ideas can be useful earlier (see also 'Planning for an integrated unit' in Chapter 11). The key idea is that all children need time to develop deep understanding of the ways in which data can be collected, summarised and displayed, so opportunities to experiment and 'play' with data are not time wasted.

Figure 8.7 shows a simple data set of nine students' heights and the impact that changing a single data point can have on the mean. The blue dot at 180 cm in the left-hand figure was changed to 173 cm in the right-hand figure. The median (red line) has remained the same, but the mean (blue line) has been shifted downwards.

The Shodor website has a useful interactive called Plop It! that could be used to explore ideas about how the mean and median change as the data change. Children could be challenged, for example, to create a data set with a given number of data points where the mean and median are identical, or to use an outlier to change the value of the mean but not the median. This activity would be suitable for children who need to be challenged mathematically, working in a small group to predict and discuss what they find out. They should be asked to provide a brief report to the class.

Mean a balancing point that provides a summary of the data

Median the middle value of an ordered set of data

Mode the most frequently occurring value

The uses of different types of 'average', the mean, median and mode, are discussed further in 'Concepts to consider' at the end of the chapter.

Measures of central tendency a collective term for summary statistics such as the mean and median

Link 8.4 Shodor: Plop It!

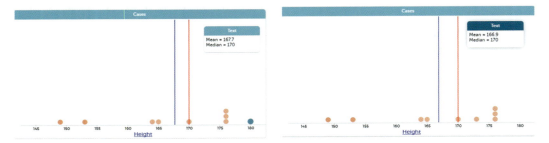

Figure 8.7 Screenshot from CODAP website showing changes to the mean and median when one data point is shifted
Source: © 2018 The Concord Consortium (concord.org), all rights reserved. This open-source software is licensed under the MIT license.

Using technology tools such as these provides a way of playing with data that is difficult to do with paper-based methods. Dealing with middle measures, such as means, medians and modes, requires considerable computation, and children get caught up with the process of calculating the different measures rather than understanding what they are doing. Using technological tools can remove the computational burden, but the technology must be accompanied by discussion and informal recording of the ideas to help children consolidate their learning.

PAUSE AND REFLECT

Understanding the mathematics to come is sometimes called 'horizon knowledge' (Ball & Bass 2009) and teachers often focus on the mathematics taught at their year level rather than the bigger picture (Mosvold & Fauskanger 2013). Why is it important that teachers in the upper years of primary school are aware of the demands of Year 7? What do teachers lower down the primary years need to take account of?

Data can be represented in many different ways, and technology makes this easy to do. Not every representation of data is helpful or correct, however, and technology tools will simply do what they are told to do. Activity 8.3 suggests ways of changing representations as part of exploring a very small data set.

ACTIVITY 8.3

Table 8.2 shows a sample of 10 students in Years 5 to 8, with their sex and height recorded. Copy the table into a spreadsheet, using a software program such as Excel. In table form, these data don't provide much information. It is difficult even to see how many males or females are included in the sample.

Use your software program to create a column graph of the data. It should look something like the graph shown in Figure 8.8, which shows a bit more information, but is still uninformative.

Table 8.2 Students' heights by sex

Sex	Height (cm)
Male	150
Male	151
Female	152
Female	153
Female	160
Male	161
Female	165
Male	165
Male	165
Male	173

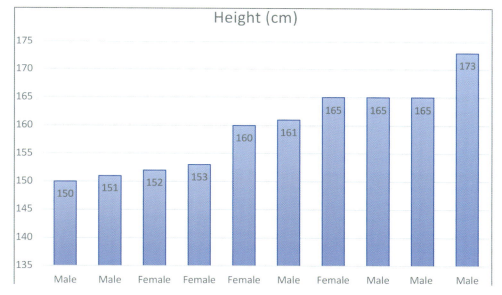

Figure 8.8 Graph of ordered heights by sex created in Excel

We need to consider what we want to know about the data – what information do we want? For example, we may want to find out whether, in this sample, girls are taller than boys. We may want to find out what height is typical of school students in Years 5 to 8. We may want to consider how the data are distributed. Each of these questions suggests a different data display.

In Excel, sort the data by sex. How does this change the graph? Is the display more helpful than the first column graph? Can we confidently answer any of the questions we have posed?

Stem-and-leaf plot a display based on splitting each data value into a 'stem' and 'leaves' – particularly useful for comparing two groups on the same attribute

A better way to look at the comparison between males and females might be a **stem-and-leaf plot**. In this instance, we will make a back-to-back stem-and-leaf plot that will show males on one side of the stem and females on the other side of the stem. Excel will not create this representation automatically, so it has to be done manually. The stem is created by looking at the data set and choosing an appropriate value that will form the backbone of the plot. This is the first digit if the data are two-digit numbers or, in this instance, the first two digits, which represent the hundreds and tens values: 15, 16, 17. The other digits then form the leaves. If you place male values on the left and female values on the right, the stem-and-leaf plot should look like Figure 8.9.

			M	Stem	F	
		1	0	15	2	3
5	5	1		16	0	5
			3	17		

Figure 8.9 Stem-and-leaf plot of students' heights by sex

There are a number of websites that will produce simple stem-and-leaf plots. Activities such as creating a stem-and-leaf plot can also help to reinforce place-value ideas.

Distribution the look or shape of the data when displayed systematically on an axis

Although the data set is too small to be able to draw firm conclusions, the **distribution** of the data suggests that boys are a little taller than girls. This form of representation is more helpful than the column graph for answering the comparison question. Although, in this instance, means could have been used to compare the data sets, sometimes the means are very similar and looking at the distribution using a stem-and-leaf plot or similar representation will provide better information.

Telling a story from the data (conclusions)

Many children persist with representations in which each data point is associated with an individual, but such thinking limits the inferences that could be drawn. Deliberate, careful teaching is needed to move thinking from the representation of individual data to a more abstract conception of data that can lead to inferences about a situation. This is what Mike is trying to achieve in Classroom Snapshot 8.3.

CLASSROOM SNAPSHOT 8.3

Mike's Year 6 class was talking about reaction times as part of a health unit. During the day, each student recorded their average reaction time using an online reaction time test (there are several available). He then created an informal graph by asking each child to place their sticky note on to an axis drawn on butcher's paper. He posed the question 'What is the typical reaction time for our class?'

Through careful, structured discussion, he led the children to the idea of looking at the concentration of data in the middle and used the 'middle half' as the boundaries. There were 24 children in the class, so he counted up six data points from the lowest value and drew a line. He then counted six down from the highest value and drew another line. He showed the children that there were 12 data points in the middle – the middle half of the data – and they agreed that the typical value lay somewhere within this range (see Figure 8.10).

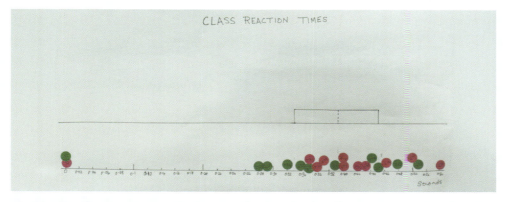

Figure 8.10 Informal dot plot showing the middle 50 per cent of the data and the median (the middle of the data)

Mike left the concrete representation with sticky notes on the whiteboard for the children to refer to, and he photographed it for future reference using his phone, transmitting the image to a folder on his laptop.

The children were then asked to explore similar information on their laptops. Mike previously had downloaded a sample of 154 responses from the Census at School site (note: you will need to visit the New Zealand site), choosing questions that included one about the reaction time the respondent had recorded, whether the students were right or left-handed, a memory test score and age in years. The children used the data exploration program CODAP (Common Online Data Analysis Program) to explore the data. Mike also asked them to ask a question and find the answer, and to identify other questions they would like to ask, as a way of assessing what they understood about identifying appropriate data and posing questions that could be answered using the data (AC9M6ST02; AC9M6ST03).

Kavitha investigated whether handedness made a difference to reaction time. Her CODAP report is shown in Figure 8.11.

Kavitha has used a representation of a 'boxplot' which shows the middle 50 per cent of the numerical data and the median, to illustrate what is typical of the three categories of right-, left- and both-handedness. Mike had shown the students a simpler 'hat plot' to develop the idea of the 'middle 50%' (Figure 8.10). Hat plots give an introduction to box-and-whisker plots in an intuitive way. They do not require complex explanations of the **interquartile range** – the key idea is that the hat represents the middle half of the data and the brim shows the **range** from lowest to highest value (Watson et al. 2008). Hat plots are not included as a formal representation in the curriculum but are useful for providing a stepping-stone to understanding. They give a visual display that tells a story and helps children to build on intuitive ideas about summarising data. They also provide a way of introducing the notion of the median as 'the middle of the middle' in a conceptual rather than

Link 8.5 CODAP

Interquartile range contains the 'middle half' of the data set

Range a measure of the spread of the data

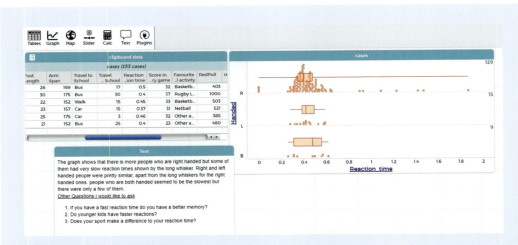

Figure 8.11 Kavitha's CODAP report
Source: CODAP <https://codap.concord.org/>

a procedural way. Kavitha's simple report shows the beginnings of statistical inference. There is a reference to the summary of the data, but the interpretation is still very individualistic, shown by the focus on the right-handed spread of values. The questions she wants to pose, however, are quite sensible showing her developing understanding of what kinds of data are useful.

CODAP has many features that cannot easily be replicated using other programs, including intuitive drag-and-drop displays. It is particularly useful for exploring the distribution of data. CODAP is free to use and has several interesting data sets available.

Developing the relationship between a real situation and a graphical representation is important, and this was the approach that Mike took by creating a concrete representation before moving into a technological solution.

ACTIVITY 8.4

Link 8.6 NRICH: Take Your Dog for a Walk
Link 8.7 Slow Reveal Graphs
Link 8.8 reSolve: Data – Making Decisions

Activities, such as Take Your Dog for a Walk (Resource 4803) from NRICH, are useful ways of developing an understanding of what a graph represents. Go to this site and try the various story activities.

Slow Reveal Graphs is another site that has resources that teachers can use to develop understanding of data representations. Each graph has a series of slides which progressively add more information to the graph. Teachers can use these resources as discussion starters.

reSolve has an inquiry called Data: Making Decisions that includes several unlabelled graphs for students to create their own stories. Download the resource and try the first student activity.

Write down your thoughts about these activities. How might you use these kinds of activities in the classroom? Find other telling-the-story activities.

Many children have difficulty understanding that a graph of distance against time shows the distance from the starting point, not the direction. Playing with dynamic graphical interfaces can help children understand what the graph is showing them. The interactive nature of this kind of activity makes it suitable for individual use – for example, as part of a series of workstations about data and graphs.

Graphing Stories is a useful website that contains videos of a variety of situations, which can be used to create graphs that tell the story of what the video is about. Many of these would be suitable for upper primary students. Try creating your own videos of different situations, such as filling bottles of different shapes at a constant rate, graphing height against time, or running up and down stairs and graphing the number of steps away from the ground against time. Videos can easily be captured using mobile phones and then saved to a folder on a computer for later use. Children could work in groups to produce their video and a related electronic report.

The conclusion step in the PPDAC cycle is crucial and requires time to develop the necessary language and conceptual understanding (Pfannkuch et al. 2010). Children need considerable experience to develop the skills of writing reports that explain what the data are telling them, and the language focus may be unusual in a mathematics lesson.

The NZ Maths site includes many useful units of work to support statistical investigations appropriate for every level of schooling. It includes examples of children's work, ideas for investigations and links to appropriate learning objects, and can be accessed from outside New Zealand.

Link 8.9 NZ Maths: Statistical Investigations Units of Work

Using data in social contexts

Data are used to problem-solve in many situations. A doctor making a diagnosis may use data of different kinds from a variety of sources, including the patient's description, the results of tests (which may include imagery and/or numbers) and a physical examination of the patient. We rarely see this as a data-driven activity, but it involves using different types of data and putting them together to answer a question – in the doctor example, 'What is wrong with this patient?'

In mathematics classes, we are trying to develop understanding of the processes involved with quantitative data – that is, data expressed as numbers – while in other subject areas we may be using a variety of other forms of data as well as numeric data. Other learning areas provide opportunities to reinforce the statistical ideas in social contexts. There are many resources available about water use including several available from Goulburn Valley Water.

Link 8.10 Goulburn Valley Water: Resources – water use

The personal water use calculator could be used as part of a unit about water that combines studies of society, English and mathematics, and also addresses the cross-curriculum priority of sustainability. Using a data set from the First Fleet or the *Titanic*, for example, links to history and English. The quantitative data must be presented in ways that are useful to support the reasoning about the social context, and sometimes data available from websites intended for education may need manipulating before presenting it to primary age students. Historical height or weight data, for example, may be recorded in feet and inches or pounds. It is useful to convert such data to metric units if the purpose of the lesson is to focus on analysing data. Explain to students that data often have to be prepared before they can be analysed. We call this process 'data cleaning'.

Children as young as those in Years 3 or 4 can draw sensible conclusions from data presented by others if the social context is suitable and the questions posed are straightforward. The text in the media may be difficult but understanding ideas such as 'the top 10 toys for Christmas' is not. This context, for example, could provide a starting point for a survey about toys, a discussion about toy safety and a design challenge to create a new toy, all of which can be undertaken by middle primary students. Technology could be used to enhance these activities.

> **TIPS FOR ONLINE TEACHING**
>
> Many of the activities suggested in this chapter lend themselves to online teaching. For example, students could collect data about 'favourites' from other people in their house and contribute these to a class folder. From the data collected, they could create graphs to show what they have found. Many of the graphing stories websites could be useful to develop skills in representing data, and students could make their own videos and challenge other students to 'tell the story'. Undertaking a media hunt for statistics in the news and critiquing the presentation can be done easily online. Resources such as CODAP are freely available. Reports about investigations could be presented using PowerPoint or similar programs. The principles of PPDAC are as accessible online as in the classroom.

Conclusion

Statistics is an important area of the mathematics curriculum. As we have developed more varieties of ways to collect and display data, and the demand for 'evidence-based' decision-making grows, it becomes increasingly important to equip children with the tools that they will need later to function in their world.

In this chapter, several ideas about teaching and learning statistics have been presented. Technology provides ways of collecting, presenting and analysing data. The use of data is likely to increase, placing greater demands on educators to develop sound statistical sense in their students. From reading this chapter and engaging in the activities, you should have begun to develop an understanding of some of the key ideas in teaching statistics and the ways in which technology can enhance this endeavour. Statistics is also intrinsically linked to uncertainty and probability, and probability forms the focus of Chapter 9.

Link 8.11 ABC Education: 'A guide to statistical literacy in the classroom'

GUIDED STUDENT TASKS

1. Media articles are a source of statistical ideas. Visit ABC Education, find the statistical literacy article 'A guide to statistical literacy in the classroom' by Jane Watson and Rosemary Callingham (22 October 2020) and choose one of the activities from the Years 7–10 section. Undertake the activity. What did you learn?

2. Collect articles from the newspaper, television or online news that use statistics. Identify what statistics are being used.
3. Look at other areas of the Australian Curriculum v. 9.0. Consider how statistics are used and presented in curriculum areas such as science or geography. How well do these uses align with the mathematics curriculum?
4. Visit the ABC Education site and find the article 'Use the news in the maths classroom' by Rosemary Callingham and Jane Watson (30 September 2020). Choose one of the activities and plan a lesson for Year 6 students to meet outcomes AC9M6ST01 and AC9M6ST02.
5. In media articles, sometimes writers use counts (e.g. 150 people attended a meeting) and sometimes percentages (e.g. 95 per cent of people were in agreement). Why would people use a count? When would a percentage be more persuasive? Which would be more impressive if the sample size was small? Discuss these ideas with a colleague.
6. Visit the website of the Bureau of Meteorology. Here you will find information relating to changes in climate over time. Information is presented in a variety of ways including charts and maps. Choose one topic and write a short article for a school magazine about the weather and climate.

Link 8.12 ABC Education: 'Use the news in the maths classroom'

CONCEPTS TO CONSIDER

There are several key ideas about statistics that should be considered. The research basis for these ideas is summarised in Watson (2006) or for a more teacher-friendly approach go to the AAMT Top Drawer for Statistics. A brief introduction is provided here for some specific concepts that may be confusing.

Data types and variables

Variables are all those things we can count or measure. They give rise to different types of data, and those described here are mentioned in the Australian Curriculum: Mathematics v. 9.0. *Categorical* data refers to some quality that can be defined, such as types of litter defined as landfill, compostable or recyclable, or kinds of pets, such as cats, dogs, birds or fish. *Numerical data* are data that can be counted or measured. Counting favourite pets in a class leads to data that are '*discrete*' – that is, there is a finite number that can be counted (although this number may be very large). Data of this kind is '*numerical discrete* data'. Variables such as time, height or weight that can be measured are '*numerical continuous*' variables where there are, at least in theory, an infinite number of possibilities between any two points on a scale. *Ordinal* data are categorical data that are placed in order, such as ranking favourite colours. Although commonly met in day-to-day life, from the perspective of teaching students about statistical processes, these have limited value. They require quite sophisticated treatment. For example, how do you decide the favourite colour of the class from the data shown in Table 8.3?

Table 8.3 Choices of favourite colours

	1st	2nd	3rd	4th
Red	4	5	7	6
Blue	6	6	3	7
Yellow	7	1	6	8
Green	2	10	5	5

The various types of data are analysed and represented differently. For example, it makes sense to create a pie chart from discrete numerical data based on the categories included. In contrast, numerical continuous data can be shown as a line graph.

Statisticians sometimes use different terms for data types (nominal, ordinal, interval and ratio data) and you can search for these if you want more information.

Distribution

Distribution in statistics refers to the ways in which the data are spread across categories or the measurement scale. Rather than looking at individual data points, we consider the aggregation of the data – its spread or clumpiness and gaps. We often talk about a 'bell curve' which is a type of symmetrical distribution, called the normal distribution, in which the mean, median and mode of the data (see below) have the same value. Distributions may be skewed, spread out or clustered.

The distribution shown in Figure 8.12 shows a spread of foot lengths from 19 cm to 32 cm. The mode of the data is 22 cm, the median is 23 cm and the mean is 24 cm. Write a brief description of this distribution without referring to the mean, median or mode values. What does this tell you about the length of students' feet in Year 5? What else would you like to know?

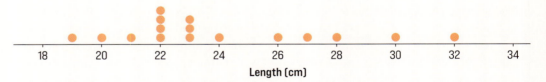

Figure 8.12 Dot plot of distribution of foot length from one class in Year 5

Average

Often, we use the term 'average' to mean ordinary or common but in statistics this term is used to indicate several 'measures of central tendency'. These are statistics that are used to summarise a set of data.

The *mode* is the category that occurs most often when the categories are counted (discrete numerical data). In Figure 8.5, the mode has a value of 9 for the category 'dogs'. If a data set has two categories with the same highest values, then the data is *bimodal*.

The *median* is the middle of the ordered data. In Figure 8.10 Mike identified the median by counting. The median is often used when the distribution is skewed or there are one or two *outliers* that are exceptionally large (or small). Median house prices provide an example, where the sale of one house for an exceptional amount would cause the mean value to shift so that the 'average' is not an accurate summary.

The *mean* is the value we remember as 'add all the numbers and divide by the number of numbers'. Using phrases such as this one is not helpful because the mean is a balance point on the scale and is often used to summarise continuous numerical data sets. For example, the mean (average) time taken to complete a 5 km Parkrun is about 31 minutes, but an Olympic champion may run it in just over 14 minutes and walkers take about 45 minutes.

For practice activities and more details, go to AAMT Top Drawer: Statistics. Work through the student activities to develop your own understanding.

Link 8.13 Top Drawer: Statistics

FURTHER READING

Bagnell, B [2006] 2018, Meaningful statistics, Article number 4936, NRICH, <https://nrich.maths.org/4936>.

English, LD 2017, *Manufacturing licorice: Modeling with data in third grade*, in 39th annual meeting of the International Group for the Pscyhology of Mathematics Education: North American Chapter, 5–8 October, Indianapolis, In.

Watson, J 2008, 'Critical numeracy in context', National Literacy and Numeracy Week NSW.

Watson, J & English, L 2018, 'Eye color and the practice of statistics in Grade 6: Comparing two groups', *Journal of Mathematical Behavior*, vol. 49, pp. 35–60.

Websites for exploration

CHAPTER 9

EXPLORING CHANCE AND PROBABILITY

LEARNING OUTCOMES

By the end of this chapter, you will:

- understand the difference between objective and subjective views of probability
- be able to use a range of random generators to determine probabilities
- be able to recognise the applications of probability in daily life
- be confident in using technology effectively to develop ideas about uncertainty.

Introduction

Uncertainty is a part of everyday life. We live with a range of situations that inherently have an element of uncertainty in them – for example, crossing the road, going on holiday, or making a major purchase – but we often ignore the embedded chance in these activities. Risk is acknowledged in many activities, and much effort is expended in identifying these risks and minimising any potential negative outcomes. In schools, for example, a risk assessment is required prior to any excursion with children. Probability is the strand of mathematics that addresses uncertainty. This chapter explores ideas relating to probability in the mathematics classroom.

Why is probability important?

Probability
a quantification of the chance of an event based on the possible outcomes

Probability is concerned with how likely it is that something will happen or that a particular outcome will be achieved. As such, it can be both objective – as in calculating the probability of tossing a six on a fair die – or subjective – as in assigning a probability to the chance of rain. In both examples, there is some uncertainty attached, and probability aims to quantify that uncertainty. Both objective and subjective views of probability are met in the primary mathematics classroom. Classical probability is concerned with determining the likelihood of a particular outcome where all the possible outcomes are known. However, in daily life, outcomes can never be known exactly, so we use different approaches. Take, for example, a 1-in-100 years flood which has a 1 per cent chance of happening in any given year. This chance is based on the number of occurrences over the past 100 years that the flood water has reached a given height using the records that we keep and is an example of the links between probability and statistics. This occurrence does not, however, mean that a severe flood may not happen more frequently because we are dealing with probabilities not certainty. You can find more information about flooding at the CoastAdapt website.

The Australian Curriculum: Mathematics v. 9.0 is concerned mainly with classical probability but this is an important precursor to understanding how we use probabilities in daily life.

As a teacher, it is important to understand the ideas of probability, but for many people these ideas are difficult to grasp. The formal ideas challenge our intuitions, even for experienced and knowledgeable people. There is a famous probability problem based on a game show called 'Monty Hall's problem'. When the problem was first presented, it caused great controversy – including among mathematicians – because the formal solution is so counter-intuitive. The video 'What is the Monty Hall problem?' by ABC Education provides an explanation.

> Theoretical and experimental classical probability are discussed in 'Concepts to consider' at the end of the chapter.

Link 9.1 CoastAdapt
Link 9.2 ABC Education: 'What is the Monty Hall problem?'

ACTIVITY 9.1

There are many websites devoted to social aspects of probability, such as gambling, weather forecasting or determining risk. You may also find newspaper articles or online blogs related to risk, uncertainty, probability and chance. Search for some of these websites or articles; some suggestions are provided below. Be aware that your computer may block some websites, especially if they are related to gambling.

- *Understanding Uncertainty*: This website includes videos, a blog and links to numerous articles about uncertainty.
- *Understanding Risk*: This is a worldwide forum that runs a series of conferences with different foci. The website provides information on risk assessment.
- *Know Your Odds*: This is a Tasmanian government website that addresses common myths and beliefs about gambling.

1. Identify the language of probability used on these websites.
2. What is the difference between expressing probability as the chance of an event and as the odds of something happening?
3. How is probability expressed mathematically? (You will see uncertainty expressed as odds and chance presented as a percentage, a fraction, a ratio or in words.)
4. Think about what makes probability tricky for children (as well as many adults). Discuss your ideas with another person.

It is worth comparing the material presented on these websites with some of those that promote gambling. How does the language used differ?

Link 9.3 Understanding Uncertainty
Link 9.4 Understanding Risk
Link 9.5 Know Your Odds

These sites indicate the pervasiveness of uncertainty and the complexity associated with expressing it. It is therefore not surprising that this is one of the trickiest areas of the mathematics curriculum. It is, however, also one of the most important, because so many everyday situations are expressed in probabilistic terms, such as the risk of dying from a particular disease, insurance and investment risks, or the odds of a particular team winning in a sporting contest.

Psychology also plays a part. We tend to exaggerate the likelihood of something unwanted happening. Even school students recognise that the choices we make are not always based entirely on evidence (Watson & Callingham 2015). The reSolve activity Rock Paper Scissors uses the fact that most people play this game predictably and that by changing your strategy you can increase your chance of winning. There is a video explanation of this game available on the ABC Education website.

Link 9.6 reSolve: Rock Paper Scissors
Link 9.7 ABC Education: 'How to win at rock-paper-scissors'

Investigative approaches to developing an understanding of probability are useful for children. Using approaches where children collect data about random events, such as coin tossing or rolling a die, helps to develop the ideas of uncertain **outcomes** using a **relative frequency** approach. Such an approach is relevant for all children because it allows them to build their knowledge on the basis of experience, and helps them to develop new, sound intuitions necessary for better understanding probability.

Outcomes the set of possible predictable events in a given situation, such as heads and tails when tossing a single coin

Relative frequency the number of times a given outcome occurs relative to other possible outcomes. This is the basis for classical probability theory.

Understanding probability

Bryant and Nunes (2012) suggest that children need to understand four key concepts in probability: randomness, sample space, quantifying probability and correlations.

Randomness does not mean disorder. In the mathematical sense, it is about a lack of predictability, and can be thought of as a measure of uncertainty. There is considerable evidence that children – and many adults – do not recognise the independence of events in a random sequence. If you toss a fair coin and get five heads in a row, the chance of getting a head (or a tail) on the next toss is still 50 per cent. Each toss is **independent** of those that have come earlier.

Randomness a situation where any particular outcome is uncertain

The concept of randomness is discussed in 'Concepts to consider' at the end of the chapter.

Sample space is essential for identifying the number of possible outcomes. Many children have difficulty identifying all possible outcomes. Although this is fairly easy when tossing a single coin with only two possible outcomes (H/T), tossing two coins has three outcomes (HH, HT, TT). There are, however, four ways to achieve these outcomes: head/head, tail/tail, head/tail and tail/head (see the example later in this chapter). Recognising all possible ways of achieving the outcomes is critical in being able to identify theoretical probabilities and quantify outcomes.

Independent events two or more events that have no dependence on each other – for example, the chance of getting six when tossing a fair die is always one in six regardless of any previous tosses

Quantifying probability is relatively straightforward for a single event based on a concrete example, such as tossing a die or a coin. It does rely on having identified all possible outcomes in the sample space, and this becomes more complex when there is more than one event, such as tossing a coin and rolling a die together.

Sample space the list of possible outcomes from an event (e.g. rolling a single die has six possible outcomes)

Understanding relationships and associations – **correlations** – can be quite complex. Although beyond the formal scope of the primary curriculum, this is a key understanding for daily life, and teachers should be aware of potential pitfalls in drawing conclusions from associations. Good examples are provided by Gigerenzer (2002), including breast cancer screening and the OJ Simpson murder trial.

Correlation the association between two independent variables

The research into school children's understanding of probability indicates that they have difficulty coming to terms with its non-deterministic nature. Unlike mathematics, where

3 + 4 makes 7, every time a probabilistic experiment is conducted, the result may be different. For example, every time a die is rolled, a number from 1 to 6 will appear, but we would be suspicious if only 6 ever appeared. Young children, in particular, need many opportunities to understand that the chance of any one number appearing when a die is rolled is a random event (Truran 1995). Very young children often ascribe the behaviour of the die to some outside force, or to the die itself, saying, 'The die's naughty', and the phrase 'It's just luck' is used by all ages as a generic description of uncertainty.

Moving from this intuitive view to an understanding that there may be a set of outcomes for which the chance of occurrence can be determined theoretically is a big step. Watson and Caney (2005) suggested that even upper primary or early high school students struggle with the tension between intuition, expected (theoretical) outcomes and the natural variation that occurs from these expected outcomes. Take, for example, rolling a single, fair, six-sided die 60 times. Many children think that the distribution of numbers that will appear will be something like representation (a) in Figure 9.1. This may be due to many experiences of rolling two dice to create addition computation problems to practice arithmetic.

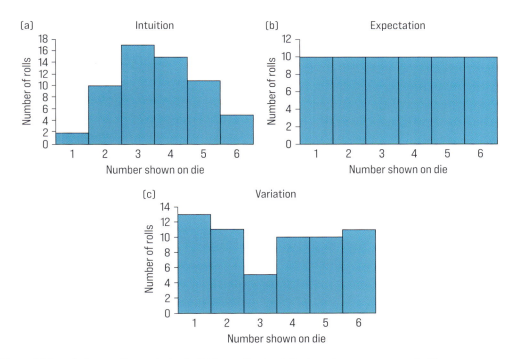

Figure 9.1 Results from rolling a single die 60 times. The 'variation' numbers were generated from an actual experiment using a spreadsheet.

The theoretical outcomes look like (b) – the expected distribution – but if an experiment is carried out, the result may look like (c) – the variation from expectation. Many children will think there is 'something wrong' with the number 3 in representation (c) but the apparent 'problem' is simply due to natural variation.

Not only do children need to come to terms with variation from **expectation**; they also have to begin to understand that rolling a die many more than 60 times will lead to observed

Expectation what is theoretically expected to happen, such as expecting 10 occurrences of each number when you toss a fair die 60 times

Simulation any created activity that aims to represent a 'real-life' situation

outcomes that are closer to the expectation. Technology can be extremely useful here because of its capacity to repeat the same action very quickly, setting up a **simulation**. It is important, however, that children have experience in using the concrete materials prior to moving into a virtual world.

The Australian Curriculum: Mathematics v. 9.0 includes outcomes for a separate strand for probability from Year 3 onwards. Young students, however, will experience the language of uncertainty much earlier such as 'Mum said we may go to the beach at the weekend'. The everyday use of the language of uncertainty is an important foundation for developing understanding.

Developing understanding of uncertainty

Although children have many intuitions about uncertainty and likelihood, often these are not well articulated or are incorrect, and these misunderstandings can persist well into adulthood. The primary years are when many of the ideas are first encountered. Recent research concluded that young children benefit from being taught probability concepts (Nunes et al. 2015). In the next sections, children's understanding of chance, uncertainty and probability will be considered as they move through the primary years. It is important to realise that children will develop at different rates and in different ways. Although most children will show typical understanding, some will not, and, as a teacher, you must be aware of this and adapt your activities accordingly. Many of the activities and ideas for teaching in the following sections include tasks that can be undertaken by children who have a wide range of understanding.

Early primary years

In the early years of schooling, the curriculum emphasis is on developing the language of uncertainty, such as 'possible', 'likely', 'maybe', 'certain' and 'impossible'. Read Classroom Snapshot 9.1 about a teacher's approach to developing these ideas.

CLASSROOM SNAPSHOT 9.1

Helen teaches a Year 1 class in a country school. She wants to introduce the idea of uncertainty through deciding whether an event is certain to happen, might happen or is impossible. For one week every day, the children take a walk to the school car park. They take note of what they see, and practise remembering so that they can talk about the visit when they get back to the classroom.

In the classroom, Helen asks the children what they saw, and they create a collection of observations for each day of the week using the whiteboard. On Friday, they review the week's observations. Helen asks, 'What things did we see every day?' The children identify objects such as trees, fences, white lines and signs. Then she asks, 'What things did we sometimes see?' This time they suggest objects such as a bird, a red car, a caterpillar and the moon in the sky. Finally, she asks, 'What things did we never see?' This question confuses the children initially, so she suggests some ideas, such as a train, a penguin and a volcano. This provides the children with imaginative prompts, and they start suggesting objects such as monkeys and dinosaurs.

One child suggests a horse, and this proposal leads to a discussion about whether they would never see a horse or if it would happen only very occasionally, which begins to establish the idea of chance. Finally, the children return to their tables and create a chart on paper divided into three parts headed NEVER, SOMETIMES and ALWAYS, using pictures cut from magazines. Later, Helen scans each child's work before they take it home to add to their electronic portfolios.

Helen is using technology to record the children's observations efficiently for effective use of the information later, but the activity could be done using butcher's paper with stickers or stamps, for example. The aim is to record the information pictorially to remove any potential literacy load for the children. She engages the children in discussion using the language that she is aiming to develop, and then reinforces the discussion by referring to the visual imagery that they created during the week. The discussion also supports the reasoning proficiency in the curriculum.

The culminating activity where children create their own charts has several purposes. Most importantly, it provides a record of what the children have done and information about how well they understood the language of never, sometimes and always, based on the activity they did during the week. Understanding the language provides a foundation for later work on predicting events. Helen has also created the sheets that the children use to move from NEVER on the left to ALWAYS on the right, replicating the direction of more formal probability number lines that the children will meet later.

The activity also gives the children fine motor skill practice through cutting out and pasting, and encourages language development through the conversations that Helen, the aide and the other children have about the pictures they choose.

The language of chance is the focus of a video 'Will it Rain Today?' on the ABC Education website, in which Flynn and Dodly prepare for a day at the beach. Children in Years 1 and 2 could watch the video and discuss the words used to describe uncertainty, such as 'not much chance', 'might' and 'likely'. Children could then make their own mini-videos about uncertainty, using simple puppets on sticks and shooting the video with a mobile phone. The activity of preparing a storyboard and writing the script also emphasises sequencing, and links mathematics to the arts. Children's books where the outcomes are uncertain are plentiful and provide another opportunity to develop appropriate language. Using children's literature gives teachers the opportunity to link literacy and mathematics activities. Whatever activity is chosen, the key element in teaching chance and probability in the early years of primary school is the discussion and development of the language of uncertainty.

Link 9.8 ABC Education: *Count Us In*, Ep 12 – 'Will it Rain Today?'

Children appear to have more difficulty with events that sit at the extremes – impossible or certain events (Fischbein, Nello & Merino 1991). They can accept the inherent uncertainty of events that might happen because of prior experiences. As they grow older, however, they are better able to make judgements and recognise that some events can be classified at or close to the extremes.

Middle primary years

The language focus is still evident in the middle primary years, but it becomes more refined. Children sequence events using uncertainty language (AC9M3P01), building on activities such as those in Classroom Snapshot 9.1. In the middle primary years appropriate children's literature can be helpful. Discussing a story in terms of 'Was that event unexpected?', 'What's the chance of ... happening?', and 'Is it likely that ... ?' helps to build familiarity with the vocabulary. There are several books that are aimed specifically at probability concepts, but many of these books move quickly into formal theoretical outcomes, which many children in the middle primary years may not be ready for. The picture book *Heads or Tails* (Muir 2018) tells the story of Maggie, a little girl who makes decisions throughout the day, based on the toss of a coin. The story can be used as a stimulus for discussing the chance of a particular outcome from a coin toss and the notion that every coin toss is independent regardless of what has been tossed before. Deciding what resources to use to develop children's understanding must always be based on professional judgement, taking account of the students and their prior experiences.

As children move into the middle primary years, identifying the possible outcomes from a particular event (AC9M4P01) becomes important to lead to the Year 5 outcome of identifying ALL possible outcomes (AC9M5P01). The capacity to identify all outcomes underpins objective notions of theoretical probability, and it is important to develop this skill. When children played a variety of board games, such as Snakes and Ladders or Ludo, they developed a sense of the possible outcomes from rolling a die, but many children now have limited experiences with these ideas. Introducing board games into the classroom for optional activities or 'free' time helps to develop these intuitive ideas. These intuitions can then be built on and discussed during mathematics time.

Developing the skills to recognise possible outcomes involves systematic counting of all possibilities, as illustrated in Classroom Snapshot 9.2. This is not probability itself, but an important underpinning capability that children need to develop.

CLASSROOM SNAPSHOT 9.2

Josie, in Year 4, has been to a shop where teddy bears are made. She chose her bear, put a red heart inside it from a choice of either plain or checked red, then chose a blue scarf from a choice of red, blue or green. She tells her story to the class and shows them her bear. The teacher, Neil, decides to capitalise on this by asking, 'How many different bears could Josie have made?'

The next day, he organises the children into pairs, and gives each pair a teddy bear outline, two hearts and three scarves, as in Josie's story. The children are asked to find the answer to the problem posed and to record their working out in any way they like. As they are working, Neil talks to them about their thinking and asks selected groups to record their approach on the whiteboard. Some groups have chosen to draw all the possible bears, some make lists, some use other kinds of symbols such as coloured lines to represent the hearts and scarves, and one pair develops a form of a tree diagram. All the children correctly answered the question by getting six possible bears.

Neil then decides to take this further and asks, 'What if there were more choices, like four different scarves or three types of heart? Could we find out how many different bears could be made then? To explore these extension ideas, Neil uses an interactive activity called Bobbie Bear, from the Illuminations website, which uses shorts and T-shirts rather than hearts and scarves. He models the original problem with Bobbie Bear, using a computer and data projector, to make the link between the two slightly different contexts, then returns to the extension problems. He encourages the children to pose their own problems.

Link 9.9 Illuminations: Bobbie Bear

In pairs, the children work on the four scarves/three hearts problem, or others posed by Neil or by themselves as he monitors each pair's progress. Again, he asks selected groups to share their work. Finally, Neil returns to the original scenario and asks the class, 'If Josie had just shut her eyes and chosen a heart and a scarf without looking, what would be the chance of her getting the bear with the plain red heart and the blue scarf?' Through discussion and showing the original solutions that the children had recorded, Neil leads the class to the total of six outcomes and that Josie had one chance in six of getting that particular outcome. At this stage he does not take this idea further.

This activity has a focus on identifying all possible outcomes (AC9M3P02, AC9M4P01, AC9M5P01). Neil uses technology together with concrete materials to enhance the ideas that he wants to develop. He builds on the intriguing story that Josie tells, and hence connects the mathematical ideas directly to the children's experiences. He also understands where the learning will need to go as the children move through school, by introducing the links between counting outcomes and probability. He chooses not to pursue this connection because only a small number of children in the class are really ready to learn this idea, and quantifying probability is not in the curriculum in Year 4.

This snapshot raises a number of pedagogical issues. These include links to real-world situations and building on these as they occur – such as when Josie told her story. There are questions around formal and informal recording of possibilities, and Neil did not follow this line of thinking although he did capture the various approaches for possible future use. The activity could have gone in different directions. Neil could have made links to algebra by moving towards a generalised approach to looking at all possibilities. Instead, he deliberately chose to build the connection to probability.

PAUSE AND REFLECT

Consider the different decisions that Neil made, such as to follow up on Josie's story; collecting but not formalising the children's different recording processes; extending the scenario and his use of technology to do this; and his decision to emphasise probability and the beginnings of quantifying chance outcomes. Think about the arguments for and against these decisions.

1. What other courses of action might Neil have taken?
2. What factors might influence these decisions?
3. What mathematical ideas did the children need in order to undertake the activity that Neil organised?
4. What do you think was the key focus of the lesson?
5. How did Neil's use of technology impact on the teaching?

Because of the mathematical potential of tasks such as Bobbie Bear, combinatorial tasks should be encouraged in the middle primary classroom. They are easy to contextualise to the current topics in the classroom, such as food combinations and decorating objects. Another source of problems is mix-and-match books such as *Flip-o-saurus* (Ball & Drehsen 2010). Children could make their own mix-and-match book and identify all the possible combinations. In this way, there could be concrete links made to other curriculum areas.

It is also important that children in these middle years begin to understand randomness in its mathematical sense. Many children think that 'anything can happen' is random, and they need to learn that a random event, mathematically, can be quantified by considering all possible outcomes. Activities such as What's in the Bag? (available from NZ Maths or from Maths300) are useful starting points for developing ideas about random samples. In What's in the Bag? the teacher or a child hides a number of coloured cubes in a bag. The aim is to work out what combination of coloured cubes was placed in the bag initially by sampling one cube at a time and then replacing it in the bag. The activity can be made more or less complex according to the experience and development of the children involved. Once the children are familiar with the task, this activity could also be used as a quick 'filler', for use between different activities, for example. An interactive version of this activity is available from the NRICH website.

Link 9.10 NZ Maths: What's in the Bag?
Link 9.11 NRICH: In the Bag

Good as these activities are, however, it is the language use that is critical. Teachers must consciously use words such as random ('Let's make a random choice'), sample ('We take a sample of one cube'), uncertain ('I am uncertain what colour will be drawn out'), and maybe ('Maybe we'll get a blue this time'). This language should be encouraged in the class discussion and talk around these activities.

Upper primary years

In the upper primary years, the emphasis in the Australian Curriculum is on beginning to quantify uncertain events, leading to ideas about theoretical probability. Children use fractions, decimals and percentages to assign a likelihood to an event occurring (AC9M6P01). They also conduct experiments using random generators such as spinners, coins and dice, and, in so doing, develop the more formal language of probability, such as sample space, frequency and outcomes. This aspect addresses experimental probability and leads to ideas about expectation in the long run. The power of technology to run very large numbers of trials quickly is useful and can be used to develop the idea that the larger the number of trials, the closer the experimental probability comes to the theoretical values (AC9M6P02). The expectations build on the experiences and activities undertaken in the lower years of the primary school.

Language is still important but becomes more complex. Activities such as ordering chance words on a line from 0–1 (or 0% to 100%) provide starting points for quantifying probability (AC9M6P01). Children in Years 5 or 6 can be encouraged to find phrases, sayings and words associated with probability in newspapers or on the internet. A class probability line can then be constructed, with each child placing a favourite word or phrase somewhere on the line. This activity could be done concretely using string across the classroom and pegging the words on to it or electronically using a spreadsheet program.

Once the words and phrases are ordered, children can begin to allocate a fraction to each one to quantify the chance of the event. As a follow-up, children could research the origins of phrases such as 'pigs might fly', 'once in a blue moon' and 'Hobson's choice' or write a story that uses chance language. The children's novel *Pigs Might Fly* (Rodda 1986) could provide a model, integrating mathematics and English in a meaningful way in the classroom. Children's literature is a source of rich language and opportunities to develop understanding (Watson 1993). It may be worth searching for books suitable for the relevant age group. A useful website is Numeracy in the News.

Link 9.12 Numeracy in the News

Simulation activities

Simulation is a way of conducting an experiment that mirrors a real situation. The further the simulation is from the actual situation, the more complex it will be for children to understand. A simulation is an abstraction, and the notion that a real situation can be modelled by something else is difficult for children to recognise. For example, adults can understand that 12 cards labelled one to 12 can model the months of the year, but children might need the actual month names on the cards to understand this idea.

In the upper primary years, children can begin to develop their own simulations (AC9M6P02). These may be concrete or technology-based and can support the investigative approaches to developing probabilistic ideas through experimentation. The unit of work 'Murphy's Law', available from NZ Maths, provides an interesting approach to building experimental probability ideas. The ideas to be explored include buttered toast always landing buttered side down, your keys always being in the opposite pocket to your free hand, and traffic lights always being red when you are in a hurry. The ideas require different simulations. Buttered toast landing buttered side down could be modelled using a coin toss, for example, assuming that the toast has an equal likelihood of landing on either side. The simulation could be compared with an actual experiment with real toast!

Work on 'how many ways' combinatorial tasks should continue in the upper years of primary school, building on work done in the lower primary years. The emphasis should be on efficient and effective recording to ensure that all possible outcomes are counted systematically. Using a book like *Flip-o-saurus* (Ball & Drehsen 2010), older primary children can be challenged to work out how many combinations can be made for a particular number of animals. Crazy Animals (available from Maths300) is one example of a rich activity that has a number of potential learning outcomes. Children make a book with three animals divided into head, body and legs. They then explore all the possible outcomes that can be made by using one head, one body and one pair of legs. If the animals are, for example, a camel, a bear and a sheep, possible combinations could be listed as 'ceap' (camel head, bear middle and sheep legs), 'beeel' (bear head, sheep middle, camel legs) or 'shamr' (sheep head, camel middle, bear legs). How many different combinations are possible? Activities like this are problem-solving exercises that also link to literacy and arts.

Leading into more probabilistic thinking, children can roll a die to make an animal at random. This activity simulates the turning of the pages and these links will have to be made explicitly. Roll 1 is the head, roll 2 is the body and roll 3 gives the legs, and the number on the die decides whether it is a camel part (1 or 2 rolled), a bear (3 or 4 rolled) or a sheep (5 or

6 rolled). From here there are several rich probability activities that could be followed, such as 'What is the chance of getting a three-part camel, a two-part camel, a one-part camel or a zero-part camel?' To answer this question, children have to identify all the possible animals (outcomes). They can simulate the process and speed it up using three dice or virtual dice (available online from several sources). A question that is more difficult to answer might be, 'How many rolls will it take to get a three-part camel?'

The notion of simulation – that is, using a random generator to create a model of a situation – is a powerful idea that upper primary children should begin to experience. Many children find the abstraction from a real situation difficult to understand once it becomes more complicated than, for example, tossing a coin to simulate whether a new baby will be a girl or a boy. Children may transfer the 50:50 chance given by a coin to other situations where the chance is not 50 per cent. To illustrate the use of simulations to solve problems, in Classroom Snapshot 9.3, the problem is a famous one called the birth month problem: 'What is the chance that if any five of us meet by chance on the beach, at least two of us will have birthdays in the same month?'

CLASSROOM SNAPSHOT 9.3

The students in Di's Year 6 class have been discussing birthdays. She poses the birth month problem and asks the children to guess the answer. Each child secretly writes a guess of the likelihood of there being two people with the same birth month on a piece of paper as a percentage or a fraction and then Di records these guesses on the whiteboard for later referral. The students in the class discuss how they might find out how accurate their guesses are. They decide to try it out for themselves using a random selection of names drawn from a container to create the groups. Di moves the class to a multi-purpose room where there is more space to move, and the children form groups of five as their names are drawn from the hat. They then compare their birth months and the number of groups in which there is a 'match' (two or more birthdays in the same month) is recorded. After doing this five times, it is clear that it will take quite a long time to generate enough data to be sure of the outcome.

The class returns to the classroom and Di introduces the idea of a simulation. Leading a discussion about what to simulate, she emphasises that there are 12 months and five people, so both need to be included. The children come up with different ideas, such as having a bag with 12 numbered counters, and drawing one counter five times; using 12 cards in the same way; using a spinner with 12 segments and spinning five times; and rolling a 12-sided die five times. They also discuss how best to record the matches and decide that a table of Match/No match recorded with tally marks would work.

The children are organised into random groups of three and each group is asked to use its chosen method 10 times. After conducting this experiment, the children are asked whether they want to change their predictions. They decide that they still cannot be sure of the outcomes.

Di then goes to an online virtual dice resource that allows the teacher to choose how many faces the dice can have. She chooses to roll five 12-sided dice. She asks the children to explain why she is using five dice (to represent the five people) and why the dice are 12-sided (to represent the 12 months). These questions reinforce the links between the real-world situation and the simulation. She rolls the dice 10 times and the children record the number of matches in 10 rolls. The class repeats this until there are 100 rolls (10 lots of 10 rolls) completed. They then repeat the virtual experiment using an interactive spinner (several are available online). They use trials of five spins of a 12-sector spinner, collecting the matches each time, and repeat this until there are 100 trials (500 spins) completed. The children then consider all the data and individually write a report about the activity and their conclusion about how likely it is that if five people meet by chance, at least two of them will have the same birth month.

There are several good reasons for Di to spend what appears to be wasted time getting the children first to model the problem by forming groups, and then to undertake a concrete simulation. Any simulation is an abstraction, and a virtual simulation – such as rolling five 12-sided dice or spinning a 12-segmented spinner – needs to be connected to the real problem in stages so that children can follow the line of reasoning. Using two different random generators – the die and the spinner – provides an opportunity for discussion about the fact that these diverse methods will produce similar results, and that the more trials are conducted, the closer the outcomes will be to a theoretical value. Calculating the theoretical value is outside the scope of the average Year 6 student, but some children may wish to look at this as a challenge. There are two good explanations of the more complex problem of finding out what size group will be needed to have a 50 per cent chance of two people having the same birthday at ABC Education.

Link 9.13 ABC Education: *MathXplosion*, Ep 8 – 'Birthday probability'
Link 9.14 ABC Education: 'Probability and the birthday paradox'

Not only do children need to collect data to simulate a situation, but they also need to be able to analyse data obtained from using a random generator. Try Activity 9.3 to think about the kinds of responses that children might give.

Theoretical probability

Theoretical probability defines the expectation of getting a particular outcome. This is trivial when we think of tossing a single coin or a **fair** die. The outcomes from a single coin toss are either head or tail so the probability of getting a head is one in two, $\frac{1}{2}$, 50:50 or 50%.

If two coins are tossed, however, the picture becomes more complex. The four possible outcomes are HH, HT, TH, TT. Mathematically, HT and TH are identical. Hence there is twice the chance of getting a head and a tail together than there is of getting either two heads or two tails. A tree diagram can show these outcomes in a systematic way. Such a diagram leads to the idea that the chance of getting two heads (or two tails) is 1 in 4, or $\frac{1}{4}$, or 25%, but the chance of getting a head and a tail is 2 out of 4, or $\frac{1}{2}$ or 50%. If these outcomes are quantified, HH and TT have a 25% probability and the combined HT (HT, TH) outcome has a 50% probability. In this instance, the theoretical outcomes are not equally likely. If we then did an experiment in which two coins were tossed four times, we would not be surprised if the results were HH, HT, TT, HH, showing variation from the expected values. Figure 9.2 shows the possible outcomes from tossing two coins together.

Fair the device being unbiased, so that is there is no external interference that would prevent the device from providing the random outcomes

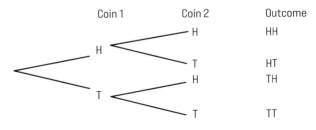

Figure 9.2 Tree diagram to show outcomes from tossing two coins

The aims for the upper primary years are for children to develop systematic ways of identifying all possible outcomes and expressing the different outcomes as fractions or percentages. This kind of activity also links to the development of proportional reasoning (see Chapter 6).

ACTIVITY 9.2

Find all the possible outcomes for tossing three coins. You could model this with three coins, use a tree diagram or use some other approach. Then, do the same thing for four coins. Record your findings or trials systematically.

For each of these situations, there is only one way of getting all heads or all tails. There are, however, several ways of getting the other combinations. Organise your findings using the diagram shown in Figure 9.3. The 1 going down the outside edges represents the single way of getting all heads or all tails. The other numbers show the number of ways of getting the other combinations. So, for two coins, there are two ways of getting the combination of HT, as described above. Look carefully at the diagram. What do you notice? Predict the next line for five coins. The total number of possible outcomes is obtained by adding the numbers in each row: two outcomes for one coin, four outcomes for two coins and so on.

1 coin				1		1		
2 coins			1		2		1	
3 coins		1		3		3		1
4 coins	1		4		6		4		1
5 coins								

Figure 9.3 Outcomes from tossing coins

This diagram is the first few rows of Pascal's Triangle. Research Pascal's Triangle and write a short paragraph about three interesting facts that you find out.

One reason for undertaking short mathematical tasks of this type is to build up your own mathematical understanding, but also to acquire some interesting mathematical 'snippets' that you can use in the mathematics classroom. Pascal's Triangle is full of interesting patterns that children in upper primary could explore.

Theoretical probability indicates the number of possible outcomes, but experimental probability begins to provide the links between statistics and probability by collecting data.

Experimental probability

Random generator
any device that, provided that it is 'fair', will generate an outcome randomly – for example dice, spinners, choosing names from a hat without looking

Tossing coins, throwing dice, choosing names from a hat are all examples of a random situation. Although there is a predicted range of outcomes, these outcomes may not all come up in the short term. Items such as dice, coins and spinners are often called random generators. Children need considerable experience with different kinds of **random generators**. We mostly use dice, coins or spinners in the classroom, but spreadsheets will also produce random numbers, and could be used to simulate dice, for example, by setting up the random number function to provide outcomes from one to six. There are many commercial spinners available, but a reasonable spinner can be constructed from a blank spinner and a paper clip (see Figure 9.4). Spinners have the advantage that they can be partitioned in any way and can be constructed to give unequal outcomes, which is not the case with dice. Asking children to predict the outcome from, say, 10 spins of a four equal-part spinner coloured red, blue, yellow and green, and then comparing their predictions with both actual and theoretical outcomes, helps build useful intuitions about probability.

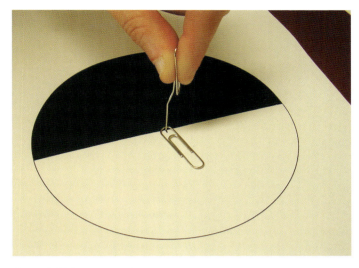

Figure 9.4 50 per cent spinner

Collecting data from random generators leads to experimental probability, which is the actual number of times a particular outcome occurs when an experiment is conducted. Undertaking experiments with different random generators develops ideas about the differences between small and large sample sizes. As our sample (the number of coin tosses, dice throws, spins etc.) becomes larger, the results obtained will be closer to the theoretical values for a particular random generator (e.g. see Figure 9.1). These ideas link to statistics, developing a sense of when a sample is big enough, which becomes important when, for example, you want to evaluate claims made in advertising or to conduct a survey. Try tossing two coins 10 times and then 100 times. Record the number of times you get two heads. How close were you to the theoretical values of 25 per cent?

Experimental probability is also related to simulation activities as discussed earlier.

Combinatorial tasks

Other useful activities for children in the primary years are combinatorial tasks done with concrete materials. English (1991) found that problems such as how many different pizzas can be made from three toppings and two bases can be solved successfully using concrete materials by children as young as 7 years through using systematic trials of all possible combinations. Walter, aged 7 in Year 1 at school, solved the problem shown below. Walter's solution is shown in Figure 9.5.

> Walter wanted to design a new train. The train must have one carriage and one engine.
> For the engine he could choose from three different colours: yellow, green and blue.
> For the carriage he could choose from orange or black.
> How many different trains could he make?

The observer noted:

> He struggled comprehending the puzzle when I read it out but when I suggested he could use his trains to work it out he did it in about 30 seconds flat.
> He lay the trains out and swapped over the trucks on each train one after the other.

Figure 9.5 Walter's solution to the 'trains' problem

Problems such as these, presented as 'puzzles', build up necessary skills for later identifying the sample space and quantifying all outcomes. The idea that for every engine there are two possible carriages is a very important underpinning to developing multiplicative thinking, and it is often referred to as the 'for each' idea. Combinatorial problems also have links to other parts of the mathematics curriculum such as algebra (see Classroom Snapshot 9.2).

PAUSE AND REFLECT

Think about the comments of the observer to Walter's problem-solving. Why might Walter have had trouble understanding the spoken problem? To what extent might we underestimate young children's mathematical capabilities by not recognising that we often use language that is complex?

To develop a sense of the difference between theoretical and experimental outcomes try Activity 9.3.

ACTIVITY 9.3

The graph in Figure 9.6 shows the outcomes from spinning a four-colour spinner 20 times.
- Make a spinner that would most likely give you similar results.
- Test your spinner and record your results in any way that you wish.
- Explain why your results are the same as or different from the ones shown here.

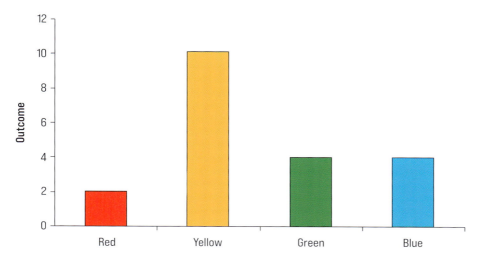

Figure 9.6 Graph of spinner outcomes

When reading a graph of the type in Activity 9.3, many children are likely to focus on the number of categories, rather than the proportion of each colour. They may make a spinner that has four equal quadrants, or one that is half coloured yellow, but the remaining proportions are inappropriately distributed. They will test their spinner, but their recording of the results may be laborious and inefficient, such as listing the outcome from each spin, rather than using a summative approach such as tally marks. Explanations for the difference between their results and those of the spinner shown on the graph are likely to focus on the physical characteristics of the spinner or the manner in which it is spun.

Later, children will develop a more sophisticated approach to reading data and interpreting the graph. They recognise the importance of the relative frequencies, and they are likely to attempt to design a spinner by colouring half yellow and the remaining half equally blue and green. Red may be placed inappropriately in either half so that the proportions are not exactly those shown in the graph. They will test their spinner and record the outcomes efficiently and systematically, and then present their findings in appropriate ways such as a table or graph. Their explanations of the different outcomes, however, are likely to be based on chance only, and the relevance of sample space will not be appreciated.

Those children who have developed a good understanding of probability outcomes will complete the task efficiently and systematically. They will manipulate the data and understand the variation that is likely to occur in small samples of 20 spins. They may express

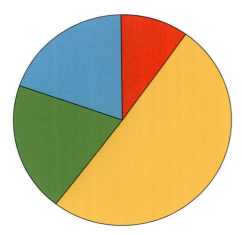

Figure 9.7 A spinner most likely to give the outcomes recorded on the graph in Figure 9.6

this informally rather than in terms of theoretical probabilities, and they are ready to learn early ideas of theoretical probability. An appropriate spinner is shown in Figure 9.7.

Activities such as designing spinners from graphed or tabulated data and the birth month problem (Classroom Snapshot 9.3) make valuable links between probability and statistics, which become important later when inferential statistics are introduced. ABC Education (search for 'Spinners') has some activities with simulated spinners that could be follow ups to use of the concrete materials.

In addition to experiments involving chance, children should have opportunities to recognise the uncertainty inherent in sampling. Discussions about the need for a sample, the difference between a sample and a population, and the notions of random and representative samples are needed before students design and carry out surveys. For example, if children want to survey the school, how should they select the sample? Should they have a random group selected from each year level – a random and representative sample – or simply rely on the chance of getting a representative group? These questions are less trivial than they may seem, because all these decisions are also affected by real-world constraints. Activities such as 'What's in the Bag?' can continue to be used in the upper primary years and extended to compare outcomes when samples of two or four cubes are chosen. This relatively simple activity can set up important discussions about the nature and size of a sample.

Representing probability

In the upper primary years, children begin to represent probability formally. They recognise that probability cannot be represented by a number greater than 1 (or 100%). They use fractions, decimals or percentages to quantify uncertainty (AC9M6P01). As well as connecting to the data aspects of statistics, probability connects to the Number and Algebra strands (see Chapters 5, 6 and 7). The representation of probability as a number can reinforce links between fractions, decimals, percentages, and ratio. Mathematically, probability is represented as:

$$P \text{ of an outcome} = \frac{f}{n}$$

where P is the probability of a favourable outcome, f is the number of favourable outcomes, and n is the total number of outcomes. If we consider the probability of tossing heads, for example, on a fair coin, this would be written as:

$$P_H = \frac{1}{2}$$

This representation is automatically in fraction form, and this can be changed to a decimal (0.5) and a percentage (50%).

PAUSE AND REFLECT

From your reading and personal experience, why is probability so tricky for primary school children? We all live with uncertainty in our lives but expressing this mathematically appears to present particular difficulties for children. How will you approach teaching probability in your classroom? How will you use technology to help you?

Chance activities can be linked to other areas of the curriculum. In many instances, these involve social situations that lead to subjective views of probability. Children are used to the inherent uncertainties of daily life, but they may find it more difficult to accept that these can be quantified. An example is the bushfire danger sign that all Australian children see on a regular basis (see Figure 9.8).

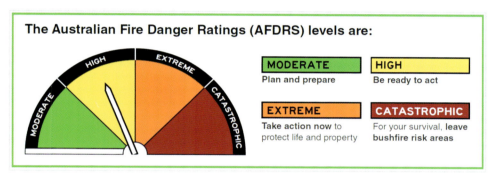

Figure 9.8 Bushfire warning sign
Source: AFAC <https://www.afac.com.au/initiative/afdrs/afdrs-overview/afdrs-design>, © 2022 AFAC

Behind this familiar object are some quite complex probabilistic ideas. The sign provides an indication of the risk associated with a bushfire should it break out. It is a measure of the likely danger and can be interpreted as a statement of conditional probability – if there is a bushfire, then it is likely to be dangerous, expressed as moderate to catastrophic. The probability cannot be quantified in the way that counting outcomes on a die is possible but, based on experience and expert opinion, a generally agreed scale can be provided and interpreted.

Australian children are used to the uncertain nature of bushfires, in which some trees are burned and others survive. A cross-curriculum unit on natural disasters can be enhanced by use of simulation tools such as Fire available from Shodor or Wildfire Simulation from The Concord Consortium.

These resources simulate a 'wildfire' (bushfire) that allows children to set the probability of the fire spreading. The Bureau of Meteorology also has useful information about bushfires. Such activities stress the cross-curriculum numeracy capability expected in the Australian Curriculum: Mathematics v. 9.0 and provide an opportunity to develop proficiencies – particularly reasoning and problem-solving.

It is useful also to discuss 'risk' with upper primary classes. Many children will have experienced the disruption due to natural disasters such as cyclones or floods. What does a 'once

Link 9.15 Shodor
Link 9.16 The Concord Consortium: Wildfire Simulation

in 20-year flood' mean? Could a 'once-in-20-year flood' occur two years running? These are important questions because they are linked to insurance, for example, about which many children will have heard discussion at home or in the community. Why are some homes insured for flood and some are not? These are social questions that have a mathematical basis, and teachers should not be afraid of discussing these kinds of issues in relation to mathematics.

> **TIPS FOR ONLINE TEACHING**
>
> There is scope for many investigations and activities in the online environment. Generating random numbers using home-made spinners (Figure 9.4) will allow students to create their own investigations. For example, they could create a spinner, conduct an experiment with 10, 50, 100 spins and create the corresponding graphs. They could then swap a graph with their online buddy and challenge the buddy to create the spinner that generated those outcomes. Accessing the many online resources, especially those in ABC Education that have Australian content, could provide another avenue. After watching 'Will it Rain Today?' students could be challenged to write their own 'uncertain' story and/or make a video that could be posted to the class folder. See Chapter 11 for other online suggestions, such as 'Greedy Pig' and 'The King's Tax' which are both games which can help to develop probabilistic ideas. Making a flipbook can also be easily adapted to online. Students can make their own books and then undertake some guided investigations. There are many online resources available such as virtual spinners, coins and cards, although students ideally should use concrete materials first.

Conclusion

Probability is one aspect of the mathematics curriculum that creates difficulties for children. It is about uncertainty, and this is different from other areas of mathematics. Children have to come to terms with ideas like, 'We can calculate a theoretical probability, but if we conduct an experiment, the results are likely to differ from the expected values.' Making a guess about the likelihood of an event is not the same as predicting an outcome based on an expected value, and it underlines the difference between subjective intuitions and objective predictions based on theory.

Despite the difficulties, this is an area of the curriculum that has potential for rich investigations and a high degree of engagement by children. As with all good teaching, it is important that children have opportunities to reflect on their learning through discussion or by writing a report of an activity. Language, and classroom talk and discussion are critically important, and the more practice children get, the better.

GUIDED STUDENT TASKS

1. Make a list of 10 words that describe uncertainty (e.g. maybe, certainly, impossible). Order these on a line from 0 (no chance) to 1 (absolute certainty). Ask a friend to undertake the same task. Compare your lists and the positions of the words on the probability line. Discuss the differences.

2. Research common sayings or phrases related to chance (e.g. Hobson's choice, London to a brick). Annotate these phrases to explain their history and meaning.
3. Write a short story for children based on probability and uncertainty.
4. Make a collection of newspaper cuttings or phrases from newspaper articles that reflect uncertainty (sports pages are a good source).
5. Talk to children of different ages about the chance of an event happening, such as 'What's the chance of sunshine tomorrow?' or 'How likely is it that I'll get a strawberry lolly if I shut my eyes and just choose one?' Listen carefully to the language that they use. How does this change as children get older and have more experience?

CONCEPTS TO CONSIDER

This section highlights some of the underlying ideas of probability. It does not claim to cover everything. There are many online resources addressing probability but choose these with some thought for what you want to learn. Many of the sites are devoted to business and stock market ideas which may not help you to teach this strand. One interesting podcast is from the BBC in the United Kingdom *In Our Time*: 'Probability', which covers something of the history of probability and the mathematics behind it.

Link 9.17 BBC's *In Our Time*: 'Probability' podcast

Probability comes from a Latin word that means to test or demonstrate and, over time, has come to mean likely, reasonable or plausible. The mathematical basis did not develop until the 18th century in the context of gambling. Where there is a finite number of possible outcomes that are known, it is possible to identify the likelihood of a particular outcome occurring. A simple example is rolling a die – we know that there are six possible outcomes so the likelihood of getting a specified number is one in six. Rolling two dice is more complex. Here the possible outcomes are far greater (36), so the likelihood of getting a particular outcome varies according to the numbers desired.

Complete the Table 9.1 and determine the probability of getting 4 when the two numbers rolled are added together. The first row and column are filled in for you.

Table 9.1 Sum of two dice

	1	2	3	4	5	6
1	2	3	4	5	6	7
2	3					
3	4					
4	5					
5	6					
6	7					

Answer these questions:

- How many possible outcomes are there?
- How many ways can you get 12? How many ways can you get 7?
- Draw a graph that shows the frequency of occurrence of each total (2 to 7).
- What is the probability of getting a total of 5? What is the probability of getting a total of 9?

Behind these kinds of activities are assumptions that the dice are fair and that the way in which they are rolled does not create bias. Describing probability in this way is the basis of *classical probability*. You can also conduct an experiment. As the number of rolls increases, the *distribution* (see 'Concepts to consider' in Chapter 8) of outcomes becomes closer to the theoretical outcomes., and the graph should look more and more like the one you drew. These are experimental outcomes. Where you can calculate (theoretical probability) or determine the outcomes through an experiment (experimental probability), the probability is said to be *objective*. The probability is determined by the *relative frequency* (the count) of each occurrence of each outcome.

In daily life we can rarely determine every possible outcome, or there may be so many that it is impossible to identify them all. In this situation we use other techniques such as modelling or comparing to long term records. This probability is said to be *subjective*, although the result should not be seen just as a guess when it is based on carefully collected data.

Conditional probability is where the likelihood of an event or outcome is dependent on the occurrence of a previous event. The Monty Hall problem described earlier is an example. This is the way that insurance companies operate – you lose your no claims bonus on your car insurance if you have an accident, because if you have had one accident you are statistically more likely to have another one. Although these ideas are outside the primary curriculum, it is useful to be aware of this way of thinking.

Randomness is a more complex idea than we think. The word means something that happens without a conscious decision or method – that is, it occurs by chance alone. Colloquially it has come to mean something unfamiliar or unknown. In mathematics, however, randomness is not haphazard but follows a known distribution of outcomes. Tossing a coin will generate a random sequence of heads and tails but over a long period of time, or taking a large sample of tosses, the distribution of heads and tails will approach 50:50. Try taking a random walk. Allocate heads to right and tails to left. From your start point, toss a coin and turn in the direction indicated. Every time you come to a junction repeat this process and turn left or right according to the toss of the coin. After 10 tosses make a note or take a photograph of where you are. Try the same process again from the same start point. Did you end up in the same place? Each toss of the coin is independent of what has happened before, so you have a 50 per cent chance each time of going left or right. You can try the same activity on a number line where you start on zero and move one unit right on heads and one unit left on tails. It is possible to determine all possible outcomes from a small number of flips. Look up One-dimensional Random Walk to find out more or watch the video 'Simple Random Walk' by Maths Partner, available on YouTube.

Link 9.18 Maths Partner: 'Simple Random Walk'

FURTHER READING

Kramer, K & Gigerenzer, G 2005, 'How to confuse with statistics or: The use and misuse of conditional probabilities', *Statistical Science*, vol. 20, no. 3, pp. 223–30.

Muir, T 2018, *Heads or tails*, Blairgowrie, Vic: Teaching Solutions.

Sutherland, R 2014, 'What the O.J. Simpson jury didn't know (and schools should teach)', *The Spectator*, 1 March, <https://www.spectator.co.uk/article/what-the-o-j-simpson-jury-didn-t-know-and-schools-should-teach/>.

Watson, J & Callingham, R 2015, 'Getting out of bed: Students' beliefs' in M Marshman, V Geiger & A Bennison (eds), *Mathematics education in the margins* (Proceedings of the 38th annual conference of the Mathematics Education Research Group of Australasia), Sunshine Coast: MERGA, pp. 619–26.

Watson, J & Fitzallen, N 2019, 'Building understanding of randomness from ideas about variation and expectation', *Statistics Teacher, American Statistical Association*, 19 September, <https://www.statisticsteacher.org/2019/09/19/building-understanding-of-randomness-from-ideas-about-variation-and-expectation/>.

Websites for exploration

CHAPTER 10
CAPITALISING ON ASSESSMENT FOR, OF AND AS LEARNING

LEARNING OUTCOMES

By the end of this chapter, you will:

- understand the notion of assessment for, of and as learning, and how these forms of assessment work together in the mathematics classroom
- have a developmental framework to assist in designing an assessment item and assessing the quality of a student's response: the SOLO model
- be aware of the use of national testing data in a positive way to support growth in mathematical understanding
- be able to use various tools to create valid assessment items.

Introduction

While the activities presented in the previous chapters all have the potential to be used for assessment purposes, this chapter specifically targets making the most of assessment in terms of identifying students' levels of understanding, better targeting future student activities and providing feedback to students and parents/caregivers. The most exciting fact about assessment in the primary classroom is that student teaching and learning tasks and assessment tasks can be united seamlessly. As teachers, we can make the most of a mathematics assessment task if it provides evidence of students' current levels of understanding, if this can be communicated positively to students and parents or caregivers, and if the students have some role to play in their own goal-setting of where to head next. For too long assessment has been driven by commercially produced closed worksheets that do not provide the flexibility and open-endedness needed for students to enter the task at a variety of levels. The over reliance on formal tests is prevalent in many educational contexts, nationally and internationally. The following discussion demonstrates the power in reducing our reliance on formal tests, which are not equitable and offer limited value for teaching.

This chapter investigates the design of assessment for learning tasks, assessing and evaluating the tasks, and providing feedback to students, parents and caregivers. The chapter considers positive strategies for utilising the online National Assessment Program – Literacy and Numeracy (NAPLAN) items, school results and individual student results as a diagnostic tool to move forward.

Assessment

Assessment generally means to identify in measurable terms the knowledge, skills and beliefs of an individual or group. While the definition appears simplistic, problems arise when one attempts to categorise assessment practices into distinct groups. We can fall into the trap of categorising assessment items as either summative or formative, and thus placing them in two separate groups. Summative means assessment at the end of a teaching period (such as a unit, term, semester or year), with the aim being to assess what the students know for reporting purposes. Formative, on the other hand, traditionally was perceived as less formal, often not warranting recording, and enabled feedback to the students and teacher to identify where they were at and where they needed to head. Educationally, we have developed our ideas of assessment greatly and are no longer so quick to categorise different forms of assessment as one or the other and to judge their value. Purposefully, this chapter is not bounded by the assigning of a particular form of assessment to define a student task.

This multi-dimensional view of assessment has led to the terms '**assessment of learning**', 'assessment for learning' and 'assessment as learning', where the power of assessment lies in the overlap in the nature of these types. One of the most exciting times for assessment in the primary mathematics classroom was during the implementation of assessment policies that focused on assessment for learning. A significant example of this was the New South Wales Board of Studies, Teaching & Educational Standards (2012) Assessment for Learning Practices document. One of the key factors was the integration of assessment tasks into the teaching and learning sequence, whereby students may not be aware that they are being assessed. This is often described as assessment tasks and teaching and learning activities being seamlessly united. Noting the importance of seamless integration of assessment with teaching and learning, we devote most of the emphasis in this chapter on assessment for learning. Teachers are asked to consider a range of informal strategies, such as classroom observations and questioning, and formal assessment strategies. These formal and informal types are included in subsequent sections.

Assessment for learning

The Australian Curriculum: Mathematics v. 9.0 adopts the principles of **assessment for learning**. Teachers are asked to integrate their assessment practices into their daily mathematics tasks in a manageable fashion. Assessment strategies should not pressure teachers or students. Goals should be articulated clearly to students, with the emphasis placed on gaining a deeper understanding as opposed to a higher mark or rank. Assessment should be inclusive and accessible to all learners and provide valuable and timely feedback to students. This is supported by the Australian Association of Mathematics Teachers (AAMT 2008) in its Position Paper on the Practice of Assessing Mathematics Learning, which stresses that students' learning of mathematics should be assessed in ways that:

- are appropriate
- are fair and inclusive
- inform learning and action (AAMT 2008, p. 1).

Assessment to identify in measurable terms the knowledge, skills and beliefs of an individual or group

Assessment of learning the process of gathering information about student achievement and communicating this information

Assessment for learning the central purposes of assessment for learning are to provide information on student achievement and progress and to set the direction for ongoing teaching and learning

Interestingly, the Australian Curriculum: Mathematics F–10 v. 9.0 states that the learning of Mathematics should aim to 'foster a positive disposition towards mathematics, recognising it as an accessible and useful discipline to study' (ACARA 2022). It is essential for assessment practices to reflect this aim, particularly in the context of assessment for learning.

Assessment for learning has also been high on the agenda of the Assessment Reform Group (2002) in the United Kingdom, which devised the following 10 principles of assessment for learning:

1. It is part of effective planning.
2. It focuses on how students learn.
3. It is central to classroom practice.
4. It is a key professional skill.
5. It has an emotional impact.
6. It affects learner motivation.
7. It promotes commitment to learning goals and assessment criteria.
8. It helps learners know how to improve.
9. It encourages self-assessment.
10. It recognises all achievements.

Classroom Snapshot 10.1 provides an example of an assessment for learning task and the feedback provided by the teacher to the students. With the introduction of the Australian Curriculum: Mathematics (ACARA 2016b), online materials were released by ACARA that assist teachers in choosing suitable assessment for learning tasks within each of Foundation to Year 10 years of schooling. Links to these can be found on the Australian Curriculum v. 8.4 Mathematics Foundation to Year 10 Curriculum website. The expected level of understanding is articulated for each year, with content descriptors, and there are work-sample portfolios for each year. The support materials for version 9.0 of the Australian Curriculum: Mathematics are under development, at this time of publication, with resource links provided to the former version 8.4 of the curriculum.

Link 10.1 Australian Curriculum (v. 8.4): Resources

CLASSROOM SNAPSHOT 10.1

Alex's Year 1 class was working on the Friends of 10 concept (see Figure 10.1). Using numeral necklaces, he previously had asked the children to find their 'friend of 10' – for example, if a student was

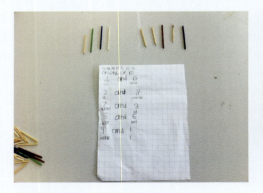

Figure 10.1 Friends of 10 activities

wearing a 2 necklace, they needed to find an 8 to match with. Alex decided he needed to assess the students' understanding of this concept before moving on. He usually wrote a series of numbers from 1 to 10 on the whiteboard and then asked the students to find the matching 'friend of 10'. This time, he decided to give the students a range of materials such as 10-frames and counters, coloured toothpicks and the Friends of Ten app. He asked them to find all the 'friends of 10' and record them. Alex observed some very interesting differences in the way students tackled the task.

Link 10.2 Friends of Ten app

PAUSE AND REFLECT

Before reading on, what do you think Alex may have observed while watching the students solve the task?

As the children manipulated the variety of materials in groups, Alex made the following observations:

- Some students counted each square covered with a counter and then counted the squares without counters by touching each square.
- Some students used the counters for the first number and then subitised to find the second number.
- Some students used the counters to find a pair such as 4 and 6, and later repeated the process using the counters for 6 and 4.
- Some students identified 3 and 7, for example, and then instantly recorded 7 and 3 without using counters.
- Some students did not use counters at all but recorded each of the 'friends of 10' in a systematic order.

As Alex was observing the children while they worked through the task, he applied his pedagogical content knowledge to provide the students in two of the groups with a harder problem. He went on to ask these students to find all the 'friends of 16' and 'friends of 20' (see Figure 10.2).

CLASSROOM SNAPSHOT 10.2

Figure 10.2 Using counters to assist in finding friends of 16

This simple activity highlights the positive nature of the assessment for learning practices. The task was part of the everyday teaching and learning sequence, the students were unaware of being 'formally' assessed, the task could be varied to suit the different levels of understanding and the teacher could make decisions concerning the appropriate direction of the activity during the lesson. This type of assessment task enables students to receive positive and constructive feedback promptly, and recorded work samples provide evidence of the students' thinking at this point.

The following activity has been explored in numerous classrooms for many years, and versions of it can be obtained from the Australian Curriculum website, the Assessment Resource Centre and the Maths300 website. These sites are examples only, as each state's documents and other national documents have similar materials.

Classroom Snapshot 10.3 targets a lower secondary school content area involving the concept of finding the volume of a cylinder (AC9M9M01). The scenario in Classroom Snapshot 10.3 is an authentic assessment for learning task, as the students had been exploring volume concepts and had focused upon the cylinder in the last week. While this concept is usually explored in the secondary years, it provides a useful teaching example for primary teachers to consider, as it puts us back in the role of student as we play around with our response to this task.

CLASSROOM SNAPSHOT 10.3

Megan wanted to assess each student's level of understanding before moving on to the next unit of work. In the past, she had produced a series of routine questions, similar to those they had completed in class. The students were usually told that they would be doing an assessment task, and the teacher was aware that some students displayed anxiety when placed in a test situation.

After some searching, she found an assessment task on the Assessment Resource Centre website, known as Mr Tall and Mr Short. Megan decided to use this activity as an assessment task, with the students being unaware of the importance of the activity for assessment purposes. The students entered the room as if for any other activity that week.

The activity began with a class vote about whether students thought a cylinder formed by rolling an A4 piece of paper lengthways (Mr Tall) would have a greater volume than a cylinder formed by rolling the paper widthways (Mr Short) or whether the volumes of the cylinders would be the same. An anonymous vote was held, and most students thought they would be the same.

Megan had prepared cardboard versions of the cylinders, with a circular face to attach to the base. The students observed as Megan filled Mr Tall with rice and then poured that rice into a measuring cylinder. Rice was then poured into Mr Short until it reached capacity, and that rice was poured into a second measuring cylinder. Most students were amazed that Mr Short held more rice and thought that Megan had tricked them somehow.

Megan made the most of the students' intrigue, stating, 'Your mission is to prove mathematically which of these containers will hold the most – Mr Tall or Mr Short. You may each have two pieces of paper, one for measuring and one for recording your response. I would like you to use your best mathematics communication skills and use diagrams to assist your explanation. You may use a ruler and a calculator. For this activity, I would like you to work individually.'

While this activity has an introduction that involves stimulating students' curiosity through a student vote and the concrete cylinder filling task modelled by the teacher, this lesson design is also suitable to the online teaching environment. The introduction can be shared and discussed through an online platform such as Zoom, and the three options voted on anonymously. The students could then work individually or in small groups if required and rejoin the class group to share their findings.

TIPS FOR ONLINE TEACHING

ACTIVITY 10.1

Before reading any further, and using the materials outlined in the scenario so far, write your own solution to: 'Which will hold the most – Mr Tall or Mr Short? Or do they have the same volume?' Make sure you clearly show why you have reached that conclusion.

Quality of student responses

The next phase in the assessment process will be considered in the context of the cylinder task. This phase occurs upon completion of any assessment task or observed student response during any mathematics activity, and it involves evaluating each student's response. It is generally straightforward when marking closed items that require a single response, but even this type of question requires the teacher to consider the complexity of the thinking required to answer the question and the process used to determine the solution. Some teachers opt to use pre-designed assessment rubrics; however, these are often general in nature and not specific to the content area being observed.

CLASSROOM SNAPSHOT 10.4

Megan considered a sample of student responses to the Mr Tall and Mr Short task, and she placed the samples into the following groups.

Group 1: These students attempted to draw the cylinders and labelled one Mr Short and one Mr Tall. A selection of unrelated measurements were recorded by the students, such as the height of each cylinder, for no specific purpose. There was no attempt to calculate the volume.

Group 2: These students drew each of the cylinders. The students attempted to use the formula, $V = Ah$, but instead multiplied the base and height of the original A4 piece of paper and came to the conclusion that the cylinders did have the same volume.

Group 3: These students focused upon substitution into the correct equation, $V = Ah$, but the radius was taken as half of the circumference (half the base length of the A4 piece of paper).

Group 4: These students used the correct formula; however, the radius was not accurately found as these students attempted to position their ruler to find the centre of the circular base. These students did not use the circumference of the circle to find the radius by dividing the circumference of the base by 2π.

Group 5: These students used the relationship between circumference and radius to find the radius accurately. The students used what is known as reversibility to find the radius (see Figure 10.3), and correctly divided the circumference of the base of the cylinder by 2π. With the correct use of the formula V = Ah, the students identified and justified that Mr Short had a greater volume than Mr Tall.

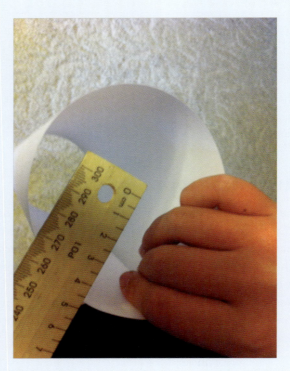

Figure 10.3 Estimating the radius of the circle

While this concept area is usually taught in the lower secondary setting, it provides a detailed example of the difference between quoting a right or wrong mark, or even a mark out of 10, and an analysis of the quality of the response indicating the level of understanding of a particular concept. One could place a numerical value on the responses of Groups 1 to 5 above, but the marks would mean nothing without the description of achievement alongside the responses.

All the previous chapters have used developmental frameworks or cognitive structures that have informed the teaching practice discussed. A variety of developmental models inform assessment. This section considers three of these: Newman's (1977) Error Analysis, Blank's (2002) questioning framework and the SOLO model (Biggs & Collis 1982). The next section provides an introduction to the developmental models to assist teachers in their interpretation of students' responses.

Across the education sector, teachers are discovering the work of Newman (1977), who suggests five prompts to assist in determining students' errors with attempting to solve word problems (White 2005). The prompts that can be used in primary and secondary contexts are shown in Table 10.1.

Table 10.1 Newman's prompts

Newman's prompts	Basic steps in finding a solution to a mathematics problem
1. Please read the question to me. If you don't know a word, leave it out.	1. Read the problem (R). (About 2 per cent of errors occur at this stage.)
2. Tell me what the question is asking you to do.	2. Comprehend what is read (C). (About 12 per cent of errors occur at this stage.)
3. Tell me how you are going to find the answer.	3. Transform the words of the problem into an appropriate mathematical strategy (T). (About 50 per cent of errors occur at this stage.)
4. Show me what to do to get the answer. 'Talk aloud' as you do it, so that I can understand how you are thinking.	4. Apply the process skills required for the chosen strategy (P).
5. Now, write down your answer to the question.	5. Encode a written answer in an acceptable form (E).

Source: Adapted from New South Wales Education Standards Authority n.d. and Newman 1977

After interviewing the student and working through the five prompts, the attempt can be coded as R, C, T, P or E, depending on where the student error took place. The sample word problem below demonstrates the use of the five prompts in the context of ducks on a pond.

Sample word problem

There were nine ducks on a pond. They were joined by some other ducks, making a total of 15 ducks on the pond. How many ducks joined the group?

- Step 1 – Decoding: Can you read the problem to me? (picks up decoding issues)
- Step 2 – Comprehension: What is the problem asking? (retelling)

   Student response: I need to find out how many ducks came to the pond.

- Step 3 – Mathematising: What mathematics do you know that could help?

   Student response: adding up (child doesn't recognise that this is a subtraction problem – intervention needed).
   OR
   Student response: If I take away the 9 from 15 it should tell me how many ducks joined. (Child can correctly turn the problem into mathematical strategy.)

- Step 4 – Process skills: Show me how you would do it.

   Student response: Child attempts to count back from 15 to 9 using fingers and answers '7'. (Child needs to move to a more efficient mental strategy.)
   OR
   Student response: Child attempts to write a vertical algorithm but takes the 5 away from 9 and gets an answer of 14. (Work with number lines might help.)

- Step 5 – Encoding: What have you found out?

   OR

Step 5 – Encoding: Draw me a picture to show what you found (usually little intervention needed for straightforward word problems).

The work of Blank (2002) provides another model for questioning that describes four levels of question types:

- Level 1: Directly supplied information
- Level 2: Classification
- Level 3: Reorganisation
- Level 4: Abstraction and inference.

The patterns and algebra questions that follow provide an example for each level of questioning (see the pattern Figure 10.4).

Figure 10.4 Triangle path pattern

- Level 1: How many matches are used for each triangle?
- Level 2: What is the pattern?
- Level 3: How many more matches are needed each time?
- Level 4: How many matches are needed for 50 triangles?

ACTIVITY 10.2

Write an appropriate question for each level in Blank's (2002) question framework.

Level	Label	Example	Add one of your own
1	Directly supplied information	7 What number is this?	
2	Classification	27 – 7 = What kind of problem is this?	
3	Reorganisation	42 = 7 × 6 How could you write this as a division problem?	
4	Abstraction and inference	If you multiply an odd number by an even number, what kind of number do you get?	

The third model considers the quality of students' responses in terms of structure, and it provides a guide to designing tasks. You will notice elements of the previous models within the description of the SOLO model that follows.

The SOLO model

The Structure of the Observed Learning Outcome (SOLO) model has been identified as extremely useful in assisting with assessment task design, evaluating the quality of the student response and determining the direction of the follow-up student activities. This model was developed by Biggs and Collis (1982) and extensively built on by researchers such as Pegg and Davey (1998), Serow (2007a) and Watson and colleagues (1995). It utilises the modes described by Piaget (see below), but also acknowledges that previously developed modes are still available to learners as they mature. While the model has been researched to a very detailed level, only its introductory global key characteristics will be explored in this chapter.

The SOLO model grew from the desire of Biggs and Collis (1982) to explore and describe students' understandings in the light of criticisms of the work of Piaget. Rather than focus on the levels of thinking of students, the emphasis in the SOLO model is on the structure of students' responses. The framework consists of two main components: the modes of functioning and the levels of the model.

The five SOLO modes represent the level of abstraction of a response. The characterisation of the SOLO modes appears similar to the Piagetian developmental stages; however, there are some fundamental differences. The SOLO model characterises the mode of functioning utilised within a response, as opposed to characterising the person as at a single developmental mode; newly acquired modes do not subsume previously acquired modes; and multi-modal functioning is possible. The modes of functioning are described below. Each has been included, but you can expect frequent observation of the first three modes of functioning in the primary setting. Basically, this means that we acknowledge the support of reactions to the physical environment, and images and verbal language, when working with written symbols and solving problems using these symbols.

Modes of functioning

The modes of functioning include the following:

Sensori-motor: The response involves a reaction to the physical environment. It is associated with motor activity, and it can be described as tacit knowledge. Examples include a child learning to walk or an adult playing sport.

Ikonic: The response involves the internalisation of images and linking them to language. There is a reliance on images, and development of language and thinking in this mode can be described as intuitive knowledge. Examples include a child developing words for images, and an adult's creation of science fiction images.

Concrete symbolic: The response involves the application and use of a system of symbols, which can be related to real-world experiences. This abstraction enables concepts and operations that are applied to the environment to be manipulated through the medium of symbolic systems – for example, written language and number problems.

Formal: The response involves the consideration of abstract concepts, as there is no longer a need for a real-world referent. The formal mode is characterised by a focus on an abstract system, based on principles in which concepts are embedded.

Post-formal: The response involves the challenge or questioning of abstract concepts and theoretical perspectives of the formal mode.

The SOLO modes represent developmental growth, with the acquired SOLO modes remaining accessible and continuing to evolve while supporting other modes.

Levels of the model

The five levels of the SOLO model, describing the complexity of the structure of a response, are prestructural (P), unistructural (U), multistructural (M), relational (R) and extended abstract (EA). The levels can be identified by observing the structure of an individual's response to a given task. While unistructural, multistructural and relational responses appear in each of the modes of functioning, a prestructural response is typified as at a lower level of abstraction than is required for a task. An extended abstract response to a task requires higher synthesis and application than is reasonably expected. The five levels are described below:

Prestructural: The response is below the target mode. In an attempt to provide a response, the learner is misled or distracted by irrelevant aspects of the task and responds in a lower mode. A typical response may be 'The square is like a box.'

Unistructural: The response is characterised by a focus on a single aspect of the problem/task. Since only one relevant piece of information is utilised, the response may be inconsistent. A typical response may be 'A square has all sides equal.'

Multistructural: The response is characterised by a focus on more than one independent aspect of the problem/task. No relationships are perceived between the components utilised. A lack of integration is evident, and some inconsistency is apparent. A typical response may be 'A square has all sides equal, four right angles, all sides are parallel, and two pairs of opposite sides.'

Relational: The response is characterised by a focus on the integration of the components of the problem/task. The relationships between the known aspects are evident, with consistency within this system. A typical response would be 'A square has all sides equal and one right angle. I don't need to say all of them, because if it has that, the others will be equal, and they will also be parallel.'

Extended abstract: The response is taken beyond the domain of the problem/task and into a new mode of reasoning.

Within each mode, there exist cycles of levels. For example, researchers have found two cycles within the concrete symbolic mode. These are acknowledged here but not discussed further in the context of this chapter.

If we revisit the five groups of responses to the Mr Tall and Mr Short assessment task in Classroom Snapshot 10.3, we can interpret the responses using the SOLO model in the following way:

- Group 3: Concrete symbolic mode – unistructural level
- Group 4: Concrete symbolic mode – multistructural level
- Group 5: Concrete symbolic mode – relational level.

The SOLO model provides a framework through which we can design questions that elicit responses at a target level or are accessible to a range of levels.

Construction of assessment tasks

The categorisation of students' responses to tasks, rather than the categorisation of the individuals, requires careful construction of assessment items. Both closed and open assessment items are applicable to the SOLO model. However, the most appropriate method for eliciting optimum responses depends upon the type of investigation being carried out. In the same manner that some students think of the equals sign as meaning 'the answer is', there are many community members who believe that mathematics assessment items and test questions only have one answer. Some people find it difficult to believe that there can be many legitimate ways of solving a problem. This is particularly evident in relation to formal algorithms.

Open-ended items, also known as free-response items or constructed-response items, require the student to 'create a response rather than select it from a list' (Collis & Romberg 1991, p. 84). 'Open-ended and free response questions … require the student to generate the correct answer, not merely to recognise it. Such assessment items would … allow for more reliable inferences about the thought processes contributing to the answer' (Alexander & James 1987, p. 23). Added to this, open-ended assessment items are enhanced further by seeking justification and clarification from the student about the way they have tackled the task.

An example of an extended open-ended activity involves students coming up with as many different designs for placing four identical cubes together as possible, with complete faces touching only and with the ability to stand freely. The Maths300 lesson The Architect's Puzzle places the student in the context of being an architect with a design scope and costing schedule. This task also illustrates the development of literacy skills within a mathematics exploration.

Task construction is considered in the remaining sections of the chapter in the context of making the most of national testing feedback and items, syllabus support material and online resources.

National testing

In political circles, school classrooms, school staffrooms and students' homes, it is common to hear discussions concerning national testing. In Australia, NAPLAN is an assessment that has been administered to Years 3, 5, 7 and 9 since 2008. While the NAPLAN assessment covers aspects of reading, writing, spelling and numeracy, this chapter is concerned with the numeracy section only. The same written assessment is undertaken across the nation each year. This, in itself, highlights issues of equity that have been debated extensively. The tests cover the main areas of the curriculum that are considered essential and common; these are described as number, algebra, function and pattern, measurement, chance and data, space and working mathematically. 'Working mathematically' is a term that describes components of working as a mathematician, such as communication, reasoning, reflection and technology application. The numeracy test contains multiple-choice items and short-response items. Generally, each item is not accessible to a range of abilities, and so is recorded as correct or incorrect. The primary tests are non-calculator for all items, and the secondary test has calculator and non-calculator sections. The NAPLAN assessment is now predominantly administered online across Years 3, 5, 7 and 9. This change in mode of delivery has been investigated with Lowrie and Logan (2015) finding that the pen-and-paper environment was more effective when applying problem-solving processes. They also found that the students found it more challenging to draw diagrams and decode information in the digital mode, suggesting that teachers will need to spend time on tasks that explicitly use these understandings and skills to assist students in coping with the higher cognitive demands.

NAPLAN describes minimum standards for numeracy in terms of skills and understandings at each particular year of schooling. An example of a standard follows:

> Students recognise common two-dimensional shapes and three-dimensional objects, describing them using both everyday language and geometric names. They sort and group them using common characteristics, draw sketches and construct reasonable models using a range of materials, drawing tools and other technology. They recognise angles both as parts of shapes and objects, and in turns.
> (Curriculum Corporation 2006, p. 6)

Figure 10.5 shows a sample of the NAPLAN student performance feedback to parents. The example provided is for a Year 3 student. The band scales are different for Years 5, 7, and 9.

The black dot indicates the individual student result and the filled triangle indicates the national average. Alongside the standards, students are reported on scales used for comparison. These initially were developed as a means of measuring growth over time; however, such results have frequently been used in the political arena to compare schools and for funding purposes. These are presented through the MySchool website. At this point, it needs to be made clear that AAMT (2008, p. 8) 'prohibits the publication of league tables of schools from their data' and that the information provided to schools should be statistically legitimate.

In contrast, for NAPLAN results to be used positively requires three levels of analysis: individual students, year trends and school trends. For example, the NAPLAN results may indicate differences between particular classes of students or general trends across a school.

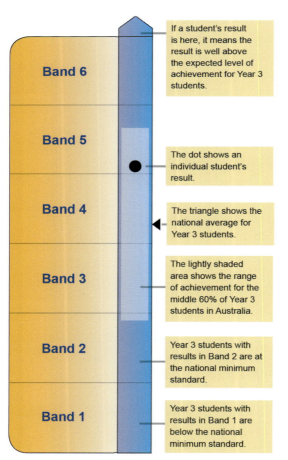

Figure 10.5 Sample NAPLAN communication to parents
Source: ACARA 2017, p. 1

CLASSROOM SNAPSHOT 10.5

In 2005, a primary school received its NAPLAN results. When compared with the rest of the state, it was performing just above the state average. The results could now be filed. The principal decided to take a closer look at the results before leaving the matter alone. When she did, she noticed that the test area that was the poorest in terms of performance across Year 5 was space and geometry. After discussions with staff, it was revealed that this was an area of shared concern, and teachers felt that they were not developing the geometrical concepts to a deeper level. This became a school focus in terms of professional development and school resourcing. The following two years of NAPLAN results indicated a growth in the area of geometrical concepts.

Figures 10.6–10.10 show some sample items from the NAPLAN public demonstration website. You will notice that they are generally closed in nature and can be adapted for classroom use.

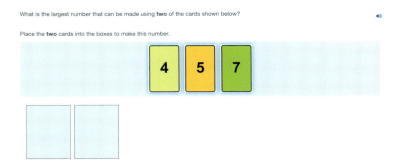

Figure 10.6 NAPLAN Drag and drop place value item
Source: NAPLAN public demonstration site, Year 5 Numeracy <www.nap.edu.au/naplan/public-demonstration-site>

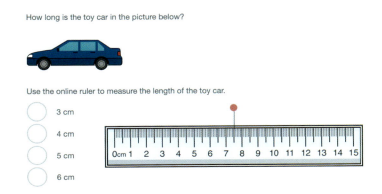

Figure 10.7 NAPLAN Measurement item showing online ruler
Source: NAPLAN public demonstration site, Year 5 Numeracy <www.nap.edu.au/naplan/public-demonstration-site>

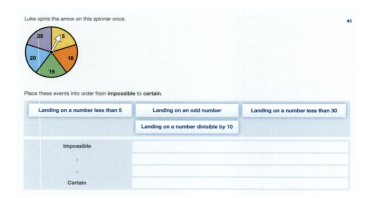

Figure 10.8 NAPLAN Drag and drop Probability item
Source: NAPLAN public demonstration site, Year 7 Numeracy <www.nap.edu.au/naplan/public-demonstration-site>

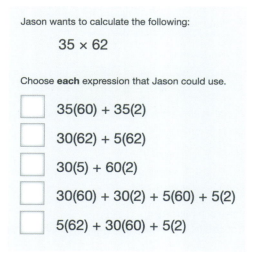

Figure 10.9 NAPLAN Addition item with multiple possible correct responses
Source: NAPLAN public demonstration site, Year 9 Numeracy <www.nap.edu.au/naplan/public-demonstration-site>

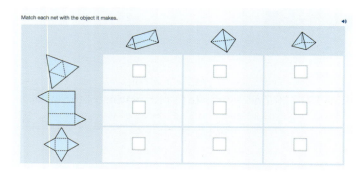

Figure 10.10 NAPLAN Geometry item
Source: NAPLAN public demonstration site, Year 5 Numeracy <www.nap.edu.au/naplan/public-demonstration-site>

Some practical strategies for developing numeracy concepts, without drilling students through NAPLAN question types, include open-ended items for exploration and providing opportunities for assessment for learning across all strands of the syllabus. This builds on the work of Sullivan and Lilburn (2004), who have developed an extensive collection of open-ended items that can be used in the mathematics classroom across all primary year levels. Examples of open-ended questions are:

- The area of the rectangle is 36 cm^2. What could the dimensions be?
- Draw as many different nets for a cube as you can.
- Provide the students with a graph which has no labels or titles. What could the graph represent?

A simple strategy for creating open-ended items provided by Sullivan and Lilburn (2004) is to take a closed question, write the answer and construct a question that uses the answer in it. For example, instead of asking the students to find the area of a rectangle with certain dimensions, give them the answer and ask them to find the dimensions (as in the first dot point example above). Another strategy involves taking a standard question and opening it up to have multiple answers (as in the third dot point example above). This strategy would also be useful in the context of opening up the multiple-choice assessment items included in the Progressive Achievement Tests, which are suitable for multiple year levels (Years 3 to 10) to assess student progress in the content areas of number knowledge, number strategies, algebra, geometry and measurement, and statistics.

Link 10.3 NZCER: Progressive Achievement Tests (PATs)

ACTIVITY 10.3

Take each of the closed sample NAPLAN items in Figures 10.6–10.10 and create an open-ended item to be used as an assessment item targeting the same concepts. You might like to match the concept covered with the appropriate outcome/s in your relevant syllabus.

The online Assessment Resource Centre provides a wealth of assessment for learning tasks that cover many of the primary topics. These are designed in a manner that is open to change to meet the interests of students in your class and the context of their community. The design of the items can also be adopted within different content areas. The discussion below and Activities 10.4–10.7 demonstrate the adaptation of the tasks.

ACTIVITY 10.4

Link 10.4 NSW Education Standards Authority: Spotty Octopus

Assessment task: Spotty Octopus

This NSW Education Standards Authority activity is based on a scenario presented to the students. It is centred around an octopus with eight legs, 16 spots and the same number of spots on each leg. The children are asked to draw a picture to solve their problem and record their answer.

Consider adaptions that could be made to the context of this question:

1. Could you use something else instead of an octopus?
2. How could you have different students doing the same structured task but at different levels?
3. Is there a way you could have some students working on a response that involves groups of three, or a larger number in the total collection to be divided?

ACTIVITY 10.5

Link 10.5 NSW Education Standards Authority: Halves

Assessment task: Halves

In this NSW Education Standards Authority task, students are asked to make a ball with any available modelling materials that can be moulded by hand. Roll the material out, make a shape, then cut the shape in half. The important component of the task is that the students are asked to reflect on how they created a half and whether the shape they made first is actually cut in half.

1. What materials could you use if modelling materials such as play dough are not available?
2. As the children's understanding of fractions progresses, what fraction concepts could be targeted when adapting this activity?
3. How could you adapt this assessment task using an online geoboard app, such as the iPhone, iPad and web app developed by the Math Learning Center?

ACTIVITY 10.6

Link 10.6 NSW Education Standards Authority: Making Number Patterns

Assessment task: Making Number Patterns

This NSW Education Standards Authority activity is described as targeting lower primary patterns and algebra; however, the structure of the assessment task could be used in the context of number patterns on the decade, off the decade, counting up or down by any number, using fraction and decimal notations of various complexities, or even algebraic patterns in the secondary context.

It is important to bear in mind that a good assessment for learning task fits seamlessly into the teaching and learning sequence. The sequence is described on the website as follows:

- Students make a number pattern that increases or decreases.
- They explain their number pattern in words and record this explanation in writing.
- Students continue their number pattern.

They then create another number pattern that has a particular number in it – for example, 10.

In the last step of the sequence, what elements could you ask the students to include in their number pattern at various stages of development?

ACTIVITY 10.7

Assessment task: What could the question be?

This NSW Education Standards Authority assessment task is applicable to many concepts in mathematics. It is often described as providing the students with a scenario – such as, 'The answer is 16. What could the question be?' Students are asked to record as many questions or word problems as possible.

Link 10.7 NSW Education Standards Authority: What could the question be?

CLASSROOM SNAPSHOT 10.6

Miss Mack began a unit on chance by playing a class game of Snakes and Ladders, then asked the students to respond to a scenario in their journals. The scenario was, 'Do you think it is harder to throw a 6 or a 4 on a die?' Two of the students' responses are shown in Figures 10.11 and 10.12.

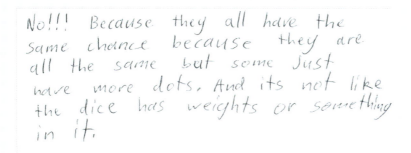

Figure 10.11 Chance student sample 1

Figure 10.12 Chance student sample 2

PAUSE AND REFLECT

Carefully consider the two responses to the task in Classroom Snapshot 10.6. What do the responses tell you about the students' understanding in relation to this task?

How would you describe the quality of the students' responses? In the light of these two answers, what chance activities would you design to follow on with?

It is possible to source stimulus items from a wide range of technological tools and use these to create an interesting investigative assessment task. For example, in a student investigation of fish growth, students compared genetically enhanced fish with non-genetically enhanced fish. The students were required to display data appropriately using TinkerPlots software, and to make generalisations based on what they had identified. The students were also required to justify their answers.

Designing assessment items for different levels of complexity

The structure of building the complexity of a task through a series of connected items was explored by Collis and Romberg (1991), who produced a selection of super items in an attempt to design assessment items that addressed issues concerning open and closed questions. The tasks contain a stem with four questions specifically targeting the levels described in increasing order of conceptual difficulty. While each of the questions may be answered independently, it is expected that a correct response to a higher-level question would be achieved after the successful completion of the earlier responses. For example:

Item A: What are the dimensions of the shape below?

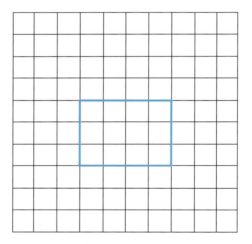

Figure 10.13 First in thread measurement Item A

Item B: What is the perimeter and area of this shape?
Item C: A rectangle has an area of 64 m². What could the dimensions be? Think about all the possibilities.
Item D: Emily stated that all rectangles with a perimeter of 20 cm have the same area. Is she correct? Why?

Assessment as learning

Assessment as learning the use of assessment information by teachers and students to guide curriculum planning that influences future student learning

The notion of assessment as learning was flagged at the beginning of the chapter, and, like assessment of and for learning, **assessment as learning** should be an element of all assessment processes. Statutory educational bodies such as the Queensland Curriculum and Assessment Authority provide practical suggestions for scaffolding assessment as learning strategies in the mathematics classroom. They particularly target ways to develop confidence in students so they will actively become involved in the development of learning goals. These include:

- learning logs or learning journals
- 60 seconds to think about how your learning is going so far
- concept maps identifying areas requiring further exploration.

Link 10.8 Queensland Curriculum and Assessment Authority: P–10 Mathematics

Conclusion

In reading this chapter and completing the activity tasks, you will have explored the importance of seamlessly integrating assessment tasks into the teaching and learning sequence. You may have also noticed that it is often not possible to place assessment for learning and assessment of learning tasks into two separate baskets. It is how the teacher designs the task, presents the task and communicates the feedback that makes all the difference. The activities in this chapter demonstrate that it is possible to adhere to assessment for learning as an underlying philosophy, thus demonstrating to many education systems that it is possible to have a valid assessment system without external national testing. We have explored NAPLAN items and communication of results, and also considered cautiously how we allocate time for familiarisation with such tasks in the classroom without practising items to the extent that test anxiety is evident. In fact, we can use these items to our advantage by considering opening them up and aiming for a deeper understanding of the underlying concepts. A theoretical framework has been introduced from which we can analyse students' responses and design follow-up activities at an appropriate level. Various technological sources of assessment stimuli have also been explored.

GUIDED STUDENT TASKS

1. There are many mathematics student workbooks for every level in the primary context. You will find many examples in schools, local libraries and online. Choose a topic, find the appropriate page/s and code the tasks as open or closed. Choose a closed task and turn it into an open-ended task. Are you able to design a practical investigative task to explore the same concept?
2. Imagine you are planning to teach a unit on transformations to a Year 5 class. What activities can you design that would assist the students in developing their interpretation and decoding skills when completing assessment items, such as NAPLAN, in the online mode.
3. Put yourself in the situation where you have decided to use a mathematics learning journal as an assessment strategy with a Year 3 class. Design three stimulus activities that act as catalysts to get the students to record their learning in rich ways.
4. Design an assessment for learning task that uses arrays to elicit what students know about multiplication concepts. Start by finding the appropriate outcomes in your relevant syllabus.

5. Some of the parents of the children in your class may be more comfortable with seeing a numerical grade on their report rather than a qualitative comment concerning their child's achievement. How will you use student work samples in the parent–teacher interview situation to discuss their child's learning? How will you communicate the validity of work samples to show where students are at in their learning of mathematics?

FURTHER READING

Flewelling, G, Lind, J & Sauer, R 2013, *Rich learning tasks in measurement and geometry for primary students*, Australian Association of Mathematics Teachers.

Serow, P, Callingham, R & Tout, D 2016, 'Assessment of mathematics learning: What are we doing?' in K Makar, S Dole, J Visnovska, M Goos, A Bennison & K Fry (eds), *Research in Mathematics Education in Australasia 2012–2015*, Singapore: Springer, pp. 235–54.

Sinclair, N & Bruce, CD 2015, 'New opportunities in geometry education at the primary school', *ZDM: The International Journal on Mathematics Education*, vol. 47, no. 3, pp. 319–29.

Swan, P 2013, *Geoboard gems*, A–Z Type.

Websites for exploration

PLANNING FOR MATHEMATICS TEACHING IN THE 21ST CENTURY CLASSROOM

CHAPTER 11

LEARNING OUTCOMES

By the end of this chapter, you will:

- be able to identify practices to consider when planning mathematics lessons
- be able to consider the role that digital technologies play in the 21st century classroom
- begin to develop strategies for planning effective mathematics lessons.

Introduction

This chapter begins with an overview of the key components of lesson planning and what this looks like in the context of a mathematics lesson. We consider approaches to planning that focus on developing a sound conceptual understanding of important mathematical concepts. We then look at how the use of technology can be planned for and capitalised on to support students' learning, including in an online environment, and within the context of a 21st century classroom. The latter part of the chapter uses classroom snapshots and case studies to show how mathematical skills, knowledge and understanding can be developed through the use of inquiry over a series of lessons.

Planning considerations

While we acknowledge that there is no 'recipe' for planning an effective mathematics lesson, we do believe that there are a number of components and considerations that should be taken into account. Lesson plans for teaching mathematics should include clear intended learning outcomes that focus on important mathematical concepts, links with the Australian Curriculum content descriptors, key questions and experiences, and opportunities for assessment. In addition, we also recommend that you anticipate student responses and/or difficulties that they are likely to encounter, and how you will differentiate the learning to accommodate a range of interests and abilities. Lesson sequences typically consist of three phases:

1. An introductory phase involving the whole class which can include revision, discussion, and introduction to new content
2. An exploratory or working phase where students may work independently, in pairs or small groups on set tasks

3. A summary or reflection phase where the whole class is involved in sharing and reflecting on the learning that has occurred.

Implementing challenging tasks
The three-phase model

Sullivan and colleagues (2015) recommended that teachers involved in the Encouraging Persistence, Maintaining Challenge project, adopted a lesson structure that was similar to the above, but required the teacher to provide little or no instructions. The three-phase model used in the project was as follows:

1. *The launch phase*: Students are given a task to read quietly with the expectation that they work individually on the task for at least 5 minutes.
2. *The explore phase*: Students continue to work on the task, but some clarification may now be given; enabling prompts, consolidating tasks and extending prompts can be utilised in this phase (see Classroom Snapshot 11.1).
3. *The summary phase*: The class regroups, and the teacher's role is to use the solutions, ideas and strategies of the students to highlight the important mathematical ideas in the task. It is useful in this phase to make use of a document camera or tablet to project student work onto an interactive whiteboard (IWB) (see Figure 11.1).

This three-phase model can happen a number of times in each lesson.

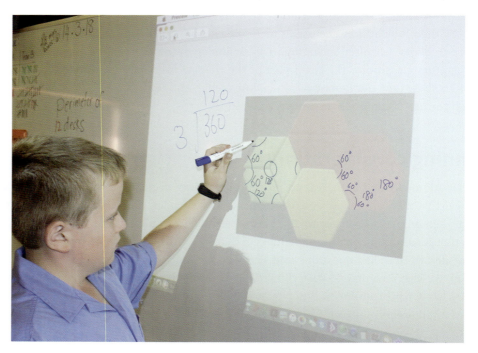

Figure 11.1 Student sharing of work projected onto IWB
Source: Courtesy of Sharyn Livy

CLASSROOM SNAPSHOT 11.1

Mrs Mitchell's Year 5 class were looking at the operations of addition and subtraction. Mrs Mitchell particularly wanted to encourage the use of mental computation and to focus students' attention on thinking flexibly about addition and subtraction, rather than applying the standard algorithm. The lesson was relevant to the content descriptor 'Use mathematical modelling to solve practical problems involving additive and multiplicative situations including financial contexts; formulate the problems, choosing operations and efficient calculation strategies, using digital tools where appropriate; interpret and communicate solutions in terms of the situation' (AC9M5N09).

The students were given individual copies of the following task:

> Show how to use a calculator with a broken '4' button to solve each of these problems:
>
> $341 + 276 =$
>
> $341 - 276 =$
>
> Give two different possibilities for each one.

After introducing the task to the students, Mrs Mitchell explained the notion of a calculator with one button broken and showed them an old calculator with one button taped over. She also explained that students could use any of the other buttons.

After the students had worked independently on the task for about 5 minutes, Mrs Mitchell noticed that one of the students, Sam, was having difficulty with getting started. She offered him an 'enabling prompt', which she had prepared earlier:

> I know that you can do the following equations in your head, but how could you do them on a calculator if the '4' button is broken?
>
> $4 + 7 \quad 4 - 2$

Students who had completed the initial task were given supplementary tasks to consolidate their learning, such as:

> How can you use a calculator with a broken '4' button to solve these problems?
>
> $441 + 246 \quad 441 - 254$

Extending prompts were also given to those students who easily completed the tasks:

> How would you use a calculator with broken '4' and '5' buttons to solve these problems?
>
> $541 + 245 \quad 451 - 254$
>
> Give two different possibilities for each one.
>
> How would you use a calculator with a broken '0' button to solve these problems?
>
> $507 + 320 \quad 2058 - 608$
>
> Give two different possibilities for each one.

After students had worked on the tasks for approximately 40 minutes, Mrs Mitchell assembled the students and seated them in front of the IWB.

Some students were selected to share their solution strategies, which were projected on the IWB for all the class to see. During the sharing, Mrs Mitchell encouraged the students to not only share their strategies, but also to justify their solutions and comment on each other's strategies.

Source: Adapted from Sullivan 2018

> **PAUSE AND REFLECT**
>
> How does this approach of differentiating the learning contrast with other ways that you may have seen used in the classroom? Why do you think teachers should encourage students to 'struggle' with the tasks prior to assisting them?

The 5 practices

Another approach that we recommend, and one that fits in nicely with the three-phase model, is the use of **5 practices** for orchestrating productive classroom discussions (Smith & Stein 2011). The five practices were designed to enable students' responses to advance the mathematical learning of the class as a whole, rather than just a sharing of ideas. The five practices are:

1. *Anticipating* likely responses to challenging mathematical tasks
2. *Monitoring* students' actual responses to the tasks (while students work on the tasks)
3. *Selecting* particular students to present their mathematical work during the whole-class discussions
4. *Sequencing* the student responses that will be displayed in a specific order
5. *Connecting* the different students' responses and connecting the responses to key mathematical ideas. (Smith & Stein 2011, p. 8)

> **5 practices** an approach to planning and teaching that involves: anticipating, monitoring, selecting, sequencing and connecting (Smith & Stein 2011)

The 5 practices approach relates to the three-phase model in a number of ways. Prior to implementing the task, the teacher should personally undertake the task and think about the responses that students are likely to produce. When the students are working on the task, the teacher's role is to monitor the students' progress and assist when required (e.g. when Mrs Mitchell gave Sam an enabling prompt). During this monitoring phase, the teacher needs to pay close attention to students' mathematical thinking and solution strategies, so that particular students' work can then be selected and shared with the class. The selection of particular work samples is guided by the mathematical goal for the lesson and the teacher's assessment of how each solution will contribute to that goal (Smith & Stein 2011). Once the work samples have been selected, the teacher needs to decide on how to sequence the students' presentations. This purposeful choice capitalises on the mathematical opportunities offered in the lesson and varies according to the teacher's goals. For example, the teacher might want to highlight the strategy that was used by the majority of the class, or to begin with a less sophisticated strategy before discussing more complex solutions. Finally, the teacher helps students to make connections between their solutions and those of other students as well as between the different areas of mathematics. Rather than discretely sharing solutions or presentations, the goal is to have student presentations build on one another to develop powerful mathematical ideas (Smith & Stein 2011).

ACTIVITY 11.1

Consider the following five work samples in Figure 11.2 that were selected by a teacher in the monitoring phase of the lesson in response to the following question:

I had a full box of chocolates, but someone ate some of the chocolates.

The box now looks like this.

How can I work out the number of chocolates I started with?

(a)   (b)

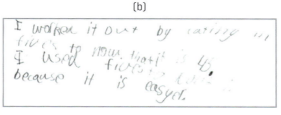

(c)   (d)

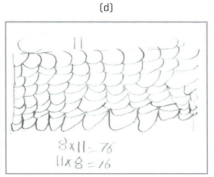

(e)

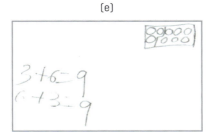

Figure 11.2 Work samples selected from the monitoring stage a–e
Source: Courtesy of Sharyn Livy

▶▶ In which sequence would you recommend that the teacher share the solutions with the class? Can you justify the reasons for your choice? (For further reading on this task, and to see how a group of pre-service teachers sequenced the students' responses, see Livy, Muir & Downton 2017).

Teaching practices that facilitate thinking

Based on extensive research conducted in 40 classrooms, Liljedahl (2021) identified that while students may appear to be 'engaged' in their mathematics lessons, there was not a lot of evidence of mathematical thinking occurring in many of the classrooms he observed. In order to address this, he identified 14 optimal practices for thinking:

1. What types of tasks we use
2. How we form collaborative groups
3. Where students work
4. How we arrange the furniture
5. How we answer questions
6. When, where, and how tasks are given
7. What homework looks like
8. How we foster student autonomy
9. How we use hints and extensions
10. How we consolidate a lesson
11. How students take notes
12. How we choose to evaluate
13. How we use formative assessment
14. How we grade.

Some, or all, of these practices can be incorporated or adapted when teaching mathematics using challenging tasks. See Classroom Snapshot 11.2 for an illustration of this.

CLASSROOM SNAPSHOT 11.2

Mrs Smith often used challenging tasks with her Year 3 class, but today she decided to introduce her students to the practices of forming collaborative groups and changing where students work. She provided the following challenging task to the class:

My dog is half my age. How old might I be and how old might my dog be?

Students were to work in groups of three to solve the task. To form the groups, Mrs Smith randomly dealt out a playing card to each student. There were three of each card. Students were required to find other students who had the same number card as they did and sit down when they had found their group (see Figure 11.3).

Placed around the room on vertical surfaces, such as the walls and windows, were seven or eight pieces of A3 paper (see Figure 11.4), with the problem written on it. Groups of three students chose an area to work in and began to solve the problem. One student had the pen and was the initial recorder, with the 'rule' being that they could only record the answers from other group members, not write their own ideas. After about 5–10 minutes, the pen was passed to another group member.

Figure 11.3 Random group allocation using playing cards

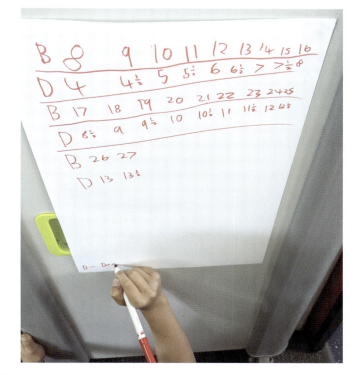

Figure 11.4 Collaborative problem solving using a vertical surface

▶▶

> After everyone had a turn with writing some possible solutions to the task, Mrs Smith invited the groups to do a 'gallery walk' and look at other groups' solutions. The class were then called back to the mat where group solutions were shared and discussed. Mrs Smith used the opportunity to make connections with the mathematics as per the 5 practices.

Preparing your lesson

Now that you have been acquainted with some guiding principles and research-informed teaching approaches, it is time to consider how to prepare your lesson plan. As mentioned previously, there is no one right way to conduct a mathematics lesson or a planning proforma that is universally accepted. However, there are some general principles that we recommend be taken into account when planning a mathematics lesson. First consider your learning goals or intentions. Every lesson should have a mathematical focus that is relevant and addresses the question: 'What should my students be able to do by the end of the lesson?' The Australian Curriculum: Mathematics v. 9.0 should guide the selection of the mathematics to be taught for any given year level. While it may be tempting to select a fun game or activity and base your lesson around that, the focus should be on developing an understanding of key mathematical concepts. Identify the key mathematical concept, then select appropriate activities, experiences and approaches that are likely to develop an understanding of that topic. We recommend the following considerations when planning mathematics lessons:

- Frame the learning intentions/objectives around the important mathematical concepts that you want students to know and understand by the end of the lesson
- Link the lesson to the Australian Curriculum: Mathematics v. 9.0 to ensure the mathematics to be taught is appropriate for the year level. In addition to the content descriptor/s, also consider how mathematical proficiency can be embedded and whether links can be made with cross-curriculum priorities and general capabilities.
- Anticipate likely difficulties or misunderstandings students may have with the concept. This will enable you to explicitly address common misunderstandings and respond effectively when misunderstandings arise, rather than being unprepared and having to respond on the spot
- Think about and document the structure and sequence of the lesson. This will assist with timing of the lesson, allow you to scaffold the learning for students and consider the logistics and organisational aspects to ensure the lesson runs smoothly. You should also consider the key questions that you could ask prior to, during and after the lesson. Key questions can help to gauge, monitor and assess students' understanding.
- Identify the resources that will be required to implement the lesson. Are the resources readily available? Do the resources need adapting for online delivery? Can digital resources be used to consolidate or extend students' understanding?
- Identify how you will determine the learning that has occurred. Think about opportunities for assessment. These might come from responses to your key questions,

completion of the lesson tasks and/or observations (see Chapter 10 for assessment guidelines and suggestions).
- Identify how you will differentiate the learning for the range of students in your classroom. Will you incorporate strategies such as enabling and extending prompts? (For more information on catering for diversity, see Chapter 12).

Teaching online

While teaching remotely or online is not a new phenomenon, the rapid shift to online teaching in schools that occurred as a result of COVID-19 restrictions, posed many challenges for teachers and students. Teachers whose mathematics classrooms were characterised by materials and hands-on approaches suddenly needed to adapt how they might represent ideas and concepts for teaching mathematics within the mediation afforded by the digital environment. In addition, as a result of lockdown, teaching staff were required to prepare and deliver their classes from home, with all the practical and technical challenges that this entailed (Hodges et al. 2020). Online learning and teaching approaches involve a diverse range of tools, resources, pedagogical approaches, roles and forms of interaction, monitoring and support (Rapantam et al. 2020) which can pose challenges for teachers whose Pedagogical Content Knowledge was developed through classroom teaching. Nevertheless, the rapid shift to online teaching also provided opportunities, resulting in an enhanced use of digital technologies to engage learners. The use of platforms such as Zoom, Microsoft Teams and Google Classroom was popular in primary and secondary schools as they provided a virtual classroom where synchronous interaction could occur between the teacher and students.

Within the platforms, the use of break-out rooms were also utilised and allowed for small group interaction. Tools such as Jamboard and Padlet could be used to complement breakout sessions, provide for brainstorming and publicly display students' work and contributions. Classroom Snapshot 11.3 shows how Padlet and Jamboard could be utilised to engage students in number talk and mathematical inquiry.

CLASSROOM SNAPSHOT 11.3

Every morning during lockdown, Ms Wong would meet with her Year 5 class at 11.00 am via Zoom for their daily mathematics lesson. Each lesson would typically begin with a 15–20 minute warm-up activity. Today the students were participating in a Number Talk where they were sharing their responses to the challenge: 'Do the following in your head 25 + 89.' Earlier Ms Wong had provided a link to a Padlet where the students could post their responses, along with their working out. She could then share her screen and display everyone's responses (see Figure 11.5). Students were called upon to explain their answers or comment on others' responses.

On another occasion, capitalising on students' home environments, Ms Wong asked students to take a photo at home that made them think of mathematics. They then posted the photo to a Padlet, together with a question or task for other students to attempt. Figure 11.6 shows an example of a photo and question that were posted. These inquiry-based prompts led to small group investigations, which culminated in reporting back to the whole class via PowerPoint presentations shared via Zoom.

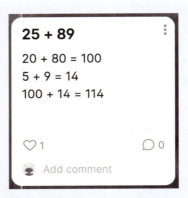

Figure 11.5 Screenshot showing an example response to 25 + 89

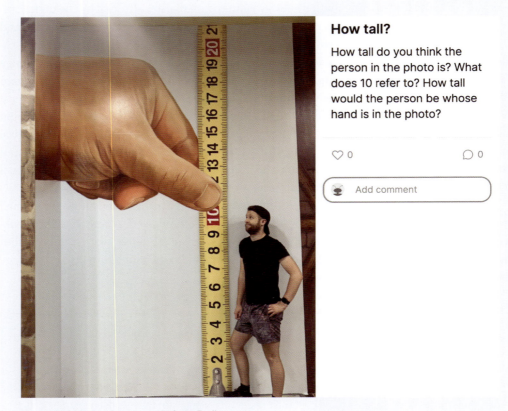

Figure 11.6 Maths shot example from Padlet

A focus on shape required the students to sort objects, such as cylinders, prisms, and pyramids, into groups. As students were learning from home, the usual access to real materials found in mathematics classrooms was not possible. It was also not reasonable to expect all students had access to the shapes at home. To cater for this, Ms Wong placed the students in Zoom breakout rooms to simulate group work, provided links to virtual online objects, and used Jamboard to record students' responses to the task (see Figure 11.7). Through completing the task using Jamboards and accessing virtual online objects, the students were able to post numerous possible solutions that did not rely on them having access to the real objects.

Figure 11.7 Shape task completed using Jamboard
Source: Jamboard

PAUSE AND REFLECT

Think of a mathematics lesson that you either taught or observed being taught in a primary classroom. Imagine that you had to adapt that lesson to teach online. What tools would you utilise? How would you adapt your pedagogical approaches? How would you ensure the participation of all students? Do you think your lesson would be as effective when taught online as compared to face to face? Why/why not?

Adapting games to the online environment

Games are often viewed as an effective way of engaging students in mathematics. Games can promote positive learning environments, enhance student motivation and generate mathematical discussion (Bragg 2006). Russo and colleagues (2018) highlight five principles of educationally rich mathematical games:

Principle 1: Students are engaged
- Mathematical games should be engaging, enjoyable and generate mathematical discussion.

Principle 2: Skill vs luck
- Mathematical games should appropriately balance skill and luck.

Principle 3: Mathematics is central
- Exploring important mathematical concepts and practicing important skills should be central to game strategy and gameplay.

Principle 4: Flexibility for learning and teaching
- Mathematical games should be easily differentiated to cater for a variety of learners, and modifiable to cater to a variety of concepts.

Principle 5: Home–school connections
- Mathematical games should provide opportunities for fostering home–school connections.

Many educational and mathematically focused games require resources, such as dice and counters, and interaction between participants. It is possible, however, for online learners to interact and participate in games, in similar ways to their in-class counterparts. Greedy Pig and The King's Tax are two games that meet the principles of educationally rich games. Below we describe how to play these games, with consideration being given to online delivery.

Greedy Pig

You will need: A die, individual paper for recording scores
Aim: To be the person with the highest score at the end of the game
How to play:
- All students stand.
- Teacher rolls the die and students add up the score. They remain standing until they want to save their total. They then sit down, retaining and recording their score.
- If a 1 is rolled and they are still standing, they receive 0 for that round.
- A new round begins once a 1 has been rolled or when everyone is sitting down.

Link 11.1 Free Online Dice
Link 11.2 Transum: Dice and Spinners
Link 11.3 Transum: Skunk

The classroom version of Greedy Pig can easily be adapted to the online environment. Using a platform, such as Zoom, turning on and off individual cameras achieves the same purpose as standing up or sitting down in the classroom. An online virtual die can be used to replace an actual die, as well as coins and spinners. A nice variation of Greedy Pig is Skunk by Transum.

The King's Tax

Figure 11.8 shows the instructions for The King's Tax as provided to students in a synchronous Zoom session.

The King's Tax

What you need
- Deck of cards (online here)
- Pen and Paper
- 2 players or a whole class!

How to Play
→ This is an adaptation of the classic probability game Greedy Pig. Instead of using dice, it uses cards. This means the probabilities change constantly, based on what cards have been turned over.
→ Begin by shuffling the deck.
→ One card is turned over. That is the amount of money each player has 'earned'. For example, a 7 is turned over, so each player has $7. After each card is revealed, players must decide if they are staying in or 'banking' their money (**they indicate this by turning off their camera**). Once you're out of a round, you can't return.
→ For those who stay in, they can add the value of the next card to their earnings for the round. For example, if a 4 is turned over next they are now on $7 + $4 = $11. They must choose to stay in or 'bank'.
→ If a **KING** is turned over, **he collects his tax**. Players who are still in get nothing for that round.
→ If a **QUEEN** is turned over, players who are still in DOUBLE their score for the current round.
→ If a **JACK** is turned over, players get a $15 bonus.

★ The winner is the player who has the most money once all four kings are revealed.

VIDEO OF THE GAME HERE

Figure 11.8 The King's Tax game
Source: Courtesy of Sharyn Livy

Similar to Greedy Pig, the game can be used to teach probability concepts and encourages mental computation. The cards provide for more possibilities to occur. In the classroom, real playing cards can be used, with students sitting down when they want to bank their money. Virtual decks of cards are a great resource for when cards are not readily available or accessible.

Link 11.4 'The King's Tax Maths Game'
Link 11.5 Deck of Cards

PAUSE AND REFLECT

In what ways do both games meet any, or all, of the 5 principles of educationally rich mathematical games?

What other games can you think of that are popular in the classroom? How would you adapt these games to play online?

Are there any games that would not easily transfer to the online environment? What is it about these games that make them unsuitable?

The first part of this chapter looked at considerations required when planning mathematics lessons. We looked at lesson structure and how to adapt lessons to online delivery – a reality that primary and secondary school teachers were faced with due to COVID-19. The next part of this chapter looks at a particular mathematics topic (place value) and demonstrates how a teacher (Mrs Knight) incorporated a range of activities and experiences to develop an understanding of place value with her Year 1 class. We then provide an example of an integrated unit of work to demonstrate how lesson planning can be sequenced to develop an understanding of statistics and probability.

Developing an understanding of place value

Developing an understanding of place value and the base-10 number system is a focus in early childhood and primary classrooms, with students in Year 1, for example, expected to 'recognise, represent and order numbers to at least 120 using physical and virtual materials, numerals, number lines and charts (AC9M1N01))'. Classroom Snapshot 11.4 describes how Mrs Knight uses a variety of classroom routines, planned activities and ICT to develop a conceptual understanding of place value in her Year 1 class.

CLASSROOM SNAPSHOT 11.4

The students in Mrs Knight's class look forward each day to recording how many days they have spent in school for the year. The days are recorded in a place value chart at the front of the classroom, with icy-pole or bundling sticks used to represent each day. When 10 days are reached, these are bundled into 10; when 100 days are reached, the bundles of 10 are bundled into 100. Each day the total is recorded symbolically, and a discussion based around the numbers is held.

Another daily routine involves the use of the hundreds chart. Each day, an interactive hundreds board is displayed on the IWB. Mrs Knight uses a variety of daily activities to focus attention on the base-10 number system. For example, on Tuesdays, students play a cover-up game where they have to identify the hidden number on the chart by using the numbers surrounding it as clues (see Figure 11.9).

1	2	3	4	5	6	7	8	9	10
11	12	13	14	15	16	17	18	19	20
21	22	23	24	25	26	27	28	29	30
31	32	33	34	35	36	37	38	39	40
41	42	43	■	45	46	47	48	49	50
51	52	53	54	55	56	57	58	59	60
61	62	63	64	65	66	67	68	69	70
71	72	73	74	75	76	77	78	79	80
81	82	83	84	85	86	87	88	89	90
91	92	93	94	95	96	97	98	99	100

Figure 11.9 Hundreds chart with covered number

Students are expected to explain how they identified the hidden number using place value terminology; for example, 'I know that number 44 is hidden because the number before is 43, the number after is 1 more than 44, 45, and the number 10 below it is 34 and the number 10 above it is 54.' Through using the cut and paste function in Microsoft Word, Mrs Knight can prepare a number of different versions, producing different numbers each day.

HOTmaths has a widget called Hundred Grid that can be used in the same way (see Figure 11.10).

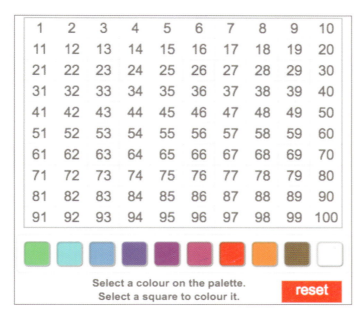

Figure 11.10 Screenshot of HOTmaths Hundred Grid widget

Number Lineup

Mrs Knight also makes regular use of games to teach place value concepts and to encourage students to work with partners or in small groups. The following game, sourced from Mathwire (Kawas n.d.), encourages students to think about how the relative value of a digit changes, depending on its placement.

Link 11.6 Mathwire: Place Value Activities

Materials

- Deck of digit cards for each set of partners (2–4 each of 0–9, depending on the level of students and the size of the numbers they will create). *Note:* Spinners with 0–9 may be used instead of cards, if desired.
- Place value mat for each player.
- Recording sheet, if desired.

Directions

- Partner A turns over the first card and decides where to place that card on their place value mat. Once the card is placed, it may not be moved.
- Partner B turns over a card and decides where to place that card on their place value mat. Again, the card may not be moved once it is placed.
- Play continues, with each partner turning over a card and deciding where to place it on their place value mat in the hope of building the largest number.

- When all slots are filled on the place value mats, partners compare numbers to see who created the larger number. That partner wins a point for the round.
- Partners record both numbers on their recording sheet and circle the larger number.
- Students clear their mats, shuffle the cards and play additional rounds, as time allows.

Variations

Students try to form numbers to meet specified criteria (which will vary from these suggestions, based on the number of digits used):

- Students try to form the smallest number.
- Students try to form a number that is closest to 500 (or 2000 or …).
- Students try to form a number that is less than 1000.
- Students form numbers and earn a different number of points, depending on the range within which the number falls (one point for numbers from 0–500, two points for numbers from 501–1000, etc.)

The interactive game Top-it from Everyday Mathematics reinforces this concept and players can challenge the computer to form the smallest five-digit number. Interestingly, the winner is the player with the smallest number, rather than the one with the largest number.

Nasty Games

Nasty Games is another favourite of Mrs Knight's class. In this game, students use dice to form three-digit numbers, with the twist being that they can place each rolled digit in any player's space (see Figure 11.11 for the game sheet).

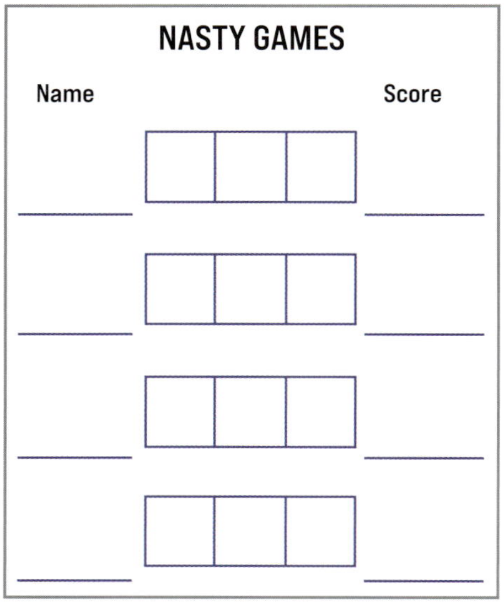

Figure 11.11 Nasty Games game sheet

It is an ideal game to play in small groups, and Mrs Knight often begins these sessions by projecting the game board on the IWB and selecting five students to play against each other while the rest of the class watches and offers suggestions. The whole-class focus allows discussion to occur around 'strategies' and the relative value of the digits. Students can then play the game in small groups and keep a tally of their scores.

> ### PAUSE AND REFLECT
>
> The example provided in Classroom Snapshot 11.2 and the examples of Number Lineup and Nasty Games were designed to provide students with opportunities to engage in exploring the key ideas associated with the place-value system. Think about how you would adapt these activities if all your students were online and attending the lesson virtually.

Planning for an integrated unit

The following case study about the teacher, James, provides an overview of one approach to developing mathematics skills, knowledge and understanding through an integrated unit. It includes a teaching sequence that develops understanding of statistics and probability, in which the use of technology in various ways is integral to the teaching. James, the teacher, particularly wants to incorporate technology because the school is emphasising technology use across all grades because of NAPLAN online.

James has a Year 5/6 class of 23 students in a country school. He decides that he wants to address the content description of statistics using a large data set from an outside source to broaden the students' experience. He goes to the Census at School New Zealand website to find a data set that provides information about students in four countries: Australia, New Zealand, the United Kingdom and Canada. He downloads this as an Excel file. Looking at the data set, and the other resources available on the websites, James realises that an integrated unit will also address the geography learning area and aspects of literacy.

Although the Census at School data set is in a spreadsheet format, James decides that his class is not sufficiently fluent in the use of Excel to be able to use it efficiently. Instead, he imports the dataset into **CODAP (Common Online Data Analysis Platform)** that has been designed for children from middle primary onwards to analyse data in an investigative environment. This specialised educational software allows children to 'drag and drop' variables onto a graph and to sort groups into categories. James creates a new file from the Census at School data. This file provides 300 cases including data about the importance of reducing pollution, saving water and ways in which children travel to school. He wants the students to pose their own **inquiry** questions, then conduct the investigation and write a report. Prior to starting the sequence of lessons, he ensures that a copy of the datafile is available in each child's online folder, and that they can find and access the CODAP site on their tablets.

CODAP (Common Online Data Analysis Platform) dynamic data software that aims to develop students' understanding of data, number, probability and graphs

Inquiry a teaching approach which investigates open-ended questions that reflect real-life problems

Lesson 1

Objectives

Lesson objectives are:

- familiarisation with the Census at School data
- the use of inquiry questions that the children will explore
- the effective use of digital technologies.

James shows the children the Census at School data set in CODAP using the IWB. He discusses the types of information provided by the file, focusing on the nature of each attribute and the units. The children are particularly interested in the travel time to school, and he promises that they will look at this in more detail later.

He then turns to a page on which he has prepared some guiding questions for the children to explore the data set for themselves (see below). Working in pairs, the children open the CODAP file (see Figure 11.12) from their tablets and work through the guiding questions. James moves around the room helping children who are having problems with the software and encouraging students to share their findings, and their ways of going about answering the questions, with the neighbouring group.

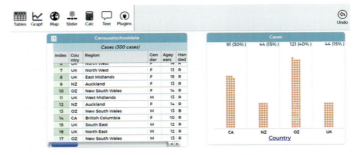

Figure 11.12 CODAP display showing the countries in the Census at School dataset
Source: The Concord Consortium, © 2018

Guiding questions

1. How many countries are there in the data set and what are their names?
2. Which student is the tallest in the data set and how tall is this student?
3. How many male and how many female students are there? What percentage of the whole group is female?
4. How many male students and how many female students are from Canada?
5. Find two new interesting facts about the students in this data set and write these into your report using the text tool.

As the children work at answering these questions, James moves around the room helping individuals with the technology where needed and making suggestions about efficient ways to find the answers to the questions. At the end of the lesson, the children report back the interesting facts they have found and save their files to their own folders. James promises the children that they may continue to work on their investigations during free-choice time – unstructured time when the children have some control over what they work on.

Lesson 2
Objectives
Lesson objectives are:

- communicate findings, using appropriate displays
- compare distributions visually.

In this lesson, James increases the difficulty of the tasks that he gives the children. He wants them to recognise differences between groups and to create data displays to compare two or more groups. He has deliberately chosen these kinds of activities to build on the children's previous work, and their emerging interest in the differences among the students from the four countries. In geography, the children have been researching information about students in the other countries, using a variety of internet resources. They have begun to create a portfolio of their own findings about the ways in which students in these other countries live. This work has increased their interest in the data set.

James uses a question-and-answer session to remind the children of their previous work and the stories they have researched in the meantime. The children work in small groups and open their own CODAP files to work on during the lesson. James puts a series of guiding questions on the IWB that will assist the children to construct data displays. The first guiding question repeats one from the last session, but also adds to the complexity by asking children to show this in different ways. As he moves around the room, he gives the children tips for improving their data displays.

Guiding questions

1. Find out how many male and how many female students are in each country. Show this information in two different ways.
2. Choose one of the 'Importance' variables. Find out two interesting facts about the students who answered this question. You might look at their age, where they come from, male and female differences, and so on. Display your findings so that someone else can understand them.
3. Compare the information that you have found with the information that another group has found. How is it the same? How is it different?

The children each create a short report of their findings and save this in their electronic portfolio.

Lessons 3 and 4
In these lessons, James decides to work on the measurement variables of height, foot length and so on.

Objectives
Lesson objectives are:

- to understand the difference between measurement (continuous) variables and discrete (categorical) variables
- to explore the relationships between two variables.

James does not expect his young class to develop a statistician's view of the types of variables or of the relationships between the variables. He knows that the children have intuitively started to try to summarise and compare variables, and he wants to help them do this in ways that are more systematic and statistically sound but do not confuse them. He also wants to see how well they can use the Data Detective PPDAC cycle (see Chapter 8) with a data set that they have not collected themselves.

Guiding questions

1. What is the smallest arm span?
2. What is the difference between the shortest and longest foot lengths?
3. Do children with the biggest feet have the longest arm span?
4. Write some 'I wonder ... ' questions about the data that you have, and find ways of answering one of these questions.
5. Write a report about similarities and differences among children in the four countries.

The children record their answers to these questions in their electronic portfolios.

Lessons 5 and 6

Before these lessons, James reviews the children's portfolios to check that they are all familiar with CODAP and have completed all the work to date. He wants to introduce the idea of average as a way of summarising the data. Although formal ideas of central tendency and spread of data are not expected until later in schooling, James recognises that having some background will be helpful to the children, and they have encountered the terms 'average', 'mean' and 'median' when looking at media reports.

Objectives

Lesson objectives are:

- to understand average as a way of summarising data
- to explore ideas about distribution of data
- to find the mean and median of a data set using technology rather than by computation.

James starts the lesson with a concrete example, using the IWB. He has created a number line with the numbers 0 to 5 equally spaced along it. He asks each child to come up and make a dot above the number that shows how many brothers and sisters they have. In this way, he creates a dot plot. Most children have one sibling and no children have five siblings. He asks the children to suggest a way of summarising the data. Ideas emerge, such as taking the most common number or using the middle number. James picks up the idea of the middle number. One child says it should be 3 because it is the middle of 0 to 5. Other children object because there are more children with one sibling and only one with four siblings.

James gradually leads the discussion to the idea of finding the data point that lies in the middle of all the data. By counting, the children establish that the middle point is 2. James explains that this is the median, and he brings up the Maths Dictionary website to help him discuss the meaning. He points out that ordering the data was done through the dot plot, and that the class counted to the middle. He then asks about other ways of summarising the data: 'Is there another kind of "middle"?'

One person says the word 'average'. James picks this up and describes this as a balance point. He demonstrates the idea using a number balance that he has borrowed from Year 1, moving the weights until they are at the middle and the balance is even. He then asks different children to come to the IWB and move the dots from the ends towards the middle, moving one place at a time. He ends up with a representation that looks similar to the one in Figure 11.13.

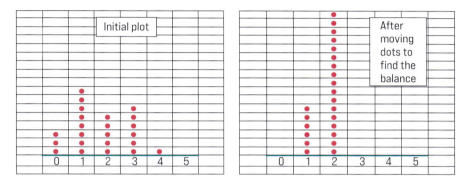

Figure 11.13 Representation of the number of siblings in James' class

He explains that the balance point is not a whole number, but lies between 1 and 2, and through questioning gets the children to recognise that it would be closer to 2. He chooses not to develop the computation aspect of the mean at this time, but he does tell the class that this average is called a mean.

The children then move to their CODAP files. They create a stacked dot plot of the age of the children in the data set. James asks them to describe the distribution of the data and to predict what the average might be. He collects their predictions on the IWB. He then shows the children where to find the median and mean in CODAP. He stresses that what the program is doing is very like what they have just seen from their class, but it is more accurate and also more hidden. The children then explore the ideas for a short time on their own. When James is happy that the groups can all create a plot and put in the median and mean, he poses some further guiding questions.

Guiding questions

1. Find the mean and median of the heights of all students.
2. Which country had the tallest students?

Lessons 7 and 8

James wants the last two lessons in this sequence to provide an opportunity for the children to consolidate what they have learned in mathematics. He sets up an investigation of the Census at School data, which they will present on a poster created in PowerPoint using a template that they have used before. The investigation is designed to complement the work they have also done in history.

Objectives

Lesson objectives are to:
- provide an opportunity for children to apply their new knowledge
- give children the opportunity to extend their understanding through an open task
- assess children's understanding of data representations.

James asks the children to continue to work in pairs, and then asks each pair to complete an investigation and prepare a poster for publication. He stresses that he will be looking for data representations through graphs, tables and the use of statistics such as means and medians, and interpretations of what they see referring to the information they have created. He reminds them of the work they have done and puts a summary page on the whiteboard of all they have explored. He also says that they can ask him to remind them about anything they may have forgotten how to do. He gives each child a printed sheet containing several guiding questions (shown below).

ACTIVITY 11.2

Investigation of the Census at School data

These questions are guiding questions only. You are free to explore the data in any way that you like but you must make sure that you use graphs, tables, a mean, a median, and make some comparisons between our country and at least one other country. Present your work on a poster using the PowerPoint template in the class folder. You have two mathematics sessions to complete this task.
- What is a typical student like?
- Investigate the students from one country (use a filter).
- Compare the students in our country with students in a different country.
- What can you say about the things that matter to students in our country? Are these the same things that matter to students in the United Kingdom?

TIPS FOR ONLINE TEACHING

This chapter has provided many examples of how classroom-based lessons can be adapted for online delivery. An important aspect teachers needed to consider when they were suddenly tasked with online teaching was to maintain the relationships they had built with their students. Synchronous Zoom and team meetings, often held first thing of a morning, helped students to maintain social connections with teachers and fellow students and enabled established routines to continue. The vast array of digital tools such as JamBoards and Padlets can provide for collaborative experiences and address feelings of isolation, which are often associated with online learning.

Conclusion

This chapter has provided some suggestions about how to plan for mathematics lessons, using contemporary practices that focus on engaging students and developing their mathematical understandings of important concepts. We have also looked at ways in which we can plan for and capitalise on ICT in the mathematics classroom, and how lessons can be adapted for online delivery. Through reading the chapter and completing the activities, you will have explored the role the teacher plays in planning for authentic mathematical experiences and what this looks like for one lesson and a sequence of lessons. The case study about James and his lessons has provided an example of how mathematics and ICT can be used in an integrated unit of work, and how digital technologies can be used to extend students' experiences.

GUIDED STUDENT TASKS

1. Write a challenging task of your own. Can you think of an enabling and extending prompt to support this task?
2. Select a content descriptor for a year level that you may teach in. Describe a lesson that you could take to address the mathematical learning relevant to the content descriptor. Think about how you could adapt the lesson to online delivery if required.
3. If you were conducting a similar lesson to James, what might you *anticipate* students might do? What would the students who are experiencing difficulty require, and what might the more capable students need?
4. Compare the use of concrete and virtual manipulatives where they have been used to teach similar concepts (e.g. 1–100 chart, tangrams). Identify the benefits and/or constraints of each model.

FURTHER READING

Liljedahl, P 2021, *Building thinking classrooms in mathematics, grades K–12*, 2nd edn, Thousand Oaks, CA: Corwin.

Livy, S, Muir, T & Downton, A 2017, 'Connecting pre-service teachers with contemporary mathematics practices: Selecting and sequencing students' work samples', *Australian Primary Mathematics Classroom*, vol. 22, no. 4, pp. 17–21.

Russo, J, Russo, T & Bragg, LA 2018, 'Five principles of educationally rich mathematical games', *Australian Primary Mathematics Classroom*, vol. 23, no. 3, pp. 30–4.

Smith, MS & Stein, MK 2011, *Five practices for orchestrating productive mathematics discussion*, Reston, VA: NCTM.

Sullivan, P, Askew, M, Cheeseman, J, Clarke, D, Mornane, A, Roche, A & Walker, N 2015, 'Supporting teachers in structuring mathematics lessons involving challenging tasks', *Journal of Mathematics Teacher Education*, vol. 18, no. 2, pp. 123–40.

Websites for exploration

CHAPTER 12

DIVERSITY IN THE PRIMARY MATHEMATICS CLASSROOM

LEARNING OUTCOMES

By the end of this chapter, you will:

- understand the complexity of primary mathematics classrooms
- be able to recognise a range of potential barriers to learning mathematics
- understand how the curriculum may be differentiated
- be able to plan for diversity in the mathematics classroom.

Introduction

Australian classrooms are becoming increasingly diverse. In addition to a wide range of mathematical abilities, primary teachers of mathematics must meet the needs of children from varied cultural backgrounds, many of whom have had different mathematical experiences. Children who have physical, intellectual, social or emotional difficulties may be included in the mainstream classroom. There may also be children who are classified as gifted and talented in one or more domains. All have the capacity to learn mathematics, and the right to experience mathematics suitable to their learning needs.

Although this chapter addresses issues relating to inclusion in primary mathematics classrooms, it does not pretend to provide a special education focus. The needs of children with specific disabilities can be highly technical, and it is well beyond the scope of this chapter to try to deal with all the detailed requirements and concerns that may be encountered. Rather, this chapter aims to help the primary teacher deal with the reality of mathematics teaching in modern classrooms, where there may be children with very diverse learning and mathematical needs. The ideas presented in this chapter will benefit all students. Many students are not categorised as having a disability but have information processing delays. These students will benefit from the same approaches as those with recognised disabilities. Teaching mathematics well is good for everyone.

Why is it important to recognise diversity?

A fundamental tenet of the Australian Curriculum v. 9.0 is that all learners should have access to the full mathematics curriculum, regardless of background (Commonwealth of Australia 2009). The rationale included in the Australian Curriculum: Mathematics v. 9.0 begins with the statement, 'Learning mathematics creates opportunities for and enriches the lives of all Australians.'

Australia has recognised the need for the curriculum to be adapted in some instances and offers advice and help to use the curriculum effectively to provide for the **diverse** needs of students – including those with a disability, gifted and talented students, and students for whom English is an additional language or dialect (EAL/D). The Australian Curriculum: Mathematics v. 9.0, in line with the overall curriculum structure, covers mathematics content, general capabilities (including literacy, numeracy, and personal and social capability) and cross-curriculum priorities, including Aboriginal and Torres Strait Islander cultures, Asia and engagement with Asia, and sustainability. The capabilities and cross-curriculum priorities can become the basis for age-appropriate adaptations to the mathematics content. Some approaches to achieving this goal are the focus of this chapter.

In the section 'Planning for Diversity' on the Australian Curriculum v. 9.0 website there are two key approaches to planning: using all three dimensions (cross-curriculum priorities, general capabilities and learning area content) and planning for individualised education programmes (IEPs).

Diversity the range of children in a particular classroom that includes low-incidence disabilities, diverse cultural groups, and social and emotional problems

ACTIVITY 12.1

Go to the Australian Curriculum v. 9.0 website and access the resources available regarding students with disabilities from the tab labelled Student diversity. Imagine that you have a Year 4 class that includes two students with an individualised education program, and several students who speak English as an additional language as well as Aboriginal students. Access the tab labelled Planning for student diversity. With specific reference to mathematics, consider how you can use the three dimensions of the Australian Curriculum v. 9.0 – cross-curriculum priorities, general capabilities, and mathematics learning area – to address the first list of dot points about how teachers can support students' diverse needs. Write one or two sentences about each dot point.

Then access the information about taking steps to personalise learning. Consider the four areas of CASE – Content (mathematics), Abilities, Standards and Evaluation – and think about how you might provide for students needing IEPs. Remember that these students are as much part of your Year 4 class as every other student and their needs should be met as far as possible in the mainstream classroom. Write one or two sentences about each aspect of CASE.

The aim of this activity is to familiarise you with the expectations of the Australian Curriculum v. 9.0, especially in mathematics.

The challenges posed by the range of different children in a single classroom are far from trivial. The philosophy of **inclusion** can be uncomfortable and difficult to implement in practice. It is the professional responsibility of teachers to ensure that all children they teach have access to the powerful learning available through mathematics.

Many students with special needs have teacher aide time allocated for classroom support. It is important that the teacher is in control of the learning program and that, as far as possible, this is in line with what the rest of the class is doing. Teachers must explain the

Inclusion policy of including all students, including those with disabilities, in mainstream classrooms wherever possible

learning objectives and aims of the lesson to the allocated aides and, wherever possible, the aide should ensure that the child participates fully with the class. Chapter 18 provides additional information about working with education support workers, including aides, in the classroom.

In addition to classroom support, there may be a range of other professional services working with individual students. These services may include speech pathologists, occupational therapists, guidance officers or school counsellors, social workers and specialists in English language support. All these people are working towards the same goal of ensuring that educational outcomes for the students in question are the best that they can be. The teacher is responsible for directing the mathematical learning of the child and therefore should discuss specific adaptations and needs with the relevant person.

Where there are a number of different support personnel, classrooms can become very crowded with additional adults either helping or observing particular students. One kindergarten teacher who had a child with a disability that had occurred at birth, and was the subject of legal proceedings, looked round her classroom one day and found that there were 11 adults in the room with 19 children. In this situation, it is sensible to seek the support of the principal or a senior teacher to manage the number of classroom visitors. Although all available support should be provided and used for those individuals that require it, this support should not detract from the mathematics or other learning of the class. The teacher described arranged with her principal that she would have one day each week free of any extra people, so that she, her kindergarten aide, and the special aide allocated to the child with a disability were the only adults in the room. This allowed the teacher to focus on the group as a whole in order to develop the social and learning needs of all children.

Differentiating the mathematics curriculum

Differentiation the ways in which teachers respond to students' learning needs

Teachers often hear that they need to **differentiate** the curriculum. What does this mean in practice? There are two key aspects to differentiation. The first is the learning environment – how the content, delivery, classroom organisation and product are changed. The second refers to individual student characteristics – their readiness to learn, interests and ways of learning. In this chapter, there are examples of all of these approaches used to allow all students' learning needs to be met. There is considerable advice about differentiation of the curriculum available from state education departments.

Teachers should always be sensitive to the mathematical learning needs of their students. For example, framing a mathematics question in terms of football teams and using 'Bombers' as a team name may be very appropriate if the school is located in an area where the Bombers are a local team. For children from refugee backgrounds, however, the name may have emotional connotations that could interfere with their understanding and response to the question. Similarly, talking about negative numbers in terms of temperature in a remote Indigenous community in the Northern Territory is likely to have less meaning than using a rope swing over the creek as an example, where the knots below the water level show negative numbers. Considering favourite pets in our class, a popular early years' activity, may not be appropriate in a class where students have a Muslim background, because dogs are unclean. Undertaking the activity of collecting data about balancing on one leg (see Chapter 8) is not appropriate for a class that includes a child in a wheelchair. Using colour as a discriminator ('Group all the red triangles together') is not suitable for children with vision impairment, or who are colour blind. Being sensitive to context is an important aspect of effective mathematics teaching, particularly when considering classroom diversity.

Students with special needs may also become tired more quickly than other class members. High expectations should always be the norm, but these should be tempered by each student's individual needs. With appropriate supports in place, all people can learn mathematics, and this is the expectation of the Australian Curriculum: Mathematics v. 9.0.

The impact of teachers' understanding and beliefs

It is important to acknowledge that teachers' beliefs about mathematics and its teaching and learning are factors to consider in diverse classrooms. For example, DeSimone and Parmar (2006) found that Year 6, 7 and 8 teachers who had students with learning disabilities in their classrooms had limited understanding of those students' mathematics learning needs. The teachers also judged collaboration with other teachers to be the most helpful way of dealing with diverse needs and felt inadequately prepared to deal with diversity. Beswick (2007–2008) reported similar findings in an Australian context and showed that many beliefs – such as 'Some people have a maths mind and some don't' – were remarkably persistent, even after appropriate professional learning. Woodcock (2021, p. 110), however, found that

> teachers who believe that inclusive education is an effective way to teach all students, provide greater positive feedback, feel less frustrated, and hold lower expectations for future failure, in comparison to their colleagues with more negative inclusive educational beliefs.

All students benefit from well-taught mathematics that has a focus on strategy use rather than recall of facts and formulae. Lessons should focus on relevant, contextualised mathematics in which high expectations by the teacher are the norm and children are actively engaged in their learning (Boaler 2008). Language is important, but it is possible for children with severe language impairment to learn to calculate accurately, even when they have difficulty with counting tasks (Donlan et al. 2007). Nevertheless, the complex language of mathematics cannot be ignored. For example, the distance round a 2D shape is referred to as the perimeter, but when applied to a circle it is the circumference. Neither of the two mathematical terms is easy for children to understand, and for those with language delays or intellectual disabilities, the words may be completely incomprehensible. There is useful advice about mathematical language and the literacy demands of mathematics on the education site of the Victorian State Government in the Literacy Teaching Toolkit which includes suggested strategies for supporting students' mathematical language development and developing understanding in mathematics. A Maths Dictionary for Kids is an interactive resource that is accessible to students and explains mathematical terms with diagrams and examples.

Link 12.1 Victorian Government: Literacy Teaching Toolkit
Link 12.2 A Maths Dictionary for Kids

> **PAUSE AND REFLECT**
>
> Why is it important to ensure that all children learn mathematics in meaningful ways so that they develop mathematically to their greatest potential? Is this simply being 'politically correct', or is it an important principle that all teachers of mathematics should follow? Share your views with another person.

Despite their best intentions, teachers can fall into the trap of 'victim blaming', such as saying 'These kids won't learn their tables'. Teachers instead should be asking themselves 'What can I do to help my students learn their tables?' Sometimes teachers use other students to manage children who have behaviour problems. For example, one teacher in a Year 1 class found herself always placing a student who could be quite disruptive with two particular girls because they managed him well. She realised that what she was doing was hindering the learning needs of the two girls, so the teacher made sure that the two girls did not always have to work with the disruptive student so that their own learning needs could be met. Teachers also can find themselves in a 'standoff' situation, where a child simply refuses to do something, or teachers may unintentionally provoke some unwanted behaviour. Read Classroom Snapshot 12.1.

CLASSROOM SNAPSHOT 12.1

Zak is in Year 6. He is very restless in class, and rarely concentrates for more than a few minutes at a time. Although he has not been diagnosed with ADHD (attention deficit hyperactivity disorder), his teacher treats him as though this is the problem. He can be disruptive with other children. Marj, the Year 6 teacher, wants the class to undertake a mathematical investigation using paper planes. She knows that Zak is likely to be difficult to control in the relatively unstructured environment of an investigation, so she has some computer activities ready for him if he starts to play up. Zak makes his paper plane but then starts roaming the classroom, annoying the other children. Marj takes him to the computer corner and shows him the activity, which is related in content to the measuring activity she has planned with the paper planes. She tells him he has until recess to work on the computer activities and suggests that he might try to finish a particular section of the game before recess. Zak settles down and works quietly and well for the next 35 minutes.

About 5 minutes before recess, Marj decides to get the class together to debrief about the activity. She asks Zak to pack up and come to the mat. Zak ignores her. Marj asks him again, and this time Zak says, 'I just want to finish this'. Marj asks him a third time, and when Zak again ignores her, she leans over and shuts down the computer. Zak immediately jumps up shouting that she has ruined his work and kicks Marj. At this point the recess bell goes, so Marj dismisses the class and takes Zak to the principal.

What has happened here? Certainly, kicking people, teacher or other students is unacceptable behaviour and Zak needs to understand the consequences. Could Marj have avoided this situation? Undertake Activity 12.2 to think about these issues.

ACTIVITY 12.2

Do you think Marj was right to turn off the computer? Why do you think this? Brainstorm some other actions that Marj might have taken and make a list of these. For example, Marj could have decided to leave Zak at the computer and talk to the rest of the class. She might have given him a personal 5-minute warning before calling the class together. The situation could have been addressed in many other ways. Consider each of the actions on your list and decide which of these you would have done. Think about your reasons for your choice. Would you use different strategies in diverse circumstances? How could you engineer the situation so that you were praising Zak for his good work? Discuss your thoughts with a colleague.

All teachers should think through their beliefs about students' mathematics learning. It is important to have a strong philosophy that underpins your approach to teaching. There are no rights or wrongs – teachers are as diverse as the children they teach, and differing views should be respected. Teachers are, however, expected to work within the policies in their particular system and school. At times, these may be at odds with your personal beliefs, but you will be expected to implement the policies regardless. This chapter aims to help you adapt the curriculum and its delivery as appropriate for a range of children with special needs within a mainstream classroom.

Practical aspects of addressing diversity in the mathematics classroom

In any classroom, teachers will make decisions, either planned or in the moment, about the mathematics learning needs of the particular group. When dealing with very diverse classrooms, however, there is a wider range of issues that need to be planned for. Children with physical disabilities typically make different demands from those with intellectual disabilities, and some children have a combination of conditions.

ACTIVITY 12.3

Although there is advice about curriculum adaptation on the Australian Curriculum v. 9.0 website, this is fairly general and may not specifically target mathematics. Using the Australian Curriculum v. 9.0 resources and any others you might find, consider what adaptations might be needed to undertake activities in Year 3 that address learning outcomes about measuring lengths, areas or capacity using formal and informal units. Think about students with a physical disability, a vision or hearing impairment, or an inability to manipulate physical objects; Indigenous students; students who do not speak English as a first language; students who have intellectual disabilities or developmental delay; students with social and emotional disabilities; and students who might be gifted and talented.

1. Which of these groups might require specific adaptations to the curriculum itself by, for example, changing the content?

2. Which of these groups might require a careful consideration of the nature of the activities that you might want to use?
3. Is technology a help or hindrance with any of the adaptations that you might need to make?

Later sections of this chapter will consider some of these challenges, but the questions are posed here to prompt your thinking about classroom diversity.

The suggestions provided here are starting points for discussions with support workers and special education teachers about catering for the mathematical requirements of diverse primary aged students. They do not pretend to provide all the answers, rather they are starting points for thinking about the issues.

In the following sections some specific student needs are highlighted. Many of these needs are 'low incidence' – that is, they are unlikely to be present in every class. It is almost certain, however, that there will be students with particular needs in every class. This chapter is not a list of possible disabilities but aims to provide suggestions for dealing with diverse needs. It should be remembered that many of the suggestions are simply good mathematics teaching and will benefit all students.

Students with physical disabilities

Many students with physical disabilities can participate intellectually in the full curriculum if suitable activities are used. Students confined to a wheelchair, for example, often need little adaptation, but some students with cerebral palsy cannot manipulate physical objects easily. Large rulers or measuring tools, calculators with large buttons and magnetic boards with numbers and symbols are all appropriate tools to allow students with physical disabilities to access mathematics learning. For example, mental computation questions can be answered by pressing calculator keys. When a teacher asks the question 'What is 7 × 6?', the response can be made by pressing the 4 and 2 keys, thus using the calculator as a communication tool rather than for computation. The calculator can be used in the same way for playing shops when learning about money, and in this way can also allow students for whom English is limited (EAL/D) to participate.

For students with very specific needs, it is worth asking the relevant support person in your school or system what adaptive technology is available and investing time in learning to use it effectively. It is beyond the scope of this chapter to detail specialised adaptive technology, but readily available mainstream resources include speech-recognition software, tablet computers, virtual manipulatives, apps for tablets and audio-technology that allows a child to listen to the teacher. Students who have difficulty writing or drawing, for example, can record their mathematical thinking using a variety of audio resources including smartphones, interactive whiteboard (IWB) facilities or computer software. Such adaptations are particularly important for students with vision impairment.

Problem-solving activities that are suitable for students with disabilities may be equally effective for students without a disability. For example, the geometry challenge Design Paper Money for the Visually Impaired (Robicheaux 1993) is an excellent task for a Year 6 class. The aim is to develop some way of differentiating paper money by snipping off corners so that people with vision impairment can easily identify the different notes. The corner cuts have to be congruent, right-angled isosceles triangles, and this alone can lead to a discussion about meaning. On the surface, this appears to be a simple task, but if it is remembered that it is not possible to distinguish between the front and back of the note, then the task becomes more complex.

Not only does a task of this kind develop visualisation skills and an understanding of symmetry and congruence, but it should also lead to a discussion about the difficulties experienced by people with vision impairment to build a more inclusive classroom. As a follow up, students could research how Australian banknotes have been developed to address this issue, and other strategies that the Reserve Bank of Australia have developed to help people with vision impairment.

The banknotes task clearly addresses problem-solving and reasoning proficiencies in the Australian Curriculum: Mathematics v. 9.0 and can also enhance the understanding of mathematical transformations. A similar problem-solving task is to design and build a scale model of a ramp for wheelchair access to the school hall, for example, with requirements for height, width or slope. Tasks of this type are challenging mathematical problems that can have immediate relevance to students who share their classrooms with fellow students with physical disabilities, and they meet the goals of the mathematics curriculum. These kinds of activities are worthwhile even if there are no students in the class or the school with the specific disability. By using these contexts, the tasks indicate the values of society and the school itself.

CLASSROOM SNAPSHOT 12.2

Sara has a Year 1 class that is learning about ordering numbers from 1 to 9. She wants to use an activity that she knows is successful. It involves students role-playing Mrs Number's children, who get mixed up. The class has to reorder them by giving directions to the students, who have placards with numbers 1 to 9 around their necks, role-playing the children.

In the class this year is Sophie, who is intellectually very capable but is confined to a wheelchair. She cannot be one of Mrs Number's students easily because of the space demands of her wheelchair, so Sara wants to find an alternative approach that will allow Sophie to participate fully. Before the lesson, she prepares some pages for her IWB showing Mrs Number and her children all mixed up. She starts the lesson as she has always done by handing out number cards to different students and lining them up in order from 1 to 9. Then they mix themselves up and the rest of the students have to give them clues. Sophie says, '3 must be next to 4', and the other students agree and give similar clues.

Then Sara moves to the IWB. First, she asks the students with the cards to line up the numbers on the IWB exactly as they have just done to show the students that the activity is the same as before but translated onto the IWB. Then she hands the cards to other students so that every child will get a turn at being one of Mrs Number's students. Sophie has the card showing 7. The class plays the game in the same way as when they role-played it, with the students who have the numbered cards moving the numbers on the IWB. The IWB is fixed low on the wall so that Sophie can access it easily. This time, as the students are playing the game, Sara asks the students to give a reason for their clue.

Sara ends the lesson by asking the class to draw a picture of Mrs Number's children, all lined up in order. For those students who clearly understand, including Sophie, Sara sets the additional challenge of drawing the children in the reverse order.

Sara is making use of the technology available in her classroom to ensure that Sophie is able to participate in the same way that the other students do. For an activity of this type, the technology use is integral to the adaptation of the activity.

She can follow up this activity with others such as Caterpillar Ordering by Top Marks. There are many resources available online that would make good follow-up activities to Mrs Number that would be accessible to students like Sophie. Many activities that require movement in the classroom, which become difficult for students with physical disabilities, can be undertaken using appropriate technology.

There are many activities that can use physical involvement and role play that are easily adaptable for students with physical disabilities. Examples include Bob's Buttons (Mathematics Centre Maths at Home), Woolly Worms (reSolve: Maths by Inquiry), or a 'Mini-Olympics' where students take part in events such as paper-plate discus, first making a guess about how far they can throw, then estimating the distance they have thrown, and finally measuring the actual distance thrown. You don't need to search for specific resources – any good quality mathematics activity site will have material that is adaptable.

Link 12.3 Top Marks: Caterpillar Ordering
Link 12.4 Maths at Home: Bob's Buttons
Link 12.5 reSolve: Woolly Worms

Students with sensory impairment

There are a number of low-incidence conditions that impact on students' mathematical learning. These include hearing and vision impairment. Typically, students with these conditions achieve less well mathematically, but it is possible to make accommodations to support students with sensory impairment.

Hearing impairment

Students with hearing impairment are more common than may be apparent. Many students suffer from intermittent hearing loss associated with 'glue ear', and many students in busy classrooms may use the support of lip reading to some extent. Students with hearing loss may also be distracted by classroom background noise, especially when working in small groups where there is a high level of conversation. Students who are deaf or hard of hearing may be up to three years behind their peers in mathematics (Brun 2018). These students do not pick up language in their environment, such as through simple counting games, and may enter school without the basic mathematical vocabulary that other children have. They also may have difficulty communicating with other students and thus miss out on collaborative activities.

When giving instructions, providing explanations or posing problems, it is sensible to stand so that light from the window falls onto your face rather than standing with your back to the window so that your face is in shadow. Similarly, if you want to write on the whiteboard, don't write and speak at the same time because a child with a hearing difficulty may need to see your face to gain the support from lip reading and expression. Many teachers in primary classrooms develop the skill of writing on an easel while they are facing the students in the class.

In mathematics, when there is a focus on mental computation presented orally, these students may miss important words and give incorrect responses because they have not heard clearly what is being said. For mental computation practice, there are any number of resources available that could be used as an alternative to oral questioning for students with hearing impairment. The important aspect is to ensure that all students can develop strategies that lead to powerful computation. To support this goal, some dialogue with the child or within groups of students is important. Voice-to-text software might be useful for one-to-one conversations with the child concerned. If a child uses Auslan and has an interpreter in the classroom, discuss the lesson with the interpreter beforehand, and slow the pace of the lesson a little to allow the hearing-impaired child to watch the interpreter as well as any work that is being completed on the whiteboard. These suggestions are practical ways to support all students.

Formal signs for numbers used by hearing impaired people may be in conflict with the ways in which hands and fingers are used to signify numbers informally. Signing even a simple algorithmic problem, such as 'How many more marbles does Sally have than Harry?' becomes very complex. Students with a hearing impairment typically do not do as well in mathematics as students without any hearing impairment (Gregory 1998). One possible reason could be the difficulty with language – especially words such as 'if' and 'because', which are common in mathematics. In addition, the specialised language – such as isosceles, hypotenuse, numerator and denominator – is complex, and may be difficult for hearing-impaired students to read or process. There are also words that have everyday meanings but are used in a specialist way in mathematics. Whole, for example, is used to denote a type of number (whole numbers) and the complete part of a fraction ('If this is one-quarter, what is the whole?'). For a child with a hearing impairment, it is difficult to separate 'whole' from 'hole'. Developing vocabulary around concepts rather than objects is more difficult for hearing-impaired and deaf students. Resources such as mathematics dictionaries can be helpful. Students who are hearing impaired may have better non-verbal reasoning skills than students with the normal hearing range (Braden 1994). This finding has implications for mathematics teaching because it suggests that introducing ideas using non-verbal signs could be helpful. Technology can support this idea by providing virtual manipulatives such as interactive number lines, shapes or patterns. A number of these issues and suggestions for addressing them are available from ttaconline.org.

Vision impairment

Although profound vision impairment (VI) or blindness is relatively uncommon, many children have some degree of VI that has not been identified. Such students may have difficulty with specific mathematical tasks. Imagine how students with little or no sight develop concepts such as 'big, bigger, biggest' or 'between'. Whereas a sighted child can see the relationships at a glance, students with VI can only explore one object at a time, and they have to hold the size of the attribute in their heads while they explore the second and then third object. This reality adds a significant cognitive load and may partly explain why students with VI typically lag behind their peers.

Mathematics is highly visual and modern texts have built on this. Concepts such as geometrical transformation are predominantly recognised visually and described using visual language (e.g. flip, slide, turn). Tactile materials will be important to use in developing these ideas and can be used with a straight stick as a reference (see Figure 12.1).

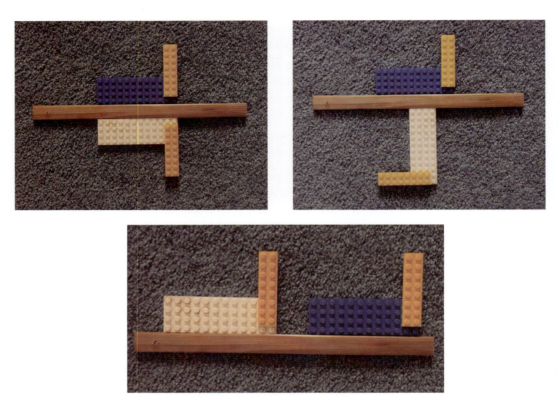

Figure 12.1 Tactile materials arranged to show mathematical transformations

Learning about right angles may require tactile frames that can be used with a set square to check whether an angle is a right angle, or the corner of a book may provide a useful reference. Circles can be represented by CDs or plates, books are rectangular and so on. Making reference to everyday objects and allowing the child to feel them is important and is often done in the early years of schooling. These kinds of adaptations may need to be continued longer for students who are vision impaired. It is critical, however, that these adaptations are recognised by the child, and the rest of the class, as 'adaptations', not babyish aids. Computer tablets can be helpful because they can magnify print to make it easier to read. This provides access to the normal range of online resources, although be aware that many mathematics sites make use of Flash™ technology that may not be accessible on tablets.

A variety of tactile materials is available, including measuring tapes and rulers, dice, clocks and talking scales. However, as students progress through school, and the mathematics content becomes more abstract and symbol based, students with severe vision impairment may be disadvantaged. Mathematical text is tricky on ordinary computers, but the handwriting-recognition software for use with tablets and computers has some potential for visually impaired students. Text-to-speech software is becoming increasingly available on tablets, but abstract mathematical text is difficult to translate. The research base for the use of technology is still limited (Klingenberg et al. 2020). Some students read Braille, and for these students access to the mathematics curriculum may require thinking ahead to ensure that Braille versions of texts or other material are available. It is important to seek specialist advice, and to talk to the child and parents/caregivers to identify the best approaches for the individual. A useful video and other resources about teaching mathematics to students who are blind or visually impaired is available from Perkins School for the Blind.

Link 12.6 Perkins School for the Blind: 'Teaching Math to Students Who are Blind or Visually Impaired'

CLASSROOM SNAPSHOT 12.3

Tom's Year 6 class is undertaking a mathematical investigation into circles, with the aim of developing understanding of the relationship between diameter and circumference.

Dan is a student in Tom's class who is visually impaired. He uses a tablet with a keyboard, and is skilled with voice-recognition, handwriting-recognition and audio-recording software for recording mathematical ideas.

Tom organises the class into groups of three students, and he gives each group a box containing a variety of circular objects and several measuring devices including rulers, tapes and string. The groups have the task of measuring across the diameter and around the edge of each object, and every child is required both to measure and to create a recording system for each measurement.

Dan's group is provided with a tactile ruler in addition to the materials that the other groups are given. With support from the other group members, Dan is able to measure the concrete objects using string and the tactile ruler. He creates a table on his tablet using the touch-sensitive screen to scribe notes, and he calculates the ratio of the diameter to circumference using a tactile calculator. Finally, he records a summary of his findings using the audio-recording facility on the tablet.

The next day, the class repeats the activity in the playground, this time creating large circles with string and chalk. The purpose is to discuss measurement error, and how this can have a big impact on small measurements but a lesser impact on larger ones. Dan participates fully by using a trundle wheel and counting the clicks that this makes, with the members of his group helping him to stay on the circle accurately.

The adaptations made for Dan are those necessary to ensure that he has access to the learning activity. The curriculum itself is not compromised or changed in any way, and the classroom expectations are the same for Dan as for any other child. In addition to mathematical outcomes, there are social outcomes for Dan and the other class members in terms of cooperation and understanding that people can be different but achieve in the same way.

Developmental dyscalculia

Developmental **dyscalculia** (DD) is defined as 'a specific learning disability affecting the development of arithmetic skills' (Kucian & von Aster 2015, p. 2). Not every child who has problems with arithmetic, such as number facts or multiplication tables, has DD. It can be thought of as the mathematical equivalent of **dyslexia**, and affects between 3 per cent and 6 per cent of the population. Many more people have trouble with arithmetic without having

Dyscalculia a specific learning disability that causes problems with arithmetic

Dyslexia a specific learning disability that causes problems with reading

DD. In addition, true DD is not associated with socio-economic status or intelligence, age or reading ability (Mazzocco & Myers 2003). Students with DD can use a calculator effectively and they should be allowed to use this tool.

Regardless of whether students have DD or other learning disorders, the teaching approach is the same. Provide a variety of rich activities using concrete materials, visual stimuli, songs and rhymes, physical activity, calculators and technology, with some written work preferably using the child's own recording rather than pre-printed worksheets. The exact nature and focus of the arithmetic activity will need to vary with age and the intent of the lesson. Students with learning disabilities, including dyscalculia, benefit from a rich learning environment.

Students with intellectual disabilities

Mathematics classrooms have always included a wide range of student cognitive abilities. Increasingly, however, students with specific difficulties, such as Down syndrome (DS), are learning mathematics alongside their age peers in mainstream classrooms. All teachers should be prepared to manage a wide range of mathematical abilities within the classroom.

The research on teaching mathematics to students with learning or cognitive disabilities suggests that visual and concrete approaches can be effective (Brady, Clarke & Gervasoni 2008). These students often need direct instruction, and there is some evidence that such students do not learn from mistakes, but rather that making the same mistake can reinforce the error (Moyer & Moyer 1985). Traditionally, students with learning disabilities have received a curriculum focused on algorithms, based on a drill and practice model. However, students with learning disabilities often benefit from being actively engaged in hands-on tasks that involve discussion and thinking about mathematics.

There is a growing body of evidence that students with DS may have developmental dyscalculia (Faragher 2017). They can deal with a range of mathematical ideas, including some that would be thought of as too abstract for a child with an intellectual disability. Despite these successes, however, they universally have difficulty with routine computational tasks. Faragher (2017) suggests that there are four implications for teaching students with DS:

1. Students with DS should be taught to use calculators, because for this group, calculators are a prosthetic in that they replace a part of the brain which does not function.
2. Throughout life there needs to be ongoing attention to numbers and number facts, using visual supports such as number lines to encourage development of alternative neural pathways.
3. Functional mathematics programs designed for students with DS should be changed to encourage the use of calculators or electronic banking approaches rather than relying of algorithms and concrete artefacts such as coins.
4. The expectation that students with DS cannot do mathematics because they cannot master number facts should change. Students with DS should experience the same mathematics curriculum as their age peers, with access to calculators or similar tools.

Some students with learning disabilities – especially those with language delay – respond to visual approaches to mathematics learning, and these can be supported by technology. Technology use makes individualised challenges available in ways that paper versions cannot. For example, the use of HOTmaths widgets such as Dot Pictures and Leaping Frog is appropriate for all students, and the challenge level can be altered as required (see Figure 12.2). Similar resources are widely available online.

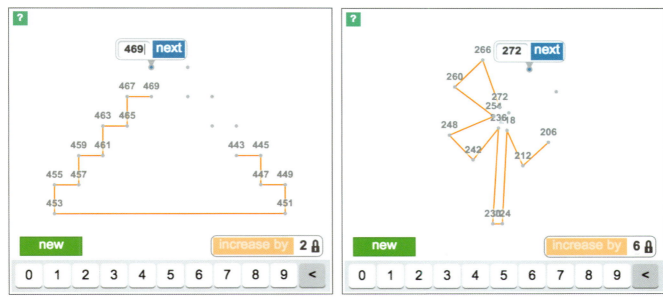

Figure 12.2 Screenshot of HOTmaths Dot Pictures widget, showing the variation possible within the one type of activity

For students with learning difficulties, the starting numbers can be made smaller and the jumps less difficult. All students are thus participating in identical activities, but the intended outcomes are chosen to be appropriate for students with special needs. There is a watch-point, however: students with learning difficulties may not respond to 'wrong' answers in the same way that other students do. They are likely to continue to repeat the same error. When working on technology tasks, it is important that all students but especially those with learning difficulties have someone with them to initiate dialogue and discussion. Technology can be a support but cannot replace the important dialogue between the child and the teacher or teacher aide. Classroom Snapshot 12.4 provides an example.

Students with intellectual impairment are also likely to have short-term memory problems (Hay & Fielding-Barnsley 2012). They will need more prompts and support, and 'wait time' is particularly important. Teachers should slow down their dialogue and allow students thinking time before jumping in with an answer. For example, asking a child to recall a number fact, such as '3 times 6' typically will need a longer time lapse before a prompt is given. Teachers and education support workers tend to 'rescue' students by giving the answer, depriving the child of the satisfaction of working it out.

CLASSROOM SNAPSHOT 12.4

Mary is in Year 5 and has DS. She is working with her aide, Katrina, with the HOTmaths Split-and-Add Robot widget.

Before the lesson, Mary's teacher has provided Katrina with a sequence of problems to start the session and then some starting numbers so that Mary can choose the second number to add. Katrina explains the task to Mary and demonstrates what the robot does, using 14 + 13. She then enters the number 13 and asks Mary, 'How will the robot split that number up?' Mary correctly answers, 'Into a 10 and a 3.' Katrina then enters the second number as 24 and asks Mary the same question. This time Mary says, 'Into a 10 and a 4.'

Katrina then starts a dialogue with Mary about the meaning of the number 24. She asks first, 'What is the number?', which Mary answers correctly. Then she asks about the meaning of the digits with questions such as, 'Where is the 20?', 'What does 20 mean?', 'What does the 4 show?' When she is satisfied that Mary knows what 24 represents, she returns to the robot and asks Mary how the robot splits numbers up, returning to the 13 and then, finally, to the 24. This time Mary correctly identifies that the robot will give a 20 and a 4. Mary then presses the release button and, as the robot splits the number up, Katrina and Mary together say the numbers that are produced (see Figure 12.3).

When Mary has worked through the questions provided by the teacher, Katrina gives her a worksheet that the teacher has prepared showing the robot before the numbers are entered (use a screenshot and provide a set of similar two-digit add two-digit problems to reinforce the strategy). Mary starts the worksheet in class and takes it home for homework to discuss with her parents what she has been doing. When she has to add numbers, she uses a calculator, but before completing the problems she has a dialogue with her aide or her parents about the number structure.

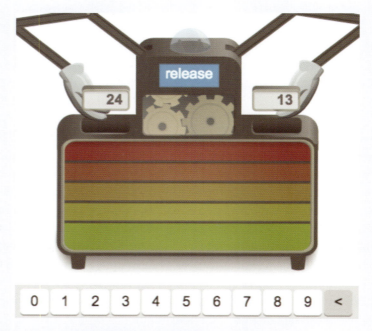

Figure 12.3 Screenshot of HOTmaths Split-and-Add Robot widget

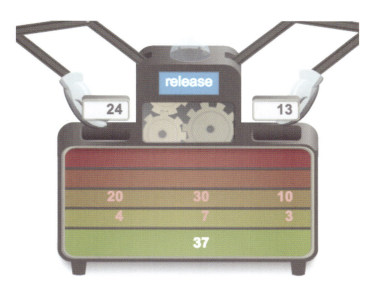

Enter two numbers and then RELEASE them.
Watch as the robot splits them and then adds them.

Figure 12.3 *(cont.)*

There are several points about this lesson that add to its effectiveness for Mary's mathematical development. First, although she is in Year 5, the task chosen is suitable for Year 4 as well as Year 5. Mary's teacher has clearly planned a sequence of numbers that she knows Mary can cope with and has constructed the early activities so that the sum does not go over the next 10. The focus at the start is on the structure of the number. She has discussed with Katrina a suitable series of questions to ask, and the importance of not letting Mary simply play with the widget. The long dialogue may seem tedious, but it is through the discussion and questions that Mary is learning. The repetition of the questions and saying the numbers aloud as they are produced also add to the learning experience for Mary. The worksheet provides reinforcement both visually in using the robot picture and mathematically by having a set of similar problems. Computation is done with a calculator. The curriculum has been modified slightly because the expected outcomes are closer to Year 2. Mary is using strategies to combine and partition whole numbers leading ultimately to efficient approaches to addition. The activity clearly fits the Australian Curriculum v. 9.0 numeracy capability element of estimating and calculating with whole numbers. Although Mary works closely with the aide, Katrina, Mary's teacher is in control of the learning experience. The use of technology in this instance is not essential – the activity could also be undertaken using Multi-Base Arithmetic blocks or bundles of straws or paddle pop sticks – but the technology provides an incentive for Mary to engage with the task. The same approach would be effective for other forms of learning disability.

Tasks that are multi-layered are valuable tools for developing mathematical understanding in students with intellectual disabilities. The circles activity described in Classroom Snapshot 12.3 is accessible to students with intellectual disabilities, but the purpose of the activity for such students would be to develop measuring skills at about a Year 4 level of using measuring instruments and recording the information systematically. Using the circles activity with students who have an intellectual disability is an example of the curriculum being adapted by changing the expected outcomes. The activity remains the same because it is an age-appropriate activity for the class as well as the individual student. Many activities described in this book can be used in this way.

Students with autism spectrum disorder or social difficulties

The number of students within this category of disability appears to be growing. For example, an estimated one in 70 people in Australia is diagnosed as having an autism spectrum disorder (ASD), and boys are four times more likely to be diagnosed than girls (Autism Spectrum Australia (Aspect) 2018). ASD impacts on the ways in which students interact with the world around them, and hence may have a big impact on their schooling.

There is a growing body of research suggesting that students who have difficulty with social interactions and communication may interact effectively with technology. In the United Kingdom, for example, software is being developed that allows students with social difficulties to interact with virtual characters to develop behaviours that they can translate into the classroom (Guldberg et al. 2010). Despite these initiatives, at present there is little specialised mathematics software available, and teachers have to use currently available resources or create their own (Leach 2010).

Routines are very important for many of these students. They need certainty, not unpredictability, so lessons should have a familiar structure. Often this is a 'whole-part-whole' structure, where the whole class is introduced to the focus of the lesson, then students work individually or in small groups on the lesson content, with a final reflection session involving the whole class. This organisation is also typical of explicit instruction approaches (see Chapter 1). Within this lesson structure, there is scope for many different activities. Lessons do not have to be confined to explication of the idea, drill-and-practice and a final summary. The lessons described in the classroom snapshots in this chapter could all be taught within this framework – for students with ASD, and many others, it is the predictability of the overall routine that is critical.

It is worth noting that many students with ASD, and others, may find classroom noise distracting or unpleasant. Lessons where coins are tossed, for example, or where there is a lot of discussion, can lead to surprisingly high noise levels. Students who find noise difficult to cope with could be encouraged to bring a pair of earmuffs to school to use when they want to concentrate. Mathematics often requires students to hold a considerable amount of information in their heads in order to solve problems, especially multi-step problems. Distractions such as noise can impair a child's ability to manage all of the information. As one student remarked 'When there's too much noise I can't hear my voice in my head.' Similar considerations apply to many online resources. When using these, it would be sensible to turn off the sound. For example, a virtual pinboard – such as that at Crickweb – can

Link 12.7 Crickweb: Virtual Pinboard

be used to set a variety of challenges at different stages of schooling, but it is accompanied by a popping sound that can cause anxiety in sensitive students. Personalised activities can be created by using IWB resources (Leach 2010) and incorporating familiar situations such as pictures or photographs from the child's environment. Mathematics activities that are accompanied by sounds and graphics when the answer is incorrect can also be distracting because the reward for getting an incorrect answer is greater than that for getting it correct. For example, a drill-and-practice activity for number bonds asked students to save their teacher from getting a custard pie thrown at them and the accompanying graphic showed a cartoon teacher covered in custard when the answer was incorrect – hardly an incentive to try to get a correct answer!

Activities that require group interactions may also be helpful for students with social difficulties. The NRICH website has a number of cooperative activities in which each member of the group has a clue that cannot be shown to anyone else. Group members may describe their clue and ask clarification questions, but no one person ever sees all the clues at once. The group works together to solve the problem. Examples from NRICH include Arranging Cubes (activity 6973) and What Shape? (activity 6986). What's My Number? from Teaching Ideas (UK) may also be useful, as is the HOTmaths A Mystical Map HOTsheet.

Link 12.8 NRICH: Arranging Cubes
Link 12.9 NRICH: What Shape?
Link 12.10 Teaching Ideas: What's my Number?

Such activities can help students with social difficulties because, although they must interact, it is within a structured framework and not too much is asked of them. The activities are educationally and mathematically sound for all students, but because some limited interaction is required, they can provide other social outcomes for students with special needs, addressing the social management element of the personal and social capability in the Australian Curriculum: Mathematics v 9.0. An example of a set of clue cards is shown in Figure 12.4. The clues in this set range from those that could be used with most middle primary students through to some that require more sophisticated understanding. The teacher could choose not to give out clues that are beyond the students' experience or might ensure that those clues are used in a group where there is a child who has this level of understanding and could explain this to others.

MIN'S NUMBER	MIN'S NUMBER	MIN'S NUMBER
Min's number is not even.	Min's number is divisible by 3.	Min's number has two prime factors.
Find Min's number.	Find Min's number.	Find Min's number.
MIN'S NUMBER	MIN'S NUMBER	MIN'S NUMBER
When you add the digits you get an even number.	Min's number is smaller than 50.	Min's number is the sum of two prime numbers.
Find Min's number.	Find Min's number.	Find Min's number.

Figure 12.4 Clue cards for a cooperative problem-solving activity

Students with behavioural problems, such as ADHD, can be tricky to manage in the primary mathematics classroom. Again, routines are important, as is controlling the amount of work presented at one time. Providing one investigative task rather than an overwhelming number of mathematics problems to solve can aid in keeping these students engaged. The same principles apply to students with ADHD as to all students. They respond to a rich mathematics curriculum where they are actively involved and have some control over their activity. Because some drill-and-practice is needed, and students with ADHD may find it difficult to sustain attention for long periods, computer activities can help to provide engaging situations. Using a variety of online activities that provide suitable practice activities may be more effective than giving a child with ADHD worksheets or rapid-response mental computation practice. There is some indication that technology use helps students with attention deficits to focus for longer (Lucangeli & Cabrele 2006), but the research is limited (see Classroom Snapshot 12.1).

Link 12.11 marjin.org: How to count from 0 to 100 in 20+ different languages

Multicultural classrooms

There are many students in Australian primary classrooms who do not speak English as a first language. These students include Aboriginal and Torres Strait Islander Australians, as well as immigrants and refugees from other countries. The principles of treating these students with respect and acknowledging their personal mathematical backgrounds are important. Successful teachers of mathematics not only understand mathematics and its pedagogy, but also demonstrate a culturally relevant pedagogy (Morris & Matthews 2011). There is further information, especially about teaching mathematics in culturally appropriate ways, in Chapter 16.

In the early years of schooling, when mathematical language is critical, it is important for students with limited English that mathematics contexts relevant to their situation are emphasised. If they know how to count in their first language, this can be celebrated and shared with the class. There are websites where counting in other languages can be explored.

Older students can carry out research projects into counting systems from other parts of the world, which are rich and diverse. These projects can provide a basis for developing understanding about why mathematics has developed in different ways across the world, and how these systems have impacted on a particular society. Geometry is another area rich in culture, from patchwork quilts from North America to Islamic tiling patterns and Pasifika weaving patterns.

When teaching mathematics, the cultural backgrounds from which the mathematics has evolved can be emphasised. It is worth asking students from an EAL/D background what their words are for particular mathematics ideas. Some cultures, for example, have no words for left and right; others label 2D shapes

Figure 12.5 A woven screen and basket in a Māori *marae*

according to the number of edges so that a question such as 'How many sides has a pentagon?' translates as 'How many sides has a five-sided shape?' Sharing these ideas with the class provides an interesting starting point for a discussion about the mathematical properties. Activities that do not have a language basis may also be useful. Figure 12.6 shows an activity from HOTmaths called X marks the spot, suitable for upper primary students. The aim is to find the correct spot following directions provided either as three-figure bearings or as compass directions. Such an activity could be undertaken by students in pairs, without the need for high levels of language, because they could point to the movement needed.

A follow up activity such as the HOTsheet Using Compass Directions could provide opportunities for language development if the same pairs of students worked together.

Examples that deliberately encompass diverse cultural backgrounds can be used as a basis for investigations – for example, in statistics. Gapminder is an interactive resource suitable for older students that allows them to investigate a variety of statistics across the world.

Figure 12.6 HOTmaths widget X marks the spot

Questioning students from other cultures

In mathematics classrooms, teachers aim to ask questions and to encourage students to ask questions about the mathematics. In some cultures, however, it is not always appropriate to ask, or respond to, direct questions. Students have to be taught explicitly that it is okay to ask and respond to questions in the classroom. Establishing culturally responsive classroom norms may take time and considerable reinforcement, but it is essential if all students are to participate in mathematical learning (Thompson & Hunter 2015). One approach is to consider the mathematics classroom as a 'family' in which members can have friendly disagreements and discussions about different approaches to solving mathematical problems (Bills & Hunter 2015). Good resources for developing mathematics in culturally responsive ways can be found at the Make It Count2 website and at the NZ Maths website. From a mathematical perspective, all students – regardless of social and cultural backgrounds – learn mathematics best when the problems are relevant to their context and understanding, there is some degree of freedom in how they respond to the mathematical problems, and they are encouraged to talk about mathematics and ask questions about mathematics.

Students who are gifted and talented

Students who are gifted in mathematics may need stimulation and extension beyond the mathematics suitable for their year group. Often teachers will carry out some pre-assessment before starting an activity, and then continue to teach regardless of the fact that some students can already do all the work. Such a practice leads to boredom and sometimes behaviour problems (Webb et al. 2011). There are two common approaches to teaching students who are gifted in mathematics: accelerating the curriculum or providing more depth and breadth. Multi-layered tasks provide opportunities for both approaches. Consider Classroom Snapshot 12.5.

CLASSROOM SNAPSHOT 12.5

Pat has posed the question to her Year 1 class, 'I was walking down the corridor when I heard a child say "19" and the teacher said, "That's correct." What question might have been asked?'

After some discussion, the students are working individually to create questions for which the answer is 19. They are recording their answers. Simon, who is gifted mathematically, initially provides random problems such as 57 ÷ 3 and 1199 − 1180. Gradually, he begins to work systematically, working from 19 + 0, 18 + 1, and so on down to 0 + 19. At this point, he continues −1 + 20, −2 + 21 and so on. When Pat asks him about what he has written, he says, 'It's a pattern that goes on forever. It's the add-ons backwards.' Pat encourages him to share his findings with the rest of the class.

The activity that Pat chose was very open-ended, and students could use any numbers with which they were comfortable. The activity allowed Simon to explore his understanding and Pat validated this through her response of sharing it with the class.

Many activities, such as those on the NRICH, reSolve: Maths by Inquiry and Illuminations websites, provide good starting points for developing a challenging program for students who are gifted in mathematics. Once again, the approach of creating a rich and varied mathematics classroom with multi-layered tasks offers opportunities for all students to participate and learn.

In some schools, students who are very capable, or gifted and talented, may participate in extension activities such as robotics (see also Chapter 14). Programs that can be undertaken individually may also be used to challenge capable students. Coding develops computational thinking and there are many activities available from Code.org. The logical thinking and mathematical concepts required can not only reinforce more formal mathematics lessons but also provide motivation and challenge for students who might otherwise become disengaged. Wherever possible, students should work in pairs or small groups so that the social and language aspects of their learning are also met.

PAUSE AND REFLECT

From what you have read in this chapter, any additional research that you have done and what you have seen in classrooms, how well do you think the diversity of students' needs are met in the primary mathematics classroom? What approaches have you seen or tried that appeared to have been successful? How can technology use enrich the mathematics classroom so that all students can participate in meaningful mathematics learning?

For students with IEPs transferring to online learning is relatively straightforward. The key issues are to ensure that the student has any relevant materials or equipment to continue their learning, and that the parent or carer understands what is expected. Preparing an advice sheet (see Chapter 18) would be useful in this situation. Ensure that the student can access any online programs at home, noting that this may need to be negotiated with the school's IT support. If the student has a dedicated teacher aide or support worker, liaise with that person, and ask them to monitor and continue to work with the student wherever possible. Doing so helps to provide continuity for the students.

For other students, the same accommodations have to be made as for all students in mainstream classrooms. It is helpful to touch base in person at least once a day using video conferencing tools, and group activities can be facilitated using 'break-out' rooms within the various programs. Challenging activities that can be accessed by students at any level of capability can still be used, and students can be asked to put completed work into their school folder so that it can be checked by the teacher.

Be realistic about outcomes. Students are likely to progress more slowly and may lose motivation. Making a series of short videos of yourself explaining concepts or ideas, or providing support at known 'sticking points', can also help students. Choose activities that can be managed by busy parents or carers. ReSolve has many good activities that are manageable in an online environment. For example, the activity called What a Load of Rubbish could be adapted so that students collect data about their household rubbish, rather than rubbish in the playground, and this could then be pooled with the class using Google docs or a similar sharing site. Where parents do not speak English, you may have access to an interpreter to translate video text, or worksheets. If not, create a group of students who can help to support each other with language difficulties. Every class will be different so flexibility is the key.

TIPS FOR ONLINE TEACHING

Conclusion

Australian primary mathematics classrooms are probably some of the most diverse anywhere in the world. The underlying equity focus is important for social and economic reasons, and it should not be dismissed as either unrealistic or unnecessary. Mathematics is critical to future success, and many students are turned off mathematics very early in their schooling. Nevertheless, however committed teachers are to catering for diversity it does make great demands on planning and thinking about teaching. The approaches to teaching mathematics to cater for diversity that are suggested in this chapter are grounded in research that indicates all students benefit from a rich and meaningful mathematics curriculum. Technology can play an important part in providing tailored resources to allow all students to participate meaningfully in mathematics.

GUIDED STUDENT TASKS

1. Identify a disability that you know little about. Find out as much as you can about that disability, especially how it might impact on mathematics learning. If there is little information specifically about mathematics, consider how the characteristics of that disability would affect a child's learning of mathematics.
2. Find a free speech-to-text app; Google Docs is one free application that has the capacity to turn spoken language into text. Imagine that you are explaining a mathematical concept to a child and record your explanation as text. Read what you said. Does it make sense? Is it accurate? Does it convey what you intended? Remember that students with hearing impairment may only have this explanation to work with. How could you improve your explanation?
3. Imagine that you are teaching early fraction concepts to a child with vision impairment. What kinds of manipulatives could you use to develop the understanding of the meaning of, for example, one-third?
4. Wait time is critical for many students with low-level processing delays. Practice waiting for a response. Ask a typical mental computation question and wait 30 seconds before giving the answer (time yourself). How did that feel? Now try waiting for 1 minute. Some students need considerable time to process information, even for number facts that we might consider trivial.
5. Go to the Code.org website and access the activities for elementary students. Work though some of these. As you do, think about the mathematical ideas that you may use such as direction, patterns, if – then statements and so on. Make a list of all the mathematics needed to undertake a group of tasks.

Link 12.12
Code.org: Grades K–5 courses
Websites for exploration

FURTHER READING

Boaler, J 2010, *The elephant in the classroom: Helping children learn and love maths*, London: Souvenir Press.

GENERAL CAPABILITIES AND CROSS-CURRICULUM PRIORITIES

CHAPTER 13

LEARNING OUTCOMES

By the end of this chapter, you will:

- be able to identify the general capabilities and cross-curriculum priorities referred to in the Australian Curriculum v. 9.0
- understand how the general capabilities and cross-curriculum priorities can be addressed through appropriate mathematics teaching
- know how to develop strategies for incorporating the general capabilities and cross-curriculum priorities into the teaching of mathematics.

Introduction

The Australian Curriculum: Mathematics v. 9.0 (ACARA 2022) is structured around six content strands: Number, Algebra, Measurement, Space, Statistics and Probability. An expectation of mathematical proficiency has been embedded into curriculum content across all strands. It is expected that students will develop and apply mathematical understanding, fluency, reasoning and problem-solving as they learn mathematical content. It is these areas that typically receive the most attention in mathematics classrooms, particularly as there are requirements to assess and report on students' progress in these strands. The Australian Curriculum v. 9.0 also identifies seven general capabilities, which encompass knowledge, skills, behaviours and dispositions, and three cross-curriculum priorities: Aboriginal and Torres Strait Islander histories and cultures, Asia and Australia's engagement with Asia, and Sustainability. However, Atweh, Miller and Thornton (2012) contend that these areas receive minimal reference in the content descriptions and elaborations, leading to the impression that they are only given lip service. This chapter will provide an overview of the general capabilities and cross-curriculum priorities and will also identify ways in which these aspects of the curriculum can be enacted into authentic mathematical experiences for students. While this chapter is current at the time of writing, it is important to acknowledge that ongoing cultural, political and intellectual debate may affect the content and nature of our curriculum, and that our curriculum is essentially a societal construction that reflects national aspirations and pressures.

General capabilities

The skills, behaviours and attributes that students need to succeed in life and work in the 21st century have been identified in the Australian Curriculum v. 9.0 as general capabilities (ACARA 2022). There are seven general capabilities:

1. Literacy
2. Numeracy
3. Critical and creative thinking
4. Digital literacy
5. Ethical understanding
6. Intercultural understanding
7. Personal and social capability.

In the learning areas of the Australian Curriculum v. 9.0, general capabilities are identified, using icons, where they are developed or applied in the content descriptions and elaborations. While literacy and numeracy are fundamental to all learning areas, numeracy development is particularly core to Mathematics. According to ACARA (2022), other general capabilities that are of most relevance to mathematics are critical and creative thinking, digital literacy and ethical understanding. These five capabilities will be discussed in the following sections, along with illustrative classroom snapshots, activities and suggestions as to how they can be embedded into authentic mathematical experiences.

Literacy

According to ACARA 'Students become literate as they develop the skills to learn and communicate confidently at school and to become effective individuals, community members, workers and citizens. These skills include listening, reading and viewing, writing, speaking and creating print, visual and digital materials accurately and purposefully within and across all learning areas' (ACARA 2016b, p. 8). At the time of writing, the literacy general capability in version 9 of the Australian Curriculum had not been revised. Instead, the icon links to the literacy progression, which describes the observable indicators of increasing complexity in the use of Standard Australian English language (ACARA 2022).

Literacy knowledge, skills and dispositions to interpret and use language for learning and communicating in order to participate effectively in society

In relation to mathematics, students require **literacy** skills in order for them to understand written problems and instructions, mathematical vocabulary, technical terminology, and metaphorical language used to express mathematical concepts and processes. Most of the content descriptors in the Australian Curriculum: Mathematics v. 9.0 include the literacy icon, which relates directly to 'Word knowledge: Understand learning area vocabulary'.

ACTIVITY 13.1

Visit the Australian Curriculum: Mathematics v. 9.0 and familiarise yourself with the general capability icons and read some elaborations for each.

Figure 13.1 Literacy skills are important to understand and express mathematical concepts and processes

Literacy demands in mathematics

Mathematical word problems, including ones in international assessment tests, such as NAPLAN and PISA (Programme for International Student Assessment), often have inherent literacy demands necessary to understand the requirements of the task. This aspect has drawn attention to the importance of explicit teaching of the literacy skills that allow students to access what is being assessed in the questions (Perso 2009). Perso uses the following example from a Year 7 NAPLAN test to discuss the literacy demands inherent in the question:

> Ben puts 7 flowers in each of 8 vases. He has 3 flowers left over. Ben wants to put 9 flowers in each vase. How many more flowers does he need?

In order to make sense of the question, students need to understand what the terms 'in each of', 'left over', 'in each', and 'how many more ... does he need?' mean. 'How many more?' can be potentially confusing for students as they often learn to associate 'more' with addition. In order to think more about teaching comprehension skills and test preparation, read Classroom Snapshot 13.1 and then complete the Pause and Reflect activity.

CLASSROOM SNAPSHOT 13.1

Three teachers at a local primary school regularly combine their three Year 5/6 classes in the school's multi-purpose room in order to teach different mathematical topics. On this day, the focus was on measurement and a number of past NAPLAN measurement questions were used as a stimulus for students to solve measurement problems. A test question was displayed on the data projector and students used individual whiteboards to record their answers.

Annie, the teacher who was leading the lesson, asked if anyone could explain what perimeter meant and a distinction was made between perimeter and circumference. Students then individually worked on the problem. Students were then asked to share their responses and strategies for working out the missing sides with the whole group.

PAUSE AND REFLECT

Would you consider Snapshot 13.1 an example of helping students understand specific mathematical vocabulary or an example of preparing them for NAPLAN testing? Do you think the wording of NAPLAN items test students' literacy skills, numeracy skills, or both?

Connecting mathematics with children's literature

Engaging students in mathematics through the use of children's literature is becoming increasingly popular. Children's literature has been shown to help students learn important mathematical concepts and skills, provide a meaningful context for learning mathematics, and facilitate students' development and use of mathematical language and communication (Schiro 1997). Sharing book experiences has been shown to particularly assist in mathematical concept development in the early years (van den Heuvel-Panhuizen & van den Boogaard 2008) and helps to promote mathematical play, discussion, disposition towards mathematics, and improved mathematical achievement (Marston 2010). There are a number of online resources that contain suggestions for incorporating picture books and stories into the teaching of mathematics – for example, the NZ Maths website has a section that includes book titles, covers and mathematical topics. Links are provided to activities that contain lesson ideas and resources.

There are also a number of teaching resource books that provide suggestions of how to link mathematics with literature (e.g. Muir et al. 2017; Thiessen 2004). In the book *Engaging with Mathematics through Picture Books*, a number of lesson ideas are included to engage children with mathematical concepts including early number, place value, measurement, shape, chance and data. Many of the books suggested are available as readings through YouTube.

ACTIVITY 13.2

Six Dinner Sid (Moore 1991) is a story about a cat named Sid who lives at six houses on Aristotle Street and is fed six dinners a day, unbeknownst to his six different owners. One day Sid becomes ill and his secret is revealed.

Look on YouTube for a reading of *Six Dinner Sid*. What mathematics would you engage students in after the reading of this story? How could you capitalise on the story to develop students' mathematical language and communication?

Link 13.1 'Six Dinner Sid'

Figure 13.2 shows an activity where students were asked to identify which number bowl is missing. Activities such as this can help develop the stable order principle, which is discussed earlier in Chapter 2.

Figure 13.2 Which number bowl is missing?
Source: Photo courtesy of Leicha Bragg

Numeracy

According to the Australian Curriculum: Mathematics (ACARA 2018), 'mathematics makes a special contribution to the development of **numeracy** in a manner that is more explicit than is the case in other learning areas. The mathematics curriculum should provide the opportunity to apply mathematical understanding and skills in context, both in other learning areas and in a real-world context'. Financial mathematics, data interpretation and design are examples of contexts that can help students become numerate through mathematics.

Numeracy knowledge, skills, behaviours and dispositions required to use mathematics in a wide range of situations

Numeracy Learning Progressions

As expected, all the mathematical content descriptors in the Australian Curriculum: Mathematics v. 9.0 include a numeracy icon, and as this book is about teaching mathematics and developing students' numeracy, this capability will only be briefly discussed here. The numeracy icons are linked to the National Learning Progressions. These progressions describe the skills, understandings and capabilities that students typically acquire as their proficiency with mathematics increases. Essentially, they describe a pathway or trajectory along which students typically progress. They are designed to help teachers identify the stage of learning reached, any gaps in skills or knowledge, and assist with planning for the next step to progress learning (ACARA 2020). The current version 3.0 of the National Numeracy Learning Progressions refers to the elements of Number sense and algebra, Measurement and geometry, and Statistics and probability. However, they are linked with the revised six content areas through clicking on the icon in the content descriptors within the Australian Curriculum: Mathematics v. 9.0 site. Figure 13.3 shows the elements and sub-elements of the National Learning Progressions.

As an example of the link between mathematics and the numeracy progressions, a Year 3 content descriptor for 'Number': recognise, represent and order natural numbers

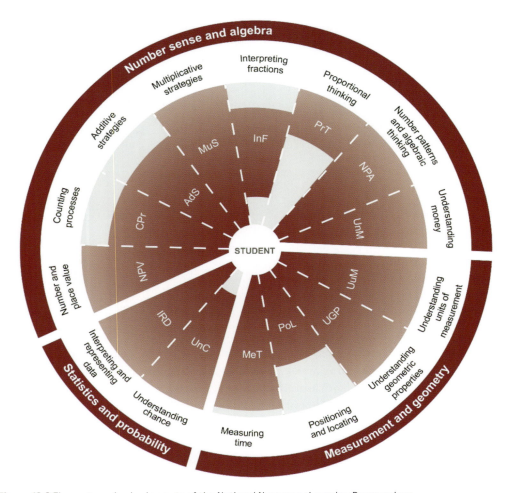

Figure 13.3 Elements and sub-elements of the National Numeracy Learning Progressions
Source: ACARA 2020, p. 5

using naming and writing conventions for numerals beyond 10 000 (AC9M3N01) links with the following level 6 learning progressions:

- Numeral recognition and identification
- Place value

Each progression is elaborated upon. For example, numeral recognition and identification contains the following description:

> Identifies, reads, writes and interprets numerals beyond 1000; applying knowledge of place value, including numerals that contain a zero (e.g. reads 1345 as one thousand, 3 hundred and 45); reads one thousand and 15 and writes as 1015; compares the size of populations of schools, suburbs, cities and ecosystems or the cost of items in shopping catalogues.

Teachers can also access the descriptions for the levels before and after. In the above example, levels 5 and 7 are also included with Level 6. This provision is useful in determining what prior learning is required, and what future learning might look like.

ACTIVITY 13.3

Select a content descriptor from the Australian Curriculum: Mathematics v. 9.0 and click on the numeracy icon. Read the learning progression extract for the relevant level. Does the extract provide you with a clearer understanding of what the content descriptor entails? Before accessing the levels below and above for the learning progression, predict what learning might come before and after for that particular mathematical concept.

Digital literacy

In addition to the Australian Curriculum: Digital Technologies, students develop digital literacy as they learn to use ICT effectively and appropriately when investigating, creating and communicating ideas and information at school, at home, at work and in their communities (ACARA 2022). Calculators allow students to make calculations, draw graphs and interpret data in ways that have previously not been possible. Digital technologies, such as spreadsheets and dynamic geometry software, can engage students and promote understanding of key concepts (see Chapter 11). The use of digital tools is explicitly mentioned in some of the mathematical content descriptions; for example, 'Solve problems involving multiplication of larger numbers by one or two-digit numbers, choosing efficient calculation strategies and using digital tools where appropriate; check the reasonableness of answers' (AC9M5N06). When relevant, the descriptor is accompanied by the Digital Technologies icon, which can be clicked on for further information. Similar to numeracy, links are provided to a continuum which shows the alignment of the continuum with the content. For example, AC9M5N06 is aligned with Level 4 (Years 5–6):

- Select and use the core features of digital tools to efficiently complete tasks.
- Troubleshoot basic problems and identify repetitive tasks to automate Levels 3 and 5 are also readily accessible to determine prior and future learning directions.

In the previous version of the Australian Curriculum: Mathematics, the Information and Communication Technology icon would typically include links to digital tools, websites or online resources. Version 9.0 has replaced the ICT icon with digital literacy and just provides continuum extracts. We think it would be useful to provide teachers with suggested websites and resources to help students progress through the continuum. For example, an interactive website that addresses part of AC9M5N06 (check the reasonableness of answers) is Estimation180. This website has hundreds of examples of quantities and measures where students are asked to provide estimates, including 'too high' and 'too low' estimates. Some of the situations come with a video where you can watch the items being counted and connect the quantity with the number. It is a very engaging website that is likely to be of interest to students. Once an estimate has been entered, students can click on the video below the image and watch (fast forwarded) footage of the cheeseballs being counted. If conducting the activity with students, pause the video at certain points and ask them if they would like to revise their estimates. Experiences such as these can help develop students' number sense, which is an important aspect of being numerate.

Link 13.2 Estimation180

In statistics, content descriptor AC9M5ST01 ('acquire, validate and represent data for nominal and ordinal categorical and discrete numerical variables, to address a question of interest or purpose using software including spreadsheets; discuss and report on data distributions in terms of highest frequency [mode] and shape, in the context of data') links to the general capability of digital literacy, with the sub-elements of 'Create, communicate and collaborate' and 'Interpret data'. The extract for 'Interpret data' is 'analyse and visualise data using a range of digital tools to identify patterns and make predictions'. An online resource that could be utilised to achieve this is the Data Graphs tool on Maths is Fun, where students can construct their own graphs and see what different functions produce. Figure 13.4 shows a screenshot with a simple graph generated from a class survey of pets owned.

Link 13.3 Maths Is Fun: Data Graphs (bar, line, dot, pie, histogram)

Figure 13.4 Screenshot from 'Make your own Graphs'
Source: Maths is Fun <https://www.mathsisfun.com/data/data-graph.php>

ACTIVITY 13.4

The following continuum extract is linked to the content descriptor AC9M5N06 for Level 4 (Years 5–6):

- Select and use the core features of digital tools to efficiently complete tasks
- Troubleshoot basic problems and identify repetitive tasks to automate

Both indicators align with Digital Literacy: Managing and Operating: Select and operate tools. Think about what this would look like in the classroom. Identify a tool that could be used in this context. What are its key features? Locate an online resource that would make a digital tool accessible to all learners, regardless of their location.

Critical and creative thinking

Critical and creative thinking is key to the development of mathematical understanding and is particularly relevant to the concept of mathematical proficiency (ACARA 2022). It is manifested in the mathematics classroom when we ask students to justify their choice of a particular strategy or in identifying the questions that need to be answered when undertaking a statistical investigation. Creative thinking is essential to mathematics problem-solving, and the Australian Curriculum: Mathematics v. 9.0 encourages students to look for alternative ways to approach and solve problems.

The AAMT Top Drawer website has a whole drawer devoted to reasoning. Simple activities that focus on similarities and differences can help develop students' abilities to reason. When comparing and contrasting, students are likely to be:

- noticing and describing
- explaining and justifying
- thinking analytically
- finding relationships
- using logic
- focusing on important features (AAMT, Top Drawer).

Critical and creative thinking the ability to collect and analyse relevant information in order to understand and solve problems

ACTIVITY 13.5

Above and below the line

Draw a horizontal line across the middle of the board.

Without speaking, write 24, 32 and 80 (or other multiples of 4) above the line and 15, 11 and 71 below the line.

Explain that the top numbers have a 'rule' and ask students if they know another number to write either above or below the line.

Link 13.4 Top Drawer: Above and below the line

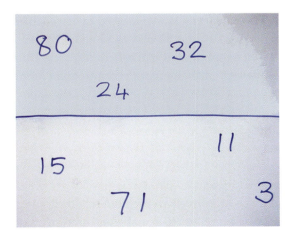

Figure 13.5 Above and below the line

Invite individuals to write their numbers on the board. When most of the students seem to know 'the rule', ask some individuals what they think the rule is. Go back to some of the answers that were sensible but wrong. For example, some students may have thought that the rule was 'evens above and odds below'.

Ask students to add other numbers to challenge and extend knowledge. For example: 'Nobody has added a negative number yet' or 'We need some numbers that are greater than 100'.

Focus the discussion on reasoning. Some possible questions are listed below:

- What is common about the numbers above the line?
- How do you know 12 belongs above the line?
- Can you see anything that all the multiples of 4 have in common? Are there any numbers that end in 2 but are not multiples of 4 to put below the line?
- Can a number ending in 3 go above the line? Why not?
- If I had the number 3407, where would it go, and why?

This activity may be used at all year levels with various categories of number (including fractions and types of integers), measurement units and shapes. It could be extended to include a third and fourth classification area in relation to the line.

Source: Top Drawer, © 2013 Education Services Australia Ltd <www.esa.edu.au>, <https://topdrawer.aamt.edu.au/Reasoning/Big-ideas/Same-and-different/Classification/Above-and-below-the-line>

PAUSE AND REFLECT

In what ways do the activities, such as Activity 13.5, encourage critical and creative thinking? What responses would you be looking for that showed evidence of critical and creative thinking?

Challenging tasks

According to Sullivan (2018), learning is enhanced when students work on problems that they do not yet know how to solve, and students need to be provided with **challenging tasks** that encourage them to persist. Chapter 11 also talks about challenging tasks and how we can plan to teach with challenging tasks. Creativity and critical thinking can be developed through providing students with challenging tasks that require them to:

- plan their approach, especially sequencing more than one step
- process multiple pieces of information, with an expectation that they make connections between those pieces, and see concepts in new ways
- choose their own strategies, goals and level of accessing the task
- spend time on the task and record their thinking. (Sullivan 2018, p. vi)

Students are also expected to explain their strategies, justify their thinking to the teacher and other students, and listen attentively to each other. Classroom Snapshot 13.2 involves a scenario where a student was expected to explain her solution following the completion of a challenging task.

Challenging tasks
tasks that require students to solve problems using their own strategies

CLASSROOM SNAPSHOT 13.2

Mrs Jones had been using challenging tasks with her Year 5 class. On this day, she gave the task as shown in Figure 13.6 to the class.

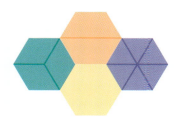

In a circle there are 360 degrees.

Work out the exact size of as many of the angles in this shape as you can.

Explain how you worked them out.

Figure 13.6 Angles task

As usual, students were given minimal instruction on how to solve the task, but enabling prompts were given to those students who were experiencing difficulty. After the students had been working on the task (or variations of) for about 40 minutes, the class were called together to present and explain their solution strategies. Maria's solution was displayed on the IWB for the class to see, and her solution showed that she correctly labelled the angles in the green parallelograms. She then explained that the opposite angle or the interior angle in the hexagon and was 120 degrees. The following exchange then occurred:

Mrs Jones: How do you know that?

Maria: It is 120 degrees. I divided 360 by 120.

Mrs Jones: Where did you get 360 from?

Maria: It is because a whole circle is 360 degrees.

[She did not, however, use this knowledge to add to her explanation.]

[The teacher continued to probe for a more detailed explanation.]

Mrs Jones: I am still not convinced how you got the answer 120.

[At this point, another student tried to help.]

Helen: It is like the red triangle, because two of those [angles] make one of those [angles].

Mrs Jones: Was that your thinking, Maria?

Maria: It is sort of like my thinking but sort of isn't.

[Another student offered his strategy.]

John: [at the board] See – here I think she divided each of these angles [pointing to the centre of the green hexagon] by three, and three times 120 is 360 and these angles would all be the same.

Mrs Jones: Why would they be the same? [referring back to the same problem]

John: I am not quite sure.

▶▶

▶▶

[At this point, Maria is looking rather concerned and later said that she thought she had the wrong answer.]

Mrs Jones: We are trying to work out why Maria's thinking is correct [reassuring Maria that she is correct but still needs to clarify].

[Then, a third student offered a suggestion.]

Chole: We could cut the green hexagon in half, and then they would be the same as two red triangles. And, we would be able to add 60 and 60 together to get 120 because the angles in one triangle equal 180 degrees.

[Finally, Maria was able to justify the answer with understanding after listening to Chloe.]

Maria: If you were able to draw a line like that it would be 60 and 60, and if you add these up [pointing to the two angles in the triangle] you get 120.

Source: Originally printed in Livy, Muir & Sullivan 2018, reprinted with permission

PAUSE AND REFLECT

It is interesting to note that Mrs Jones persisted with probing Maria further with the expectation that she should explain her thinking. How do you think Maria felt about this? What would you do as a teacher? Do you think that such exchanges and experiences encourage the development of critical and creative thinking?

Ethical understanding

Ethical understanding
a personal and socially oriented ethical outlook that influences the management of context, conflict, and uncertainty and includes an awareness of the influence of one's values and behaviours on others

Students develop **ethical understanding** as they learn to understand and act in accordance with ethical principles (ACARA 2022). This involves acting with regard for others and having a desire and capacity to work for the common good. The mathematics curriculum provides opportunity to 'explore ethical issues' and 'explore ethical concepts' (ACARA 2022), in a range of contexts. Examples of these contexts are rational inquiry including sampling, collecting, analysing and interpreting data and statistics; being alert to intentional and accidental errors or distortions and questions of validity in propositions and inferences and interrogating financial claims and sources. The Statistics strand in the Australian Curriculum: Mathematics v. 9.0 is linked with ethical understanding such as in Year 8: 'Investigate techniques for data collection including census, sampling, experiment and observation, and discuss the practicalities and implications of obtaining data through these techniques (AC9M8ST01)'. The following continuum extract shows the alignment of the continuum with this content:

> Analyse the relationships between values, ethical perspectives and ethical frameworks when responding to ethical issues. (ACARA 2022)

Obtaining secondary data from sources such as the internet and newspapers can provide interesting contexts for discussing the use of statistics and their ethical considerations.

The Numeracy in the News website contains a repository of newspaper articles, teacher discussion ideas and student questions all based on interpreting, analysing and critiquing secondary sources of information. As an example, see a report on a study involving pregnant women and smoking: 'Smoking mums alarm'. With relation to the smoking article, students could be asked to investigate the following:

Link 13.5 Numeracy in the News: 'Smoking mums alarm'

- How many cigarettes would a person smoke in 30 pack-years?
- What questions would you ask the researchers about the matching of men and women with lung cancer with healthy men and women?
- Write a conditional probability statement relating the chances of contracting lung cancer for women who smoked 60 pack-years compared to those who did not smoke.
- Summarise why the headline focuses on women smokers.

Investigations such as these are not trivial and relate to the other general capabilities of literacy, numeracy, creative and critical thinking, and personal and social capability.

Incorporating the general capabilities in online teaching

Classroom Snapshot 13.3 details an account of an online problem-solving project whereby Year 5 students worked in groups to collaboratively solve problems in a computer supported collaborative learning environment (Symons, Pierce & Redman 2016). Two different exchanges are provided to show the contrast between working as individual group members and as collaborative group members. After reading the vignette, take time to think about and consider the Pause and Reflect questions.

CLASSROOM SNAPSHOT 13.3

Collaborative online problem-solving

As part of a research project, students in Mr Smith's Year 5 class worked in small groups to collaboratively solve mathematical problems using the Edmodo online social learning platform. All 'discussions' occurred online and out of class. The first exchange involves four students whose problem involved estimating and then calculating the length of a toilet roll without unrolling it.

Sally: Hi, my answer is 9112 cm. I got this by measuring 1 sheet and I searched how many sheets are on a new toilet paper roll. I multiplied the sheet's measurement with the number of sheets that are on a new toilet roll. This is how I got 9112 cm.

Jessica: My answer was 2090 cm. All I had to do was look on the packet with the toilet rolls in it, and on the packet it said how many sheets were on each roll and how long each sheet was. When I found how long and how many sheets there were, I just multiplied and then I got my answer, 2090!

Nathan: Hi, my answer is 9110 cm. I got this answer because I searched in Google for how long one piece and one block is. Then I estimated it altogether.

Krystal: My answer is 17 100 cm. I found this out because it said on the packet of toilet rolls. All I had to do was multiply 180 by 95 to get 17 100 cm.

In the exchange, it appears that rather than collaborating, the students tended to independently state their responses to the problem, along with an explanation of how they came to their answer.

In the following exchange, a different group of students were discussing online their approaches to solving a problem related to the relative rates animals aged compared to humans. Specifically, they were asked to consider the commonly stated claim that 'a human life year is equivalent to five cat years'.

Olivia: What does it mean by saying how old? Could someone help me?

Zander: It means what age is your cat.

Chris: We should also put more animals like elephants and giraffes.

Olivia: Yeah but first we need to do the cats and the other animals that Mr Smith has given us, so we should be talking about that first and then do the other animals in a different Excel document. So how would we be doing the cat one first? Let's discuss the cat one first.

Olivia: I still kinda don't get it when it says by human years. Could anyone help me please?

Zander: What do you mean? You just go up by one. I'm confused.

Olivia: So, what we should do in my opinion is for the cat we could work it out with the strategies that Mr Smith showed us and like for the camel as well and then who should put all of them together?

Zander: I am 20 years old in camel years.

Olivia: Yeah, the same.

Zander: I'm going to do the section where you have to show how old your family is if they were lorikeets.

Olivia: I'm not really sure about that section, but soon I would be doing the cat years and for the cat years it goes by 5s, yeah?

Olivia: So, like 5, 10, 15 and so on. What does it need to go up again?

In contrast to the toilet paper discussion, the above exchange demonstrates more evidence of collaboration and group cohesion, rather than individual reporting, which was characteristic of the first exchange.

Source: Adapted from Symons 2017

PAUSE AND REFLECT

We often make assumptions that when students work in groups, they do so in a collaborative manner. What strategies could you use as a teacher to encourage students to work collaboratively as a group, rather than a collection of individuals? How could the use of digital technologies assist with this?

What general capabilities can you see enacted within this snapshot?

Cross-curriculum priorities

There are three **cross-curriculum priorities** in the Australian Curriculum v. 9.0 (ACARA 2022):
- Aboriginal and Torres Strait Islander histories and cultures
- Asia and Australia's engagement with Asia
- **Sustainability**.

While version 9.0 of the Australian Curriculum Cross-Curriculum of Aboriginal and Torres Strait Islander Histories and Cultures essentially retains the same organising ideas, some of the descriptions of the organising ideas have been revised. The terms 'First Nations Australians' and 'First Nations Peoples' are now used collectively to describe Aboriginal Peoples and Torres Strait Islander Peoples. These terms encapsulate the cultural diversity that existed before colonisation and ensure the culturally sensitive and appropriate identification of the essential aspects of Aboriginal and Torres Strait Islander Histories and Culture (ACARA 2022).

In relation to the Australian Curriculum: Mathematics v. 9.0 (ACARA 2022), students can engage with and value the history and cultures of Australian First National Peoples. The Australian Curriculum v. 9.0 states that 'many First Nations Australians are adept at pattern recognition and algebraic thinking, which informs their cultural expressions, ways of caring for Country/Place and the development of material culture' (ACARA 2022). For many First Nations children, mathematics is an intuitive process and mathematical concepts are well grounded prior to their first year of formal schooling. Content elaborations incorporate 'identified themes in Australian First Nation Peoples' mathematical thinking understandings, and processes, in contexts that can be taught across the content strands and through the year levels' (ACARA 2022).

In version 9 of the Australian Curriculum, the organising ideas of the cross-curriculum of Asia and Australia's engagement with Asia, have been revised to: Knowing Asia and its diversity; Understanding Asia's global significance; Growing Asia-Australia engagement. Essentially the sentiments of these ideas have not been altered significantly, with the focus still being on the interrelationships, diverse backgrounds and experiences and global implications. The Australian Curriculum: Mathematics v. 9.0 'provides opportunities to promote students' awareness of the significant contributions of Asian culture to the historical development and application of mathematical ideas and approaches' (ACARA 2022). Students can learn about the understandings and applications of mathematics in Asia through investigating and exploring concepts such as the development of the Hindu-Arabic and Chinese numeral systems, and the use of tools such as abacuses and counting boards for calculation and solving equations (ACARA 2022).

The sustainability cross-curriculum priority explores the knowledge, skills, values and world views necessary for people to act in ways that contribute to a sustainable future (ACARA 2022). In mathematics, students can be encouraged to explore issues of sustainability through developing skills in mathematical modelling, statistical investigation and analysis. These skills are essential for identifying and exploring sustainability issues and proposed solutions (ACARA 2022). Mathematical understandings can also be applied 'to model, measure, monitor and quantify change in social, economic and ecological systems over time' (ACARA 2022).

> **Cross-curriculum priorities** a dimension of the Australian Curriculum v. 9.0 that develops knowledge, understanding and skills related to Aboriginal and Torres Strait Islander histories and cultures, Asia and Australia's engagement with Asia, and/or Sustainability
>
> **Sustainability** study of how natural systems function, remain diverse and produce everything needed for the ecology to remain in balance

Mathematics also has practical applications across other curriculum areas, particularly in English, science and history. For example, practical work in the sciences requires the capacity to organise and represent data in a range of forms, perform unit conversions, and use and interpret rates. Making sense of history involves interpreting and representing large numbers and a range of data such as immigration statistics, mortality rates, correlation and causation, and imagining timelines and time frames.

Make it Count: maths and Indigenous learners

Make it Count is a website for educators working with First Nations Peoples in mathematics education. It is a teaching and learning resource and a professional learning tool, and it and offers resources for improving the mathematics and numeracy learning outcomes of First Nations' learners. The site contains a number of 'Significant Episodes', which are stories about how teachers have implemented the project into their classrooms and the impact it has had on changing their practice and enhancing student learning. The episodes can be used to promote discussions with colleagues. A number of resources are included, along with links to Maths300 lessons, which participants found to be particularly successful and engaging for First Nations learners.

ACTIVITY 13.6

Visit the Make it Count website. Find and read the Significant Episode: 'Getting Ready in Numeracy'. How do programs like this make a difference to student learning? What actions by the teacher may have helped improve Anthony's attitude toward mathematics?

If the World Were a Village

If the World Were a Village (Smith 2006) is a picture book that promotes 'world-mindedness' by imagining the world's population as a village of just 100 people. It can be used as a stimulus for children to think about life in other nations, including Asia, and to investigate aspects of sustainability. As an example, one of the pages in the book is devoted to nationalities. Of the 100 people in the global village:

- 61 are from Asia
- 13 are from Africa
- 12 are from Europe
- 8 are from South America, Central America and the Caribbean
- 5 are from Canada and the United States
- 1 is from Oceania (an area that includes Australia, New Zealand, and the islands of the south, west and central Pacific) (Smith 2006, p. 8).

Aspects such as school and literacy, air and water, money and possessions, and food are also addressed. Not everyone is well fed: 'There is no shortage of food in the global village. If all the food were divided equally, everyone would have enough to eat. But the food isn't divided equally' (Smith 2006, p. 17).

- 50 people do not have a reliable source of food and are hungry some or all of the time.
- 20 other people are severely undernourished.
- 30 people have enough to eat.

The statistics in *If the World Were a Village* can be used to enhance mathematics skills. For example, the numbers of villagers can be expressed as percentages or fractions (e.g. 20 per cent of people are severely undernourished). Students can be directed to use graph-making software to create pie or bar graphs from one of the topics in the book. The free Create a Graph tool could be used for this or CODAP, if students have access.

Other considerations

Although not included as a cross-curriculum priority in the Australian Curriculum v. 9.0, STEM (Science, Technology, Engineering, Mathematics) and STEAM (Science, Technology, Engineering, Arts, Mathematics) are certainly considered as cross-curriculum concepts. STEM education is a term which is used to 'refer collectively to the separate disciplines within its umbrella … and also to a cross-disciplinary integrated approach to teaching these subjects aimed at increasing student interest in STEM-related fields and improving students' problem-solving and critical analysis skills' (Australian Education Council 2015, p. 5). See Chapter 14 to find out more about STEM and how it can be implemented in the primary classroom.

> **TIPS FOR ONLINE TEACHING**
>
> Many of the activities suggested in this chapter can be adapted for online delivery. Incorporating the general capabilities and cross-curriculum priorities in the classroom supports an inquiry-based teaching approach and inquiry can occur at home. For example, students could work on inquiry-based sustainability activities which involve the whole family. Practical investigations could be undertaken involving collecting data on how much rubbish was generated in the home over a week, how much milk was consumed, how much toilet paper was used, and so on. Groups could be given different investigations to undertake, with regular catch-ups and reporting of results occurring through scheduled Zoom or teams meetings. The general capabilities relate directly to the skills, behaviours and attributes that students need to succeed in life and work, so isolated online tasks such as drill-and-practice routines would not be appropriate online teaching experiences for students in this context.

Conclusion

This chapter has provided some suggestions on how the general capabilities and cross-curriculum priorities can be incorporated into authentic mathematical learning experiences. Links with the Australian Curriculum: Mathematics v. 9.0 can easily be sourced through clicking on the relevant icons that are included in the content descriptors. Teaching and learning mathematics is made more meaningful when it occurs in a context that is relevant, and the general capabilities and cross-curriculum priorities provide a range of contexts for students to investigate. ICT can be capitalised on to access a wealth of statistics and information that is current and easily accessible. It is hoped that teachers will capitalise on these resources and contexts to engage students in rich mathematical investigations.

GUIDED STUDENT TASKS

1. Visit the Australian Curriculum: Mathematics v. 9.0 online site. Familiarise yourself with the different icons for the general capabilities and the cross-curriculum priorities. Explore the suggestions for a range of icons and year levels.
2. There are currently no related icon links to personal and social capability in the Australian Curriculum: Mathematics v. 9.0. Have a look at the other curriculum areas and try to find reference to this capability. Can you think of some suggestions for where this capability could be included in mathematics content descriptors?
3. Explore websites that are dedicated to reporting statistics and data (e.g. the ABS). Identify data sets and statistics that are relevant to the general capabilities and the cross-curriculum priorities.

FURTHER READING

Website for exploration

Livy, S, Muir, T & Sullivan, P 2018, 'Challenging tasks lead to productive struggle!', *Australian Primary Mathematics Classroom*, vol. 23, no. 1, pp. 19–24.

Muir, T, Livy, S, Bragg, L, Clark, J, Wells, J & Attard, C 2017, *Engaging with mathematics through picture books*, Albert Park, Vic: Teaching Solutions.

Perso, T 2009, 'Cracking the NAPLAN code: Numeracy and literacy demands', *Australian Primary Mathematics Classroom*, vol. 14, no. 3, pp. 14–18.

Sullivan, P 2018, *Challenging mathematical tasks*, South Melbourne, Vic: Oxford.

CHAPTER 14

STEM IN THE PRIMARY SETTING

LEARNING OUTCOMES

By the end of this chapter, you will:

- have developed an understanding of the STEM education strategy that is prevalent nationally and internationally
- be able to design student learning tasks that are inspired by STEM-related careers for targeted mathematics outcomes and open investigations
- understand what coding means for the primary mathematics context and how it relates to STEM-related learning tasks
- have developed an awareness of robotics activities in the primary setting
- consider the debate that surrounds the STEM strategy in relation to primary mathematics education
- have developed an appreciation and understanding of tasks that measure and explain sustainability issues over time and explore the world through aspects of mathematics.

Introduction

STEM is an acronym for science, technology, engineering and mathematics. The term was first used in 2001 by the United States National Science Foundation to refer to the group of career fields and also as a basis for a career-oriented curriculum based on integrating knowledge from these separate disciplines. The aim was to develop students to become flexible problem-solvers and, at the same time, to stimulate interest in STEM-based careers (White 2014). Since then, STEM has become a keyword in many discussions and policy papers about curriculum in Australia and other parts of the world. The development of young Australians who are well prepared to take up a career of STEM is reflected in the agreed National STEM School Education Strategy (Department of Education, Skills and Employment Education Council 2015) 'which focusses on foundation skills, developing mathematical, scientific and digital literacy, and promoting problem solving, critical analysis and creative thinking skills'. Strongly entwined with this strategy is our responsibility, as primary educators, to design tasks that enable students to develop an understanding of sustainability issues and instil a sense of responsibility to take action through informed choices. One essential component of making the informed choice lies in having the mathematical understanding to explore our changing world in a flexible and adaptive manner.

This chapter considers some practical applications of STEM in the primary classroom with a particular emphasis on STEM's relationship to mathematics outcomes and the integrity of the mathematics as taught in the STEM context. This will extend to an exploration of Education for Sustainability (EfS) in the primary mathematics classroom, and opportunities for STEM tasks that are based on inquiry within the EfS space.

STEM in schools

In 2016, the Australian Government released a document outlining the intended strategy for engagement in STEM-related pathways and careers. The Australian **STEM education strategy** 2016–2026, introduced earlier in the chapter, describes five areas of action. These are communicated in the ACARA STEM Connections Project Report (ACARA 2016a, p. 4), being:

> **STEM education strategy** an approach that is cross-disciplinary with an aim to increase student interest in STEM pathways and related fields while improving students' problem-solving and critical analysis skills

1. increasing student STEM ability, engagement, participation and aspiration
2. increasing teacher capacity and STEM teaching quality
3. supporting STEM education opportunities within school systems
4. facilitating effective partnerships with tertiary education providers, business and industry
5. building a strong evidence base.

Discussions around STEM in primary and secondary classrooms have become more prevalent over the past 15 years as the impact of the STEM agenda and strategy unfolds. There are differing views on the nature of STEM activities, and whether STEM is merely a defined example of integration across the curriculum or if it is more appropriately recognised as a stand-alone learning experience. No matter where one sits in this debate, activities that bring integrated real-world problems into the classroom are a worthwhile addition to our teaching and learning tasks. Like many aspects of mathematics education, it is best to consider the merits of each learning opportunity, of which many exist within the STEM realm of possibilities.

> **STEM education** the teaching of the science, technology, engineering and mathematics disciplines under the same umbrella

It appears that in many education circles, **STEM education** has become a buzz term, with most educators knowing what the acronym stands for, but having little understanding of what it means for each of the four learning areas. The design of STEM activities and subsequent implementation in the primary classroom remains a hurdle for many teachers (Hudson et al. 2015). There is a general lack of shared understanding in the education sector as to the practical implications of STEM, and how these relate to the implementation of the national curriculum. Different schools have taken varied positions on how STEM will be addressed. Some schools have specialist STEM teachers, and STEM is treated as a separate component in the curriculum.

The ACARA STEM Connections Project, from which the five areas of action are taken, targeted the Years 9 to 10 context. The fifth strategy above seeks a strong evidence base, and this is particularly an area of need for STEM in the primary context. It is reported that teachers involved in the study 'found that Mathematics was the most difficult learning area to plan for in this project' (ACARA 2016a, p. 10). Despite the secondary setting of the project, these teachers described the identification of incidental mathematics teaching moments as crucial to the project approach. The project-based learning model used in the Connections Project enabled the students to be connected to their learning as the tasks directly related to real-world settings that built on their individual real-world experiences. This is a fundamental principle of constructivism that underpins the project-based strategy and fits well with the STEM agenda.

STEM education has come to mean a project-based teaching approach characterised by open-ended problems that children work in groups to solve. There is a design element (engineering), usually something to be made (technology), a testing or evaluation phase (science) and mathematics to underpin all these stages.

One approach to STEM education is to work with local industries. Industry partners are more familiar in the secondary sector than the primary sector. As partner linkages are a positive strategy for connecting students to STEM-related careers, it would be wise to commence this in the primary years. In primary schools, tapping into parents as a resource can provide many opportunities for accessing expertise in areas such as trades, engineering, technology-based careers and science fields. It is also motivating to connect with students' older siblings who may be training or studying in one of the STEM pathways to share their experiences and assist in the facilitation of problem-based learning tasks.

PAUSE AND REFLECT

Where have you experienced STEM education? Did you go to a school that emphasised STEM, or have you seen applications of STEM in schools that you have visited? Think about STEM and identify what strengths there might be in integrating all the science, technology and mathematics curriculums into a STEM subject. Where does engineering fit in a primary classroom? Do you think STEM can be addressed effectively?

STEM and primary mathematics

Although STEM has been taken up successfully by many schools and teachers, there have been some warnings about this approach. English (2016) articulated a concern that if the focus on STEM outcomes is too intense, it may diminish opportunities to advance mathematics. Fitzallen (2015) suggested that the essential supporting nature of mathematics in STEM is often neglected, and the focus in classrooms is on the development of the idea rather than the mathematical aspects of both the design and the evaluation of that design. Blackly and Howell (2015, p. 104) indicated that the challenges of teaching through STEM have not entirely been met and primary teachers in particular 'have defaulted to the notion of S.T.E.M. rather than STEM' – that is, the different disciplines have been separated with only cursory attention paid to the integrated nature of STEM. As integrated STEM education has developed, there has been a shift in focus and the engineering and technology aspects have been emphasised (Blackly & Howell 2015). Moore and Smith (2014) described two approaches to integrating STEM education. The first related to context and design challenges based in engineering and technology, which acted as a motivator for learning mathematics. The second approach used engineering outcomes as part of the intended learning, and mathematics skills were developed incidentally.

Classroom Snapshot 14.1 shows a teacher using the first of these two approaches to motivate her students to undertake some meaningful mathematics.

CLASSROOM SNAPSHOT 14.1

Mrs Thompson was finding the motivation levels in her Year 5/6 class to be of concern. This was particularly evident during her mathematics time slot. She had recently been reading about the emphasis on STEM in Australia and decided to put in a concerted effort to bringing this into her classroom. Mrs Thompson thought that one way of getting the class motivated could involve bringing some trade topics into her lessons. She was struggling with the balance between what she expected to cover from the curriculum and what the trade topic could motivate the children to solve.

The school was located in Sydney, and the students were all aware of the light rail scheme being built. There were lots of concrete trucks going in and out of the construction site, and one of the parents of the children in the class was a carpenter on the project. Mrs Thompson phoned

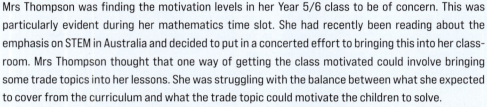

Figure 14.1 Concrete, mortar and render composition ratios for different purposes
Source: Cement Australia

the parent and he volunteered to come in with some tools and examples to show the students what was involved. He left the class with a real-world problem to solve. He needed to create a concrete section that was 8000 mm × 2500 mm × 345 mm inclusive of a 450 mm × 450 mm beam that was along one side. The students were asked to calculate the amount of concrete required, and then research the components that make up concrete, and work out the amounts of each component required. The students were asked to illustrate their work and demonstrate their mathematical thinking.

Mrs Thompson's concern about the balance between mathematical content and problem-solving skills was answered with this real-world problem, and she noted that she had covered the measurement outcome, so she made a note of this in her program. The submissions also indicated where the students were at in relation to some concepts in the areas of measurement, geometry and number. The students' final work provided some qualitative assessment for learning evidence.

ACTIVITY 14.1

Before bringing this real-world problem into the classroom, Mrs Thompson realised that some of her students would struggle with the reasoning required to calculate the quantities needed for the concrete. She thought that a series of introductory tasks would help build her students' confidence and competence.

Using the above guidelines for making cement for different purposes, design three different tasks that connect to real-world problems. Design tasks that could be undertaken by children having different levels of understanding. This activity relates to the development of proportional reasoning and Chapter 6 may provide some help.

The problem-based learning approach advocated for STEM education has been welcomed, and the next section considers this approach in the context of primary mathematics.

Problem-based learning and STEM

Problem-based learning (PBL) is an approach where students are immersed in a topic by experiencing how to find a solution to an open-ended problem or task. The approach has been used in areas such as medical studies, teacher education, social science and science. STEM tasks lend themselves to the PBL pedagogy due to the following characteristics of the approach adapted from Boud (1985):

- The problem is presented at the start of the teaching and learning sequence.
- Students are encouraged to take responsibility for their own learning.
- Crossing the boundaries of key learning areas is enabled.
- A focus on the process exists.
- Collaboration between facilitator and students is fostered.
- Students' individual level of understanding and prior experiences is recognised when designing the problem.

Problem-based learning (PBL)
a student-centred pedagogy where students develop their understanding of concepts through tasks that involve solving an open-ended problem

- Communication during the task is an expectation and is an important component of the problem-solving process.
- Teachers are viewed as facilitators rather than content experts.

The key to a successful STEM teaching episode is the problem addressed. This needs a context and should address significant mathematical content as well as the other three STEM areas. The problem needs to be carefully developed, with the different aspects of STEM addressed explicitly. One example could be 'Licorice Lines' from reSolve: Maths by Inquiry. In this project, children are asked to make by hand 'licorice' sticks from modelling dough and to make these as similar as they can. They then manufacture the 'licorice' sticks in a factory, and compare the two products to answer the question 'Which process will make the sticks more consistent? How can we test this?' The mathematics is integral to solving the problem and draws on measurement and statistics understanding.

To be successful in a problem-based approach, children in primary schools need to develop problem-solving skills. English (2016, p. 359) synthesised recent work in STEM education and presented a list of required elements for effective problem-solving as:

- a substantial and flexible grasp of foundational mathematics ideas and processes
- general skills that are of a cognitively high level
- an understanding of conceptual models that underlie processes or systems, which in turn requires the ability to interpret complex representations within given contexts
- the ability to interpret quantitative data in different complex forms in unfamiliar, multiple domains
- the ability to solve a range of novel problems.

The first of these elements indicates the importance of mathematics. Mrs Thompson in Classroom Snapshot 14.1 recognised the need for mathematical skills and ensured that her students were well prepared.

Although teachers recognise the importance of problem-solving in the context of mathematics, finding the mathematics in problem-based learning contexts is more challenging. Beswick and colleagues (2012) showed that it was possible to address almost all the mathematics curriculum through projects that took a strong problem-solving focus, but that teachers often did not recognise how they could develop the mathematical ideas.

There are two major watchpoints when it comes to teaching mathematics in PBL contexts. First, the mathematics within the chosen context must be explicitly recognised and then developed as the problem scenario is being developed (see Activity 14.1). Unless the mathematics is explicit, it may be missed by children. Second, many contexts that lend themselves to PBL in primary classrooms draw on computation and measurement or, sometimes, statistics. The mathematical aspects of algebraic, geometric or probabilistic reasoning may become overlooked or contrived. Teachers using the PBL approach need to review their programs regularly to ensure that all strands of the mathematics curriculum are addressed.

Culturally responsive STEM pedagogies

The integrated STEM education approach provides a vehicle for developing culturally responsive pedagogy. Pedagogically, working in groups to solve problems is appropriate for many different cultures. We often talk about constructivism as learning by building on students' life experiences, each child's culture plays a very important role in relation to lived experiences. There is no need for activities that include cultural links to be considered as additional tasks to the curriculum being followed. In contrast, on reflection after teaching a culturally responsive task, it can be observed that a range of objectives is met, often across mathematical strands and across different key learning areas.

Think about the problem of weaving a mat with a three-colour, repeating design to cover a specified area. Although we may not think of this as an engineering problem, the design process and the scaling up encourage engineering thinking. Science content may be addressed through dyes used to create the colours and technology through making the mat. Mathematically, this challenge draws on geometric reasoning, measurement and possibly computational tasks. In appropriate locations, the local community could be invited to share their expertise and provide examples of weaving techniques.

One strength of STEM is that it can cross cultural boundaries. STEM curriculums have been developed in other parts of the world, and we can learn from their experience.

The United Kingdom experience

The United Kingdom's STEM outcomes, over a 30-year period, have resulted in some key lessons that Australia should consider in its own approach to support STEM education. Pauline Hoyle (2016) provides a set of recommendations to increase the likelihood of secondary school students choosing STEM-related careers based on their STEM journey. Of particular interest to this chapter in regard to the practicalities of the primary context are the following measures described by Hoyle (2016, p. 9):

- a need to value STEM subjects to the same level that success in sport is valued (in relation to school culture)
- provision of funding for professional development for teachers in the STEM area, which would include all primary teachers
- access to online STEM teaching materials and ideas, and information about STEM-related pathways
- access to STEM experts (in the primary setting this could involve regular involvement of parents in STEM-related careers)
- an understanding of STEM across the curriculum
- identification of clear pathways for STEM knowledge and skills to assist both teachers and students, which should include suggestions for how to use these in context.

In the Australian Curriculum v. 9.0, STEM is addressed within the curriculum areas of mathematics, science and technologies, and is supplemented by inclusion in the general capabilities, namely: numeracy, critical and creative thinking, and information and communication technology. In addition, engineering is a key component of digital technologies, science, and, of particular interest to this chapter, mathematics. Because primary teachers teach the whole curriculum, they are ideally placed to recognise and implement STEM activities within the more flexible arrangements of the primary classroom. Our role as primary mathematics teachers is to provide authentic learning experiences that draw upon STEM-related contexts where students have ownership of their solutions to identified problems in this area.

> ### PAUSE AND REFLECT
>
> STEM education requires an integrated approach to curriculum. Many schools have a dedicated numeracy and literacy block early in the day when children are fresh. How can these two expectations be resolved? If STEM is only taught outside the 'important' curriculum times, does that downplay its importance? Does the emphasis on STEM demand a different approach to thinking about curriculum delivery in school? Discuss your thoughts with a colleague.

Implementing STEM in the primary classroom

Despite the challenges of implementing STEM in primary classrooms, there are many successful examples. In this section, some aspects of STEM are considered in relation to the mathematics experienced.

Integrating engineering design

When investigating STEM initiatives, there are many more initiatives that cross the boundaries of mathematics, science and technology, than engineering. This is not surprising when you consider that primary teachers do not have an engineering curriculum to fulfil; hence, engineering could be perceived as an extra-curricular activity. Despite this, English (2016, p. 85) stated that 'engineering-based experiences can develop young students' appreciation and understanding of the roles of engineering in shaping the world, and how engineering can contextualize mathematics and science principles to improve achievement, motivation, and problem-solving'. In the Australian Curriculum, **engineering design** tasks fit into the design and technologies (version 8.4) content. In this content area, teachers are asked to provide learning experiences where students design and produce products. It is here that mathematics concepts have an important role to play; as to design and produce products effectively requires the relevant mathematical understanding that underpins the task. This is also true for science concepts that may be embedded in the task.

The task set in Classroom Snapshot 14.2 is an example.

Engineering design an iterative process where problems are defined by specific criteria and constraints leading to multiple solutions that are evaluated and assessed systematically in consideration of optimisation

CLASSROOM SNAPSHOT 14.2

Mr Daly, a Year 5 teacher, was wrapping up a measurement topic in mathematics. At the same time, the class was working on persuasive text types. Like most children, the class was always excited about food-related activities. In nearby Guyra, there was a very large tomato farm that was bringing industry and employment to the area. As part of a science excursion, the children had recently visited the tomato farm. Mr Daly decided to bring in all the aspects described above to create a problem-based learning experience where the children needed to work in teams of four. The team needed to choose a tomato-based product and then, using manufacturing principles, design suitable packaging, including a logo that had geometric elements. The team then presented their design in a 2-minute video alongside a written design portfolio.

The students were given the following brief.

Tomato product

Design challenge: Design a product that can be mass-produced using tomatoes as the key ingredient. The product should consider high nutritional value and be suitable to market to families. The team needs to consider cost analysis, packaging and branding.

Design brief: Who are you choosing as your target audience? Your brief should be a team decision based on your knowledge of the tomato farm and your research of this industry.

Outcomes: At the end of your team work, you will be expected to present your team design portfolio, an example of your packaging and the logo you have designed in a 2-minute edited video presentation. These videos will be viewed by managers at the tomato farm and feedback provided to the class.

In this scenario, the engineering design elements are included in the packaging and logo, and the science elements through the tomato farm experience, growing conditions and nutritional value. Technology is involved in the video production and could include a prototype of the packaging. The mathematics included is potentially extensive. Geometric reasoning is needed for the logo design and the packaging, measurement skills are developed throughout the project, statistics could be used to undertake market surveys, and a range of other measurement and computational skills will be needed. This example includes both of Moore and Smith's (2014) approaches to STEM.

Evidence-based practice in STEM

A group of mathematics education researchers (Fitzallen et al. 2018) are unlocking the potential of STEM activities embedding statistics concepts in the primary setting. One of their activities that considers data representation in STEM tasks uses the context of catapults to engage Year 4 students, while developing a range of mathematics concepts with a focus on data representation. The activity enables the student to tell the story of the data by creating their own data representations. The student activity requires a simple pre-made catapult structure for each group, or each group could be given the same materials to make their own catapult structure in a prior STEM-related activity targeting the area of engineering. The catapult lesson may include:

- a class discussion and internet exploration to familiarise themselves with catapults, including historical aspects
- a play with the catapult designed to throw a ping pong ball on a spoon
- class consensus concerning an appropriate question to explore
- a discussion regarding the rules that would need to be followed to make a trial of the catapult fair (test conditions)

- the process of trial, improve, and retrial
- designed data representation to answer the group question.

Fitzallen and colleagues (2018, p. 5) found that a group of Year 4 students they observed came up with the following question to lead their investigation: 'What is the typical distance a ping pong ball travels when launched from a catapult?' While the students explored the concept of average, or mean, the data representations provided ways to further explore this statistical idea by considering appropriate graphical representation. In this study, the students predominantly presented the data in case-value plots, frequency bar charts and tables/tallies (p. 4). Further stressing the point that 'there will be times when explicit instruction will be needed to help students transition from case-value plots to frequency plots for measurement data' (p. 5).

PAUSE AND REFLECT

Inquiry tasks, such as the catapults task above, have the potential to develop many mathematical concepts during the pedagogical sequence. The concepts may be different for different children in the class. Write a list of all the mathematical concepts that could be addressed through the catapult activity.

Inquiry pedagogy

Li and colleagues (2020) completed a systematic review of publications targeting STEM education and identified four main areas of interest being the most prevalent. These are policy, goals, policy, evaluation and assessment. Li and the research team also found that community had a general interest in pedagogical approaches that would support STEM education across primary and secondary sectors. In this book, we have explored a number of pedagogical frameworks. In this chapter, we present the work of Fielding-Wells, Dole and Makar (2014), who have investigated the effectiveness of inquiry pedagogy to promote conceptual understandings of proportional reasoning. It becomes evident in their work that the problem context, important to the pedagogical process, fits nicely with the STEM space. Their approach to inquiry focuses the student on the mathematical thinking required and their choice in finding a solution to what the researchers describe as an ill-structured question (p. 4) that is posed. During the learning process, the students are placed in the position where they need to analyse, explain and defend their mathematical decisions throughout the solution process.

There are five phases described by Fielding-Wells, Dole and Makar (2014, p. 7). These are summarised as:

- *Discover*: 'Hook to engage students', in relation to purpose and context of the inquiry and linking the inquiry question to children's prior experience and knowledge.
- *Devise*: Students develop a plan to address the inquiry question. They develop their plan while thinking about the evidence they will need to support their conclusion to

the inquiry. They may need to trial plans while focusing on the mathematics they may need to commence the process.
- *Develop*: At this stage the students carry out their plan. They collect evidence along the way, and gradually apply deeper mathematical thinking as they trial and revise their plan as it grows in sophistication.
- *Defend*: Students report their processes, solutions and conclusions while evaluating their process and reasoning along the way.
- *Diverge*: Connect and transfer their learning through the inquiry to other areas and new problems within the area of inquiry.

ACTIVITY 14.2

In Further Reading, we have included the link to the evidence-based study of Inquiry Pedagogy described above. The study is in the context of comparing a Barbie Doll to human physical structures. Is Barbie a human? (Fielding-Wells, Dole & Makar 2014, p. 13). Using the five phases above, how would you facilitate this Barbie inquiry task in a Year 5 classroom? What leading, probing and prompting questions would you use? What resources would you make available to the students? Finally, locate the journal article online, and compare the researchers' sequence to your sequence. What were the similarities and differences?

TIPS FOR ONLINE TEACHING

The Barbie inquiry task can be adapted for online learning by developing and exploring 'the hook' session over Zoom; devising, planning and possibly trialing in Zoom break-out groups, carrying out the plan individually, back into the same break-out groups to defend their evidence and response, back into the class Zoom group for short presentations of their findings, and lastly, an individual activity where the knowledge is transformed or transferred to a different topic. Adaptions need to consider that the students will not have the same Barbie and, in fact, may include action characters of many different proportions. While the final results will be different, the shared process and mathematical discussion is one of the most important components of the sequence.

Coding

While there is a push for STEM education outcomes generally, the technology component has prompted debate about the value of **coding** in the primary curriculum. Coding is commonly used to represent programming to solve problems. As used today, however, coding does not require high-level computer programming skills. Modern programs such as Scratch have been developed with a 'drag-and-drop' interface.

Scratch was launched in 2007 by the Lifelong Kindergarten Group at the MIT media lab. The goal is to provide an appealing environment for young people to develop programming skills (Resnick et al. 2009). Resources and ideas for parents and educators are freely available from the website. The approach taken is suitable to a range of ages (targeting children 8

Coding a common term used to represent programming to solve problems

to 16 years) and includes games, interactive stories, simulations, animations, and avenues to share and discuss what they have produced with other interested young creators. The interactive medium also has the facility for users to work on other students' projects and to work collaboratively with each other. The remixing that is possible pushes design ideas that bit further, with group ideas being pooled in the development of one online project. It is interesting to note that while the developers of Scratch have provided a forum 'to nurture a new generation of creative, systematic thinkers comfortable using programming to express their ideas' (Scratch 2022). This highlights an important role that primary education has to play in the STEM agenda. It appears as important to facilitate opportunities for creative thought and systematic thinking, as much as building links with industry partners and fostering knowledge of STEM-related career pathways.

Scratch uses a series of programming blocks, with similarities to building blocks, that students can put together in a relaxed environment without complicated programming language. There are many tutorials, guides and activity cards to assist in using Scratch in the classroom. Many have connections to mathematics outcomes. Consider the examples shown in Figures 14.2 and 14.3.

Figure 14.2 Scratch Make it Fly card example 1
Source: Scratch <https://scratch.mit.edu/ideas>

Figure 14.3 Scratch Make it Fly Card example 2
Source: Scratch <https://scratch.mit.edu/ideas>

ACTIVITY 14.3

Go to the Scratch website. Undertake one of the tutorials. Try one of the examples under tips. Now create a new Scratch program. Reflect on how easy or difficult you found this. What mathematical thinking did you use? Write a paragraph about your experience with Scratch. If you are able, ask a primary age child to try out Scratch. How did your experience differ from that of the child? Discuss Scratch and its uses with a colleague.

Previous research on coding (then called programming) indicated that mathematics outcomes were ambiguous (Benton et al. 2017). A recent project in the United Kingdom explicitly addressed mathematical outcomes using Scratch. The study found that children could program to demonstrate, for example, place value, but that teachers who were less familiar with the program found teaching in this way more difficult (Benton et al. 2018). It should be noted that, despite the use of technology and the need for students to design the designated programs, this project was not actually a STEM project. Science was not integrated into the study, and while the design and production of the program and the focus on mathematics did meet some aspects of STEM, this was not intended to be a real-world experience for students.

Another place that also offers coding applications is LEGO® Education. LEGO® also offers robotics, which is used in some schools to develop a range of skills.

Robotics

The use of **robotics** in primary classrooms has grown rapidly over the past 10 years. Robotics provides a novel and real-world context for problem-based learning tasks that have the added advantage of ticking every box when it comes to targeting science, technology, engineering and mathematics in the same learning sequence. When writing about the educational market and adoption of educational robotics kits, Kee (2011, p. 16) provided the following snapshot of topics that can be covered using these resources:

- mathematics of gearing
- levers, pulleys and simple machines
- electronics
- sensors and actuators
- software flowcharting and artificial intelligence
- datalogging
- automated systems.

Robotics the branch of technology that deals with the design, the construction, the operation, and application of robots

All these topics potentially address significant mathematics, but as with coding, the teacher still needs to translate these into curriculum outcomes.

Dependent upon the budgetary constraints of a school, most robotic products fall into two categories. The expensive option is modular systems, which are kits that can be built in varied configurations for different purposes. The less expensive option provides only a single configuration. After budget considerations, it is necessary to consider the teaching and learning affordances of the kit. Many schools have opted for LEGO® Mindstorms

Link 14.1 VEX Robotics
Link 14.2 Fischertechnik

systems; however, other common kits are VEX and Fischertechnik. All are widely available in Australia. Once the choice of a system is made, primary schools can choose to embed robotics into the curriculum or have a robotics program that is an extracurricular activity. When set up as an extracurricular activity, program outcomes may include displays of built robots, robotic competitions or presentations. The disadvantage of robotics as an extracurricular activity is that only those children interested in the area or able to participate are involved.

When considering the potential of robotics as a problem-solving tool, Castledine and Chalmers (2011) found that 'robotic activities assisted students to reflect on the problem-solving decisions they made' (p. 19) and that LEGO® robotics activities 'required careful teacher scaffolding'. The ability to reflect on their problem-solving processes enables the learners to assess, modify and adjust their actions. With problem-solving being one of the key proficiencies underpinning the Australian Curriculum: Mathematics v. 9.0, robotic activities in the primary setting potentially have an important role to play.

Generic reflective questions can prompt students during robotic activities to think about their problem-solving. Castledine and Chalmers (2011, pp. 24–5) provide five reflective questions for students that were asked during a robotic activity that involved a race:

1. How did you calculate the secret distance time for the robot?
2. Explain how you used your trial runs. What strategies did you use?
3. What strategies did you change during your trial runs?
4. What new strategies did you learn?
5. Where else in your life could you use these strategies?

Robotics are motivating and interesting for most children. Consider Classroom Snapshot 14.3 as an example of one teacher introducing robotics into her classroom.

CLASSROOM SNAPSHOT 14.3

St Angela's Primary School invested funds in LEGO® robotics kits for middle to upper primary students. Ms Jenkins was a Year 5 teacher, and while she was intrigued to use the kits, she had no idea where to begin. She decided to seek some advice from colleagues one lunch break. This was becoming a critical issue, as since the purchase of the kits had been announced at a recent school assembly, her students were constantly asking questions about when they would be using them. One teacher suggested that the LEGO® company might have an education website with examples of some areas the robotics could be used in her classroom. This was sound advice, as LEGO® had provided a grid with ACARA syllabus connections for each primary year group. One example for a Year 5 measurement and geometry outcome is shown in Table 14.1. The outcome ACMMG112 is represented by AC9M5M04 (Australian Curriculum: Mathematics F–10 v. 9.0), 'estimate, construct and measure angles in degrees, using appropriate tools including a protractor, and relate these measures to angle names'.

Ms Jenkins had the starting point she needed, and she was able to wait until the appropriate time in her program to embed the robot activities. The activities were cross-curricular incorporating

Table 14.1 LEGO® connections to the ACARA syllabus

Content descriptions	Elaborations	LEGO® Education	Teacher notes
Geometric reasoning Estimate, measure and compare angles using degrees. Construct angles using a protractor. (ACMMG112)	Measuring and constructing angles using both 180° and 360° protractors. Recognising that angles have arms and a vertex, and that size is the amount of turn required for one arm to coincide with the other.	Estimate the angle at which the robot turns x rotations, positioning the robot at 0° before program run. Draw the angle the robot turned, measure the correct angle of turn and compare this to estimation. Repeat for numerous angles, measuring and comparing angles in degrees, e.g. difference in degrees, acute vs. obtuse.	Build basic robot and use pen attachment to draw different angles. Students identify the vertex and arms of the angles and understand how the start and end of the program represents each arm and the construction of the angle.

Source: Excerpt from LEGO® Education website <https://education.lego.com/en-au/curriculum>

technology and science. She added two writing tasks to the learning sequence that involved a creative writing task about the robot each group created and a procedural text type task, where each group shared the design and making procedure they employed. The children worked in groups to design robots that could be programmed to create different angles.

STEM and robotics have a place in primary classrooms, and how it is implemented may depend on the school context. STEM activities, however, do not have to involve expensive robotics.

Education for Sustainability (EfS) in the Mathematics Classroom

There has been recent debate on the level of attention given to EfS with such a strong strategic agenda directed at STEM education (Smith & Watson 2019). For our world to be sustainable, it relies on the interrelationships of four key systems: economic, ecological, social and political. Any small change to one of these systems will have an impact on other systems. It is the notion of small change that highlights the importance of equipping our students with tools to take positive action towards their vision of a sustainable future. In the primary mathematics classroom, we can explore this natural component of STEM to develop individual responsibility for our environment and, at the same time, develop higher order mathematical concepts and skills. For example, measuring change over time, in various forms, is one strategy for investigating students' own environment and making decisions that relate to beneficial change. Contextual stimulus could be drawn from:

- poverty, equity and participation
- consumption
- population and density
- climate change
- pollution and waste
- resources
- biodiversity.

For more information on these sustainability issues as they relate to education read *Education for Sustainability in Primary Schools* (Taylor, Quinn & Eames 2015).

CLASSROOM SNAPSHOT 14.4

It was a special day for a Year 2 class in Armidale, New South Wales. Most winters, there will be a day or two that the temperature and conditions are just right for a covering of snow. On this cold Monday morning, the students arrived, chattering about the amount of snow they had in their yards at home and the structures they made. Most students talked about the snowman they made. They shared how tall they thought their snowman was, and what they used for facial features and other decorations.

The teacher, Miss Edwards asked: Do you think the snowmen will still be there when you get home?

One student responded: No, I didn't put a coat on mine, so it won't get too warm.

Miss Edwards asked what others had done to protect their snowman from melting, and most had the same idea. She realised that this was a good opportunity to connect their measurement and graphing concept development to the idea of glacier melts and global warming, with the notion of insulation.

The teacher created a practical student-centred lesson that involved freezing a rubber glove filled with water (tied with a rubber band) in the freezer, and co-designing a class investigation answering the inquiry question, 'Do glass hands (the frozen gloves filled with water look like glass hands) need to stay warm to stay around?' The activity involved measuring the size of the melt on concrete over a set amount of time when the frozen hands were in the shade, in the sun, or covered with a jumper in the shade and then in the sun. The diameter of the melt was measured over time in the different situations, then tabulated, and then represented graphically on a digital graphing tool. The students presented their group evidence, and their final response to the question.

PAUSE AND REFLECT

What mathematical concepts are potentially developed in this activity?
How does this activity connect to a discussion of global warming?
What relationship is made between the insulation and the snowman melting or not?

ACTIVITY 14.4

There are many opportunities to explore EfS issues in the primary mathematics classroom. For example, in the measurement and geometry strand, you may develop the following different lesson ideas:
- Designing a solar passive home and floor plan for the home
- The fuel used for certain foods to travel the distance to our table
- Package design for using less resources
- Placement of charging points for electric cars.

Choose one of these lesson ideas and create a student-centred lesson sequence that develops the mathematical idea, as well as providing opportunities for developing the students' toolkit to take action for sustainability.

Conclusion

While a focus on STEM is important for our national need to address shortages in students choosing STEM-related pathways in senior secondary and post-school settings, there appears to be a different educational focus in the primary context when compared to the secondary context. Whereas school industry partnerships and providing teaching and learning sequences that explicitly foster students' engagement in STEM pathways is very important in secondary education, primary students benefit from engaging motivating activities that promote critical thinking, develop problem-solving skills, and provide a contextually rich environment for developing specific mathematical contexts. Teachers don't need to get too concerned about the open investigative tasks where the students find their own way through a problem. There are times for these and times for tasks that are designed with specific concepts in mind. Inquiry pedagogy, with the five phases, provides a framework to assist the teacher in guiding and supporting students through the inquiry process. The 'big ideas' often explored in very open questions, sometimes described as ill-structured, provide an innovative starting point for exploring the greater issues of sustainability within the mathematics classroom. Under the STEM umbrella, as teachers, we are granted the opportunity to be creative and explore the role we play and the change we can create as humans to keep the balance in our world. Part of this is developing the desire and responsibility in our students to take action and fulfil the vision they want for their future world.

GUIDED STUDENT TASKS

1. Imagine you are about to focus on graph interpretation with a Year 5 class. What stimulus could you use from STEM-related contexts to inform your tasks? Take one example and design the student task in context.
2. Download Scratch and work through a sequence described in one set of guide cards.

3. Explore the LEGO® Education website. Choose one Year level to design a one-week unit for targeted outcomes that use robotics as a learning tool. Use the problem-based learning approach to start the learning process with an overarching real-world problem.
4. Choose one STEM-related career and write a list of tasks that involve the application of mathematical concepts in that task. Take one of these tasks and use it as a stimulus for a student-centred mathematics lesson.
5. Look through the online news for today on your device. Find a news item that relates to a sustainability issue that would be of interest to primary age students. Design a STEM lesson with a focus on a mathematical concept that also explores the context and issues related to the sustainability issue.

FURTHER READING

Castledine, A & Chalmers, C 2011, 'LEGO Robotics: An authentic problem solving tool?', *Design and Technology Education: An International Journal*, vol. 16, no. 3, pp. 19–27.

Department of Education, Skills and Employment Education Council 2015, *National STEM School Strategy: A Comprehensive Plan for Science, Technology, Engineering and Mathematics Education in Australia*, <https://www.education.gov.au/education-ministers-meeting/resources/national-stem-school-education-strategy>.

English, LD 2016, 'STEM education K–12: Perspectives on integration', *International Journal of STEM Education*, vol. 3, no. 3, pp. 1–8, <https://www.researchgate.net/publication/296626399_STEM_education_K-12_perspectives_on_integration>.

Fielding-Wells, J, Dole, S & Makar, K 2014, 'Inquiry pedagogy to promote emerging proportional reasoning in primary students', *Mathematics Education Research Journal*, vol. 26, pp. 47–77.

Fitzallen, N, Watson, J, Wright, S & Duncan, B 2018, 'Data representations in a STEM context: The performance of catapults', *ICOTS10*, <https://iase-web.org/icots/10/proceedings/pdfs/ICOTS10_4B2.pdf?1531364264>.

Serow, P 2015, 'Mathematics and sustainability in primary education' in N Taylor, F Quinn & C Eames (eds), *Education for sustainability in primary school: Teaching for the future*, Rotterdam: Sense Publishers, pp. 177–94.

Websites for exploration

SURVIVING AS AN 'OUT OF FIELD' TEACHER OF MATHEMATICS

CHAPTER 15

LEARNING OUTCOMES

By the end of this chapter, you will:

- be aware of issues pertinent to 'out of field' teachers of mathematics
- know about strategies offered to assist 'out of field' teachers of mathematics
- realise the positive side to teaching mathematics as a primary-trained teacher
- be aware of examples of teachers' critical pedagogical content knowledge that has a high impact on students' growth and development across the main strands of the curriculum.

Introduction

It is not unusual to find a regional, rural or remote school without a qualified secondary mathematics teacher. In fact, such a dire shortage exists in the supply of qualified secondary mathematics teachers in our schools that, in Australia, nearly 50 per cent of teachers employed to teach junior secondary mathematics do not possess the appropriate qualifications, and 32 per cent of teachers teaching senior secondary mathematics do not meet the tertiary mathematics content requirements to teach in the area (Vale 2010, p. 17). Interestingly, disadvantaged schools are hit harder by a lack of qualified secondary mathematics teachers. According to Thompson (2021), 'in more affluent schools, out-of-field teachers taught just 16% of students. More qualified maths teachers taught 54% of these students. In contrast, in more disadvantaged schools, out-of-field teachers taught 28% of students. More qualified maths teachers taught just 31% of students.' To make matters worse, the percentage of students studying advanced courses in mathematics at senior secondary levels is declining. While governments are introducing policies to reduce the higher education fees of mathematics programs, the benefits will not be felt for a considerable time, and a large number of secondary schools will have to accept that they will need to support 'out of field' mathematics teachers. This chapter tackles some essential pedagogical content knowledge to assist 'out of field' teachers of mathematics in the junior secondary context. A real-life scenario will provide the stimulus to commence this chapter.

CLASSROOM SNAPSHOT 15.1

Ella completed her Bachelor of Education (Primary) course and had prepared herself for the possibility of not finding employment in Sydney. In the final semester, she began applying for positions in rural areas of New South Wales. In mid-January the following year, Ella received notification that she had been granted an interview at a central school (K–10, ages 5 to 16 years) as a primary teacher. She did some investigating and found that the school was organised across two campuses, with K–6 students on one site and a 7–10 campus approximately two kilometres away on the other side of town. The primary campus had one class per year group and appeared to be adequately resourced, with a mix of experienced and early-career teachers.

During the interview, Ella communicated her philosophy of teaching and her professional teaching experiences during her studies. In relation to her course, members of the interview panel were keen to know more about her primary mathematics curriculum major and her elective major in environmental science. The following week, the principal of the school phoned Ella and began by stating that the interview panel had decided not to give her the primary position. The principal went on to add that the school would be delighted if she would take the position of mathematics and science teacher in the secondary campus. While Ella was surprised, her thoughts were on the fact that she had been offered a teaching position for her 'first year out'. She hadn't stopped to think about the learning curve she was about to face, teaching outside her primary teaching area.

This classroom snapshot is continued in Classroom Snapshot 15.2.

The difficulty faced by teachers in Ella's position is often described in terms of a combination of limited mathematical content knowledge that is closely linked to pedagogical content knowledge. While primary teachers often come into the secondary sector with a kit of sound practical teaching strategies, their existing qualifications have not given them the opportunity to develop a deep conceptual understanding where the connections among concepts are the focus (Askew 2008; Vale 2010). It is interesting to note that programs that have been specifically designed to support 'out of field' teachers of mathematics through further professional learning 'drew on their general pedagogical [content] knowledge as practising teachers and was enhanced by classroom and school-based enquiry' (Vale 2010, p. 19). Thompson (2021) describes two groups of 'out of field' teachers that require different types of professional learning opportunities. These groups are described as 'teachers that have the maths skills required but not enough understanding of maths teaching methods and practices' and teachers that 'have the pedagogical background, but weaker maths skills'. The need for professional development opportunities is echoed by 70 per cent of mathematics teachers who describe that 'they need professional development in maths pedagogy and instruction, as well as assessment' (Thompson 2021).

PAUSE AND REFLECT

When faced with the proposition of teaching in an unfamiliar teaching area, teachers often resort to teaching in the same manner as they were taught. How would you describe your own mathematics experiences in the secondary setting? What can you remember about the strategies used by your own secondary mathematics teachers? What characteristics in your teachers did you find supported your learning?

Community beliefs about mathematics teaching and related issues

The disappointing reality is that many members of the general public believe that secondary mathematics teaching means working through a textbook from beginning to end, with the most important classroom instruction being similar to 'Class, please turn to page 102 and complete questions 1 to 6 showing all working.' This provides a sad contrast to Sullivan's (2011, pp. 60–1) strategies for systematic planning for teacher and learning in mathematics. The first of the four strategies targets 'creating possibilities for engaging students in mathematics', and the issues identified by Sullivan are summarised as follows:

- examining 'big ideas' that underpin curriculum strands
- examining the proficiencies – namely, understanding, fluency, problem-solving and reasoning – and creating opportunities to experience and explore these
- emphasising numeracy and practical student tasks in teaching and assessment
- promoting decision-making, connected experiences and usefulness
- selecting engaging student tasks and building these into a lesson
- exploring the mathematical content within mathematics tasks and developing strategies for learning knowledge as required
- examining strategies for heterogeneous classes that will enable all students to engage and develop, including specific ways to support students having difficulty and students requiring extending.

If the issues summarised above were addressed, the mathematics classroom would be a far cry from the textbook-reliant classrooms that still exist. However, this requires a paradigm shift to move from instructional top-down mathematics teaching to student-centred teaching, where the students are empowered to develop their own mathematical ideas. This procedural approach is particularly apparent in junior secondary mathematics classrooms, as many schools are allocating their experienced teachers of mathematics to senior classes, 'leaving teachers from other subject areas such as science to cover the gaps in junior and middle school mathematics teaching' (Australian Council of Deans of Science 2006, p. 58).

For **'out of field' teachers**, there is frequently a considerable amount of **mathematical content knowledge**, **pedagogical content knowledge** and knowledge of students to explore while teaching full time. It is essential for these teachers to find a suitable 'mentor' in the school, who will take the time to have professional discussions concerning these issues and other school-based issues that arise. Preferably, the mentor should be a mathematics teacher; however, this may not be possible. Professional relationships can extend beyond your own key learning area, and in some schools this has led to programs targeting numeracy and literacy within all key learning areas.

In remote areas, professional associations, such as the Association of Australian Mathematics Teachers, and affiliated state-based associations, such as the Mathematics Association of New South Wales, are invaluable. The Mathematics Education Research Group of Australasia offers membership into a community of practice that supports mathematics education researchers and teachers of mathematics across all sectors. Professional

'Out of field' teacher of mathematics a teacher of mathematics who has not completed the minimum requirements to be registered to teach secondary mathematics; these teachers may be qualified to teach in the primary years or in secondary areas other than mathematics

Mathematical content knowledge understanding the necessary mathematics beyond the immediate demands of the curriculum

Pedagogical content knowledge the complex blend of content and pedagogical knowledge that provides the basis for classroom decisions made on a day-to-day basis

reading concerning curriculum issues, research, teaching strategies (including information and communication technology), professional development opportunities and conference information can be accessed online.

CLASSROOM SNAPSHOT 15.2

With only two weeks to prepare for her new classes, Ella contacted the school to find out which classes she would be teaching. She was surprised to hear that she had been allocated Years 7–10 mathematics, Years 7–10 science, one Year 7 music class, an interest elective (two hours per week) in home science and a Year 9 home room group. The reality of the situation had now hit, and on closer inspection she realised that her Year 8 and 9 classes were multi-grade. Ella's first port of call was the syllabus documents. In relation to mathematics, there appeared to be many topics. Ella was confused about where she should start and for how long she needed to teach each unit. Where would it end?

When Ella went to her new school to begin getting her room organised, she spoke to the principal and was encouraged to discover that he was a former mathematics and science teacher. He suggested that she contact him whenever she had any questions related to what she was teaching and how she was teaching, no matter how trivial she thought the questions seemed. Ella survived the first term by having an on-site mentor, a school environment that encouraged working as a team and the professional support provided by her mathematics association.

CLASSROOM SNAPSHOT 15.3

The members of a small group of teachers in a regional community were asked to join a professional learning study where groups of mathematics teachers were requested to develop their own professional learning project based upon the group's identified needs. The teachers were familiar with the term 'dynamic geometry software (DGS)'. They had opened DGS software and had a little play; however, they had no idea how to incorporate DGS into the teaching and learning sequence. As a group, they decided to make 'the meaningful use of DGS in the mathematics classroom' the aim of their professional learning proposal. The proposal involved three phases:

1. a professional development session with a DGS expert to facilitate engagement in student-centred DGS activities as a group and discuss the experience
2. as a team, teachers incorporating three DGS activities into their next two- to three-week unit
3. sharing of students' work samples, the teaching experience, evaluation and planning suitable DGS activities for the following unit.

With this shared focus among the team of secondary teachers, they had moved from 'retreatism' (Serow & Callingham 2011) to using DGS as a key component of student-centred tasks. Over the period of two school terms (20 weeks), the teachers were growing in their confidence to:

- develop lessons that explored GeoGebra basics, such as writing your name, designing a picture using the reflection tool, and exploring the resultant quadrilateral when joining the mid-points of the sides of any quadrilateral using the segment tool
- construct figures using their properties to form 'robust' figures (when dragging points on the shape, the shape remains in that class of figures)

- turn a written open-ended task into a student-centred DGS task
- create templates that could be opened by students to lead them through an exploratory task.

The last point is illustrated in Figure 15.1, showing all text that would appear when the students click on the action buttons. The italicised text shows what the students wrote after the constructions, 'dragging' and measuring had been completed.

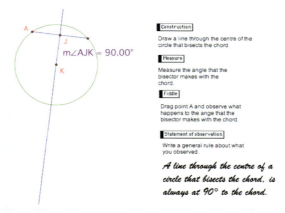

Figure 15.1 Circle geometry student work sample
Source: Serow & Inglis 2010, p. 13

Senior secondary teachers introduced the first derivative by exploring the change in gradients of tangents to the curve using DGS. For the first time in their experienced teaching career, these teachers witnessed an understanding of the gradient function.

Algebraic relationships were taken a step further and represented on DGS by the students when suitable. This didn't require moving to the computer room; instead, the teachers began using the data projector as a catalyst for student discussion.

On reflection, this group of four teachers – of whom two were 'out of field' – developed in their content knowledge and pedagogical knowledge (including using technology as a teaching tool) as the intervention targeted a teacher-recognised area of need. It was embedded in their classroom practice over a six-month period.

Secondary lesson structures

For the 'out of field' teacher of mathematics, it is heartening to know that lesson-planning skills developed in other settings can be transferred to the secondary mathematics situation. Keeping this in mind reduces the risk of falling into the trap of teaching secondary mathematics in the instructional procedural manner we sometimes hold in the memory banks of our own experiences at school. In addition, there are education advocates who promote the lesson structure of 'I do, we do, you do', thus focusing on worked examples and following procedural steps with often shallow conceptual understanding of the reasons behind the procedures.

With this method, sometimes referred to as explicit instruction, students are unable to find their way to a solution when placed in unfamiliar context or different task-types.

Although a multitude of combinations of lesson components exist, a few key techniques will help you get started. Considering typical secondary mathematics lesson components, we have formed the following six categories to assist lesson planning:

- short questions at the start of the lesson or the presentation of a scenario
- a clear introduction to focus the lesson
- student tasks
- sharing and discussion
- homework setting and correcting
- the conclusion to the lesson.

Short questions at the start of the lesson or the presentation of a scenario

This lesson component has a few functions, with the short questions usually taking 5 to 10 minutes to complete. The short questions can assist in:

- transitioning the students from their activities prior to beginning the mathematics lesson
- gathering information concerning students' current level of understanding of concepts that will be developed (assessment for learning)
- focusing the students on the topic to be explored
- leading into the introduction of the lesson
- automaticity of mathematical facts to relieve the short-term memory.

Some teachers find online question banks useful, using a stimulus task from the media, or generating questions from the class randomly using a die. Scenarios can lead into a contextual investigation grounded in real-life situations, with a strong emphasis on enquiry-based learning.

A clear introduction to focus the lesson

While it may take only 1 minute, this is a very important component of the lesson. In an attempt to lead the students to the development of the mathematical idea, it is important to communicate the intention of the lesson clearly, and hopefully in an intriguing manner. This could be as simple as, 'Today we are going to explore one of the techniques that builders use in their constructions. Let's begin by looking at a few pictures of builders at work.' This could be the introductory component to a lesson exploring Pythagoras' theorem.

Student tasks

The student tasks can take on various forms and have a range of purposes. One of the most effective student tasks are those that develop the mathematical idea by doing the task. This is very different to the student being shown a procedure and then following the procedure to complete a series of similar questions.

Tasks that develop the mathematical idea

The tasks in Figures 15.2 and 15.3 explore coefficients of x^2 and the addition or subtraction of a constant term. Again, it is evident in the design of these student tasks that the students have ownership of the mathematical ideas as opposed to explaining the relationships and procedures and asking the students to repeat the process.

Student Task Card: Investigating Parabolas

1. Work in pairs and open a new page in GeoGebra.
2. On the same axes, graph the following:

    $y = x^2$

    $y = 2x^2$

    $y = \frac{1}{2}x^2$

    $y = 5x^2$

3. On a second set of axes, graph the following:

    $y = x^2$

    $y = -x^2$

    $y = -2x^2$

    $y = -\frac{1}{2}x^2$

    $y = -5x^2$

4. What do you notice about the graphs in section 2?
5. What do you notice about the graphs in section 3?
6. What generalisations can you make about the coefficient of x^2 and how it changes the graph?

Student Task Card: Investigating Parabolas 2

1. Work in pairs and open a new page in GeoGebra.
2. On the same axes, graph the following:

    $y = x^2$

    $y = x^2 + 1$

    $y = x^2 + 2$

    $y = x^2 - 1$

    $y = x^2 - 3$

    What do you notice?

3. On the same axes, graph the following:

    $y = -x^2$

    $y = -x^2 + 1$

    $y = -x^2 + 2$

    $y = -x^2 - 1$

    $y = -x^2 - 3$

    What do you notice?

4. On the same axes, graph the following:

    $y = 2x^2 + 1$

    $y = -\frac{1}{2}x^2 - 3$

    $y = -2x^2 - 1$

    $y = \frac{1}{3}x^2 + 2$

    What do you notice about the constant in each graph and the graph drawn?

    What generalisations can you make about the coefficient of x^2 and the constant and how they change the graph?

Figure 15.2 Design your own Investigating Parabolas Task 1

Figure 15.3 Design your own Investigating Parabolas Task 2

Tasks that utilise the mathematical idea in a problem-solving context

The task in Figure 15.4 can be used with any suitable recipe. The idea of extending the exploration to include profit and a break-even point turns it into a task that explores additional mathematical concepts. Often, tasks that use recipes as stimulus stop at the cost and ratio calculations.

Numbers to 10

THE ANZAC BISCUITS BUSINESS

You decide to make Anzac biscuits to sell for a fundraising drive. This recipe makes 10 large biscuits.

ANZAC BISCUITS
- 1 cup plain flour (200 g)
- 1 cup rolled oats (regular oatmeal) uncooked (150 g)
- 1 cup desiccated coconut (150 g)
- 1 cup brown sugar (200 g)
- 1/2 cup butter (100 g)
- 2 tbsp golden syrup or honey (40 g)
- 1 tsp bicarbonate of soda (bicarb) (5 g)
- 2 tbsp boiling water

TASK 1   Decide on the numbers

Determine the quantity of ingredients needed. Number of biscuits you want to cook = _____

TASK 2   Research the costs

Use supermarket brochures, the internet or visit a supermarket to find the cost for each ingredient.

Ingredient	Amount needed	Cost
Flour		
Oats		
Coconut		
Brown sugar		

Ingredient	Amount needed	Cost
Butter		
Golden syrup		
Bicarb		

TASK 3   Calculate the cost

Calculate the total cost of biscuits.

TASK 4   Calculate the profit

You will need to make a profit of at least 40% to make the venture worth your while.

How much do you need to sell each biscuit for to make at least 40% profit?

TASK 5   Break even

Calculate the number of biscuits you need to sell to *break even* (to make back the costs).

TASK 6   Profit

If you sell all your biscuits, how much profit will you make?

Figure 15.4 HOTmaths The ANZAC Biscuits Business HOTsheet

Sharing and discussion

This component of the lesson is just as important as the student tasks, and it is often not included. Due to the period structure of most secondary school timetables, running out of time can mean that the discussion simply doesn't happen. One way around this is to make the discussion of the key ideas of the previous lesson flow after the short questions in the next lesson. Each student in a class will benefit from the sharing of ideas in the mathematics classroom. Even if more able students have mastered the concepts previously, they are given the opportunity to express their findings and converse at their level of understanding. You may witness other students moving from informal to formal descriptions of mathematical concepts during pair, small-group or whole-class discussions. Moving students from an implicit to an explicit focus is facilitated by mathematical conversations where students are prepared to take mathematical risks.

Homework setting and correcting

It can be difficult to determine the stage of the lesson at which it is best to introduce this component. There is no hard and fast rule, but some teachers find it easier to state homework expectations before the conclusion of the lesson. This avoids problems related to students packing up their equipment as the teacher attempts to get them to record homework details. While many schools have homework policies, there is no need to set mathematics homework each night if it is not suitable for the next lesson or if it is not a useful revision task. Mathematics homework for 'homework's sake' creates negativity and boredom. When the homework is achievable, is related to classroom experiences, engages students in varied contexts and/or is a form of communication between school and home, homework tends to have a positive impact.

Conclusion to the lesson

The conclusion is the 'punch' in the lesson. It should be a time for the students to clarify their thoughts briefly on the 'big mathematical ideas' of the lesson. It can take many forms, including a journal entry, a discussion, a brainstorm, a concept map or a diagram, to name only a few. You may wish to design an activity that uses a mathematics dictionary to clarify language and start a conversation.

ACTIVITY 15.1

Imagine you have completed a coordinate geometry unit with a Year 10 class. While engaged in the unit, the students formulated various formulas and generalisations. Find three different illustrated definitions of mid-point. How do they vary? What do they have in common? Are there any inconsistencies?

Issues to think about in the secondary context within each strand

When a teacher first begins targeting a new key learning area, it takes quite some time to get a handle on the important issues. This section highlights a range of concepts that require meaningful consideration in the classroom.

Statistics and probability

Watson (2006) has carried out extensive explorations of students' statistical and probability understanding. Based on this work, the following concepts require some explicit attention at the secondary level:

- sampling in terms of size, representation and randomness
- graphing and data representation to tell the story beyond the mechanical labelling
- averages in terms of what they actually represent
- summarising data
- chance and likelihood concepts, including language used to describe likelihood, exploring single and compound events, and early conditional elements
- the beginnings of statistical inference in the form of justifying conclusions by referring to data
- variation concepts, which are recognised as underpinning many statistical relationships in terms of describing distributions.

Students at the secondary level yearn for opportunities to explore mathematical concepts related to real-life examples. The exploration of data and statistics concepts is open to a wealth of examples. For example, even a trip to a decommissioned prison could enable the collection of stimulus material captured as an image on a mobile device. A secondary mathematics teacher recently collected images that included presentations of data relating to the ageing population in prison, titled 'Growing old behind bars: Why it matters', and the hidden costs of incarceration, titled 'Full impact of incarceration'. Both topics provided opportunities for in-depth mathematical investigations while fostering interest in current debates at a local and international level.

All teachers of mathematics should aim to contextualise mathematics tasks to draw out the key mathematical ideas from real-world problems as much as possible. Simple strategies that make use of extra-curricular school activities provide a good source of stimulus material. These could be drawn from the mathematics behind running a stall at the school fete, measurements of a running track, football scores and league tables, or local-interest stories such as problem traffic areas near the school.

Space

At this stage of schooling, the students are required to focus upon the relationships among figures and properties; however, many secondary students are still at the level of understanding where they focus on individual properties. Some students will focus on visual cues, and activities will need to target properties before relationships among them become the focus.

Students at this stage benefit from tasks in which they identify the relationships themselves. As in the circle geometry example in Figure 15.1, if exploring relationships among parallel lines and the angles formed by a transversal, it would not be suitable to explain the relationships, provide worked examples and ask students to complete 20 similar questions. The students will gain more by being asked to draw five different pairs of parallel lines (different lengths, different distances apart and in different orientations) and cut each pair with a transversal. The students can then investigate all the angles formed and describe any relationships they find. After sharing what they have found, formal names for the relationships – such as alternate angles, corresponding angles and co-interior angles – can be introduced. At the same time, students will be revising angles at a point and angles on a straight line. This task could be done on paper or using a form of dynamic geometry software on personal devices.

Number

Just as we have witnessed the shift to a greater emphasis on mental computation in the primary context, this is also pertinent to the secondary context. When visiting secondary classrooms, it can be disappointing to find students relying completely on their calculators for simple computations. As mentioned earlier, students' working memory is better placed on the 'big idea' at hand. It is essential for secondary students to continue developing their mental computation skills across each of the strands.

> **PAUSE AND REFLECT**
>
> Consider strategies for using online quizzes to enhance mental computation in your class. What could a regular schedule look like in your classroom? How would this schedule differ in the online learning environment?

Algebra

Again, focusing on the relationships is key to the development of algebraic concepts. It is interesting to note that the strand that uses symbols to represent values relies strongly on concrete materials and explorations to develop these notions. Taking the time in the early years of secondary to work with real-life algebraic relationships, where the students explore the number patterns, describe the relationships, represent them and manipulate them, will have more impact than completing a multitude of repetitive similar questions. Solving equations with the equal arm balance and then moving to the visual is worth the time it takes to organise.

Measurement

Measurement in the secondary context gradually becomes a web of connections requiring knowledge of concepts across all strands. It is useful to draw students' attention to the connections, and then give them time to reflect on all the strategies and knowledge that they have brought to the task. Presenting questions in an interesting context enhances engagement in measurement lessons. Taking the time to physically explore relationships is important.

ACTIVITY 15.2

When do you think it would be appropriate to use an online interactive software that explores the relationship between volumes of prisms and volumes of pyramids? During which lesson component/s would you incorporate it?

There are many online videos demonstrating this relationship above. Locate one and think about how you could use it to assist students' understanding of the concept. Explore your options for using it at different times in the lesson; sometimes the conclusion is a good place to include the video for comparison to the class results.

In all content strands, tasks that ask the students to use reversibility techniques require them to focus on the relationships among the elements rather than follow procedures. These tasks often begin with what we may see as the answer to a traditional problem, where the students are required to reverse their thinking in order to solve the problem. An example of this comes from the Maths300 website and targets the concept of the area of a triangle. The students are provided with the area of a triangle and are required to find the possible dimensions of the triangle that will result in that area. The task enables movement of the corners of the triangle, followed by an animation to show the rectangle to which the area of the triangle is equal.

Sample secondary sequence

The teaching sequence described in Serow (2007a) was designed with two main elements in mind: using the van Hiele (1986) teaching phases (introduced in Chapter 4) as the teaching and learning framework, and the embedding of dynamic geometry software and other suitable technology. The two-week teaching sequence (eight sessions of 40 minutes' duration) is appropriate to a secondary mathematics class targeting classifying, constructing and determining quadrilateral properties. An outline of the teaching sequence and sample student responses to tasks is provided next.

> **TIPS FOR ONLINE TEACHING**
>
> This student-centred and technology-rich teaching sequence is easily adapted to the online learning environment where students can use group communication tools to share their responses and gradually move from informal to more technical language through student discussion using online learning tools.

Session 1: Information phase – mechanics and recall

Students work through simple constructions using a form of DGS and brainstorming known quadrilaterals. Constructions involve the following tasks:

- Write your name using GeoGebra.
- Create a person and reflect the person. Measure a selection of corresponding sides and angles. What do you notice when you drag one of your people?
- Create a house design using the six quadrilaterals: kite, trapezium, square, rectangle, rhombus and parallelogram.

At this stage, in most cases, the students will construct their figures using the line tool. This will be extended in later phases. When the students are asked to drag (drag test) the quadrilaterals they have formed in this way, they will notice that the constructions are not robust. This becomes the motivation for the following phase.

Session 2: Explicitation phase – robust templates and recording

Students create robust templates for each of the six quadrilaterals on separate DGS pages. If the drag test allows the figure to remain as intended, the construction will involve known properties of each figure. Discussions will begin to occur on relationships among figures – for example, comments such as 'this is really strange – when I drag the parallelogram it is sometimes a rectangle, square or rhombus'. This activity will involve constructions such as parallel lines, perpendicular lines and transformations. It is essential for the students in this phase to describe their construction within a textbox on the DGS page and to record the properties for each quadrilateral in a teacher-designed table.

Session 3: Directed orientation phase – irregular quadrilateral and mid-point construction

Students are instructed to:

- create any irregular quadrilateral using the line tool
- construct the mid-points
- join the mid-points to construct another quadrilateral
- answer the question 'What do you notice?'
- investigate the properties of this shape to justify what they have found and record their justification in a text box.

Session 4: Free orientation phase – further exploration of properties and figures

Students design a spreadsheet where the six quadrilaterals are contained in the first column and the first row contains all possible properties of quadrilaterals. Particular care needs to be taken to include diagonal properties such as 'diagonals meet at right angles'. The students record the properties of each figure by ticking the appropriate cell. There is an element of surprise in the classroom when the students notice that the square has the maximum number of ticks.

Session 5: Free orientation phase – diagonal starters game design

This activity is designed to reinforce diagonals as a property and not merely a feature of the quadrilaterals. Students are given the challenge to create the diagonal formation needed for each of the quadrilaterals. The aim is for the students to construct templates for younger students to complete the figure and explore the properties.

Session 6: Free orientation phase – concept maps and flowcharts

Students create concept maps and flowcharts using suitable software. The chosen software will vary according to school accessibility. Figures 15.5 and 15.6 show student samples of a concept map and flowchart using Inspiration software.

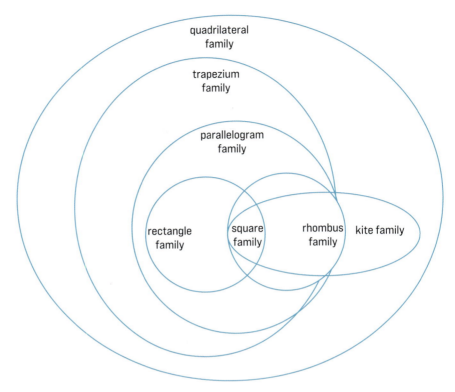

Figure 15.5 Sample of student's concept map
Source: Serow 2007a

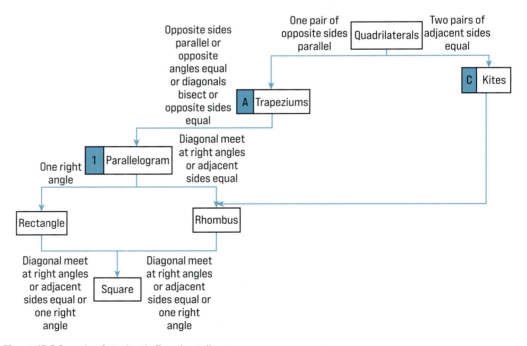

Figure 15.6 Sample of student's flowchart diagram
Source: Serow 2007a

Session 7: Free orientation phase – property relationships consolidation

Using DGS, students explore and record the relationships among properties. For example, students may record the relationship among opposite sides parallel, opposite sides equal and opposite angles equal. Figure 15.7 shows an example of a student's record of property relationships.

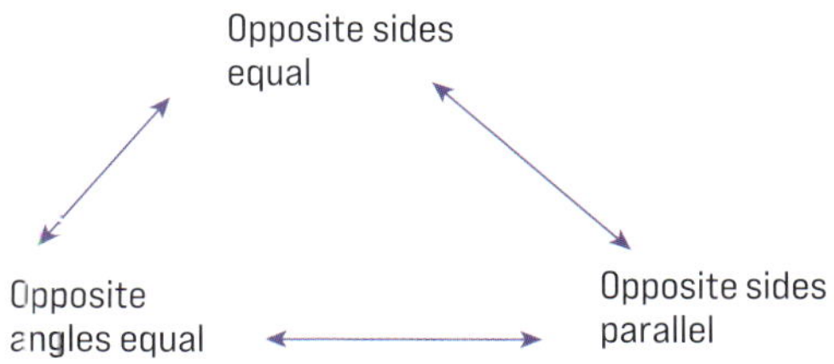

Figure 15.7 Sample of student's property relationships summary
Source: Serow 2007a

Session 8: Integration phase – information booklet design

Students organise the constructions they have made, justifications, tables, spreadsheets, concept maps and flowcharts to produce an information booklet to explain what they know about the relationships among quadrilaterals and quadrilateral figures. Students are instructed to include an overall summary of their findings.

Session 9: Integration phase – sharing and routine questions

This phase involves class sharing of booklet designs and routine questions involving known properties and relationships. A main feature of the teaching sequence presented is the integration of dynamic geometry software using the van Hiele (1986) teaching phases as a framework for maintaining students' ownership of their mathematical ideas. This is facilitated via student-centred tasks that acknowledge students' individual experiences and the progression from informal to formal language use. The teaching sequence combines a range of effective teaching practices that make use of the potential of the technological tools currently available to secondary students.

Conclusion

While it is essential for governments and universities to consider the long-term effect of the demand for teachers with a strong mathematics background, the education community can provide avenues for assisting 'out of field' teachers of mathematics in the secondary setting. Suitable mentoring programs, in-service education that directly impacts on classroom practice, and accessing online information and tools will assist in creating a community of practice where mathematical and pedagogical content knowledge is developed and shared. Essentially, societal attitudes towards mathematics teaching are impacting the number of people considering a career as a mathematics teacher. For this attitude to change, we need to begin by considering the experience that the school-age generation is having in the mathematics classroom. With a student-centred approach based on investigation, exploration and relevance to the world around them, motivation to continue in a mathematics career should keep growing.

GUIDED STUDENT TASKS

1. Planning is an essential component of all student-centred teaching. One way forward is to design one carefully planned innovative task per week per secondary year group you teach. During a teacher education program, it is useful to start your collection of tasks in preparation for professional experience and your future teaching positions.
2. There are many aspects of primary education that will support your teaching in the secondary setting. Cooperative learning strategies are often used in secondary classrooms. Search and collect a variety of cooperative learning tasks to complement your lessons. Can you identify other teaching strategies that you consider suitable to both primary and secondary mathematics teaching? In what ways do you think a primary education teaching background is beneficial to teaching in the secondary context?
3. Similar to the student tasks cards earlier in this chapter, design three consecutive activity cards to investigate statistics concepts. Attempt to use real-world situations as stimulus for the tasks.
4. Have a play with online dynamic software, such as GeoGebra. Devise a series of small tasks designed to familiarise students with the software in the secondary setting.
5. Think about your own strategy for continuing to develop mental computation strategies in secondary age students. How will you maintain a balance between using mobile devices appropriately, but at the same time mindfully?
6. How would you respond to a question frequently asked by secondary students in the mathematics classroom, when will we ever us this?

FURTHER READING

Goos, M, Vale, C & Stillman, G 2016, *Teaching secondary school mathematics: Research and practice for the 21st century*, Crows Nest, NSW: Allen and Unwin.

Hobbs, L & Törner, G (eds) 2019, *Examining the phenomenon of 'teaching out-of-field': International perspectives on teaching as a non-specialist*, Rotterdam: Springer.

Thompson, S 2021, '1 in 4 Australian Year 8s have teachers unqualified in maths – this hits disadvantaged school even harder', ACER Discover Article, <https://www.acer.org/au/discover/article/1-in-4-australian-year-8s-have-teachers-unqualified-in-maths-this-hits-disadvantaged-schools-even-harder>.

Weldon, PR 2016, 'Out-of-field teaching in Australian secondary schools', *Policy Insights*, no 6, Melbourne: Australian Council for Educational Research (ACER).

Websites for exploration

TEACHING MATHEMATICS BEYOND THE URBAN AREAS

CHAPTER 16

LEARNING OUTCOMES

By the end of this chapter, you will:
- explore challenges and rewards when working in remote locations in Australia and small Pacific Island nations
- discover teaching strategies that assist in maintaining a positive learning environment in remote and small Pacific nation classrooms
- understand the importance of the relationships among and between parents, students, teachers and other community members
- discover how to make the most of available resources, including online sources of teacher reference material.

Introduction

One of the most rewarding and professionally invigorating experiences a teacher can have is working beyond the city in regional, rural and remote communities. Whether these communities are situated in rural and remote Australia, or in a developing Pacific Island nation, the teaching of mathematics requires a thoughtful responsiveness to culture, context and the creation of communities of inquiry (Hunter et al. 2018).

If you have ever taught in a remote area, one of the first things you may have noticed is the importance of community and parental involvement. Relationship building is the key to success at all levels. While mathematical content knowledge and pedagogical content knowledge remain important ingredients, elements of pedagogical content knowledge are further extended to enable concept development when working in a climate of limited resources, reduced availability of technological tools and access, and fewer role models in terms of mathematics career paths. Often, lower rates of school attendance impact on individual student growth in mathematics, and it is essential to implement strategies to improve attendance rates and close the gap in mathematical opportunities.

This chapter considers issues common in the mathematics classroom in rural and remote areas of Australia and small Pacific Island country contexts such as Nauru and Tuvalu. Classroom snapshots capture real classroom situations within the context of primary and early secondary mathematics teaching (Stage 4, Ages 13 to 14 years). Many of the issues discussed, such as resources, can also be found in suburban and regional centres; however, their prevalence and the need to address them are often exacerbated in remote areas. This chapter explores strategies for making the most of available resources and the invaluable professional experience of working in these areas.

Rural and remote areas

While approximately two-thirds of Australia's population lives in major cities, outside the major cities Australia has the lowest population density compared with the rest of the world, according to the Australian Institute of Family Studies (AIFS 2011). Despite this, it can be a shock for some early career teachers to find that they have received a teaching position in areas often described as 'the bush', 'the country' or any place out of 'the city' that requires venturing into an unknown environment. For statistical purposes, Australia's areas are divided into major cities (69%), inner regional (20%), outer regional (9%), remote (1.5%) and very remote regions (0.8%). While there is little difference in terms of family composition, similar to Pacific Island households, very **remote areas** have a higher proportion of their households described as multi-family. Everyday family life involves the extended family, and this should also include the school community and communication.

Remote area a location far away from an urban centre or large regional town

The AIFS (2011) has identified that, 'Access to services and educational aspirations are generally more limited in outer regional areas'. In addition, it has found that geographic area does affect the type of after-school activities in which students engage, with children from remote areas spending more time outdoors. Children from urban areas spend more time on a range of extra-curricular activities. There are also 'differences in children's developmental outcomes across geographic areas, with children in major cities doing better on physical development and learning outcomes measures than children in other areas' (AIFS 2011). Issues such as sleep deprivation, appropriate school clothing, transportation and lunch provision are daily concerns faced by some students in many areas of the world.

To further complicate the educational setting, home schooling due to illness or mandated due to a pandemic situation, such COVID-19, is difficult due to restricted bandwidth in many remote locations, or in some cases, no internet access at all. With the growing delivery of mathematics lessons through the online environment, many students are disadvantaged due to their inability to access the online material or contribute to synchronous online discussion and tasks. Instead, teachers often resort to finding a written task that comes close to meeting the same outcomes, often missing the essence of the online student-centred investigation that students with more reliable bandwidth are engaged in.

A review of inclusive education by Powell (2012) suggests that challenges remain in relation to equity in access to education due to remoteness. As educators, we are asked to respond to different settings and different needs of learners by adapting the content of our teaching, as well as making decisions about the strategies we employ to enable all children to have access to quality education. Vale and colleagues (2016, p. 114) state that the development of this responsiveness to different environments should be an essential component of 'teacher education where we prepare teachers who are adaptable and ready to implement equitable and socially just pedagogies appropriate for the students in their school community'.

While equity in access issues have been reported in varied arenas, it is not our task as teachers in these areas to placidly accept the gap in educational opportunity; rather, our role is to respond in a culturally responsive manner, developing and using strategies that reduce the gap. The solutions are not one-size-fits-all. We do know that sitting back and accepting the difficulties as unworkable is not the answer, though. For example, it would not be acceptable for a school to acknowledge that a community does not have a resident female scientist when noticing the scientific interest shown by a female student. Instead, the school should grasp the opportunity and search for an online mentoring/partnership program where female science professionals are linked with students who have an interest or potential in this area.

Being flexible

Many schools beyond the inner regional centres do not have access to key learning area specialists, and you will most likely find that music lessons, information skills, physical education and languages are planned and delivered to your class by you alone. As a consequence, the amount of planning required is increased, and release from face-to-face teaching is sometimes minimised. There is also a need to be more flexible with playground supervision responsibilities in smaller schools. One strategy for making the most of teacher time outside is an edible school garden project that can extend to a wide range of key learning areas. In mathematics, for example, a range of number, measurement, statistics, chance, patterns and algebra, and geometry concepts can be explored with the school garden as a catalyst for student activities. Student tasks of this nature lend themselves to education for sustainability links in the mathematics classroom (Serow 2015). These could include:

- developing algebraic relationships through tile patterns on square garden beds
- pen and paper-scaled garden designs
- dynamic geometry software constructions to create garden designs
- experimental chance activities through seed germination counting from the original number of seeds
- experimental chance activities through the analysis of produce from a transect of plants
- array activities in the context of plant rows and columns
- design and collection of data concerning students' fruit and vegetable preferences
- following a recipe and measuring substances to create a meal using fresh produce from the garden
- comparing fast food preparation time with meal options that focus on fresh foods.

Integrated programs present many challenges and rewards in out-of-city settings. They particularly lend themselves to making links to personal stories, the land and the community, and to varied ways of tackling problems. In some remote settings, English will be a second language, and it is not uncommon for some children to have up to four languages at their disposal by the age of five. Bilingual and multilingual classrooms have the potential to be rich and engaging in terms of culture, and all languages should be celebrated and incorporated into classroom activities.

In remote schools, teacher turnover is high, and it is difficult to recruit experienced teachers (Sullivan 2011). Due to these two key factors, schools are often faced with professional knowledge moving out of a school each time a teacher vacates a position. Sustainable practices are required to reduce the impact on the school community, which often will have put considerable effort into professional development and positive change. Strategies for reducing the impact of teacher turnover will be explored in Chapter 17, which targets mathematics key learning area coordination. Classroom Snapshot 16.1 provides a scenario of a school that recently addressed this issue.

CLASSROOM SNAPSHOT 16.1

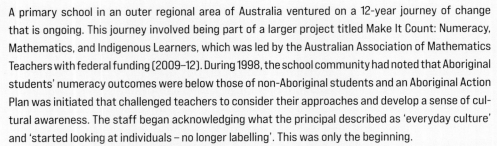

A primary school in an outer regional area of Australia ventured on a 12-year journey of change that is ongoing. This journey involved being part of a larger project titled Make It Count: Numeracy, Mathematics, and Indigenous Learners, which was led by the Australian Association of Mathematics Teachers with federal funding (2009–12). During 1998, the school community had noted that Aboriginal students' numeracy outcomes were below those of non-Aboriginal students and an Aboriginal Action Plan was initiated that challenged teachers to consider their approaches and develop a sense of cultural awareness. The staff began acknowledging what the principal described as 'everyday culture' and 'started looking at individuals – no longer labelling'. This was only the beginning.

The school took a closer look at teacher and student engagement, and worked with Chris Matthews and Tyson Yunkaporta, Aboriginal academics who are educational leaders in this field. As community engagement was high on the list of school priorities, they began with community links. To illustrate, one of these took the form of building communication of the current mathematics focus between school and home. For example, when the students were targeting a particular mathematics topic at school, a small, related, practical task would be sent home for completion that involved family members and discussion. The teachers shared the Eight Ways approach (Yunkaporta 2009) with the students, and always began lessons with a 'Yarn Up' (story sharing) that often included a pre-assessment. They had begun to teach 'through culture and not about culture'.

Yunkaporta's 'eight ways came from Indigenous research, which is research done by and for Aboriginal people within Aboriginal communities, drawing on knowledge and protocol from communities, Elders, land, language, ancestors and spirit' (Yunkaporta 2009, p. 1).

The Eight Ways model (Yunkaporta 2009, pp. 4–7) includes the following elements:

- story sharing
- learning maps
- non-verbal learning
- symbols and images
- land links
- non-linear processes
- deconstructing/reconstructing
- community links.

The *Make It Count Correspondence Newsletter* became a regular publication; this was requested by Aboriginal parents. There was a sense of a 'learning together culture' evolving, where a common purpose had been struck. While there are over 600 students on two campuses, through Eight Ways they have a common language that has enabled them to continue to grow.

This project brought about careful planning of each mathematics unit (K–6) using the Eight Ways pedagogical structure. The school removed individual student texts and adopted a student-centred approach that uses varied materials (including information and communication technology). As each unit was designed by classroom teachers for their particular groups of students, the teachers have noticed that the students are engaged and generally enjoying mathematics. Each unit is stored on an online database to enable transfer of information, further development and individualisation.

Figure 16.1 Using concrete materials and everyday items

Teachers made the following observations about their own changes in practice:

Teacher 1: The thing that I've enjoyed about it is that the way we've been teaching it works for all kids … I like the yarn-up, for example – we give them a bit of an understanding of what it's about in everyday terms, if you're talking about angles, you talk, you know, where angles are, or volume, where they have volume in their everyday life, where it … you know, where it happens, where it occurs … How it, what it means to them, so I suppose then they're constructing that knowledge, building on that knowledge that they already have … therefore it's deeper based, I suppose.

Teacher 2: When we were developing the program, we did a lot of collaborative planning … that really helped me to understand how to connect the outcomes and indicators with the activities, and using the Eight Ways of learning to create different ways of teaching maths, I guess … we do a lot of hands-on assessment, which I find is

> really good with Kindergarten. And … I guess it's just really helped me to understand – I found assessment a really hard thing to sort of understand while I was at university, because we just didn't do much of it, so I didn't really know how it [would] fit in … with the 3D shapes for the assessment, it might be like sorting them into the different groups, or making them out of play dough, things like that, so it's really hands-on …
>
> **Teacher 3:** For me, a lot more hands-on activities. Maths really moved away from worksheets and … concentrated on different – differentiation and also hands-on activities and concrete materials and things like that. So that's what it has meant. It's changed, it's really changed a lot of the ways we're teaching maths … Also involved a lot of technology, and incorporating things like that – which is using the smartboards more, making up sort of … notebooks on a concept, so you still have it there at your fingertips … and taking them outside, and doing really good yarn-ups and things like that – which were always things we were doing in maths before, but really consolidating that … and having it there ready at your fingertips as soon as you're ready to go.
>
> In relation to communication and professional sharing, the following comment was made:
>
> **Teacher 4:** You know, really [high-]quality assessments, and we're emailing those to each other. Which is … that's probably the first time in my career that we've really shared stuff like this too. Like, teachers always did it, but they'd do it on their own and … it just wasn't a culture of sharing. It wasn't that people wouldn't share, it's just that you were doing different things at different times and it didn't happen so much. So that's been really positive, I think.

Supporting best practice for teaching Indigenous students

Recognising the 'performance gap between Indigenous young people and their non-Indigenous peers', the Australian Association of Mathematics Teachers (AAMT) has a publication called *Make It Count Blueprint for Supporting Best Teaching of Mathematics for Indigenous Learners* (AAMT 2013), which summarises some approaches to improving mathematics outcomes for Indigenous students that have been generated by research. These include:

- establishing a classroom environment that is predictable for students
- working with integrated curriculum in which there is a clear focus of mathematics development
- student learning groups
- cross-age tutoring in which older students are cast in the familiar role of helping educate younger children
- 'dialogic' teaching in which educators have a dialogue with students and build narratives about and with mathematics. (AAMT 2013)

AAMT supports the notion that there is no single approach that leads to successful mathematical development for all students. Partnerships are stated as being key to future progression. They are described as occurring on two levels, 'school, parent, family, and community' and 'professional learning communities as educators' (AAMT 2013). Sarra and Ewing (2021) reinforce the importance of acknowledging students' culture and making this culture visible whilst planning and providing mathematical learning experiences.

Very young children take many stories from school to home and vice versa. We can make the most of this communication medium by linking our classroom explorations with simple home tasks. Figure 16.2 shows children's collections of four objects brought to school from home while targeting the numeral 4 that week. As a class, they added four exercise books and four pencils to the collections.

Figure 16.2 Communication between school and home

Considering classroom structures

When most of a teacher's personal experiences have been in single-grade classes, it can be a challenge to begin teaching in a multi-grade or multi-age class structure. Multi-grade classes have students from different grades within the same classroom. They may range from two grades together up to seven grades together, depending on the size of the school and how the school classes are structured. The determining factor for which classes will be grouped together in small schools is often the number of students in each grade. Multi-grade classes are very common in the remote areas of Australia. Cornish (2006, p. 10) outlines a number of factors that impact on teaching in a multi-grade class:

- number of grades in the class
- number of different classes (where one teacher is responsible for more than one class)
- size of the class
- teacher's experience
- teacher's preparation to teach a multi-grade class
- teacher's attitude to teaching a multi-grade class
- resources available
- curriculum documents
- mandatory requirements in terms of assessment and curriculum
- amount of flexibility available to the teacher
- support from educational professionals
- community support
- absenteeism of students
- absenteeism of teachers.

ACTIVITY 16.1

Think about the scenario of teaching a Year 5/6 class of students in a remote school where casual teachers are not available. The Year 3/4 teacher is sick, and her class of students will be joining your class. You have been in this position before, so you have started compiling a collection of open-ended mathematics tasks that can be the centre of an innovative large-class lesson sequence. Figure 16.3 is an example of a HOTmaths HOTsheet activity that is included in your file. Find five other open-ended tasks that could be added to the collection.

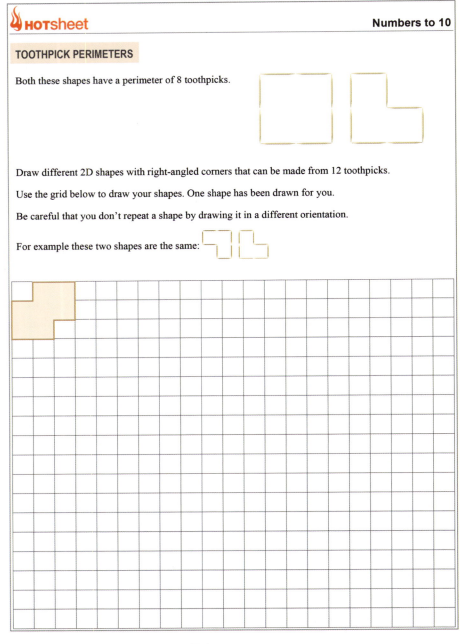

Figure 16.3 HOTmaths Toothpick Perimeters HOTsheet

While absenteeism of students in remote areas and in many Pacific Islands is a frustrating and a continuing issue, absenteeism of teachers affects all members of the community. In many remote areas, there is no such thing as a supply list of available casual teachers. In fact, if a teacher is away, it usually means allocating the students to other classrooms until the teacher returns to work. If this happens at a crucial time within the sequence of the activities, it can impact upon the continuity of the unit of work. When this occurs, the class sizes are generally so large that planned resources do not 'stretch' to cater for the additional students in the class and the planned activity is abandoned.

Multi-grade classes

In contrast to multi-grade classes, Cornish (2006) describes multi-age classes as a 'mixed-age by choice, by philosophical preference, and reflecting a well-thought-out approach to teaching and learning based on the idea that diversity leads to educational benefits'. This notion is not reflected in mono-grade systems, where 'the most effective way to organise a schooling system is to reduce diversity by grouping the students into classes based on their age and assumed similarity of development'. While it is not necessary to go down the track of multi-age classrooms, teachers of mathematics can organise multi-grade and mono-grade classes from the principle of targeting the individual needs of each student and carefully considering the structure of tasks and how developmentally appropriate the tasks are for each student in the class.

There are various ways of structuring the class to cater for students' individual needs. Bear in mind that teachers can use a combination of strategies based on the children in the class, the concepts being targeted and the context of the school community. Common ways of structuring mathematics lessons for multi-grade classes are described below (with each having its positive and negative elements):

- splitting the timetable to have different subjects for different grades – for example, mathematics activities for the Year 1 students while the Year 2 students are doing English activities
- mathematics at the same time for each grade
- a combination of whole-class teaching followed by separate mathematics tasks for each grade
- running topics on a cycle and teaching to the whole class, considering developmental differences among the students
- placing students into smaller learning groups – ability or non-ability groupings – across or within grades
- peer-tutoring strategies.

Tensions exist in each of these structures. When splitting the timetable, the teacher has multiple planning and resourcing responsibilities. Also, due to the increase in organisation, teachers can find that they spend more time organising and administrating than facilitating mathematics discussion and enabling the students' mathematical ideas to be expressed explicitly by the students. One of the most important skills the teacher of mathematics has is the ability to 'draw out' the key mathematical ideas from the students. The gradual shift from informal to formal language requires investigation, reflection and discussion. This is difficult to maintain across different groups doing different subjects at the same time.

Interestingly, students' mathematical developmental journeys can be upset by curriculum mapping that is not sequential – for example, if topics are mapped over a two-year sequence, every second year the concepts have the potential to be out of sequence for many of the students. One way forward is to take a more flexible, mixed-methods approach. In multi-grade classes, it may be suitable to have some strands where sub-strands are the same for each grade due to the accessibility of open-ended tasks to be completed at different levels. Some sub-strands also lend themselves to task modification, where the central idea of the task is the same, but the tasks can be attempted at varied levels of understanding.

ACTIVITY 16.2

Consider the concepts mapped out for each year group in the mathematics syllabus applicable to your setting. Choose any content strand, and look for follow-on key ideas that, if they were swapped, would impact upon the developmental sequence. Three examples are provided below. The first example is from the Australian Curriculum: Mathematics F–10 v. 9.0, in the fractions and decimals context:

- Recognise and extend the application of place value to tenths and hundredths and use the conventions of decimal notion to name and represent decimals (AC9M4N01).
- Interpret, compare and order numbers with more than 2 decimal places, including numbers greater than one, using place value understanding; representing these on a number line (AC9M5N01).
- Apply knowledge of place value to add and subtract decimals, using digital tools where appropriate; use estimation and rounding to check the reasonableness of answers (AC9M6N02).

National testing

As flagged in Chapter 10, national testing in Australia (NAPLAN) has been linked to teaching to tests, narrowed pedagogy, de-skilling of teachers, anxiety among participants, distribution of test results and the interpretation of results. Some interpretations have led to social comparisons that are detrimental to many school communities. The wider community should consider snapshots in context, along with the appropriateness of having one measure to determine numeracy levels across the extremes that exist in Australia and other nations (Jorgensen 2010). Australia is geographically vast, and the population is widely dispersed, so one needs to question the suitability of a one-size-fits-all policy and national testing. Skills tested in NAPLAN should be incorporated into teaching and learning experiences beyond preparation for the test to ensure that they are transferable to different contexts that lead to a deeper understanding. All 'children deserve the right to have mathematics assessment tasks that allow them to demonstrate "what they do know", engage them, and consider their interests in an environment that does not cause stress'. (Serow, Callingham & Tout 2016, p. 251).

Professional development in remote areas requires considerable attention, particularly in the area of mathematics education in the secondary context, where most teachers are teaching 'out of field'. Issues surrounding this reality were presented in Chapter 15. Beswick and Jones (2011) report on the need to provide a professional learning model 'designed to meet the specific needs of teachers and schools in the cluster and to establish relationships that would form the basis of ongoing contacts'. The importance of professional development is also emphasised by Jenkins, Reitano and Taylor (2011). Nicol, Archibald and Baker (2010) identify the critical aspects of culturally responsive mathematics education as:

- grounded in place
- connected to cultural stories
- focused on relationships
- inquiry based
- requiring personal and collective agency.

Resourcing

Problems associated with accessing quality mathematics resources are not unique to remote areas. While it can be a problem in terms of funding and availability, there are many schools in regional and urban areas that do not have adequate funding allocated to the mathematics key learning area. It is very disappointing when one visits a school that has identified mathematics development as an area requiring attention to find that motivation does not extend to making it a funding priority.

> **PAUSE AND REFLECT**
>
> Consider a situation where you are teaching a Year 4 class at a school that has not provided an equitable funding strategy, and mathematics resources are at a critically low level. What would you consider to be an essential starter pack of resources? What key elements would you include in your justification to the school executive?

In terms of resources, there are many options beyond commercially produced material that can be sourced and organised. Organising the resources is the key to reducing teacher time required, by having the equipment ready to go for the appropriate teaching activity. Take, for example, resources that could be used for developing place-value concepts. It is not necessary to hold back on using concrete materials if the commercially produced base-10 materials (see Figure 16.4) are not in the school.

It is possible to:

- make your own 10-frames using recycled cardboard and objects such as stones and pebbles (see Figure 16.5)

Figure 16.4 Developing understanding of place value using base-10 materials

Figure 16.5 Making your own 10-frames

- use paddle-pop sticks and rubber bands when investigating two-digit numbers (see Figure 16.6)
- cut palm leaves into sections with 10 leaves per stem to make an interesting display for whole-class investigations
- use egg cartons to make individual 10-frames by cutting off the two egg compartments on one end of the carton. Use bottle caps for counters and ask the students to individually decorate their cartons in their own particular style (creative arts link).

In some very remote areas, access to simple and everyday hands-on materials, such as counters, are not available. One option is to collect natural items of similar size and colour to use for activities such as grouping. An example of using shells is in Figure 16.7.

Figure 16.6 Exploring place value through paddle-pop stick bundling

Figure 16.7 Using uniform shells for grouping activity

Schools in remote areas, and particularly in small Pacific Island nations, have limited – if any – access to photocopiers. Even if innovative mathematics tasks can be accessed on the internet, there can be a problem with printing and copying. There are many activities designed for copying recording sheets that can still run smoothly and provide an innovative catalyst for student discussion without requiring photocopying.

CLASSROOM SNAPSHOT 16.2

Jessica found an interesting activity called Brainy Fish (New South Wales Department of Education and Training 2008, p. 28), targeting addition and subtraction strategies. The task required pairs of students to play on a game board (which was an outline of a fish with various one- and two-digit numbers). Each pair had a die and a spinner that pointed towards the following instructions:

- Double it.
- Double it plus 1.
- Double it, take away 1.
- How many more to make 10?

Each student was provided with counters to put over the numbers as they played the game. The students then took it in turns to roll the die, spin the spinner, follow the instruction and colour in the number on the fish that was the result of following the instruction – for example, if the student rolled a 2 then spun double it, they would need to colour in 4. The winner was the first student to place three counters in a row.

Jessica did not have access to a photocopier but thought the students would find the activity stimulating and appropriate to their developmental stages. She decided to draw the fish on the board for the students to copy into their books, have one spinner and one die for the students to take turns to throw and spin, and complete the activity as a class activity with discussion along the way. At a later date, when learning chance concepts, the students made their own Brainy Fish spinners and they repeated the game in pairs.

In the Measurement and Geometry strand, a wide variety of everyday materials can be used as manipulatives. These include plastic straws and sticky tack, packaging of all kinds, paper, card and adhesive tape.

CLASSROOM SNAPSHOT 16.3

A Year 6 class in a small remote area school was completing a unit on the volume of a rectangular prism. Textbooks were in short supply, and the school did not have a photocopier due to a lack of access to servicing for the machine.

The teacher, David, began with some short revision questions and a worked example, then proceeded to draw some rectangular prisms on the board for the students to copy and work out the volume. The students began moving in their seats, chatting and disrupting one another.

Figure 16.8 Practical measurement experiences

David decided that he had to tackle this in a different way. He looked around the room and found five different rectangular prisms – packages that stored items or were ready to be thrown away.

The class was divided into five groups, and each group was provided with a rectangular prism package (two large cardboard boxes, a tissue container, a long-life milk carton, and a staples box), a ruler, pencils, calculator and a book in which to record their solutions.

Student discussions concerned which dimensions were important, measuring techniques, rounding measurements, perspectives when drawing, organising the recording of the solution, estimation and determining the appropriateness of calculator solutions. The rectangular prisms were rotated between groups, with most groups completing three tasks.

PAUSE AND REFLECT

What characteristics of this lesson in Classroom Snapshot 16.3 changed the learning environment?

CLASSROOM SNAPSHOT 16.4

Kathy had been exploring length units in a Year 4 class on a small Pacific Island. The children were enjoying the practical activities she had facilitated throughout the teaching and learning sequence. It was time to assess the children on their understanding of the formal units – metres and centimetres.

The school had a culture of end-of-term tests and yearly exams driving teaching assessment, and many of the students had experienced failure and negative feedback as a result of the reliance on formal tests.

Kathy decided to continue with her student-centred teaching and learning practices, and assessed the students with an activity known as Towering Metres (New South Wales Department of Education and Training 2004), where the students needed to create a tower that was exactly 1 metre

Figure 16.9 Towering metres

in height. Kathy was surprised that by observing, listening to and interacting with the students, she had a window through which to view understanding of a metre as a unit of length, measuring techniques with a tape measure and metre ruler, and use of language to compare lengths. She was particularly interested to observe one group's determination to add 1 centimetre of cardboard to the top of the tower when it was repeatedly measured to be 99 centimetres instead of 1 metre. Kathy noticed that the student-centred activity targeting the concept of metre as a unit of length provided valuable assessment evidence.

As with the exploration of measurement concepts indicated in the scenario in Classroom Snapshot 16.4, the exploration of statistics concepts provides a wonderful opportunity to use freely available resources – in fact, in the primary setting, the investigations are enhanced through the collection of data about everyday events. As illustrated in Chapter 8, collecting, displaying and analysing data concerning students' lives, the environment, body measurements and sporting competitions make use of readily available resources.

Figure 16.10 Real-life statistics experiences

Simple spreadsheets should be introduced with a purpose. This could include organising a class or school celebration using local merchandise, setting up a market stall or organising a school café – thus providing opportunities for literacy in terms of sourcing recipes or creating promotional material. Some primary schools in remote areas are closely linked to secondary schools offering TAFE-delivered education and training programs. Real-life experiences such as these enable links to be formed with the hospitality programs, which may assist in providing a smoother transition between primary and secondary school, with purposeful connections between feeder schools and local secondary schools.

It is essential in any mathematics classroom to avoid a situation where a textbook series is driving your lesson planning and teaching. Engaging activities often come in 'small packages' that are driven by student activity and experiences rather than glossy products. Students gain more from developing their own display materials in the form of models and posters than from purchased resources on display. This is evident in Figure 16.11, which shows students' images of cubes in the world around them and their own 3D constructions, beginning with student-designed nets of cubes.

Figure 16.11 Students' creations on display

Conclusion

This chapter has focused on engaging students via open-ended practical tasks. While many areas have limited internet access, some remote areas have established connections that lend themselves to the techniques described in the content chapters of this book. The world has expanded for many students in remote areas through the use of connected classrooms (linking classrooms in real time through class video streaming, screen sharing and interactive whiteboard sharing).

Through reading this chapter and completing the activity tasks, you will have explored issues related to teaching out of urban areas and further afield in remote and rural locations. While there are many challenges, such as remoteness, fewer professional development opportunities, fewer role models with regard to careers in mathematics and science, varied class structures and a smaller pool of experienced teachers, there are many positives to a teaching career in a remote setting. In regional and particularly in remote settings, the community is closely related to the school, forming an invaluable resource. With lateral thinking, resources can be sourced from online and using everyday materials. Flexibility in planning and open-ended tasks will assist in catering for individual developmental needs in multi-grade classrooms.

GUIDED STUDENT TASKS

1. There are many reasons teachers take on a position in a remote but, despite the rewards, there are many challenges. Compile three lists in relation to working in a remote area: one with positive factors, one with negative factors, one with major challenges. Finally, write a statement in relation to your readiness to teach in a remote location.

2. Think about a well-planned lesson you have taught that uses particular interactive technology on either a hand-held device or a laptop. You are teaching in a remote area where there is a power outage for the morning. You still wish to address the concepts of the lesson – how will you adapt it?
3. One of the strategies described in this chapter to support Indigenous students is an integrated curriculum in which there is a clear focus on mathematics development. Imagine if you are designing a unit around a school café for Year 6. What would the mathematics development look like for the teaching of fractions, percentages and decimals?
4. Some students in your class have shared with you that their parents don't like the way you are teaching subtraction, addition, multiplication and division. They would like to see their children doing a formal algorithm to solve all the problems as opposed to mental computation and strategies such as the open number line. It is not possible for most parents to travel to the school, so how will you communicate with the parents to address this issue? What would the form of your communication be? What would you include in your communication?

FURTHER READING

Hunter, R, Hunter, J, Anthony, G & McChesney, K 2018, 'Developing mathematical inquiry communities: Enacting culturally responsive, culturally sustaining, ambitious mathematics teaching', *Set: Research Information for Teachers*, no. 2, <https://doi.org/10.18296/set.0106>.

Perso, T 2005, *Improving Aboriginal numeracy: A book for education systems, school administrators, and teacher educators*, Adelaide: Australian Association of Mathematics Teachers.

Sarra, G & Ewing, B 2021, 'Culturally responsive pedagogies and perspectives in mathematics' in M Shay & R Oliver (eds), *Indigenous education in Australia: Learning and teaching for deadly futures*, Abingdon, Oxon: Routledge, pp. 148–61.

Serow, P, Callingham, R & Tout, D 2016, 'Assessment of mathematics learning: What Are we doing?' in K Makar, S Dole, J Visnovska, M Goos, A Bennison, & K Fry (eds), *Research in mathematics education in Australasia 2012–2015*, Singapore: Springer, pp. 235–54.

Toumu'a, R, Sanga, K & Johansson, S (eds) 2016, *Weaving education, theory and practice in Oceania*, Selected papers from the second Vaka Pasifiki Education Conference, Tonga: Institute of Education, The University of the South Pacific.

Vale, C, Atweh, B, Averill, R & Skourdoumbis, A 2016, 'Equity, social justice and ethics in mathematics education' in K Makar, S Dole, J Visnovska, M Goos, A Bennison & K Fry (eds), *Research in Mathematics Education in Australasia 2012–2015*, Singapore: Springer, pp. 97–118.

Websites for exploration

DIGITAL TECHNOLOGIES IN THE MATHEMATICS CLASSROOM

CHAPTER 17

LEARNING OUTCOMES

By the end of this chapter, you will:

- be familiar with the TPACK and SAMR frameworks as ways of interpreting digital technology implementation
- develop strategies for evaluating and reflecting upon your own use of technology
- develop strategies for selecting and evaluating the use of online resources and digital tools
- understand what a community of practice is and how to establish one within your school
- understand how to engage parents with their children's learning online.

Introduction

Schools are technology rich. Teachers routinely now use digital tools for reporting, communications within school and with parents, for maintaining class records, for preparing materials and so on. Some schools use online teaching programs or electronic textbooks. With NAPLAN moving to become fully online (see Chapter 19), there is a need for both teachers and students across the primary years to be confident and creative users of digital technology. Each chapter in this book has included examples and strategies for integrating digital tools into the teaching of mathematics across a range of mathematical content areas.

ACTIVITY 17.1

Make a list of as many ways as possible in which digital technology tools are used in school settings. Think about schools that you have visited or where your own or friends' children go.

When you have developed your list, classify the uses as 'Administration', 'Communication', 'Teaching-related activities' (e.g. planning, reporting), and 'Pedagogical use', such as students creating reports, podcasts or using e-textbooks. Do not restrict your thinking at this stage only to mathematics but consider the broader picture.

Which of these categories is largest? How many of the pedagogical strategies apply to mathematics? Share your thinking with a colleague.

The technology world changes very rapidly. Hence the need for advice and guidance for teachers to make judgements for themselves about the quality of resources. Both pre-service and in-service teachers will vary considerably in terms of their confidence with integrating technology, so this chapter will discuss two frameworks that are helpful in understanding an individual's uptake and use of digital technology. The **TPACK** (Technological, Pedagogical and Content Knowledge) framework will be considered, and readers will also be introduced to the **SAMR** (Substitution, Augmentation, Modification, Redefinition) model.

These frameworks form a useful basis from which teachers can develop a shared understanding of what knowledge is required for teaching with digital tools, before developing a consistent approach to integrating these tools in their classrooms and lessons and teaching online.

TPACK a framework through which an individual's technology knowledge can be evaluated

SAMR a framework through which technology use can be assessed and evaluated

The TPACK framework

Technological Pedagogical and Content Knowledge (TPACK) is a framework that builds on Shulman's (1987) formulation of pedagogical content knowledge and describes how teachers' understanding of technology and pedagogical content knowledge interact with one another to produce effective teaching with technology (Koehler & Mishra 2008). As Figure 17.1 shows, there are seven components to the framework.

The model addresses the knowledge that individuals need for successful integration of digital technology tools. Teachers should address all components, emphasising that not only content and pedagogical knowledge are important: digital technologies also have to be understood.

The framework is useful because it shows that there is a relationship between technology, content and pedagogy, and the purposeful way in which they are combined by a teacher can lead to effective integration of digital tools into the classroom, resulting in better outcomes for students. It is sometimes assumed that merely adding digital tools will improve students' learning outcomes; the TPACK framework illustrates that it is not simply enough to add technology – many elements need to be considered.

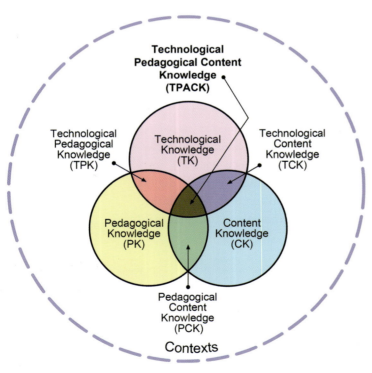

Figure 17.1 TPACK framework
Source: Reproduced by permission of the publisher, © 2012 by tpack.org

PAUSE AND REFLECT

Think about what the implications of TPACK are for teaching mathematics. Visit tpack.org and read the descriptions for each element of the framework at the 'What is TPACK' tab. Write your own explanation of TPACK. How would you rate your own TPACK across all components with respect to mathematics? Are there some components that you are stronger in than others? Be honest!

Auditing your digital technology skills

Although most people today have basic computing skills, there may be some aspects of technology with which you are less familiar or less confident about using. Activity 17.2 will help you to recognise areas of technology use that you may need to seek some support or practice in using.

ACTIVITY 17.2

Conduct a self-audit of your digital technology skills using the following rating scale and questions. Put a tick in the box to indicate your level of confidence (VC – very confident; C – confident; SC – somewhat confident; U – unsure; NC – not confident).

Table 17.1 Digital technology skills audit

Skills or knowledge	VC	C	SC	U	NC
Basic word processing skills					
Use of spreadsheets					
Use of presentation software (e.g. PowerPoint)					
Use of IWB for presenting or whole-class sharing					
Use of software for planning and structuring lessons					
Use of software facilities (e.g. recording, saving work)					
Creation of animations					
Use of specialist software (e.g. Geogebra, CODAP)					
Knowledge of interactive websites for mathematics					
Knowledge of appropriate apps for mathematics					
Using CAD or design software					
Using coding programs (e.g. robotics, Scratch, Studio Code)					
Other (please name)					

Table 17.1 in Activity 17.2 provides a starting point for thinking about your own skills and knowledge. The table can be extended to provide further information to assist program leaders to identify the staff expertise within a school and areas for future professional learning. The following questions may be useful to consider:

- In which areas of digital technology use are you most confident?
- Do you have an interactive whiteboard (IWB) in your classroom? How confident are you with using the IWB? How would you typically use the IWB?
- Are there any particular websites that you use regularly in your teaching of mathematics? Please list some.
- Do you make use of blogs, wikis or online communities in your classroom?
- Do you have a smartphone or tablet and, if so, do you regularly download apps?
- Have you attended any professional learning focused on the use of digital technology within the last 12 months?
- With what areas of digital technology use would you like more support? Consider both technical knowledge and pedagogical knowledge.

The SAMR model

Link 17.1 'How to Apply the SAMR Model with Ruben Puentedura'

The SAMR (Substitution, Augmentation, Modification, Redefinition) model was designed by Dr Ruben Puentedura to guide teachers towards effective implementation of technology into their classroom programs. Figure 17.2 shows a visual representation of the model. You may also look for the video 'How to Apply the SAMR Model with Ruben Puentedura', available on YouTube, to listen to Dr Puentedura explain the concept behind SAMR.

The SAMR model can be seen as a tool for assessing and evaluating technology practices and their impacts in a classroom setting, with a focus on teachers' abilities to redefine previous or traditional tasks, and develop new tasks using new technological tools (Kihoza et al. 2016). Like the TPACK framework, it is generic in nature but can be applied to any learning area, including mathematics.

SAMR has been criticised as being too linear and implying that schools and teachers should always aspire to the Redefinition level. Used in conjunction with TPACK, however, it is a useful tool to see whether you are making the most of the technological tools available to you.

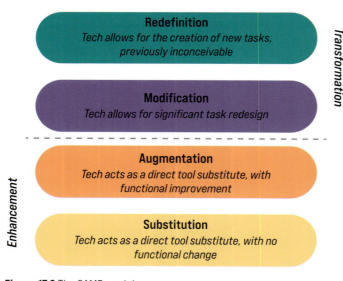

Figure 17.2 The SAMR model
Source: Dr. Ruben Puentedura <http://www.hippasus.com/rrpweblog/>

ACTIVITY 17.3

How would you classify the following activities in terms of the SAMR model? For each activity, decide whether it is primarily Substitution, Augmentation, Modification or Redefinition?
- Teacher converts a paper worksheet to an electronic one for access on a tablet.
- Students practice NAPLAN online (see Chapter 19).
- Students justify their solutions to a problem-solving task using Explain Everything.
- Students complete an ePortfolio of a term's work using an e-book creator program.
- Teacher uses an interactive app to round decimals up or down.
- Students use the internet to plan a budget for a school trip.
- Students use an Excel spreadsheet to record the results of a coin tossing experiment.
- Students watch a series of videos on Khan Academy on properties of quadrilaterals.
- Students work in small groups to create an informational video on how to use bridging 10 as a mental computation strategy.
- Students use CODAP (see Chapter 8) to work out whether or not arm span is related to height.

Link 17.2 Explain Everything
Link 17.3 Khan Academy
Link 17.4 CODAP

These two frameworks, TPACK and SAMR, can provide information about how a particular digital technology is being used, but there are many resources available. How teachers choose an appropriate resource is a different issue. Table 17.2 provides a list of possible mathematics learning activities, along with some educational technologies that could support each activity. The types of activities are derived from the Australian Curriculum: Mathematics v. 9.0 and the technology use is based on suggestions from Grandgenett et al. 2011. Table 17.2 is far from exhaustive, but it does provide a starting point for thinking about the kinds of digital technologies that are available in classroom.

Table 17.2 Mathematical activity types

Activity type	Brief description	Example technologies
Pose a conjecture	The student poses a conjecture such as 'Taller people have bigger feet'.	CODAP to analyse data, word processing to design a survey, spreadsheet to collect data
Justifying a finding	The student develops a mathematical argument such as 'All triangles tesselate because the angles add to 180°'.	Dynamic geometry software (Geogebra, Geometers Sketchpad), word processing, computer drawing programs
Categorise	The student examines a concept of same, or not same (different) based on criteria that they decide such as 'Animals that have legs and animals that do not have legs'.	Computer images, drawing programs, interactive sorting games, word processing to create a report, concept mapping software
Representations	Students explain the relationships apparent in a mathematical representation such as a table, formula, chart, diagram, graph, picture, model, animation and so on.	Data visualisation software, 2D and 3D animations, video, Global Positioning Devices (GPS), Computer Aided Design (CAD) visualisation software, spreadsheets

Table 17.2 (cont.)

Activity type	Brief description	Example technologies
Estimate	Students approximate a mathematics value by exploring relationships such as 'Predicting a multiplication pattern from a given start point'.	Calculators, spreadsheets
Create a mathematical model	Students identify how a tessellating shape grows and record their findings using photographs (see the Sphinx at the Mathematics Centre)	Digital cameras, video, interactive graphing program, specialised word processing,
Computational thinking	Students use coding software to solve problems using logical sequencing.	Coding apps (e.g. Scratch (scratch.mit.edu), Studio Code (studio.code.org)); robotics

Source: Adapted from Grandgenett et al. 2011, p. 23

Link 17.5 Mathematics Centre: Sphinx

CLASSROOM SNAPSHOT 17.1

Oakfields College is a technology-rich K–12 school. They have built a dedicated 'middle school' for students in Years 5 to 7. As well as individual classrooms for each class group, there are central shared areas with smaller break-out rooms for students and teachers to work collaboratively. These spaces are equipped with the latest IWB technology and laptops stored on charging trolleys for students to access as they wish. All the students also have a tablet, purchased through the school so that they are all the same. The middle school staff are concerned, however, that they may not be using the technology in mathematics as well as they might like. They decided to work together to audit their technology use in mathematics, and to share ideas. Using the SAMR framework, they set up a spreadsheet on one of the IWBs and list their current use and things they have heard about but are not currently using. The table they create looks like the one in Table 17.3.

Table 17.3 Examples of technology use classified using SAMR

Use of technology	Purpose	SAMR Classification
Electronic textbook	Provide examples for homework and classwork	S
Use of school LMS	Maintain records	S/A
Online student folders	Collect student work	S/A
Email	Communicate with parents about maths	S
Internet research		
GeoGebra		
CODAP		
CAD program		
Animation programs		

Use of technology	Purpose	SAMR Classification
Videos		
Coding	Some students only	R
Photographs	Records of student work	A

They realise that they could be more creative in their use of technology, and that many possible uses are being overlooked. They decide to work in pairs to plan and trial a new use of technology. The Year 5 teachers decide to investigate GeoGebra to create nets of 3D objects and then develop an algorithm or flow chart to sort and classify 2D shapes and 3D objects. The Year 6 teachers focus on undertaking a statistical investigation using the PPDAC (problem, plan, data, analysis and conclusion) cycle with the CODAP (common online data and analysis program), asking the students to use PowerPoint or a similar program to present their results. In Year 7, teachers plan a research project for their students focusing on square numbers and square roots.

When they revisit their spreadsheet after trialling their lessons, they find that the use of technology is mainly at the Modification level of the SAMR framework, with some aspects Redefining tasks in mathematics. More importantly, the students have been enthused and motivated by the increased technology use. The teachers agree that the extra time they had to spend thinking through these new approaches, and learning to use new software, was worth it for the improved outcomes for students.

Evaluating digital resources

As well as evaluating your own confidence with, and knowledge of, digital technologies, it is also useful to evaluate the quality of the digital resources that you are considering using with your students. Does the resource, for example, really help to develop students' understanding of the skills and concepts you are targeting, or are they only electronic versions of activities that are not pedagogically appropriate for today's mathematics classroom? The two activities that follow provide different approaches to identifying appropriate software. Activity 17.4 identifies software and then asks you to consider how you might use it in the classroom.

ACTIVITY 17.4

From Table 17.2, choose one of the types of software that you are not familiar with. Search the web for examples of 'child-friendly' software. Think about how you might use this software in a mathematics classroom. Develop a lesson plan, including student learning outcomes, using the software to teach a particular mathematics concept to a Year 3/4 class. Consider your lesson plan using TPACK and SAMR and decide where each component of your lesson fits on these two frameworks. Identify areas that you may need more help with using TPACK, for example, understanding how to use the software yourself or how you would teach the use of the software to the students. Share your thinking with a colleague.

Activity 17.5 takes the opposite perspective. In this activity you start from the concept or idea that you want the students to develop and search for software that could support this development.

ACTIVITY 17.5

1. Sketch the Venn diagram in Figure 17.1, and label each circle 'content', 'technology' or 'pedagogy'.
2. Think about a particular topic in mathematics, for example, angles, and the appropriate year level you want to teach. Write this in the content part of the circle, then identify two or three learning outcomes that you want students to achieve and note these also in the content circle.
3. In the technology circle, write down what technology you could use to help students understand.
4. In the pedagogy circle, write down how you will use the technology and other teaching approaches.
5. In the overlapping parts, identify what skills, knowledge and understanding you will draw on to incorporate technology into your teaching of the topic.

It is not necessary to totally apply the TPACK or SAMR frameworks to every mathematics lesson you teach. Whether you apply it regularly or from time to time, it may help you to think more strategically about how you are implementing digital technology in your classroom. Through considering TPACK and SAMR, the emphasis remains on 'how' to teach, not 'what' to teach. This integrated approach is in contrast with keeping technology separate, which tends to result in considerations such as 'What technology are we going to use today and what skills does it require?', rather than 'How am I going to teach my students?'

Although time consuming, it is worth thinking carefully about your choice of digital mathematics tools. McAnelly (2021) suggests considering value, ease of use, how well does the tool align with the curriculum, can the tool be accessed by all students equally, and is it of good quality.

As an example, consider any of the commercial mathematics programs available online. How much does it cost? Are there discounts for school use? (Value). How intuitive is the interface or does it take time to learn? (Ease of use). Is it aligned closely to the Australian Curriculum: Mathematics v. 9.0 or is it based on another curriculum? (Curriculum alignment). Can all students access it in school? Out of school? What about students with disabilities (see Chapter 12) (Equity). Is it mathematically accurate? Are the diagrams or pictures unambiguous and easy to read by all students? Does it focus on skill development or mathematical thinking (Quality)? It is surprisingly difficult to find a single program that ticks every box.

Leading teaching with digital technologies within your school

Even as a new graduate, you may find yourself in a situation where you are called upon to take the lead in developing a whole-school approach to teaching with digital technologies. This next section looks at ways of supporting teachers and/or school leaders in developing and sustaining a whole-school approach to the effective integration of digital technology into both general teaching practice and, particularly, mathematics teaching.

> **PAUSE AND REFLECT**
>
> Imagine that you are teaching in a small school in a regional area. There are only four teachers and the other three have been teaching for many years. Their understanding of digital technology is limited. You are asked to lead the introduction of digital technologies across the school.
>
> How would you feel about this situation? Where could you go to get help and support? How would you start? Discuss this scenario with a colleague.

The scenario described in the Pause and Reflect section is not that unusual especially in rural areas. This situation provides both opportunities and challenges. One approach to developing a technological focus is to create a community of practice.

Developing a community of practice

The term '**community of practice (CoP)**' was used by Lave and Wenger (1991) to describe the social learning that occurs when practitioners who share a common interest collaborate over a period of time, sharing ideas, best practices and resources. CoPs enable practitioners to take collective responsibility for managing the knowledge they need, and it can serve to create a direct link between learning and performance. It has been shown that schools that have a focused CoP can make a difference to mathematics outcomes (Callingham et al. 2017). While CoPs can evolve naturally, within the context of introducing digital technology use in a school, a CoP can be created specifically with the goal of gaining knowledge in teaching with technology. Through the process of sharing information and experiences with the group, members can learn from each other, and have the opportunity to develop themselves both personally and professionally (Lave & Wenger 1991).

According to Wenger (2006), there are three elements that distinguish a CoP from other communities:

- *The domain*. A CoP is something more than a club of friends or a network of connections between people. It has an identity defined by a shared domain of interest. Membership therefore implies a commitment to the domain, and a shared competence that distinguishes members from other people.
- *The community*. In pursuing their interest in their domain, members engage in joint activities and discussions, help each other, and share information. They build relationships that enable them to learn from each other.
- *The practice*. Members of a CoP are practitioners. They develop a shared repertoire of resources: experiences, stories, tools, ways of addressing recurring problems – in short, a shared practice. This takes time and sustained interaction.

Table 17.4 is adapted from Wenger (2006). It illustrates what a CoP might look like in a school community with a focus on developing a shared understanding of teaching mathematics effectively with digital technologies.

Community of practice (CoP) provides social learning that occurs when practitioners who share a common interest collaborate over a period of time, sharing ideas, best practices and resources

Table 17.4 Example of a CoP in a school community

Focus	Catalyst
Problem-solving	How can I incorporate the use of technology in my classroom without access to an IWB?
Requests for information	How can I get access to Geometer's Sketchpad or GeoGebra?
Seeking experience	Does anyone know how to use the graphing feature in CODAP?
Reusing assets	How can I use the save features in EasiTeach to save lessons?
Coordination and synergy	How do I know what other classes are doing? How can we find time to meet and plan collaboratively?
Discussing developments	What do others think might be the best coding software for us? What alternatives should we consider?
Documentation projects	Here is a lesson that I conducted with my Year 5 class – I would love to receive feedback from other teachers.
Visits	I would love to see how other Year 1 teachers are using apps with their classes – is it possible to organise some inter-school visits?
Mapping knowledge and identifying gaps	I'm not aware of what I don't know … could we conduct an audit of staff skills and identify areas in which we are strong and which need attention?

Source: Adapted from Wenger 2006

The point of a CoP is that there is shared accountability and focused activity among the members. There is another example of a CoP in action in Classroom Snapshot 19.3.

Classroom Snapshot 17.2 has a focus on the level of individual expertise that may be available but unrecognised in a school.

CLASSROOM SNAPSHOT 17.2

The following provides an explanation of an example resource that was set up by a Year 4 teacher, Miss Brown. The students were required to carry out a 'jump strategy' for subtraction using the IWB. Miss Brown pre-recorded instructions for those students who needed reminding of what the 'jump strategy' meant, along with instructions on how to save their file when they had completed the activity. The pre-recording of this enabled Miss Brown to work with the rest of the class, as any difficulties could be overcome through accessing the pre-recorded tutorial. Miss Brown is explaining what she did to other teachers.

Miss Brown: I've set this up really to be an independent activity, so I don't need to be here as the students can do this on their own. What I want them to focus on during this lesson is just to consolidate the use of the jump strategy for subtraction. So I have highlighted how we go about doing that, and the students are well aware of this strategy and use it a lot in their daily mathematics. And here I've listed just the instructions of how to actually complete this activity.

So the first thing you notice it says is to think about the jump strategy for subtraction, just to remind yourself. So I made a quick recording in case students were unsure.

The next recording focuses on recalling the steps for how to make a recording of what they do on the Smartboard.

Miss Brown: You come down to Start, All Programs, go across to Science and Technology, and notebook software.

When you've done that, go to Setup box, just drag it down to the bottom and press record then you'll be able to integrate that on the whiteboard. So what you need to do is to remember to press Record when you find your file name and it will record your working out. I'd like you to focus on just using your jump strategy for today's lesson and if you'd like revision of the jump strategy, come back up to slide number two, where it will explain 67 take away 42 and you'll see, in outline, using the MAB blocks. The next line of working is where I've subtracted the tens and now we're left with two tens and seven units. So 27. And then the next line I've subtracted the units again, so here the units will be two. Taking away two units and left with five. So the answer of 67 take away 42 is 25.

Remember you also need to save your recording and save your filename, so I'll show you an example here. Here I've labelled the file as 'Miss Brown 47 take 33', and then I'll show you how to upload that on to your page.

Okay, that was just a quick demonstration to remind the students of the steps to go through and that's enough of a refresher really for them now to go ahead and work through the whole thing independently. We can then use it as an authentic assessment of their thinking throughout the term and compare that to initial assessments of how they might have approached subtraction at the start and at the end of the term.

So now I can just change that for anything. So you know, I've done the similar things for addition, similar things for multiplication and division. And the fact that you can tape yourself explaining it to the students means that those students who need a refresher feel that they can quickly go and listen to that, or if they are doing it independently, take a set of headphones and feel confident in doing that too.

Classroom Snapshot 17.2 highlights an example of the type of expertise that individual staff members may have, which can then be accessed by other teachers. It may well be that, within a given school, little is known about the digital technology skills possessed by other teachers or about resources that may have been developed and could be shared with other staff. In order to investigate and document the skills and knowledge held by staff members, an information and communication technology (ICT) audit of staff skills could be carried out, similar to that in Activity 17.2. This may be one of the earliest activities undertaken through the community of practice (see also Classroom Snapshot 17.1).

CoPs also undertake professional reading and share their thoughts about the theoretical and practical implications. Some starting points for professional discussions are provided below.

Professional reading

Depending upon the expertise identified, the audit may reveal that there are members of staff who would be suitable and willing to lead professional learning in particular areas. It may also be necessary to source professional learning from outside the school, such as by attending conferences or arranging school visits. One easily accessible and legitimate form of professional learning that can occur as a CoP involves professional reading. As a school leader, or member of the CoP, you could suggest accessing particular articles and establish a reading group to respond to those articles on a regular basis. Following are some articles and readings that could be used as starting points for reading groups (full details in Further Readings):

- Attard and colleagues (2020) reviewed the domain of teaching and learning with digital technologies. The wide-ranging review considered diverse aspects of teaching with digital resources. Points for discussion could include how technology use changes classroom dynamics and the use of digital learning objects.
- Calder (2022) considered coding and how this facilitated thinking, by using ScratchMaths. Students in the middle primary years solved problems based on geometric and spatial thinking. Points for discussion could include how the teachers interacted with the students to support their thinking; how the technology fostered collaboration among students; and the teachers' pedagogical approaches.
- Darragh & Franke (2022) and Darragh (2022) investigated the use of commercial online mathematics instructional programs in schools. Discussion points might include how the use of these platforms impacts on teachers' planning and programming, and what should the balance be between online and traditionally classroom-focused mathematics learning and teaching.

Links 17.6–17.9
Readings links

Policy and curriculum documents

Link 17.10 Studio Code: Courses
Link 17.11 Grok Academy
Link 17.12 Scratch

The Australian Curriculum: Mathematics v. 9.0 recognises the increased use of technology in schools. In many areas of mathematics there is mention of the use of computational thinking, which is the development and use of algorithms to underatke specific tasks. This kind of thinking is used in coding and STEM activities such as robotics. It is worth accessing Studio Code, Grok, Scratch or similar resources and trying some of the activities to develop understanding of this kind of thinking. All these websites have substantial free resources for education. Other sources for reading can be found in the Further Reading sections throughout this book. You may also consider other avenues for discussion, which could be based around collaborative viewing of particular websites including YouTube, Teachers TV and TED Talks.

ACTIVITY 17.6

View the TED Talk by Sugata Mitra, 'Build a School in the Cloud'.

1. What implication does his message have for today's schooling practices?
2. How well do you think our schools are preparing our students for the future?
3. How important do you think it is that all students have equitable access to technology?
4. How would a 'curriculum of big questions' impact on mathematics?

Discuss your responses with a colleague, a parent and an experienced teacher. How do their responses differ?

Link 17.13 Ted Talk: 'Build a School in the Cloud'

Involving the community and learning online

Parental involvement in a child's education is positively correlated with academic achievement (Muir 2012b). It can be difficult, however, to involve parents in their child's mathematical education (Wadham, Darragh & Ell 2022). During the lockdowns caused by the COVID-19 pandemic parents became a critical part of schooling. The experiences of parents during this time were varied (Darragh & Franke 2022) with some feeling very unsupported. Vale and Graven (2022), however, found that teachers had three views of the role of parents: a hindrance to mathematics learning; a collector of resources and communication between school and home; and a partner in the learning process. Over the disrupted period, teachers' views shifted towards the recognition of parents as partners.

Parents are an integral part of the school community, and therefore should be included and encouraged to actively participate in their children's education. An inclusive approach to school decision-making and parental involvement creates a sense of shared responsibility among parents, community members and teachers. Such considerations become even more important when learning has to be delivered online.

It can sometimes be challenging to encourage parents to participate in their children's mathematical education, as many often find themselves in unfamiliar territory when they attempt to work with their children on mathematics (Wadham, Darragh & Ell 2022). One way to address this issue is to provide parents with information, workshops and take-home activities to help familiarise them with the mathematical content and pedagogical approaches that are part of today's classroom. It is also reasonable to expect that many parents would be unfamiliar and/or not confident with using the digital technology that is so readily available and accessible to their children.

CLASSROOM SNAPSHOT 17.3

The school has mandated a particular online mathematics instructional program for use in all classrooms. Assessment is also completed online and Richard, a Year 4 teacher, was struck by how many of his students seemed to have made a lot of progress when they were following the program during home schooling. He asked parents for their impressions. Mr Jones, the father of a moderately capable student called Peter, wrote the following email to Richard:

▶▶

> I was not able to completely supervise Pete during home schooling because I was working from home myself. One day I asked Pete about his maths, which he had completed seemingly in record time. He said it had been completed and posted. When I looked at his workspace, I noticed that he had a calculator. I asked whether he was using this, and he said it was OK because it was technology like the maths program they were following. Please would you let me know whether this is OK?
>
> Richard checked Pete's progress on the maths program. He realised that the activity that Pete had been doing was a practice activity involving addition and subtraction with carrying and decomposition, and that in this case the use of the calculator was not helping Pete develop understanding of the process. He resolved to develop maths activities that were more meaningful and engaging while the students had to learn online. Richard also brought up the issue of how the online platform was being used and the unreliable data about student progress at the next staff meeting.

Classroom Snapshot 17.3 emphasises the challenges posed by technology. It is not the technology itself but how it is used that becomes the issue. When parents are actively involved with their children's mathematics learning, technology use can enhance the learning. The following suggestions could be used as starting points for involving parents in school-based activities designed to inform them and make them more comfortable with both mathematics education and the role played by technology:

Host a maths night or maths afternoon. Set up a number of games and activities in the school's hall or gymnasium. Invite parents to participate with their children. Set up a number of computers and an IWB, and have children instruct parents on their use.

Take-home numeracy activities. A number of schools have weekly take-home numeracy bags, which encourage parents and children to complete mathematical activities at home. This experience can be especially valuable if the purpose of each activity is included and links to digital technologies can be made with suggestions for websites that reinforce the concept.

Publish newsletter links to websites. A regular feature of the newsletter could be 'Website of the Week', which would encourage parents to visit websites with their children and build up their own bank of online resources.

Host 'Appy Hour'. Once a month or once a term, host an 'Appy Hour', where participants share afternoon tea along with their favourite apps. A database could be established where the apps are named and described, with selected ones being included in the weekly school newsletter.

It seems logical to expect that if any change or practice is to be sustained in a school community, parents will have an integral role to play in helping this to occur. The above suggestions are starting points for actively involving parents and making them part of the school's community of practice. Many of these activities can be adapted for online learning.

> ## PAUSE AND REFLECT
>
> Read the article by Daniel (2020) which was written early in the pandemic. Daniel suggests some approaches that could be taken by schools and systems to help with remote learning. Reflect on the following:
> - How could you use asynchronous learning in mathematics?
> - What resources might you recommend to a school that wants to have a plan for online learning?
> - What kinds of activities could you use to ensure your students remained engaged with mathematics?
> - What advice would you give to parents helping their children learn mathematics at home?

Link 17.14 Daniel 2020, 'Education and the COVID-19 pandemic'

Record your reflections in a journal or as an e-note and discuss them with a colleague. Revisit these ideas from time to time.

Conclusion

Effective implementation of digital technologies into the mathematics classroom requires teachers to be confident with their own knowledge and use of ICT, along with an understanding of what effective implementation looks like in practice. This chapter has provided an overview of the teacher knowledge required for effective teaching with technology, and some practical suggestions on how teachers can become aware of this knowledge and audit their own technological skills and expertise. Frameworks such as the TPACK and SAMR models provide a useful reference for teachers to make considered decisions about the most effective ways of capitalising on ICT to enhance students' experience and learning opportunities. Teachers also need to recognise that changes in teacher practice are more likely to occur if they are supported and can see positive impacts from new pedagogies and practices.

GUIDED STUDENT TASKS

1. Conduct a self-audit of your own ICT skills. What can you do to increase your capacity to implement ICT into your teaching of mathematics?
2. Next time you are looking for digital resources, apply an evaluative framework to your selection. To what extent are they user friendly, pedagogically sound and focused on substantive mathematics?
3. Join a CoP – either within your school or take advantage of those that are online.
4. Identify useful apps or programs for teaching online. Make a list of these.

FURTHER READING

Daniel, J 2020, 'Education and the COVID-19 pandemic', *PROSPECTS*, vol. 49, pp. 91–6.

Darragh, L & Franke, N 2022, 'Lessons from lockdown: Parent perspectives on home-learning mathematics during COVID-19 lockdown', *International Journal of Science and Mathematics Education*, vol 20, pp. 1521–42.

Harris, JB, Hofer, MJ, Schmidt, DA, Banchard, MR, Young, CY, Grandgenett, NF & Van Olphen, M 2010, '"Grounded" technological integration: Instructional planning using curriculum-based activity type taxonomies', *Journal of Technology and Teacher Education*, vol. 18, no. 4, pp. 573–605, <http://activitytypes.wm.edu/HarrisHofer&Others-InstructionalPlanningUsingLATsTaxonomies.pdf>.

McAnelly, N 2021, 'How to select effective digital math tools', Edutopia, <https://www.edutopia.org/article/how-select-effective-digital-math-tools>.

Muir, T 2012, 'Numeracy at home: Involving parents in mathematics education', *International Journal for Mathematics Teaching and Learning*, <https://www.cimt.org.uk/journal/muir.pdf>.

CHAPTER 18

EDUCATION SUPPORT ROLES

LEARNING OUTCOMES

By the end of this chapter, you will:
- understand the range of education support roles
- be able to recognise effective ways of working with education support workers
- plan for mathematics learning that involves education support workers in productive ways
- understand the role of numeracy coaches.

Introduction

Schools are complex workplaces. In addition to teaching staff there are many other people involved in supporting children's learning, including learning mathematics. Every school has administrative staff to undertake important and necessary paperwork that keeps a school running. In addition, there may be other professionals and volunteers who come into schools for specified reasons. These include numeracy or mathematics coaches; educational psychologists, counsellors and guidance officers; social workers; school chaplains or other religious leaders; speech, occupational and other therapists; specialists in hearing impairment or blindness; teacher aides, teaching assistants, education support workers and Aboriginal Education Officers; volunteer help such as parent help, grandparent help or other volunteers; and occasional visitors. The number of people who come into schools and classrooms can be overwhelming to beginning teachers but knowing what roles these people can play in helping children learn mathematics can help.

Regardless of whether they provide professional or volunteer support, most jurisdictions in Australia specify requirements for entry into a school, such as a Working with Children (or Vulnerable People) check. Each jurisdiction has its own expectations, and these may not be transferable between Australian states and territories. Pre-service teachers should check the requirements before practicum placements or entering a school as a volunteer.

In this chapter, the focus is on working with the people who are most often in classrooms – teaching assistants and parents or other volunteers. It will also consider the support that can be provided by other specialists and how you can best work with them. It does not explicitly cover staff whose roles are to work with students having specialised physical or intellectual needs (see Chapter 12). Support staff have a variety of titles, depending on the jurisdiction or school. In this chapter, the term 'education support worker' will be used to cover all the professional and volunteer personnel that a beginning teacher might meet.

What are education support workers?

Education support workers (ESWs), or learning support staff, have been defined as 'school staff whose main function is to assist the work of teachers' (Masdeu Navarro 2015). They come from a variety of backgrounds and training and may be employed as permanent, contract or casual staff, on a full-time or part-time basis. Many pre-service teachers work or volunteer in classrooms to provide teacher support and have insight into the different ways in which schools make use of the extra hands in classrooms.

Professional ESWs provide general classroom support predominantly in early years' classrooms (Green 2022). In the upper years of primary school, and into high school, ESWs mainly provide support to focus students with special needs (see Chapter 12). Education support workers do not teach whole classes, although they may work with small groups of children in ways that require pedagogical decisions (Fernandez & Hynes 2016). Sometimes this support occurs in a separate room to the main classroom, to reduce distractions for students who may be experiencing difficulties. They may also provide practical support, such as putting up classroom displays, or making teaching aids. Professional ESWs may also help with behaviour management.

Although not trained as teachers, in Australia most jurisdictions require ESWs to have undertaken some training, such as a certificate level qualification. The boundaries between professional classroom ESWs and teachers are becoming increasingly blurred (Green 2022). Professional classroom ESWs are undertaking training and professional development at increasing rates. Some schools now routinely provide openings for ESWs to have focused professional learning opportunities or include ESWs in professional learning activities within the school. Increasingly, ESWs play a pedagogical role in classrooms. Nevertheless, the classroom teacher oversees the learning and teaching program. It can, however, be daunting for a beginning teacher to have to plan and work with a highly experienced ESW. During practicum placements it is useful to discuss these issues with both experienced teachers and ESWs.

Education support workers are valued by teachers (Masdeu Navarro 2015). The findings about the impact on student attainment, however, are mixed. Some studies report strong effects on students' reading and, to a lesser extent, mathematics, but others have found that ESW support made little difference to mathematics outcomes (Hemelt et al. 2021). Classroom ESWs generally ask more closed questions and have shorter 'wait times' when they ask a question in mathematics. They are also more likely to tell students how to perform a computation. Taken together, these practices may lead to students recognising that all they need to do is say nothing and the ESW will 'rescue' them (Radford, Blatchford & Webster 2011). It is worth discussing these ideas with the ESW and explaining that all students need to struggle with mathematics concepts to develop fluency and understanding. The key is providing activities that ensure that students have to work hard, in a cognitive sense, but at a level that they can reach – an example of using Vygotsky's (1978) Zone of Proximal Development (ZPD). Vygotsky, a Russian psychologist, identified social aspects of learning and described the ZPD as:

the distance between the actual developmental level as determined by independent problem solving and the level of potential development as determined through problem-solving under adult guidance, or in collaboration with more capable peers. (Vygotsky 1978, p. 86)

The ESW and the teacher are examples of more-knowledgeable others with whom the student interacts during learning. How these interactions occur is at the heart of social constructivism (see Chapter 1).

Education support workers want the best outcomes for students and often worry that they are not doing enough to support them, especially in mathematics (Reaburn 2015). Many ESWs lack confidence in their own mathematical knowledge or revert to using algorithms that they were taught, regardless of whether these are what is current practice (Houssart 2013). There is, however, growing evidence that ESWs can be used effectively to encourage mathematics learning with some training (Kalogeropoulos et al. 2020). The key to success appears to be close working relationships between ESWs and teachers and a collaborative and cooperative approach to classroom planning. Agreement on key aspects of classroom life, such as routines and behaviour management, and a recognition of the different roles of the teacher and the ESW lead to effective working interactions.

PAUSE AND REFLECT

Think about your own experiences and what you may have observed ESWs doing. Have there been occasions when the ESW has, deliberately or inadvertently, contradicted the teacher? As a teacher, what are your aims for working with a professional classroom ESW? What specific actions might you need to do to achieve these aims?

Students develop understanding at different rates, and, at times, most students will have a period when they just 'don't get it'. Often ESWs work with those students requiring additional support. Having a more knowledgeable adult can help students move to the next level of understanding. It is important, however, that all students have opportunities to interact with their teacher and expecting the same group of students always to work with the ESW is counterproductive. The ESW is a support person, not an alternative teacher. Consider the exchange between an ESW and a student shown in Classroom Snapshot 18.1.

CLASSROOM SNAPSHOT 18.1

ESW: Hi Alex – can we please go through the fraction work that you did yesterday? I want to understand your thinking. Please explain to me what you are thinking here. [pointing to the fractions in Alex's picture (Figure 18.1)].

Alex: Well ... 3 is smaller than 4 and 4 is smaller than 5 ... so, I put them in order from small to big.

ESW: I can see your thinking, but we are talking about fractions. Do you know what a fraction is?

Alex: They are numbers. Parts of something?

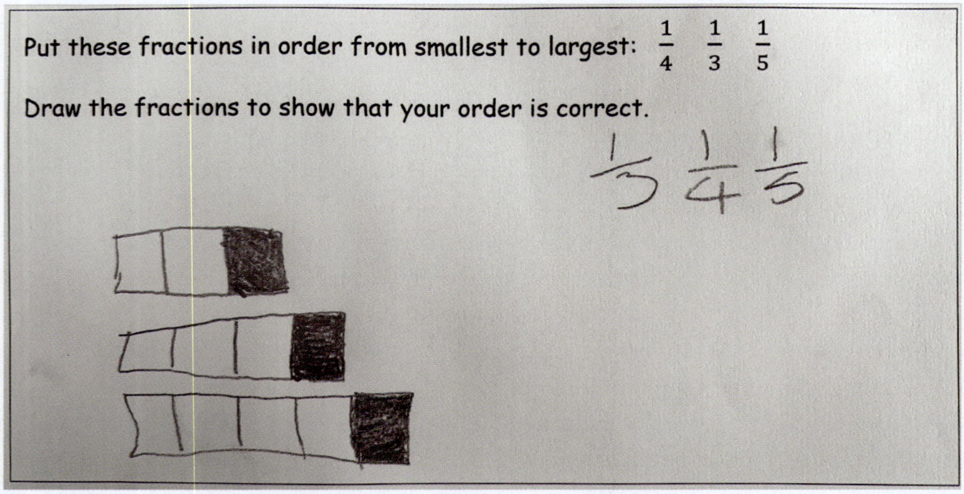

▶▶

> Put these fractions in order from smallest to largest: $\frac{1}{4}$ $\frac{1}{3}$ $\frac{1}{5}$
>
> Draw the fractions to show that your order is correct.
>
> $\frac{1}{3}$ $\frac{1}{4}$ $\frac{1}{5}$

Figure 18.1 Alex's representations of $\frac{1}{3}$, $\frac{1}{4}$ and $\frac{1}{5}$

ESW: Yes, they are numbers, correct! Please explain more. What sort of parts and what do you mean by 'something'?

Alex: Something that's cut up into pieces.

ESW: Cut up into what sort of pieces?

Alex: Pieces – like a cake or a pizza.

ESW: Do you think that all those pieces should be equal?

Alex: They're equal ... I made the bits the same size. [pointing]

ESW: Looking at your pictures that you have drawn, can you tell me about this one [pointing to $\frac{1}{3}$]?

Alex: It's cut into 3 pieces, and I coloured in one piece asked.

ESW: Well done! What about this one? [pointing to $\frac{1}{4}$].

Alex: It's cut into 4 pieces, and I coloured in one piece.

ESW: And this one? [pointing to $\frac{1}{5}$]

Alex: It's cut into 5 pieces, and I coloured in one piece.

ESW: How did you know how many pieces something should have been cut into?

Alex: Because this part tells me ... [pointing to the denominator]

ESW: Great! Do you remember its name?

Alex: Denominator.

ESW: How did you know what had to be coloured in?

Alex: This number at the top tells me [pointing to the numerator].

ESW:	Remember it's the numerator. This is the numerator [pointing] and this is the denominator [pointing]. We do not say the top number and bottom number when talking about fractions – we call them the numerator and the denominator. Can you remember that?
Alex:	Yep.
ESW:	Do you think all the pieces should be the same size or what you are cutting into pieces (the whole) should be the same size?
Alex:	The pieces should be the same or it wouldn't be fair when you had cake!
ESW:	Ok. Let's imagine these strips of paper are 'cakes' [shows 3 strips of paper of equal length]. All these 'cakes' are all the same size.
Alex:	Cakes are round!
ESW:	Cakes can be many shapes ... do you think you could cut this rectangle 'cake' into thirds (3 pieces)? It may help you to understand this question you have just done. [pointing]

[Alex does cut it into thirds but not equally].

ESW:	Are they all the same size?
Alex:	No ... it's not easy ... can you please help?
ESW:	Yes, I can see how that could be tricky!
	[work together to complete]
ESW:	Can you make this 'cake' into quarters? [hands a new strip of paper]
Alex:	Yeah, that's easier. [successfully folds and cuts into quarters]
ESW:	Great work! Which piece out of the $\frac{1}{3}$ and the $\frac{1}{4}$ is bigger?
Alex:	This one [pointing to $\frac{1}{3}$]
ESW:	Why?
Alex:	I don't know ... They should be the same size ...
ESW:	The reason is, we are cutting cakes (the whole) which are same size into different size pieces. If you had three people eating this cake, they would get bigger slices of the cake compared to if four people were eating the other cake ... Do you see what I mean?
Alex:	Yeah ...
ESW:	What slice of 'cake' would you want?
Alex:	One third because it is bigger ...
ESW:	Great! Do you see if there are more people to share with you get less cake?
Alex:	Yes
ESW:	What do you think will happen when we cut this cake into 5 pieces?
Alex:	The bits will be smaller ...

It is clear that Alex has some good developing conceptual understanding about fractions but still needs to visualise them as concrete objects (the cake or the strips of paper). The ESW is gradually leading Alex to a more nuanced and abstract understanding through questioning and working with Alex to create a representation of one third, and the recognition that to compare fractions the same 'whole' is needed. Alex's misconception is similar to that shown in Figure 6.6.

> **PAUSE AND REFLECT**
>
> In what ways did the ESW assist Alex with understanding fundamental fraction concepts?
> At the end of the session, how confident would you be that Alex's misconception was addressed?

Mathematical language is dense and difficult for many students. For the best reasons, ESWs may try to simplify complex language for weaker students. For example, they may call a 'rectangle' an 'oblong' or name a 'rhombus' as a 'diamond'. Ultimately this practice is not in the students' best interests because it reduces the mathematical meaning. Successful schools have agreed correct mathematical terms, and these are used consistently across the school (Callingham et al. 2017). This language includes terms such as commutative or distributive properties. Education support workers need to recognise that they too must emphasise the correct mathematical language. It is worth having a discussion with the ESW to clarify this point, and to reiterate that while they may provide a simple explanation, they should use correct terminology. For example, it is acceptable to say, 'This is a sphere. It looks like a ball', but it is not correct to say, 'A sphere is a circle'. Doing so closes down opportunities for students to develop the concept of a 3D object called a sphere. Because ESWs often work with small groups or individuals, they may have longer and more detailed exchanges about mathematics than the teacher is able to do (see Classroom Snapshot 18.1). Hence, ESWs carry great responsibility for developing students' mathematical vocabulary. Teachers, especially pre-service teachers and beginning teachers, may make the assumption that ESWs always use correct mathematical terms but it is worth having this conversation.

Where ESWs lack confidence in their own mathematical knowledge, they may feel that mathematics is too hard for many students. This is a matter of beliefs (see Chapter 12) and is as important when ESWs are working with students as it is when teachers teach. If a teacher is working with a professional ESW in their class, being aware of the ESW's thinking about mathematics is useful. This need for awareness reinforces the critical nature of building a good relationship with the ESW and planning collaboratively for students' success.

Working with ESWs

There is a difference between working with professional classroom ESWs and classroom volunteers. For example, it is reasonable to ask a professional classroom ESW to remove a disruptive student from the classroom, in line with school protocols, but this can never be the role of any volunteer help. In this section, some ways of working productively with classroom ESWs, professional and volunteer, will be explored.

ACTIVITY 18.1

Make a list of the different ways that you have experienced ESWs being used in classrooms. Think about your own experience, maybe as parent help or during volunteer work, and what you may have seen or discussed during practicum or as an employee. Include a wide range of classrooms across the primary years. Categorise the activities as general practical support or pedagogical practice. How does the work of a classroom based ESW change from Kindergarten to Year 6? How does it differ between volunteer help and professional ESWs? Share your thoughts and experiences with another pre-service teacher or colleague.

Working with professional ESWs

In the classroom, ESWs may support the work of teachers in many ways, but teachers and ESWs have different roles and areas of responsibilities. Table 18.1 outlines these areas and is a useful framework to refer to help ensure a productive collaborative working relationship (adapted from Kearns 2020).

Table 18.1 Comparing the roles of teachers and ESWs

Teacher	ESW
Establishes teaching and learning routines	Discusses routines with teacher and applies them in the classroom
Develops individual education plans, learning support plans, and/or individual behaviour management plans	Assists in the delivery, monitoring and assessment of individuals' respective plans
Plans lessons based on curriculum and learning outcomes; identifies appropriate teaching strategies, daily goals and learning intentions	Works with individuals and small groups as directed by the teacher
Identifies appropriate learning materials and resources to be used to support student learning	Prepares and uses learning materials and resources as directed by the teacher
Determines assessment requirements including reporting and documentation requirements; identifies assessment tools and strategies	Undertakes student assessment, such as observations, under the direction of the teacher
Provides written and verbal feedback to parents/carers	Only provides feedback to parents/carers in consultation with teacher

In practice, it is likely that there would be flexibility in terms of the roles and responsibilities of the teacher and the ESW, but it is important for the teacher to be well prepared in order to capitalise on having an extra assistant in the room. For example, sometimes it might be preferable for the ESW to move around the class during mathematics activities while the regular teacher works with groups of students who are struggling mathematically. It is important that all students work directly with the class teacher at some time, and that students needing support are not always working with an ESW. Education support workers may also help with behaviour management – having a second adult in the room can help to prevent conflicts emerging. Regularly reviewing roles and responsibilities can help to maintain a satisfying and respectful relationship between the teacher and the ESW.

Classroom Snapshots 18.2 to 18.4 each address different ways of working with professional ESWs in primary classrooms. They are all based on real situations observed or experienced.

CLASSROOM SNAPSHOT 18.2

Nathaniel is a beginning teacher in a small school in regional Australia. The school is located in a rural area and has a very high proportion of migrant and refugee families who do not speak English at home, and a high Aboriginal enrolment. Nathaniel is lucky to have been allocated an ESW, Taylah, for the whole morning period to support his work in a combined Year 1 and Year 2 class. At the start of the year, Nathaniel discussed with Taylah how they would work together. The school takes a case management approach to every student, and teachers keep daily records of progress. Taylah undertakes some of this daily monitoring by undertaking quick 'on-the-run' assessments, devised by Nathaniel, such as asking students to count on from any number across the decade, skip counting by 2 from any number and so on. Taylah records the outcomes on a class record sheet. Nathaniel uses this information to help him form groups for ongoing mathematics learning. During the mathematics block, Taylah works with a small group of students identified as still having difficulty with counting, many of whom do not speak English at home. Nathaniel provides challenge material to the three students who have already mastered counting on and skip counting by 2 and by 5, including across 100. He spends his time working with the middle group of students, who are split into two groups, with an emphasis on those students who have the ideas but are not entirely secure in their understanding. During the lesson he makes sure that he monitors what each group is doing and brings students back on task when needed.

Nathaniel is working with Taylah to enhance teaching, rather than expecting routine tasks. The 'light' assessment that Taylah does, under Nathaniel's direction helps Nathaniel make pedagogical decisions about next steps for the students in his class. Although he is a beginning teacher, Nathaniel is ensuring that he makes the pedagogical decisions that will impact on the teaching and learning program and that he also undertakes the critical assessment for reporting purposes. He does listen to Taylah, however, and the discussion that they had at the start of the year has set up a productive partnership.

CLASSROOM SNAPSHOT 18.3

Nancy is a beginning teacher in a large inner-city school in a lower socio-economic area. She has an ESW, Mandi, to work in her Year 3 room for three hours each week, one hour on each Tuesday, Wednesday and Friday mornings before lunch. The school has an emphasis on presentation, in the belief that having attractive and entertaining classrooms helps children learn. Mandi, the ESW, is very creative and good with arts and crafts so Nancy asks her to update the classroom displays each week, and to prepare special displays for particular units of work. Mandi prepares a spectacular display of geometry in art and architecture. The other teachers are very impressed but Nancy notices that the students in her class only give the display cursory attention. Nevertheless, the display remains for several weeks.

In Classroom Snapshot 18.3 Nancy and Mandi are working together in a different way from Nathaniel and Taylah. Partly this reflects the more limited time that Mandi spends with Nancy's class. She is not able to get to know the students as well as Taylah does. Nancy is also reacting to the school's emphasis on presentation, capitalising on Mandi's talents. Mandi's support is less pedagogically focused but does take pressure off Nancy to devise suitable classroom displays.

CLASSROOM SNAPSHOT 18.4

Norm, who has been teaching for one year, has a Year 5 class in a small school in an outer suburb of a sizeable town. There is one student, Fay, who is moderately capable in mathematics but gets easily frustrated. The ESW, Sal, works in Norm's class once a week. The class is working on the relationship between decimal notation, fractions and percentages, using squared paper, collections of objects, double number lines, number expanders (see Chapter 6) and so on to create appropriate representations of given numbers. Sal, at Norm's request, is working with Fay's group, with a focus on Fay who is struggling to make the connections between the various representations. Suddenly, Fay jumps up and shouts 'This is rubbish!'. She throws the materials onto the floor. Sal quietly takes Fay to another part of the classroom, and then, when she hasn't calmed down, moves her outside the classroom in line with agreed school protocols. Later Sal makes a note about the incident in the school record book and discusses Fay's 'meltdown' with Norm.

In this scenario, Norm has anticipated that Fay might become disruptive. He has a good working relationship with Sal, the ESW, and Sal knows that if Fay does have a meltdown, the agreed school approach is to remove her from the classroom. The ESW is here being used mainly for behaviour management, although she works with a group of students rather than being allocated solely to Fay.

PAUSE AND REFLECT

Think about these three classroom snapshots. They reflect different philosophies of education in the schools. The three teachers, Nathaniel, Nancy and Norm, are reacting to these philosophies by making use of the ESW resources provided in ways that they believe are most productive. In the same situations what might you have done? Is Nathaniel making the best use of his ESW by using her to undertake some on-the-run assessments, and placing her with the weakest group? What do you think about Mandi's geometry display? Is it appropriate for Year 3? What about Sal's response to Fay's behaviour? Should she have made Fay pick up the materials she had thrown around? There are no rights or wrongs, simply an opportunity to reflect on some different approaches.

These scenarios indicate some of the varied ways that ongoing support of mathematics teaching in the classroom can be helpful to teachers.

Volunteer ESWs

Working with volunteer help in classrooms is very different from working with professional ESWs. Some volunteer ESWs do become embedded in the school and may work with a particular teacher for many years on specific tasks. One volunteer ESW worked for over 30 years in a Year 3 and 4 classroom and became responsible for the craft work in the room, devising and carrying out projects across the school year, with the collaboration and approval of the teacher and the school. She would work with a small group and engage them in conversation as they worked, much of which had a mathematical basis involving measurements and geometric concepts such as tessellation. This situation, however, is very rare and depends mainly on the teacher and volunteer ESW developing an ongoing relationship. Far more common is parent or grandparent help, where a child's parent or grandparent comes into the classroom occasionally, usually on a rostered basis. Schools may have restrictions on volunteer help. For example, many schools do not have any volunteers in classrooms in Term 1, to allow classes to settle into school routines. Sometimes schools restrict the number of days that volunteers can work in classrooms, such as having no parent help on Fridays because this is usually assembly day.

Volunteer ESWs' presence in the classroom cannot be relied upon to the extent of professional ESWs. They may forget the day or time that they agreed to come into the classroom or turn up unexpectedly. All teachers need to be flexible and accommodate volunteers wherever possible. Often volunteers do not want to work with mathematics. They may feel ill-equipped to answer students' questions or to guide them appropriately. Many experienced teachers have an advice sheet that they give to volunteer ESWs with suggestions for prompts when they are working with mathematics groups. Ideas might include mathematics games that they could play, the mathematical language used in the school with its meaning, or questions that could be asked such as 'Can you do it another way?' or comments such as 'That's interesting. Can you explain that to me?'

However competent volunteer helpers are, they should never be expected to supervise a class or manage difficult behaviours. The role of volunteer ESWs in classrooms is usually limited to working with small groups on a specific task under the supervision of the teacher.

CLASSROOM SNAPSHOT 18.5

Ailine is a shy student who is new to the school and is having trouble making friends. Her mother offers to come into Ailine's Year 1 class as parent help. She explains that she was a teacher in Tonga but has recently come to Australia with her Australian husband and family. She has all the necessary checks to work in the school. Ailine's teacher, Tara, asks her to work with a small group to practice connecting numerals with their written English words. Tara chooses the group carefully, with two girls who have talked with Ailine and two quiet boys that she can trust to behave with Ailine's mum. She provides each child with a sheet divided into ten sections, each having a digit 0 to 9 in the corner. She asks Ailine's mum to get the children to draw the given number of objects in each box, and to write the English word for the number. As Tara works with the rest of the class, she keeps an eye on Ailine's mum's group. The students are all highly engaged with the activity and are talking animatedly with Ailine's mum and apparently saying words in Tongan language. Tara is intrigued and finishes the lesson a bit early so that groups can report back. The students show their drawings and words to the class. They have used objects and animals from Tonga such as one turtle and five frangipani flowers. They also explain that Ailine's mum taught them some of the number names in Tongan: *noa* (0), *taha* (1) and so on. Tara calls Ailine to join the group and together, with some help from Ailine's mum, they manage to count from 0 to 9 in Tongan language. At the next break time, Tara is pleased to see that several students are talking to Ailine about Tonga and what it is like there.

What is going on here? The activity that Tara chose for her volunteer is very appropriate. It has a mathematical basis and targets an aspect that some students struggle with. To some extent, however, Ailine's mum has gone beyond the brief and teaching students the Tongan words could have been confusing. Rather than discussing this with Ailine's mum or completely ignoring it, Tara chose to react positively to this situation, and this seems to have helped Ailine. The outcome was less mathematical than social. Next time that Tara is faced with a volunteer ESW, however, she should think carefully about the instructions that she gives the ESW to ensure that the mathematical outcomes that she wants are met.

Students' mathematics work is often ignored in classroom displays. Many classrooms have posters about mathematics but little else. There is no reason, however, that students' mathematical work should not be on display, and imagine the impact that the display might have had on the students if Mandi (Classroom Snapshot 18.3) had been able to draw on students' own work. Mathematical activities that lead to students' own work as the basis for a display can be supported by professional and volunteer ESWs.

ACTIVITY 18.2

Imagine that you are the teacher of Nancy's Year 3 class (see Classroom Snapshot 18.3). Devise a geometry unit for the class that will draw on their experiences of living in a city and involves concrete materials that they can manipulate. The outcome of the unit should be work that can be published in the classroom, and may include photos, drawings, diagrams, models and writing about their geometric thinking. How could an ESW, professional or volunteer, support such a unit in both practical and pedagogical ways? Create a journal entry about the unit you have planned, and the support that an ESW could give, and share this with colleagues.

Nancy may have missed an opportunity to connect geometry with her students' experiences because Mandi was so good at creating classroom displays. Rather than start from the students and their interests, Nancy has let Mandi dictate the content and nature of the display. Students love to see their own work exhibited and are more likely to bring their parents into the classroom to show off what they have been doing, breaking down barriers between school and home. The ESW, Mandi, could still have created the display but using material produced by the students.

There are very good reasons for having parent help as volunteer ESWs in classrooms. Where parents are involved in school, outcomes for their students are improved (Desforges

2003). However, students who have most difficulties with mathematics are often those whose parents are least involved. That is frequently because the parents had poor experiences in mathematics themselves and lack confidence to help their children. They are less likely to volunteer for classroom help. One way of recruiting volunteers for mathematics support is to ask for help to make up mathematics games. There are many good resources for games. Dr Paul Swan has a good selection of activities that can be downloaded free of charge. By asking parents to help in this way, you can build their confidence with mathematics, and the games could be sent home for parents to play with their children.

Link 18.1 Dr Paul Swan

Another common way in which volunteer ESWs are involved is with excursion support, when more adults are needed for supervision. It is important to explain clearly what the purpose of the excursion is and your expectations for support. Prepare an excursion sheet for each ESW detailing what to do in an emergency including the school phone number, and make sure you complete all the necessary paperwork, including a risk analysis, well before you go. It is useful also to let the front desk staff know when you are going and where, so that if there is an emergency they will not leave the caller waiting.

CLASSROOM SNAPSHOT 18.6

Josie has been teaching for three years and has a Year 3/4 class in a K–10 school in a regional city. She decides to take the class on a mathematics excursion to the local park. The park is about 5 minutes' walk from the school along a quiet suburban street. Josie prepares well for the excursion. She visits the park several times, identifying different areas that could be used for the measurement and geometry activities that she wants to include, such as measuring the perimeter of a flower bed and identifying 2D shapes and 3D objects in the environment. She prepares a worksheet to guide students on the day. Josie completes all the necessary paperwork and obtains permission for the outing. The school allocates a professional ESW who has basic first aid qualifications to support her, and Josie also asks three volunteers, all of whom have worked in her classroom before. She carefully explains what the excursion will involve, and the learning outcomes that she wants from the outing. Josie thinks carefully about the groups she will allocate to the ESWs, breaking up students who might argue with each other. She has two difficult students in her group, and allocates another one to the professional ESW. The volunteer ESWs have students they know or have worked with before. She prepares her class for the excursion by making sure they know how to use the equipment such as a trundle wheel or string as a go-between (see Chapter 3). Before the outing, Josie collects enough clipboards and pencils for each student and enough equipment for each of the five groups. The ESW collects the excursion first aid kit. Josie puts all these materials in a small tow-along cart.

PAUSE AND REFLECT

Think about the preparation that Josie has put into this excursion. Is there anything she has missed? What might you have done differently? Had you thought that a small excursion like this would need so much planning, or do you think Josie has over-prepared?

Classroom Snapshot 18.7 continues Classroom Snapshot 18.6.

CLASSROOM SNAPSHOT 18.7

It is the day of the mathematics excursion. The students are excited but attentive when Josie reminds them of their expected behaviour and the purpose of the excursion. They walk to the park, led by the professional ESW's group with Josie bringing up the rear so that she can observe all the students. When they reach the park, they gather in the rotunda and Josie hands out the clipboards, with the worksheets and pencils, and asks every student to write their name on their sheet. She gives the equipment to the ESW in charge of the group. She explains that the rotunda is their 'home base' and if anyone has an accident, the group should immediately come to the rotunda. She also promises some 'free play' time on the play equipment before they leave.

Josie's group remain to work in the rotunda area and the other groups disperse to their designated spots to start work. Josie can see all the groups from the rotunda, and they are all engaged and occupied. Suddenly, Josie realises that one of the groups led by a volunteer ESW is running to the rotunda. A dog appears to be chasing them, although dogs are not allowed off leash in the park. The volunteer ESW, one of the mothers, is very distressed, shouting about dogs being unclean and that this is an insult to her and her children. Some of Josie's group pick up on this and start calling names. Josie realises that she needs to get the situation under control quickly. The other groups are still working well so she decides not to call the whole group together. Instead, she asks all the students in her group and the distressed volunteer's group to come into the rotunda, to sit down with their legs crossed, hands in laps and to be silent and mindful for a minute. Josie has used this strategy in class when the students become over excited, and the familiar routine helps calm the students down. During the silent period, Josie ensures that the volunteer ESW is alright, gives her a drink of water, and promises to discuss the incident when they get back to school, reassuring her that this was an unexpected incident and that no insult was intended to the volunteer's Muslim beliefs.

She makes it clear to the students that name calling and insults are not acceptable, that this is against the school values and that they will follow up as a class later. Josie then asks the students to get their clipboards out and starts a conversation about the shapes in the environment that they can see. By the time the other groups join them, all the students are back on task. They collect the equipment up, place the clipboards in the cart and have 10 minutes free play in the fenced play area before returning to the school.

Back at school, Josie suggests that the volunteers go to the staff room for a drink. She flags with the students that the next day they will have a discussion about social skills but thanks the students for their generally good behaviour and gets each student to say what they enjoyed most about the excursion. After the bell goes, Josie makes a point of catching up with the distressed volunteer ESW. She explains that dogs are not allowed off leash in the park and that this dog must have slipped its leash. She had not anticipated that there might be a dog loose in the park but no insult was intended, and Josie herself was upset by the incident. The volunteer ESW accepts Josie's explanation. Later Josie debriefs with the junior school principal.

Josie seems to have rescued a potentially serious situation. The learning objectives for the excursion have been met by most students, and those that were disrupted have experienced similar activities before. She has tried to leave the students on a high by focusing on what they enjoyed, but she has also flagged that there are some matters for discussion later. She has tried to rebuild her relationship with her volunteer ESW.

ACTIVITY 18.3

Think about Josie's reactions to this incident. There is an immediate response to manage the situation in the park. Then there is recovery from the situation in the classroom. Later there will need to be some rebuilding of behaviour and reinforcement of the school's values. How well do you think Josie has reacted? What specific actions do you notice that may have helped with each level of reaction? For example, Josie used a familiar routine to settle the students in the park and made sure to follow up with the volunteer ESW afterwards. Make a list of Josie's behaviours at each stage and identify a negative action that Josie has avoided.

Working with volunteer ESWs can put pressure on teachers, especially beginning teachers. Parents, particularly, can make judgements about teachers' practices and there is a risk of such opinions becoming part of school gate gossip, or parents may become overly familiar when they run into teachers in the supermarket. Matters such as this should always be discussed with a more experienced colleague, such as a mentor teacher or the principal, who may be able to suggest strategies to reduce this stress. Striking the balance between professionalism and friendship is a balancing act.

There are many ways that parents can be engaged with the classroom. Some good ideas can be found in *The Guardian*'s article 'Top tips for teachers on engaging parents in learning'. Even if members of the school community cannot be volunteers in classrooms they may provide other forms of education support, such as coaching sports teams, making equipment, or spring-cleaning the school grounds. All these activities support the classroom teacher and come about through building good relationships with parents and volunteer ESWs.

Link 18.2 *The Guardian*: 'Top tips for teachers on engaging parents in learning'

PAUSE AND REFLECT

Imagine that you are a teacher with a Year 6 class. Often there is little ancillary support in upper primary classrooms. What would be your ideal working arrangements with professional and volunteer ESWs to support students' mathematics learning? Consider both practical and pedagogical support, and how you would justify a request to the school or to parents/volunteers for this assistance.

Working with other ESWs

As indicated at the start of this chapter, there are many other people involved in education support. In this section the work of some of these ESWs is briefly outlined, with specific reference to their support of mathematics learning. Specialists, for example in hearing impairment or blindness, are generally called in by the school when there is a student who has particular needs, and there is more information about this kind of specialist help in Chapter 12. Here only general support available to all students and teachers is considered.

Link 18.3 Tasmanian Department for Education, Children and Young People: Parent Fact Sheets

Teachers can refer individual students to specialist support, but it is sensible first to discuss the issues with a more senior colleague. The Tasmanian Department for Education, Children and Young People has a parent fact sheets page that has a useful list of roles and the kinds of support they can provide. If you think there is an individual student in your class who is at risk of falling behind or is having difficulties, seek advice Education support workers are there to support learning and teaching.

Education psychologist or school counsellor

Most schools have access to the services of an education psychologist. They are trained to undertake a variety of support roles, including assessments of cognitive and developmental functioning. Between 5 and 8 per cent of students have some level of disability with respect to mathematics, and many more students have negative feelings about mathematics (Gould 2019). The school psychologist can help to diagnose specific problems and provide advice about individual education programs or support for individual students.

Social worker

Social workers can help in cases of need, or where there are attendance issues. They can access resources for students who do not have basic materials such as rulers or exercise books. Students who are hungry cannot learn mathematics, or any other subject, and a surprisingly large number of students come to school without breakfast, for example. Social workers can liaise between the school and the family and other community agencies.

Numeracy or mathematics coach

In contrast to some of the other supports, a mathematics or numeracy coach usually has a whole school focus on quality teaching. Research has shown that schools successful in mathematics work consistently across the school to develop programs that support mathematics learning (Callingham et al. 2017), and some schools may use a coach as part of that process.

CLASSROOM SNAPSHOT 18.8

Northern Primary School is struggling to improve its numeracy outcomes. The school is small, situated on the edge of a regional town and has a large Aboriginal enrolment. The school works hard to engage with parents but has had limited success in enthusing them about numeracy. The school decides to employ a numeracy coach to both work with teachers to improve students' outcomes and to help the school community more generally understand the importance of numeracy. After getting to know the school, Lola Preston, the coach, suggests having a community numeracy day with each class responsible for an activity that will be run by the students on the day. Teachers are very doubtful about this approach, but Lola finds appropriate activities that are suitable for students to run. These range from making groups of objects and number dot-to-dots for the lower classes to measurement activities for the older students. Each class works with Lola until the teachers and the students are familiar with the activity and can explain it to those who visit from the community.

On the day, workstations are set up outside and students are rostered to work at their class station. When they are not at their own class workstation, they are free to visit other classes and are given a sheet that will be stamped to say they have visited. The day is a great success, with a large proportion of parents visiting the school. The students continue to talk about it for several weeks. Because of the greater engagement of the community and the students, Northern Primary decides

> to build the day into its school calendar. The second time the event is held, Lola has less work to do because many teachers have found their own activities and students are keen to be involved.
>
> After two years of encouraging the greater involvement of the community, the school's NAPLAN outcomes have improved, and they have added value to students' growth trajectories.

A mathematics or numeracy coach may work with individual teachers, small groups, and the whole school staff to change and improve pedagogy. The coach may be someone from inside the school, released from regular teaching duties, or may be appointed to the school from elsewhere. Sometimes coaches have several schools that they work with, and these coaches often run extended professional learning sessions for teachers from several schools together, which also supports professional dialogue across schools. Mathematics coaches may teach demonstration lessons, team teach in classrooms, or observe mathematics lessons with the aim of modelling best practice and providing advice. Developing a good relationship with the mathematics coach can be productive for everyone involved.

Conclusion

It is impossible in a single chapter to cover in depth all the myriad roles of ESWs. These will vary from school to school, system to system, and across states and territories in Australia. Overseas teaching will be different again in terms of the ESWs available. The key idea is that teachers recognise that that they are not alone in the teaching and learning endeavour. If support is offered, accept it gladly but use it judiciously.

GUIDED STUDENT TASKS

1. Find a job description for an ESW on the web. Make sure that this is from Australia rather than overseas. Compare the qualifications, duties and responsibilities with the AITSL Graduate Standard for teachers. What additional responsibilities does a teacher have? How else do the roles of an ESW and a teacher differ?
2. Prepare an advice sheet for volunteer ESWs for mathematics. Include suitable prompts and probes that will help students to make connections. Also include advice about 'wait time' and the difference between explaining what a student needs to do (e.g. you need to put this number together with this one and make a different larger number. That's addition.) and telling a student how to do it (e.g. write the start number on the number line. Now jump forward 10 …).
3. Choose any of the content chapters in this book. Make a list of mathematical terms that you find, and any others that you think are relevant. Write a 'plain language' statement next to each one. Imagine you are working with a professional ESW. Practice the conversation that you could have to introduce the correct mathematical language.

4. Talk to someone who has worked in a classroom as a professional or volunteer ESW. If you have this experience yourself, offer to be that person for a colleague to talk to. Find out from the ESW what the teacher explained about working in mathematics support. What additional information would have been helpful to the ESW?

FURTHER READING

Evidence for Learning 2019, 'Making best use of teaching assistants: Seven recommendations to support schools make the best use of teaching assistants', *Evidence for Learning*, 26 September, <https://evidenceforlearning.org.au/education-evidence/guidance-reports/teaching-assistants>.

Gould, K 2019, 'Math challenges? A school psychologist could help', *The Conversation*, 21 July, <https://theconversation.com/math-challenges-a-school-psychologist-could-help-111488#>.

ACKNOWLEDGEMENT

Thank you to Peta Corkery for providing the script and image for Classroom Snapshot 18.1.

CHAPTER 19

BECOMING A TEACHER OF MATHEMATICS

LEARNING OUTCOMES

By the end of this chapter, you will:

- better understand the purpose of LANTITE and NAPLAN
- be able to recognise strategies to reduce mathematics anxiety in students
- better understand the AITSL standards in the context of mathematics
- understand ways to evaluate evidence to address the AITSL standards
- be able to recognise the effectiveness of learning communities
- be able to recognise some of the challenges of teaching online in the primary school context.

Introduction

Graduate teachers of primary mathematics face a range of professional issues as they bridge the divide from being a student to becoming a teacher. Some of these issues occur only at this stage of professional life; others are ongoing. This chapter considers some of the key issues that concern pre-service and early graduate teachers, all within the context of teaching primary mathematics.

Undertaking the Literacy and Numeracy Test for Initial Teacher Education Students (LANTITE) is one issue that this chapter addresses. The Australian Government introduced LANTITE because of concerns about teachers' personal literacy and numeracy. Universities have adopted different strategies for initial teacher education students to meet the requirement to achieve the appropriate professional standard in LANTITE. For many people, adults and children, the thought of having to do a mathematics test is a source of anxiety, so consideration is given to dealing with mathematics anxiety, especially in relation to NAPLAN, because some schools and parents have indicated both staff and students becoming stressed about the testing (Wyn, Turnbull & Grimshaw 2014).

Evidence-based education is widely discussed but what constitutes evidence is an issue for beginning teachers. Graduating students must provide evidence about the effectiveness of their teaching and demonstrate how they meet the Graduate Standards of the Australian Institute for Teaching and School Leadership (AITSL). In classrooms, teachers need evidence of learning. Some of the challenges of collecting appropriate evidence of teaching and learning will be considered.

As a professional teacher, ongoing professional learning is an expectation. Ways in which graduate teachers of primary mathematics can become part of a professional learning community or network will be canvassed. Building a portfolio of experience and expertise will help teachers to meet the standards set by AITSL for graduate teachers but also on an ongoing basis. More importantly, ongoing professional learning ensures that teachers become the best possible teachers of mathematics so that their students achieve the best possible outcomes.

In recent times, online delivery of the mathematics curriculum has been necessary because of disruption due to COVID-19 (OECD 2020). There are also eschools, distance education provision and support for students unable to be schooled in regular classrooms because of illness or other factors. Challenges are associated with presenting the mathematics curriculum in this way and some strategies for doing so effectively will be outlined.

Mathematics anxiety and the challenge of tests

Anxiety about mathematics

Many initial teacher education students feel **anxious** about mathematics. There is good evidence, however, that everyone can (and does) operate mathematically. Some of this anxiety relates only to tests or examinations of mathematics but may go beyond this to having a fear of any mathematical activity. There are suggestions that about 20 per cent of the population has some level of anxiety about mathematics (Buckley 2013). How often have you heard 'I was never any good at maths'?

Mathematics is important in daily life and its role in underpinning many of the developments in technology has been emphasised in many government reports. As a teacher, it is your responsibility to ensure that every child in your class learns mathematics. More importantly, helping students to feel positive about mathematics and to have belief in their ability to do mathematics is critical. Reflect on how you learned mathematics and create your own mathematics journey in Activity 19.1.

Mathematics anxiety feelings of fear or helplessness when faced with mathematical situations, including mathematics tests

ACTIVITY 19.1

Feelings about mathematics change throughout your life. Think about your own mathematics journey. Remember what you felt when you were doing mathematics in primary school, in high school or at university. Make a picture of your mathematics journey across time. Some examples are provided in Figure 19.1. The first of the two examples shown is from a woman who became a chemical engineer. The second belongs to a male pre-service primary teacher. Notice how both these examples have become much more positive as they entered their professional life.

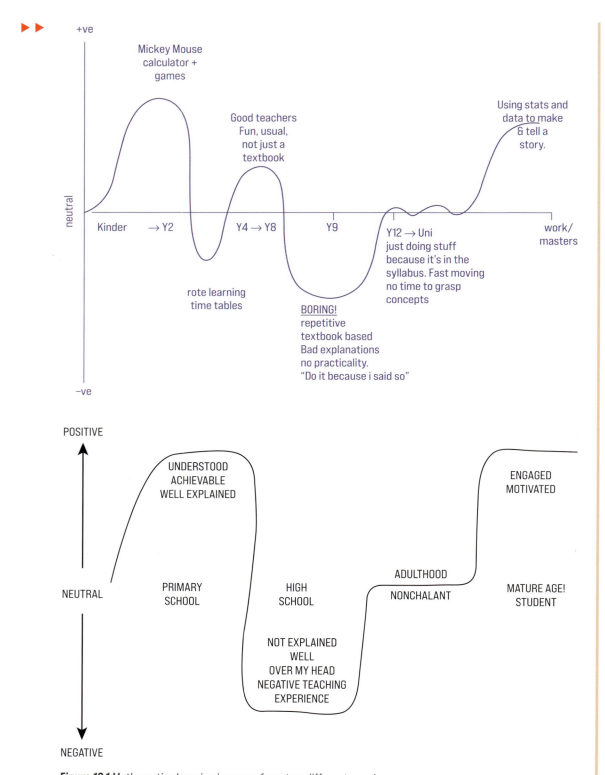

Figure 19.1 Mathematics learning journeys from two different people

There are some similarities in these two profiles. In both, the authors were positive about mathematics when it was well explained. When mathematics was presented as a series of disconnected skills, the charts show negativity. Both are very positive about mathematics in their professional lives. Being anxious or negative about mathematics can change. There is no such thing as a 'maths brain' and everyone can learn mathematics.

PAUSE AND REFLECT

Look at the times when you were most positive about mathematics. What was happening then? Make a list of all the factors that influenced your feelings about mathematics when you felt good about it. Do the same for those times when you were most negative about mathematics. Being enthusiastic about teaching mathematics has the greatest influence on students' outcomes (Callingham et al. 2017), more so than knowing a lot of mathematics. How enthusiastic were your teachers when you enjoyed mathematics?

As a teacher, write down at least two actions that you can take to help your students avoid negative feelings about mathematics.

One aspect of mathematics anxiety is based on tests and examinations. The next sections consider two tests that you will meet as a pre-service and beginning teacher: LANTITE and NAPLAN.

What is LANTITE?

All students enrolled in an Australian initial teacher education course are required to reach the expected standard in both numeracy and literacy. The Australian Government introduced LANTITE to ensure that teachers have high levels of personal numeracy and literacy so that they can nurture the important mathematical skills, knowledge and understanding in their classrooms. LANTITE provides a consistent measure of initial teacher education students' numeracy across Australia.

Personal numeracy is defined in the LANTITE Assessment Framework as: 'interpreting and communicating important non-technical mathematical information, and using such information to solve relevant real-world problems to participate in an education community, to achieve one's goals, and to develop one's knowledge and potential as a teacher' (ACER n.d., p. 21). The test does not test abstract mathematics, such as trigonometry or algebra skills, but does address the kinds of mathematics used every day by education professionals.

Your own institution will have advice for you about preparing and sitting LANTITE. The best way to be prepared is to become familiar with the format and nature of the test and the questions asked. If you are studying off-campus or online, it is possible to undertake LANTITE at home. If this option is available to you, be very aware of the particular conditions and expectations of undertaking LANTITE in this mode (see Figure 19.2). Undertake Activity 19.2 to become more familiar with LANTITE.

Figure 19.2 Students can take LANTITE at home. Note the cleared desk.

ACTIVITY 19.2

Link 19.1 LANTITE

Go to the LANTITE website. These questions are designed to help you explore the site.

1. Who is eligible to take LANTITE?
2. How many times may a student attempt LANTITE?
3. How do students sit the test?
4. What are the test dates for the current year?
5. What are the proficiency bands for numeracy?

There are several sets of practice questions available. Download the Numeracy Practice Test. Try all the questions and then access the answers. If you are registered for the test with an account, you may try the practice material online. It is worth doing this to familiarise yourself with the way that the online calculator works, and how the test is presented. Download the Worked Examples and check your answers against these. Identify which areas of mathematics you found difficult. Try working backwards from the answer to work out your mistakes. If you are still unsure, seek help from another student, a lecturer at your institution, your student support services, or another person who is knowledgeable about mathematics.

Before you take the LANTITE test read carefully the instructions on the website. Give yourself enough time to get to the venue but on the morning of the test do not try to do last-minute revision. Last minute cramming is actually unhelpful because it interferes with your thinking and can lead to confusion. The aim is to be cool, calm and collected about LANTITE.

NAPLAN (National Assessment Program – Literacy and Numeracy)

All students in Australia in Years 3, 5, 7, and 9 undertake the NAPLAN tests. From 2023, these tests will be undertaken in mid-March so that results can be sent back to schools earlier than has been the case. The tests are gradually being moved online, and this provides an added level of complexity for many students, especially those in Year 3. The online tests are adaptive – that is, after each group of questions, students are presented with the next set of questions that most closely aligns with their numeracy capability. Thus, not every student receives an identical test. Such testing is different from the traditional pen-and-paper test where every student answers the same set of questions. The tests, both online and paper, are created in such a way that students can be tracked over time and both their individual progress monitored and that of the school or system.

There is evidence, however, that some students and teachers find NAPLAN very stressful (Thompson 2013; Wyn, Turnbull & Grimshaw 2014). An Australian study (Callingham et al. 2017) showed that schools successful in achieving strong growth in their students recognised both positive and negative aspects of NAPLAN. They downplayed NAPLAN for their students and limited practice to some sample tests in the week or so leading up to NAPLAN. They treated NAPLAN as 'one test on one day' and used the data obtained from the test alongside other evidence gathered from internal school processes. Growing concerns about the use of NAPLAN data and the stress on students and teachers have led to changes, but many argue that the system needs more change (Wilson et al. 2021). It is beyond the scope of this chapter to consider all the issues in detail.

Some advice about working with NAPLAN items is provided in Chapter 10, but in this chapter the focus is on reducing any anxiety in students caused by mathematics tests.

CLASSROOM SNAPSHOT 19.1

Richard has been teaching for two years but this is his first experience of teaching a Year 3 class. He is aware that his students will undertake NAPLAN online early in the year and he wants to prepare them as well as he can. In a previous school, he saw teachers and students becoming very stressed about the NAPLAN tests and he wants to avoid that. He talks to colleagues and is relieved to find that they downplay NAPLAN to the students apart from ensuring that the students recognise and are familiar with the test format. However, he recognises that his Year 3 students are likely to be

▶▶ very unfamiliar with the online testing environment and wants to make sure that this does not cause additional stress.

Richard realises that sitting in silence, working alone and having to wear headphones may be issues for his class, because they usually work cooperatively and are encouraged to discuss their work with other students. He decides to explain the NAPLAN format to the class and he gives them five NAPLAN Numeracy questions on paper to familiarise them with working in silence on their own. He also talks with the numeracy coordinator at his school about arranging for his class to undertake a trial of the online environment, and to do this as a whole class. When they have used technology in the past, the students have usually been in small groups so having all the students at computers with headphones on is a different experience. Before the trial test, Richard uses the public demonstration site to show the students the various question formats. He allows the students to interact with the test on the interactive whiteboard and on the computer.

During the online trial Richard checks that every student understands how to answer the different formats and makes a note of questions that they had trouble understanding. Some students are obviously less familiar with technology and Richard arranges for these students, with support from an education support worker, to have extra access to the technology to familiarise them with the device being used by the school.

Richard discusses the experience of trying the test with his class. They talk about the language used in the questions and the different formats such as drag and drop, draw a line and enter your answer. He works hard to make the experience a positive one for all the students.

The school schedules the online NAPLAN assessments over several days during the online testing window. Numeracy is the last test to be completed and Richard is aware that the students may be feeling tired by the time that they get to undertake the assessment. He makes sure that during the test window his program includes physical and outside activity, and he allows students opportunities for 'free choice' after each assessment and gives them time to 'debrief'.

In these ways, Richard is reducing the stress on his students by ensuring that they are as well prepared as they can be and that they have opportunities for a range of activities during the period when the tests are scheduled.

PAUSE AND REFLECT

Think about your experiences in schools with NAPLAN, as a student, as a teacher or teacher's aide, as a pre-service teacher on practicum, or as a parent. Write down all the words you have heard to describe NAPLAN. Organise these words into positives and negatives. Focus on the positive aspects of NAPLAN and draw a picture (or series of pictures) to illustrate these. Now consider the negative aspects. For each negative, write down one action that you can take to minimise the impact.

NAPLAN is widely criticised on many grounds, but if the data are used sensibly, there are positive outcomes for schools and students. If NAPLAN becomes a source of mathematics anxiety, then the potential benefits will be reduced. Explore NAPLAN through Activity 19.3.

ACTIVITY 19.3

Go to the NAPLAN website. Start by accessing the school support material. Find the Minimum Standards for Year 3 and Year 5.

Compare the Working Mathematically standards for these two year levels. How do they change? What additional expectations are there for Year 5 that are not included in Year 3? For one dot point from each year level, consider how you would develop students' mathematical thinking to meet that particular standard. What kinds of activities will develop students' confidence and capacity to solve problems and use mathematics?

Go to the Tests section. Try the online tests on the public demonstration site for all year levels (including Year 7 and Year 9). An example item is shown in Figure 19.3.

Link 19.2 NAPLAN: National minimum standards – numeracy

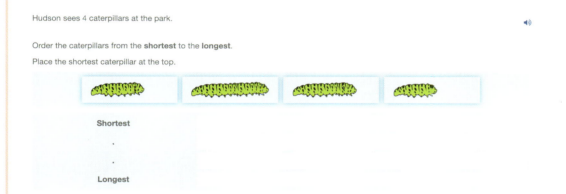

Figure 19.3 Year 5 NAPLAN numeracy item
Source: NAPLAN public demonstration site, Year 5 Numeracy <www.nap.edu.au/naplan/public-demonstration-site>

How did you do? Did you notice any unfamiliar language or diagrams, such as triangles presented in different orientations to those usually shown? Try out the online tools, such as the ruler and calculator. Look at the accessibility options as well. How do these change the experience of taking the test?

Now look at the parents/carers support pages. Write a short paragraph to explain to a parent/caregiver what is the best help that they can give a primary school child with NAPLAN numeracy to reduce any anxiety. Try this explanation out on a friend.

There are many ways to assess mathematics, and the chapter about assessment provides some ideas. NAPLAN is a tool used by systems and the important issue for teachers is to make use of the data to improve the experience of mathematics for their students.

Using evidence to inform teaching is an important aspect of teachers' work in schools today. This evidence can be used at many levels. At the school level, data may inform the development of programs across the year groups. Within the classroom, knowing what your students can do is important for tailoring your own classroom program to meet the needs of your class. Finally, there is the evidence that you will need to collect about the effectiveness of your teaching. The next section, Evidence-based teaching, has a focus on the kinds of evidence that you can collect to meet professional standards.

Evidence-based teaching

Evidence-based teaching the process of collecting and analysing data from a variety of sources to inform planning and programming at school and classroom level

Several studies have shown that using **evidence** to differentiate teaching in classrooms leads to productive outcomes for students (e.g. Goss et al. 2015). For graduate and early career teachers this expectation can be overwhelming. It is, however, part of the core business of a teacher.

As a teacher, the aim is to be efficient and effective. Evidence that you collect to inform your teaching may also be the basis for evidence of the effectiveness of your teaching, because it provides indications of learning. Collecting information through a range of assessment activities should be the basis for future planning. Unless assessment involves some decision and action, it has limited impact on learning.

Addressing the AITSL standards

The Australian Institute for Teaching and School Leadership (AITSL) was set up by the Federal Government as the body charged with supporting teaching in schools. It provides accreditation for ITE programs and a set of teacher standards for different career stages. One of the major challenges for graduating teachers is the need to provide evidence that they have met the requirements of the Graduate Standards for AITSL, including evidence about the effectiveness of their teaching. Many of the standards can be addressed through your final practicum placement. The AITSL requires all students to undertake a Teaching Performance Assessment (TPA) in their final year. The form that this takes is decided by your institution, but all TPAs have been reviewed and endorsed by the AITSL.

Do not treat this task as simply an assessment requirement for your course. The kinds of activities included are the daily work of teachers, and this is an opportunity to demonstrate what you know and can do. Get to know the AITSL Graduate Standards through the activity provided here. The focus is on mathematics.

ACTIVITY 19.4

Link 19.3 AITSL: Australian Professional Standards for Teachers

Go to the AITSL website. From the home page the standards are listed under the Teacher Standards tab. There are seven standards each of which has a number of sub-headings.

Think specifically about a practicum you have undertaken, or maybe your final placement if you are in your final year. The seven standards are listed in Table 19.1. Copy this table and for each standard, with a specific focus on mathematics, identify what evidence would contribute towards demonstrating competency. You may find the AITSL website useful for examples. Some ideas are provided in Table 19.1, but you should provide much more detail. For example, where Table 19.1 suggests assessment information, identify exactly what you did (or will do) to identify your students' needs and/or progress. There are many other sources of information and other chapters in this book will also provide ideas.

Table 19.1 AITSL standards (2017) and examples of evidence

Standard	Examples of types of evidence
1. Know students and how they learn	Assessment information, informal and formal conversations such as conferencing with individual students, small group and whole class discussion
2. Know the content and how to teach it	Lesson and unit plans linked to curriculum outcomes and expectations (use the Australian Curriculum: Mathematics v. 9.0), learning progressions, sources of activities
3. Plan for and implement effective teaching and learning	Lesson and unit plans including pre- and post-assessment strategies
4. Create and maintain supportive and safe learning environments	Handing out and collecting back equipment, valuing all students' input and thinking
5. Assess, provide feedback and report on student learning	Assessment strategies, examples of written and oral feedback that has a focus on where to next
6. Engage in professional learning	Documented attendance at mathematics PL sessions, professional association membership (e.g. local mathematics association, mathematics conference attendance)
7. Engage professionally with colleagues, parents/carers and the community	Discussions about mathematics learning and teaching with colleague teachers, at staff meetings, with peers and other community members

Developing as a teacher will be an ongoing process throughout your career. The AITSL website has many resources to download and useful 'Illustrations of Practice' to watch. Make use of these resources and cultivate the habit of collecting the kind of information that will allow you to address the standards. Some systems require you to undertake a set number of hours of professional learning, so keeping records of relevant events and training sessions that you attend can become very important. As you progress through your career, you will be required to maintain your teacher accreditation and this evidence may be used for reaccreditation purposes. One approach is to use a professional portfolio.

Developing a professional portfolio

There are many ways of developing and maintaining a professional portfolio, but these days the expectation is that portfolios should be electronic. There are many tools available for eportfolios and most universities provide access to portfolio tools. The portfolio that you start during your pre-service teacher education should not be considered as just a requirement of your course. Rather these tools are the start of a professional journey that will grow and change with you as you develop further in your career.

As well as your curriculum vitae, your portfolio can, and should, contain a variety of evidence that showcases your work as a teacher. This evidence might include formal accreditation (such as being a sports coach), lesson plans and evaluations, records of professional learning such as attendance at the local mathematics association conference, membership of relevant professional associations, and work samples from your university course or students. There are several examples of beginning teacher portfolios on the web (search for 'teaching portfolio' or 'AITSL standards portfolio' to find several examples). AITSL also has a set of templates that can be used to show how you met the graduate standard, which may be as simple as documenting your result for specific units during your initial teacher education program.

ACTIVITY 19.5

Examine your personal portfolio. If you do not yet have one, you could create one using one of the many platforms available or the one recommended by your institution. List all the items that you have in it. Decide which AITSL standard each addresses and identify any gaps. Do you have examples from mathematics in it? If not, you should aim to include some mathematics examples because it is an important part of the work of a teacher in the primary school. Make sure that your mathematics examples come from different strands of the curriculum and from different year levels. The purpose is to build up a resource from which you can draw for different purposes such as job applications or accreditation. Look at several of the examples on the web and critique these as if you were responsible for judging whether or not they provided well rounded evidence against the AITSL standards. What examples are there from mathematics or numeracy? Are the portfolios effective at 'telling the story' of a professional journey, especially in relation to mathematics or numeracy?

Classroom Snapshot 19.2 is an example of a beginning teacher who had to modify a lesson 'in the moment'. She used an unexpected situation to collect evidence of her capacity as a teacher to meet the next level of the AITSL standards.

CLASSROOM SNAPSHOT 19.2

Jay is a first-year teacher working in a remote country school. She plans a unit on volume and capacity for her Year 6 class. Her objective is to build to the idea that the volume of a cuboid is the area of the base multiplied by the height so that the students will be able to calculate the volume of a rectangular prism when they meet it in Year 7.

She begins the lesson by giving the students centimetre grid paper and asking them to colour in an area of 12 square centimetres. She plans to then give the students some centicubes and get them to build up the volume in layers.

Only a short time into the lesson, the noise level is high and most of the class are off task. She realises that they have only a hazy understanding of area – some are trying to measure a 12 cm length using a ruler. Others are colouring in alternate squares to create a pattern, and some students are just sitting and waiting to be told or shown how to do the task.

Jay realises that to continue with the lesson she has planned will be a waste of time. She calls the class together and explains that the lesson isn't going according to plan and that she wants them to put their pencils down. She promises that they will go back to the activity at another time. As an alternative, she gives students a sheet of paper and asks them to write or draw pictures to tell someone else what area is, an activity that she had in the back of her mind in case the lesson fell apart. The class settles down and at the end of the lesson, Jay collects their work.

Reflecting on her actions that evening Jay realised that she had made assumptions about her students' prior knowledge. She had based a pre-assessment on the Year 5 expectations of the Australian Curriculum: Mathematics v. 9.0. Although the students were supposed to be able to practical problems involving areas of regular shapes (AC9M5M02) in Year 5, they obviously didn't really understand the concept of area. This insight was reinforced when Jay looked at the work that they had completed to explain area to someone else. Jay planned a couple of lessons dealing with area as an idea, and then aimed to repeat her abandoned lesson to develop the concept of volume. Jay decided to record her thoughts, and to keep examples of the students' work and her new lesson plans as evidence of her developing flexibility in teaching.

Jay is demonstrating her capacity to think on her feet. Many beginning teachers struggle with these kinds of 'contingencies' (Rowland 2013) and continue with the lesson planned. Jay chose to change what she was doing, and, at the same time, she collected useful information about her students' levels of understanding of a pre-requisite concept of area. Things do not always go to plan in the mathematics classroom, regardless of how well planned, or experienced, the teacher may be. In this case, Jay had anticipated that some students might struggle with the concept of volume and had an idea for another activity to give to those students. When the whole class was disengaged, she chose to use her 'emergency' activity as the basis for the lesson. Adding her reflections and lesson plans to her professional portfolio provides Jay with powerful evidence of her capacity to teach and meets several AITSL standards.

PAUSE AND REFLECT

When have you seen teachers change their lesson plans in response to some unexpected event in the class? Have you ever had to do this? Why was Jay's strategy effective? Discuss this classroom scenario with an experienced teacher and ask what advice they would have for a beginning teacher.

Evidence of learning

Evidence of learning can come from a variety of sources including classroom observation, discussion with students individually or in groups, special assessment tasks, tests, assignments and so on. Wherever possible, a variety of sources of evidence should be used before making major decisions about a particular student. Chapter 10 provides a wealth of ideas for developing rich assessment tasks that will identify students' understanding.

All students develop differently. Although it is a worthy aim to cater for every individual difference, in reality there will be groups of students within your class that, while they have varied patterns of development, will be similar enough to think of as a group. The key aspect, however, is not to see these groups as fixed. Using evidence appropriately means being flexible so that students may be in varied groups for diverse purposes. You may group students to encourage discussion or develop problem-solving skills. The key is to use rich tasks with a 'low-floor, high-ceiling' approach to allow all children to engage and grow at their own level. Examples and ideas can be found at websites including NRICH, reSolve: Maths by Inquiry, Maths300 and youcubed. Sometimes you will want to group by ability. Grouping by ability is not always as effective as it seems (e.g. Boaler, Wiliam & Brown 2000; Clarke & Clarke 2008; Attard 2015) and should be used for specific purposes rather than as an everyday classroom practice.

> **PAUSE AND REFLECT**
>
> How have you grouped students for learning mathematics? What evidence did you collect? List different approaches to grouping students for mathematics learning that you have seen. Which seemed to you to be the most effective for all students?

If you are going on a practicum placement, ask your colleague or mentor teacher how students are grouped in the class. If you are teaching a specific unit of work, plan a rich assessment task that will give you understanding of students' knowledge of the mathematics topic that you are teaching. If the groupings are not the same as those of your colleague/mentor teacher, discuss the similarities and differences. Sometimes students who are 'good at maths' are really only good at arithmetic – they recall tables and other number facts easily and can apply standard algorithms. Often these students are less comfortable when placed in an open-ended problem-solving situation, whereas students who are perceived to be less 'good' at mathematics may have insightful ways of going about solving a problem.

Some considerations about using students' data

Students' work samples create powerful evidence about students' mathematics learning. Collecting and using these and other information such as individual NAPLAN or other test scores, requires careful thought. Some schools will not give pre-service students access to individual student records for confidentiality reasons. Check with colleague/mentor teachers what information you can access and how this may be used. For example, you may be able to look at individual students' records but not to include them as part of your evidence about particular students. Work samples from students may be similar – you can use them to inform your teaching but not keep them as part of a portfolio.

If work sample collection is encouraged, either during practicum or when you are teaching, check the conditions for their use. Is parent and/or student permission needed for you to use work samples as part of a portfolio? Can you use them but only to provide a descriptive account of an individual without showing the actual work? The answers to these kinds of questions may determine the nature of what you do to demonstrate your capacity to meet AITSL standards.

Even if you are able to use work samples as part of a portfolio, these must be de-identified. Change the student's name and do not give the name of the school from which the sample is collected. Keep work samples confidential – don't post them on social media sites, for example, or in any situation where they can be accessed openly by anyone. All of the work samples in this book have been collected with appropriate permissions and have been stored in password-protected files. Maintaining students' confidentiality and privacy is an important professional consideration today.

Graduating as a teacher is the beginning of a professional journey that has many possibilities. You will be expected to maintain professional accreditation, undertake ongoing professional learning, and to engage with a variety of professional activities in school and in the wider community. Possibilities for professional engagement proliferate. Some will be mandated by your school or system, while others will allow you to follow your own interests. The focus in this section is mathematics and its teaching, rather than more general opportunities.

Professional learning communities

There is no single definition of a **professional learning community**, but it is generally accepted that key elements include a collaborative approach to critically evaluating teaching practice within a framework of shared values with a focus on student well-being and achievement (DuFour 2004; Ingvarson 2018). There is personal accountability within the group to improving teaching. All members contribute to developing the culture of improvement.

Professional learning community a group that comes together with a shared purpose and interest in improving learning and teaching (of mathematics)

Beginning teachers have an important part to play because of the recency of their academic experience. You may remember particular readings or activities from your course that can inform discussion, for example. You may have experienced a situation during practicum placements that provides a scenario for discussion.

Consider Classroom Snapshot 19.3, which describes how a school changed its approach to teaching patterns and algebra.

CLASSROOM SNAPSHOT 19.3

A group of upper primary teachers is discussing the recent NAPLAN results for Year 5. Looking at the trends over time, they notice that the Year 5 cohort is consistently doing less well on questions that involve pattern and algebra. Kate, a Year 6 teacher, makes the point that this strand provides a foundation for the more abstract thinking that children will experience when they move on to high school. Sam, one of the Year 5 team, agrees but says that the children come into his class with limited understanding about mathematical patterns. He says, 'I'm not trying to avoid responsibility or run down colleagues in the lower part of the school, but maybe we should discuss this with them.'

Following this meeting, the upper primary team leader talks to the principal about setting aside a full staff meeting to discuss the mathematics program with a focus on pattern and algebra. At the staff meeting, all teachers bring with them their yearly mathematics programs so that they can identify the pattern and algebra components. Following a sharing session, it is obvious that this strand of the curriculum is not being addressed as well as it could be.

A representative from each year group is nominated to be part of a working party under the leadership of the numeracy coordinator to identify what is needed to improve the teaching of pattern and algebra across the school. Damien, a beginning teacher, volunteers to be the Year 3 representative because he has a particular interest in teaching mathematics.

The working group first identifies all the relevant outcomes from the Australian Curriculum: Mathematics v. 9.0. They recognise that although they believe that they do address the content, they may not emphasise the patterning aspects. Each person in the group is assigned a task to follow up for the next meeting. Damien and the Kindergarten (Foundation) and Year 1 representatives undertake to research concrete materials and their use that could be helpful. Kate (Year 6) and the Year 4 teacher agree to look for articles and readings about children learning patterns and algebra. Sam (Year 5) and the Year 2 teacher look for activities and professional learning opportunities that could be used across year groups to develop understanding of patterns and algebra.

When the group reconvenes, they share all that they have found. The working group realises that although they do have materials in the school, the increased emphasis will require the purchase of additional concrete materials. They look at the articles and the activities and decide which of these would be suitable for particular year levels as professional reading or as classroom activities. Each person in the group agrees to trial an activity in their classroom before sharing all the information with their colleagues. There is discussion about specific professional learning, but the teachers decide that unless a teacher wants to follow this up personally, they will not recommend specific professional learning at this time because they recognise the expertise within the group.

In year level groups, the representatives report back to their colleagues. They provide readings and examples linked to the curriculum outcomes, and describe the activity that they tried and how the children responded. Finally, a submission is made to the principal for funds for equipment purchase. The year level programs are rewritten to specifically include pattern and algebra, and the new program is ready for the new school year.

This is an example of a school creating a group for a special purpose. It has many of the elements of a professional learning community:

- Data are used sensibly to identify an issue rather than to blame teachers or students.
- Members are accountable to the group and to the wider group of colleagues.
- The focus is on improving student learning – in this instance in patterns and algebra.
- Members of the working group share a purpose and vision for patterns and algebra.
- Members look outside their immediate environment to identify useful resources.
- There is mutual trust and respect between all members including the first-year teacher, Damien.
- The school leaders support the group by providing time and resources, and taking an interest in the group's progress.

The working group took time to carefully research the problem and identify ways in which it could be addressed. There was no suggestion of a quick fix for Year 5 students. Instead, the school took nearly a year to work through what was needed and to involve all teachers.

> **PAUSE AND REFLECT**
>
> How do staff meetings happen in schools that you are familiar with? When the school wanted to make a change in its mathematics teaching, how was this discussed and enacted? How often did teacher meetings focus deeply on learning and teaching mathematics? How much time was allocated to administrative tasks (such as organising the school disco or athletics carnival)?

Classroom observation

Many schools have adopted peer observation as one way of sharing best practice. Sometimes the observation is carried out by the mathematics coordinator or a numeracy coach, sometimes by other classroom teachers. The observation may be formal, with specific aspects of practice agreed beforehand, or quite casual, such as someone wanting to watch how you teach a specific concept after discussing this with you, or the principal 'dropping in' from time to time. Some beginning teachers may find the number of people coming in and out of their classrooms rather confronting. The aim of peer observation is not to judge the quality of teaching, but rather to share good ideas about learning and teaching practices. It is also a very useful practice if you are having trouble teaching an idea or topic, or you are wanting to bring in a new approach to teaching. Modern classrooms are not hidden behind closed doors. More than ever, multi-purpose facilities provide opportunities for team teaching or shared activities. Don't be concerned about these practices; embrace them as collegial and enlightening.

TIPS FOR ONLINE TEACHING

Although teachers in primary schools were thrown into online teaching unexpectedly due to COVID-19, there are many situations where this is the norm. Students who are unable to attend school because of illness or remote location are often catered for using online learning.

Research into effective online classrooms and pedagogy is still in its infancy. Although there are many websites that include online resources, simply telling students to access a website and undertake a particular activity is neither motivating nor effective. Young students need to feel connected to their teacher and their class, so finding ways to do this online are important. Some teachers use an online meeting in real time every day. This meeting is less about what you want the students to do and more about building relationships, sharing news and 'show and tell'. You could make this mathematics focused, for example by setting an age-appropriate task such as a mathematics scavenger hunt. You can find several examples and ideas by searching online. After an appropriate interval, one or two days, ask each student to share their most interesting find, or use online breakout rooms for small group sharing. If you are also using a chat function, especially with older students, try to have someone with you at class meetings or whole class teaching to monitor the chat. It is almost impossible for one person to manage the technology, provide clear instructions, and monitor chat in real time.

Being highly organised is very important. Ensure your students have access to a dedicated mathematics folder where you place work. Set up a folder for each student to post their work, and access this regularly.

It might be worth having set times that you check their folders and communicating this to the students. Provide feedback to the students every day by marking and commentating on their work. Make short videos about the key points. There is some anecdotal evidence that students prefer their own teacher explaining concepts rather than using another website such as Khan Academy.

Online teaching needs to be explicit. Students must understand what the learning intentions are for the unit or lesson. Knowing this helps to keep the students on track, and you can encourage them to revisit the learning intentions often. Set tasks that involve students, rather than drill and practice worksheets. Many of the suggestions in this book can be adapted for online learning.

Online teaching also needs to be in shorter and more focused segments. An activity that could take 30 minutes in a classroom is better broken down into two or three tasks, each with its own learning intention. For example, the discussion in Classroom Snapshot 8.2, about the conditions for collecting data about balancing on one leg, could be turned into a short survey where the students have to vote on the conditions. From the vote a data collection sheet could be created and the students then collect their data individually with the help of a parent or older sibling, or by having a pairs of students working together via a video link. The learning intentions for these two activities are first, to decide on what and how the data should be collected, and second, to collect the data consistently. Moving this lesson online has the same intended outcomes but the lesson is broken into shorter segments that students can undertake asynchronously.

CLASSROOM SNAPSHOT 19.4

Trudy Dawson has a Year 4 class that are learning online. She has set up a learning space using the school's preferred platform with a weekly folder and a series of subfolders for different subjects. In the mathematics folder she places the activities that she wants the students to engage with during that week. She also has an 'Ask Miss Dawson' folder where students can ask any question they like about any subject. She monitors this at least twice a day and works hard to ensure that students do not wait too long for a response. Trudy would like to meet with her students every morning, but the school has found that the wifi cannot cope with every class being online at the same time. Instead, they have organised a timetable so that classes know when their online timeslot is scheduled. This works well for Trudy's class. She always team teaches this part of the day with the Year 3/4 teacher who monitors the class, including any chat or 'hands up' emojis, while Trudy is engaging with the students. Trudy returns the favour during the Year 3/4 online session.

The class is studying a measurement unit, with the aim of developing understanding of different types of units and using scaled instruments. The previous week she asked students and their carers to collect as many different measuring tools as they can from around the house. She expects to see rulers and measuring tapes, weighing scales, cup and spoon measures, measuring jugs and so on. Today's meeting is about students showing the tools that they have found and explaining how they work. After greeting the students, Trudy opens the meeting by setting up the learning intention saying, 'In our meeting today we want to learn about different measuring tools and how they work'. Then she asks students how many people found a tool for measuring length. The students use the 'hands up' function and the co-teacher indicates that 12 students have put their hands up. Trudy chooses one of these students to explain what they have found. The meeting progresses with other tools, and towards the end, Trudy shares her screen and shows the students where they can find a short video explaining the activity she has set, which involves making measurements with their tools and the learning intentions for that activity.

After the meeting, Trudy reviews the recording and the chat and realises that two students did not engage at all during the class. One had not been online and the other had been online but had not contributed at all. Trudy makes a note of these two students and later rings their carers to find out why they had not been part of the meeting. The parent of the student who was online but did not contribute told Trudy that her daughter was struggling with online learning and missing her friends. Trudy organises a face-to-face discussion with the student and suggests to her mother that she organise a group chat with her daughter's friends so they can undertake the activity together. The other student is sick, so Trudy makes a note to mention this at the next class meeting.

Online teaching is different but just as intense as face-to-face classroom teaching. Using collegial support during real-time meetings is very helpful. Such support could come from another teacher, as in Classroom Snapshot 19.4, or from an education support worker or teacher's aide. As with any teaching, there is no substitute for good preparation and organisation.

Conclusion

All graduate teachers have concerns as they move into the professional world. This chapter has addressed some of these. Issues such as mathematics anxiety and maintaining a portfolio will be met throughout your career; others, such as LANTITE, are located at a particular time. Quality mathematics teaching in the primary school deserves ongoing consideration and you will need to be proactive about identifying opportunities for professional learning. This ongoing professional learning opens other doors and shifts in career focus, such as becoming a numeracy specialist or numeracy coach. As you become more experienced, the issues that concern you will change but long-term engagement with mathematics education will support both your own development and that of your students. The first term with your own class is a steep learning curve. This quote is from a beginning teacher at the end of his first term.

> I started out feeling very confident – I could do this. Very rapidly I had complete cognitive overload. There was so much information and so many things going on that I felt quite overwhelmed. I had terrific support from my mentor teacher and principal. I had to accept some well-deserved criticism which is always difficult. I found that reflecting on what I was doing became essential. We had so much about reflective practice in our course and I had always kind of dismissed it, but I began to realise that it is really important. I am now feeling much better able to cope as we start Term 2 and am sure that this is where I really want to be.

GUIDED STUDENT TASKS

1. Go to the ACER website and read some of their research articles about professional learning communities.
2. Talk to teachers about collecting evidence against the AITSL standards. Ask what kinds of evidence they suggest you focus on.
3. Develop a rich task (see Chapter 10 for ideas) that will identify a wide range of students' knowledge and understanding of a specific aspect of mathematics. Choose a topic that you are less familiar with and discuss this with other teachers online or face to face.
4. Plan a lesson that you could teach online or choose a Classroom Snapshot from this book and adapt it for online learning.

FURTHER READING

Brown, C, McMahon, J & McDonald, S 2016, *Teaching maths – What does the evidence say actually works?*, Online: The Conversation Better Teachers Series, 16 September 2016.

Ingvarson, L 2017, *School improvement and a strong professional learning community*, ACER research development series, 6 January, Melbourne: Australian Council for Educational Research.

Organisation for Economic Co-operation and Development (OECD) 2020, *Education responses to COVID-19: Embracing digital learning and online collaboration*, <https://www.oecd.org/coronavirus/policy-responses/education-responses-to-covid-19-embracing-digital-learning-and-online-collaboration-d75eb0e8/>.

Sullivan, P 2011, *Teaching mathematics using research-informed strategies*, Melbourne: Australian Council for Educational Research.

Terada, Y 2020, '7 high-impact, evidence based tips for online teaching', *Edutopia*, 9 October, <https://www.edutopia.org/article/7-high-impact-evidence-based-tips-online-teaching/>.

Wilson, R, Piccoli, A, Hargreaves, A, Ng, PT & Sahlberg, P 2021, *Putting students first: Moving on from NAPLAN to a new educational assessment system*, The Gonski Institute Policy Paper #2–2021, Sydney: UNSW Gonski Institute.

Wyn, J, Turnbull, M & Grimshaw, L 2014, *The experience of education: The impacts of high stakes testing on school students and their families*, Sydney: Whitlam Institute.

Websites for exploration

REFERENCES

Alexander, L & James, HT 1987, *The nation's report card*, Cambridge, MA: National Academy of Education.

Allen, E 2011, 'Scandal of the primary pupils who can get full marks in maths without even knowing their times tables', *Mail Online*, 7 September, <http://www.dailymail.co.uk/news/article-2034442/Pupils-passing-maths-exams-good-marks-dont-know-times-tables.html>.

Allmond, S, Wells, J & Makar, K 2010, *Thinking through mathematics: Engaging students with inquiry-based learning: Book 3*, Carlton South, Australia: Curriculum Press.

Askew, M 2008, 'Mathematical discipline knowledge requirements for prospective primary teachers, and the structure and teaching approaches of programs designed to develop that knowledge', in P Sullivan & T Wood (eds), *Knowledge and beliefs in mathematics teaching and teaching development* (The international handbook of mathematics teacher education), vol. 1, Rotterdam: Sense, pp. 13–36.

Asplin, P, Frid, S & Sparrow, L 2006, 'Game playing to develop mental computation: A case study', in P Grootenboer, R Zevenbergen & M Chinnappan (eds), *Identities, cultures, and learning spaces*, Proceedings of the 29th annual conference of the Mathematics Education Research Group of Australasia, Canberra, Adelaide: MERGA.

Assessment Reform Group 2002, *Assessment for Learning: 10 Principles – Research-based principles to guide classroom practices*, Bristol: Assessment Reform Group, <http://methodenpool.uni-koeln.de/benotung/assessment_basis.pdf>.

Assessment Resource Banks 2011, <http://arb.nzcer.org.nz>.

Attard, C 2015, *Ability grouping and mathematics: Who benefits*, Engaging maths, <https://engagingmaths.com/2015/08/16/ability-grouping-and-mathematics-who-benefits/>.

Atweh, B, Miller, D & Thornton, S 2012, 'The Australian Curriculum: Mathematics – world class for déjà vu' in B Atweh, M Goos, R Jorgensen & D Siemon (eds), *Engaging the Australian National Curriculum: Mathematics – Perspectives from the field*, University of Queensland: MERGA, pp. 1–18.

Australian Association of Mathematics Teachers (AAMT) 2008, *Position paper on the practice of assessing mathematics learning*, <http://www.aamt.edu.au/content/download/9892/126724/.../aamt-assess-bw.pdf>.

———2013, *Make it count: Blueprint for supporting best teaching of mathematics for Indigenous learners*, <http://www.aamt.edu.au/Media/Files/Make-It-Count-Blueprint>.

Australian Association of Mathematics Teachers & Early Childhood Australia (AAMT & ECA) 2006, Position paper on early childhood mathematics, Adelaide, SA & Watson, ACT: Authors.

Australian Children's Education and Care Quality Authority 2018, *National Quality Standard*, <https://www.acecqa.gov.au/nqf/national-quality-standard>.

Australian Council of Deans of Science 2006, The preparation of mathematics teachers in Australia: Meeting the demands for suitably qualified mathematics teachers in secondary schools, report prepared by K Harris & F Jensz, Melbourne: Centre for the Study of Higher Education, University of Melbourne.

Australian Council for Educational Research (ACER) n.d., *Literacy and Numeracy Test for Initial Teacher Education Students Assessment Framework*, <https://teacheredtest.acer.edu.au/files/Literacy-and-Numeracy-Test-for-Initial-Teacher-Education-Students-Assessment-Framework.pdf>.

Australian Curriculum Assessment and Reporting Authority (ACARA) 2016a, *ACARA Stem Connections Project Report*, <https://www.australiancurriculum.edu.au/media/3220/stem-connections-report.pdf>.

———2016b, *ACARA Curriculum*, <https://www.acara.edu.au/curriculum>.

———2017, *NAPLAN 2017 student reports: Student report information for parents brochure*, <https://www.nap.edu.au/docs/default-source/default-document-library/naplan-2017-student-report-information-for-parents-brochure5e3404344b146909a44fff0000c50d63.pdf?sfvrsn=2>.

———2018, *ACARA Curriculum*, <https://www.acara.edu.au/curriculum>.

———2020, *National Numeracy Learning Progression: Version 3.0*, <https://www.ofai.edu.au/media/iiwbecoj/national-numeracy-progression-v3.pdf>.

———2022, *Australian Curriculum version 9.0*, <https://v9.australiancurriculum.edu.au/>.

Australian Education Council 2015, *National STEM school education strategy*, <www.educationcouncil.edu.au>.

Australian Institute of Family Studies (AIFS) 2011, 'Families in regional, rural and remote Australia', Fact sheet, <http://www.aifs.gov.au/institute/pubs/factssheets/2011/fs201103.html>.

Australian Institute for Teaching and School Leadership Ltd (AITSL) 2017, *Australian Professional Standards for Teachers*, <https://www.aitsl.edu.au/docs/default-source/general/australian-professional-standards-forteachers-20171006.pdf?sfvrsn=399ae83c_12>.

Australian Public Service Commission (APSC) 2021, 'Choosing numerals or words', *Australian Government Style Manual*, <https://www.stylemanual.gov.au/grammar-punctuation-and-conventions/numbers-and-measurements/choosing-numerals-or-words>.

Autism Spectrum Australia (Aspect) 2018, 'Autism prevalence rate up by an estimated 40% to 1 in 70 people', <https://www.autismspectrum.org.au/news/autism-prevalence-rate-up-by-a-estimated-40-to-1-in-70-people-11-07-2018>.

Back, J 2012, *Difficulties with division*, NRICH, <https://nrich.maths.org/5450>.

Ball, DL & Bass, H 2009, 'With an eye on the mathematical horizon: Knowing mathematics for teaching to learners' mathematical futures', Paper presented at the 2009 Curtis Center Mathematics and Teaching Conference, Oldenburg, Germany, <http://www.mathematik.tu-dortmund.de/ieem/cms/media/BzMU/BzMU2009/Beitraege/Hauptvortraege/BALL_Deborah_BASS_Hyman_2009_Horizon.pdf>.

Ball S & Drehsen B 2010, *Flip-o-saurus*, New York: Abbeville Press Inc. US.

Banks, S 2011, 'A historical analysis of attitudes toward the use of calculators in junior high and high school math classrooms in the United States since 1975', MA thesis, Cedarville, OH: University of Cedarville, <http://digitalcommons.cedarville.edu/cgi/viewcontent.cgi?article=1030&context=education_theses>.

Benton, L, Hoyles, C, Kalas, I & Noss, R 2017, 'Bridging primary programming and mathematics: Some findings of design research in England', *Digital Experiences in Mathematics Education*, vol. 3, pp. 115–38.

Benton, L, Saunders, P, Kalas, I, Hoyles, C & Noss, R 2018, 'Designing for learning mathematics through programming: A case study of pupils engaging with place value', *International Journal of Child-Computer Interaction*, vol. 16, pp. 68–76.

Beswick, K 2007–2008, 'Influencing teachers' beliefs about teaching mathematics for numeracy to students with mathematics learning difficulties', *Mathematics Teacher Education and Development*, no. 9, pp. 3–20.

Beswick, K, Callingham, R & Muir, T 2012, 'Teaching mathematics in a project-based learning context: Initial teacher knowledge and perceived needs' in J Dindyal, LP Cheng & SF Ng (eds), *Mathematics education: Expanding horizons*, Proceedings of the 35th annual conference of the Mathematics Education Research Group of Australasia, eBook, Singapore: MERGA, Inc., pp. 114–21.

Beswick, K & Jones, T 2011, 'Taking professional learning to isolated schools: Perceptions of providers and principals, and lessons for effective professional learning', *Mathematics Education Research Journal*, vol. 23, no. 2, pp. 83–105.

Biggs, JB & Collis, KF 1982, *Evaluating the quality of learning: The SOLO taxonomy*, New York: Academic Press.

Bills, T & Hunter, R 2015, 'The role of cultural capital in creating equity for Pāsifika learners in mathematics', in M Marshman, V Geiger & A Bennison (eds), *Mathematics education in the margins*, Proceedings of the 38th annual conference of the Mathematics Education Research Group of Australasia, Mooloolaba, Qld: MERGA, pp. 109–16.

Björklund, C, van den Heuvel-Panhuizen, M & Kullberg, A 2020, 'Research on early childhood mathematics teaching and learning', *ZDM Mathematics Education*, vol 52, pp. 607–19.

Blackly, S & Howell, J 2015, 'A STEM narrative: 15 years in the making', *Australian Journal of Teacher Education*, vol. 40, no. 7, pp. 102–12.

Blank, M 2002, 'Classroom discourse: A key to literacy', in K Butler & E Silliman (eds), *Speaking, reading and writing in children with learning disabilities: New paradigms in research and practice*, Mahwah, NJ: Lawrence Erlbaum, pp. 151–73.

Blanton, ML & Kaput, JJ 2004, 'Elementary grades students' capacity for functional thinking', in MJ Hines & AB Fuglestad (eds), *Proceedings of the 28th annual conference of the International Group for the Psychology of Mathematics Education*, vol. 2, Bergen, Norway: PME, pp. 135–42.

Boaler, J 2008, 'Promoting "relational equity" and high mathematics achievement through an innovative mixed ability approach', *British Educational Research Journal*, vol. 34, no. 2, pp. 167–94.

Boaler, J & Chen, L 2016, 'Why kids should use their fingers in math class', <https://www.theatlantic.com/education/archive/2016/04/why-kids-should-use-their-fingers-in-math-class/478053/>.

Boaler, J, Wiliam, D & Brown, M 2000, 'Students' experiences of ability grouping – disaffection, polarization and the construction of failure', *British Educational Research Journal*, vol. 26, no. 5, pp. 631–48.

Booker, G, Bond, D, Sparrow, L & Swan, P 2010, *Teaching primary mathematics*, 4th edn, Sydney: Pearson.

Boud, D 1985, *Problem-based learning in education for the professions*, Pennsylvania State University: Higher Education Research and Development Society of Australasia.

Braden, JP 1994, *Deafness, deprivation and IQ*, New York: Plenum Press.

Brady, J, Clarke, B & Gervasoni, A 2008, 'Children with Down syndrome learning mathematics: Can they do it? Yes they can!', *Australian Primary Mathematics Classroom*, vol. 13, no. 4, pp. 10–15.

Bragg, L 2006, 'Students' impressions of the value of games for the learning of mathematics', *Proceedings of the 30th conference of the international group for the psychology of mathematics education*, International Group for the Psychology of Mathematics Education, Cape Town, South Africa, pp. 217–24.

Bruce, T 1991, *Time to play in early childhood education*, London: Hodder & Stoughton.

Brun, D 2018, 7 tips for teaching maths to deaf learners, June 19, <https://mathsnoproblem.com/blog/learner-focus/tips-for-teaching-maths-to-deaf-learners/>.

Bruner, JS 1961, 'The act of discovery', *Harvard Educational Review*, vol. 31, no. 1, pp. 21–32.

Bryant, P & Nunes, T 2012, *Children's understanding of probability*, London: Nuffield Foundation, <http://www.nuffieldfoundation.org/news/childrens-understanding-probability>.

Buckley, S 2013, *Deconstructing maths anxiety: Helping students to develop a positive attitude towards learning maths* (ACER Occasional Essays), Melbourne: ACER, <https://research.acer.edu.au/learning_processes/16>.

Calder, N 2022, 'Mathematics and coding: How did coding facilitate thinking?' in N Fitzallen, C Murphy, V Hatisaru & N Maher (eds), *Mathematical confluences and journeys* (Proceedings of the 44th Annual Conference of the Mathematics Education Research Group of Australasia, July 3–7), Launceston: MERGA, pp. 98–105.

Callingham, R 1993, 'Cemetery maths', *Australian Mathematics Teacher*, vol. 49, no. 3, pp. 38–9.

——2008, 'Dialogue and feedback: Assessment in the primary mathematics classroom', *Australian Primary Mathematics Classroom*, vol. 13, no. 3, pp. 18–21.

Callingham, R, Beswick, K, Carmichael, C, Geiger, V, Goos, M, Hurrell, D, Hurst, C & Muir, T 2017, *Nothing left to chance: Characteristics of schools successful in mathematics* (Report of the Building an Evidence Base for Best Practice in Mathematics Education Project), Hobart: University of Tasmania.

Carle, E 1994, *The very hungry caterpillar*, New York, US: Puffin.

Carpenter, TP, Fennema, E, Franke, ML, Levi, L & Empson, S 1999, *Children's mathematics: Cognitive guided instruction*, Portsmouth, NH: Heinemann.

Castledine, A & Chalmers, C 2011, 'LEGO Robotics: An authentic problem solving tool?', *Design and Technology Education: An International Journal*, vol. 16, no. 3, pp. 19–27.

Chua, B & Wu, Y 2005, 'Designing technology-based mathematics lessons: A pedagogical framework', *Journal of Computers in Mathematics and Science Teaching*, vol. 24, no. 4, pp. 387–402.

Clarke, D & Clarke, B 2008, 'Is time up for ability grouping?', *Curriculum and Leadership Journal*, vol. 6, no. 5, (electronic resource).

Clement, J, Lochhead, J & Monk, G 1981, 'Translation difficulties in learning mathematics', *American Mathematical Monthly*, vol. 88, pp. 286–90.

Clements, DH 1999, 'Subitising: What is it? Why teach it?', *Teaching Children Mathematics*, vol. 5, no. 7, pp. 400–5.

Clements, DH & Sarama, J 2021, *Learning and teaching early math: The learning trajectories approach*, 3rd edn, New York: Routledge.

Collis, KF & Romberg, TA 1991, 'Assessment of mathematical performance: An analysis of open-ended test items', in MC Wittrock & EL Baker (eds), *Testing and cognition*, Englewood Cliffs, NJ: Prentice Hall, pp. 82–130.

Commonwealth of Australia 2009, Shape of the Australian Curriculum: Mathematics, Canberra: Commonwealth Government, <http://www.acara.edu.au/verve/_resources/Australian_Curriculum_-_Maths.pdf>.

Cornish, L 2006, 'What is multi-grade teaching?', in L Cornish (ed.), *Reading EFA through multi-grade teaching: Issues, contexts and practices*, Armidale, NSW: Kardoorair Press, pp. 9–26.

Cotton, T 2010, *Understanding and teaching primary mathematics*, London: Pearson.

Cowan, R 2011, *The development and importance of proficiency in basic calculation*, London: Institute of Education, <http://www.ioe.ac.uk/Study_Departments/PHD_dev_basic_calculation.pdf>.

Crews, D 1996, *Ten black dots*, New York: Harper Collins.

Curriculum Corporation 2006, *Statements of Learning for Mathematics*, <http://www.nap.edu.au/naplan/statements-of-learning.html>.

Dale, P 2007, *Ten in the bed*, London: Candlewick Press.

———2010, *Ten out of bed*, London: Walker Books.

Daniel, J 2020, 'Education and the COVID-19 pandemic', *PROSPECTS*, vol. 49, pp. 91–6.

Darragh, L 2022, 'Teacher agency and professionalism in the context of online mathematics instructional platforms' in N Fitzallen, C Murphy, V Hatisaru & N Maher (eds), *Mathematical confluences and journeys* (Proceedings of the 44th Annual Conference of the Mathematics Education Research Group of Australasia, July 3–7), Launceston: MERGA, pp. 170–7.

Darragh, L & Franke, N 2022, 'Lessons from lockdown: Parent perspectives on home-learning mathematics during COVID-19 lockdown', *International Journal of Science and Mathematics Education*, vol 20, pp. 1521–42.

Day, L, Stephens, M & Horne, M 2017, 'Developing learning progressions to support mathematical reasoning in the middle years – algebraic reasoning' (Symposium: Learning progressions to support mathematical reasoning in the middle years – introducing the Reframing Mathematical Futures II Project), in A Downton, S Livy & J. Hall (eds) *40 years on: We are still learning!*, Proceedings of the 40th annual conference of the Mathematics Education Research Group of Australasia, Melbourne: MERGA, pp. 663–6.

Department of Education and the Arts, Tasmania 1994, *K–8 Guidelines: Measurement*, Hobart: Department of Education and the Arts, Tasmania.

Department of Education, Employment and Workplace Relations (DEEWR) 2009, *Belonging, being and becoming: The Early Years Learning Framework for Australia*, <http://www.deewr.gov.au/Earlychildhood/Policy_Agenda/Quality/Documents/Final%20EYLF%20Framework%20Report%20-%20WEB.pdf>.

Department of Education, Skills and Employment Education Council 2015, *National STEM School Education Strategy (2016–2026)*, <https://www.dese.gov.au/australian-curriculum/support-science-technology-engineering-and-mathematics-stem/national-stem-school-education-strategy-2016-2026>.

Department of Education and Training, NSW 2003, *Fractions, pikelets and lamingtons*, Sydney: Department of Education and Training Professional Support and Curriculum Directorate.

Department of Education and Training, WA 2004, *First steps in mathematics: Number*, Melbourne: Rigby Harcourt Education.

Desforges, C 2003, The impact of parental involvement, parental support and family education on pupil achievement and adjustment: A literature review. Research report No. 433. Department of Education and Skills.

DeSimone, JR & Parmar, RS 2006, 'Middle school mathematics teachers' beliefs about inclusion of students with learning disabilities', *Learning Disabilities Research and Practice*, vol. 21, no. 2, pp. 98–110.

Donlan, C, Cowan, R, Newton, EJ & Lloyd, D 2007, 'The role of language in mathematical development: Evidence from children with specific language impairments', *Cognition*, no. 103, pp. 23–33.

DuFour, R 2004, 'What is a "professional learning community"?', *Educational Leadership*, vol. 61, no. 8, pp. 6–11.

Eather, J 2018, *A maths dictionary for kids 2018: Add, addition*, <http://www.amathsdictionaryforkids.com/dictionary.html>.

English, LD 1991, 'Young children's combinatoric strategies', *Educational Studies in Mathematics*, vol. 22, no. 5, pp. 451–74.

——2016, 'Targeting all of STEM in the primary school: Engineering design as a foundational process', in *Proceedings of ACER Research Conference 2016, Improving STEM Learning: What will it take?*, pp. 84–8.

Ewing, B 2011, 'Direct instruction in mathematics: issues for schools with high indigenous enrolments: A literature review', *Australian Journal of Teacher Education*, vol. 36, no. 5, <http://dx.doi.org/10.14221/ajte.2011v36n5.5>.

Faragher, R 2017, 'Hypothesis of developmental dyscalculia and down syndrome: Implications for mathematics education', in A Downton, S Livy & J Hall (eds), *40 years on: We are still learning!*, Proceedings of the 40th Annual Conference of the Mathematics Education Research Group of Australasia, Melbourne: MERGA, pp. 245–52.

Fernandez, H & Hynes, JW 2016, 'The efficacy of pullout programs in elementary schools: Making it work', *The Journal of Multidisciplinary Graduate Research*, vol. 2, no. 3, pp. 32–47.

Fernández, JM & Velazquez, A 2011, 'A contexts for column addition and subtraction: Reflect and discuss', *Teaching Children Mathematics*, vol. 17, no. 9, pp. 540–8.

Fielding-Wells, J, Dole, S & Makar, K 2014, 'Inquiry pedagogy to promote emerging proportional reasoning in primary students', *Mathematics Education Research Journal*, vol. 26, pp. 47–77.

Fischbein, E, Nello, MS & Merino, MS 1991, 'Factors affecting probabilistic judgements in children and adolescents', *Educational Studies in Mathematics*, no. 22, pp. 523–49.

Fisher, J 2010, *Moving on to key stage 1: Improving transition from the early years foundation stage*, Maidenhead: Open University Press.

Fisher, KM 1988, 'The students-and-professors problem revisited', *Journal for Research in Mathematics Education*, vol. 19, no. 3, pp. 260–2.

Fitzallen, N 2015, 'STEM education: what does mathematics have to offer?', in M Marshman (ed.), *Mathematics Education in the Margins*, Proceedings of the 38th annual conference of the Mathematics Education Research Group of Australasia, Sunshine Coast, June 28–July 2, Sydney: MERGA, pp. 237–44.

Fitzallen, N, Watson, J, Wright, S & Duncan, B 2018, 'Data representations in a STEM context: The performance of catapults', ICOTS10, <https://iase-web.org/icots/10/proceedings/pdfs/ICOTS10_4B2.pdf?1531364264>.

Flores, MM 2010, Using the concrete-representational-abstract sequence to teach subtraction with regrouping to students at risk for failure. *Remedial and Special Education*, vol. 31, no. 3, pp. 195–207, <https://doi.org/10.1177/0741932508327467>

Gelman, R & Gallistel, C 1978, *The child's understanding of number*, Cambridge, MA: Harvard University Press.

Gigerenzer, G 2002, *Reckoning with risk*, Harmondsworth: Penguin.

Goss, P, Hunter, J, Romanes, D & Parsonage, H 2015, *Targeted teaching: How better use of data can improve student learning*, Melbourne, Vic: Grattan Institute.

Gould, K 2019, Math challenges? A school psychologist could help. *The Conversation*, <https://theconversation.com/math-challenges-a-school-psychologist-could-help-111488#>

Gould, P, Outhred, L & Mitchelmore, M (2006), 'One-third is three-quarters of one-half', in P Grootenboer, R Zevenbergen & M Chinnappan (eds), *Identities, cultures, and learning spaces*, Proceedings of the 29th annual conference of the Mathematics Education Research Group of Australasia, Canberra, Adelaide: MERGA, pp. 262–70.

Grandgenett, N, Harris, J & Hofer, MJ 2011, 'An activity-based approach to technology integration in the mathematics classroom', *NCSM Journal of Mathematics Education Leadership*, vol. 13, no. 2, pp. 19–28.

Green, A 2022, *Examining the work and training of teacher aides*, Institute of Teacher Aide Courses, <https://www.itac.edu.au/blog/teacher-aides-literature-review>.

Gregory, S 1998, 'Mathematics and deaf children', in S Gregory, P Knight, W McCracken, S Powers & L Watson (eds), *Issues in deaf education*, London: David Fulton, pp. 121–7.

Guldberg, K, Porayska-Pomsta, K, Good, J & Keay-Bright, W 2010, 'ECHOES II: The creation of a technology enhanced learning environment for typically developing children and children on the autism spectrum', *Journal of Assistive Technologies*, vol. 4, no. 1, pp. 49–53.

Hay, I & Fielding-Barnsley, R 2012, 'Social learning, language and literacy', *Australasian Journal of Early Childhood*, vol. 37, no. 1, pp. 24–9.

Haylock, D & Cockburn, A 2008, *Understanding mathematics for young children*, London: Sage.

Hemelt, SW, Ladd, HF & Clifton, CR 2021, 'Do teacher assistants improve student outcomes? Evidence from school funding cutbacks in North Carolina', *Educational Evaluation and Policy Analysis*, vol. 43, no. 2, pp 280–304.

Higgins, J 1990, 'Calculators and common sense', *The Arithmetic Teacher*, vol. 37, no. 7, pp. 4–5.

Hodges, C, Moore, S, Lockee, B, Trust, T & Bond, A 2020, 'The difference between emergency remote teaching and online learning', *Educause Review*, 27 March, <https://er.educause.edu/articles/2020/3/thedifference-between-emergency-remote-teaching-and-online-learning>.

Hodgson, T, Simonsen, L, Lubek, J & Anderson, L 2003, 'Measuring Montana: An episode in estimation', in DH Clements & G Bright (eds), *Learning and teaching measurement*, Reston, VA: National Council of Teachers of Mathematics, pp. 221–30.

Hong, LT 1993, *Two of everything*, Morton Grove, IL: Albert Whitman & Company.

Houssart, J 2013, '"Give me a lesson and I'll deliver it": Teaching assistants experiences of leading primary mathematics lessons in England', *Cambridge Journal of Education*, vol. 43 no. 1, pp. 1–16.

Hoyle, P 2016, 'Must try harder: An evaluation of the UK government's policy directions 1 in STEM education', *Improving STEM Learning: What will it take?*, Proceedings of ACER Research Conference 2016, pp. 1–11.

Hudson, P, English, L, Dawes, L, King, D & Baker, S 2015, 'Exploring links between pedagogical knowledge practices and student outcomes in STEM education for primary schools', *Australian Journal of Teacher Education (Online)*, vol. 40, no. 6, pp. 134–51.

Hunter, R, Hunter, J, Anthony, G & McChesney, K 2018, 'Developing mathematical inquiry communities: Enacting culturally responsive, culturally sustaining, ambitious mathematics teaching', *Set: Research Information for Teachers*, no. 2, <https://doi.org/10.18296/set.0106>.

Hurst, C & Hurrell, D 2014, 'Developing the big ideas of number', *International Journal of Educational Studies in Mathematics*, vol. 1, no. 2, pp. 1–18.

—— 2021, 'Specialised content knowledge: The convention for naming arrays and describing equal groups problems', *International Online Journal of Primary Education*, vol. 10, no. 1, pp. 19–31.

Ingvarson, L 2018, *Developing a professional learning community* (ACER research development series, 2 February 2018), Melbourne: Australian Council for Educational Research.

Jenkins, K, Reitano, P & Taylor, N 2011, 'Teachers in the bush: Supports, challenges and professional learning', *Education in Rural Australia*, vol. 21, no. 2, pp. 71–85.

Jorgensen, R 2010, 'Issues of social equity in access and success in mathematics learning for Indigenous students', in C Glascodine & KA Hoad (eds), *Teaching mathematics? Make it count. What research tells us about effective mathematics teaching and learning* (conference proceedings), Melbourne: ACER, pp. 27–30.

Kalogeropoulos, P, Russo, J, Russo, T & Sullivan, P 2020, 'Effectively utilising teaching assistants to support mathematics learning: Some insights from the Getting Ready in Numeracy (G.R.I.N.) program', *International Electronic Journal of Mathematics Education*, vol. 15, no. 3, <https://doi.org/10.29333/iejme/8314>.

Kawas, T. n.d., 'Place value activities', <http://mathwire.com/numbersense/placevalue.html>.

Kearns, K 2020, *Supporting education*, 3rd edn, Southbank, Vic: Cengage.

Kee, D 2011, 'Educational Robotics—Primary and Secondary Education [Industrial Activities]', *IEEE Robotics & Automation Magazine*, vol. 18, no. 4.

Kihoza, P, Zlotnikova, I, Bada, J & Kalegele, K 2016, 'Classroom ICT integration in Tanzania: Opportunities and challenges from the perspectives of TPACK and SAMR models', *International Journal of Education and Development using Information and Communication Technology*, vol. 12, no. 1, pp. 107–28.

Klingenberg, OG, Holkesvik, AH & Augestad, LB 2020, 'Digital learning in mathematics doe students with severe visual impairment: A systematic review', *British Journal of Visual Impairment*, vol. 38, no. 1, pp. 38–57, <https://doi.org/10.1177/0264619619876975>

Koehler, MJ & Mishra, P 2008, TPACK Framework diagram, <http://www.tpack.org>.

Konold, C & Miller, CD 2005, *TinkerPlotsTM: Dynamic data exploration* [computer software], Emeryville, CA: Key Curriculum Press.

Kucian, K & von Aster, M 2015, 'Developmental dyscalculia', *European Journal of Pediatrics*, vol. 174, pp. 1–13, <https://doi.org/10.1007/s00431-014-2455-7>

Lave, J & Wenger, E 1991, *Situated learning: Legitimate peripheral participation*, Cambridge: Cambridge University Press.

Leach, C 2010, 'The use of smartboards and bespoke software to develop and deliver an inclusive, individual and interactive learning curriculum for students with ASD', *Journal of Assistive Technologies*, vol. 4, no. 1, pp. 54–7.

Leeper, M & Muir, T 2019, *Developing early maths through story: Step-by-step guide for using storytelling as a springboard for maths activities*, Strawberry Hills, NSW: Teaching Solutions.

Li, Y, Wang, K, Xiao, Y & Froyd, JE 2020, 'Research and trends in STEM education: A systematic review of journal publications', *International Journal of STEM Education*, vol 7, <https://doi.org/10.1186/s40594-020-00207-6>.

Liljedahl, P 2021, *Building thinking classrooms in mathematics, Grades K–12*, 2nd edn, Thousand Oaks, CA: Corwin.

Livy, S, Muir, T & Downton, A 2017, 'Connecting pre-service teachers with contemporary mathematics practices: Selecting and sequencing students' work samples', *APMC*, vol. 22, no. 4, pp. 17–21.

Livy, S, Muir, T & Maher, N 2012, 'How do they measure up? Primary pre-service teachers' mathematical knowledge of area and perimeter', *Mathematics Teacher Education and Development*, vol. 14, no. 2, pp. 91–112.

Livy, S, Muir, T & Sullivan, P 2018, 'Challenging tasks lead to productive struggle!', *APMC*, vol. 23, no. 1, pp. 19–24.

Lowrie, T & Logan, T 2015, 'The role of test-mode effect: Implications for assessment practices and item design', in CV Yu (ed), *In pursuit of quality mathematics education for all*, Proceedings of the 7th ICMI-East Asia Regional Conference on Mathematics Education, vol. 12, pp. 649–56, Philippines: Philippine Council of Mathematics Teachers Educators (MATHTED, Inc.)

Lucangeli, D & Cabrele, S 2006, 'Mathematical difficulties and ADHD', *Exceptionality*, vol. 14, no. 1, pp. 53–62.

Ma, L 1999, *Knowing and teaching elementary mathematics: Teachers' understanding of fundamental mathematics in China and the United States*, Mahwah, NJ: Lawrence Erlbaum.

MacDonald, A 2018, *Mathematics in early childhood education*, South Melbourne, Vic: Oxford University Press.

MacGregor, M & Stacey, K 1999, 'A flying start to algebra', *Teaching Children Mathematics*, vol. 6, no. 2, pp. 78–85.

Malola, M, Symons, D & Stephens, M 2020, 'Supporting students' transition from additive to multiplicative thinking: A complex pedagogical challenge', *Australian Primary Mathematics Classroom*, vol. 25, no. 2, pp. 31–6.

Marston, J 2010, 'Developing a framework for the selection of picture books to promote early mathematical development', in L Sparrow, B Kissane & C Hurst (eds), *Shaping the future of mathematics education*, Proceedings of the 33rd annual conference of the Mathematics Education Research Group of Australasia, Freemantle, WA: MERGA.

Masdeu Navarro, F 2015, 'Learning support staff: A literature review', *OECD Education Working Papers, No. 125*, Paris: OECD Publishing, <https://doi.org/10.1787/5jrnzm39w45l-en>.

Mazzocco, MM & Myers, GF 2003, 'Complexities in identifying and defining mathematics learning disability in the primary school-age years', *Annals of Dyslexia*, vol. 53, no. 1, pp. 218–53.

McAnelly, N 2021, 'How to select effective digital math tools', Edutopia, <https://www.edutopia.org/article/how-select-effective-digital-math-tools>.

McIntosh, A 2004, 'Developing computation', *Australian Primary Mathematics Classroom*, vol. 9, no. 4, pp. 47–9.

McIntosh, A & Dole, S 2005, *Developing computation*, Hobart: Department of Education, Tasmania.

Moll, C, Amanti, C, Neff, D & Gonzalez, N 1992, 'Funds of knowledge for teaching: Using a qualitative approach to connect homes and classrooms', *Theory Into Practice*, vol. 31, no. 2, pp. 132–41.

Moore, I 1991, *Six Dinner Sid*, New York, US: Simon & Shuster.

Moore, TJ & Smith, KA 2014, 'Advancing the state of the art of STEM integration', *Journal of STEM Education*, vol. 15, no. 1, pp. 5–10.

Morris, C & Matthews, C 2011, 'Numeracy, mathematics and Indigenous learners: Not the same old thing', in *Proceedings of the ACER Research Conference*, 2011, Melbourne: ACER, <http://www.acer.edu.au/documents/RC2011_-_Numeracy_mathematics_and_Indigenous_learners-_Not_the_same_old_thing.pdf>.

Mosvold, R & Fauskanger, J 2013, 'Teachers' beliefs about mathematical knowledge for teaching definitions', *International Electronic Journal of Mathematics Education*, vol. 8, no. 2–3, pp. 43–61.

Moyer, MB & Moyer, JC 1985, 'Ensuring that practice makes perfect: Implications for children with learning disabilities', *The Arithmetic Teacher*, vol. 33, no. 1, pp. 40–2.

Mozelle, S 1989, *Zack's alligator*, New York: HarperCollins.

Muir, T 2005, 'When near enough is good enough: Eight principles for enhancing the value of measurement estimation for students', *Australian Primary Mathematics Classroom*, vol. 10, no. 2, pp. 9–14.

——— 2012a, 'What is a reasonable answer? Ways for students to investigate and develop their number sense', *Australian Primary Mathematics Classroom*, vol. 17, no. 1, pp. 21–8.

——— 2012b, 'Numeracy at home: Involving parents in mathematics education', *International Journal for Mathematics Teaching and Learning*, <https://www.cimt.org.uk/journal/muir.pdf>.

——— 2018, *Heads or tails*, Blairgowrie, Vic: Teaching Solutions.

Muir, T, Bragg, L & Livy, S 2015, 'Two of everything: Developing functional thinking in the primary grades through children's literature', *Australian Primary Mathematics Classroom*, vol. 20, no. 1, pp. 35–40.

Muir, T, Callingham, R & Beswick, K 2016, 'Using the IWB in an early years mathematics classroom: An application of the TPACK framework', *Journal of Digital Learning in Teacher Education*, vol. 32, no. 2, pp. 63–72.

Muir, T, Livy, S, Bragg, L, Clark, J, Wells, J & Attard, C 2017, *Engaging with mathematics through picture books*, Albert Park, Vic: Teaching Solutions.

Mulligan, J 2017, 'In search of mathematical structure: Looking back, beneath and beyond – 40 years on', in A Downton, S Livy & J. Hall (eds) *40 years on: We are still learning!*, Proceedings of the 40th annual conference of the Mathematics Education Research Group of Australasia, Melbourne: MERGA.

Mulligan, JT & Mitchelmore, MC 1997, 'Young children's intuitive models of multiplication and division', *Journal for Research in Mathematics Education*, vol. 28, no. 3, pp. 309–30.

——— 2009, 'Awareness of pattern and structure in early mathematical development', *Mathematics Education Research Journal*, vol. 21, no. 2, pp. 33–49.

——— 2016, *Pattern and Structure Mathematics Awareness Program (PASMAP): Book one – Foundation and Year 1*. Australian Council for Educational Research.

Myller, R 1990, *How big is a foot?* New York: Random House.

New South Wales Board of Studies, Teaching & Educational Standards 2012, *Assessment for Learning Practices*, Sydney: NSW Government, <http://syllabus.bostes.nsw.edu.au/support-materials/assessment-for-as-and-of-learning>.

New South Wales Department of Education and Training 2003, *Teaching about angles: Stage 2*, Sydney: NSW Department of Education and Training, Professional Support and Curriculum Directorate.

——— 2004, *Teaching measurement: Stage 2 and 3*, Sydney: NSW Department of Education and Training, Curriculum K–12 Directorate.

——— 2008, *Developing efficient numeracy strategies: Stage 2*, Sydney: NSW Department of Education and Training, Curriculum K–12 Directorate.

New South Wales Education Standards Authority n.d., 'Assessment', <https://educationstandards.nsw.edu.au/wps/portal/nesa/k-10/understanding-the-curriculum/assessment>.

Newman, MA 1977, 'An analysis of sixth-grade pupils' errors on written mathematical tasks', *Victorian Institute for Educational Research Bulletin*, no. 39, pp. 31–43.

Nicol, C, Archibald, J & Baker, J 2010, *Investigating culturally responsive mathematics education*, Toronto: Canadian Council on Learning, <http://www.ccl-cca.ca/pdfs/FundedResearch/201009NicolArchibaldBakerFullReport.pdf>.

Northcote, M & Marshall, L 2016, 'What mathematics calculations do adults do in their everyday lives? Part 1 of a report on the Everyday Mathematics project', *Australian Primary Mathematics Classroom*, vol. 21, no. 2, pp. 8–17.

Nunes, T, Bryant, P, Evans, D, Gottardis, L & Terlekts, ME 2015, *Teaching mathematical reasoning – probability and problem solving in the classroom*, Oxford, UK: Oxford University and Nuffield Foundation.

NZ Maths 2010, *Geometry information*, <http://nzmaths.co.nz/geometry-information>.

Organisation for Economic Co-operation and Development (OECD) 2020, *Education responses to COVID-19: Embracing digital learning and online collaboration*, <https://www.oecd.org/coronavirus/policy-responses/education-responses-to-covid-19-embracing-digital-learning-and-online-collaboration-d75eb0e8/>.

Pegg, J & Baker, P 1999, 'An exploration of the interface between van Hiele's levels 1 and 2: Initial findings', *Proceedings of the 23rd International Group for the Psychology of Mathematics Education*, vol. 4, Haifa: Israel Institute of Technology, pp. 25–32.

Pegg, J & Davey, G 1998, 'A synthesis of two models: Interpreting student understanding in geometry', in R Lehrer & C Chazan (eds), *New directions for teaching and learning geometry*, Mahwah, NJ: Lawrence Erlbaum, pp. 109–35.

Pegg, J, Graham, L & Bellert, A 2005, 'The effect of improved automaticity of basic number skills on persistently low-achieving pupils', in HL Chick & JL Vincent (eds), *Proceedings of the 29th Conference of the International Group for the Psychology of Mathematics Education*, vol. 4, Melbourne: PME, pp. 49–56, <http://www.emis.de/proceedings/PME29/PME29RRPapers/PME29Vol4PeggEtAl.pdf>.

Perry, B, Dockett, S & Harley, E 2012, 'The Early Years Learning Framework for Australia and the Australian Curriculum: Mathematics: Linking educators' practice through pedagogical inquiry questions', in B Atweh, M Goos, R Jorgensen & D Siemon (eds), *Engaging the Australian Curriculum: Mathematics – perspectives from the field* (conference proceedings), Sydney: Mathematics Education Research Group of Australasia, pp. 153–74.

Perso, T 2009, 'Cracking the NAPLAN code: Numeracy and literacy demands', *APMC*, vol. 14, no. 3, pp. 14–18.

Pfannkuch, M, Regan, M, Wild, C & Horton, NJ 2010, 'Telling data stories: Essential dialogues for comparative reasoning', *Journal of Statistics Education*, vol. 18, no. 1, pp. 1–38, <http://www.amstat.org/publications/jse/v18n1/pfannkuch.pdf>.

Piaget, J 1936, *Origins of intelligence in the child*, London: Routledge & Kegan Paul.

Powell, D 2012, 'A review of inclusive education in New Zealand', *Electronic Journal for Inclusive Education*, vol. 2, no. 10, Article 4, <http://corescholar.libraries.wright.edu/cgi/viewcontent.cgi?article=1147&context=ejie>.

Przychodzin, AM, Marchand-Martella, NE, Martella, RC & Azim, D 2004, 'Direct instruction mathematics programs: An overview and research summary', *Journal of Direct Instruction*, vol. 4, no. 1, pp. 53–84.

Radford, J, Blatchford, P & Webster, R 2011, 'Opening up and closing down: How teachers and TAs manage turn-taking, topic and repair in mathematics lessons', *Learning and Instruction*, vol. 21, no. 5, pp. 625–35.

Rapantam C, Botturi, L, Goodyear, P, Guardia, L & Koole, M 2020, 'Online university teaching during and after the Covid-19 crisis: Refocusing teacher presence and learning activity', *Postdigital Science and Education*, vol. 2, no. 3, pp. 923–45.

Reaburn, R 2015, 'The practice of teacher aides in Tasmanian primary mathematics classrooms' in M Marshman, V Geiger & A Bennison (eds), *Mathematics education in the margins*, Proceedings of the 38th annual conference of the Mathematics Education Research Group of Australasia, Sunshine Coast: MERGA, pp. 516–23.

Resnick, M, Maloney, J, Monroy-Hernandez, RN, Eastmond, E, Brennan, K, Millner, A, Rosenbaum, E, Silver, J, Silverman, B & Kafai, Y 2009, 'Scratch: Programming for all', *Communications of the ACM*, vol. 52, no. 11, <https://doi.org/10.1145/1592761.1592779>

Robicheaux, R 1993, 'How can we design paper money for the visually impaired?' *The Arithmetic Teacher*, vol. 40, no. 8, pp. 479–81.

Rodda, E 1986, *Pigs might fly*, Sydney: Angus & Robertson.

Rowland, T 2013, 'The knowledge quartet: The genesis and application of a framework for analysing mathematics teaching and deepening teachers' mathematics knowledge', *Sisyphus – Journal of Education*, vol. 1, no. 3, pp. 15–43.

Russo, J, Russo, T & Bragg, LA 2018, 'Five principles of educationally rich mathematical games', *Australian Primary Mathematics Classroom*, vol. 23, no. 3, pp. 30–4.

Ruthven, K 1998, 'The use of mental, written and calculator strategies of numerical computation by upper primary pupils within a "calculator-aware" number curriculum', *British Educational Research Journal*, vol. 24, no. 1, pp. 21–42.

Ryan, J & Williams, J 2007, *Children's mathematics 4–15: Learning from errors and misconceptions*, Maidenhead: Open University Press.

Sarra, G & Ewing, B 2021, 'Culturally responsive pedagogies and perspectives in mathematics' in M Shay & R Oliver (eds), *Indigenous education in Australia: Learning and teaching for deadly futures*, Abingdon, Oxon: Routledge, pp. 148–61.

Sayre, A & Sayre, J 2003, *One is a snail, ten is a crab*, London: Walker Books.

Schiro, M 1997, *Integrating children's literature and mathematics in the classroom: Children as meaning makers, problem solvers, literacy critics*, New York: Teachers College Press.

Scratch 2022, 'Discuss Scratch', <https://scratch.mit.edu/discuss/>.

Serow, P 2007a, 'Incorporating dynamic geometry software within a teaching framework', in K Milton, H Reeves & T Spencer (eds), *Mathematics: Essential for learning, essential for life*, Proceedings of the 21st biennial conference of the Australian Association of Mathematics Teachers, Adelaide: Australian Association of Mathematics Teachers, pp. 382–97.

——2007b, 'Utilising the Rasch model to gain insight into students' understandings of class inclusion concepts in geometry', in J Watson & K Beswick (eds), *Mathematics: Essential research, essential practice*, Proceedings of the 30th annual conference of the Mathematics Education Research Group of Australasia, Adelaide: Mathematics Education Research Group of Australasia, pp. 651–60.

——2015 'Education for sustainability in primary mathematics education', in N Taylor, F Quinn & C Eames (eds), *Educating for sustainability in primary schools: Teaching for the future*, Rotterdam: Sense, pp. 177–94.

Serow, P & Callingham, R 2011, 'Levels of use of interactive board technology in the primary mathematics classroom', *Technology, Pedagogy and Education*, vol. 20, no. 2, pp. 161–73.

Serow, P, Callingham, R & Tout, D 2016, 'Assessment of mathematics learning: What are we doing?' in K Makar, S Dole, J Visnovska, M Goos, A Bennison & K Fry (eds), *Research in Mathematics Education in Australasia 2012–2015*, Singapore: Springer, pp. 235–54.

Serow, P & Inglis, M 2010, 'Templates in action', *Australian Mathematics Teacher*, vol. 66, no. 4, pp. 10–16.

Shulman, LS 1987, 'Knowledge and teaching: Foundations of the new reform', *Harvard Educational Review*, vol. 57, no. 1, pp. 1–22.

Shumway, J 2011, *Number sense routines*, Portland, ME: Stenhouse.

Siemon, D 2007, *Developing the 'big' ideas in number*, <https://www.edu.vic.gov.au/edulibrary/public/teachlearn/student/devbigideas.pdf>.

——2017, 'Targeting "big ideas" in mathematics', *Teacher Magazine*, <https://www.teachermagazine.com.au/articles/targeting-big-ideas-in-mathematics>.

Siemon, D, Beswick, K, Brady, K, Clark, J, Faragher, R & Warren, E 2015, *Teaching mathematics: Foundations to middle years*, 2nd edn, South Melbourne, Vic: Oxford University Press.

Siemon, D, Bleckly, J & Neal, D 2012, 'Working with the big ideas in number and the Australian Curriculum: Mathematics', in B Atweh, M Goos, R Jorgensen & D Siemon (eds), *Engaging the Australian National Curriculum: Mathematics – perspectives from the field*, Sydney: Mathematics Education Research Group of Australasia, pp. 19–45, <http://www.merga.net.au/node/223>.

Siemon, D & Callingham, R 2019, 'Researching mathematical reasoning: Building evidence-based resources to support targeted teaching in the middle years' in D Siemon, T Barkatsas & R Seah (eds), *Researching and using progressions (trajectories) in mathematics education*, Leiden, NL: Brill Sense, pp. 101–24.

Siemon, D, Callingham, R, Day, L, Horne, M, Seah, R, Stephens, M & Watson, J 2018, 'From research to practice: The case of mathematical reasoning', in J Hunter, P Perger & L Darragh (eds), *Making waves, opening spaces*, Proceedings of the 41st annual conference of the Mathematics Education Research Group of Australasia, Auckland: MERGA, pp. 40–9.

Simon, M 2000, 'Constructivism, mathematics teacher education, and research in mathematics teacher development', in LP Steffe & PW Thompson (eds), *Radical constructivism in action: Building on the pioneering work of Ernst von Glasersfeld*, London: Routledge Falmer, pp. 213–30.

Skinner, BF 1968, *The technology of teaching*, New York: Appleton-Century-Crofts.

Smith, C & Watson, J 2019, 'Does the rise of STEM education mean the demise of sustainability education?', *Australian Journal of Environmental Education*, vol. 35, pp. 1–11.

Smith, D 2006, *If the world were a village*, Crows Nest, NSW: Allen & Unwin.

Smith, MS & Stein, MK 2011, *Five practices for orchestrating productive mathematics discussion*, Reston, VA: NCTM.

Sowder, J 1990, 'Mental computation and number sense', *The Arithmetic Teacher*, vol. 37, no. 7, pp. 18–20.

Steen, LA 1999, 'Numeracy: The new literacy for a data-drenched society', *Educational Leadership*, vol. 57, no. 2, pp. 8–13, <http://www.ascd.org/publications/educational_leadership/oct99/vol57/num02/Numeracy@_The_New_Literacy_for_a_Data-Drenched_Society.aspx>.

Steinle, V & Stacey, K 2001, 'Visible and invisible zeros: Sources of confusion in decimal notation', in M Mitchelmore, B Perry & J Bobis (eds), *Numeracy and beyond*, Proceedings of the 24th Annual Conference of the Mathematics Education Research Group of Australasia, Sydney: MERGA, pp. 434–41.

Sullivan, P 2011, 'Teaching mathematics using research-informed strategies', *Australian Education Review*, no. 39, <http://research.acer.edu.au/aer/13>.

——2018, *Challenging mathematical tasks*, South Melbourne, Vic: Oxford.

Sullivan, P, Askew, M, Cheeseman, J, Clarke, D, Mornane, A, Roche, A & Walker, N 2015, 'Supporting teachers in structuring mathematics lessons involving challenging tasks', *Journal of Mathematics Teacher Education*, vol. 18, no. 2, pp. 123–40.

Sullivan, P & Lilburn, P 2004, *Open-ended maths activities: Using 'good' questions to enhance learning in mathematics*, Melbourne: Oxford University Press.

Swan, P & Marshall, L 2009, 'Mathematics games as a pedagogical tool', *Proceedings: CoSMEd 2009 3rd International Conference on Science and Mathematics Education*, Penang, pp. 402–6, <http://www.recsam.edu.my/cosmed/cosmed09/AbstractsFullPapers2009/Abstract/Mathematics%20Parallel%20PDF/Full%20Paper/M26.pdf>.

Symons, D 2017, *Using online collaborative learning spaces in primary mathematics education*, unpublished doctorate thesis, University of Melbourne.

Symons, D, Pierce, R & Redman, C 2016, 'Exploring collaborative online problem solving as opportunity for primary students' development of positive mathematical identity', Paper presented at the 2016 annual AARE Conference, Melbourne, Victoria.

Taylor, N, Quinn, F & Eames, C (eds) 2015, *Educating for sustainability in primary schools: Teaching for the future*, Rotterdam: SensePublishers.

Thiessen, D (ed.) 2004, *Exploring mathematics through literature*, Reston, VA: NCTM.

Thomas, N & Mulligan, J 1994, *Dynamic imagery in children's representations of number*, <http://www.merga.net.au/documents/RP_Thomas_Mulligan_1994.pdf>.

Thompson, G 2013, 'NAPLAN, MySchool and accountability: Teacher perceptions of the effects of testing', *The International Education Journal: Comparative Perspectives*, vol. 12, no. 2, pp. 62–84.

Thompson, S 2021, '1 in 4 Australian Year 8s have teachers unqualified in maths – this hits disadvantaged school even harder', ACER Discover Article, <https://www.acer.org/au/discover/article/1-in-4-australian-year-8s-have-teachers-unqualified-in-maths-this-hits-disadvantaged-schools-even-harder>.

Thompson, Z & Hunter, J 2015, 'Developing adaptive expertise with Pasifika learners in an inquiry classroom', in M Marshman, V Geiger & A Bennison (eds), *Mathematics education in the margins*, Proceedings of the 38th annual conference of the Mathematics Education Research Group of Australasia, Mooloolaba: MERGA, pp. 611–18.

Truran, KM 1995, 'Animism: A view of probability behaviour', in B Atweh & S Flavel (eds), *Proceedings of the Eighteenth Annual Conference of the Mathematics Education Group of Australasia*, Darwin: Mathematics Education Group of Australasia, pp. 537–41.

Tucker, K 2014, *Mathematics through play in the early years*, 3rd edn, London: SAGE.

Vale, C 2010, 'Supporting out-of-field teachers of secondary mathematics', *Australian Mathematics Teacher*, vol. 66, no. 1, pp. 17–24.

Vale, C, Atweh, B, Averill, R & Skourdoumbis, A 2016, 'Equity, social justice and ethics in mathematics education' in K Makar, S Dole, J Visnovska, M Goos, A Bennison & K Fry (eds), *Research in Mathematics Education in Australasia 2012–2015*, Singapore: Springer, pp. 97–118.

Vale P & Graven, M 2022, 'Teacher views of parent roles in continued mathematics home learning' in N Fitzallen, C Murphy, V Hatisaru & N Maher (eds), *Mathematical confluences and journeys*, Proceedings of the 44th Annual Conference of the Mathematics Education Research Group of Australasia, Launceston: MERGA, pp. 514–21.

Van de Walle, JA, Karp, KS & Bay-Williams, JM 2013, *Elementary and middle school mathematics*, 8th edn, Boston, MA: Pearson Education.

——— 2017, *Elementary and middle school mathematics*, 9th edn, Essex, England: Pearson.

van den Heuvel-Panhuizen, M & van den Boogard, S 2008, 'Picture books as an impetus for kindergartners' mathematical thinking', *Math. Think. Learn*, vol. 10, pp. 341–73.

van Hiele, PM 1986, *Structure and insight: A theory of mathematics education*, New York: Academic Press.

von Glasersfeld, E 1996, 'Introduction: Aspects of constructivism', in CT Fosnot (ed.), *Constructivism: Theory, perspectives, and practice*, New York: Teachers College Press, pp. 3–7.

Vygotsky, LS 1978, *Mind in society: The development of higher psychological processes*, Cambridge, MA: Harvard University Press.

Wadham, B, Darragh, L & Ell, F 2022, 'Mathematics home-school partnerships in diverse contexts', *Mathematics Education Research Journal*, vol 34, pp. 679–99.

Watson, JM 1993, 'Pigs might fly!!', *Australian Mathematics Teacher*, vol. 49, no. 2, pp. 32–3.

——— 2006, *Statistical literacy at school: Growth and goals*, Mahwah, NJ: Lawrence Erlbaum.

Watson, JM & Callingham, R 1997, 'Data handling: An introduction to higher order processes', *Teaching Statistics*, vol. 19, no. 1, pp. 12–17.

——— 2015, 'Getting out of bed: Students' beliefs' in M Marshman, V Geiger & A Bennison (eds), *Mathematics education in the margins* (Proceedings of the 38th annual conference of the Mathematics Education Research Group of Australasia), Sunshine Coast: MERGA, pp. 619–26.

Watson, JM & Caney, A 2005, 'Development of reasoning about random events', *Focus on Learning Problems in Mathematics*, vol. 27, no. 4, pp. 1–42.

Watson, JM, Collis, KF, Callingham, RA & Moritz, J 1995, 'A model for assessing higher order thinking in statistics', *Educational Research and Evaluation*, vol. 1, no. 3, pp. 245–75.

Watson, JM, Fitzallen, NE, Wilson, K & Creed, JF 2008, 'The representational value of hats', *Mathematics Teaching in the Middle School*, vol. 14, no. 1, pp. 4–10, <http://www.keycurriculum.com/docs/PDF/TinkerPlots/MTMS_Representational-Value-of-Hats.pdf>.

Watson, JM & Kelly, BA 2006, 'Development of numerical and graph interpretation skills: Prerequisites for statistical literacy', *Journal of the Korea Society of Mathematical Education*, vol. 10, no. 4, pp. 259–88.

Webb, JT, Amend, ER, Webb, NE, Goerss, J, Beljan, P & Olenchak, FR 2011, 'Misdiagnosis and dual diagnosis of gifted children', *Articles for Professionals*, New York: SENG.

Wenger, E 2006, 'Communities of practice: A brief introduction', <http://www.ewenger.com/theory>.

Whitacre, I, Henning, B & Atabaş, S 2020, 'Disentangling the research literature on number sense: Three constructs, one name', *Review of Educational Research*, vol. 90, no. 1, pp. 95–134.

White, A 2005, 'Active mathematics in classrooms: Finding out why children make mistakes – and then doing something to help them', *Square One*, vol. 5, no. 4, pp. 15–19.

White, DW 2014, 'What is STEM education and why is it important?', *Florida Association of Teacher Educators Journal*, vol. 1, no. 14, pp. 1–9, <http://www.fate1.org/journals/2014/white.pdf>.

Wild, CJ & Pfannkuch, M 1999, 'Statistical thinking in empirical enquiry', *International Statistical Review*, vol. 67, no. 3, pp. 223–65.

Williams, E & Shuard, H 1982, *Primary mathematics today 3rd edition for the age of the calculator*, Harlow: Longman.

Wilson, R, Piccoli, A, Hargreaves, A, Ng, PT & Sahlberg, P 2021, *Putting students first: Moving on from NAPLAN to a new educational assessment system*, The Gonski Institute Policy Paper #2-2021, Sydney: UNSW Gonski Institute.

Woodcock, S 2021, 'Teachers' beliefs in inclusive education and the attributional responses toward students with and without specific learning difficulties', *Dyslexia*, vol. 27, no. 1, pp. 110–25.

Worthington, M 2018, 'Funds of knowledge: Children's cultural ways of knowing mathematics', in V Kinnear, M-Y Lai & T Muir (eds). *Forging connections in early mathematics teaching and learning*, Singapore: Springer, pp. 239–58.

Wright, RJ 1994, 'A study of the numerical development of 5-year-olds and 6-year olds', *Educational Studies in Mathematics*, no. 26, pp. 25–44.

Wyn, J, Turnbull, M & Grimshaw, L 2014, *The experience of education: The impacts of high stakes testing on school students and their families*, Sydney: Whitlam Institute.

Yunkaporta, T 2009, '*Aboriginal pedagogies at the pedagogical interface*', PhD thesis, Townsville: James Cook University.

INDEX

5 practices for lesson preparation, 236–8
10-frames, 25, 26–9, *see also* hundreds square

A Lion in the Night (Allen), 87
ABC Education website, 191, 192, 195, 201, 206
Aboriginal and Torres Strait Islander histories and cultures, 293–4
absenteeism, 339
abstraction principle, 17
accommodation, 16
accreditation, 2
activities
  extra-curricular, 332
  open-ended, 223, 227
addition, 32, 104–5
  Classroom Snapshots, 293–4
  commutativity principle, 104
  meanings of, 108
  mental computation strategies, 33
  and multiplication, 34, 110
  parts-of-a-whole problems, 104
additive thinking, 110
algebra
  in curriculum, 142, 152, 153, 157
  in primary classroom, 141
  issues to think about, 325
  and multiplicative thinking, 136
  pronumerals in, 164
  and proportional reasoning, 134–7
  secondary mathematics, 325
  tasks, 321–2
algebraic reasoning, 141
algebraic thinking, 146
algorithms, 103–4
All Nursery Rhymes website, 22
angle turners, 59–60
angles, 41, 58
  challenging tasks, 288–90
  in curriculum, 85–6
  and triangles, 46–7
anxiety about mathematics, 383–5
apps
  counting, 22
  geometry, 89, 282–3
  math learning, 29
  patterns, 145
  use of, 362
area, 41, 46–7, 53
  activities, 54
  circles, 47
  Classroom Snapshots, 56–7
  formulae, 161–2
  and perimeter, 55, 67–8
arithmetic, 100

arithmetic blocks, 130
arithmetical strategies, 18
arrays, 33, 45, 110, 119
Asia and Australia's engagement with Asia, 293
assessment
  as learning, 213, 230
  Blank's questioning framework, 220–1
  and curriculum, 213–16
  described, 213
  developmental models, 218
  for learning, 213–16
  national testing, 223–7
  Newman's Error Analysis, 218–19
  of learning, 213
  and online teaching, 217
  quality of student responses, 217–23
  Structure of the Observed Learning Outcome (SOLO) model, 221–3
Assessment Reform Group, 214
Assessment Resource Centre, 227
assessment tasks
  and complexity, 230
  construction of, 223
  examples, 227–9
assimilation, 16
Attard, C, 360
attributes of objects, 42, 52–65
Atweh, B, 279
Auslan interpreters, 265
Australian Association of Mathematics Teachers (AAMT), 14, 213, 224, 317, 336
Australian Bureau of Statistics website, 48, 49
Australian Children's Education and Care Quality Authority (ACECQA), 14
Australian Curriculum Assessment and Reporting Authority (ACARA), 298
Australian Curriculum: Mathematics F–10 v. 9.0
  and assessment, 213, 214
  background, 19
  calculators, 115
  computation, 109, 110, 111, 116
  content strands, 279, 324–6
  cross-curriculum priorities, 279, 293–4
  diversity, 257
  Foundation Year, 20–1, 36, 142
  fractions, 122
  general capabilities, 280, 283, 285, 287, 290

  geometry, 36, 69, 76, 80, 86
  mathematical modelling, 5, 133
  measurement, 46, 52, 64
  multiplication and division, 33
  numbers, 31, 102
  patterns and algebra, 142, 152, 153, 157
  percentages, 132
  probability, 191, 194
  and robotics, 310
  secondary mathematics, 324–6
  statistics, 166, 167, 169, 179, 286, 290
  STEM, 303
  strands, 7
  teaching approaches, 3
  technology use, 285
  Year 1, 5, 31, 36, 52, 142
  Year 2, 21, 33, 111, 116
  Year 3, 52, 102, 116, 152, 167, 283
  Year 4, 46, 52, 110, 116, 152, 153, 156
  Year 5, 132, 310
  Year 6, 5, 52, 107, 133, 142
  Year 7, 46
  Year 8, 46
Australian Institute for Teaching and School Leadership (AITSL), 390, 392
  Graduate Standards, 390–1
Australian Institute of Family Studies (AIFS), 332
Australian Mathematics Sciences Institute, 151
Australian population, 332
autism spectrum disorder, 272–4
averages, 179, 188–9

balance scales, 60, 152
bar graphs, 174
behavioural problems, 260–1, 274
behaviourism, 3
Belonging, Being & Becoming: The Early Years Learning Framework for Australia (DEEWR), 19
Beswick, K, 259, 302, 341
Biggs, JB, 221
binary system, 119
binomial data, 188
bisect, 80
Blackly, S, 299
Blank, M, 220
Blank's questioning framework, 220–1
Blanton, ML, 160
booklets, 329

books
- counting in, 23
- geometry, 87
- and money, 64
- patterns, 149, 150
- probability, 195, 196, 198, 199
- using, 282–3
- world mindedness, 294–5

box-and-whisker plots, 183
boxplots, 183
Bragg, L, 150
Braille, 267
bridging 10 strategy, 33
Brunner, JS, 4
Bryant, P, 192
Bugs and Buttons app, 145
Bureau of Meteorology, 207
bushfires, 207–8

cakes, 54
calculators
- broken multiplication key, 34
- counting on, 34
- decimals, 131
- and patterns, 153
- use of, 114–15, 262, 285

Calder, N, 360
cameras, 94
Caney, A, 193
capacity, 41, 57–8
cardinal numbers, 39
cardinal principle, 17
cardinality, 39
Carpenter, TP, 32
Castledine, A, 310
categorical data, 169, 174, 187
cause and effect, 168
Census at School data, 254
challenging tasks, 234–8, 288–90
Chalmers, C, 310
children, *see* students
circles, 47, 266–7
circumference, 47
classroom observation, 397
Classroom Snapshots
- 10-frames, 27–8
- addition, 105, 106
- area, 56–7, 161–2
- assessment, 214–16, 217–18, 225–7, 229
- behaviour problems, 260–1
- challenging tasks, 288–90
- classroom changes, 1–2
- decimals, 130
- diversity, 263–4, 266–7, 276, 293–4
- dynamic geometry software (DGS), 318–19

Education for Sustainability (EfS), 311–13
education support workers, 367–70, 371–3, 374–8, 379–80
equivalence, 151–2
estimation, 48–50, 65–6
fractions, 124
games, 343–4
geometry, 73–4
Indigenous students, 334–7
isometric projections, 78
length, 345–6
lesson preparation, 235, 238–40, 246–9
literacy, 281–2
matchstick activity, 158–60
measurement, 37
money, 64
multiplication, 116–17
NAPLAN, 387–8
numbers, 24, 263–4
online teaching, 241–3, 397–9
out of field teachers, 316, 318–19
patterns, 149–50, 153, 155–6
place value, 246–9
probability, 194–5, 196–7, 200–1
professional learning, 395–6
proportional reasoning, 135–7
quadrilaterals, 81
relationships, 149–50
road mats, 13
statistics, 171–3, 182–4
STEM education, 300, 310–11
symmetry, 95
teacher education students, 392–3
technology use, 354–5, 358–9, 361–3
volume, 344–5
classrooms
- diversity in, 261–76
- education support workers in, 257–8
- groupings within, 394
- multicultural, 274–5
- multi-grade, 337–40
- structures, 337–8

Clements, DH, 18, 25
clocks, 61
clothesline activities, 22
clue cards, 273
CODAP (Common Online Data Analysis Program), 183, 184, 249
coding, 307–9

cognitive guided instruction (CGI), 32
coin tosses, 196, 201, 202, 210
Collis, KF, 221, 230
colour vision, 259
column graphs, 174
combinatorial tasks, 203–6
commas in numbers, 102
Common Online Data Analysis Program (CODAP), 66
communities
- beliefs about teaching mathematics, 317–19
- and Indigenous students, 336
- involving, 361–3
- professional learning, 395–7

community of practice, 357–60
commutativity principle, 33, 104, 107, 110
comparing and ordering, 42
complexity, 230
composite units, 31
computation, 100, 103–4
- in curriculum, 109, 110, 111, 116
- online teaching, 117

computational thinking, 360
computer tablets, 266
concept maps, 327
conceptual understanding, 101
conclusion to lessons, 323
Concrete, Representational, Abstract (CRA) sequence, 24
conditional probability, 207, 210
cones, 99
congruent figures, 80
conservation, 51
constructivism, 3, 16
continuous data, 169
Cornish, L, 339
correlations, 192
Count Me in Too Learning Framework in Number, 18
counting
- apps, 22
- arithmetical strategies, 18
- beyond 10, 29–30
- early, 16
- on calculators, 34
- resources, 18, 25
- rhymes and songs, 22
- sequencing activities, 22–4
- skip, 30, 34, 111
- strategies, 30–1
- trusting, 17

counting back, 18, 30, 33
counting on, 18, 30, 33
counting principles, 17

Cowan, R, 115
creative thinking, 287–8
crisis of thinking, 75
critical thinking, 287–8
cross-curriculum priorities, 293–4
cross-sections of objects, 78, 99
cubes, 78
Cuisenaire rods, 104, 106
culturally responsive education, 302–3, 341
currency converters, 64
curriculum
    differentiation, 258–9
    see also Australian Curriculum: Mathematics F–10 v. 9.0
curriculum mapping, 340
cylinders, 99

Darragh, L, 360
data
    analysing, 175
    categorical, 169
    collection, 168, 170–3, 203
    definition, 168
    distribution, 179, 182, 188
    in social contexts, 185–6
    reading, 205
    recording, 170, 173–4, 175
    representing, 175–82, 183
    students' work samples, 394–5
    summarising, 175, 179
    telling a story from, 182–6
    types of, 169, 174, 185, 187–8
data cards, 173
decimal number expanders, 129
decimals
    as fractions, 133
    and calculators, 131
    and fractions, 129
    and money, 131–2
    multiplying by 10, 130
    and place value, 139
    and probability, 206
    understanding, 129–31
denominators, 139
DeSimone, JR, 259
developmental dyscalculia, 267–8
diagonals, 80
diamonds, 81
dice, 193, 199, 201, 209
dictionaries, 259
differentiation of curriculum, 258–9
digital literacy, 285–6
digital resource evaluation, 355–6
digital technologies, *see* technology use
direct teaching, 6

disabilities, *see* intellectual disabilities; learning disabilities; physical disabilities
discontinuity, 76
discovery learning, 4
discrete data, 187
discussion in lessons, 323
dissect, 80
distance, 185, 306
distance education, 383, *see also* online teaching
distribution of data, 179, 182, 188
distribution of outcomes, 210
distributive property in multiplication, 116–17
diversity
    in classrooms, 261–76
    in curriculum, 257
    and online teaching, 277
    recognising, 256–8
division, 33, 112–14
    fractions as, 126
    in curriculum, 33
    learning stages, 113
    meanings of, 112
    notation, 113
    rules, 114
Dole, S, 33, 306
dot patterns, 25
doubling strategies, 33
Down syndrome, 268–72
drawing programs, 25
drill and practice, 115–17
dynamic geometry software (DGS), 83–5, 95, 318–19, 326–9
dyscalculia, 267–8
dyslexia, 267

early childhood mathematics pedagogy, 14
Early Years Learning Framework (EYLF), 12, 20, 35–6
edges, 77
Education for Sustainability (EfS), 311–13
education psychologist, 379
education support workers
    described, 366
    excursion supporters, 376–8
    in classrooms, 257–8
    mathematical content knowledge of, 370
    mathematical knowledge of, 370
    and mathematical language, 370
    numeracy or mathematics coach, 379–80
    parents as, 375, 378
    professional, 371–3

    requirements for entry into schools, 365
    roles of, 371
    specialist, 378–9
    and students, 367–70
    teacher aides, 257
    and teachers, 366–7
    training for, 366
    use of, 367
    volunteer, 374–8
    working with, 370–80
eFlashApps, 22
Eight Ways model, 334–5
emergent counting, 18
engineering design, 310–11
English, 199
English, LD, 203, 299, 302, 304
English as additional language or dialect (EAL/D) students, 262, 274–5, 333
equality, 151–6
equals sign, 164
equations, 152, 157, 164
equivalence, 126, 127, 139
    definition, 156
    and equality, 151–6
estimation
    meaningful, 50–1
    measurement, 41, 47–50, 65–6
    resources, 285
Estimation180 (online resource), 285
ethical understanding, 290–1
Euler's theorem, 77
Every Child Counts video, 17
evidence
    of learning, 393–4
    of teaching effectiveness, 382
evidence-based teaching, 305–6, 382, 390
Excel (spreadsheets), 181
excursions, 376–8
expectations (probability), 193, 201
experiences, everyday, 12
experimental probability, 202–3
explicit teaching, 5–6

faces, 77
factor trees, 114
factors, 111–12
fairness, 201
Faragher, R, 268
Fielding-Wells, J, 306
figurative counting, 18
fires, 207–8
First Nations Peoples, 293, 294
First Steps Framework, 18
Fisher, J, 15

Fitzallen, N, 299, 306
five practices for lesson preparation, 236–8
floods, 207
floor plans, 87
flowcharts, 327
formative assessment, 213
formulae
   applying, 45
   area, 161–2
   area and volume, 46–7
   using, 55
fraction notation, 113
fraction walls, 126
fractions
   as decimals and percentages, 133
   as division, 126
   as operators, 125, 127
   common, 139
   and decimals, 129
   equivalent, 126, 127, 139
   in curriculum, 122
   and language, 139
   meanings of, 125–9
   and probability, 198
   representations of, 301–2
   understanding, 123
Franke, N, 360
frequencies, 192, 210
function machines, 150
functioning, modes of, 221–2
funding, 341
funds of knowledge, 15
Fuse (online resource), 145

Gallistel, C, 17
gambling, 191
games
   examples, 244–6, 247–9
   geometry, 82–3, 89
   percentages, 133
   principles of, 243–4
   probability, 196
   resourcing, 343–4
Gelman, R, 17
general capabilities, 280, 283, 285, 287, 290
generalisations, 142, 156–63
geoboards, 55
GeoGebra (software), 83, 84, 159, 318–19
Geometer's Sketchpad, 84
geometric thinking, 36, 305
geometry
   apps, 282–3
   concepts, 70–1

games, 82–3
   in curriculum, 36, 69, 76, 79, 80, 85–6
   online teaching, 72, 82, 83
   outside classroom, 71–2
   resources, 91–3
   theoretical frameworks, 72–6
   van Hiele teaching phases, 96, 282–3
   van Hiele theory, 72–3, 326
   see also dynamic geometry software (DGS)
gifted students, 275–6
Gigerenzer, G, 192
Goulburn Valley Water, 185
Gould, P, 124
Grandgenett, N, 353
Graphing Stories website, 185
graphs, 174, 175–82, 183, 205
Graven, M, 361
Greedy Pig game, 244
group interactions, 273
growing patterns, 146
guess-and-check approach, 156
Guinness World Records website, 48, 49

hand prints, 54
Handshake Problem, 162
hat plots, 183
Heads or Tails (Muir), 64, 196
hearing impairment, 264–5
hefting, 60
home schooling, 332
homework, 323
HOTmaths tools
   addition, 104, 293–4
   algebra, 321–2
   angles, 47
   compass, 275
   counting, 25
   geometry, 82, 83, 91–3
   hundreds square, 29, 148, 247
   measurement, 44, 51, 338
   multiplication, 34, 112
   numbers, 269
   patterns, 161
   statistics, 174, 178
   time, 62
Howell, J, 299
Hoyle, P, 303
hundreds square, 29–30, 146–8
Hurrell, D, 122
Hurst, C, 122

ICT Games website, 45
If the World Were a Village (Smith), 294–5

Illuminations website, 134, 152
   area, 46
   factors, 112
   numbers, 25
   probability, 197
inclusion, see diversity
independent events, 192
index notation, 119
Indigenous students, 293, 334–7
industries, working with, 299
inferences, 182
informal units, see non-standard units
information and communication technologies (ICT), 285, see also technology use
inquiry-based approaches to measurement, 65–6
inquiry pedagogy, 249, 306–7
instrument reading, 45
integers, 103
integrated programs, 333
intellectual disabilities, 268–72
interactive whiteboards (IWB)
   10-frames, 27–8
   geometry, 78
   measurement, 45
   patterns, 155–6
   use of, 358–9
   see also Classroom Snapshots
interpreters, 265
interquartile range, 183
introduction to lesson, 320
intuition, 192
investigations, 5
irregular shapes, 84
isometric projections, 78

Jones, T, 341
journals, 156

Kahoot!, 136
Kaput, JJ, 160
Kee, D, 309
Khan Academy website, 47, 129
Kid Pix (drawing program), 25
King's Tax game, 244
knowledge
   funds of, 15
   prior mathematical, 38–9, 317, 370

language
   and fractions, 139
   impairment, 259
   and levels of thinking, 74, 90
   mathematical, 185

language (cont.)
  of mathematics, 81, 259, 264, 281
  of probability, 194–5, 198
  and numbers, 102
  other than English, 274
Lave, J, 357
learning
  discovery, 4
  evidence of, 393–4
  needs, 258
  numeracy progressions, 19, 283–5
learning disabilities, 267–8, 269
learning support staff, see education support workers
Learning Today website, 152
LEGO® robotics, 309, 310
length, 41, 53, 345–6
lesson preparation
  5 practices for, 236–8
  area, 161–2
  categories to assist, 320
  challenging tasks, 238–40
  components, 319–23
  dynamic geometry software (DGS), 326–9
  for challenging tasks, 234–8
  integrated unit, 249–54
  online teaching, 241–3
  place value, 246–9
  planning considerations, 233, 240–1
  secondary mathematics, 319–23
  sequence examples, 305
  teaching sequence, 326–9
  three-phase model, 234–6
lesson sequences, secondary mathematics, 326–9
Li, Y, 306
Lilburn, P, 226, 227
Liljedahl, P, 238
literacy
  demands in mathematics, 281–2
  digital, 285–6
  in curriculum, 280
  skills, 280
Literacy and Numeracy Test for Initial Teacher Education Students (LANTITE), 38, 382, 385–7
Literacy Teaching Toolkit, 259
literature, childrens, see books
lived experiences, 303
Livy, S, 55, 150
location, 282–3

Logan, T, 224
Lowrie, T, 224
Lyncean Education website, 61

Ma, L, 55
MacDonald, A, 14
MacGregor, M, 146, 151
Maher, N, 55
Makar, K, 306
Make It Count: Numeracy, Mathematics, and Indigenous Learners project, 334
Make it Count website, 294
manipulatives, 66, 344
mass, 41, 60–1
matchstick activity, 158–60
Math Doodles (app), 89
Math Playground (online resource), 54, 150
Mathwire (online resource), 247
mathematical content knowledge, 317
  of education support workers, 370
mathematical development
  beyond number, 35–8
  number activities and strategies, 22–31
  number sense, 101–3
  operations with numbers, 31–5
mathematical modelling
  in curriculum, 5, 133
  number operations, 31
mathematical models, 129
mathematics
  anxiety about, 383–5
  and problem-based learning, 301–2
  and STEM, 299–301, 304–7
  teachers' beliefs about, 259–61
mathematics coaches, 379
Mathematics Education Research Group of Australasia, 317
mathematics journals, 156
mathematics pedagogy, 14
Maths Dictionary for Kids, 259
Maths is Fun (online resource), 286
maths nights, 362
Maths300 website, 78
Mathsframe website, 23
Matthews, Chris, 334
McAnelly, N, 356
McIntosh, A, 33, 101
mean, 179, 189
measurement
  area and volume, 46–7
  attributes, 42, 52–65
  and conservation, 51

  early development, 37–8, 41
  estimation, 41, 47–51, 65–6
  in curriculum, 46, 52, 64
  inquiry-based approaches to, 65–6
  issues to think about, 325
  learning sequence, 41–5
  online teaching, 66
  resources, 42, 45
  secondary mathematics, 325
  with non-standard units, 57, 59, 60, 64
measures of central tendency, 179
median, 179, 189
mental computation strategies, 30, 33
mentors, 317
metric units, 52
Miller, D, 279
Mitchelmore, MC, 124, 142
mix-and-match books, 198
mode, 179, 188
money, 41, 52, 64–5, 131–2, 262–3
Monty Hall's problem, 191
Moore, TJ, 299, 305
Muir, T, 55, 150
Mulligan, JT, 142, 147
multi-age classes, 339
multibase arithmetic blocks, 130
multicultural classrooms, 274–5
multi-grade classes, 337–40
multiplication, 33, 109–12
  and addition, 34, 110
  as arrays, 34–5, 110, 119
  as scaled up, 109
  distributive property, 116–17
  in curriculum, 33, 110, 111
  and factors, 111–12
  times tables, 110, 115
  with larger numbers, 116–17
multiplicative proportionality, 122
multiplicative thinking, 110, 122–3, 136
Murphy's Law, 199

Nasty Games, 248
National Assessment Program – Literacy and Numeracy (NAPLAN), 223–7, 281–2, 340, 387–90
National Center for Education Statistics (NCES), 174
National Library of Virtual Manipulatives website, 56
National Numeracy Learning Progressions, 19, 283
National Quality Framework, 14

National STEM School Education Strategy, 297
national testing, 223–7, 340–1, *see also* National Assessment Program – Literacy and Numeracy (NAPLAN)
negative numbers, 107, 258
nets, 77
Newman, A, 218
Newman's Error Analysis, 218–19
newsletters, 362
noise, 272
non-standard units, 42–4, 57, 59, 60, 64
normal distribution, 188
NRICH website
   decimals, 130
   fractions, 127
   group interactions, 273
   hundreds square, 148
   numbers, 101, 102, 117
   patterns, 154
   proportional reasoning, 136
   statistics, 177, 184
NSW Education Standards Authority, 228
number bars, 104, 106
number charts, 29–30, 146–8
number frameworks, 17–19
number lines, 33, 108, 130, 132
number sentences, 108
number slides, 131
number systems, 118
numbers
   big ideas in, 122
   Classroom Snapshots, 263–4
   commas, 102
   early concepts, 16–17
   early operations with, 31–5
   in curriculum, 20–1, 31, 102
   index notation, 119
   issues to think about, 325
   and language, 102
   linking with quantities, 24–5
   negative, 107, 258
   operations with whole, 103–14
   part-whole, 123–37
   patterns with, 146–8, 149–50
   place value, 35, 100, 107, 119, 129
   properties of, 103
   recall of number facts, 117
   relationships between, 149–50
   secondary mathematics, 325
   sense of, 101–3
   signs for, 265
   understanding, 16
   see also counting; hundreds square
numeracy
   activities, 362
   definition, 283
   in curriculum, 283
   personal, 385
   progressions, 19, 283–5
numeracy coaches, 379
Numeracy in the News website, 199, 291
numerators, 139
numerical continuous variables, 187
numerical data, 187
numerical discrete data, 187
Nunes, T, 192
nursery rhymes, 22
NZ Maths
   decimals, 130
   geometry, 79, 87
   measurement, 51, 53
   probability, 199
   statistics, 174, 185

odds, 191
one-to-one principle, 17
online teaching
   and assessment, 217
   computation, 117
   and diversity, 277
   and general capabilities, 291
   geometry, 72, 82, 83
   involving parents, 361–3
   lesson preparation, 241–3
   measurement, 66
   need for, 383
   part-whole numbers, 137
   patterns, 163
   probability, 208
   problem-solving, 293–4
   secondary mathematics, 326
   and social connections, 254
   statistics, 186
   STEM education, 307
   sustainability, 295
   tips for, 397–9
open-ended activities, 223, 227, 301, 394
operators, fractions as, 125, 127
order irrelevance principle, 17
ordering, 42
ordinal data, 187
ordinal numbers, 24
out of field teachers of mathematics, 2, 315–16, 317–19
outcomes, 192, 196–7, 206–8, 210
Outhred, L, 124
outliers, 170, 179, 189

parabolas, 321
parallel lines, 75, 99
parallelograms, 80
parents
   as education support workers, 375, 378
   involving, 361–3
Parmar, RS, 259
part-part-whole relationships, 16, 25, 31
part-whole numbers, 123–37
parts-of-a-whole problems, 104
Pascal's Triangle, 202
Pattern and Structure Mathematical Awareness Program (PASMAP), 142
pattern-recognition activities, 25
patterns
   growing, 146
   in curriculum, 142, 152, 153, 157
   in early years, 143–6
   online teaching, 163
   recognising, 136, 154–6
   repeating, 145, 152
   resources, 162
   and rules, 154
   and structure, 142–3
   and transformations, 152
   with numbers, 146–8, 149–50
pedagogical content knowledge, 317
pedagogical practices, 14
peer observation, 397
percentages, 132–4, 206
perceptual counting, 18
perfect squares, 103
perimeter, 55, 67–8
pets, 258
photocopiers, 343
physical disabilities, 262–4
pi, 47
pictograms, 169
pie charts, 174, 178
place value, 35, 100, 107, 119
   lesson preparation, 246–9
   numbers less than 1, 129, 139
play, 12, 14, 15–16
play dough, 61
playing cards, 45
populations, 168
portfolios, 391–3, 394
Powell, D, 332
PowerPoint, 26

PPDAC (Problem, Plan, Data, Analysis, Conclusion) cycle
  analyse, 175–82
  conclusions, 182–6
  described, 5, 167
  plan, data, 170–4
  problems, 169–70
practice, 115–17
prime factors, 114
prime numbers, 114
prisms, 78, 99
probability
  books, 195, 196, 198, 199
  classical, 210
  conditional, 207, 210
  and decimals, 206
  described, 209–10
  experimental, 202–3, 210
  and fractions, 198
  games, 196
  importance of, 190–2
  in curriculum, 191, 194
  in early primary years, 194–5
  issues to think about, 324
  language of, 194–5, 198
  middle primary years, 196–8
  online teaching, 208
  quantifying, 192
  representing, 206–8
  secondary mathematics, 324
  social aspects, 191
  theoretical, 201–2, 210
  understanding, 192–4
  upper primary years, 198–9
problem-based learning
  described, 301
  and STEM, 301–2
problem-solving
  asking questions, 169–70
  online teaching, 293–4
  skills, 302
  and statistics, 167
  tasks, 321
  understanding questions, 218–21
procedural understanding, 101
professional associations, 317
professional learning
  and education support workers, 366
  for out of field teachers, 317
  mentors, 317
  need for, 383
  remote areas, 341
  technology skills, 360
professional learning communities, 395–7
professional portfolios, 391–3, 394

Progressive Achievement Tests (PAT), 227
project-based teaching approach, 299
pronumerals in algebra, 164
proportional reasoning, 121–2, 134–7
protractors, 59
psychology, 192
Puentedura, Ruben, 352
puzzles, 54, 204
pyramids, 78, 99

quadrilaterals, 73–4, 80–1, 326–9
quantitative data, 185
questions
  asking, 169–70
  Blank's questioning framework, 220–1
  and children from other cultures, 275
  closed, 230, 366
  Newman's Error Analysis, 218–19
  open-ended, 223, 226
  start of lesson, 320

random generators, 202
randomness, 192, 210
range, 183
ratios, 125
recall of number facts, 110, 115, 117, 269, 394
relationships between numbers, 149–50
relative frequencies, 192, 210
remote areas, 332–3
  multi-grade classes, 337–40
  professional learning, 341
  resourcing, 341–7
repeated equivalent groups, 111
repeating patterns, 145, 152
reSolve website, 111, 154, 184, 192, 302
resources, 2, 341–7
  evaluating digital, 355–6
  robotics, 309
responses, quality of student, 217–23
reversibility techniques, 326
rhymes, 22
risk, 191, 207
road mats, 13
robotics, 309–11
Romberg, TA, 230
rote learning, 3
routines, 272
rulers, 44
  broken, 45

rural areas, 332–3, *see also* remote areas
Russo, J, 243
Ryan, J, 45

sample spaces, 192
samples, 168, 180, 203, 206
SAMR (Substitution, Augmentation, Modification, Redefinition) model, 350, 352–3, 354–5
Sarama, J, 18
scales, 45, 63, 152
  making, 61
school communities, involving, 361–3
school counsellors, 379
schools
  integration of technology in, 356–63
  requirements for entry into, 365
  transition to, 14–15
  see also education support workers
sciences, 294
Scootle (online resource), 34, 144
Scratch (online resource), 307–9
secondary mathematics
  curriculum strands, 324–6
  lesson preparation, 319–23
  lesson sequences, 326–9
  online teaching, 326
  out of field teachers, 315–16, 317–19
sensory impairment, 283–5
sequencing activities, 22–4
Serow, P, 326
shapes, 35–6, 84
sharing in lessons, 323
Shodor website, 179
Shuard, H, 113
Shulman, LS, 350
Shumway, J, 26
Siemon, D, 16, 17, 31
simulation, 194, 199–201
Six Dinner Sid (Moore), 24, 282
skills audits, 351–2
skip counting, 30, 34, 111
Slow Reveal Graphs (online resource), 184
Smith, KA, 299, 305
social capabilities, 273
social connections, 254
social difficulties, 272–4
social workers, 379
songs, 22
Sophie's Prize (Marston), 64
sound, 272
space, 35–6, 69, 324–5

spatial awareness, 35–6, 41, 51, 86
spinners, 201, 203, 205
spreadsheets, 169, 173, 174, 180, 346
square numbers, 103
stable order principle, 17, 20
Stacey, K, 146, 151
standard units, 44
standards (AITSL), 390–1
start of lessons, 320
statistical inferences, 168
statistics
   developing understanding of, 168
   importance of, 166
   in curriculum, 166, 167, 169, 179, 286, 290
   issues to think about, 324
   online teaching, 186
   and problem-solving, 167
   resources, 184
   resourcing, 346
   secondary mathematics, 324
   technology use, 169, 180–2
   and variation, 166
   see also data; PPDAC (Problem, Plan, Data, Analysis, Conclusion) cycle
STEAM (Science, Technology, Engineering, Arts, Mathematics), 295
STEM (Science, Technology, Engineering, Mathematics) education
   and culturally responsive pedagogies, 302–3
   described, 295, 297, 298
   evidence-based practice in, 305–6
   implementing, 304–7
   in curriculum, 303
   in schools, 298
   in United Kingdom, 303–4
   and primary mathematics, 299–301
   and problem-based learning, 301–2
   strategy, 298
   working with industries, 299
stem-and-leaf plots, 182
Structure of the Observed Learning Outcome (SOLO) model, 221–3
student-centred approaches, 3
student tasks in lessons, 321–2
students
   and education support workers, 367–70
   engaging, 238–40, 317, 346
   evidence of learning, 393–4
   from refugee backgrounds, 258
   Indigenous, 293, 334–7
   quality of responses, 217–23
   samples of work, 394–5
   talented, 275–6
   who are gifted, 275–6
   with autism spectrum disorder, 272–4
   with behavioural problems, 260–1, 274
   with developmental dyscalculia, 267–8
   with English as additional language or dialect (EAL/D), 262, 274–5
   with intellectual disabilities, 268–72
   with learning disabilities, 258, 267–8, 269
   with physical disabilities, 262–4
   with sensory impairment, 283–5
   with social difficulties, 272–4
   with special needs, 259
subitising, 16, 25–6, 39
subtraction, 32, 105–9
   commutativity principle, 104, 107
   meanings of, 106, 108
   mental computation strategies, 33
Sullivan, P, 226, 227, 234, 288, 317
summary statistics, 179
summative assessment, 213
support staff, see education support workers
sustainability, 293, 295
symmetry, 80, 95

tactile materials, 266
take-home activities, 362
talented students, 275–6
tally marks, 174
tangrams, 51, 54
targeted teaching, 6
TeachableMath (online resource), 59
teacher aides, 257
teacher-centred approaches, 3
teacher-directed approaches, 3
teacher education, 2
   and LANTITE, 385–7
teacher education students
   anxiety about mathematics, 383–5
   professional portfolios, 391–3
teachers
   absenteeism, 339
   being flexible, 333–6
   beliefs about mathematics, 259–61
   and education support workers, 366–7, 370–80
   roles of, 371
   shortage of secondary mathematics, 315
   technology skills, 351–2, 360
   turnover, 334
teachers of mathematics
   and mentors, 317
   out of field, 2, 315–16, 317–19
teaching
   direct, 6
   evidence-based, 382, 390
   explicit, 5–6
   inquiry pedagogy, 306–7
   project-based approach, 299
   targeted, 6
Teaching and Learning About Decimals website, 129
teaching mathematics
   approaches, 3–7
   community beliefs about, 317–19
   content knowledge (mathematical), 38–9
   culturally responsive, 341
   curriculum mapping, 340
   engaging students, 238–40, 317, 346
   issues to think about, 324–6
   and learning needs, 258
   multi-grade classes, 337–40
   resourcing, 341–7
   teaching sequence, 326–9
   van Hiele teaching phases, 96, 282–3
   see also Classroom Snapshots; online teaching; secondary mathematics
Teaching Performance Assessment (TPA), 390
technological pedagogical content knowledge (TPACK) framework, 350–1
technology
   auditing skills, 351–2
   evaluating digital, 355–6
   integrating in schools, 356–63
   and professional learning, 360
   selecting, 356
technology frameworks, 350, 353
technology use
   activities, 353
   challenges, 361–3
   and children with physical disabilities, 262

technology use (cont.)
    and community of practice, 357–60
    and Early Years Learning Framework (EYLF), 20
    examples, 354–5
    in curriculum, 285
    multiplication, 116–17
    proportional reasoning, 136–7
    and sound, 272
    statistics, 169, 180–2
    and students with autism spectrum disorder, 272–3
    and students with intellectual disabilities, 269
    see also calculators
temperature, 41, 63
Ten in the Bed (Dale), 149
tessellations, 88–9
theoretical probability, 201–2
Think Boards, 128
thinking
    and teaching practices, 238
    see also specific types of thinking e.g. geometric thinking
thinking, levels of
    crisis of thinking, 75
    and figures, 96
    hierarchical nature, 74
    and language, 74, 90
    level reduction, 75
    progression, 75
    van Hiele theory, 36, 72–3
Thomas, N, 147
Thompson, S, 315, 316
Thornton, S, 279
three-dimensional (3D) objects, 70, 76, 99

three-phase model for lesson preparation, 234–6
time, 41, 46, 52, 61–3
time zones, 63
times tables, 110, 115
timetables, 339
Top Drawer resource, 125, 189, 287–8
Topmarks website, 23, 264
Tower of Hanoi, 162
transformations, 70, 80, 152, 282–3
transition to school, 14–15
tree diagrams, 201
triangles, 46–7
trusting the count, 17
two-dimensional (2D) figures, 70, 76, 80–5
Two of Everything (Hong), 150

uncertainty, 191, 194–208, see also probability
understanding, 76
United Kingdom, 303–4
units
    metric, 52
    non-standard, 42–4, 57, 59, 60, 64
    standard, 44

Vale, C, 332
Vale, P, 361
value, 41, 64–5
Van de Walle, JA, 53, 59, 61
van Hiele, PM, 76
van Hiele-Geldof, Dina, 90
van Hiele levels of thought, 36
van Hiele teaching phases, 96–283, 326

van Hiele theory, 72–6
variables, 150, 187–8
variation, 166, 193
vertices, 77
victim blaming, 260
virtual characters, 272
vision impairment, 259, 265–7
Visnos (online resource), 127
visualisation, 70
volume, 41, 46–7, 57–8, 344–5
volunteer education support workers, 365, 374–8
Vulnerable People check, 365
Vygotsky, LS, 366

Watson, JM, 193, 324
weight, 60–1
Wenger, E, 357
What's in the Bag? (activity), 198
whole number operations, 103–14
Will it Rain Today? (video), 195
Williams, E, 113
Williams, J, 45
word problems, 5, 219–21, 281
work samples, 394–5
Working with Children check, 365
world mindedness, 294–5
Wright, RJ, 18

x in algebra, 164

YouTube, 22, 282
Yunkaporta, Tyson, 334

Zack's Alligator (Mozelle), 56
zero, 118